Pro ASP.NET Web Forms Techniques, Second Edition

ALEX HOMER

APress Media, LLC

Pro ASP.NET Web Forms Techniques, Second Edition

Copyright ©2004 by Alex Homer
Originally published by Apress in 2004

ISBN 978-1-59059-317-2   ISBN 978-1-4302-0662-0 (eBook)
DOI 10.1007/978-1-4302-0662-0

Trademarked names may appear in this book. Rather than use a trademark symbol with every occurrence of a trademarked name, we use the names only in an editorial fashion and to the benefit of the trademark owner, with no intention of infringement of the trademark.

Technical Reviewers: David Beauchemin, Matt Bullock, Mathew Gibbs, Praveen Hari, John Kauffman, Ajoy Krishnamoothy, Robert Oliver, David Schultz, Kevin Spencer, Kent Tegels, Gary Vartanoff

Editorial Board: Steve Anglin, Dan Appleman, Gary Cornell, James Cox, Tony Davis, John Franklin, Chris Mills, Steven Rycroft, Dominic Shakeshaft, Julian Skinner, Martin Streicher, Jim Sumser, Karen Watterson, Gavin Wray, John Zukowski

Assistant Publisher: Grace Wong

Project Manager: Beth Christmas

Copy Editor: Anne Friedman

Production Manager: Kari Brooks

Production Editor: Lori Bring

Proofreader: Thistle Hill Publishing Services, LLC

Compositor: Kinetic Publishing Services, LLC

Indexer: Rebecca Plunkett

Artist: Kinetic Publishing Services, LLC

Cover Designer: Kurt Krames

Manufacturing Manager: Tom Debolski

Contents at a Glance

Contents

About the Author

Alex Homer is a computer geek and Web developer with a passion for ASP.NET. Although he has to spend some time doing real work (a bit of consultancy and training, and the occasional conference session), most of his days are absorbed in playing with the latest Microsoft Web technology and then writing about it. Living in the picturesque wilderness of the Derbyshire Dales in England, he is well away from the demands of the real world—with only an Internet connection to maintain some distant representation of normality. But, hey, what else could you want from life? You can contact Alex through his software company, Stonebroom Limited: alex@stonebroom.com.

Introduction

ASP.NET MAKES IT EASY to create interactive and intuitive interfaces for Web applications, and attractive and exciting Web pages. The server-based postback architecture, combined with the comprehensive array of server controls that are provided as part of the .NET Framework, allow developers to quickly build browser-based interfaces for Web sites and Web applications—using much the same event-driven approach as in "traditional" executable programs developed in languages like Visual Basic, Delphi, and C++.

This is a completely new and different way of working from previous versions of ASP, and the underlying principles and workings of server-based events, which occur in response to actions made by the user in the page, can prove to be difficult to grasp in their entirety. However, constructing ASP.NET pages, especially with some of the tools that are available or under development now, is very much easier and often less error-prone than in classic ASP.

Besides, a completely server-based approach to user interaction does have its downsides. In high-latency scenarios, or over slow network connections, the need to hit the server every time the page content needs to be modified can intrude on the workings of an application or reduce the perceived responsiveness of a Web site.

Although the ASP.NET philosophy tends to engender a server-based mechanism, where postbacks to the server are used to generate and update the pages, some of the server controls (notably the Validation controls) also encompass client-side interactivity through JScript that is sent to the client for execution there. And there is no reason why a developer cannot add to this functionality for other controls by handling client-side events in the same way as has become the norm in most Web sites and Web applications today.

What Is This Book About?

So, based on the title and the preceding preamble, you can safely assume that this book aims to examine the possibilities for developing user interfaces that are driven by ASP.NET. It attempts to discuss and explore a range of techniques and approaches predominantly for creating Web sites and Web pages that are as follows:

- Intuitive and easy to use

- Attractive and full-featured

- Interactive where this is appropriate

- Based (loosely) on real-world scenarios

- Able to fulfill a predefined set of design requirements

- Fun, memorable, and provide user satisfaction

The example pages are, for the most part, elements of an overall application that—while being somewhat optimistic as regards consumer buying patterns—form the basis for the kind of Web site/application that is becoming one of the basic ingredients of the World Wide Web today. I'll be building a site that allows the user to choose, customize, and purchase a new car or truck from the world-famous Xrox Car Company.

To do so, I focus on the steps of requirements-analysis and design (though not in extreme detail), followed by planning and mapping out the site. While this seems like the natural way to get started, it's often skimped on or even omitted, thereby allowing a site to develop in a haphazard and unpredictable way. While this is not always categorically wrong, it does make site development and maintenance that much more difficult. Even the most simplistic starting plan can reduce development and maintenance time, as well as avoiding many common frustrations that result from the "no plan" approach.

Once the basic design in is place you'll see the development of the various resources that make up the complete site. Of course, repetition is commonplace in a Web site, and so to make the book as useful as possible I've taken some liberties to try and cover as many useful topics as possible. It means that you will look at a range of things, such as the following:

- A central "Home page" that makes navigating the whole site easy

- How to display the products available from the site from a back-end database

- Interactive content that is driven either by server-side or client-side code, or both

- Creating graphics on the fly and animations to liven up the site

- A "login" feature that recognizes users and provides optional personalization

- An online order facility with order tracking and status reports via email

- Some ASP.NET development tools that are available now, or are on the way

What I won't be doing is concentrating on the back-end data processing tasks in any more detail than I need to in order to get the site running. On the grounds that I don't have thousands of pages available here, this book concentrates on the user interfaces, and on using fairly simple data access techniques. Of course, that doesn't mean I won't be doing it "properly," it just means that you won't see detailed discussions of the workings of all of the .NET data access classes, or the long diatribes on catching and reporting concurrency errors.

All ASP.NET code you see listed in the book, with the exception of simple abstract snippets that demonstrate a specific principle or just show the syntax, is available for download in both VB .NET and C#. The listings you see in the book are mostly written using VB .NET syntax, but they avoid the use of language-specific features wherever possible, so that the code can easily be converted to other languages by any reasonably capable developer who prefers to work in a different language. Where there is an obvious difference between VB .NET and C# in the way that a specific feature is implemented, I show the C# version as well. Meanwhile, the client-side code is predominantly written in JavaScript/JScript. The code has been tested on version 1.1 of the .NET Framework, as well as on version 1.0, for which it was originally written. Where there are issues or differences between the versions, I document these in the code or chapter.

You can download all the code for this book from: http://www.daveandal.net/books/7868/. You can also run many of the examples online on my server from the same URL. The sample code for this book is also available to readers at http://www.apress.com/ in the Downloads section.

Who Is This Book For?

As is becoming clear, ASP.NET and the accompanying .NET Framework class library are far more comprehensive—and complex—than anything available in ASP 3.0 or earlier (or, in fact, in other environments like PHP and JSP). The result is that it's not possible for every ASP.NET book to cover an introduction or brief tutorial to ASP.NET as well as the more advanced content that forms the core of this book.

Mind you—this is a good thing from your point of view, as you don't want to pay for material that covers topics you're already familiar with. What it does mean is that you *do* need to be familiar with ASP.NET and, to some extent, the .NET Framework classes to be able to use this book successfully. I assume that you have already installed and are using ASP.NET to build pages, perhaps using a text editor or with Visual Studio .NET or another development tool.

> **NOTE** *The downloadable samples provided for this book cannot be loaded directly into Visual Studio .NET. To provide maximum compatibility with all development tools and editors, and to maximize readability, the samples do not implement the code-behind approach demanded by Visual Studio .NET.*

I also assume that you have a reasonable grasp of using a database to drive a Web site. I explain the data access code I use, how it works, and discuss alternatives where appropriate. But I won't be covering the basic techniques for setting up and administering your database.

What This Book Is Not

- It's not a dry reference book on any particular area of the technologies.

- It's not an academic text that follows every thread or aspect of any one technology.

- It's not about hardware performance or software configuration for ASP.NET.

- It's not about SQL programming, server optimization, or data access theory.

- It's not aimed at system or database administrators—it's aimed at developers.

What This Book Is

- It is a practical approach aimed at achieving useful goals without drowning in complexity.

- It is a guide to many of the useful and powerful interface-oriented features of ASP.NET.

- It is an exploration of a process for designing and building an interactive Web site.

- It is a useful introduction to many peripheral techniques, such as drawing and email.

- It is a demonstration of how easy ASP.NET makes building great Web sites.

- It is, I hope, informative, useful, and fun to read.

What Do You Need to Use This Book?

Providing that your level of experience and knowledge meets the not-excessive requirements of the earlier sections, the only other things you need are:

- A development environment. At minimum your favorite text editor, or perhaps Visual Studio .NET, Microsoft ASP.NET Web Matrix, or any other suitable tool from a third party manufacturer. For details of Web Matrix, check out the Apress book *Web Matrix Developer's Guide* (ISBN: 1-59059-092-9), or the free PDF document available from http://www.daveandal.net/books/webmatrix/.

- Internet Information Server and the .NET Framework installed and configured on a server that you can access. Alternatively, if you are using Web Matrix, you can take advantage of its built-in Web server. I also recommend that you install the complete version of the .NET SDK that includes all the reference material, as it makes it easy to look up specific items when you aren't using Visual Studio .NET.

- A database such as Microsoft SQL Server or MSDE, although you can use any other SQL database system—or even a desktop database such as Microsoft Access—as long as there is a .NET Data Provider available so that it can be accessed via ASP.NET. For development and experimentation you can run the database, IIS and .NET, and your chosen development environment on the same machine. This often makes debugging easier as well.

So, if you have parted with your hard-earned cash and are ready to start building sites, all that remains is to say thank you. Or, if you're still standing amongst the shelves of the computing section in the bookstore, go on—shell out—you know it's worth it! I'm sure you will find this book interesting, stimulating, and useful. Please let me know, as your feedback really is appreciated (whether good or bad) and helps me a great deal when planning future books (alex@stonebroom.com).

CHAPTER 1

Getting Started

THERE'S A SAYING THAT GOES something like "you can't make an omelet without breaking eggs." OK, so perhaps if you subscribe to the same school of culinary arts as this particular author (take it out of the freezer and put it in the microwave), then perhaps it's possible to avoid the physical experience of egg-breaking yourself. But someone has had to do it somewhere down the line—unless that someone started breeding chickens that lay omelets directly, of course.

But what has all this to do with building a Web site or Web application? Well (as you probably guessed from the title and introduction) this book is about designing and building interfaces for your applications using ASP.NET as the driving force. In the culinary terms I started out with, this comes down to a simple question that you will keep coming back to at almost every stage of your ASP.NET application design process: "can you build an ASP.NET Web application without using server controls?"

The answer to any technical question posed to a programmer is almost invariably "it depends," but in general you can safely say that somewhere down the line, most of your ASP.NET pages will contain at least a sprinkling of these clever little beasts. After all, they form the core around which many ASP.NET page design techniques are wrapped—rather like (to continue the culinary introduction) the rice and chicken in a tortilla. Although comparing server controls to the contents of a flour or corn pancake may be stretching the allegory just a little too far.

So, following this customary off-topic wandering, what are you actually going to be looking at in this chapter? As the title suggests, the aim here is to think about how you can get started building an interactive Web site or Web application based on ASP.NET, which provides an interesting and usable interface for your users. You'll look at:

- Why ASP.NET provides a great environment for building interactive pages and sites

- The fundamental ways that ASP.NET makes building dynamic pages easier

- The built-in features of ASP.NET that you can use in your pages and applications

- The impact and reasoning behind using client-side and server-side processing

- How to approach designing a site to get the most from ASP.NET

I start with the basics of the design approach—pen and paper—and from there, by the end of the chapter, you should be in a position to start constructing the first of your pages. However, first you look at how ASP.NET provides new tools and enables new techniques that you can take advantage of to make building these pages much quicker and easier than ever before.

Why ASP.NET?

The fact that you are reading this probably means that you are already a confirmed ASP.NET developer, and looking to see how you can get the most from the techniques you've learned from other books and publications. Alternatively, you may be thinking about trying ASP.NET to see if it is any better than your current development environment when it comes to building high-performance dynamic Web sites and applications.

If you fall into the first category, then you should find the following sections useful in giving you guidance about how to plan your site to take full advantage of ASP.NET. If you fall into the second category, then you may find that you need something more introductory to start with. However, the overall approach to the design of the site should still give you more ideas about what ASP.NET can do—and how easy it makes it to accomplish.

A Note on Terminology

In the not-so-distant past, it was easy to differentiate a Web *site* from a Web-based *application*. *Web sites* used mainly static HTML pages to display information, while *Web-based applications* were ordinary applications that had often been converted from an executable running locally on your machine into something that is executable across the Internet.

However, the continuing trend towards making *everything* Web-enabled means that most new applications are designed and built with a remote interface that allows them to run over HTTP. And many Web sites constructed today are much more interactive than their predecessors—providing dynamic access to back-end systems both for exposing and collecting information.

So, if both Web sites and Web-based applications are really becoming just interfaces to some back-end data store, aren't they same thing? Should we stop thinking about them as two different things, and approach both the same way as far as design and implementation are concerned?

Certainly, there will always be some Web sites that are not "interactive" (they just present information), but it's also fair to say that some Web-based application interfaces only present information as well—in other words they are not really "interactive" either.

Is It a Bird? ... Is It a Plane? ... No, It's a Wapplisite!

So, I propose dropping the distinction. It's time that we moved away from thinking about the two as different things and treated them the same way. What's important is the level of interactivity that they expose. But what do we call them? In this book, you'll generally find I refer to just "the site" or "the application," and both should be taken to mean much the same thing.

One word that has been in circulation for a while is a combination of the words "Web" and "application": *Weblication*. However, this doesn't encompass the fact that we are also dealing with Web sites. So, my new favorite word, and my pitch for everlasting fame (online glossary and dictionary Webmasters please take note) is *Wapplisite*. If you should happen to see this popping up in the remainder of the book, instead of the more cumbersome phrase "Web application or Web site" you'll now know exactly what I am referring to. And, as a bonus, you get value for money because there is more room for useful words on each page.

ASP.NET Fundamentals

Before you get started looking at how to put together the recipe for a site, it's worth exploring in some detail why and how ASP.NET can provide the ingredients you need to make the task as easy and as productive as possible. The answers center around the fundamental change in the way that ASP.NET allows you to approach the whole concept of creating distributed applications that work across the Web using HTTP as the only transport mechanism.

Event-Driven Applications

Modern applications that are built to run on a "window-based" interface to the operating system need to be *event-driven*, rather than *procedural*, in the way that they work (here I use the term "window-based," with a lower-case "w," to indicate that it applies to systems other than Microsoft Windows).

Procedural-based applications (generally with text rather than GUI interfaces) follow an execution path that is predefined, using menus that are effectively conditional statements that execute the code in a specific order, depending on a user intervention that occurs only when the application prompts for input.

On the other hand, an event-driven application generally provides and displays several interface elements at a time (one or more window, each of which can contain more than one control or input element). The user can interact with the elements whenever and in whatever order they wish. As they do so, the elements raise events that are handled by the code in the application.

However, providing an event-driven environment has always been a difficult task in a Web application. Web browsers were never designed to act as application interfaces. Their original purpose was to display (and allow editing of) information that is delivered in the form of structured HTML-encoded documents.

OK, so they have always offered a range of simple "form controls," such as the <input> and <textarea> elements, but it's only over the last few years that they have developed to include features such as client-side scripting, executable applets and ActiveX controls, and programmatic access to the content of a page that allows something other than a basic data-input form.

Programming Dynamic Pages on the Web

The traditional approach to building a Web application is to provide a page containing the form controls that collect the user's input, and then have the user submit (or post) this page to a separate dynamic page that handles this user's input. There are plenty of existing technologies that can achieve this, for example scripting languages such as Perl, PHP, JSP, and ASP. Another approach is to build executables that interact with the Web server directly, using technologies like ISAPI (Internet Server Application Programming Interface) or the CGI (Common Gateway Interface).

Irrespective of the technology that is used, however, the basic technique is the same. The code in the dynamic page has to retrieve the values sent from the previous page, process them as required, and then, step by step, generate the output required to create the returned page that is sent to the client (see Figure 1-1).

Figure 1-1. The traditional dynamic Web programming cycle

Yes, it works, but is it the best approach? The code in the page is executed in a procedural way in that execution starts at the top of the page and continues until the page is complete. In other words, this model for handling the user's input means that you are simply responding to a single event (that of the page being submitted to the server), and you have to generate output as the execution proceeds. It can lead to a tangle of intermixed code, HTML, and other content—making maintenance and debugging a nightmare, and often prevents the page from being extended or adapted without a huge redesign effort.

Event-Driven Programming on the Web

What you really want is a clean and easily extensible model that allows you to react to specific events as users interact with the interface you provide in their browser. As in traditional event-driven programming environments, the goal is to create a form containing the controls and content, and then react to events that are raised for the individual controls (Figure 1-2).

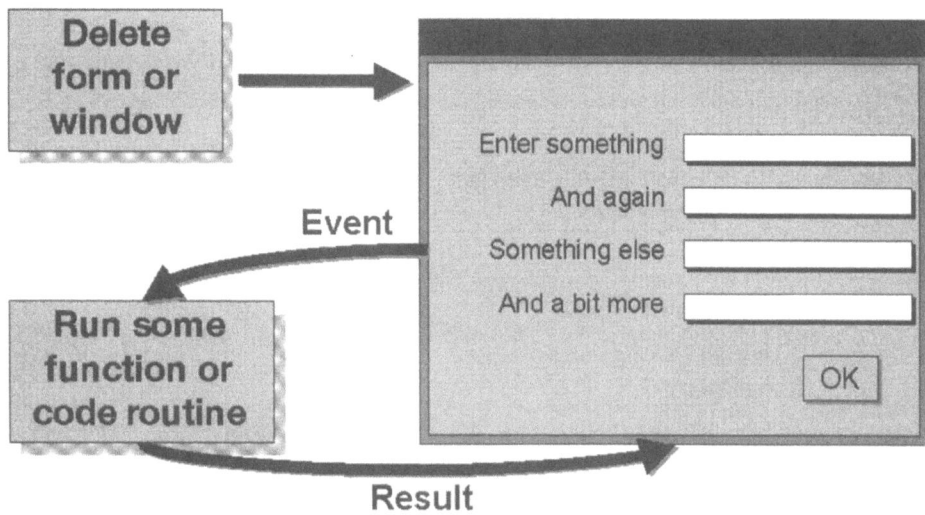

Figure 1-2. The event-driven programming cycle

In this scenario, you only need to execute code in response to specific events, and generate output to update the areas of the page that need to be changed. Of course, to some extent, this isn't directly achievable using a Web browser and a Web server, because there is no persistent connection in the stateless environment that HTTP provides. The user still has to submit the page to your server for processing, whereupon it is processed in a procedural manner.

However, ASP.NET does provide an architecture that allows you to get close to your stated requirements. It is achieved through the *postback architecture* on which ASP.NET is built, and the features that are implemented as part of this overall architecture. To get the most from ASP.NET, it's important to be familiar with this architecture, and you'll be looking at this in some detail.

But before then, you need to explore the underlying construction and processing of ASP.NET pages in relation to their script-based predecessors. In particular, it's important to realize just how different these underlying processes are, and how they provide the environment we're looking for to create applications that are truly event-driven.

The ASP.NET Page As a Compiled Class

In previous versions of ASP, and in other Web server scripting environments such as JSP and PHP, code is executed as it occurs within the page, in the order that the page-parsing engine and the script interpreter encounter it. Anything that is not server-side script code is simply fed back to the client, via the Web server, "as is." So, for an ASP 3.0 page, for example, the process might look something like Figure 1-3.

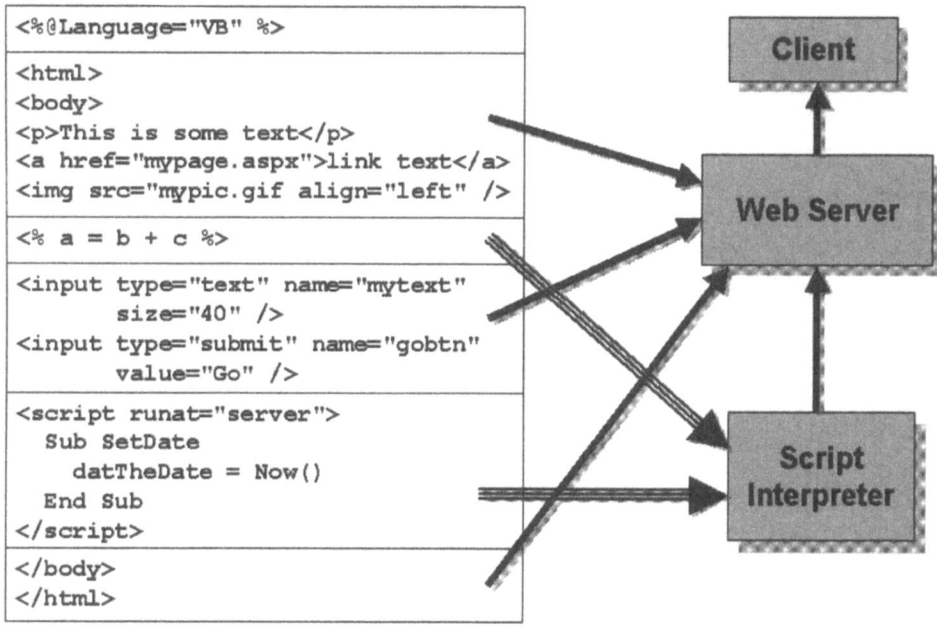

Figure 1-3. How an ASP page is interpreted

However, in ASP.NET, the process is completely different. The appropriate .NET Framework language compiler converts every page into a *class* file, using MSIL (Microsoft Intermediate Language) code. Content that is not server-side code is converted into a series of output.Write statements within the class, in much the same way as you might have used Response.Write in ASP 3.0 (this is similar to the way that JSP pages are converted to servlets by most Java application servers). In extremely simplified form, what ASP.NET is actually executing looks something like the following (I've added the comments to indicate what's happening):

```
Public Class MyPage_aspx
  Inherits System.Web.UI.Page    '<-- the base class for the page
  ...

  'your own server-side code and event handlers go here
  Sub Page_Load()
    ...
  End Sub
  'routines to create the server-side controls declared in the page
  Private Sub BuildControlMyControl1
    ...
```

```
      End Sub
      Private Sub BuildControlMyControl2
        ...
      End Sub
      'routine to build the complete tree of controls for the page
      Private Sub BuildControlTree
        ...
      End Sub
      'routine to create the output to send to the client
      Private Sub Render_Control1    '<-- rendering the complete page
        ...
        output.Write("<html><body><h1>Welcome to my page</h1>")
        ...
        'tell each individual control to render itself to the output
        ChildControl.RenderControl(output)
        ChildControl.RenderControl(output)
        ...
        output.Write("</body></html>")
        ...
      End Sub
    End Class
```

Obviously, this process means a performance hit when compared to simply executing the server-side code as in ASP 3.0, but ASP.NET also writes this code to a disk file within the folder \Winnt\Microsoft.NET\Framework\[version]\Temporary ASP.NET Files\ using a randomly generated file name and with the .dll file extension. It becomes a .NET assembly that is then executed by the Framework the next time that this page is requested, without having to be parsed and compiled again.

You can view the contents of these compiled assemblies using the ildasm tool that is provided with the Framework. An easier way to confirm what is going on is to look at the code that the compiler has generated when a compilation error occurs in a page (Figure 1-4).

Within the code that will form the class file (once you sort out the compilation error) you'll see any server-side code that you placed in the page, plus the code that builds the complete tree of objects that make up the final class. The point to take away from this is that everything you place within an ASP.NET page becomes an object, and not just some arbitrary text or HTML that will be sent to the client as it stands. The class exposes a Page object, and within that a host of objects that represent every server control, every block of text and other content, and every other object that is referenced (Figure 1-5).

Why is this useful? You'll see more as you look at server controls shortly, but what it does mean is that now—to send this page to a client after it has been compiled—all ASP.NET has to do is execute the MSIL code within this assembly. This is something that the Framework is optimized to do very quickly, and so you get great performance.

Figure 1-4. Viewing the compiled source for a page

All the extra work involved in building the tree of objects that make up the page only has to be done once, the first time it is requested by any client. Of course, if the source code for the page is edited, the compiled assembly file is automatically invalidated and removed, so the next request for the page will generate a new assembly. Furthermore, as the assemblies are written to disk, the MSIL code also survives a server reboot.

Figure 1-5. Everything in the page is an object

The ASP.NET Postback Architecture

As I assume that you have already experimented with ASP.NET, built a few pages, and understand the basic way it works, I won't present a tutorial or a full reference to the technology here. Having looked at the underlying processing model, what I want to do is make sure you grasp the fundamentals of the various features on which you will depend when building interactive pages using ASP.NET.

Posting to the Same Page

As I mentioned earlier in this chapter, the usual approach to handling user input before ASP.NET arrived had been to use two separate pages—a static page containing a <form> section, which has its action attribute set to point to a dynamic page that handles the values posted from that form. The second page might display a confirmation message, or contain another <form> section to collect more values from the user (Figure 1-6).

Figure 1-6. Posting values to a different page in ASP

However, one technique that has grown in popularity is to create a single dynamic page that contains not only the <form> section, but also the server-side code that handles the input and generates a suitable page to return to the client. The form is posted back to this same page each time (Figure 1-7). This often makes the overall design of the site easier to manage, but it adds complexity to the page itself. The code has to decide if this is the first request by the client for this page, or if it is the result of the client submitting the page (in which case there are values that have been posted to the server).

both.asp

```
<form action="both.asp">
<input type="text"
        name="txtThis"/>
<input type="submit" />
</form>

<%
strText = Request("txtThis")
If strText <> "" Then
  Response.Write(strText)
End If
%>
```

Figure 1-7. Posting values back to the SDame page

Server-Side ASP.NET Forms

ASP.NET includes the concept of a *server-side form*, where the <form> element is itself a server control that contains the runat="server" attribute. In this case, you have no choice but to post back to the same page—ASP.NET prevents the action attribute from being set to a different page. In fact, all you need to declare is the <form> control element itself and allow ASP.NET to fill in all the attributes that are required when it creates the control at runtime:

```
<form runat="server">
... form controls here ...
</form>
```

This is where the term *postback architecture* comes from, because you always post the values from a server-side ASP.NET <form> to the same page that contains the <form> declaration. If the page you are creating is called both.aspx, the simple definition above produces the following output and sends it to the client:

```
<form name="_ctl0" method="post" action="both.aspx" id="_ctl0">
... form controls here ...
</form>
```

Notice that as well as setting the action attribute to the current page, it also sets the method to "post" so that the values will be available in the Form collection. In ASP 3.0 (and, of course, in HTML) the default for the method, if not specified, is the value "get." In this case the values are sent as part of the query string when the form is submitted, and they appear within the ASP QueryString collection.

What the postback architecture gives us is the ability to create a page containing HTML form controls, and have that page displayed all the time so that users can interact with it and submit the values they enter to the server—but all the time seeing the same page. It becomes more like the event-driven approach that I discussed earlier, and certainly resembles a normal window-based application more closely than the earlier technique of having a separate page that handles the submitted values.

However, replicating the behavior of a normal executable application window is still a way off. There are three obvious limitations:

- The form still has to be submitted to the server in full each time for processing

- The values of the controls are not normally maintained when the postback occurs

- The user sees a page reload each time

ASP.NET attempts to answer these limitations for us in various ways. You look at these ways next.

Emulating Individual Control Events

Although you have a page that appears like an event-driven window-based application interface, there is still the limitation that it is only reacting to a single event—the page being submitted to the server. However, recall that your page is compiled into a class file that gets executed by the .NET Framework. This means that code in the page, and in the ASP.NET runtime processor, can provide an extra layer of capabilities on top of the simple Request and Response objects that are used in ASP 3.0 and earlier.

In effect, the code you write can tell from the request (you'll see how later) if this is a postback, or if this is the first time that the page has been loaded. It can also tell which control on the page caused the page to be submitted, and even if the current value of any control has changed since the page was sent to the client. This means that ASP.NET can expose a whole range of different events, depending on what interaction took place client-side in the page.

For example, the page can expose a Click event for the control that was clicked to cause the page to be submitted, or a Change event if the currently selected value in a list control is different from that selected when the page was sent to the client. All this is baked into the architecture, and you don't have to do anything to implement it yourself. Just write event handlers to react to the individual events.

For example, the following code creates an ASP.NET server-side form containing four controls: a text box, a drop-down list, a check box and a **Submit** button:

```
<form runat="server">
<asp:textbox id="MyText" text="OriginalValue"
             ontextchanged="MyChangeCode" runat="server" />
<asp:dropdownlist id="MyListBox"
                  onselectedindexchanged="MyChangeCode" runat="server">
  <asp:listitem text="Option 1" value="Value1" runat="server" />
  <asp:listitem text="Option 2" value="Value2" runat="server" />
  <asp:listitem text="Option 3" value="Value3" runat="server" />
</asp:dropdownlist>
```

```
<asp:checkbox id="MyCheckBox"
              oncheckedchanged="MyChangeCode" runat="server" />
<asp:button id="MySubmitButton" text="Submit"
            onclick="MyClickCode" runat="server" />  
</form>
```

I have attached an event handler to one of the events of each control, for example the OnTextChanged event for the text box control, and the OnClick event of the **Submit** button. You can handle these events by inserting an event handler into the server-side code section of the page. In fact, I've included two event handlers—one for the "change" events from the text box, list, and check box controls, and a separate one for the "click" event from the button:

```
<script runat="server">
Sub MyChangeCode(objSender As Object, objArgs As EventArgs)
  divResult.InnerHtml += "Change event detected for control '" _
                         & objSender.ID & "'<br />"
End Sub
Sub MyClickCode(objSender As Object, objArgs As EventArgs)
  divResult.InnerHtml += "Click event detected for control '" _
                         & objSender.ID & "'<br />"
End Sub
</script>
```

Now, if I change the values in the three controls and submit the page by clicking the **Submit** button, the following is displayed:

```
Change event detected for control 'MyText'

Change event detected for control 'MyListBox'

Change event detected for control 'MyCheckBox'

Click event detected for control 'MySubmitButton'
```

Other events can be handled in a page; these are only a few examples. And, as well as client-initiated events like those you've just seen, there are also server-initiated events that you can handle. Examples are the Page_Load event, or events such as OnDataBound that occur for data-bound controls.

Server-Side and Client-Side Event Handling

What is important to grasp is that all the events you saw in the previous code listing are *handled server-side*, in the ASP.NET code, even though they represent actions that *occurred client-side* in the browser. Some occur immediately, because they cause a postback to occur (as is the case with the Click event for the **Submit** button).

Others occur belatedly, such as the Change events for the other controls. This is because they can't be raised on the server until a postback occurs.

Of course, there's nothing to prevent a page from containing the usual client-side event handlers as well; for example you can still write client-side code that is executed in response to a form being submitted or a button being clicked. That code can manipulate the controls on the page, or the page content via Dynamic HTML. But this is an entirely separate process from handling events on the server. Client-side code can't be used to handle ASP.NET-specific events.

This can be a confusing state of affairs until you start to get it straight in your head. There are three ways that events can occur and be handled:

- Events that are *initiated on the client* and *handled on the client*. These include, for example, the OnClick event for an HTML <input> element, the OnChange event for an HTML <select> list, and the OnSubmit event for an HTML <form> element.

- Events that are *initiated on the client* and *handled on the server*. These include, for example, the OnTextChanged event for an ASP.NET text box control and the OnCheckedChanged event for an ASP.NET CheckBox control.

- Events that are *initiated on the server* and *handled on the server*. These include, for example, the Page_Load event or the OnDataBound event for a data-bound control.

Where things often get complicated is when you come to events like OnClick or OnChange. If you declare a text box element using an <input> server-side control and define a value for the onchange attribute, what you are actually doing is specifying a client-side event handler for this element:

```
<input type="text" id="txtThis" onchange="MyChangeCode()" />
```

When this is rendered in the browser, the attribute is still present and the browser expects to find a client-side event handler named MyChangeCode:

```
<input name="txtThis" id="txtThis" type="text" onchange="MyChangeCode()" />
```

If you want to specify a server-side event handler for this control, you have to use the onserverchange attribute:

```
<input type="text" id="txtThis" onserverchange="MyChangeCode" />
```

When this is rendered to the client, no event handler attribute is included:

```
<input name="MyText2" id="MyText2" type="text" />
```

However, when the page containing this element is posted back to the server, a "change" event will be raised and ASP.NET looks for a server-side event handler named `MyChangeCode`.

Specifying Both Server-Side and Client-Side `OnClick` *Event Handlers*

The `OnServerXxxxxx` events are only defined for the HTML server-side controls (controls from the namespace `System.Web.UI.HtmlControls`). The ASP.NET Web Forms controls (controls from the namespace `System.Web.UI.WebControls`) generally have specifically named events such as `OnTextChanged` and `OnCheckedChanged`, which can't be confused with the standard client-side events that are defined in HTML.

The ones that differ, and cause most confusion, are the ASP.NET Web Forms `Button`, `ImageButton`, and `LinkButton` controls. These do have an `OnClick` property, but the matching event is handled *server-side*, and *not* client-side. This is due to the way that the Web Forms controls work internally. When they see an `OnClick` attribute in the control declaration, they use it to set up a connection for the event server-side, and they do not render the attribute to the client. So you can specify a handler in an ASP.NET page for one of these controls, using something like:

```
<asp:Button id="btnDoIt" Text="Do It" runat="server"
            OnClick="ServerClickCode" />
```

In this case, the event handler named `ServerClickCode` is executed *on the server* when the page is posted back. This postback happens automatically anyway, when the button is clicked, because ASP.NET renders this control as an `<input type="submit" />` element in the page it creates.

If you want to run code on the client when the button is clicked but before the page is submitted, one trick you can use with the `Button` control is to manually add a client-side attribute to the element that the ASP.NET control creates:

```
btnDoIt.Attributes.Add("onclick", "clientClickCode()")
```

What this does is add an `onclick` attribute to the `<input>` element itself without affecting the way ASP.NET processes the event. When the button is clicked this time, the client-side code defined in the `onclick` attribute is executed. After that, the form is submitted to the server and ASP.NET executes the server-side code in the event handler that is defined for the `OnClick` property of the control. So, effectively, you can arrange for an event to be raised on both the client and the server. I hope the following code makes this clearer:

```
<%@Page Language="VB" %>
<html>
<head>
<script language="JavaScript">
<!--
// client-side script section
function clientClickCode() {
```

```
    alert("Event executed on client");
}
//-->
</script>
</head>
<body>
<form runat="server">
  <!-- declare Button control with server-side event property -->
  <asp:Button id="btnDoIt" Text="Do It" runat="server"
              OnClick="ServerClickCode" />
</form>
</body>
</html>

<script language="VB" runat="server">
' server-side script section
Sub Page_Load()
  ' add client-side "onclick" attribute to element when page loads
  btnDoIt.Attributes.Add("onclick", "clientClickCode()")
End Sub
Sub ServerClickCode(o as Object, e as EventArgs)
  Response.Write("Event executed on server")
End Sub
</script>
```

The same approach works with the other two controls I mentioned earlier, the
ImageButton and the LinkButton. The ImageButton control is rendered on the client as
an <input type="image" /> element, and this automatically submits the form it's on
when clicked. The process is exactly the same as with a Button control. When you add
your own onclick attribute to the element, the code that gets rendered on the client
from an ImageButton looks like this:

```
<input type="image" name="btnTest" id="btnTest" src="myimage.gif"
       border="0" onclick="clientClickCode()"/>
```

However, the LinkButton control works in a different way, as you'll see in more
detail in the next chapter. It relies on a client-side script function that is automatically added to the enclosing <form>, and which causes the form to be submitted
when the link created by the control is clicked. It works by specifying a JavaScript
URL (a function name preceded by the word javascript:) as the href attribute of an
<a> element.

So your onclick attribute can be added as well, and will execute your client-side
event handler before the function defined in the href attribute. Again, this is the kind
of result that is rendered in the browser from the control when you add your own
onclick attribute to the element:

```
<a id="btnTest" onclick="clientClickCode()"
   href="javascript:__doPostBack('btnTest',")">test</a>
</form>
```

Of course, you can use the Attributes collection to access any attributes of an element that an ASP.NET control creates, and add any attribute you want to the output of the control. You'll see more examples later in the book as you build your sample Web site.

So, after all this, you should be able to see how the ASP.NET approach to server-side programming in a Web page is extremely innovative when compared to previous technologies, and also gives us the clean and extensible structure that everyone is looking for. You can handle individual events for controls, and benefit from the kind of event-driven programming technique that you want. More to the point, this also reduces the code that you have to write, as well as making it much simpler to develop and maintain dynamic pages.

Control Values and Viewstate

The second major issue with building dynamic pages, once you adopt the "one-page" approach using postbacks to the same page, has always been how to maintain the values of the controls as the user submits data for processing. In ASP 3.0 and earlier (and in most other dynamic page generation technologies), the values that the user enters into the HTML controls on the page disappear each time the page is reloaded, unless you specifically write code to reinstate them.

The usual approach has been to simply insert the values from the Request.Form or Request.QueryString collection into the appropriate controls as you rebuild the page:

```
<input type="text" name="txtThis"
       value="<% = Request.Form("txtThis") %>" />
```

Of course, it gets more complicated with list controls and radio buttons, as you then have to figure out which one was selected and add a selected="selected" attribute to the appropriate <option> element, or a checked="checked" attribute to the appropriate <input type="radio"> element.

ASP.NET does away with all this messing about. When a page is posted back to the server, ASP.NET automatically extracts the values of the controls from the request and populates these controls with the values that they contained when the page was submitted. This feature alone can save a great deal of coding when you are providing pages that behave like a proverbial window-based executable application.

This is because ASP.NET implements a new concept called *viewstate*. No doubt you've already seen the hidden-type <input> control that ASP.NET automatically adds to a server-side <form>:

```
<form name="_ctl" method="post" action="test.aspx" id="_ctl">
  <input type="hidden" name="__VIEWSTATE" value="dDwxNzI5M...qQThw" />
  ... other controls here ...
</form>
```

The viewstate contains an encoded representation of two aspects of the current page: the *control tree* that makes up the page (which means that it can prevent spoofing by only allowing the viewstate to be posted back to the same page as that in which it was created), and the *values of various controls* on the page. Viewstate can be enabled or disabled for a page, or individually for each control. By default, it is enabled and persisted for all the controls on a server-side <form>.

When the page is posted back to the server, it can extract from the viewstate the values that were in the controls when the page was last generated by ASP.NET, and compare these with the current values. This is how it can detect if the user has changed the value of a control—as in the earlier example of the OnTextChanged and OnCheckedChanged events. It's also how it detects if this is a postback, or if it is the first time that this client has loaded the page.

Viewstate is also used to store values that are required for more specific purposes. For example, when you use an ASP.NET DataGrid control and take advantage of the automatic paging feature it provides, viewstate is required to store details about the current page and which page should be shown next.

Using Viewstate As a Storage Medium

Viewstate also has the advantage of being independent of things like ASP.NET Sessions, or other server-dependent techniques of storing user-specific data, because it is encoded within the page that is submitted to the server each time. And while server controls automatically persist their values to the viewstate, and extract these values when a postback occurs, you can also use this feature yourself to pass values between pages. It is a useful alternative to hidden-type <input> controls or the query string.

To add a value, which must be a String, to the viewstate for a page, just use:

```
ViewState("keyname") = ValueToStore
```

You extract the value when the page is reloaded using:

```
ValueExtracted = CType(ViewState("keyname"), String)
```

In C#, the equivalent is:

```
ViewState["keyname"] = ValueToStore;
ValueExtracted = (String) ViewState["keyname"];
```

If there is no value in the viewstate for the key name you provide, you get nothing returned. As with the Request.QueryString and Request.Form collections, the returned value is an empty string in this case.

To store objects that are not of type String, and which cannot be automatically cast into a String, you must serialize them into a String first and then resurrect them after extracting them from the viewstate. So an Integer type can be stored directly, whereas a DataSet cannot. However, you could serialize a DataSet object to a String containing an XML representation of the data, store it in the viewstate, and then extract it afterwards and read it back into a DataSet.

Disabling Viewstate

Viewstate applies to many types of controls, not just the HTML form controls. For example if you set the text or content of a <span> or <div> element that contains the runat="server" attribute in your server-side code, this will be maintained across post-backs by default, using the viewstate. Likewise, the complete contents of a DataGrid control placed on a server-side <form> will be persisted.

However, there are often occasions where you don't actually need the viewstate to be persisted between postbacks. In these cases, the processing needed to generate it, decode it upon postback, and pass it twice across the network can be avoided by disabling it. For a complete page, including all the controls on it, you can add an instruction to the Page directive:

```
<%@Page Language="VB" EnableViewstate="False" %>
```

Some content is always stored in the hidden control named "__VIEWSTATE", even when viewstate is turned off for the page as a whole. This is the encoded representation of the control hierarchy, which is used to ensure that the page is correctly posted to the same one as it was generated by, in order to give some protection against a user spoofing the server by submitting a different page.

If viewstate is disabled in the Page directive, it cannot be "turned back on" for individual controls. However, you can leave viewstate enabled for the page as a whole, and then selectively disable it for individual controls to limit the viewstate size:

```
<span id="status" enableviewstate="false" runat="server" />
```

For "status" elements, perhaps an <asp:Label>, <span> or <div> that you use to display interactive messages or feedback, be sure to add the enableviewstate="false" attribute so that the existing values are removed when the page is regenerated on the server each time.

Preventing a Page Reload

The third issue I mentioned earlier about the way that ASP.NET attempts to provide a rich event-driven architecture over the Web is the problem of page reloads. No matter how clever the server-side processing is, the user still goes through the process of submitting the whole page, and then waiting for it to be reloaded.

One way to get around this is to use some component or browser feature on the client that can submit a request to the server and receive the response without actually reloading the visible page. Some developers implement this using a Java applet or even the XMLHTTP object that is part of the MSXML parser. However, it is always hard work, and usually limited to occasions where the server is only returning specific values. In other words, it is like calling a remote function or method on the server, receiving the result in the response, and using it to update some value in the page.

In ASP.NET, a new feature called *smart navigation* has been added. It only works at the moment in Internet Explorer 5 and above, as it uses the MSXML parser and Microsoft's own brand of Dynamic HTML to update the page being viewed in the client's browser.

Simply adding the SmartNavigation attribute to the Page directive automatically enables smart navigation:

```
<%@Page Language="VB" SmartNavigation="True" %>
```

This causes ASP.NET to add a hidden <iframe> element to the page, as well as to access a special client-side script file stored within the aspnet_client\system_web\ folder that is created within the default Web site on your server when ASP.NET is installed:

```
<IFRAME ID=__hifSmartNav NAME=__hifSmartNav STYLE=display:none
        src="javascript:smartnav=1"></IFRAME>
```

Now the client immediately reaps the benefits. When the client requests a page, the client-side script code that implements smart navigation automatically requests the new page behind the scenes, without allowing the existing page to be submitted to the server. When the client's browser receives the response from the server, it figures out which parts of the page have changed, and updates just these parts by injecting the new content into the DHTML object model for the page.

Smart navigation doesn't always produce "invisible" page reloads; a lot depends on how much of the page has changed. However, it certainly makes it appear a lot more like a "real" window-based application (rather than a Web page). It also has by-product advantages, such as the fact that it prevents long pages being scrolled back to the top each time the user hits a **Submit** button.

ASP.NET Server Controls

I talked about ASP.NET server controls in the previous sections of this chapter, and no doubt you are already pretty familiar with them and how they are used. However, there are a few points worth mentioning here—in particular when you should actually consider using them and when an ordinary declarative HTML control will do the job.

Any controls or elements declared in your ASP.NET pages that are *not* marked with the runat="server" attribute are not server controls. The HTML that declares them becomes part of the various string values that the output.Write statements in the compiled class file (which implements the page) send directly to the client.

However, server controls are implemented within an ASP.NET page as objects that become part of the control tree for that page. They are individually constructed by the compiler, and compiled into the page itself as a separate object. This obviously has an impact on the performance of the page, so you should really only use them when necessary. In general this is when:

- You need to access them in your server-side code, perhaps to set their property values, or react to events that they raise.

- You want to use controls from the System.Web.UI.WebControls namespace (controls that are prefixed with "asp:") that are not available as normal HTML controls. These controls must be defined with the runat="server" attribute. Examples are the DataGrid, Calendar, and AdRotator.

You should *not* need to use a server control:

- When the element is only used to run some client-side script, such as opening a new browser window or interacting with the content of the page through Dynamic HTML.

- For a **Submit** button that only submits the <form>, and you don't need to interact with the button itself in your server-side code.

- For a hyperlink that opens another page, and you don't need to set the properties for the hyperlink on the server.

- When there is no requirement to access the properties, methods, or events of the control.

Server-Side Data Binding

I mentioned that I often choose to use an ASP.NET server control when there is no equivalent HTML control. Of course, all the server controls actually emit HTML (and sometimes JavaScript)—because that's all the browser understands.

Some specialist controls can emit other types of output, for example the controls from the Microsoft Mobile Internet Toolkit (MMIT) can emit WML instead of HTML.

What makes some of the ASP.NET Web Forms controls special is that they can automatically emit a series of HTML elements that make up more complex compound output, rather than just a single control. One simple example of this is the <asp:checkbox> control, which outputs a <span> element for the caption of the check box as well as the <input type="checkbox"> element itself.

Where the ASP.NET server controls really become useful is for building complex output such as lists. There is a range of list controls from the simpler Repeater and CheckBoxList to the more complex DataList and DataGrid. These can be bound to data sources on the server, and they automatically create a list of items based on the contents of the data source.

The techniques for formatting the output that several of these controls generate is also easy to grasp, yet at the same time extremely powerful. By using templates for each part of the list, it's easy to create attractive lists in an ASP.NET page with minimum effort.

Other Useful ASP.NET Features

As you work through building the example site for this book, you'll be taking advantage of as many of the useful features of ASP.NET as you can, and learning how they make the whole process easier, faster, and less error prone. Among these techniques are:

- Using the ASP.NET Session object to store user-specific values

- Using ASP.NET built-in caching features to improve performance and site efficiency

- Using the authentication and authorization features that ASP.NET provides for Web pages

I touch on these briefly next, before moving on to look at the design for the example site.

ASP.NET Sessions

Like ASP 3.0 and earlier, ASP.NET provides both an Application and a user-specific Session object that you can use to store values that you want to persist across postbacks. These are useful, though they do absorb resources on the server and may not be an ideal solution for a site with very heavy traffic. One advance over ASP 3.0, however, is that cookie-less sessions can now be maintained using URL munging, where the session identifier is encoded into the URL itself rather than depending on the client supporting cookies.

The actual session content, the data, can also be stored in several ways. Rather than always storing it on the server that responds to the request (a problem in a Web farm where requests may be passed to different servers each time), the data can be stored on a specific server using the new ASP.NET State Server service, or even in a SQL Server database table.

Sessions provide an alternative to viewstate for storing data that has to be passed between pages. This approach avoids the extra overhead in bandwidth use that comes from storing it within the page in a hidden-type <input> control. However, it does add extra loading to the server-side processing as the session is located and "opened" with each request.

To avoid or reduce the overhead connected with using sessions in ASP.NET, you can disable session support for individual pages that don't need to access session data (in ASP 3.0 sessions could only be enabled or disabled at application level for all pages). You can also specify that session access is read-only for specific pages, which reduces the overhead somewhat by avoiding the extra stage of writing the data back to the session when page execution is complete.

ASP.NET Caching

ASP.NET provides a rich caching environment that you can take advantage of when building applications. As well as a global cache for each application, within which you can store values with predefined expiring conditions and triggers, you can take advantage of *output caching*. This is a great way to speed up delivery of pages that are always the same, or that do not vary much between each other (based on parameter values sent in the request).

When output caching is enabled for a page, the resulting HTML and content that ASP.NET generates by executing the page is cached automatically for a period defined by the OutputCache directive in the page. All subsequent requests for this page are met by ASP.NET simply sending back the output it created from executing the page that last time until the cached page expires.

Of course, this is only going to work if the content is not supposed to be different for each request, based on some value sent from the client in a <form> or in the query string. However, caching can be configured to take this into account, and a different copy of the page is generated and cached when the values sent from the clients differ.

While some care is required when configuring output caching to take into account the requirements for different clients and different request values, it's clear that it can be hugely beneficial in improving performance.

ASP.NET Authentication and Authorization

One area where Web developers have always had to build quite complex custom code routines is when you need to protect some or all of a site by demanding that the user log in by presenting some type of credentials. ASP.NET makes it much easier to implement this type of feature in any Web site or application through a range of built-in security features.

The most common security for public Web sites is *forms-based authentication*, which depends on a specially encoded cookie being delivered to the client, which is then used to access secured pages. Forms-based authentication is easy to implement using the objects that are part of the .NET Framework, and I demonstrate it in the example application in this book.

For intranet sites, another option that ASP.NET provides is integration with the built-in Windows authentication features, using the accounts and groups that are defined within Windows itself. Finally, there are also features that allow ASP.NET sites to take advantage of Microsoft's own Passport authentication service.

All the topics I've been discussing are covered in depth in other publications that are devoted to ASP.NET itself, and so I haven't gone into great detail here. For more information, check out: *Moving To ASP.NET: Web Development with VB .NET* (Apress, ISBN 1-59059-009-0).

Designing an Interactive Web Site

Having spent time looking at why you should choose ASP.NET as the foundation for your Web sites, and seeing some of the extremely useful features it provides, I can move on to show you the process I used to design the example site you'll see being developed throughout the remainder of this book. I start with a look at the overall aims of the site, the general approach to planning it, and the design I came up with for the basic structure.

The Overall Site Design

Designing a Web site is a process that you can tackle in many different ways. However, more than many other kinds of application that you might build, the design process involves two completely different areas of expertise. A competent programmer can build the back-end interfaces, components, and logic code, and probably put together a half-reasonable user interface as well. But, for a public Web site, there needs to be input from one or more people who have at least a modicum of flair for graphical design.

I don't profess to be accomplished in this area, and for others in the same position it might prove beneficial to employ an outside agency or contractor who is expert in this field. However, even when you separate the graphical design from the physical development process, both the basic structural design of a site and its actual appearance should be based on something that meets the requirements of both the site owner and the visitors who will use it.

Requirements Analysis

As with any other software project, a good place to start is with *requirements analysis*. There are plenty of authoritative textbooks out there that describe the complete process for collecting the information required and pulling it all together into a cohesive plan. And while this is no doubt extremely necessary for applications that have to manage the day-to-day running of your corporation, the process for gathering requirements for a Web site is harder to specify in absolute terms.

You might decide to ask visitors to an existing site what they feel is wrong with it, and what they would like to see. It's also a good idea to ask your staff the same questions, plus any existing customers or users who you can track down directly. You might also decide to take a look at competitors' sites, or even just surf around looking at different kinds of Web sites to see if their approaches would suit your requirements.

Even after all this, you may still end up with a mixed set of requirements. It's just too easy to end up with a list that contains things like "we want it to look like this but in red," or "we ought to have a page where you can read product reviews." All this is useful input, but it needs to be carefully separated out into the two areas I mentioned at the start: the structure and workings of the site versus the physical appearance and "look and feel."

The Basic Site Structure

So, having said all that, how do you get started once the opinions, preferences, bright ideas, and other input have all been collated? My favorite approach involves the minimum of tools—a pen and lots of paper. Step one is then to get down on paper the overall structure for the site, showing the main pages you think will be required to give the features you want, and how they are related and linked to each other.

Next, you can add in other features if required, for example those miscellaneous requirements such as a page to display the terms and conditions of trading, or a contact page. What's important is to make sure that the pages you don't include in the first iteration are not "foundation" pages. In other words, that they are pages or features that you can add later without causing a complete redesign of the original structure.

Of course, you can never be sure that future requirements won't upset the applecart and prompt a major redesign. But it's usually possible from the requirements analysis to tell which features are the most important and form the basis for the complete site. They're usually the ones at the top of everyone's list, and crop up most often in discussions about the site requirements.

The Xrox Car Company

OK, so it's time to take the plunge. Table 1-1 shows the completed list of the requirements I used to start designing and building the **Xrox Car Company** site.

Table 1-1 Xrox Car Company Web Site Requirements

Feature	Description	Notes on Description
Home Page	Display news about the company	Show special offers and new models Display details of events that might interest visitors and customers Provide a list of car models that links to more details pages about each one Include links to Terms and Conditions, Contact page, and so on
Page for Each Car Model	Show options, colors, and extras available for that model	Display vehicle image in chosen color Allow visitors to customize the vehicle and see the cost of that customized version Show the credit (hire-purchase) terms and calculate the payments required Provide a link to reviews about that model Provide a link to allow visitors to place an order for the car they choose
Page to Compare Model Features	Allow visitors to choose different sets of features to compare	Economy, Performance, Standard Features, Running Costs, and so on Use graphical displays, pie charts, line graphs, and bar charts Open from "Home" page, and possibly from individual model pages (to be decided)
Order Page	Collect data on the configuration already specified by the customer	Collect payment and delivery information Send email order acknowledgement Process order and send email confirmation Maybe print invoice as well?
Future Extensions	Allow visitors to configure site style and appearance	Personalization Provide a Search feature although everything should be easy to find anyway

This is probably a far simpler set of requirements than many "real-world" sites during their design phase, but it is compact enough for me to have a chance of building it all without requiring a book six inches thick to describe it. It also includes all the major user interface implementation features that I want to be able to investigate in this book.

So, coming back to your pen and paper (and just to prove that I do actually follow my own advice) Figure 1-8 shows the first working sketch I made for the **Xrox Car Company** site based on the requirements listed earlier:

Figure 1-8. The Xrox Car Company high-level structure view

The design is a fairly common approach for any site that has multiple products to sell. The main functionality is in the dynamic page that will generate the details of each vehicle model based on a key or ID value that is passed into the page appended to the query string in the usual way. The Home page will also be interesting to build in that it needs to obtain the data for the news, events, and special offers from the back-end database that I'll be using to power all this.

The Data Source

Having just slipped into the narrative the topic of a database, this is also something that you need to consider before the design proceeds too far. In the **Xrox Car Company** example site, you have the luxury of being free from any existing constraints on the nature and source of the data that will drive the site. You can provide a set of data structures, tables, and columns that suit your requirements because you're building the database as well as the site.

Of course, this isn't always the case. Often you have an existing database or other data source that you need to connect to and access. This book is about user interfaces, not data management, so I don't consider data integration issues in any detail here. However, in general you can extract data from existing data stores using either SQL statements or (preferably) stored procedures to get almost any combination of table and column values. This might not be as efficient as in a database specifically designed and structured to suit the Web site you're building, and you may consider using some kind of data replication or staged bulk data transfer process to fill a more suitable database from the "production" data store that contains the original data.

Client-Side Processing

One focus of this book is a detailed examination of how you can distribute the processing load in a data management application to the client, using client-side scripting and objects such as an XML parser instantiated on the client machine. This approach not only relieves the server of considerable processing load by minimizing postbacks, but also produces a more interactive interface in the browser and better-perceived performance by the client.

In the **Xrox Car Company** application, I'm focusing on the use of the ASP.NET Web Forms controls, and other server controls, so most of the interaction with the pages will produce a postback to the server. However, you can still consider including client-side processing where it provides appreciable improvements in either interactivity or perceived performance.

For example, you can get far better control over the location and appearance of pop-up windows if you open them using client-side script rather than an ordinary hyperlink. However, this means that clients that don't support client-side scripting (or where it is disabled) won't be able to open the window. You can get around this problem by implementing a client-side script check within the application, and changing the behavior of the pages to suit each client.

The Home Page

Now that you have an idea about the structure of the site, you can start to look at the individual pages in more detail. It's here that the second set of requirements collected earlier come into play, as you can start to think about what the pages might look like as well as what they contain and how they might be implemented. The sketch of the **Home** page layout is shown in Figure 1-9.

Figure 1-9. The Xrox Car Company "Home" page

It would be nice if the graphical banner was animated in some way, and perhaps animation will be implemented using a client-side script where it is available. The example also omits the "login" controls in the first iteration, though it's useful to have an idea about how they will be integrated into the site later.

The list of text links at the bottom will appear on every page of the site, so you need to build some kind of reusable control for this. The most obvious approach, and one you'll implement, is to create it as a User Control that you can insert into any page.

The remainder of the page content is generated dynamically from your database, containing the news, events, and special offers in the left column and a list of car models in the right column. You should consider using different background colors to separate them visually. Even though these lists are dynamically generated, the data doesn't change very often—perhaps daily at the most—so this page is a good candidate for output caching to improve performance.

The Ingredients for the Home Page

The ingredients you need for the Home page are:

- Something eye-catching and graphical for a banner at the top.

- Some "button" controls to open the other pages linked from the Home page. You should consider dynamically changing the page to use "submit" buttons, rather than the Web Forms Button control, if the client doesn't support client-side scripting (you see why in the next chapter).

- A list-type control for the news and events section, probably a DataList or Repeater. Items displayed here might contain links to open other pages containing detailed reviews or more information on any topic shown in the list.

- A control to display a list of car models, again probably a DataList or a Repeater. Each car image and model name will be a link to the detail page for that model.

- A server-side ‹form› and two text box controls for the "login" section, when you decide to implement this.

- A User Control for the reusable page footer, probably one that displays the current page link in a different color to aid navigation.

The Car Model Details Page

This page is at the heart of the sample application, and is the one that visitors will use the most. It is nice to provide a lot of information about each vehicle, and allow visitors to specify complex configuration options and "add-on" extras (so that they spend more money!). You could implement different pages for each model of vehicle; for example one for the colors, one for the engine details, and one for the finance packages that are available.

The Color Options Section

I chose a more compact approach that I think makes the site feel more like a one-stop operation. Users can more easily see where they are and what options are available. I chose to use a frameset that holds three different pages, and in one of these pages I incorporated a tabbed dialog appearance. Figure 1-10 is the sketch I produced, showing what the page will look like when a user chooses the color of the new car.

Figure 1-10. The Xrox Car Company "Color Options" page

An image of the car and a brief description (marketing "blurb") are shown in the top frame, with a link to open a page where reviews about the car are displayed. In the central frame the tabbed "dialog" page shows the different areas of customization and detailed information that are available for each model. Visitors can choose the color scheme they are interested in here, and the site responds by changing the color of the image in the top frame to match so they can see what their new car will look like.

The lower frame contains the calculated cost for the vehicle with the currently selected options, and the finance terms for the vehicle. There's also the all-important button to allow them to place their order whenever they are ready.

Using a Frameset

One immediate issue that many readers may raise here is that using frames is "old-fashioned," and they are no good on many kinds of simple Web-browsing devices. They also make navigating the site more complicated and prevent the **Back** button from working properly in the browser. It's a formidable list of objections, but frames also have some distinct advantages.

The goal is to make the page as interactive as possible, but it is obviously going to be a big page (source-code wise), and will require quite a lot of processing on the server each time it's requested. By breaking it up into three frames, and only reloading the ones that actually need to be changed, you can reduce the bandwidth usage and processing effort.

Frames also allow the user to carry on interacting with the page in one frame while the other frame is reloading. This is ideal for the sample's lower frame, which can go off and recalculate the price while the user decides what other extras he or she can afford.

Other Approaches

In some respects, smart navigation could help to minimize the page reloads that the user would see if you didn't use frames, but this still requires the complete page to be sent from the server to the client each time. While the user wouldn't see the page reloading, the server would still have to work just as hard, and the time taken for the page to be delivered over the network would not be reduced. On top of this, smart navigation only works in Internet Explorer 5.0 and later at present.

Alternatively, you might decide to use <iframe> elements to build separate areas of the page that could be refreshed individually. This has the advantage over using a <frameset> in that it has less impact on navigation, but (despite being defined in the HTML 4.0 recommendations) the <iframe> element is relatively Internet Explorer-specific. Until version 6.0, Opera and Navigator did not recognize it.

The Ingredients for the Color Options Section

So, the ingredients you need for this page can be divided into three sections: one for each frame within the page. For the top frame you need:

- A panel of some kind to hold the description, perhaps within a table that fills the window or in an ASP.NET Panel control.

- A button of some type, perhaps a clickable image, to show reviews for this model.

- An Image control to display the picture of the vehicle, and you'll change the color that is displayed as visitors select a color in the central frame.

- Possibly another button to open the "Compare Features" page, if you decide to implement a link from this page to it.

For the central frame you need:

- A tabbed dialog or "tabstrip" control to display the five "option section" tabs.

- A few RadioButton controls to display the color style options.

- An ASP.NET Table control, with TableRow and TableCell controls to create the table of vehicle colors dynamically as the color style is selected.

For the lower frame you need:

- Some Label controls to display the price and finance terms.

- A button of some type, perhaps a clickable image, to start the "order" process.

The Engine Options Section

Each model is available with a choice of engines, and the second tabbed page in the central frame will show these options (see Figure 1-11). For each one, you'll display the technical specifications of the engine, and you'll update the price and finance details in the lower frame when a visitor chooses an engine for his or her new car:

Figure 1-11. The Xrox Car Company "Engine Options" page

The Ingredients for the Engine Options Section

For this page, as well as the controls specified for the top and bottom frames, and the tab strip in the central frame, you need:

- A RadioButtonList control to show the engine options, which will be different for each model.

- A list control of some type to show the engine specifications. It might be a DataGrid or a DataList, or you may even resort to using XSLT to build the display if the specifications are provided in XML format.

The Optional Extras Section

Probably the most complex of the central frame pages will be the **Optional Extras** page. Each model will have a range of optional extras available for it, and users will be able to choose the ones they want from the list in this window. Again, as they do so, the price and finance terms in the lower frame will be updated to reflect the current selection (Figure 1-12).

Figure 1-12. The Xrox Car Company "Optional Extras" page

The Ingredients for the Optional Extras Section

For now, until you investigate the types of optional extra that are available, assume that you can use drop-down lists and/or option buttons to select each one. So, the list of requirements looks like this at the moment:

- A selection of DropDownList controls to display options when there are many different variations.

- A selection of RadioButtonList controls for options when there are only a few variations.

- Some clickable Image controls to display details and help for each optional extra category—probably in a pop-up window.

- Possibly some Validation controls to check user input and make sure the combination of options chosen is valid.

The Model Details Section

The Model Details page is designed to show details of a whole range of vehicle features that are not configurable. At the moment there isn't a definitive list of what they will all be, but it's likely to be things like the overall dimensions of the vehicle, the car's weight, fuel tank capacity, the number of seats, and so on.

The actual appearance of the display will again be decided once there are more actual data details, but the ideal is probably to provide a list divided into sections like those listed in the previous paragraph. It would also be nice to display these in such a way that the visitor can expand and collapse the sections to show the details (Figure 1-13).

Figure 1-13. The Xrox Car Company "Model Details" page

The Ingredients for the Model Details Section

To implement a collapsible list, there is a range of options. You might use any of the following:

- A TreeView control of some type, or perhaps two side by side. A client-side version would provide a highly responsive interface here.

- A list control such as a DataList or DataGrid, with child list controls to show the individual values for each section.

- An ASP.NET Xml control that uses an XSLT style sheet to transform the data into a collapsible list format that relies on client-side script.

- Alternatively, a simple list control such as a Repeater or DataList if you decide to avoid the expand/collapse feature.

The Finance Options Section

The Finance Options section is relatively simple from the user interface point of view, but involves complex server-side or client-side processing to calculate the values as the user selects the required payment plan. For speed and interactivity, it would be nice to perform the calculation client-side and update the totals in the lower frame without requiring a postback. However, as the previous sections will probably rely on a postback to obtain the values, this might not be possible.

Other opportunities are to use a Web Service to fetch the payment terms calculated on the server, but this is likely to be browser version-specific. In the long term it might be better just to force a page reload for the bottom frame and calculate the new terms on the server each time. Either way, the design for the page as a whole looks like the what you see in Figure 1-14.

Figure 1-14. The Xrox Car Company "Finance Options" page

The Ingredients for the Finance Options Section

As far as controls go, the only requirements are the following:

- A text box to enter the monthly payment amount.

- One or more Validation controls to check that a valid value has been entered.

- A DropDownList to select the number of months for the finance package to run.

- A Button control (probably a **Submit** button) to calculate the new terms.

The Compare Features Page

The goal is to make sure that your customers purchase a vehicle that is right for them, and that meets all their needs. The best way to do this is to allow them to compare various features of the range of vehicles directly, within the same page. It also gives you a chance to explore how ASP.NET can create charts and other graphical output directly using the Drawing classes that are included in the Framework class library.

The **Compare Features** page will consist of a list of models, a list of comparison types, and an area where a chart or other graphic that reflects the chosen model comparisons is displayed. It will also allow the user to compare as many models from the range as they wish (Figure 1-15).

Figure 1-15. The Xrox Car Company "Compare Features" page

The Ingredients for the Compare Features Page

To implement this page, you are going to need:

- A CheckBoxList control where the user selects the models to be included in the comparison.

- A RadioButtonList control (or individual RadioButton controls) to select the type of comparison required.

- An Image control to display the results of the comparison.

- Possibly a Button control to initiate the process, or it could be done directly when a comparison type is selected.

The Order Pages

One section of the site that hasn't had much attention to so far is how to actually place an order for a vehicle after the visitor has configured it and decided on the most suitable finance package. The process of building up and placing the order is intertwined with the way that you store details of the vehicle as the user configures it.

The focus of this book (as I've already said several times) is on the user interface design and construction, and not on the back-end processing. However, your dynamic site requires a back-end database, and this will be used to store vehicle configurations and order data, as well as supplying data for the user interface. In later chapters, as you build the pages for the site, you'll see how to connect to and work with this database.

The actual design and appearance of the order pages themselves is going to follow a fairly predictable path, as they will contain a series of text boxes, drop-down lists, and buttons that collect the remaining data needed to place an order.

Along the way, you'll be providing the visitor with a username and password that identifies them, and so you'll also implement a "login" dialog so that users can come back and buy more cars without having to fill in all the information again. This will be achieved using ASP.NET forms-based security techniques, and I'll examine this, together with the various pages and code used to create the login dialog and place the order, later in the book.

Other "Peripheral" Pages

The other pages you'll be implementing on your site are fairly simple, and probably not interactive. They include Terms and Conditions, About, and Contact pages, and possibly pages to display news, events, reviews, or features concerning the site or the products. At the moment, all of these are "peripheral" pages, in that they will not form part of the foundation structure of the site. They are simply opened from links on other appropriate pages. So, as far as design goes, you can put off any final decisions until you get the main parts of the site working.

What is known is that most of these pages will probably carry the same footer as the main site pages, and perhaps a header graphic that also appears on most of the pages on the site. You'll be adding these pages to the example application, but I won't be spending any time discussing them in detail, as they are unlikely to add anything extra to your exploration of user interface design and implementation.

Is It All Actually Achievable?

One thing you can see as the process goes along is that you can stay relatively relaxed for now about the exact techniques you'll use to build the pages. Rather than tying everything down too precisely yet, exploring the possibilities is useful in finding issues that might arise later, while allowing the design to evolve (and hopefully improve) as it becomes clearer in your mind.

The one risk is that something you plan to do will prove to be impossible when you actually start writing code, and there is nothing to protect you from this except experience and a thorough knowledge of ASP.NET and the server controls it provides. Usually, nothing is actually *impossible*, though it may turn out to be difficult to achieve, or hit performance so badly that it has to be abandoned.

The point here is that you haven't spent a huge amount of effort on the actual design process for the individual pages yet, and so backtracking and adapting the design is an acceptable option. You still have the original design for the overall site layout and structure in place to fall back on, and from there you can explore other possible approaches to implementation.

All in all, however, I'm fairly well satisfied with the design as it exists now, and I'm ready to crank up a computer and start building some pages. The cookbook is open to the appropriate recipe, the oven is hot, and it's time to get cooking.

Summary

In this first chapter, I started out by considering why ASP.NET provides such a great environment for building interactive user interfaces for Web applications and Web sites (or Wapplisites). At the heart of this is the event-driven programming model that the combination of server-side controls and the postback architecture provides. It makes it easier than ever before to build applications that look, feel, and work more like the traditional executable applications that were built before the Web was invented.

I also spent quite some time exploring the topic of the ASP.NET page-processing model, and the use of server controls. This was followed by a brief review of some of the other features that ASP.NET provides to make it easier to build high-performance applications.

Following this, I moved on to look at some of the basic principles involved in designing a Web site that will take advantage of the features of ASP.NET. The first steps involved analyzing requirements for the site, and then planning the overall structure.

All this is done without too much concern over the appearance of the site or the technical implementation, as it's more important to get the foundations right first.

Then I followed up by trying to plan the pages themselves, or at least the ones that form the core of the site. This is an iterative process, as you'll see, because it's difficult at this stage to combine the need for an attractive appearance and intuitive layout with the technical details of how the pages will actually be implemented. However, until you have a feel for the appearance and layout of the pages, it's even harder to try and envisage how they might be implemented—a kind of vicious circle that you often only escape from through trial and error.

The chapter ended with some sketches and lists of ingredients for the main pages you'll be building, but these are still somewhat vague specifications. What's important is that you have somewhere to start the construction process, and a relatively well-defined path to follow. Through the remaining chapters of this book, you'll be able to see whether the original design was anywhere near to meeting the original requirements, or whether some of the pages need to be redesigned to suit the needs of the users, requirements imposed on us by the data store, or the limitations of ASP.NET itself.

In summary, this chapter covered:

- Why ASP.NET provides a great environment for building interactive pages and sites

- The fundamental ways that ASP.NET makes building dynamic pages easier

- The built-in features of ASP.NET that you can use in your pages and applications

- The impact and reasoning behind using client-side and server-side processing

- How to approach designing a site to get the most from ASP.NET

Before starting to build the pages, however, the next chapter will help you get a better understanding of how the output generated by the ASP.NET Web Forms server controls can vary depending on the client that hits your site.

CHAPTER 2

Browser Compatibility with ASP.NET Server Controls

As YOU GET USED TO USING ASP.NET, it becomes very easy to throw together attractive and usable Web sites and applications by just dropping a few server controls, such as the DataGrid, Hyperlink, or Label, onto your pages. To get the appearance you want, you only have to set a few common properties, and leave the rest to the wonders of the ASP.NET runtime framework. After all, Microsoft has sorted out the issues of generating the appropriate HTML output from its server controls, so you don't need to worry about it.

In fact, this isn't always the case, and you *should* worry about the output that you are sending to the clients that access your pages. OK, so it's only in a few circumstances that it does affect the visible appearance or the workings of the page, but it's extremely useful to be aware of just what's going on behind the scenes when you use these controls.

The topics I'll be covering in this chapter are:

- A simple test application for examining the output generated by server controls

- How Microsoft defines which are "up-level" and which are "down-level" clients

- How the style attribute and <font> elements are used in up-level and down-level clients

- Working with more complex controls like the DataList and DataGrid

- How controls are affected by the lack of client-side scripting capabilities

- How the Panel control completely changes its output for the two types of client

- How output caching can affect browser compatibility

I start by looking at what it actually means to say that the ASP.NET Web Forms server controls are "intelligent."

Built-In Intelligence

During the Beta development cycle of ASP.NET, Microsoft suggested that many of the Web Forms server controls would be "intelligent." They would change their output depending on the client type accessing the page—allegedly to provide a better user experience in modern browsers. However, it turned out that the only visible evidence of this in the release version was in the validation controls, which provide client-side interactivity via Dynamic HTML in Internet Explorer 5 and later. Controls such as the Calendar, which would have benefited tremendously from some client-side code, failed to live up to the original high expectations.

But while there is little obvious evidence of the server controls being intelligent, there is stuff going on inside them that does affect the output they generate, depending on the type of client that hits the page. In the main (with a couple of interesting exceptions that I'll come to later), the differences are confined to the controls from the namespace System.Web.UI.WebControls (the controls prefixed "asp:"), and to the way that the visible appearance of the control is generated through the browser's rendering process.

As an example, Figure 2-1 shows a DataList control that sets the size for the text in the header, item, and alternating item rows to different sizes. You can see that in Navigator on the left, the sizes are not set correctly when the control is rendered in the page.

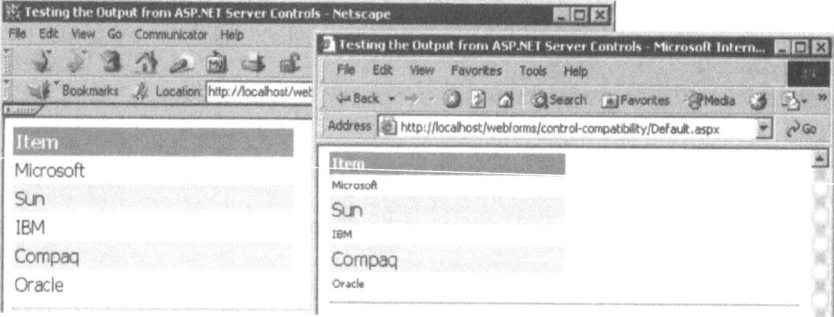

Figure 2-1. The DataGrid *control in Navigator and Internet Explorer*

The code used to create the control (omitting the section that generates the actual values) is shown next. You can see that I set the fonts for each row to specific pixel sizes. If I only test the page in Internet Explorer, I'll never know that it doesn't provide the effect I want in other browsers:

```
<asp:datagrid id="dgrTest" runat="server"
            forecolor="#000000"
            backcolor="#ffffff"
            cellpadding="3"
            gridlines="none"
            width="50%"
            font-name="tahoma,arial,sans-serif"
            font-size="14px">
```

```
<headerstyle forecolor="#ffffff"
             backcolor="#808080"
             font-name="tahoma,arial,sans-serif"
             font-size="12px"
             font-bold="true"
             wrap="false" />
<itemstyle   font-name="tahoma,arial,sans-serif"
             font-size="10px" />
<alternatingitemstyle font-name="tahoma,arial,sans-serif"
             font-size="16px"
             backcolor="#ffff00" />
</asp:datagrid>
```

A Test Application

I'll come back to look at this example later to see why the appearance is different and how to cure this. In the meantime, to demonstrate the controls and techniques I'll be exploring in this chapter, I built a simple test application that allows you to see the output created for different browsers, including those that you don't actually have installed. The code for this application is available to download from http://www.daveandal.com/ books/7868/ along with all the samples for this book (the zip file contains instructions for installing the sample files). You can run this example on your server, and modify it to experiment with other controls. Alternatively, you can just run it online directly from my server from the same URL.

The page you see in Figure 2-2 shows a list of the test pages I've provided, options to select the browser type you want to "pretend to be," and a button to fetch the page.

Figure 2-2. The example page for experimenting with server controls

After you request the page, the content is shown below these controls in the same page (Figure 2-3). It includes the user agent string that was sent to the test page, the content of the page rendered (as it would be if opened directly), the source (HTML and text) that was created by the page and returned to the browser, and the actual source code of the original test page file on disk.

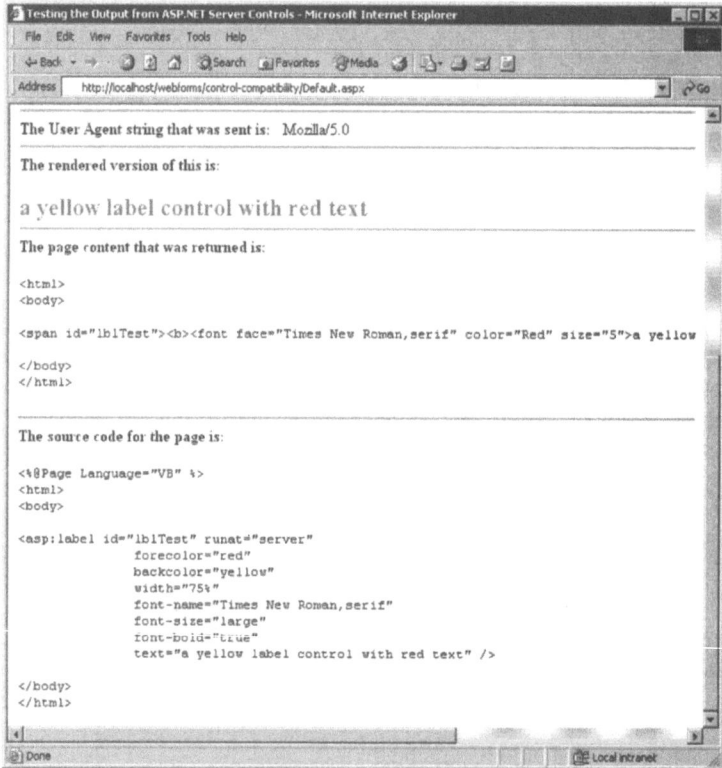

Figure 2-3. The output generated for a Label *control when pretending to be Netscape 6.0*

The list of pages that are available includes those that demonstrate working with the TextBox, Hyperlink, Calendar, Label, DataList, DataGrid, LinkButton, RequiredFieldValidator, and Panel controls. In later sections, I'll use all these to see how the output they generate affects the appearance of the page in different browsers.

The browsers that you can "pretend to be" in the sample application when sending the request to the test page are:

- **Current Browser**—the user-agent string of the browser you're using to run the test application is passed to the test page you request. This is the default.

- **Internet Explorer 6.0**—the user agent string sent to the test page is: **"Mozilla/4.0 (compatible; MSIE 6.0)"**

- **Internet Explorer 4.0**—the user agent string sent to the test page is: "Mozilla/4.0 (compatible; MSIE 4.0)"

- **Netscape 6.0**—the user agent string sent to the test page is: "Mozilla/5.0" (note that it's not 6.0 as you might expect).

- **Netscape 2.0**—the user agent string sent to the test page is: "Mozilla/2.0"

- **Opera 6.0**—the user agent string sent to the test page is: "Opera/6.0"

- **Unknown Browser (no script)**—the user agent for this option is just this: "Unknown Browser (no script)." It allows you to test your pages with what ASP.NET specifies as the default for browsers or other clients that it does not recognize, such as Web crawlers and spiders.

One interesting feature in Opera 6.0 is that you can tell it to pretend to be another browser. In the **File | Quick Preferences** menu, you can tell Opera to send a specific user-agent string to the server, and pretend to be Mozilla 3.0, 4.78, or 5.0, or Internet Explorer 5.0. In theory, Opera can support all the features of these browsers, and so you can see the different pages that are generated depending on the browser type.

Use a Selection of Browsers

One point to be aware of from the start is that the control appearance you see is generated *by the actual browser you are using to run the test page*. In other words, if you open the application in Internet Explorer and view a page pretending to be Navigator, you'll see IE's version of the rendered output. Navigator may render the same output differently.

So, while you do get the convenience of seeing what the server controls generate as output, you still need to make sure that this actually produces what you want in that particular browser. Of course, Microsoft has done a good job of tailoring the output for each client to give the closest result possible, but it's always worth a final check. I use Internet Explorer 6.0, Navigator 4.5, Opera 6.0, and Amaya 6.0 (the W3C reference browser) on the same machine with no problems. You can get the various browsers from the following sites on the Web:

- Internet Explorer: http://www.microsoft.com/windows/ie/default.asp

- Netscape Navigator: http://home.netscape.com/computing/download/index.html

- Mozilla: http://mozilla.org/

- Opera: http://www.opera.com/

- Amaya: http://www.w3.org/Amaya/

Viewing the Test Pages

Starting with a simple example, the test page asp-textbox.aspx contains a formatted text box. The TextBox control must be placed on a server-side <form>, and the code is simply:

```
<form runat="server">
<asp:textbox id="txtTest" runat="server"
    font-name="Arial,sans-serif"
    font-size="16px"
    font-bold="true"
    forecolor="red"
    backcolor="yellow"
    columns="30"
    width="75%"
    text="a yellow text box with red text" />
</form>
```

In Internet Explorer, using the **Current Browser** setting, this creates an <input type="text"> element that includes the style attribute to get the formatting specified in the code (Figure 2-4):

```
<input name="txtTest" type="text" value="a yellow text box with red text"
      size="30" id="txtTest" style="color:Red;background-color:Yellow;
                                    font-family:Arial,sans-serif;
                                    font-size:16px;font-weight:bold;width:75%;"
/>
```

However, when you run the same page in Navigator or Opera (or specify a user-agent string other than Internet Explorer 4.0 or 6.0), you get different output from the control:

```
<input name="txtTest" type="text" value="a yellow text box with red text"
      size="30" id="txtTest" />
```

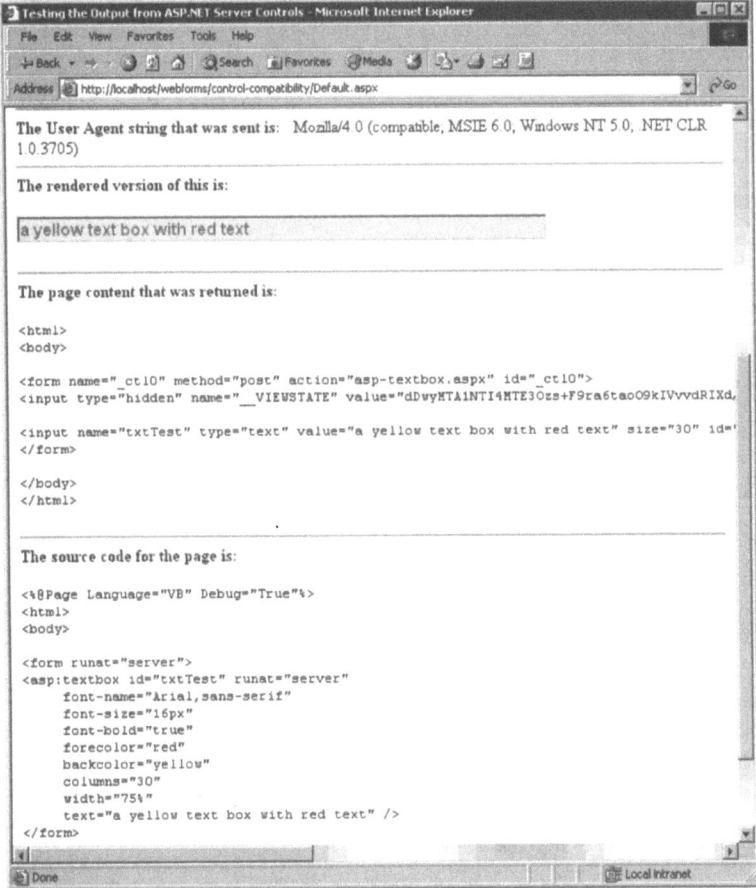

Figure 2-4. A TextBox *control in Internet Explorer*

There is no style attribute, so the page contains a simple version of the <input> element that just specifies the name, type, value, size, and id attributes (Figure 2-5). The font used is the default, and the text box is not 75 percent of the page width— and there's nothing you can do to change this behavior.

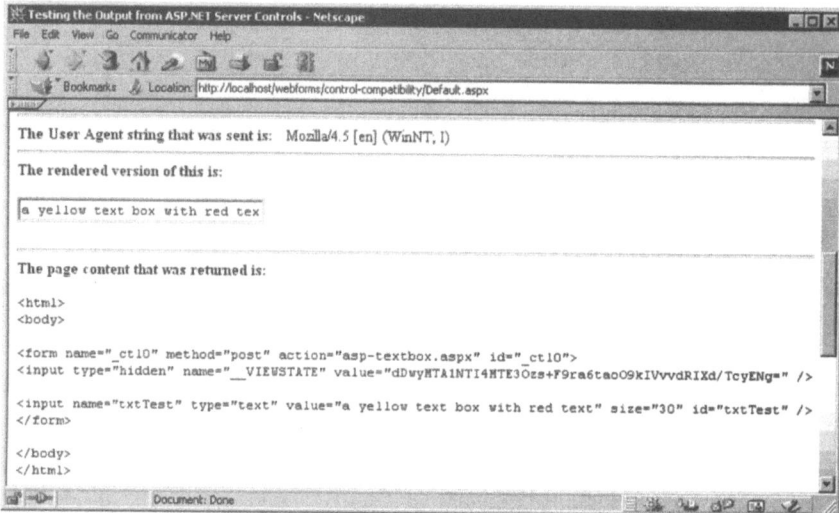

Figure 2-5. A TextBox *control in Navigator*

The Hyperlink Server Control

The next test page demonstrates a hyperlink <a> element, created by an ASP.NET Hyperlink server control. The code in the test page asp-hyperlink.aspx contains the following definition of a Hyperlink server control:

```
<asp:hyperlink id="lnkTest" runat="server"
               navigateurl="not-there.htm"
               forecolor="red"
               backcolor="yellow"
               font-name="Times New Roman,serif"
               font-size="large"
               font-bold="true"
               width="75%"
               text="a yellow hyperlink with red text" />
```

In Internet Explorer 5.0 and 6.0, as with the TextBox control, you get a style element that specifies the appearance and the width of the link:

```
<a id="lnkTest" href="/output-test/test-pages/not-there.htm"
   style="color:Red;background-color:Yellow;
          font-family:Times New Roman,serif;font-size:Large;
          font-weight:bold;width:75%;">a yellow hyperlink with red text</a>
```

However, in Navigator, Opera, and the other browsers, the control generates a <b> and a <font> element within the hyperlink instead:

```
<a id="lnkTest" href="/output-test/test-pages/not-there.htm">
   <b><font face="Times New Roman,serif" color="Red" size="5">
   a yellow hyperlink with red text</font></b></a>
```

This makes sense, as the <b> and <font> elements have been around for a long time and are widely supported. Notice also that the size attribute of the <font> element is set, but this can only be a number (where 1 is the smallest font size and larger numbers give larger sizes). If you look at the ASPX page code, you'll see I specified that the font-size property of the element should be "large". In IE this was interpreted as a font-size:Large style selector, whereas in other browsers this becomes a size="5" attribute of the <font> element.

The rendered output generated by the Hyperlink control in these two cases is shown in Figure 2-6—where you can see that only IE displays the proper width and background color.

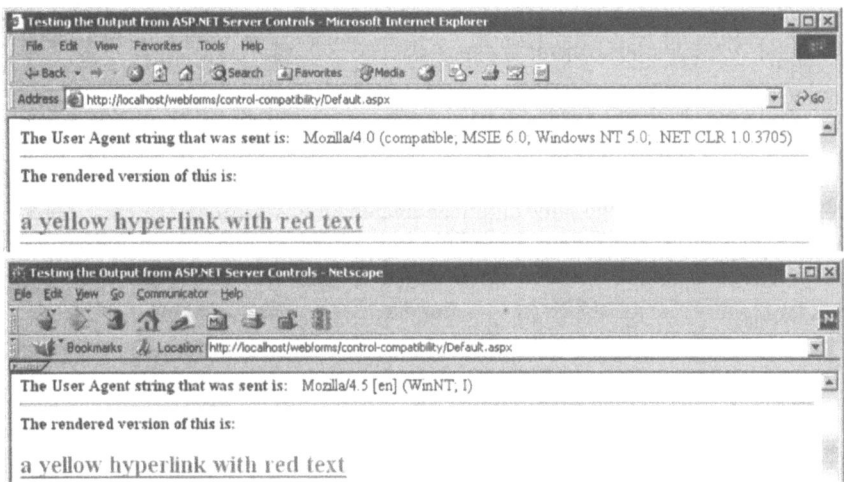

Figure 2-6. A Hyperlink *control in Internet Explorer and Navigator*

Note that, if I specify the font-size property as a specific pixel or point measurement (for example "16px" or "12pt"), it does not appear at all in the <font> element for non-IE browsers. In this case, the text of the hyperlink appears in the default font size for the page. The value for the font-size attribute has to be one of "xx-small", "x-small", "small", "smaller", "medium", "large", "larger", "x-large", or "xx-large".

You might be wondering about specifying one of these values for the font-size property in the earlier TextBox example, rather than the value "16px" used in that test page. Don't bother—it makes no difference. In HTML, you can't use a <font> element to set the size of the text within an <input type="text"> element, so the server control just ignores it.

Viewing the same page in Opera 6.0 (again with the **Current Browser** setting for the User Agent string) provides output almost identical to Navigator's. But remember that Opera always uses the default link color for the underline, though you can turn off the display of the underline in this particular browser if you wish (Figure 2-7).

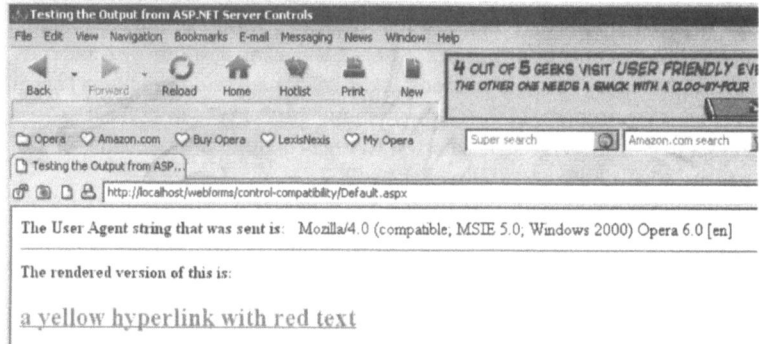

Figure 2-7. A Hyperlink *control in Opera 6.0*

And what about Amaya? If you haven't tried this browser, you'll probably be surprised at the way it renders things that are familiar to Windows developers in a totally different way. Figure 2-8 shows the same Hyperlink test page in Amaya 6.0 for Windows NT/2000/XP, for which the same output as created for Navigator and Opera is generated. Notice that Amaya indents hyperlinks from the left margin automatically.

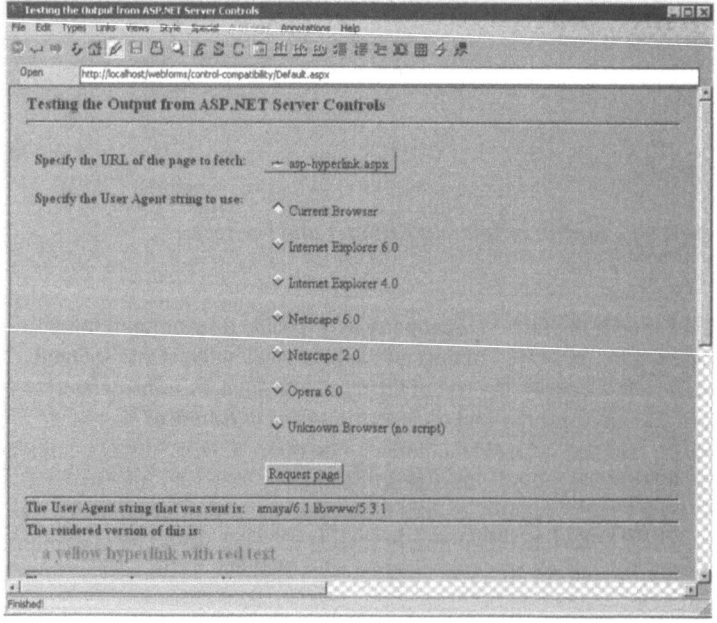

Figure 2-8. A Hyperlink *control in Amaya*

You might be interested to test all your pages against Amaya, as it is a good way to detect errors that other browsers have a neat habit of ignoring. Amaya also follows the original principles of the World Wide Web when it first came into being by allowing you to edit the page that is displayed. You can turn off this feature, and enable "normal" mode where single-clicking a link opens it, using the commands in the **Edit** and **Special** menus.

But Navigator Understands the Style Attribute!

Of course, just because ASP.NET doesn't send a style attribute to other browsers doesn't mean that they don't know what it is. In fact, all three of our "non-IE" browsers will happily display a yellow background and large bold red text that is specified in a style attribute. However, none of them understand the width selector, or at least they don't implement it for a hyperlink <a> element.

Of course, by specifying a different User Agent string, you can "pretend to be" another browser. If you open the hyperlink.aspx page in Navigator and select the Internet Explorer 6.0 User Agent string, the output generated by the control will include the style attribute. ASP.NET will think that it's serving the page to Internet Explorer 6.0. Figure 2-9 shows the results of doing this in the other three of our test browsers.

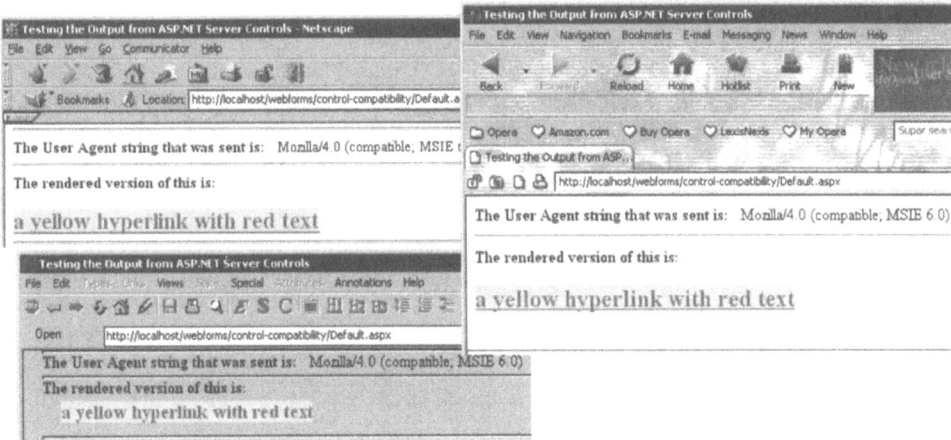

Figure 2-9. Pretending to be Internet Explorer 6.0 in other browsers

So, is the server control misbehaving? It really comes down to the fact that the ASP.NET Web Forms server controls only support two "modes" for formatting (and, in fact, for other output generation). The client accessing the page is classed as being either Internet Explorer 4.0 and above (called an *up-level* client), or it's "one of the rest" (a *down-level* client). You'll see more about this later in the chapter.

The alternative would be to detect and generate specific output for lots of types of browsers, and for the different versions of each one. The problem is that they vary quite considerably in their published and actual support for different elements and attributes, even between versions of the same browser, making it very hard to satisfy them all. Of course, there's nothing to stop you from building your own server controls that inherit from the ones provided, and adding specific browser support yourself.

The Calendar Control

Before moving on to look at the next main option for controlling formatting, take a quick look at the Calendar control. While the automatic use of client-side interactivity that was originally mooted for inclusion in the control never materialized, it does perform in two different modes for "up-level" (Internet Explorer 4.0 and above) and "down-level" (all other) clients. I used the following code to create a calendar using the ASP.NET Calendar control:

```
<asp:calendar id="calTest" runat="server"
              BackColor="#ffff80"
              BorderColor="#c0c0c0"
              BorderStyle="ridge"
              BorderWidth="5" />
```

Figure 2-10 shows the results of the four browsers I'm using. You can see that only Internet Explorer displays the "ridge" border. The others quite happily display the main part of the calendar, except for Amaya—which has problems with the background color.

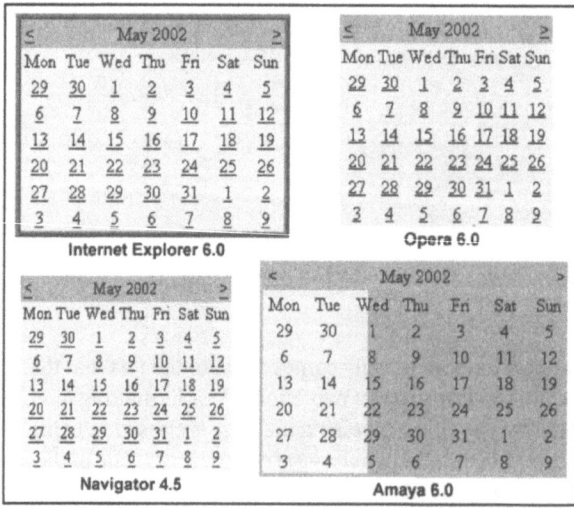

Figure 2-10. The Calendar *control in four different browsers*

The actual output generated by the Calendar control for "up-level" browsers contains a raft of style selectors within the style element of the HTML <table> and each table row and cell. You can see the border-style:Ridge selector that creates the raised border for the calendar:

```
<table id="calTest" cellspacing="0" cellpadding="2" bordercolor="Silver"
       border="0" style="background-color:#FFFF80;border-color:Silver;
                         border-width:5px;border-style:Ridge;
                         border-collapse:collapse;">
  <tr>
    <td colspan="7" style="background-color:Silver;">
    ...
    <td align="Center" style="width:14%;">
      <a href="javascript:__doPostBack('calTest','857')"
         style="color:Black">7</a></td>
```

Unlike the controls you've looked at so far, the Calendar control does not try to achieve a similar appearance for "down-level" clients by using <font> elements. Instead, it still generates a series of style selectors for the style attribute, but with a reduced set for the main <table> element. The border-style selector is omitted, so the browser does not attempt to display the raised border in this case:

```
<table id="calTest" cellspacing="0" cellpadding="2" bordercolor="Silver"
       border="0" bgcolor="#FFFF80">
...
  <td align="Center" width="14%">
    <a href="javascript:__doPostBack('calTest','857')"
       style="color:Black">7</a></td>
```

What happens if you pretend to be Internet Explorer in the other three browsers? Navigator 4.5 fails to do any better, although later versions (Navigator 6.0 and Mozilla 6.0) do work fine (Figure 2-11). Opera gets very close, with just a problem in one place with the "ridge" border. However, Amaya doesn't handle the style attributes too well at all.

Figure 2-11. Pretending to be Internet Explorer 6.0 with the Calendar *control*

To check if it's the output from the control that is the problem in Amaya (which is very strict in its interpretation of HTML), I saved the HTML generated by the page as an .htm file and loaded it into Mozquito—an XHTML validation tool that is available from http://www.mozquito.org/. It wasn't too happy with the attributes in the <form> for some reason, but otherwise reported that the structure of the document was correct according to the XHTML 1.0 strict recommendations from W3C. So you can't blame the server control in this case.

Specifying Up-level or Down-level Clients

I've spent enough time looking at the basic issues of style attributes and <font> elements for simple controls. However, before going on to explore more complicated controls, I need to quickly investigate the situation with regard to specifying if a client is an "up-level" or "down-level" one.

The ASP.NET Page directive accepts an attribute named ClientTarget, which specifies if the Web Forms server controls on the page should perform the browser detection you've been seeing earlier on in this chapter. The default, if omitted, is "Up-level," but it can be set to "Down-level" to prevent the controls from creating different output that is specially tailored to up-level clients:

```
<%@Page ClientTarget="Down-level" Language="..." %>
```

In fact, the values that you can use for this property of the Page depend on the contents of the web.config file. The values "Up-level" and "Down-level" are the defaults, but you can add your own. For full details, look up "<clientTarget> element" in the .NET SDK Help file.

You can investigate the effect of this using the two test pages in your sample application named asp-label.aspx and asp-label-down-level.aspx. They both define a Label control using the code:

```
<asp:label id="lblTest" runat="server"
          forecolor="red"
          backcolor="yellow"
          width="75%"
          font-name="Times New Roman,serif"
          font-size="large"
          font-bold="true"
          text="a yellow label control with red text" />
```

Without the ClientTarget attribute in the @Page directive (or if it is set to "Up-level"), the output is a <span> element 75 percent of the window width, with a yellow background and large bold red text (Figure 7-12).

Figure 2-12. The Label *control for an "up-level" client*

This is the output created by the page asp-label.aspx in Internet Explorer 6.0. It contains the style attribute that is usually delivered to "up-level" clients. However, the page asp-label-down-level.aspx has the ClientTarget="Down-level" attribute added to the Page directive. In this case, the page always creates the "down-level" output shown next:

```
<span id="lnkTest"><b><font face="Times New Roman,serif" color="Red" size="5">
a yellow label control with red text
</font></b></span>
```

There is no style attribute, and it's back to the <b> and <font> elements to create the appearance. So now the page looks the same in Internet Explorer 6.0 as it would in "down-level" browsers (Figure 2-13).

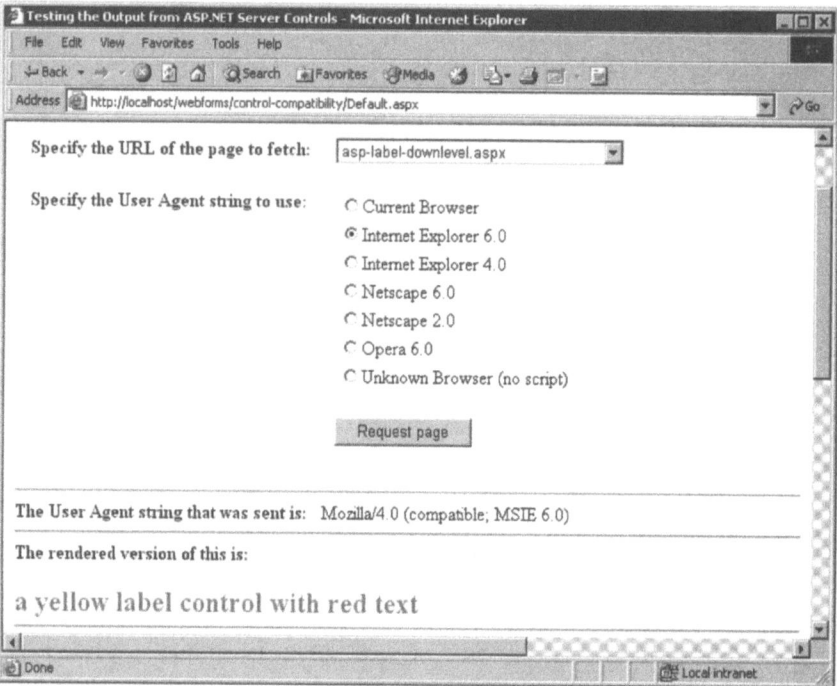

Figure 2-13. The Label *control when a "down-level" client is specified*

Thankfully, there are ways that you can get a more compatible appearance across different client browsers by using CSS styles directly instead of having the server control create them for us. This topic is covered in more detail in the next chapter.

The Definition of "Up-level" and "Down-level"

The .NET SDK contains a definition of how a client is identified as being up-level or down-level. It says that browsers and client devices are considered to be up-level if they support at least the following:

- ECMAScript (JScript, JavaScript) version 1.2

- HTML version 4.0

- The Microsoft Document Object Model (MSDOM)

- Cascading style sheets (CSS) version 1.0

Down-level browsers and client devices only need to support HTML version 3.2. More details can be found in the version 1.0 SDK at:

```
ms-help://MS.NETFrameworkSDK/cpguidenf/html/
cptskDetectingBrowserTypesInWebForms.htm
```
or in the version 1.1 SDK at:
```
ms-help://MS.NETFrameworkSDKv1.1/cpguidenf/html/
cptskDetectingBrowserTypesInWebForms.htm
```
 I also discuss ways that you use code to detect if a specific client is up-level or down-level in the section of this chapter that looks at output caching.

List Control Formatting and Templates

The Web Forms server controls include several that are predominantly used to create "lists" or "tables" of information. These include the DataGrid, DataList, and Repeater controls. They can be used with templates that specify the output to be generated by the control. In most cases an object such as a DataSet, DataReader, Array, Hashtable, or Collection provides the data through server-side data binding. Templates are predominantly used to specify which "fields" or "columns" in the data are to be shown. However, they can also be used to control the formatting and appearance of the data.

 The DataGrid and DataList (by default) create output that is an HTML <table>. The format of each row and cell can be specified separately using the syntax you already met for the simpler controls. For example, the test page named asp-datalist.aspx contains this definition of a DataList control:

```
<asp:datalist  id="dlTest" runat="server"
               forecolor="#000000"
               backcolor="#ffffff"
               cellpadding="3"
               gridlines="none"
               width="50%" >
  <itemstyle   font-name="tahoma,arial,sans-serif"
               font-size="12"
               backcolor="#ffffff" />
  <alternatingitemstyle font-name="tahoma,arial,sans-serif"
               font-size="2"
               backcolor="#ffff00" />
  <itemtemplate>
    <%# Container.DataItem %>
  </itemtemplate>
</asp:datalist>
```

 The data source is a single-column array, and you can use the sample application to view the code that creates it and binds it to the control. In the code above, you can see that I've specified quite a few attributes that affect the control's output, including the appearance of the table itself and the font name and size for the item and alternating item rows.

 So what does the output from this page look like in the various browsers? All can display the specified styles without a problem (except that Amaya doesn't recognize the font name), and the table appears at the correct width of 50 percent of the page width. However, notice in Figure 2-14 that the text in the alternating item rows in Internet Explorer is extremely small compared to the other browsers.

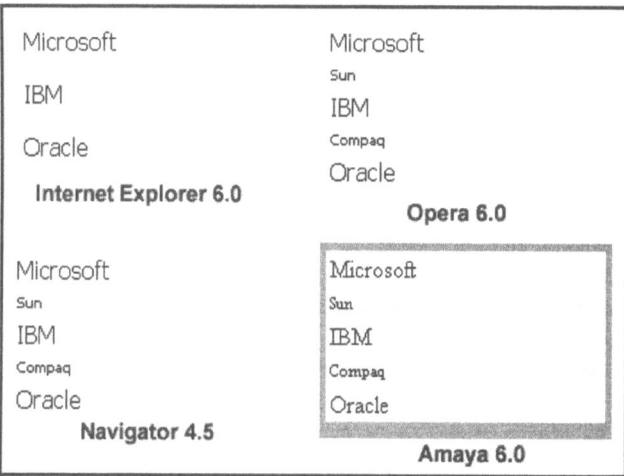

Figure 2-14. The DataList *control rendering in different browsers*

The Output from the DataList Control

Looking at the actual generated output from the control explains why this is the case. The next listing shows the output generated for Internet Explorer, and you can see that all the formatting is provided by style attributes—as you saw with the simpler controls earlier on. Notice also how the list controls convert the color that was specified using hexadecimal values (for example "#ffff00") into the color names. However, the text size for the alternating item rows is set to 2pt:

```
<table id="dlTest" cellpadding="3" border="0"
       style="color:Black;background-color:White;width:50%;">
  <tr>
    <td style="background-color:White;font-family:tahoma,arial,sans-serif;
               font-size:12pt;">
      Microsoft
    </td>
  </tr><tr>
    <td style="background-color:Yellow;font-family:tahoma,arial,sans-serif;
               font-size:2pt;">
      Sun
    </td>
  </tr><tr>
    <td style="background-color:White;font-family:tahoma,arial,sans-serif;
               font-size:12pt;">
      IBM
    </td>
```

```
    </tr><tr>
      <td style="background-color:Yellow;font-family:tahoma,arial,sans-serif;
                 font-size:2pt;">
        Compaq
      </td>
    </tr><tr>
      <td style="background-color:White;font-family:tahoma,arial,sans-serif;
                 font-size:12pt;">
        Oracle
    </td>
    </tr>
</table>
```

The reason for this can be seen in the original code. I specified the `font-size` property for the item and alternating item rows as:

```
font-size="12"      'for item rows
font-size="2"       'for alternating item rows
```

These numbers were interpreted as 12pt and 2pt by the control. But when the target browser is a "down-level" client, the situation is different.

The next listing shows the output from the control when the browser is Navigator, and you can see that the font name, color, and size are now specified with `<font>` elements instead of a style attribute on the opening `<td>` tag. The font sizes are also translated into the appropriate number of the size attribute for the `<font>` element—and as 1 is the lowest, this is used for the alternating item rows where Internet Explorer used 2pt:

```
<table id="dlTest" cellpadding="3" border="0" bgcolor="White" width="50%">
  <tr>
    <td bgcolor="White"><font face="tahoma,arial,sans-serif"
        color="Black" size="3">
      Microsoft
    </font></td>
  </tr><tr>
    <td bgcolor="Yellow"><font face="tahoma,arial,sans-serif"
        color="Black" size="1">
      Sun
    </font></td>
  </tr><tr>
      <td bgcolor="White"><font face="tahoma,arial,sans-serif"
          color="Black" size="3">
        IBM
    </font></td>
  </tr><tr>
      <td bgcolor="Yellow"><font face="tahoma,arial,sans-serif"
          color="Black" size="1">
        Compaq
      </font></td>
```

```
        </tr><tr>
         <td bgcolor="White"><font face="tahoma,arial,sans-serif"
            color="Black" size="3">
            Oracle
         </font></td>
       </tr>
    </table>
```

In fact, the control has managed the differences between the up-level and down-level clients very well. In the up-level version, the <table> element contains the style attribute:

```
style="color:Black;background-color:White;width:50%;"
```

On the other hand the down-level version uses attributes of the <table> element to achieve the same overall background color and width:

```
<table id="dlTest" cellpadding="3" border="0" bgcolor="White" width="50%">
```

The cells within each table row for the up-level client are formatted with the following style attribute on each <td> element. There is no need to specify the font color as this is done in the style attribute for the <table> element:

```
style="background-color:White;font-family:tahoma,arial,sans-serif;font-size:12pt;"
```

However, the down-level client receives a <td> element with a series of appropriate attributes plus a <font> element within the cell that also sets the font color:

```
<td bgcolor="White"><font face="tahoma,arial,sans-serif" color="Black" size="3">
```

Adding Templates to the DataList Control

One way of getting around the issue of the font size in a list control is to abandon (or override) the settings made by the style attribute in up-level clients with a <font> element within each cell, producing output that is the same as that created automatically for down-level clients. You do lose some control over the font size, in that you can then only set it to the numeric values that are supported by a <font> element. However, it does mean that you get the same overall appearance in all browsers.

The test page named asp-datalist-format-item.aspx demonstrates this, by adding specific formatting elements to the templates within the definition of the DataList control. Instead of an ordinary array as the data source, I also switched over to using a Hashtable. This allows me to store two values for each item (as the Key and Value). I also removed the font-size attributes from the declaration of the <itemstyle> and <alternatingitemstyle> as they will now be specified within the templates for these rows.

The next listing shows just the templates used in our DataList control for this example:

```
<itemtemplate>
  <%# DataBinder.Eval(Container.DataItem, "Key", _
                      "<font size='1'>{0}</font>") %>
  <%# DataBinder.Eval(Container.DataItem, "Value", _
                      "<font size='1'>${0:f2}</font>") %>
</itemtemplate>
<alternatingitemtemplate>
  <%# DataBinder.Eval(Container.DataItem, "Key", _
                      "<font size='4'>{0}</font>") %>
  <%# DataBinder.Eval(Container.DataItem, "Value", _
                      "<font size='4'>${0:f2}</font>") %>
</alternatingitemtemplate>
```

The idea is simple enough, I want to insert a <font> element manually into each cell and specify the required font details. Do this by taking advantage of the Eval method of the DataBinder that is actually performing the binding of the data to the control. Specify the data item itself as Container.DataItem, the name of the column or field you want to bind to, and a string that defines the format of the output. The string, "<font size='1'>{0}</font>", will generate a <font> element with the actual value for the cell inserted where the {0} placeholder is within the format string.

Of course, this doesn't prevent you from carrying out other formatting of the value itself, for example in the second column you can format the value as a fixed two decimal places number, and include the dollar currency symbol within the <font> element as well. The only downside is that using the DataBinder.Eval method is marginally less efficient in execution at runtime than just using Container.DataItem (as you did in the previous example page).

Now, when this row is generated by the control for an up-level client, the actual output is:

```
<td style="background-color:White;font-family:tahoma,arial,sans-serif;">
  <font size='1'>Microsoft</font>
  <font size='1'>$49.56</font>
</td>
```

For a down-level client, you get the usual switch from a style attribute to separate attributes of the <td> element, and the <font> element that wraps the entire content. However, inside this are the same set of elements and values that you get for the up-level client:

```
<td bgcolor="White">
  <font face="tahoma,arial,sans-serif" color="Black">
    <font size='1'>Oracle</font>
    <font size='1'>$41.10</font>
  </font>
</td>
```

The result is that all the browsers now provide the same appearance (with Amaya's exception of not recognizing the font name)(Figure 2-15).

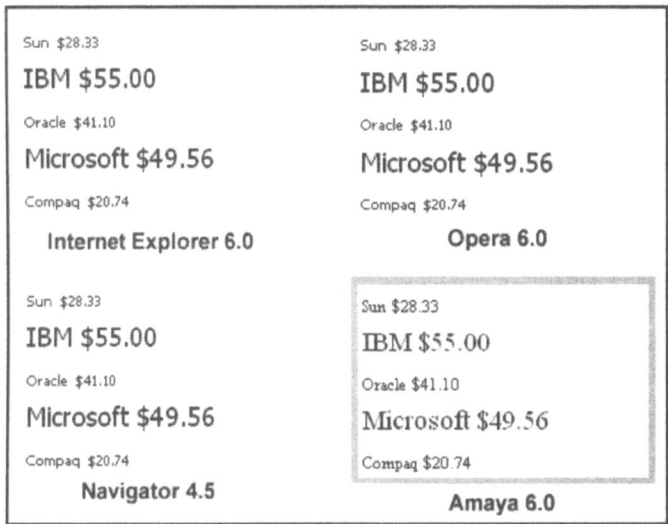

Figure 2-15. Using templates to manage the output appearance

One point worth mentioning is that many experienced Web page builders avoid any white-space between the *<font>* element and the enclosing *<td>* element in tables (or in fact in any container-type control such as a *<div>*, *<span>*, etc.). This is because any white-space characters here, be they spaces, tabs, carriage returns, and so on, are formatted in the default page or parent container font. This can upset the layout, often in unpredictable ways. However, the ASP.NET server controls that create tables often do insert unwanted white space (though not always). Sometimes you can prevent this by removing all the spaces and carriage returns from the content of your templates within source code of the page.

More Complexity—The DataGrid Control

Having seen one way that the DataList can be persuaded to generate a common appearance for the content in both up-level and down-level browsers, you'll look at a slightly more complex example. The DataGrid control works in a similar way to a DataList, but offers far more in the way of features. For example it can provide paging and sorting with only minimal extra development effort. However, the same issues arise with regard to formatting the output to suit all types of browser.

Figure 2-16 (Figure 2-1 repeated from the start of the chapter) shows the same page in two different browsers—Internet Explorer and Navigator (the result in Opera is the same as in Navigator). You can see that the formatting instructions we provide in the declaration of the DataGrid control do not provide the same output in Navigator as they do in Internet Explorer:

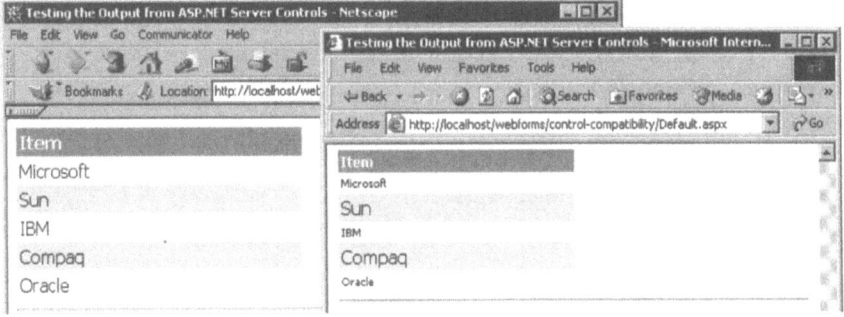

Figure 2-16. A DataList *control in Internet Explorer and Navigator*

The reason for this is just the same as was encountered with the DataList component earlier. The control declaration in the page looks like this:

```
<asp:datagrid id="dgrTest" runat="server"
              forecolor="#000000"
              backcolor="#ffffff"
              cellpadding="3"
              gridlines="none"
              width="50%"
              font-name="tahoma,arial,sans-serif"
              font-size="14px">
  <headerstyle forecolor="#ffffff"
               backcolor="#808080"
               font-name="tahoma,arial,sans-serif"
               font-size="12px"
               font-bold="true"
               wrap="false" />
  <itemstyle font-name="tahoma,arial,sans-serif"
             font-size="10px" />
  <alternatingitemstyle font-name="tahoma,arial,sans-serif"
                        font-size="16px"
                        backcolor="#ffff00" />
</asp:datagrid>
```

You can see that I am formatting the content using fixed pixel values for the font-size properties of the header, item, and alternating item rows. The result in Internet Explorer contains the usual set of style attributes that set the visible appearance:

```
<table cellspacing="0" cellpadding="3" border="0" id="dgrTest"
       style="color:Black;background-color:White;
              font-family:tahoma,arial,sans-serif;font-size:14px;
              width:50%;border-collapse:collapse;">
```

```
<tr nowrap="nowrap"
    style="color:White;background-color:Gray;
           font-family:tahoma,arial,sans-serif;font-size:12px;
           font-weight:bold;">
  <td>Item</td>
</tr><tr style="font-family:tahoma,arial,sans-serif;font-size:10px;">
  <td>Microsoft</td>
</tr><tr style="background-color:Yellow;
               font-family:tahoma,arial,sans-serif;font-size:16px;">
  <td>Sun</td>
  ...
</tr>
</table>
```

In Navigator and other down-level browsers, you get a mixture of attributes on the <table>, <tr>, and <td> elements, plus <font> elements within each cell:

```
<table cellspacing="0" cellpadding="3" border="0" id="dgrTest"
       bgcolor="White" width="50%">
  <tr nowrap="nowrap" bgcolor="Gray">
    <td><font face="tahoma,arial,sans-serif" color="White"><b>Item</b></font></td>
  </tr><tr>
    <td><font face="tahoma,arial,sans-serif" color="Black">Microsoft</font></td>
  </tr><tr bgcolor="Yellow">
    <td><font face="tahoma,arial,sans-serif" color="Black">Sun</font></td>
  ...
  </tr>
</table>
```

Specifying Column Information in a DataGrid Control

The DataGrid control doesn't need to be provided with any information about the structure of its data source if that data source exposes the values as an array or a collection. It automatically creates a column for each "field" within the items of the data source. The previous example used a simple array of string values as the data source, and the header displays the word **Item** automatically.

However, you can exert more control over the output of the DataGrid by specifying what columns you actually want to display, and how you want them to appear. In the test page named asp-datagrid-format-item.aspx you add an autogenerate-columns="false" attribute to the declaration of the DataGrid control itself, and then specify a <columns> element that defines the columns you want to display. In the next listing you can see I removed the font-size attributes from the <itemstyle> and <alternatingitemstyle> elements):

```
<asp:datagrid id="dgrTest" runat="server"
              forecolor="#000000"
              backcolor="#ffffff"
              cellpadding="3"
              gridlines="none"
```

```
                width="50%"
                font-name="tahoma,arial,sans-serif"
                font-size="14px"
                autogeneratecolumns="false" >
    <headerstyle forecolor="#ffffff"
                backcolor="#808080"
                font-name="tahoma,arial,sans-serif"
                font-size="12px"
                font-bold="true"
                wrap="false" />
    <itemstyle font-name="tahoma,arial,sans-serif" />
    <alternatingitemstyle font-name="tahoma,arial,sans-serif"
                        backcolor="#ffff00" />
    <columns>
      <asp:boundcolumn headertext="Key" datafield="Key"
                    dataformatstring="<font size='4'>{0}</font>" />
      <asp:boundcolumn headertext="Value" datafield="Value"
                    dataformatstring="<font size='1'>${0:f2}</font>" />
    <columns>
</asp:datagrid>
```

In this example, I'm using a Hashtable as the data source, which contains two values for each item—the key is a company name and the value is a number. Each <asp:boundcolumn> element specifies the column name to use in the header row (the headertext) and the "field" from the data source item to display in that column (the datafield). To get the formatting I want, I'm using the dataformatstring attribute to enclose the value for that cell in a <font> element with a specified size.

Now the result in each row of the table is the same for each browser, with just the header text being different (and, of course, Amaya's inability to recognize the font name)(Figure 2-17).

Figure 2-17. The result of specifying column details in different browsers

To get the same size for the header text, I could replace the font-size="12px" attribute in the <headerstyle> element with a value that works better across both up-level and down-level browsers. For example, using font-size="10" causes the DataGrid to create a style attribute in up-level browsers that contains font-size:10pt, while down-level browsers receive a <font> element that includes the attribute size="2". If the user has the text size setting of the browser set to **Medium** (usually this is an option in the **View** menu), the headers will appear in the same size.

Formatting Within a TemplateColumn *in a* DataGrid *Control*

Often when working with the DataGrid control, the limitations of the <asp:boundcolumn> element prevent you from achieving exactly what you want. The usual solution in this case is to use an <asp:templatecolumn> element for one or more of the columns, and within this provide templates in exactly the same way as you do for a DataList (or Repeater) control.

The next listing, taken from the test page asp-datagrid-template-format-item.aspx shows this approach. Each column declaration is now an <asp:templatecolumn>, containing a <headertemplate> and an <itemtemplate> (you could provide an <alternatingitemtemplate> and <footertemplate> template as well, if required). Inside each template place the controls that will create the visible output—in this case <font> elements with the appropriate size attribute that enclose each call to the DataBinder.Eval method that generates the value for the cells:

```
<columns>
  <asp:templatecolumn>
    <headertemplate>
      <font size="2">Key</font>
    </headertemplate>
    <itemtemplate>
      <font size="4">
        <%# DataBinder.Eval(Container.DataItem, "Key") %>
      </font>
    </itemtemplate>
  </asp:templatecolumn>
  <asp:templatecolumn>
    <headertemplate>
      <font size="2">Value</font>
    </headertemplate>
    <itemtemplate>
      <font size="1">
        $<%# DataBinder.Eval(Container.DataItem, "Value", "{0:f2}") %>
      </font>
    </itemtemplate>
  </asp:templatecolumn>
</columns>
```

The result from this example page (asp-datagrid-template-format-item.aspx) is the same as what you saw in the previous example—though now with the same size font in the header rows due to the explicit definition in the <headertemplate> shown in the listing. You can view the complete source code and the actual HTML and other content that is created by viewing this test page in the application provided as a sample.

What If There's No Client-Side Script Support?

As you'll no doubt be aware, several of the ASP.NET Web Forms server controls generate output that contains, and depends on, client-side JavaScript. As an example, the LinkButton control generates an <a> element that uses client-side JavaScript to submit the form containing it. The example page asp-linkbutton.aspx declares a LinkButton control, which must be placed on a server-side <form>. The code in the test page is shown next:

```
<form runat="server">
  <asp:linkButton id="lnkTest" runat="server"
                  forecolor="red"
                  backcolor="yellow"
                  width="50%"
                  font-name="Times New Roman,serif"
                  font-size="larger"
                  font-bold="true"
                  text="a yellow link button with red text" />
</form>
```

In Internet Explorer, as expected, you get a style attribute that defines the formatting of the <a> element The href attribute, shown below, calls a JavaScript function named __dopostback that ASP also inserts into the page:

```
 href="javascript:__dopostback('lnkTest',")"
```

You can see the JavaScript function in Figure 2-18.

Figure 2-18. The client-side script function for posting back the page in Internet Explorer

In down-level browsers, the only difference is that the formatting of the `<a>` element is set using `<b>` and `<font>` elements, as you discovered is the case with the controls examined earlier. The `href` is the same as the output for up-level clients, as is the JavaScript code (Figure 2-19).

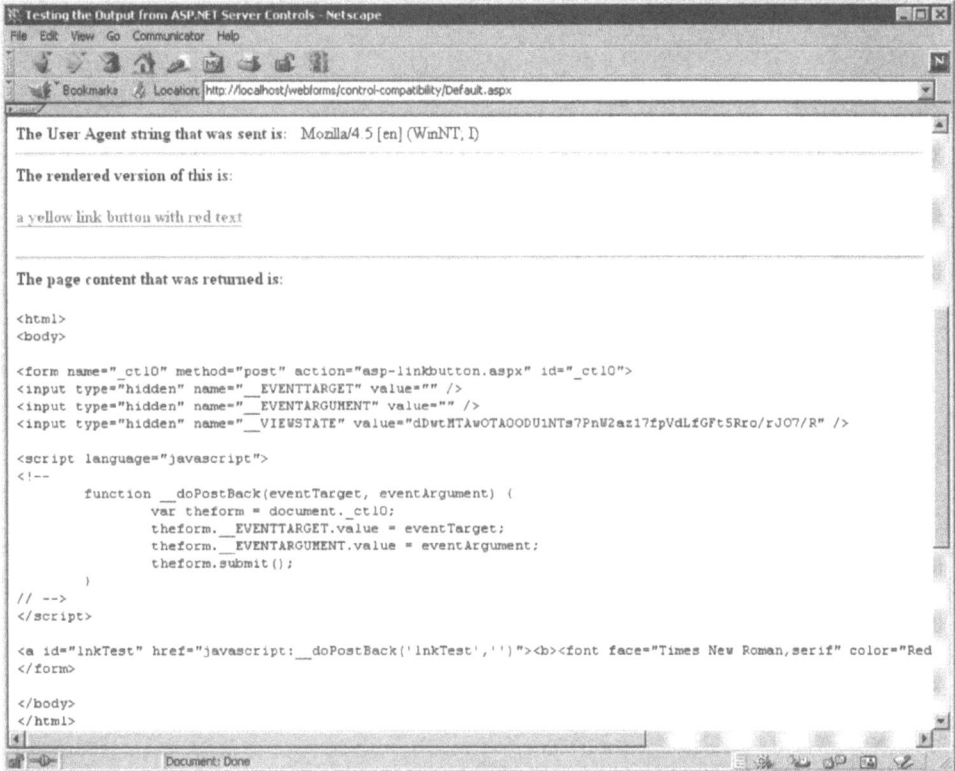

Figure 2-19. The client-side script function for posting back the page in Navigator

But what happens in clients that don't support JavaScript? OK, so most browsers do support JavaScript, but it's also possible that the user may have disabled script execution in their browser. In this case, clicking the link will have no effect. You might expect the control to recognize one or both of these situations, but it doesn't.

Example: A LinkButton in Amaya

For example, if you open the test page in a browser that doesn't support script, you'll see that the same output is generated and so the link does not function. Figure 2-20 shows what happens in Amaya (which does not support client-side scripting)—you can see the error message in the status bar at the bottom of the window.

Figure 2-20. The LinkButton does not work in Amaya without client-side script

Likewise, if you disable Active Scripting in the **Tools | Internet Options | Security | Advanced** dialog in Internet Explorer, the page generates the same client-side JavaScript code as before, but the link no longer works.

You can use the test page named `asp-linkbutton-uatype.aspx` to determine if ASP.NET thinks that the browser you are using does or does not support client-side scripting. The only difference between this page and the one you've just been using is that it queries two properties of the `Request.Browser` object to see if it thinks that `javascript` is available for the current client, and to get the "alias" or short type description for the client.

```
JavaScript supported: <% = Request.Browser("javascript") %><br />
Reported type: <% = Request.Browser("type") %>
```

The results for Internet Explorer and Amaya are shown in Figure 2-21.

The User Agent string that was sent is: Mozilla/4.0 (compatible; MSIE 6.0; Windows NT 5.0; .NET CLR 1.0.3705)

The rendered version of this is:

a yellow link button with red text

JavaScript supported: true
Reported type: IE6

The User Agent string that was sent is: amaya/6.1 libwww/5.3.1
The rendered version of this is:
a yellow link button with red text
JavaScript supported: false
Reported type: Unknown

Figure 2-21. Displaying browser properties from the Request.Browser *object*

ASP.NET populates the properties of the Request.Browser object by matching a set of patterns in the <browserCaps> section of the machine.config and any applicable web.config files with the User Agent string sent by the browser. The machine.config file is in the folder: C:\WINNT\Microsoft.NET\Framework\[version]\CONFIG\.

Updates to this section of the file can be obtained from cyScape, Inc. at http://www.cyscape.com/browsercaps/.

Solving the "No Script" Problem

The problem of lack of client-side scripting support affects not only the LinkButton, but other controls as well. If you look back at the output generated by the Calendar control, you'll see that it uses the same technique as the LinkButton to cause a post back to the server when a date is selected. On top of that, several other controls (the CheckBox, RadioButton, TextBox, and some list controls) support a property called AutoPostback. This adds the same kind of JavaScript function and element attributes to the controls as we've seen for the LinkButton control. None of these will work without client-side script support.

So, should Microsoft have made the controls more intelligent? It would certainly have made them more complex, and might also have prevented them from working properly in some browsers if the <browserCaps> file is not up to date. For example, newly released or beta versions of browsers may not be properly detected, and in this case functionality would be lost even when the client in question probably supports it.

So, you have a choice—you can avoid using the LinkButton and Calendar, and the AutoPostback feature of some of the other Web Forms controls—but this reduces the functionality of your application in all clients, when only a minority may not have client-side scripting available. Alternatively, you could just use it and hope for the best, perhaps including a message for clients that don't support scripting by using a <noscript> element:

```
<noscript>
  NOTE: this page requires a browser that supports JavaScript
</noscript>
```

When Scripting Is Supported but Disabled

But even this is no help if the client supports JavaScript but has it disabled in the browser options. In this case, you might resort to using a common trick with a redirection that detects if scripting is actually available and enabled:

```
<html>
<head>
<meta http-equiv="refresh" content="1;url=no-client-script.aspx %>" />
<title>Checking for Active Scripting Support</title>

<script language="JavaScript">
<!--
function jumpScripting() {
// jump to page using client-side JavaScript—if jump not executed
// then client does not have scripting available or it is disabled
window.location.href='client-script-ok.aspx';
}
//-->
</script>
</head>
<body onload="jumpScripting()">
Checking support for Active Scripting...
</body>

<noscript>
  Your browser does not support client-side script.
  <a href="no-client-script.aspx">Click here to continue</a>
</noscript>
</html>
```

The JavaScript code in this page will automatically load the page named client-script-ok.aspx if scripting is supported and enabled. If the code is not executed, the <meta> element will instead load the page no-client-script.aspx after one second. And if the browser does not support script at all, the <a> element will display a normal hyperlink to load the page no-client-script.aspx. You'll see this technique used in our example site in the next chapter.

The ASP.NET Validation Controls

Having discussed the shortcomings of client-side JavaScript detection in the previous sections, I need to mention the situation with regard to the ASP.NET validation controls. In fact, these are more intelligent than the other controls I've been discussing—though still not as intelligent as they could be.

If you've used the validation controls before, you'll know that—like most Web Forms controls—they generate different output for up-level and down-level clients. For up-level clients (basically Internet Explorer 4.0 and above), they take advantage of the ability to change the content of a page dynamically while it is displayed, using Dynamic HTML.

As you move the input focus from one visible UI control in the page (such as a text box) to another (by clicking or tabbing), any validation control attached to that visible control is activated. If the validation fails, the text content of the validation control is displayed in the page. You can see this if you open the test page named `asp-validator.aspx` in Internet Explorer 4.0 or above. The page contains a text box to which is attached a `RequiredFieldValidator` control (Figure 2-22).

Figure 2-22. The `RequiredFieldValidator` *control in Internet Explorer*

If there is an invalid value in any control on the page (that has a validator attached), the form cannot be submitted. Instead, the `ValidationSummary` control placed in the page displays a summary of the errors (Figure 2-23).

The relevant part of the source code for this page is shown in the code that follows. You can see the declaration of the `TextBox`, `RequiredFieldValidator`, `Button`, and the `ValidationSummary` controls:

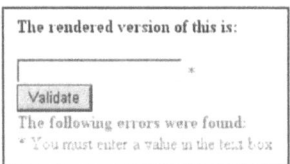

Figure 2-23. The output from the `ValidationSummary` *control*

```
<form runat="server">
<asp:textbox id="txtTest" text="delete this" runat="server" />
<asp:RequiredFieldValidator
        id="valRequired" runat="server"
        ErrorMessage="* You must enter a value in the text box"
        ControlToValidate="txtTest"
        Display="dynamic">
*
</asp:RequiredFieldValidator>
<br />
<asp:button text="Validate" runat="server" />
<asp:ValidationSummary
        id="valSummary" runat="server"
        HeaderText="<b>The following errors were found:</b>"
        ShowSummary="true"
        DisplayMode="List" />

</form>
```

Viewing the output that is generated from this page for an up-level client, it's possible to get an idea of how it works. I haven't listed it all here, but in essence there is a client-side `<script>` element that loads a JavaScript code file from the server's aspnet_client folder. There are also a couple of other client-side script sections that handle the events raised by the controls in the page to display the asterisk and the error message.

The `<input>` element that submits the page to the server calls a function within these script sections to validate the values in the controls on the page, and either submit the page to the server or cancel the submit event if any of the values are invalid:

```
<input type="submit" name="_ctl1" value="Validate"
       onclick="if (typeof(Page_ClientValidate) == 'function')
               Page_ClientValidate(); " language="javascript" />
```

The Validation Controls in Down-level Clients

The same page when loaded into a down-level browser does not, however, perform the same way. Instead, the page is always submitted to the server, and it's only there that the validation is carried out. If a control contains an invalid value, the returned page contains the asterisk and the error message. In appearance (other than the asterisks not appearing as you move from one control to another), the result is the same as for an up-level client—but requires a postback to the server.

The page also contains the same `<input>` element as that generated for up-level clients. Of course, in this case the separate client-side script functions are not loaded from the server. This means that the code in the onclick attribute does not detect the function named Page_ClientValidate—the statement typeof(Page_ClientValidate) will return "null"—and the page is always submitted to the server for validation.

If you want to see all the code that is generated, run the test page asp-validator.aspx in different browsers, or select different User Agent string values. You can also open the WebUIValidation.js script file from the \aspnet_client\system_web\[version]\ subfolder in your default Web site to see the functions that it provides for performing validation.

So what happens in a browser that doesn't support scripting when you use the validation controls? The great thing is that it actually does still work in exactly the same way as in down-level clients that do support scripting. The code in the onclick event attribute of the `<input>` element does not execute, but the page is still submitted to the server for validation there. And the controls still work in an up-level client that has scripting disabled—though again only in the same way as they do in a down-level client.

The ASP.NET Panel Control

There is one ASP.NET Web Forms control that exhibits an interesting change of behavior when used with different clients. The Panel control is used to create a separate section within a page, representing the kind of effect that is obtained by controls of the same name in environments such as Visual Basic 6.0. By adding style attributes, you can generate a section of the page that looks like a "panel"—useful for grouping related controls or other output together.

The test page, named `asp-panel.aspx`, contains the following code to create a panel with a grooved border, some text content, plus a TextBox and Button control. In this case, to make it easier to concentrate on the working of the Panel control itself, I've used `<b>` and `<font>` elements within the content rather than confuse the matter by using just the properties of the Panel control:

```
<body bgcolor="silver">
<center>
<form runat="server">
<asp:panel id="pnlTest" runat="server"
           forecolor="black"
           backcolor="silver"
           bordercolor="darkgray"
           borderwidth="5"
           borderstyle="groove"
           width="50%" >
  <font face="Arial,sans-serif" size="2">
    <b>A test panel</b><p />
    Enter some text:
    <asp:textbox id="txtTest" runat="server" text="some text" /><p />
    And click this button:
    <asp:button runat="server" text="click me" /><p />
  </font>
</asp:panel>
</form>
</center>
</body>
```

In Internet Explorer, it looks like what you see in Figure 2-24.

Figure 2-24. The Panel *control in Internet Explorer*

Looking at the code that the Panel control generates, you can see that the content of the panel is enclosed in a `<div>` element that defines the style for the foreground

and background colors, and the grooved border. It also specifies, in response to the
width="50%" attribute, that the <div> should be 50 percent of the page width:

```
<body bgcolor="silver">
<center>
<form name="_ctl0" method="post" action="asp-panel.aspx" id="_ctl0">
<input type="hidden" name="__VIEWSTATE"
        value="dDwtMTczMzcxMDE3Mjs7PjvcvBfJpdIovdPOMh4rCi0ehaBU" />
<div id="pnlTest" style="color:Black;background-color:Silver;
                         border-color:DarkGray;border-width:5px;
                         border-style:Groove;width:50%;">
  <font face="Arial,sans-serif" size="2">
    <b>A test panel</b><p />
    Enter some text:
    <input name="txtTest" type="text" value="some text"
           id="txtTest" /><p />
    And click this button:
    <input type="submit" name="_ctl1" value="click me" /><p />
  </font>
</div>
</form>
</center>
</body>
```

The Panel Control in Down-level Clients

However, if I open the same page in Navigator and Opera, I get different results. The
content is no longer centered within the panel, although the panel itself does appear
as 50 percent of the width of the page. I also lose the space below the button in
Navigator (Figure 2-25).

Figure 2-25. The Panel *control in Navigator and Opera*

A more surprising feature of the output is visible if you look at the code that is
generated by the Panel control in these cases. Instead of a <div> element, you get
a single-row HTML <table> that contains one cell:

```
<body bgcolor="silver">
<center>
<form name="_ctl0" method="post" action="asp-panel.aspx" id="_ctl0">
<input type="hidden" name="__VIEWSTATE"
        value="dDwtMTczMzcxMDE3Mjs7PjvcvBfJpdIovdPOMh4rCi0ehaBU" />
<table id="pnlTest" cellpadding="0" cellspacing="0" bgcolor="Silver"
        border="5" width="50%">
<tr><td><font color="Black">
  <font face="Arial,sans-serif" size="2">
    <b>A test panel</b><p />
    Enter some text:
    <input name="txtTest" type="text"
            value="some text" id="txtTest" /><p />
    And click this button:
    <input type="submit" name="_ctl1"
            value="click me" /><p />
  </font>
</font></td></tr></table>
</form>
</center>

</body>
```

This is because the <div> element (defined in HTML 3.0) was a relatively late addition to many browsers, as well as behaving quite differently in different browsers. For example, some browsers do not support setting the width of a <div>, and some don't support background colors. It's also possible to specify a background image for a Panel server control, but as some browsers don't support background images for a <div>, they would not be able to display this image either.

Therefore, to maximize compatibility across as many browsers as possible, Microsoft designed the Panel control to generate a <table> in down-level clients. The HTML <table> will generally support the setting of the background color and/or a background image. Most browsers also allow you to specify the width of the table (or the columns within it) as well. So it will, in most cases, give a similar appearance to the <div> element used in up-level clients.

So the reason that the <center> element in the page does not provide centered output in Navigator and Opera is that this "property" is not inherited from the page itself by a table cell in HTML, whereas it is inherited by a <div> element. The same applies to any <font> settings that are active in the page or another container control that holds the Panel element.

What this does mean is that you will quite often get a difference in appearance between browsers when using a Panel control, and it's well worth keeping your eye open for this. However, there are a couple of useful attributes you can add to the Panel control declaration that affect the output in down-level clients as well as up-level ones. Add an align attribute to control the horizontal alignment of the content in down-level clients:

```
align="center"
```

This will force the Panel control to add this attribute to each <td> element in the resulting <table> for down-level clients, centering the content. Unfortunately, however, some of the other obvious and useful attributes don't work as expected. A prime example of this is:

```
wrap="false"
```

In up-level clients it adds the attribute nowrap="nowrap" to the <div> element, preventing the content from wrapping if the <div> is narrower than the content or the page width. In down-level clients, it adds the same attribute to the <table> element, but *not* to the <td> element. In most browsers, this does not prevent the content from wrapping if it is wider than the table or the page width.

Don't Get Caught Out by Output Caching

So far, I've concentrated on what differences there are in the output of the ASP.NET Web Forms server controls between up-level and down-level clients—and some of the ways that you can make sure that you get the appearance you want in different browsers. However, there is one great feature of ASP.NET that can break all your hard work.

ASP.NET can automatically perform caching of the output that it generates by executing a page, and then send this cached output to other clients that request the same page. This saves the page from being executed every time, and can considerably reduce server loading and resource usage. While I don't have the space to discuss the workings of output caching in full, there is an unfortunate side effect when supporting different types of client.

The page asp-panel-cache-all.aspx contains an OutputCache directive that instructs ASP.NET to cache the page for 10 seconds. The rest of the page is just a simple declaration of a Panel control into which you write the date and time that the page was executed:

```
<%@Page Language="VB" Debug="True"%>
<%@OutputCache Duration="10" VaryByParam="none" %>
<html>
<body>

<asp:panel id="pnlTest" runat="server">
  Page executed: <% = Now() %>
</asp:panel>
</body>
</html>
```

If you open the page in Internet Explorer, then immediately afterwards in Navigator (or use the appropriate User Agent string options in the example page to load it first for Internet Explorer and then for Navigator), you get the result shown in Figure 2-26.

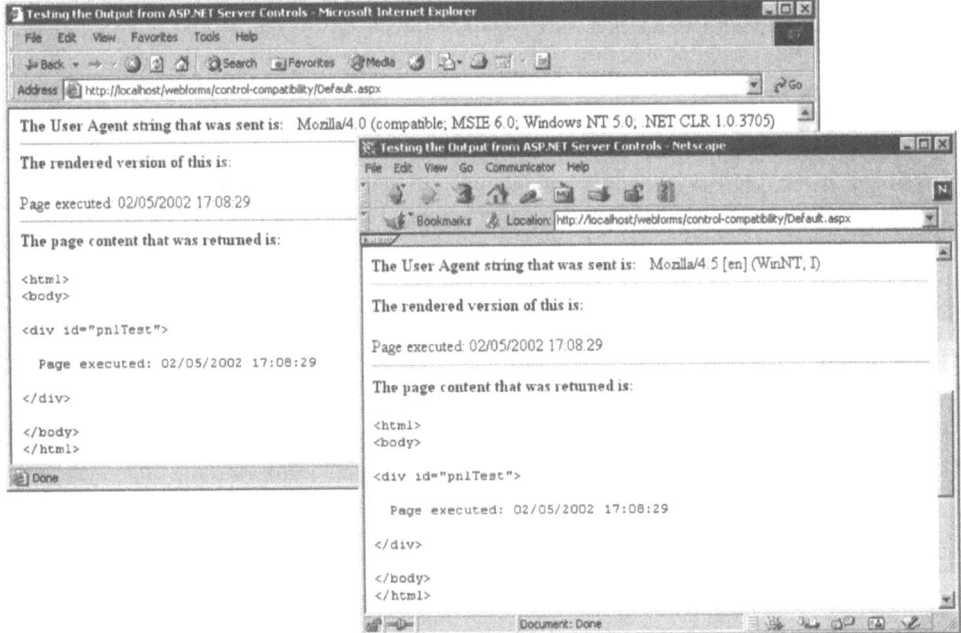

Figure 2-26. Output caching can upset browser recognition

Notice that Navigator receives the up-level page designed for Internet Explorer this time, because this is what is cached by ASP.NET. If the output depended on features that are specific to Internet Explorer, Navigator might fail to display the content correctly.

Caching by Browser Version

To get around this, if you expect to receive hits from different clients, you may prefer to set up output caching so that it still sends the appropriate page to up-level and down-level clients. The easiest way to do this is to add the attribute VaryByCustom="browser" to the OutputCache directive:

```
<%@OutputCache Duration="10" VaryByParam="none" VaryByCustom="browser" %>
```

Now, as you can confirm by running the test page asp-panel-cache-by-browser.aspx, the cached page is only sent to the same browser that it was originally created for. Each browser creates a specific copy of the page, and all these different copies are cached.

In the test page the output is cached for 10 seconds, and served from the cache every time during that period when you reload it in the *same browser* (or specify the same User Agent string setting). However, changing to a different browser (or changing the User Agent string setting) causes the page to be reexecuted and a separate copy is cached. If you then go back to the first browser within 10 seconds you'll see that the originally cached copy of the page is served again.

Of course, this means that you will cache lots of pages that are the same—every different version of every different browser will cause a copy of the page to be cached. In reality, there are only two different pages that need to be cached—one for up-level clients and one for down-level clients. You can achieve this by extending the custom caching approach you just used.

Caching by Client Target

You create a function that returns a string value within the global.asax file for your site. This value should be different only for situations where you want a separate copy of the page to be cached. If it returns the same value for more than one client request, the same page from the cache will be used for all these requests. So, if you can decide whether your client is up-level or down-level, and just return one of two values, you'll only get two copies of the page cached.

The function I used for the test page is shown next. Note the declaration has to be a Public function that overrides GetVaryByCustomString, and which takes the HttpContext and a String as the two parameters:

```
Public Overrides Function GetVaryByCustomString(context As HttpContext, _
                                        arg As String) As String

  If (arg = "clientlevel") Then
    Dim iEcmaVersion As Decimal = 0
    Dim iDomVersion As Decimal = 0
    Dim iMajorVersion As Integer = 0

    Try
      iEcmaVersion = Request.Browser("EcmaScriptVersion")
      iDomVersion = Request.Browser("MSDomVersion")
      iMajorVersion = Request.Browser("MajorVersion")
    Catch
      Return "downlevel"
    End Try

    If iEcmaVersion >= 1.2 _
    And iDomVersion >= 4 _
    And iMajorVersion >= 4 Then
      Return "uplevel"
    Else
      Return "downlevel"
    End If
  End If
End Function
```

In the function, you collect three values from the Request.Browser object for the current client: the ECMAScript version, the MSHTML DOM version, and the major version of the browser. Then you can do a test to see if it meets the criteria laid down earlier in this chapter of supporting at least ECMAScript version 1.2 and the MSHTML DOM (version 4.0 or above for Dynamic HTML support). To test for HTML 4.0 and CSS support is more difficult, as these are not available as properties of the Request.Browser object. Instead, I demand that the major version be at least 4.0.

This works because only Internet Explorer supports the MSHTML DOM version 4.0, and you know that Internet Explorer 4.0 and above support HTML 4.0 and CSS. An alternative would be to demand a major version of 4.0 and above if the browser type is "IE," or 5.0 and later for other browsers (as the main version 5 and 6 browsers from other companies do support HTML 4.0 and CSS):

```
...
If (Request.Browser("browser") = "IE" And iMajorVersion >= 4) _
Or (iMajorVersion >= 5) Then
  Return "uplevel"
Else
  Return "downlevel"
End If
...
```

Once this function is complete, you can specify it in the VaryByCustom attribute of the OutputCache directive in the pages:

```
<%@OutputCache Duration="10" VaryByParam="none"
             VaryByCustom="clientlevel" %>
```

Now the page is only cached for the appropriate client type. All requests from Internet Explorer get the same up-level cached page, while all requests from other clients get the same down-level cached page. I provided a test page named asp-cache-by-level.aspx that you can use to experiment with, but you will have to copy the function GetVaryByCustomString into your global.asax file first. This override also prevents the previous example from working until you remove the function from global.asax again.

Summary

I've tried in this chapter to help you come to grips with the way that the ASP.NET Web Forms server controls generate different output depending on the type of client accessing the page. While in most cases you can leave it to the control to generate the output you want, understanding what it is doing and why is a useful addition to your Web design and development skills.

In fact, there are occasions when knowing about all this stuff actually means that you can provide a better and more uniform output across different types of client browser. All that is really involved is two things: knowing when your property settings and other page content may affect the output that is generated, and how to get around this.

Usually, all that's involved in providing the best user experience possible is to add a few extra elements, or make minor modifications to the control's property settings, to satisfy the needs of all your down-level clients. In particular, when using the more complex server controls such as the DataList and DataGrid, a little extra care when declaring the controls, their properties, and the templates they include can make all the difference.

I haven't looked at all the server controls that are included with ASP.NET, or covered all the ways that the output might affect every browser. Such a comprehensive study might sound useful, but in fact would be extremely repetitive because so many of the issues are the same across several controls. Instead, I looked at the areas where you do need to be aware of the issues, including:

- A simple test application for examining the output generated by server controls

- How Microsoft defines which are "up-level" and which are "down-level" clients

- How the style attribute and <font> elements are used in up-level and down-level clients

- Working with more complex control like the DataList and DataGrid

- How the controls are affected by the lack of client-side scripting capabilities

- How the Panel control completely changes its output for the two types of client

- How output caching can affect browser compatibility

Having looked at some of the important issues involved in using the ASP.NET Web Forms server controls, I move on in the next chapter to consider how I'll be putting the design for the example site into practice. I'll still be doing groundwork to some extent, covering issues like checking the client's browser capabilities and designing the sample pages to provide the most compatible and accessible output possible.

Laying the Foundations

IN THE PREVIOUS TWO CHAPTERS, I've discussed recipes and ingredients for the sample Web site. You know what you want to achieve, and examined some of the techniques that you will take advantage of within the pages. Of course, there are several other factors to consider when building the site. Among these factors, two important points are achieving as wide-ranging browser compatibility as possible, and providing optimum accessibility for all types of user.

In this chapter, you'll get the groundwork done for the site by looking in some detail at the two issues highlighted in the previous paragraph, and I'll show you some interesting approaches that achieve both aims. I'll also discuss the technical requirements for the site, in terms of ASP.NET sessions and client-side scripting support. More importantly, I'll show you how to implement checks for these features, and ensure that your visitors can use the site to the fullest extent. By the end of this chapter, you should have all the remaining ingredients to build your "Home" page.

So, in this chapter, I cover:

- The client-side technical requirements for the Xrox Cars Web site

- Some of the major issues to consider with browser compatibility

- How the example site checks for sessions and client-side scripting support

- Some important issues for making sites accessible to all visitors

Once you have seen where you can obtain the samples for this chapter and the book as a whole, I'll continue by looking at the technical requirements for the site.

Obtaining the Example Files

All the examples you see in this book can be obtained from my Web site to run on your own server. The code is available in VB.NET and C#, and can be download from http://www.daveandal.com/books/7868/. Alternatively, you can just run the examples online directly from our server at the same URL, or download them from the Apress Web site at http://www.apress.com/.

Installing the Xrox Car Company Site

After downloading the example files, you must configure them for your server. The tasks required are as follows:

- **Install the files into a subfolder of your Web site**. Unzip the files using the Use folder names, Restore Folders, or Restore Directories option of your zip file manager software to re-create the correct folder tree within the sample files. It doesn't matter what the subfolder is called, though I used "webforms", as you'll see in the screenshots.

- **Create virtual applications** for the xroxcars and cookieless-xroxcars folder. In Internet Services Manager (available from Start | Programs | Administrative Tools), expand the tree in the left window to reveal the xroxcars folder, right-click it, and select Properties. In the Application Settings section of the Directory page, click the button marked Create next to the Application name text box, then click OK to close the Properties dialog. Then repeat this for the cookieless-xroxcars folder.

- **Install the database**. I've provided SQL scripts and instructions for creating the database in the folder named database of the samples. I've also provided a SQL Server 2000 compatible database backup that you can restore instead of running the SQL scripts. Be sure to create a new Logon named anon, with a blank password, before restoring the database or running the scripts.

Then navigate to the folder you just created, for example http://localhost/ webforms/, where a menu provides access to all the example, as shown in Figure 3-1.

Figure 3-1. The main menu page for the examples

Xrox Cars Client-Side Technical Requirements

We all know that software comes with a set of "minimum requirements"—usually the platform, operating system, version, and other prerequisite software that must be available. In some cases, this specification is easy. For executable applications, it could be as simple as "requires Windows 2000 or Windows XP." If the user has purchased the product, it's reasonable to expect that he or she read the label on the side of the box.

With a Web site, things should be easier. As long as the site conforms to the specifications laid down for the World Wide Web (basically, it is written in HTML), it should work no matter what platform, operating system, version, or Web browser the visitor is using. After all, that's the whole principle of the Web.

Nevertheless, as we are all so aware these days, it's not that simple. Rarely will pages written to HTML 2.0 standards provide a site that is visually acceptable in today's competitive world. You need to take advantage of features in more recent browsers such HTML 3.2 or HTML 4.01, client-side scripting, CSS style sheets, cookie support, and more.

There are plenty of other Web-based technologies that you can use as well, but the level of client-side support (and user acceptance) tends to taper off as you get to the more esoteric features. For example, you can only use graphics filters and the Remote Data Service in Internet Explorer 4 and later. And many users may have features such as Java applets and Flash graphics disabled in their browser, or blocked by a proxy server or firewall.

So, can you build attractive, interactive, and accessible sites that do work in most browsers and other Web-based clients while sticking within the limitations of the more widely accepted features of the Web? I believe that the answer is "yes," and I aim to prove it with the site you're building here. To give you an idea, Figure 3-2 shows the completed "Home" page.

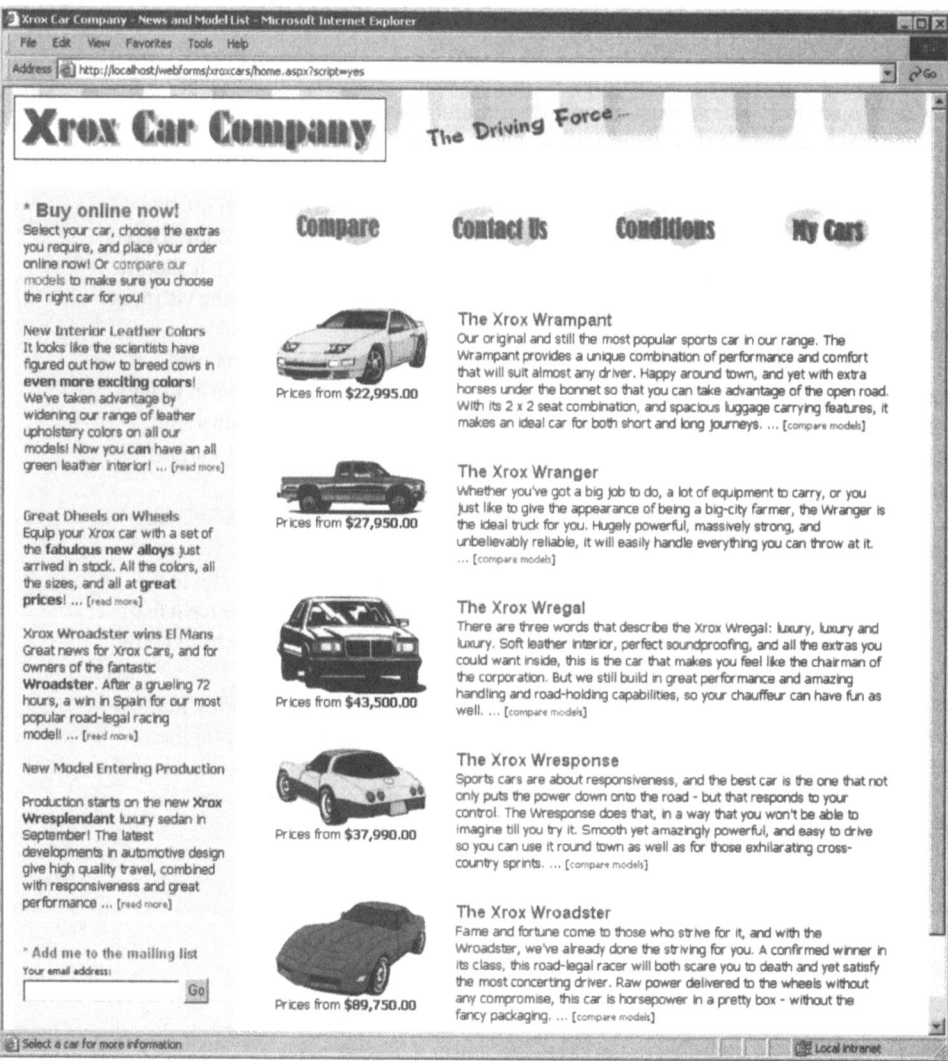

Figure 3-2. The Home page of the Xrox Cars example site

What "Standards" Are Supported or Required?

The "Home" page you see in Figure 3-2, like the rest of the site, uses markup that is generally compatible with HTML 3.2. However, it does include other elements and attributes that are not part of HTML 3.2, but that do not affect the output in HTML 3.2 clients. You'll see many such examples throughout this chapter. The HTML recommendations insist that a client should ignore any elements and attributes that it doesn't recognize, so it's acceptable to include this "extra" markup.

The "animated banner" feature explored later in this chapter requires Cascading Style Sheets version 2.0 (CSS2) support, but the page will still work for CSS1 clients and clients that don't support CSS at all. I also use CSS style sheets to implement the formatting of text and other content, but include extra formatting elements so clients that do not recognize CSS at all will still produce an acceptable appearance.

Some features of the site depend on support for ASP.NET sessions, and I also include client-side code written in JavaScript 1.0 in some of the pages. You can't manage without session support in this application (this is a design decision taken when planning the site), but the pages are designed to work without client-side script as much as possible. I'll look at all these issues when building the individual pages, explain the design decisions, and see how to implement the features to support as many different types of client as possible.

ASP.NET Sessions

When building an interactive site that has to collect and store information provided by the user, as is the case with the example site, you have to find a way to save this data between page requests. I mentioned a few of the options that are available in Chapter 1, such as using hidden-type form controls, storing it in the viewstate of the page, or using ASP.NET sessions.

I chose the last of these, ASP.NET sessions, as being the most suitable for the site. Why? Well, a lot of information is going to be collected from each user about the car he or she wants to purchase, and so storing this in the page each time will be laborious and will increase the size of the page. It will also absorb extra bandwidth, as the complete set of values will be sent over the network twice with each page request/ response made by the user.

Instead, it makes sense to store the values on the server between requests, and access these values only when required. And the easiest way to store values that are specific to each user is by using the ASP.NET Session object.

ASP.NET is very good at managing sessions automatically, far better than previous versions of ASP where sessions could just occasionally "get lost" between requests. ASP.NET is also more efficient, with session support adding less of an overhead to the processing and loading of the server. There is still some extra overhead required to manage sessions, however, but the savings in bandwidth and page size can make up for this. It also, of course, saves the processing that the code would have to carry out to handle the values any other way.

Requirements for Session Support

For ASP.NET to be able to handle sessions properly, there are two things that must be considered:

- Does the client support cookies? If not you must use the cookie-less session features of ASP.NET to provide session support through "URL munging."

- Will the site run on a Web farm or in a multiple-server environment? If so, you have to ensure that the configuration of the site and servers properly supports sessions for each user.

You look at both of these issues next.

Cookies, Cookie-less Sessions, and URL Munging

ASP.NET uses a "session cookie" (a cookie that only remains on the client for 20 minutes or until the browser is closed down) to connect each client with the session information stored on the server. A unique session ID is stored in the cookie, and the Expires property of the cookie is updated each time a request is received so that it will only expire 20 minutes after the last page request from that user (you'll see how you can configure the timeout yourself later).

Session configuration in ASP.NET is through the machine.config file (stored in your Winnt\Microsoft.NET\Framework\[version]\config\ folder), and web.config files placed in the Web site root folder and subfolders. The default within the <system.web> section of these files is:

```
<sessionState mode="InProc" cookieless="false" timeout="20" />
```

This configuration causes the session data to be stored in memory on the server that handles the request, in much the same way as in ASP 3.0 and earlier (mode="InProc"). It also defines the way that sessions will be identified—in the default case using a cookie because the cookieless attribute is set to "false". The final attribute is, of course, the time-out for sessions, and it can be edited as required.

However, the behavior can be changed in various ways. For example, if the client does not support cookies (in which case the default configuration will not provide session support), you can change it to force ASP.NET to use cookie-less sessions through a process called *URL munging*. All that's required is to change the value of the cookieless attribute to "true". Then the session ID is automatically inserted into the URL when the response is sent to the client, for example:

```
http://.../cookieless-xroxcars/(s3vs5y55dsmkrqubtrvzvw55)/home.aspx
```

The session ID is also inserted into each hyperlink on the page automatically by the ASP.NET process:

```
<a href="cookieless-xroxcars/(s3vs5y55dsmkrqubtrvzvw55)/news.aspx">
  read this news article
</a>
```

The only issue is that this setting can only be used in machine.config (where it applies to the whole machine) or in a web.config file that is in the root directory of a Web site or in a virtual application root directory. You'll see the ramifications of this when you look at the example application later on.

The Session ID and Session Timeout

The ID used by ASP.NET for each user's session can be obtained from the read-only Session.SessionID property. You might want to use this ID to store data or identify specific sessions in some custom code of your own. However, in general, you should not need to concern yourself with the actual ID, as ASP.NET manages all this for you automatically.

The session timeout can be changed in ASP.NET by editing the value for timeout in the machine.config or web.config files on your server. It can also be changed within your code by setting the Session.Timeout property to an integer value for the number of minutes that a session should remain available after the last request from a client. A common scenario is to set it to something like 10 minutes to reduce the number of sessions that are stored on a busy server, but take care that you don't annoy your users.

For an application that handles sensitive data, such as the Web interface to your bank account, short session timeouts are usually acceptable (and are a good idea for security reasons to prevent users leaving a browser open after logging in). However, they might take more than 10 minutes to read and absorb a complex page (or stop to answer the phone or make a cup of coffee). For more mundane tasks, users might be upset if this means that they have to start all over again.

Session Support Across Multiple Servers

The second issue I mentioned earlier is how ASP.NET manages sessions when there is more than one server responding to requests. This is common in a Web farm or server cluster. If the session data is stored only on the machine that responds to the initial request, subsequent requests from this user must be routed to the same server every time. If not, the request will start a new session on the server it is directed to, and this new session won't contain the current session data.

Some Web farm software, routers, and load-balancing algorithms allow for affinity to be enabled. In general, this works by detecting the client's IP address and using this to decide which server in a cluster or Web farm will receive the request. In Windows Application Center and Windows 2000 Load Balancing, affinity divides requests among servers based on their Class "C" IP address space.

> **NOTE** *Class "C" address spaces use the first three of the four values in the "dotted format" IP numbering system as the address mask. In other words, all clients that have the same values for these parts of their IP address fall into the same Class "C" address space. As an example, the Class "C" address space (namespace mask) for the IP address 194.75.229.98 is 194.75.229.*

Other techniques exist—including using a cookie that is sent to the client to indicate which server should respond to the next request that is received. However, all these techniques mean that the effectiveness of load balancing for the cluster can be compromised, and that a server failure can disrupt existing sessions.

Instead, ASP.NET allows us to centralize the session data so that any server in a cluster or Web farm can respond to the request, and then get the session data for that client from the central store. The two types of "central store" you can use are the ASP.NET State Service or a SQL Server database. Both hit performance, being less efficient than the default "InProc" session data storage method, but the effects can be minimized (as you'll see later).

Using the ASP.NET State Service

The ASP.NET State Service uses one or more separate servers that are dedicated to storing session data, and these are assigned as the *session store*. The dedicated State Service runs on these servers, and all the other servers connect to it to obtain the session data each time. In machine.config or a web.config file, change the entry for the <sessionState> element within the <system.web> section. Set the mode to "StateServer" and add an attribute to specify the IP address of the server that is running the ASP.NET State Service. For example:

```
<sessionState mode="StateServer" cookieless="false" timeout="20"
              stateConnectionString="tcpip=194.75.229.123" />
```

The State Service is installed by default with ASP.NET, but not automatically started. It can be started from the command line by typing:

```
net start aspnet_state
```

However, you probably want to go into the Properties dialog for this service (go to Start | Programs | Administrative Tools | Services) and change the Startup type to Automatic. Cookie-less sessions can still be used when the ASP.NET State Service is holding the session data.

Using SQL Server for Session Support

Rather than using the ASP.NET State Service on a Web farm or server cluster, you can use a SQL Server database to hold the session data in a table. This technique can also improve reliability for very busy sites, as two SQL Server machines can be clustered to give some redundant backup in case of failure.

A SQL script file named InstallSqlState.sql is provided with ASP.NET (stored in the Winnt\Microsoft.NET\Framework\[version]\ folder) that you can execute to create the required database, table, and procedures within your SQL Server. Then it's just a matter of setting the mode attribute in machine.config or a web.config file to "SQLServer", and adding the sqlConnectionString attribute that specifies how to connect to the SQL Server database:

```
<sessionState mode="SQLServer" cookieless="false" timeout="20"
    sqlConnectionString="data source=194.75.229.123;user id=uid;password=pw" />
```

Cookie-less sessions can still be used when SQL Server is holding the session data.

Maximizing Performance When Using Sessions

No matter how they are implemented, sessions do hit the performance of ASP.NET. For "InProc" sessions this hit is reasonably low, and is generally acceptable in exchange for the advantage of automatic per-user state support that sessions provide. And, since ASP.NET uses an MTA thread pool to read and update session state (as opposed to an STA thread pool in classic ASP 3.0) when using the "StateServer" and "SQLServer" methods, it provides better system throughput than classic ASP. There is no thread affinity in the MTA thread pool, and hence no blocking and contention.

However, irrespective of how you actually implement the session storage, you can limit the loading imposed on the server by only accessing the session data when required, and by accessing it in read-only mode when possible. By "accessing the session data," I don't mean reading and writing it in code. What I mean is reducing the work ASP.NET has to do behind the scenes to manage the session data for us. Every request for an ASP.NET page raises a series of events on the server, and the appropriate modules that make up the ASP.NET runtime handle these events.

Two events that are executed by default for every page manage the values stored in a user's session. Near the start of the page execution cycle, before any of your own code in the page is executed, the session data is fetched from the state store (either "InProc", "StateServer", or "SQLServer") ready for use in the page. Then, once the page has been rendered and sent to the client, the session data is written back to the state store so any changes are persisted and are available for the next request.

If you have a page that does not use any of the session data, you should indicate this by adding the attribute EnableSessionState="False" to the page:

```
<%@Page Language="VB" EnableSessionState="False" %>
```

Then the two processes that load and save session state are not executed for this page (the default if this attribute is omitted, is for session data to be loaded and saved each time). You'll also get a compiler error if you try to access the user's session in code when sessions are not enabled for the page.

Alternatively, if you want to read session values but not *write* (update) them, you can use the value "ReadOnly" for the EnableSessionState attribute. This means that ASP.NET avoids the processing step required to write back (update) the stored session data:

```
<%@Page Language="VB" EnableSessionState="ReadOnly" %>
```

You use these attributes in the pages of the example site where appropriate—you'll see them in the code listings later in this chapter, and throughout the remainder of the book.

Client-Side Scripting

A client-side script that runs within the browser can produce an interactive user experience that can never be matched by posting back to the server—for example, changing the value or selection in <form> controls as the user interacts with the page, or moving the input focus to a specific control. If the user's browser supports Dynamic HTML or CSS2, then there are even more opportunities to make the page interactive by changing the content within the page dynamically without requiring a postback to the server. An example might be showing or hiding controls as the user makes selections in the page.

However, there are some browser clients that do not support client-side scripting, and there are also situations where support for it is not appropriate. An obvious example is a "page reader" designed to allow blind or partially sighted people to hear the content of the page read to them. There are also many users who still prefer text-based browsers such as Lynx (http://lynx.browser.org/).

Security is a big issue with Web browsers these days, and some users also disable client-side scripting in their browsers to protect against malicious activity in the pages they view (although, in general, client-side scripting is perfectly safe). So, for all these situations, you should make sure that your pages work without client-side script support wherever possible. Reduced interactivity might be a direct result, but the pages should still work (i.e., not appear to be "broken").

In the example site, I make only marginal use of client-side scripting in the "Home" page. It's limited to the animated banner at the top of the page, and opening a new window for the "Configure" page where the user can select the optional extras for the new car before placing an order. Where client-side script is disabled or unavailable, a static banner replaces the animated one, and the links to open the new window become "normal" <a> elements. The vehicle configuration page does use client-side script a great deal, however it still works (albeit less intuitively) when client-side scripting is not available.

Users and User IDs in the Xrox Car Company Site

I want to allow visitors to interact with the site by choosing a vehicle, and then configuring it by adding optional extras. Having done so, I will give them the opportunity to place an order for the vehicle, or save their selected configuration and come back to it later. I'll also allow them to come back and view orders they have previously placed and cars that they bought in the past. All this will happen when they select the My Cars link in the "Home" page.

While you won't be looking at these features until much later in the book, it's clear that there needs to be some kind of login system so that you can tell which cars and configurations belong to each particular visitor. So, I decided to automatically allocate *every* visitor a user ID as soon as he or she enters the site, and store it in the ASP.NET session. This user ID value is used to track the configuration options that the user makes when deciding to purchase a car, and allows users to save configurations and come back and edit them.

However, it may put users off if they are asked to log in straight away, as this may deter them from browsing the site and being tempted by special offers. Instead, you can store a user's ID in a cookie with a long Expires value on his or her machine. If a visitor arrives who doesn't already have a user ID cookie, you can use a temporary randomly generated user ID and then store this in a cookie, as well as storing it in the user's current session. You could alternatively use a GUID, or the unique ASP.NET session ID, but random generation is extremely unlikely to create the same temporary ID twice.

This means that the visitor doesn't have to provide any login details to enter the site or configure vehicles. Just use the user ID as a key in the database for any data saved for this user. Only when the user comes to place an order, or view existing orders or cars (using the My Cars link) will there be a prompt to either register with the site, or enter the password that matches the current user ID.

And, to make it more user friendly, you can allow visitors to select their own user ID when they register, and simply copy any data stored against their temporary ID to their new registered ID (and update their user ID cookie). Then, when they visit the site in the future, the code will use their own registered ID for access to their saved information.

Of course, if they destroy the cookie on their machine or use a different machine to access the site (or if their browser does not support cookies), they will start off with a new temporary randomly generated user ID. However, they can use the My Cars link to access the login dialog and then log in using their registered user ID and password. This means that they are reconnected to the saved data.

Checking for Sessions and Scripting Support

What if you decide that you need to change the behavior of the site to handle clients that don't support cookies (by using cookie-less sessions) and clients that don't support client-side scripting (by changing the way that the page works)? Of course, to be able to do this, you have to be able to detect whether each client does provide cookie and scripting support.

The techniques have been described in other books, and I also mentioned the client-side scripting detection code used in this application in the previous chapter of this book. The sample site has a default.aspx page that carries out two specific tasks:

- It stores a value in the user's session, which you can look for in the next ("Home") page to see if a session is available.

- It redirects the client to the "Home" page, adding a name/value pair to the query string if client-side script is supported. Then, if you can find this name/value pair within the Request.QueryString collection in your "Home" page, you know that client-side scripting is both available and enabled.

However, before you look at the code in detail, you also need to take into account how you will identify users who come back to the site to view their current orders, their own vehicle details, and any configurations that they may have saved during previous visits. As you saw earlier, the site depends on a user ID that is saved in a cookie, or if none is available it needs to create a new one for every visitor.

Client Capabilities and User ID Detection

Figure 3-3 shows the overall process implemented to collect a user ID from each visitor as he or she enters the site (or to create a new one), and at the same time detect if the client supports sessions and scripting.

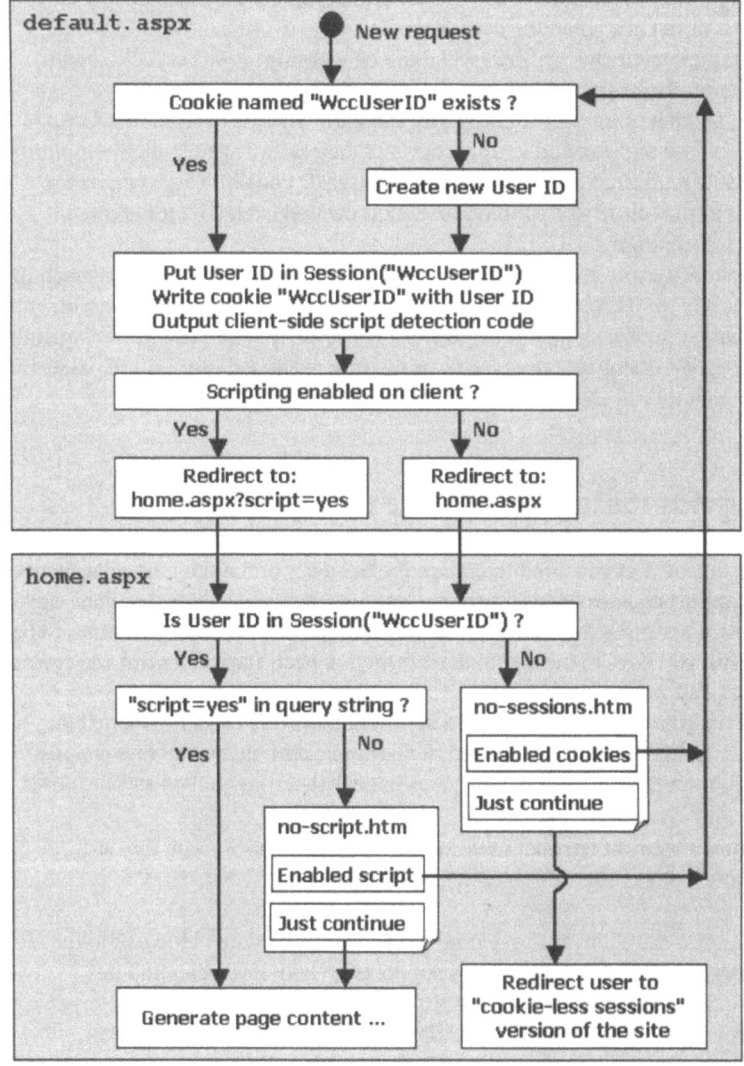

Figure 3-3. An outline of the client detection and cookie handling process

Most of the work is done in the two pages `default.aspx` and `home.aspx`, with the other two pages (`no-script.htm` and `no-sessions.htm`) only there to act as warnings that scripting or cookie support is not available, and to give the user a choice of what to do about it. You look at the code itself in detail next.

The Code in `default.aspx`

The next listing shows the server-side code `<script>` section for the page `default.aspx`. You declare a `String` variable to hold a user ID that you'll need within the site as a whole, and a `DateTime` variable that you set to the current date and time. Then look to see if the user's browser sent a cookie with the request that contains the existing ID for this user. If you don't find one, generate a new unique value using the date and a random number between 0 and 999.

Now that you know what the user ID is, either an existing one or one just created, write it back to the client by creating a new cookie named `WccUserID` that applies to the whole site (`Path = "/"`), and which has a long `expires` value (five years from now). Store the user ID in this user's session:

`default.aspx`

```
<%@Page Language="VB" EnableViewState="False" EnableSessionState="True"%>
<script runat=""server"">
Sub Page_Load()
  ' declare string to hold user ID
  Dim sUserID As String = ""

  ' get current date and time
  Dim dNow As DateTime = Now()

  ' get UserID from long-expiry cookie if possible
  Dim oCookie As HttpCookie = Request.Cookies("WccUserID")
  If Not oCookie Is Nothing Then
    sUserID = oCookie.Value
  End If
  If sUserID = "" Then
    ' no value, so create new UserID
    Dim oRandom As New Random()
    sUserID = "~" & dNow.ToString("yyMMddhhmmss") _
              & oRandom.Next(0, 999).ToString()
  End If
  ' update UserID cookie
  oCookie = New HttpCookie("WccUserID", sUserID)
  oCookie.Path = "/"
  oCookie.Expires = dNow.AddYears(5)
  Response.Cookies.Add(oCookie)
```

```
    store UserID in Session object
  Session("WccUserID") = sUserID

End Sub
</script>
...
```

The HTML and Content in default.aspx

The remainder of the default.aspx page contains the output that the user will see, and the client-side script detection code. As I indicated towards the end of the previous chapter, you can use a <meta> directive (element) to redirect the client to another page—in this case after one second to the page no-script.htm. However, default.aspx also contains a client-side script section that will be executed as the page loads, and which redirects the client to the page home.aspx, with the name/value pair "script=yes" appended to the URL if client-side scripting is available and enabled:

default.aspx

```
...
<!doctype html public "-//IETF//DTD HTML 2.0//EN">
<html>
<head>
<meta http-equiv="refresh" content="1;url=no-script.htm" />
<title>Checking for Client Scripting Support</title>

<script language="JavaScript">
<!--
function jumpScripting() {
// jump to page using client-side JavaScript—if jump not executed
// then client does not have scripting available or it is disabled
window.location.href='home.aspx?script=yes';
}
//-->
</script>
</head>
...
```

The <body> section of the page contains some text that is displayed as the next page is loading, plus a <noscript> section. Only clients that do not implement client-side scripting at all should display the contents of this section, and it is included in case the client does not implement the <meta http-equiv="refresh"> directive placed in the <head> section of the page. Within the <noscript> element you provide some text information about the site, plus links to some locations from which script-enabled browsers can be obtained:

```
...
<body onload="jumpScripting()">
<font size="2" face="Tahoma,Arial,sans-serif">
Checking for script support in your browser... </font>
<noscript>
  <p><font size="2" face="Tahoma,Arial,sans-serif" color="#ff0000">
  <b>Please note:</b></font></p>
  <p><font size="2" face="Tahoma,Arial,sans-serif">Your browser does
  not support Active Scripting or client-side JavaScript, or it is
  disabled in your security settings. For best results, you should
  enable this before using the application. If not, you will be
  unable to take full advantage of the features of this site. Some
  will require extra requests to the server, or involve extra steps
  on your behalf.</p>
  <p><font size="2" face="Tahoma,Arial,sans-serif">
  Suitable browsers can be downloaded from:
  <ul>
   <li><font size="2" face="Tahoma,Arial,sans-serif">
     <a href="http://www.microsoft.com">http://www.microsoft.com</a></font>
   </li>
   <li><font size="2" face="Tahoma,Arial,sans-serif">
     <a href="http://www.netscape.com/">http://www.netscape.com</a></font>
   </li>
   <li><font size="2" face="Tahoma,Arial,sans-serif">
     <a href="http://www.opera.com/">http://www.opera.com</a></font>
   </li><p />
   <li><font size="2" face="Tahoma,Arial,sans-serif">
     However, in the meantime, you can still:</font>
   </li>
   <li><font size="2" face="Tahoma,Arial,sans-serif">
     <b><a href="home.aspx">Continue to Xrox Car Company</a></b></font>
   </li>
  </ul>
  </font>
</noscript>
</body>
</html>
```

Note that, as the sample site will generally work OK without client-side script, you can also provide a link at the bottom of the page where the user can enter the site anyway. Figure 3-4 shows what the page looks like in Amaya, which does not support client-side scripting at all and so displays the contents of the <noscript> section.

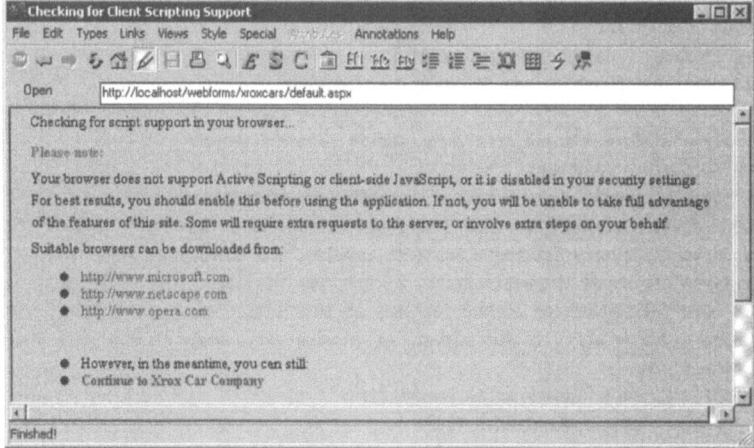

Figure 3-4. Accessing the site with a browser that does not support client-side scripting

The no-script.htm *Page*

The default.aspx page you've just seen contains a <meta> directive that will be executed by the browser if it does not support scripting, but does react to a redirection directive:

```
<meta http-equiv="refresh" content="1;url=no-script.htm" />
```

Amaya does not process <meta> redirection directives, which is why you saw the <noscript> section in Figure 3-4. However, most other browsers do process this directive, and so are redirected to the page no-script.htm. This allows you to display a more informative message, and provide the user with a couple of options. Here's the complete listing of that page:

no-script.htm

```
<!doctype html public "-//IETF//DTD HTML 2.0//EN">
<html>
<head><title>Client-side Scripting Not Available</title></head>
<body>
<h3><font size="4" face="Tahoma,Arial,sans-serif">
Client-side Scripting Not Available</font></h3>
<font size="2" face="Tahoma,Arial,sans-serif" color="#ff0000">
<b>Please note:</b></font><br />
```

```
<font size="2" face="Tahoma,Arial,sans-serif">
Either you entered the site directly without starting from the
<a href="default.aspx">default page</a>, or your browser<br />
does not support Active Scripting or client-side JavaScript.
It might be disabled in the options<br /> page for security settings.
For best results, you should enable this before using the application.
<br /> If not, you will be unable to take full advantage of the features
of this site. Some features will<br />require extra requests to the
server, or involve extra steps on your behalf.</font><br />
<ul>
 <li><font size="2" face="Tahoma,Arial,sans-serif">I have
      <a href="default.aspx">enabled client-side scripting</a>
      and I want to use the application</font></li>
 <li><font size="2" face="Tahoma,Arial,sans-serif">I want to
      <a href="home.aspx">continue into the site</a> anyway</font></li>
</ul>
</body>
</html>
```

You can see that there is a link to default.aspx for visitors to use if they originally entered the site elsewhere (in which case they will not have a user ID in their session and so will be redirected here by certain pages that require a user ID). There is also a second link to default.aspx that they can use once they have enabled scripting in their browser.

The default.aspx page will then check for scripting support again, and (provided that it is now available) redirect them to the "Home" page. The final link allows a visitor to go to the "Home" page using a browser that does not support client-side scripting, or without enabling script support if that is the way he or she prefers to work (Figure 3-5).

Figure 3-5. The warning page when client-side scripting is disabled in the browser

Enabling and Disabling Client-Side Scripting

You can test the redirection feature in default.aspx page in most browsers that do support client-side scripting by turning it off. In Navigator 6, client-side script can be disabled in the Edit | Preferences | Advanced dialog (Figure 3-6).

Figure 3-6. Setting client-side scripting options in Navigator 6

In Internet Explorer 5 and 6, client-side script can be disabled in the Tools | Internet Options | Security | Custom Level dialog. You can also elect to be prompted, and then choose whether to allow script to run or not as the page is displayed each time (Figure 3-7).

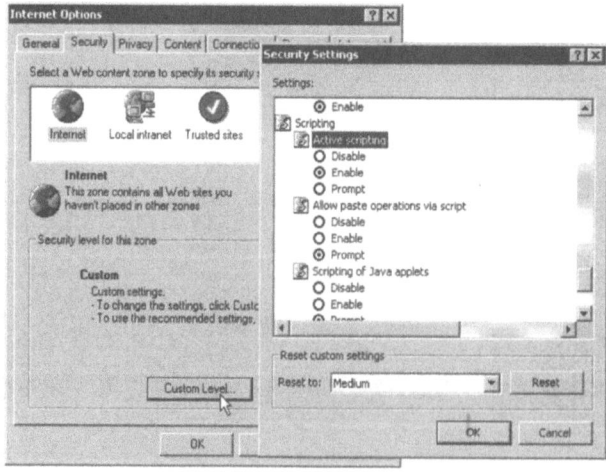

Figure 3-7. Setting client-side scripting options in Internet Explorer 5 and 6

Interestingly, when you disable client-side script in Navigator 6 or Internet Explorer 6, the contents of the <noscript> element in default.aspx are displayed. So users will see this flash up when they first enter the site, but only for the one second until the <meta> directive loads the "No Script" page.

The Detection Code in home.aspx

You'll be looking at the "Home" page (home.aspx) in detail in the next chapter. However, to complete the session and scripting detection, I'll show you the code in home.aspx that carries out the remainder of the task now. The next listing shows this code:

home.aspx

```
Sub Page_Load()
  ' get UserID from Session put there by default.aspx
  ' if not there, browser does not support Sessions (cookies)
  ' or did not load default.aspx first
  If CType(Session("WccUserID"), String) = "" Then
    Response.Clear()
    Response.Redirect("no-sessions.htm")
    Response.End
  End if

  ' get value of "script" from query string *or* Session to see
  ' if browser supports client-side scripting and it is enabled
  If Request.QueryString("script") = "yes" _
  Or CType(Session("WccCanScript"), Boolean) = True Then
    bCanScript = True
    Session("WccCanScript") = "True"      ' store in Session
  End If

  ...
  ... {remainder of Page_Load event handler code is here}
  ...

End Sub
```

You can see from this that two sets of checks are performed as the page is loaded each time. The page collects the user ID from the session, where it was stored by default.aspx. If it can't find a user ID, it means either that the client has entered the site without loading default.aspx first, or that the browser does not support cookies. The code redirects them to a page named no-sessions.htm, which you'll look at very soon.

Secondly, the page looks in the query string for the name/value pair "script=yes", or in the session for the value WccCanScript="True". If the client is just entering the site from default.aspx, the name/value pair will be in the query string. If the client is coming back to the "Home" page from another page, the value will be stored in the session instead.

If either of these values do exist, you know that the client's browser supports client-side scripting, and so set a page-level `Boolean` variable named `bCanScript` to `True`, and update the session value `WccCanScript`. Now, in any page of the site, you can extract the user's ID from their session, and check if the browser supports client-side scripting.

The `no-sessions.htm` *Page*

Providing that your client's browser supports cookies, and cookies are not disabled or blocked in the browser's security options, the user will now be looking at your "Home" page. However, if the browser does not support standard (cookie-based) sessions, the user will now be looking at the page `no-sessions.htm`.

The next listing shows `no-sessions.htm`. Provide your visitor with a similar explanation of the problem as in the `no-script.htm` page, together with a link to go to `default.aspx` if he or she entered the site elsewhere (so no user ID was created and stored in the session). You can also provide a link that the user can use to go back to `default.aspx` after enabling cookies in the browser:

`no-sessions.htm`

```
<!doctype html public "-//IETF//DTD HTML 2.0//EN">
<html>
<head><title>Cookie Support Not Available</title></head>
<body>
<h3><font size="4" face="Tahoma,Arial,sans-serif">
Cookie Support Not Available</font></h3>
<font size="2" face="Tahoma,Arial,sans-serif" color="#ff0000">
<b>Please note:</b></font><br />
<font size="2" face="Tahoma,Arial,sans-serif">
Either you entered the site directly without starting from the
<a href="default.aspx">default page</a>, or your browser<br />
does not support cookies, or they have been disabled in your security
settings. You must<br />either enable cookies before using the
application, or use the alternative version that does<br />
not require cookie support.</font><br />
<ul>
    <li><font size="2" face="Tahoma,Arial,sans-serif">I have
        <a href="default.aspx">enabled cookie support</a>
        and I want to use the application</font></li>
    <li><font size="2" face="Tahoma,Arial,sans-serif">I will use the
        <a href="/webforms/cookieless-xroxcars/default.aspx">alternative
        version</a> of the application</font></li>
</ul>
</body>
</html>
```

Cookie-based or Cookie-less Sessions?

What you use for the final link in the no-sessions.htm page depends on what you decide to do about clients that don't support cookies, and for whom you therefore cannot support cookie-based sessions in the site. You could simply turn them away, but that certainly isn't good business practice. A better alternative is to take advantage of the "cookie-less sessions" feature I discussed earlier in this chapter. You could:

- Set up the site to always use cookie-less sessions for all clients. The downside to this is the ugly URL that users see in the browser, and the extra work that ASP.NET has to do to modify all the links and URLs for each page.

- Provide a mirror copy of the site that uses cookie-less sessions, to which you redirect visitors that do not support cookies.

As you can see from the final link in the previous listing, and in Figure 3-8, I chose the second option for the sample site. As long as you are aware of a few minor issues when coding the pages (you'll look at these for the "Home" page in the next chapter), the two copies of the site will be identical and so can be mirrored on the same server, on separate clustered servers, or even in different geographical locations.

Figure 3-8. The warning page when cookies are disabled in the browser

Of course, in the "Home" page where you redirect the client to the no-sessions.htm page, you could just redirect them straight to the "cookie-less" version of the application. However, recall that users might enter the site somewhere other than default.aspx, and so it makes sense to give them the option to use the default version of the site (as in our example).

> **NOTE** *Remember that you have to create a separate virtual application for the cookie-less version of the site if you want to run both cookie-based and cookie-less versions on the same server. The sample files contain the appropriate* web.config *file for cookie-less session support in the folder* cookieless-xroxcars, *and you must configure this folder as a virtual application root as discussed at the start of this chapter.*

Enabling and Disabling Cookie Support

You can test the site, or your own session detection code, by disabling cookies in your browser. In Netscape 6, this is done in the Privacy & Security section of the Preferences dialog. You can disable cookies altogether or have the browser prompt you before accepting one (Figure 3-9).

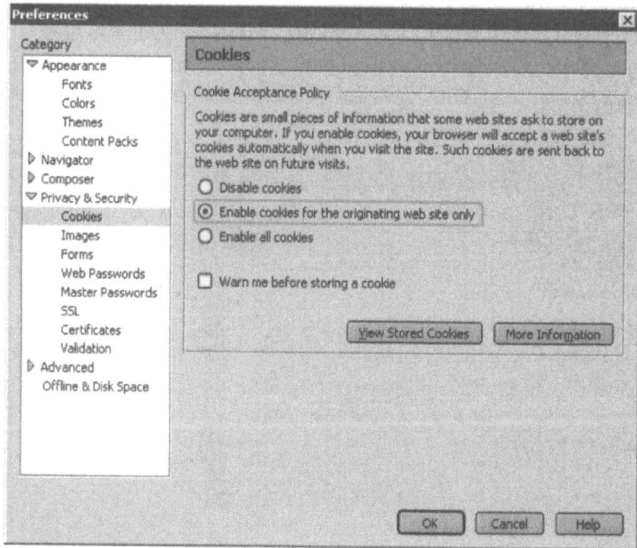

Figure 3-9. Controlling cookie acceptance in Navigator 6

In Internet Explorer 6, cookie support is configured in the Privacy page of the Internet Options dialog. As well as "general" settings such as High, Medium, and Low, you can use the Advanced dialog to specify exactly how cookies should be handled (Figure 3-10).

Figure 3-10. Controlling cookie acceptance in Internet Explorer 5 and 6

First-party cookies are those that come from the same domain as the page itself. Third-party cookies are those sent by other domains, perhaps when the browser loads an image from a different domain into this page. Turning off third-party cookies is the same as de-selecting the Enable cookies for the originating Web site only option in Netscape 6.

> **NOTE** *Notice that Internet Explorer also has an option to allow per-session cookies while blocking other (persistent) cookies. The difference between per-session cookies and persistent cookies is that the latter are stored on disk, while per-session cookies are automatically destroyed when you leave the Web site.*

Cross-Browser Compatibility Issues

As time progresses, you should expect the issues of browser compatibility that used to make life so hard for Web developers to become much less of a problem. All the major browser manufacturers have committed to follow the current and emerging recommendations from the World Wide Web consortium (the W3C at http://www.w3.org/). However, things are still made awkward by several factors:

- You should still attempt to support older and less well-known browsers where possible.

- Not all browsers interpret the recommendations in exactly the same way.

- A proportion of visitors will have special needs, for example they are blind or have difficulties using a standard keyboard and mouse. They are likely to be using a special browser, and you should endeavor to provide as much extra support as you can for these clients.

- There are lots of different display mediums appearing, such as pocket PCs, mobile phones, WebTV, and many more. Some of these (in particular mobile devices) may require something other than HTML, or may support only a subset of HTML.

I haven't attempted to answer the last of these issues in this book, or in the example site, though I will concentrate on the first three.

Browsers for Testing Your Pages

It's extremely difficult (if not impossible) to test your pages on all the different browsers that you may encounter on the Web. Not only are there many different manufacturers and individual versions, but most have incremental updates available as well. And even this doesn't account for how they perform on different operating systems. Netscape browsers are available to run on a very wide range of platforms, and Internet Explorer has long been a popular browser on the Apple Mac.

I have tested the sample pages in the following browsers running on Windows 2000:

- Internet Explorer 6.0, as required by and installed with the .NET Framework.

- Netscape 6.2.2, which implements a version of the Mozilla rendering engine.

- Netscape Navigator/Communicator 4.5, which uses a highly non-standard rendering engine and includes many features not found in other browsers.

- Mozilla 1.0 Release Candidate 2, available from http://www.Mozilla.org/. Although only at version 1.0, it is fundamentally a "version 6" browser that renders content with a version of the same rendering engine as Netscape 6.

- Opera version 6.02, available from http://www.opera.com/.

- Amaya 6.1, released in April 2002 by the W3C as a reference and test browser for HTML and CSS.

It's difficult to use earlier versions of many browsers, because you can't install them once a later version is in place. Internet Explorer is a good example of this, and in mid-2002 I was unable to find a machine where I could test pages with Internet Explorer 4. One possible solution is to make a test page available on the Web and get as many users as possible to access it and report problems. I regularly do this on my own Web site (http://www.daveandal.com/) when building new sample applications.

Having said all this, it's good to see that some uniformity is beginning to appear. The four main players (Microsoft, Netscape, Opera, and Mozilla) have "version 6" browsers available that are remarkably compliant with HTML 4.01 and CSS2 recommendations, and pages generally work the same on these browsers.

Standing out from the crowd is Amaya. It does not support many "modern" features, such as frames, client-side script, cookies, and other features. However, it does provide a good guide to what your pages might look like in some of the more basic browsers and rendering engines.

Other User Agents

I also test the pages in two other user agents. Technically these are browsers, though they tend to be used mainly by people who have a disability, or who don't want to take advantage of the usual graphical appearance that (almost without exception these days) Web sites provide. I use:

- Lynx version 2.8.3, which is a text-only browser available from
  `http://lynx.browser.org/`. Figure 3-11 shows the Home page of the Xrox Car Company site in Lynx.

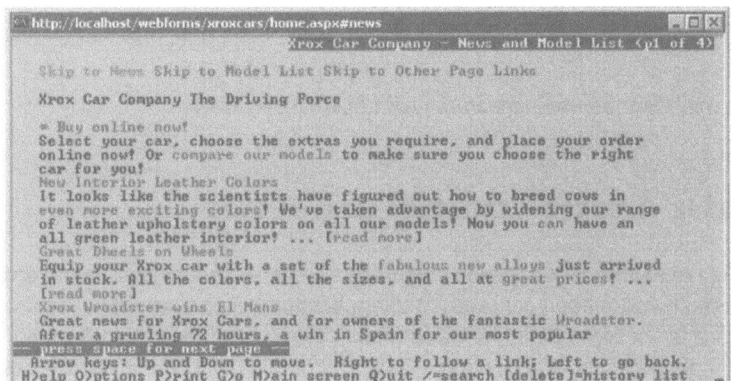

Figure 3-11. The Xrox Cars "Home" page in Lynx

- IBM Home Page Reader (HPR) version 3.02, which is a special user agent that reads Web pages aloud for people who suffer from impaired vision. A trial version can be obtained from `http://www-3.ibm.com/able/hpr.html`. It's a great way to see (or hear) how your Web site actually appears to some visitors. You can see what the Xrox Car Company Home page looks like in HPR 3.0 in Figure 3-12, where the word currently being read out is highlighted.

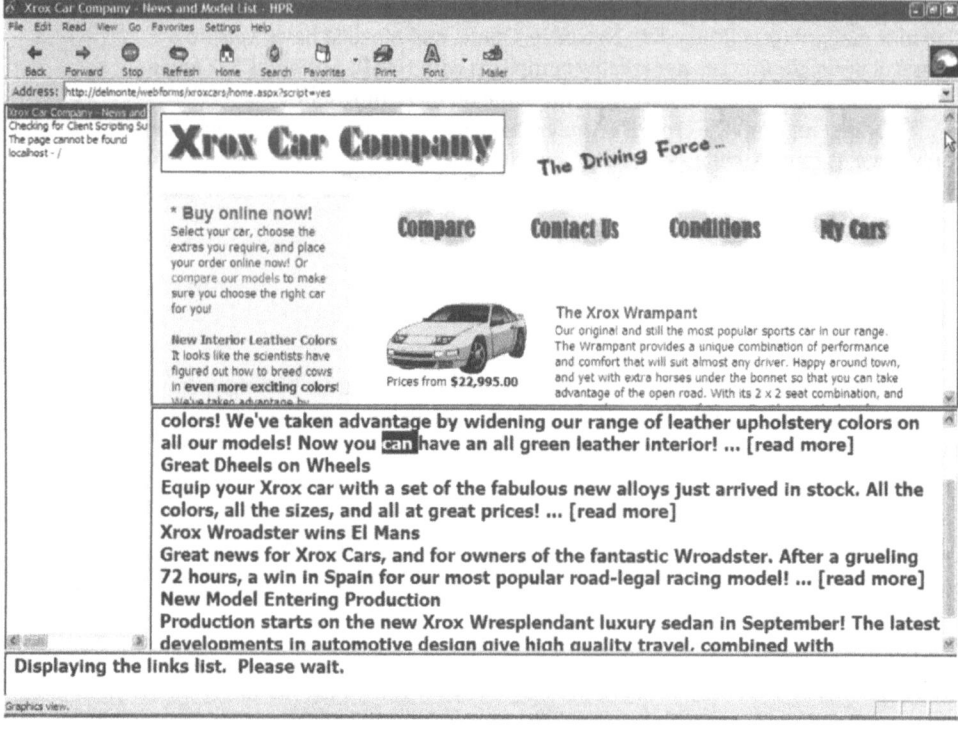

Figure 3-12. The Xrox Cars "Home" page in the IBM Home Page Reader

Solving Browser Compatibility Issues

Having talked about the browsers themselves, what are the main issues involved when you come to build pages and Web applications? As discussed earlier, almost all browsers in use today (with the exception of some special devices such as mobile or cellular phones) support HTML 3.2—or a broad subset of it. So the usual types of formatting used, including tables, <font> elements, direct formatting, and structure elements (such as <b>, <br>, <h1>, and so on) are going to work fine.

Almost every browser will recognize <span>, and most recognize <div>. And without exception "active" elements such as <a>, <input>, <select>, and <textarea> will work fine. Frames are less universally compatible, and certainly Amaya and Lynx do not support them directly. However, they do provide support for navigating between frames; so if you do need to use them you can generally get away with it (I discussed the design decisions as regards frames towards the end of Chapter 1).

The other good news is that most recent browsers recognize a few extra attributes, which are technically not part of the HTML 3.2 standards. Examples are topmargin and leftmargin for a <body> element, and face for a <font> element.

> **NOTE** *You can view and download the full recommendations for HTML 3.2, and other versions of HTML, CSS, and other recommendations from the W3C Web site at* http://www.w3.org/.

As you move towards the more esoteric presentation methods, however, support becomes less universal. ActiveX controls will only work in Internet Explorer (or with a special "ActiveX wrapper" plug-in installed in other browsers such as Netscape 6), and many non-mainstream browsers won't load Java applets either. Thankfully it's becoming commonplace for many new sites to avoid these, both for compatibility reasons and because most "savvy" users consider them to be a security risk and so block them in their security settings.

Techniques for Maximizing Compatibility

For your purposes, the main areas where there are issues to resolve in the site, and in sites that rely on similar feature sets, are:

- Declaring and linking to the CSS style sheets used in your pages

- Specifying font styles, types, and sizes

- Getting the layout of page sections and individual elements to be the same

- Making script-driven animations and other "actions" work correctly in all scriptable clients

- Coping with the often-indeterminate behavior of Navigator/Communicator 4.x

I'll look at some solutions next, and you'll see more details when I explore the code for the various pages in our site later in the book.

Declaring and Linking to CSS Style Sheets

In general, the recommendation for using CSS is to *link* to the style sheet rather than inserting the individual style definitions into the page within a <style> section. This not only makes it easier to change the styles later, and have all pages use the same style, but it also allows the browser to decide whether or not to download the style sheet at all. On top of this, the browser can download the style sheet once and cache it, thereby improving response times and reducing bandwidth usage.

For example, there would be no point in Lynx downloading a style sheet, as it only displays text. If you insert the style information into the page, you are just making the page bigger for no reason, and with no benefit for some clients.

The recommended way to link to a style sheet is with a <link> element placed within the <head> section of the page:

```
<link rel="stylesheet" title="Default" href="stylesheets/wccStd.css" />
```

You can also provide more than one style sheet for a page. Add the title attribute to each one, and all those that carry the same value for this attribute are combined—effectively the individual style selectors are inherited from all these style sheets. If you provide more than one style sheet, but don't want them to be combined, use the title attribute to indicate the purpose of each one. The value "Default" for this attribute indicates the style sheet that is used by default, and in some browsers the user can choose from the other linked style sheets as well.

When using more than one style sheet, change the rel attribute from "stylesheet" to "alternate stylesheet", and be sure to include a different value for the title attribute for each <link> you include. As an example, you could have added links to six of the standard style sheets that are available from W3C to our existing style sheet link in the "Home" page of our example site:

```
<link rel='"stylesheet" title="Default" href="stylesheets/wccStd.css" />
<link rel="alternate stylesheet" title="Modernist"
      href="http://www.w3.org/StyleSheets/Core/Modernist" />
<link rel="alternate stylesheet" title="Midnight"
      href="http://www.w3.org/StyleSheets/Core/Midnight" />
<link rel="alternate stylesheet" title="Ultramarine"
      href="http://www.w3.org/StyleSheets/Core/Ultramarine" />
<link rel="alternate stylesheet" title="Swiss"
      href="http://www.w3.org/StyleSheets/Core/Swiss" />
<link rel="alternate stylesheet" title="Chocolate"
      href="http://www.w3.org/StyleSheets/Core/Chocolate" />
<link rel="alternate stylesheet" title="Steely"
      href="http://www.w3.org/StyleSheets/Core/Steely" />
```

Then, in Mozilla, you would be able to choose which style sheet to apply to the page (Figure 3-13).

While the W3C style sheets are mainly "decorative," you might also decide to provide alternative style sheets that use a simpler color range (or even just two colors), or that change the text size or layout, so that visitors who suffer poor vision can more easily use the pages.

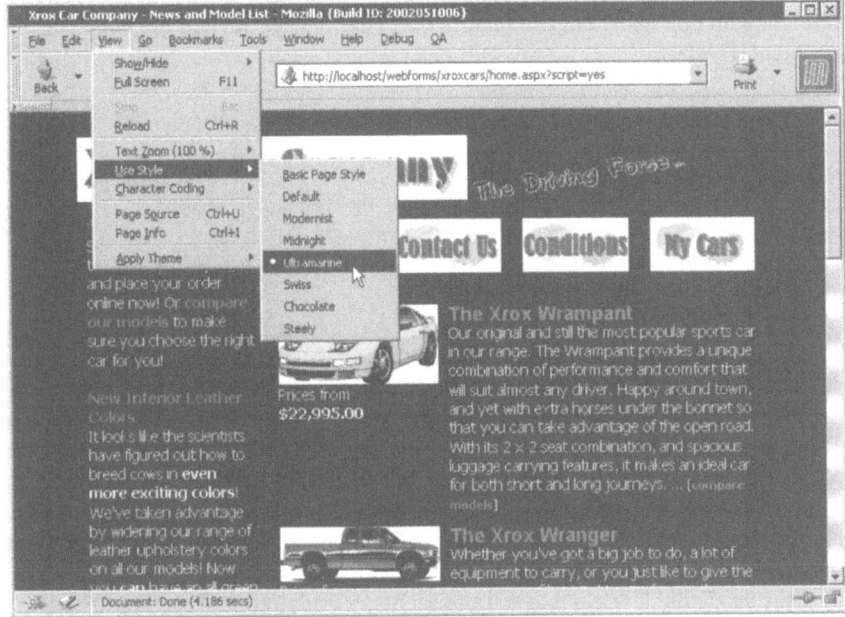

Figure 3-13. Choosing the style sheet to apply in Mozilla

Font Styles, Types, and Sizes

You saw in the previous chapter how the ASP.NET server controls vary their output depending on the type of client (up-level or down-level) that accesses the page where they are used. In general, there are two approaches to specifying the font style, type, and size: you can use CSS style sheets or the more universally acceptable <font> element.

CSS is the better solution, giving finer control over the appearance of text. You can specify the font family, color, and size (to within very fine limits, such as by pixel, point, or em). You can also specify things like the padding and margin widths (top, bottom, left, and right), the alignment, the text decoration (underlined, strikeout, and so on), and whether elements should be visible, hidden, or not occur within the rendered output at all (display:none).

In CSS2, you can also add definitions for the positioning and layout, such as absolute positioning (specifying the top, left, width, and height), the z-order, and you can animate the images using script (many of these features also work as "Dynamic HTML" in Internet Explorer 4 onwards).

However, CSS as a whole only works properly (with some minor exceptions) in Mozilla 1.0, Internet Explorer 4.x and later, Netscape 6.x and later, and Opera 3.x and later. In earlier browser versions, it's difficult to rely on getting the appearance you actually want just by using CSS.

Probably the easiest way to get maximum compatibility is to combine <font> elements with CSS styles. For example, in our "Home" page, there is the following section of HTML:

```
<font face="Arial,Helvetica,sans-serif" size="4" color="#b50055">
<span class="large-red-text"><b>* Buy online now!</b></span><br /></font>
<font face="Tahoma,Arial,Helvetica,sans-serif" size="2">
<span class="body-text">Select your car, choose the extras you require,
and place your order online now! Or </span><a class="std-link""
href="compare.aspx">compare our models</a><span class="body-text"> to make sure
you choose the right car for you!</span></font>
```

The innermost nested formatting instructions take precedence, so in the example the CSS styles take preference over the <font> elements. However, if you had placed the <font> elements within the <span> elements instead, the <font> elements would take precedence.

Any aspects of the formatting that are not specified in the innermost instruction are inherited from the parent (enclosing) element in line with the inheritance rules of CSS. So, if our body-text style class did not define the font color, it would be inherited from the enclosing <font> element.

So, after all this, it's clear that you can get better overall control over the appearance of our pages in a wide range of browsers by using a combination of nested <font> elements and CSS styles. When our "Home" page is viewed in our six test browsers, you can see that all of them produce acceptably similar output (Figures 3-14 and 3-15).

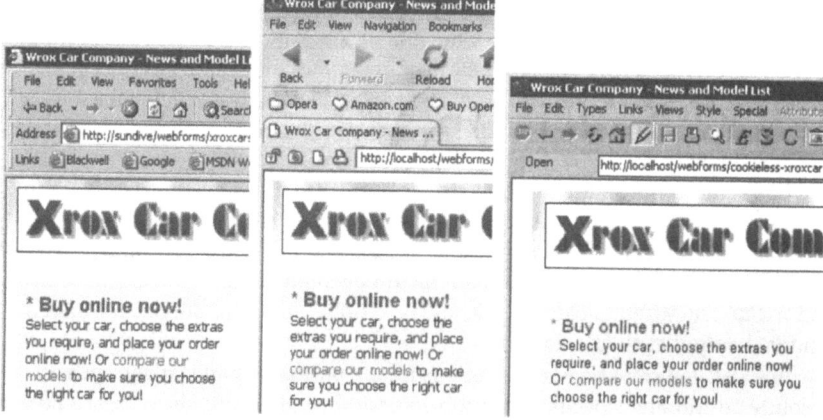

Figure 3-14. A section of the "Home" page in Internet Explorer, Opera, and Amaya

Figure 3-15. A section of the "Home" page in Mozilla, and two different versions of Netscape

One problem is that font size can only be specified in fairly broad steps in a `<font>` element, as numbers from 1 to 7 (or as relative sizes against a `<basefont>` definition using +1, -2, and so on). So you may have to juggle the CSS `font-size` selectors to match this if you want to get exactly the same font size in all browsers.

Using Predefined Font Sizes

Better still is to do as I did in the example site—use the predefined font sizes in the CSS style sheet. These were discussed in the previous chapter, and the values available are `"xx-small"`, `"x-small"`, `"small"`, `"smaller"`, `"medium"`, `"large"` ,`"larger"`, `"x-large"`, and `"xx-large"`. The big advantage with these is that it allows visitors to change the size of the text size displayed in the browser window using the features of their browser.

For example, in Internet Explorer, they can use the Text Size item on the View menu to enlarge the font size if they have problems reading small text. You can see the effect in Figure 3-16 if you compare it with the previous ones.

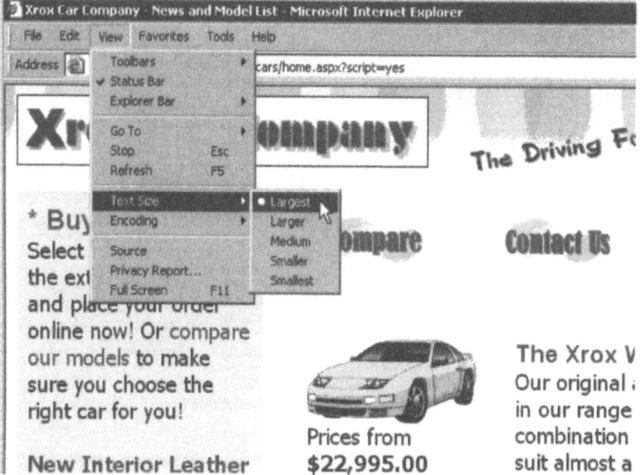

Figure 3-16. Changing the size of the text while viewing the page

If you define the font sizes in your style sheet using absolute values (such as "12px" or "10pt"), the user will not be able to resize the text when viewing the page.

Font Names and Colors

One point to remember, especially if you only test your pages on one operating system (for example, only on Windows 2000 as I have already owned up to doing!) is that font names are often O/S-specific. I prefer a sans-serif font for the sample pages, and so specify our font-family as:

```
font-family:Tahoma,Arial,Helvetica,sans-serif;
```

The browser will use the first one it recognizes. If none of them are actual font names on the platform where the browser is running, it will use the "generic" font names to give a font that has the same basic properties. The generic font names are "serif", "sans-serif", "cursive", "fantasy", and "monospace".

In a <font> element, use the face attribute to specify the same series of fonts:

```
<font face="Tahoma,Arial,Helvetica,sans-serif" size="2" color="#cc3333">
```

It's also worth using numeric values for any colors you specify, rather than the color names. While most modern browsers do recognize a series of standard color names, you can be certain that all of them will be able to interpret the color from its hexadecimal equivalent (as seen in the <font> element listed above). You might also like to stay with using just the 216 "browser-safe" colors, rather than mixing your own.

A search of the Web for "browser-safe colors" will bring up plenty of sites that list the safe colors and their hexadecimal equivalents (Google found 8,400 such sites!). A reference that I use most often is at the W3C: http://www.w3.org/MarkUp/Guide/Style.

ASP.NET Server Controls and the CssClass Property

You may recall from the previous chapter that the ASP.NET server controls are clever enough to change the output they generate based on the client type—either "up-level" or "down-level." The examples in that chapter used specific combinations of style elements to control the appearance of the output. Or, to put it another way, I specified values for the many different attributes of the controls that affect the appearance when rendered.

For example, in the demonstration of the ASP.NET Label control, I used this code to declare the control (color names are used here so that you can more easily see how they relate to the output that the control generates):

```
<asp:label id="lblTest" runat="server"
           forecolor="red"
           backcolor="yellow"
           font-size="large"
           font-bold="true"
           bordercolor="black"
           borderwidth="3"
           text="a yellow label control with red text" />
```

For up-level clients (basically, Internet Explorer 4 and above), the control generates a <style> element that combines all the specified attribute values specified:

```
<span id="lblTest" style="color:Red;background-color:Yellow;border-
color:Black;border-width:3px;border-style:solid;font-size:Large;font-
weight:bold;">a yellow label control with red text</span>
```

And the appearance is much as you would expect (Figure 3-17).

a yellow label control with red text

Figure 3-17. The styled Label *control in Internet Explorer*

However, when you access the same page with a "down-level" client, such as Netscape 6, you get totally different output generated (as discussed in the previous chapter). Instead of a style attribute you only get a nested <font> element (Figure 3-18).

```
<span id="lblTest"><b><font color="Red" size="5">a yellow label control with red
text</font></b></span>
```

Obviously, this cannot provide the formatting information required to produce the yellow background and black border.

a yellow label control with red text

Figure 3-18. The styled Label *control in Netscape 6*

However, all of the ASP.NET Web Forms controls that create visible output in the page expose a property named CssClass. You can set this to the name of the CSS class defined in a style sheet (or in a <style> section within the page), and it will be added as the class attribute of the element(s) generated by the control.

So, first create a style sheet or a <style> definition within the page like this:

```
.body-text {
  font-size:large; font-weight:bold;    color:red; background:yellow;
  border-width:3;  border-color:black;  border-style:solid;
}
```

Then define your server control like this:

```
<asp:label id="lblTest" runat="server"
          cssclass="body-text"
          text="a yellow label control with red text" />
```

Now, irrespective of the type of client that hits the page, the output of the control is just:

```
<span id="lblTest" class="body-text">a yellow label control with red text</span>
```

The only issue now is what happens if the client does not support CSS? The solution is easy—you declare your server control with specific properties for the appearance, *and* set the CssClass property:

```
<asp:label id="lblTest" runat="server"
           forecolor="red"
           backcolor="yellow"
           font-size="large"
           font-bold="true"
           bordercolor="black"
           borderwidth="3"
           cssclass="body-text"
           text="a yellow label control with red text" />
```

Now, in an "up-level" client, you get both a class attribute on the `<span>` element, and a full set of `style` selectors that mirror the individual attribute values specified for the server control. Following the CSS rules for the inheritance of style values, the selectors in the `style` attribute override the selectors for the CSS "body-text" style. But, because you used values for the server control attributes that replicate the styles defined for "body-text", the result is the same:

```
<span id="lblTest" class="body-text" style="color:Red;background-color:Yellow;
border-color:Black;border-width:3px;border-style:solid;font-
size:Large;font-weight:bold;">a yellow label control with red text</span>
```

However, in any other browser, you get a combination of the class attribute on the `<span>` element, and a nested `<font>` element:

```
<span id="lblTest" class="body-text"><b><font color="Red" size="5">a yellow label
control with red text</font></b></span>
```

This means the result in browsers that are classed as "down-level," but which do support CSS, is much better. For example, the result in Netscape 6 appears in Figure 3-19.

a yellow label control with red text

Figure 3-19. The same Label *control in Netscape 6 with style added through a CSS class attribute*

It will still give us at least large red text in clients that don't recognize CSS at all. But while this seems like the best of both worlds, there are a couple of points to bear in mind:

- As the `<font>` element is nested inside the `<span>` element, all of the formatting it specifies (which could at most be the face, color, and size) takes precedence over the selectors in the CSS style "bodytext".

- Applying styles to individual elements "hard-coded" into the page like this makes it much harder to maintain and update the page in the future than when using only a linked style sheet to specify the formatting and styles.

Layout of Page Sections and Individual Elements

Most graphically oriented sites try to achieve a pleasing display that is as near to the printed page as possible. However, the nature of the display in a Web browser often gets in the way. Some issues we often come up against are:

- Specifying page widths, and coping with different screen resolution and text sizes

- Removing excess white space around full-width banners and other elements

I'll briefly consider these topics next.

Different Screen Resolutions and Text Sizes

Many sites attempt to achieve the "same as the printed page" effect by using only a fixed-width area within the browser window. In general there is no excuse for this, and it is a constant source of annoyance for many users. They are forced to scroll the page to read content, while half of the browser window is empty.

Often the reason this approach is taken is to limit the length of the lines of text on the screen, because long lines are harder to read. This is why newspapers and magazines break the content into columns. But there is no reason why you can't use columns in your Web pages as well. Our preferred approach is to create the complete page within a two- or three-column table, and use each column for different parts of the content.

The left column is the natural area for a menu bar if you use one on your site, but it works equally well with other content—as you can see from the "Home" page of the example Xrox Car Company site shown near the start of this chapter. The one disadvantage is that the user has to wait for all the content of the table to be received before the browser can render any of it.

It is possible, in browsers that support CSS2, to arrange for fixed width tables to be progressively rendered, by adding the style selector "table-layout:fixed" to the <table> element and specifying values for the width and height selectors for every <td> element in the first row. But if the content is all in two or three cells in one row of the table, progressive rendering will not make any difference.

I prefer to set the column widths using percentage values where possible, so that the columns are spaced evenly irrespective of the browser window width:

```
<table width="100%" border="0" cellspacing="10" cellpadding="10">
 <tr>
  <td width="25%" rowspan="2" bgcolor="#ffffaa" valign="top">
    ... left-hand column contents ...
  </td>
  <td width="75%">
    ... left-hand column contents ...
  </td>
 </tr>
</table>
```

However, if you have a menu bar in one column, you may prefer to set this column to a specific width. Just bear in mind the effects that setting fixed column sizes may have when the user resizes the text within the page. Test your pages with browser window widths from 640px up to 1280px (the common range of screen resolutions), and with different text sizes selected in the browser options or View menu.

Removing Excess White Space in Page Margins

I briefly mentioned in the previous chapter how unwanted white space can affect your page layout. There are a couple of areas worth bearing in mind: setting the page margins and preventing excess characters creeping into formatted elements.

Quite a few browsers, such as Navigator 4 and Opera 6, do not recognize the leftmargin, rightmargin, and topmargin attributes for a <body> element. And Netscape 6 and Mozilla 6 do not recognize the rightmargin attribute. This is understandable, as these attributes are not part of the latest HTML recommendations. Instead, a good solution is to use CSS to define the style for the <body> element (as well as specifying zero for the leftmargin, rightmargin, and topmargin attributes):

```
body {
  font-family:Tahoma,Arial,Helvetica,sans-serif;
  font-size:x-small;
  padding-left:0;
  padding-right:0;
  padding-top:0;
}
```

This removes the white space from the left, top, and right of the page in Opera 6, though has no effect in Navigator 4. It also fails to remove the right margin white space in Netscape 6 and Mozilla, but it's a simple technique that is certainly worth including in your pages if you aim to achieve full-width display.

Removing Excess White Space from Text in Block Elements

The other point to consider is how white space affects text that is placed in a containing element such as a table cell or <div>. For example, consider the following screenshot from a test page that contains a two-row table (Figure 3-20).

The Wrampant provides a unique combination of performance and comfort that will suit almost any driver. Happy around town, and yet with extra horses under the bonnet so that you can take advantage of the open road. With its 2 x 2 seat combination, and spacious luggage carrying features, it makes an ideal car for both short and long journeys.

Whether you've got a big job to do, a lot of equipment to carry, or you just like to give the appearance of being a big-city farmer, the Wranger is the ideal truck for you. Hugely powerful, massively strong, and unbelievably reliable, it will easily handle everything you throw at it.

Figure 3-20. Extraneous white space in a table cell

You can see that the last line of text in the first table cell has extra white space above it. To understand why, I'll examine the source code that creates this table:

```
<table cellpadding="5">
<tr>
 <td><font size="2" face="Tahoma">
 The Wrampant provides a unique combination of performance and comfort
 that will suit almost any driver. Happy around town, and yet with extra
 horses under the bonnet so that you can take advantage of the open road.
 With its 2 x 2 seat combination, and spacious luggage carrying features,
 it makes an ideal car for both short and long journeys.</font>
 </td>
</tr>
<tr>
 <td><font size="2" face="Tahoma">
 Whether you've got a big job to do, a lot of equipment to carry, or
 you just like to give the appearance of being a big-city farmer, the
 Wranger is the ideal truck for you. Hugely powerful, massively strong,
 and unbelievably reliable, it will easily handle everything you
 throw at it.</font></td>
</tr>
</table>
```

Look at the closing `</td>` tags. In the first cell of the table, you allowed unformatted white space to exist between the closing `</font>` tag and the `</td>` tag. The layout rules for browsers stipulate that any number of consecutive white space characters (carriage returns, spaces, tabs, and so on) should be replaced by a single space when rendering the page.

However, this space character is outside the formatted content you placed in the cell. So, as the overall physical size of the default font for the page is larger that the size 2 "Tahoma" font that you specified for the text in the table cell, the baseline of the last line of text moves down to accommodate this larger character.

The solution is shown in the second row of the table listed above—make sure that there are no extraneous characters between the closing tag of the formatting element and the closing tag of the block element that holds it. An equally valid way to code the page, if you don't like having the `</td>` tag at the far right of the content, is like this:

```
...
 and unbelievably reliable, it will easily handle everything you
 throw at it.
 </font></td>
</tr>
...
```

Many Web page editing tools, and several of the ASP.NET server controls, automatically format your source code and insert white space before a `</td>` tag, so check for this if you find layout problems like this occurring.

The visible effect of this extra white space is worse in Internet Explorer and older versions of Navigator. It also applies to other elements and types of content. For example, if you apply CSS styles using a <span> element, make sure there is no white space after the closing </span> tag and the closing tag for any containing element (such as a table cell, <div>, <li>, etc.).

Script-driven Animations and Other "Actions"

I've already decided that I want to include "something different" in the "Home" page to attract the viewer's attention, as well as demonstrating a few techniques that combine client-side and server-side code in ASP.NET. The "Home" page contains a banner at the top, which is animated in Internet Explorer 4.x and above, Netscape 4.x and above, and Mozilla 1.0.

> **NOTE**   *I also planned to include the animation feature for Opera 6.0, which implements the CSS2 recommendations in the same way as Internet Explorer 6, Netscape 6, and Mozilla. However, at present (in version 6.02), Opera has problems with the absolute positioning of images through client-side script. Once this is cured, you'll be able to use the standard CSS2-based version of the banner in Opera as well. You can use the test page I provide with the samples (dom2-test-banner.htm in the* xroxcars *folder) to test for support in your version of Opera.*

I only show the animation once in each session, the first time that the visitor opens the "Home" page. After that, and in all the other pages (and in other browsers), I use a static representation of the banner instead.

You'll look at the implementation of the banner itself in the next chapter. Here, I want to briefly look at the different categories of support for such animations in the different browsers. Table 3-1 shows the four categories into which almost all browsers fall.

Table 3-1. The Common Techniques Available for Script-based Animations

Browser	Techniques for script-based animation
Internet Explorer 6.x Netscape 6.x Mozilla 1.0 Opera 6.x (in future revisions)	Support for CSS2 and JavaScript 1.0. Use standard HTML DOM2 methods to interact with the page content.
Internet Explorer 6.x Internet Explorer 5.x Internet Explorer 4.x	Support for Microsoft Dynamic HTML and JavaScript 1.0 (using the JScript interpreter). Use DHTML methods against the MSHTML rendering engine to interact with the page content.
Netscape Navigator 4.x	Support for Netscape-specific Dynamic HTML features such as Layers.
Most other browsers	No support for dynamic interaction with the page content.

So, you can build client-side script powered animations into pages for all of the most recent and common browsers, and therefore accommodate a high percentage of the total numbers of visitors. The problem is that you need to code the animation (and some of the other "actions" that you might need to accomplish) in three different ways, to suit the first three categories.

In essence, you can write JavaScript code so that it detects certain features of the client as it runs, and have it modify its behavior automatically. In other situations, especially when using images or building complex scripts, it's often easier to code three different versions and then just send the appropriate one to the client.

You'll see some examples of detecting the client type in ASP.NET, and delivering appropriate content, in the next chapter when you look at our page banner in more detail. In the meantime, it's useful to explore the overall techniques for detecting the abilities of the browser in client-side code.

Client-Side Browser Feature Detection

The traditional way to identify a browser in client-side code is to query the properties of the navigator object that is exposed by the root window object. For example:

```
var sBrowserName = window.navigator.appName;
var sVersion = window.navigator.appVersion;
```

However, this requires some complex parsing and decision constructs to figure out which kind of features the client supports. An easier and generally more accepted approach is to check if the client implements various object model collections and/or methods.

Only Internet Explorer version 4.x and later implements the document.all collection for accessing the contents of a rendered page. And only Navigator 4.x implements the document.layers collection for accessing the <layer> elements contained in a page. Meanwhile, any browser that supports the DOM Level 2 and CSS2 will support the document.getElementById method.

So, you can use detection code like the following—note that, as Internet Explorer 5.x implements the getElementById method, you have to check for this when looking for CSS2 and DOM2 compliant browsers:

```
if (document.all) {
  //
  // code for Internet Explorer 4.x and above goes here
  //
}
if (document.layers) {
  //
  // code for Netscape Navigator 4.x only goes here
  //
}
if (document.getElementById && !document.all) {
  //
  // code for DOM2 and CSS2 compliant clients goes here
  //
}
```

Internet Explorer versions 4.x and 5.x implement a fairly compliant version of CSS, extended to include a great many features that are now part of CSS2. One annoying difference is that the technique for getting a reference to an element using its id property is different to that used in CSS2. In Internet Explorer 4.x and later, you can access the all collection that is exposed by the document object:

```
var oElementRef = document.all['my-element-id'];
```

In CSS2 and DOM Level 2 compliant clients, we have to call the document object's getElementById method instead:

```
var oElementRef = document.getElementById('my-element-id');
```

Coping with Navigator/Communicator 4.x

Before I finish this section, I'll very quickly summarize some of the compatibility problems that arise when supporting Navigator 4.x clients—especially early versions up to 4.5. You'll see how to implement support in the example site in the coming chapters, but the main points to watch out for are:

- Navigator does not fully inherit <font> settings into things like lists (<ul> and <ol>) and table cells, leaving text in a default font and size inside these elements. It's wise to include extra nested <font> elements to ensure that the correct formatting is applied to these elements.

- If HTML controls are placed within the cells of a <table>, the <form> and </form> tags also have to be within the table, otherwise the controls may not be rendered. However, the <form> tags can be placed between the corresponding <table> and <tr> tags if required, for example:

```
<table>
 <form runat="server">
  <tr>
   <td>
      ... table contents here ...
   </td>
  </tr>
 </form>
</table>
```

- A client-side <script> section cannot be placed within a <table>. In reality, this is a limitation only when using the ASP.NET RegisterClientScriptBlock method, which insists on placing the client-side <script> section immediately after the opening <form> tag—therefore conflicting with the limitation described previously (I discuss the RegisterClientScriptBlock method towards the end of Chapter 8).

- Textbox `<input>` elements and lists do not always display text in the same size as their surroundings, and it's often necessary to specifically format the text for these elements one size larger than the surrounding elements.

- Positioning text and other content at absolute positions requires a completely different approach, using `<layer>` elements, to that adopted in other browsers. Each `<layer>` contains its own document object, complete with a hierarchy of all the other objects normally found within the document object. So accessing elements within a `<layer>` requires more code than is required to access any element within the page directly, as is possible with the DOM Level 2 and CSS2.

Making Sites Accessible to All Visitors

The final topic for this chapter—and one that is extremely important—is how to make your Web pages accessible to visitors who suffer from various types of disability. For example, have you any idea how your pages might be used by a blind user, or how easy it might be for someone who cannot use a mouse to access them?

Providing optimum accessibility often means adding extra elements or attributes to your pages, or just using the existing ones in a more sensible way to make the page more intuitive for visitors. It makes us "good players" in the field of the World Wide Web, and much of what's involved is generally just good practice anyway. However, there is an even more persuasive reason for considering how universally accessible your site actually is, as you'll see next.

Why Provide Universal Accessibility?

It's long been the case that companies and government departments have to provide facilities for disabled people to be able to use their facilities. This varies from installing wheelchair ramps at shop doorways, to making written contracts and forms available in Braille or large-print formats.

While the Web was just a communication network for scientists, and a playground for computer geeks, no one bothered about universal accessibility that much. However, now that it has become a major feature in almost everyone's life, a primary distribution channel for governmental and commercial information, and an access portal for a huge array of services, people are realizing that the laws and regulations governing accessibility in the physical world can also be applied to the Internet.

What this means is that we really do have a duty to comply with the recommendations, and there have already been several lawsuits in places like the United States and Australia against sites that are unusable by blind or disadvantaged visitors. A United States government department called the Access Board (http://www.access-board.gov/) has published a document called the *Section 508 Standards for Electronic and Information Technology*, and it applies to both hardware and software (see http://www.access-board.gov/sec508/guide/ for more details). It lays down exactly how we should aim to provide universal access for all visitors to our Web sites.

A Summary of Techniques for Accessibility

I strive to provide good accessibility for visitors in all the Web sites I build, and the example Xrox Car Company site is no exception. In the following chapters, you'll see how to implement various accessibility features. However, I'll summarize them here as a reference point, and so that you have a feeling for what is involved.

Accessibility centers on making it as easy as possible for people to navigate to and within the pages we create, to read and understand the content, and to do so with the minimum of extra effort compared to the more usual techniques such as clicking with a mouse. Special user agents, browsers, and other access software designed for use with different types of disabilities depends on some or all of the following guidelines to make pages more easily accessible.

Assisting Navigation

- Include a meaningful <title> element in every page so that software and users can tell immediately if the page covers what they are looking for. Remember that, if they are using an aural page reader, they don't want to have to wait while it reads the contents to find out that it is the wrong page.

- Provide "skip to" links as the first items in every page, allowing users with text browsers or page readers to jump directly to the area of the page that interests them. You'll see in detail at how you can provide "skip to" links in the "Home" page discussed in the next chapter.

- Try and make the structural layout of every page similar if this is appropriate for the content, for example put menus in the same place on each page.

- Avoid self-referring links, in other words links that load the same page again. If you use a common menu bar or footer section, you should arrange for it to exclude the current page among the links.

- Try and lay out the content of any tables you use so that they can be read from left to right, and still make sense. Use <th> elements for the heading row, or add a scope attribute to identify if the cell contains data that applies to the row (scope="row") or column (scope="col").

- For HTML <form> controls, always place the caption for a textbox or list to the left of the control. For a radio button or checkbox, place it to the right of the control. If the layout of a form is complex, use <label> elements to contain the caption, and in each one set the for attribute to the name or id (which should be the same) of the control it applies to.

- Avoid meaningless text in hyperlinks, such as "click here." Instead, indicate in the text of the link what the target actually is.

Identifying Elements

- Include a `name` and a `title` attribute in all `<frame>` elements, and a `title` attribute in all interactive elements, such as `<a>`, `<input>`, `<select>`, `<textarea>`, and so on.

- Include an `alt` attribute in every image element you use, with a brief but meaningful text description of the image. If the image does not contribute to the meaning of the page, for example, a spacer image, bullet, or horizontal rule image, include `alt=""` (an empty string) so that access software knows that it can be ignored.

- Include an `alt` attribute in each `<area>` definition of a client-side image map, and try and avoid using server-side image maps—which access software cannot usually describe to the user in any kind of meaningful way.

- Where an image contributes a lot towards the meaning of a page, use the `longdesc` attribute to point to a text file or Web page that contains a full description of the image.

General Recommendations

- Use the standard generic font sizes, such as `"x-small"` and `"large"` rather than fixed sizes, allowing visitors to enlarge the font in their browser if required.

- Provide alternative text content where possible, for example *inside* the declaration of an `<object>` element or `<applet>` element, but *outside* any contained elements such as `<param>`. This text will be available to the client if the software does not load the object or applet.

- Avoid generating important content through client-side scripting, where this content is not available if clients do not or cannot execute the script. Use a `<noscript>` section to provide alternative content if necessary.

- Try accessing your pages in Lynx, to see if they are usable in a text-only browser.

- Try accessing your site in one of the "page reader" applications, such as the IBM Home Page Reader you saw earlier in this chapter. Close your eyes or turn off your screen and see if you can navigate through your own site!

Summary

This chapter has ranged far and wide over many varied topics, mainly in order to prepare you for the task of building the first of the pages for your site. As you've seen, the task of building a site that conforms to current standards, works well in most browsers, and is accessible for disadvantaged visitors is not like falling off a log.

There are a lot of things to keep in mind, and a lot of different techniques available. And you still need to make it look attractive!

In this chapter I've attempted to round out the topics I started in the previous two chapters, such as figuring out what standards to support (basically HTML 3.2 and CSS), deciding on the technical requirements to impose on our visitors' browsers, and the way to detect if each browser is suitable. I also looked at how to take advantage of features in more recent browsers to make your pages work even better.

The third topic I spent time investigating was that of general browser compatibility. With so many different makes, versions, and operating systems out there, you can never be sure that you've covered everything. However, I have tried to show you how you can cover most bases, along with some useful techniques that work in most browsers.

I finished the chapter with a brief summary of accessibility issues, both how they are panning out legally and how we can all be better "Net citizens" by following the (generally common-sense) guidelines.

The topic areas I covered were:

- The client-side technical requirements for the Xrox Cars Web site

- Some of the major issues to consider with browser compatibility

- How the example site checks for sessions and client-side scripting support

- Some important issues for making sites accessible to all visitors

And at last, in the next chapter, you can start building some pages and see some results for all the work you've put in so far. You'll get started on the "Home" page for the example Xrox Car Company Web site, and you'll see many of the techniques from this and the previous chapters put to good use.

CHAPTER 4

The Home Page

IT'S TAKEN A WHILE TO GET THIS FAR, but at last you're in a position to start building the "Home" page for the Xrox Car Company site. In this chapter you'll look at how it works, the coding techniques I used, and how ASP.NET server controls make the task so much easier than in ASP 3.0 and earlier. Building on much of the theory and design issues covered in earlier chapters, you'll produce a page that satisfies all the original criteria, and that works well in each of the "test" browsers I described in the previous chapter.

As you'll see, the "Home" page can be easily divided into separate logical sections. I'll describe each of these sections in turn so that you can follow the design, and see how each section is implemented. The data access techniques in this page are relatively simple, so I'll also discuss this aspect as you explore each section of the page.

However, I don't have room to cover every section of the "Home" page in detail in this chapter. The animated banner, page footer, and mailing list sections of this page will carry over to the next chapter. Meanwhile, in this chapter, you'll see:

- The overall structure of the "Home" page

- How to specify the styles and appearance of the page, and each page section

- How to provide additional accessibility and navigation features for specialist clients

- The section containing the links to other pages

- The "News and Special Offers" section of the page

- The list of car models and descriptions

- How the page changes behavior for script-enabled and non-script-enabled clients

I start with a look at the overall page structure.

The Overall Page Structure

In Chapter 1 I showed you the first sketches of the design for the example site, and decided that the "Home" page would be divided into sections. The main sections identified were (Figure 4-1):

- Some kind of animated page banner that will attract visitors' attention when they first come to the site (possibly with a facility to log in, if this is implemented later on).

- News about the company, the cars themselves, and any other special offers or features that you want to draw visitors' attention to.

- A list of links that make it clear to visitors what other features the site offers, such as comparing models, contact details, terms and conditions, and so on.

- A section showing the full range of vehicles, including a short description of each one and links to see more about that vehicle.

- A page footer containing a set of text links to other pages, plus the copyright notice and the email address of the Webmaster.

Figure 4-1. The original pen-and-paper sketch of the "Home" page

Moving from initial design into a more in-depth study of the implementation details, one more feature was added—controls where visitors can add themselves to the mailing list. This is a common feature on many sites, and it is easy to implement using ASP.NET server controls. So, the design now translates into the high-level layout shown in Figure 4-2.

Figure 4-2. The layout of the content of the "Home" page

Figure 4-3 shows the finished page, so that you can see how well it compares to the original design (the page footer is off-screen at the bottom in this screenshot).

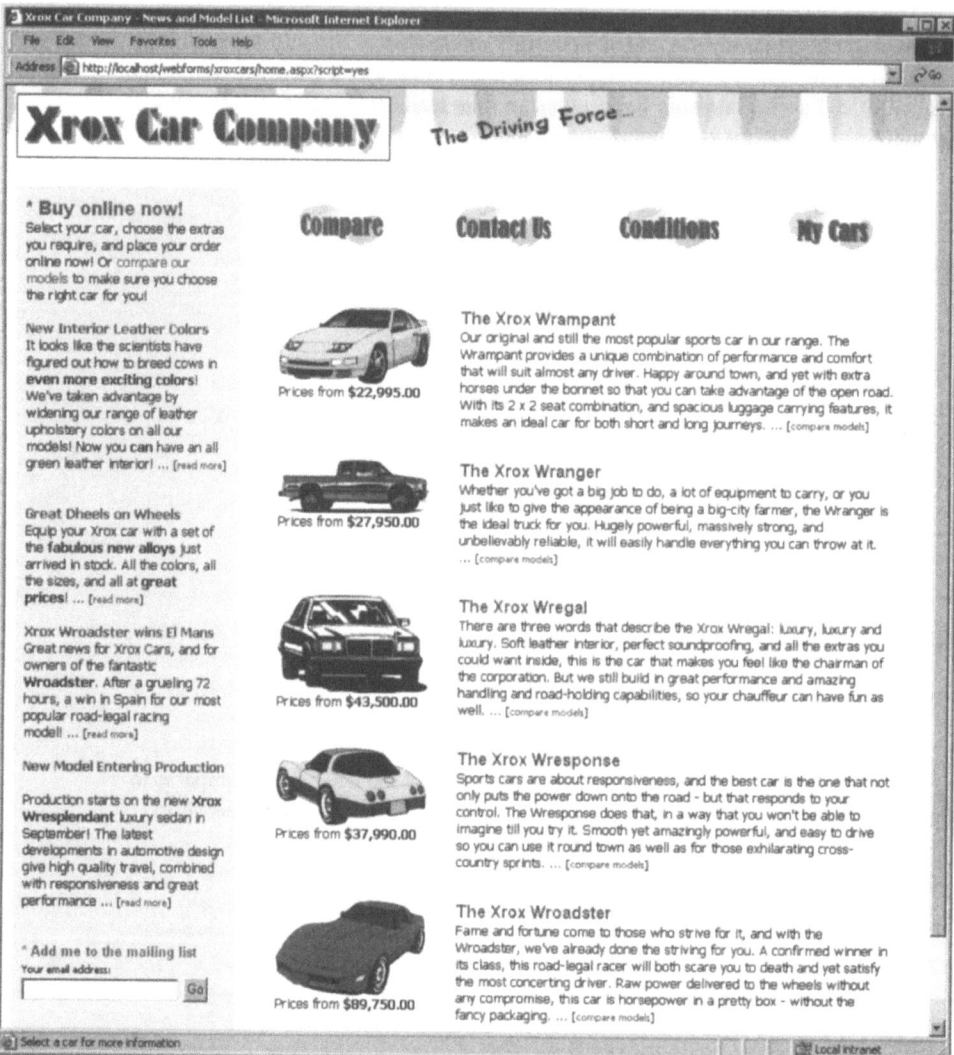

Figure 4-3. The finished "Home" page

Creating the Page Structure

You could create this layout of logically separated page sections (or "blocks") using CSS and absolute positioning, though this has limitations. In particular, it makes it hard to guarantee that the content (which is drawn from a database, and so will change regularly) will fit neatly into each section. The "absolute position" approach also means that the page sections and content will probably not resize well to fit different browser window sizes and screen resolutions. The other issue with CSS to bear in mind is that support is, at best, "patchy" in many older browsers, and can also confuse non-graphical user agents that do not recognize CSS at all.

Another approach could be to use an HTML frameset and individual frames to create the outline structure of the page. One advantage this would have is that you could enable scrolling on separate sections of the content, which would be useful if— for example—there were a lot more news items to show but you wanted to maintain the narrow left-hand "column" appearance. Users could scroll each section (the news or the list of models) separately. However, multiple frames can make navigation more difficult, and upset the working of the "Back" button (I discussed the pros and cons of frames in Chapter 1).

In the end, I decided to go with the time-honored approach of using an HTML table to break the page into separate sections. By specifying percentage values for the column widths, and some judicious use of the cellpadding, cellspacing, and nowrap attributes of the table and its individual cells, you can create a structure that works well in almost all current and older browsers. It also resizes well for different browser window sizes, from around 600px to 1200px wide.

The HTML Table for the Outline Structure

The next code listing shows the main HTML outline for the "Home" page, including the <head> and <body> elements, and the HTML table that used to create the basic display structure. I've replaced the main "content" sections and various other features with "placeholders" so you can see the page structure more clearly. I cover all these sections in more detail later in this and the next chapter.

Notice that I removed any white space (margins) from the sides and top of the page in the opening <body> tag, then specified the width of the main <table> as "100%" so that it fills the page completely. This allows the page banner to completely fill the page width with no white space above it, while the cellspacing and cellpadding attributes of the <table> provide the necessary white space around and between the content sections within each cell of the table:

```
home.aspx
<!doctype html public "-//W3C//DTD HTML 3.2 Final//EN">
<html>
<head>
... links to style sheet (and other stuff) go here ...
</head>
<body id="BodyTag" runat="server" leftmargin="0" topmargin="0"
      rightmargin="0" bgcolor="#ffffff" class="body-text">
... "Skip to" links go here ...
... animated banner is here ...
<table width="100%" border="0" cellspacing="10" cellpadding="10">
<form runat="server">
<tbody>
  <tr>
   <td width="25%" rowspan="2" bgcolor="#ffffaa" valign="top">
```

```
     ... News and Special Offers section ...
  </td>
  <td width="75%" wrap="nowrap">
     ... Links to Other Pages ...
  </td>
 </tr>
 <tr>
  <td valign="top">
     ... List of Models and Descriptions ...
  </td>
 </tr>
</tbody>
</form>
</table>
... page footer goes here ...
</body>
</html>
```

The first cell uses rowspan="2" so that it spans the two sections for the page links and model list, as shown in the page layout schematic (Figure 4-2). I also specify that it should be 25 percent of the page width, and have a light yellow background to lift it out from the rest of the rest of the page content. The second column fills the remaining 75 percent of the page width. I also set the nowrap attribute so that the column will not shrink to too small a width—the entire page content is still visible without scrolling in 640 x 480 screen resolution.

The <form> Section

Notice also that I included a pair of <form> tags within the table, but outside the content, as discussed in the previous chapter. This form is used to submit the visitor's email address, if he or she decides to join the mailing list. Because the page is using the ASP.NET postback architecture, you only need to set the runat="server" attribute, and ASP.NET provides the rest of the required attributes. As an example, the ASP.NET process automatically creates output like the following when a page containing a server-side <form> is executed:

```
<form name="_ctl0" method="post" action="home.aspx?script=yes" id="_ctl0">
<input type="hidden" name="__VIEWSTATE"
value="dDwtMjgOOTUwMzc4Ozs+u6uIRM6eSAupZaljlW1AdRVS2KY=" />
```

You can see the method and action have been set (the page is posted back to itself, and the query string script=yes is persisted as well). The hidden-type <input> element that holds the viewstate for the page is also included in the form. In the example "Home" page, I use the ASP.NET Validation controls to check that the user's input is valid (as you'll see when you look at the mailing list section of the page in the next chapter). In this case, the actual output looks like this:

```
<form name="_ctl0" method="post" action="home.aspx?script=yes"
language="javascript" onsubmit="ValidatorOnSubmit();" id="_ctl0">
<input type="hidden" name="__VIEWSTATE"
value="dDwtMjgOOTUwMzc4Ozs+u6uIRM6eSAupZaljlW1AdRVS2KY=" />
```

You can see that the Validation controls change the attribute list for the `<form>` element by adding the `language` attribute and an `onsubmit` event handler declaration that these controls rely on to perform client-side validation.

The `<body>` Element As a Server Control

One point that might have prompted a question in your mind is why I added the `runat="server"` attribute to the opening `<body>` tag. After all, there is no dedicated ASP.NET server control for a `<body>` element. However, I want to be able to manipulate the `<body>` element in the server-side code as the page is being created.

The reason is that I want the client-side script within the animated banner to be executed once the page has finished loading, and this is accomplished by specifying the name of the function that provides the animation as the `onload` attribute. However, I only want to animate the banner once—the first time the visitor accesses the "Home" page. After that, the visitor will see a static version of the banner instead, and so I won't need the `onload` attribute to be set.

ASP.NET includes many dedicated server controls, but these are mainly for the "interactive" elements found in HTML. For example, there are specific server controls for text boxes, lists, hyperlinks, and radio buttons. But you can specify that **any** element becomes a "server control" simply by adding the `runat="server"` attribute to it (as I did with the `<body>` element in the preceding listing):

```
<body id="BodyTag" runat="server" ...>
```

The `HtmlGenericControl` Class

When ASP.NET finds an element that has the `runat="server"` attribute, but for which there no specific server control in the class library, it uses the `HtmlGenericControl` class to implement this element. The `HtmlGenericControl` class is defined within the `System.Web.UI.HtmlControls` namespace. Compared to the more specialist server controls in the class library, `HtmlGenericControl` has quite a limited set of members (properties, methods, and events). These members apply to any control that is generated from this class—irrespective of the actual element type (tag name). The most useful of these members are shown in Table 4-1.

Table 4-1. The Commonly Used Members of the HtmlGenericControl *Class*

Member	Description
Attributes property	Returns a collection of all the attribute name/value pairs for the opening tag of the control.
Controls property	Returns a ControlCollection object that references all the child controls defined for this control.
Disabled property	Sets or returns a Boolean value indicating if the control is disabled (has a disabled="disabled" attribute).
EnableViewState property	Sets or returns a Boolean value indicating if the control will persist its viewstate, and the viewstate of any child controls it contains, between requests.
ID property	Sets or returns the programmatic identifier of the control.
InnerHtml property	Sets or returns the entire content between the opening and closing tags of the control, as it will be rendered in the page.
InnerText property	Sets or returns just the text content between the opening and closing tags of the control, as it will be rendered in the page.
Page property	Returns a reference to the Page instance that contains this control.
Parent property	Returns a reference to the parent control for this control within the page's control hierarchy, if it has a parent.
Style property	Returns a collection of all the cascading style sheet (CSS) properties (selectors) that are applied to this control when rendered.
TagName property	Sets or returns the tag name of the element that this control generates.
Visible property	Sets or returns a Boolean value that indicates if the control will be rendered when the page is generated.
FindControl method	Searches through all the child controls of this control to find a specific one using its ID value.

> **NOTE** *A full list of the members for the* HtmlGenericControl *can be found in the* *.NET SDK. For version 1.0, the URL is:* ms-help://MS.NETFrameworkSDK/ cpref/(html/frlrfSystemWebUIHtmlControlsHtmlGenericControlClassTopic.htm
> *In version 1.1, the URL differs only that "v1.1" is added to the path:*
> ms-help://MS.NETFrameworkSDKv1.1/cpref/(html/ frlrfSystemWebUIHtmlControlsHtmlGenericControlClassTopic.htm

Effectively, what this means is that you can generate **any** kind of HTML element using the HtmlGenericControl class. For example, you can create a paragraph of text using this code:

```
<script runat="server">
Sub Page_Load()
  Dim MyPara As New HtmlGenericControl("p")
  MyPara.Attributes.Add("align", "center")
  MyPara.InnerHtml = "This is a new paragraph with TagName '" _
                     & MyPara.TagName & "'."
  Page.Controls.Add(MyPara)
End Sub
</script>
```

This creates a new HtmlGenericControl with the tag name "p", adds an align="center" attribute to it, sets the content to the value of the InnerHtml property, and then adds it to the Controls collection of the page so that it is displayed after any other controls. The HTML that this code creates is:

```
<p align="center">This is a new paragraph with TagName 'p'.</p>
```

Of course, in the "Home" page, you aren't creating the <body> control from scratch (as you did in the previous listing). But the "Home" page code does demonstrate how you can get server-side access to any element in the page if required, simply by defining it as a server control (by adding the runat="server" attribute).

Setting the Styles for the Page

In the previous chapters, I've spent quite a lot of time discussing the ways that you can apply styles and text formatting to your Web Form pages and the output from ASP.NET server controls. In the Xrox Car Company site, it's been decided that maximum support for all kinds of browser and user agents is required, and you do this with a combination of CSS styles and the traditional <font> element. You'll see <font> elements used in several places within the HTML declarations later in this chapter and in other chapters.

I also set the base font size for the page using a <basefont> element within the <head> section of the page:

```
<basefont size="2" />
```

While this is only useful for relative sizes within <font> elements, it's worth putting it onto every page where you might use <font> elements. It can save a lot of effort trying to fix wayward output later on if you decide to include a relative font size, for example <font size="-2"> or <font size="+1">.

Specifying the CSS Style Sheet

To specify the CSS styles, include them in a separate style sheet and then link this to all the pages in your site using <link> elements. However, there is an issue that needs to be addressed first. You already know that you need to declare the sizes for the text in your pages using the generic "size names," such as x-small and xx-large, rather than as specific pixel or point sizes (I discussed this in the previous chapter). Unfortunately, not all browsers can agree on the actual display size that these generic sizes represent.

Browsers based on the Netscape and Mozilla engines render these generic sizes "one smaller" than most other browsers, for example they render small in the same size as Internet Explorer and Opera render medium. So, if you want to get the same text size in both kinds of browser, you need to provide a different style sheet for each one!

You could go even further and fine-tune the stylesheets for each different type of browser, but this is generally unnecessary. Two will suffice—with the one for Netscape/Mozilla-based clients and any clients that ASP.NET does not recognize (through its browser-detection process) specifying a text size "one size larger" than the style sheet for other clients.

The Standard Style Sheet

For example, the following listing shows the style sheet named wccStandard.css that is used in the Xrox Car Company site for browsers that are recognized by ASP.NET *other than* the Netscape/Mozilla-based ones. There are definitions for the basic page text (body-text) plus a version in a dark red color, definitions for large text in the default color (black) and dark red, and a definition for small text (such as that used above the "mailing list" text box). There is also a fixed-point-size definition only used for the tree view controls in the **Model Details** page, where an even smaller font (less than the small-text style) is required:

wccStandard.css

```
.body-text {
  font-family:Tahoma,Arial,Helvetica,sans-serif;
  font-size:x-small;
  padding-left:0; padding-right:0; padding-top:0;
}

.body-red-text {
  font-family:Arial,Helvetica,sans-serif; font-size:x-small; color:#b50055
}

.large-text {
  font-family:Arial,Helvetica,sans-serif; font-size:small;
}
```

```
.large-red-text {
  font-family:Arial,Helvetica,sans-serif; font-size:medium; color:#b50055
}

.small-text {
  font-family:Tahoma,Arial,Helvetica,sans-serif; font-size:xx-small;
}

.fixed-small-text {
  font-family:Tahoma,Arial,Helvetica,sans-serif;
  font-size:8pt;
}
```

I also specify the style and colors for hyperlinks and remove the underline when the link is not active, and prevent it changing to purple after being visited (these might be contentious issues from the navigation usability point of view, but they do preserve the appearance of the page better). I also include a definition that makes the link change to red and become underlined when the mouse hovers over it. These three definitions for "standard-sized" text links are then repeated for large links (such as the model names in the "Home" page) and small links (such as the **read more** links in the "News" section):

```
.std-link {
  font-family:Tahoma,Arial,Helvetica,sans-serif;
  font-size:x-small; text-decoration:none;
}

.std-link:visited {
  color:#0000ff;
}

.std-link:hover {
  color:#ff0000; text-decoration:underline;
}

.large-link {
  font-family:Arial,Helvetica,sans-serif;
  font-size:small; text-decoration:none;
}

.large-link:visited {
  color:#0000ff;
}

.large-link:hover {
  color:#ff0000; text-decoration:underline;
}
```

```
.small-link {
  font-family:Tahoma,Arial,Helvetica,sans-serif;
  font-size:xx-small; text-decoration:none;
}

.small-link:visited {
  color:#0000ff;
}

.small-link:hover {
  color:#ff0000; text-decoration:underline;
}
```

The Netscape/Mozilla Style Sheet

To provide the two different sets of font sizes, I've chosen to provide a different linked style sheet for Netscape/Mozilla-based clients and all other clients. You could define both "sets" of styles in one style sheet using different style names, but this would mean that you would have to dynamically change the class attribute for each element in the page depending on the browser type. By using two separate style sheets, you just need to link the correct one to your page depending on the browser type.

So, the Netscape/Mozilla style sheet (named wccLarge.css) is identical to the one I've just shown, except that each font-size selector is "one larger." For example, the body-text style is defined as:

wccLarge.css

```
.body-text {
  font-family:Tahoma,Arial,Helvetica,sans-serif;
  font-size:small;
  padding-left:0; padding-right:0; padding-top:0;
}
```

This means that you must detect the client type when the site is first accessed, and see which style sheet you should send to the client. Once you've decided, you can specify the correct one in the <link> element within the <head> section of your page.

Detecting the Client Type

Within the server-side script section of the page, declare a String variable named sStyleSize that will hold part of the name of the style sheet for the current client, and set the default value to "Standard":

home.aspx

```
<script runat="server">
' page-level variable to client browser type
Dim sStyleSize As String = "Standard"
```

In the `Page_Load` event handler for the "Home" page, after the code you looked at in the previous chapter that checks for ASP.NET sessions and client-side scripting support, include code that extracts the current browser "type" (the manufacturer/browser name) and the major version number (such as 4 or 6):

```
Sub Page_Load()
  ...
  ... code to get UserID from Session (put there by default.aspx)
  ... and get value of "script" from query string *or* Session to see
  ... if browser supports client-side scripting and it is enabled
  ...
  ' get the browser type and version
  Dim sUAType As String = Request.Browser("Browser")
  Dim sUAVer As String = Request.Browser("MajorVersion")
```

As you saw in Chapter 2, the information to populate the `Request.Browser` collection comes from the user agent string that is exposed by the browser. Netscape and Mozilla browsers do not specifically include the manufacturer's name in their user agent strings, and so they are both treated as being `Netscape` by the browser detection process, and exposed as such by the `Request.Browser("Browser")` property.

Notice that, if the browser type cannot be determined, use the larger size text styles as a precaution in case the client renders them too small to be easily read by the visitor. After figuring out which style sheet to use, store the string name (either `"Standard"` or `"Large"` in the user's ASP.NET session as well as in the page-level variable named `sStyleSize`:

```
  ' specify appropriate style sheet for <link> element
  ' cannot server-side <link> control element as the
  ' presence of an ID attribute stops some browsers
  ' from loading the style sheet! Netscape and Amaya
  ' require larger font sizes to be specified
  If sUAType = "Netscape" Or sUAType = "Unknown" Or sUAType = "" Then
    sStyleSize = "Large"
  End If
  Session("WccStyleSize") = sStyleSize    ' store in Session
  ...
  ... code to build rest of dynamic page content goes here
  ...
End Sub
```

Linking to the Correct Style Sheet

Now that you have the correct style sheet name part, you can populate the `<link>` element in the page with the full style sheet `href` value. You want the page to contain one of the following two `<link>` elements, depending on the browser you are serving this page to:

```
<link rel="stylesheet" type="text/css" href="stylesheets/wccStandard.css" />
```

or

```
<link rel="stylesheet" type="text/css" href="stylesheets/wccLarge.css" />
```

Having seen the earlier discussion about using an HtmlGenericControl for the `<body>` element of the page, so that you can dynamically add an onload attribute, it would also seem to be a good way to add the appropriate href attribute to the `<link>` element. In the page, you could declare the server control as:

```
<link id="lnkStyle" rel="stylesheet" type="text/css" runat="server" />
```

Then, in your Page_Load event handler you could add the appropriate href attribute:

```
lnkStyle.Attributes.Add("href", "stylesheets/wcc" & sStyleSize & ".css")
```

This is what I tried first, but unfortunately a problem came up in Netscape 4.x. Some minor versions seem to ignore the `<link>` element if it has an id attribute before the href attribute. But you need one to be able to access the control in the server-side code, and ASP.NET automatically places it before any dynamically added attributes.

While this effect was not 100 percent repeatable in tests, I decided to use the more traditional (ASP 3.0 style) technique for inserting the href attribute value instead. Simply place the variable inside an ASP "render block" (a pair of `<%` and `%>` tags). OK, so it's not as elegant as the first suggestion, but it works fine and avoids any issues that may arise when an id attribute is included:

```
<link rel="stylesheet" type="text/css"
      href="stylesheets/wcc<% = sStyleSize %>.css" />
```

In other pages of the site that use the same style sheets, you can simply extract the value for the style sheet "name part" from the user's session. You don't need to query the Request.Browser object properties again. For example, in the **Compare Features** page (compare.aspx), use:

compare.aspx

```
  get style sheet size from Session
sStyleSize = CType(Session("WccStyleSize"), String)
```

Then use the same <link> element definition as in the "Home" page, which takes this value and selects the correct style sheet.

Providing Accessibility Navigation Aids

It's very easy to forget how the majority of visitors to your site just click away with their mouse devices on anything that looks interesting, without really worrying too much about where these links are within the page. Stick some nice big graphic on the middle of the page, and visitors can click on it to see what it's all about.

But, if a visitor is not lucky to be as physically able as the majority of visitors, he or she may well be using a non-graphical user agent or specialist client. Then, navigation goes from being a happy point-and-click affair to something that requires a lot more effort. For a simple example, look at the "Home" page in the Lynx text-only browser (Figure 4-4).

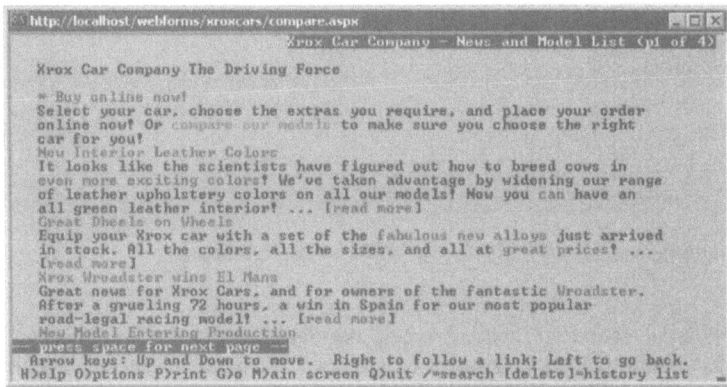

Figure 4-4. Viewing the "Home" page in the Lynx browser

The content looks fine. The alt attribute defined for the banner graphic shows up at the top of the page, so the user can tell what the site "name" is. However, all the user sees on this first section ("**p1 of 4**" because Lynx breaks each page down into sections based on the size of the DOS window) is the first few "News" items. To see what vehicle models are offered, and the links to other pages on the site, users have to scroll through the sections looking for what they require. And that's assuming that they have been here before, remember the page and site layout, and know where to find what they're looking for!

For visitors with poor or no vision, and who rely on a "page reader" client, things are even worse. The page reader will announce the site name and slogan, using the alt attributes from the banner graphics, and then start to read the list of "News" items—pausing on each "read more" hyperlink as it goes. You can tell what the user will hear by looking at the lower section in the screenshot of the IBM Home Page Reader (Figure 4-5).

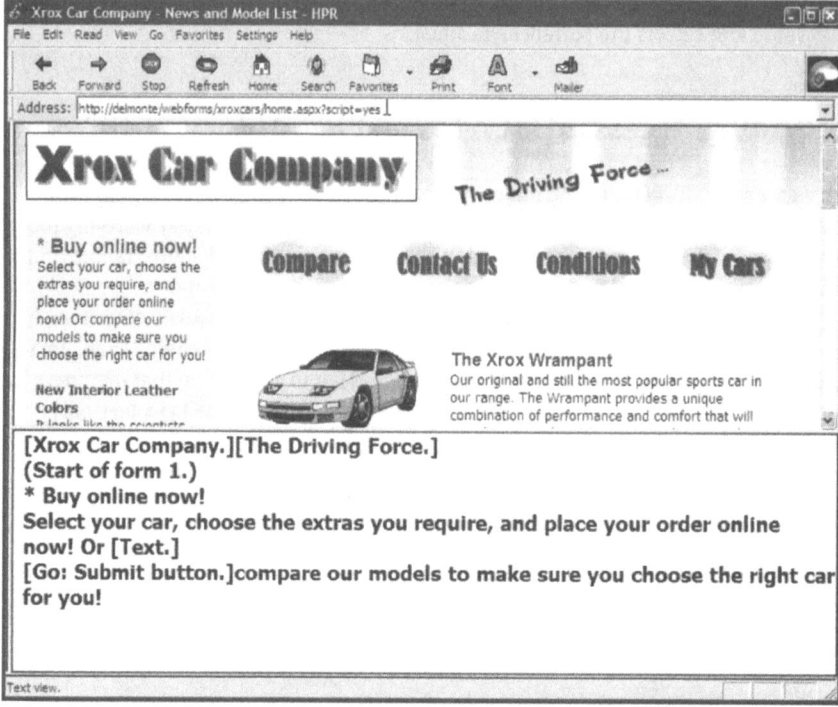

Figure 4-5. Viewing the "Home" page in the IBM Home Page Reader

Obviously you need to do something to help visitors using these types of user agents find the content they are looking for on the page. The generally accepted way to do this is with "skip to" links.

Implementing "Skip To" Links

It's clear from the previous section that you aren't making life easy for visitors who use these kinds of clients. Some sites are even worse than the sample site, for example they may have a myriad of links to other pages at the top of each page, or long "menu bars" down the left side of the page. How long will your visitor sit listening to these links being read out on every page, or spend scanning each page for useful content in a text-only browser? And maybe they might even decide to start a legal action based on Section 508 (see the end of the Chapter 3) because your site is obviously not "properly accessible."

In fact, I removed some content from my "Home" page when I took the preceding screenshots to demonstrate just how these often ignored issues affect some disadvantaged visitors. In the actual "Home" page, and in every other page, I include "skip to" links that appear as the first items in the page. They allow the visitor to go directly to specific parts of the page. In Figure 4-6, which shows the "Home" page in Lynx (after I put them back into the page), you can see these links above the site name.

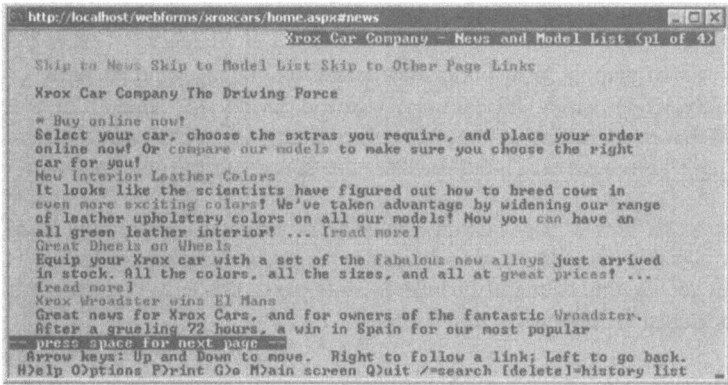

Figure 4-6. The "skip to" links viewed in the Lynx browser

When the same page is opened in the IBM Home Page Reader, these links are read to the user first—as you can see in the lower section of Figure 4-7. In the case of visitors who suffer vision problems and depend on aural browsers like this one, "skip to" links are probably one of the most useful navigation aids you can provide.

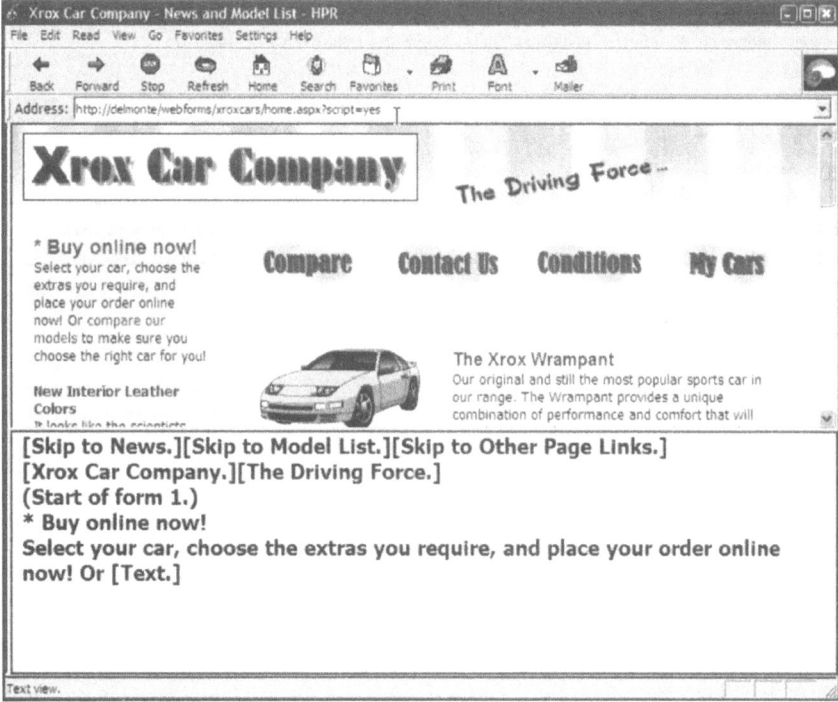

Figure 4-7. The "skip to" links viewed in the IBM Home Page Reader

The Source Code for the "Skip To" Links

Obviously, the set of "skip to" links to include depends on the page content, and which sections you feel visitors will want to navigate to directly. For example, in a simple page that contains only a menu bar and content, you would probably provide just a single "skip to content" link. You'll see this in some of the other pages on the example site.

However, in the "Home" page (as you've seen in the previous figures) three links are provided, allowing the visitor to skip directly to the "News" section, the list of models, or the section that contains the links to other pages. The following listing shows the code used to implement these links:

```
<div style="position:absolute;height:0px;"><font size="1" color=#ffffff">
<!-- skip links for aural page readers -->
<layer visibility="hidden">
<a href="#news" style="color:#ffffff;font-size:1px;text-decoration:none">
  <img width="1" height="1" hspace="0" vspace="0" src="images/_blnk.gif"
      border="0" style="height:0" alt="Skip to News" />
</a>
<a href="#models" style="color:#ffffff;font-size:1px;text-decoration:none">
  <img width="1" height="1" hspace="0" vspace="0" src="images/_blnk.gif"
      border="0" style="height:0" alt="Skip to Model List" />
</a>
<a href="#links" style="color:#ffffff;font-size:1px;text-decoration:none">
  <img width="1" height="1" hspace="0" vspace="0" src="images/_blnk.gif"
      border="0" style="height:0" alt="Skip to Other Page Links" />
</a>
</layer>
</font></div>
```

Among all the included elements, you should be able to pick out the three <a> elements that have, as their href attributes, the names of three ordinary HTML anchor elements located elsewhere within the page. The first of these, for example, points to "#news", which is an anchor element named news located in the table cell that contains the "News" items:

```
...
<td width="25%" rowspan="2" bgcolor="#ffffaa" valign="top">
  <a name="news" />
  ... cell content goes here ...
```

The same technique is used to provide anchors named models and links in the relevant table cells that contain these sections of the page content.

Hiding "Skip To" Links in Graphical Browsers

One issue that often puts site designers off implementing "skip to" links (besides laziness, of course) is that they want the page content to appear flush with the top of the browser window, as does the banner in the "Home" page. However, if the visible page content is contained within a table or other block element, these "skip to" links can cause extra white space to appear at the top of the page.

The common approach to solving this problem is to use single pixel transparent GIF images within the hyperlink, as was done in the preceding code, and even specify the width and height as zero rather than one pixel. However, this still forces white space to appear as a narrow band above any block-level element(s) that follow. It's worse in some browsers than in others (for example, Internet Explorer 6 shows more white space that Netscape 6).

You might be tempted to set the CSS style for the images to prevent them upsetting the display, for example using "visibility:hidden" or "display:none". However, doing this is an own-goal, because then the browser or page reader will ignore them. After all, you've told it that they aren't visible or that they aren't part of the page, so why would the browser display them?

Getting rid of the unwanted white space altogether, in all browsers, therefore involves a more cunning approach. I found that a combination of settings does the trick in all browsers I could find to test the page. You might decide to implement only a subset of these settings (after all, I have gone somewhat to extremes here), but if you do, make sure you test the page in all your target browsers:

- Remember to include the alt attribute on the <img> element, as this is the sole reason for using "skip to" links in the first place!

- Make sure that the <img> element contains the minimum height and width sizes (preferably one pixel in case a browser decides that the image will be omitted with zero height and width).

- Set the horizontal and vertical spacing attributes (hspace and vspace) to zero for the <img> element, and include the attribute border="0" on the <img> element to hide the border.

- Include a style="height:0" attribute on the <img> element to reduce the height to zero in browsers that support CSS.

- For the <a> element, specify a style that reduces the text to a minimum size, set the color to that of the page or banner background, and remove the underline to help it disappear if none of the other settings hide it.

- Wrap this lot in a <layer> element with the visibility="hidden" attribute for Navigator 4, which doesn't properly recognize the CSS settings. It's unlikely that any text-based browser or aural page reader will use the Navigator 4 rendering engine.

- Then, to make sure that any following relatively positioned elements are not misplaced, wrap all this in a <div> element that is absolutely positioned with zero height. Maybe even include a <font> element inside the <div> to enforce the text sizes specified for the <a> elements as an extra precaution.

> **NOTE**   *Some browsers, notably Opera, still place white space above, and to the left
> and right of the banner. However, as you discovered in the previous chapter, this is
> because Opera does not allow the page margin to be reduced to zero.*

Remember Those "title" and "alt" Attributes

One other point worth reinforcing here is to remember the "rules" about alt and
title attributes that I discussed at the end of the previous chapter. They are vital for
non-graphical user agents, and also make it easier for graphical browser users as
well. For example, if you use icons to represent links or options, you can use the alt
and title attributes to provide extra information (the meaning of the link as text).

In HTML 4, almost every element (including all visual elements) accepts the
title attribute. Some elements will not actually display this in a graphical browser,
though most do. More important, however, is that any suitably equipped user agent
will be able to read these title attribute values, and it might find ways to present this
information to the user so that it makes life much easier.

As an example, I include the title attribute in the <td> element that creates the
table cell holding the links to other pages on our site:

```
<td width="75%" wrap="nowrap" title="Links to other pages">
```

Within this cell are the links themselves, made up of images and hyperlinks
like this:

```
<a title="Compare Models" href="compare.aspx">
<img src="images/btn_compare.gif" width="100" height="49"
    alt="Compare Models" border="0" /></a>
```

I've set the alt attribute of the image, and the title attribute of the hyperlink, to
the same text values. The result is that when the mouse moves over the table cell it
displays the title of the cell, but when over the link images it displays the title of the
<a> element or the alt value of the <img> element (Figure 4-8).

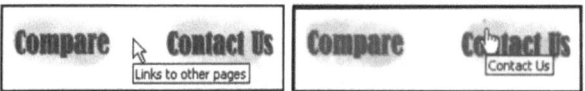

Figure 4-8. The effect of setting the alt *and* title *attributes*

This could well prove useful in a "page reader" user agent. It could indicate that
the table cell it is currently "reading" contains "**Links to other pages,**" and then read
the title/alt values for each link in turn. It doesn't require that much extra effort,
and yet provides a far more accessible interface.

However, one point to watch out for is that child elements or other contained elements often inherit the title value. For example, if you set the title attribute of a table cell (as just demonstrated), but then use <a> elements as hyperlinks without setting their own title attributes, the value of the title attribute from the table cell will be displayed when the mouse pointer is over the hyperlink.

So, if the cell has the title **"Main news section,"** a text-only hyperlink within it saying **"New Leather Colors"** will display the text **"Main news section"** as the pop-up tool-tip for this link. To avoid this, you have to set the title attribute of the hyperlink—probably to something more suitable like **"Read more about this topic."**

The Links to Other Pages

The "Home" page contains prominent links to the other main sections of the site as four clickable images. I used images to maintain the "look and feel" of the page, and they are implemented (as you saw in the previous section) simply as a combination of <a> and <img> elements (Figure 4-9).

Figure 4-9. The links to other pages from the Home page

This whole section is a single cell within the main table that provides the structure for the page. However, to achieve the desired layout, these four images must be equally spaced within the table cell (between the "News" section and the right edge of the page). You get this effect by inserting them into a <table> within the existing table cell. The following listing shows the HTML source for this section (I'll discuss the validation summary control located in this section when it's time to examine the way that the mailing list feature works):

```
...
<!-- cell in main page table -->
<td width="75%" wrap="nowrap">
  <table width="100%" border="0" cellpadding="0" cellspacing="0"
        title="Links to other pages">
    <tr>
      <td align="center">
        <a name="links" />
        <a title="Compare Models" href="compare.aspx">
          <img src="images/btn_compare.gif" width="100" height="49"
              alt="Compare Models" border="0" /></a>
      </td>
```

```
        <td align="center">
          <a title="Contact Us" href="contact.aspx">
            <img src="images/btn_contact.gif" width="100" height="49"
                 alt="Contact Us" border="0" /></a>
        </td>
        <td align="center">
          <a title="Terms and Conditions" href="tandc.aspx">
            <img src="images/btn_tandc.gif" width="100" height="49"
                 alt="Terms and Conditions" border="0" /></a>
        </td>
        <td align="center">
          <a title="My Cars" href="secure/mycars.aspx">
            <img src="images/btn_mycars.gif" width="100" height="49"
                 alt="My Cars" border="0" /></a>
        </td>
      </tr>
      <tr>
      <td colspan="4" align="center">
        ... a validation summary control is declared here and this is ...
        ... discussed in next chapter in connection with mailing list ...
      </td>
      </tr>
      </table>
    </td>
    ...
```

So there is nothing really exciting or unexpected here—it's just a conventional use of HTML elements. Set the alt attribute for each one as well as specifying the width and height. If the browser window is less than 640px wide, this table cell (with the nowrap attribute) will control how wide this cell is and how wide the cell below is, which holds the list of models. So the browser can figure out these dimensions, plus the height of this cell, from the width and height attributes—without waiting to load the images.

Why not use ASP.NET server controls here? The reason is that you don't need to access the elements in the server-side code, so they don't have to be server controls (no runat="server" attribute). By using "normal" HTML elements, you avoid the extra processing overhead that server controls would require.

The ASP.NET Hyperlink Control

However, if you did need to access the page link elements on the server, perhaps to change the image depending on whether a visitor has registered with us in the past, you would probably use ASP.NET Hyperlink controls here. A simple definition such as the following will cover your requirements for each of the clickable images:

```
<asp:Hyperlink id="lnkCompare" runat="server"
            NavigateUrl="compare.aspx"
            ImageUrl="images/btn_compare.gif"
```

```
        Tooltip="Compare Models"
        Text="Compare Models"
        Width="100"
        Height="49" />
```

In an "up-level" client (Internet Explorer 4 and above), the resulting HTML that this control generates is:

```
<a id="lnkCompare" title="Compare Models" href="compare.aspx"
style="height:49px;width:100px;"><img title="Compare Models" src="PlayButton.gif"
alt="My Hyperlink" border="0" /></a>
```

In a "down-level" client, the control generates similar visual output, setting the title and alt attributes of the <a> and <img> elements as required. However, there is one area where the control could have been a bit more intelligent. The image width and height were specified in the properties of the Hyperlink control, but these are ignored when output is generated for "down-level" clients.

The reason is that there is no style attribute generated in this case (behavior you'd expect after seeing the way that the controls work in different browsers in Chapter 2). However, you would probably also expect the control to go that extra distance and use the values you provide to set the height and width attributes of the <img> control. Unfortunately, it doesn't. And to make matters worse, you can't access the <img> element in code to add these attributes dynamically (because the HTML elements generated by the control are not themselves server controls).

Setting the "title" and "alt" Attributes

You can't actually tell by looking at the output generated by the Hyperlink control in the previous example because you used the same values for the Tooltip and Text properties, but it is important to set both properties. The value you supply for the Tooltip property is used to set the title attribute for the <a> and <img> elements. However, the value you provide for the Text property is used in different ways depending on the type of link you're creating.

If you don't provide a value for the ImageUrl property, the control will generate a simple <a> element and use the value of the Text property as the text for the hyperlink. However, when you **do** provide a value for the ImageUrl property, the control generates the nested <a> and <img> elements you've seen earlier, and then uses the value of the Text property as the alt attribute of the <img> element. This is what most non-graphical and specialist user agents will use to "describe" the image to the user.

The "News and Special Offers" Section

The section that shows news, events, special offers, and so on sits at the left side of the sample "Home" page, with a light yellow background separating it from the remainder of the page content. The section heading ("Buy online now!") and the first paragraph of text are static—they are declared within the HTML source of the page.

However, the remaining news items are generated dynamically from a database each time the page is accessed.

This book is not really aimed at teaching you about data access techniques, and so you're not going to be building complex *n*-tier data access components. Instead, you'll use code in the pages to directly access stored procedures within the database. In this book, I'm more interested in how to display the data rather that how to manipulate it behind the scenes.

Only a précis of each news item is shown in this section of the page, but the heading and the "read more" hyperlinks can be used to view the complete item (you'll see an example of this in the Chapter 5) (Figure 4-10).

The Data Access Code for the "News" List

The XroxCars database (which you can install from the downloadable samples) contains a table named tlbNews, which itself contains four columns. The NewsID column is a numeric (int) column that forms the primary key, and it is also an Identity column (unique values for this column are generated automatically as rows are added to the table). The remaining three columns, NewsTitle, NewsPrecis, and NewsText, are all of type varchar (the values are "text" strings).

The GetNewsList Stored Procedure

The database also contains a stored procedure named GetNewsList that returns all the news items from the tblNews table:

```
Stored procedure: GetNewsList
SELECT NewsID, NewsTitle, NewsPrecis FROM tblNews ORDER BY NewsID DESC
```

This is a simple approach, and means that the page will show all the news items in the database table every time, in reverse of the order in which they were added. You would have to add and delete rows to change the items that are displayed. Instead, you may prefer to include extra columns in the table that define when each news item should be shown from (DisplayFrom), when it should no longer be displayed (DisplayUntil), and even the order in which the news items should be displayed (DisplayOrder). For example:

```
SELECT NewsID, NewsTitle, NewsPrecis FROM tblNews
WHERE DATEDIFF(day, DisplayFrom, getdate()) >= 0
AND DATEDIFF(day, DisplayUntil, getdate()) < 0
ORDER BY DisplayOrder DESC
```

I'm using Microsoft SQL Server as the database, and so I can use the classes and objects from the System.Data.SqlClient namespace to access this stored procedure (and any other necessary data). To use these classes in your page, you must import the appropriate namespaces. Visual Studio .NET imports these into your projects automatically, but when using other editors you will probably have to add them yourself:

```
<%@Import Namespace="System.Data"%>
<%@Import Namespace="System.Data.SqlClient"%>
```

To use any other database, you will need to import the OleDb or Odbc namespaces instead:

```
<%@Import Namespace="System.Data"%>
<%@Import Namespace="System.Data.OleDb"%>
```

Using the ODBC Data Access Classes

The classes that implement the namespace System.Data.Odbc are **not** part of the standard .NET installation in version 1.0, and must be downloaded and installed separately from the Microsoft Universal Data Access Web site at http://www.microsoft.com/data/. This also installs a separate SDK that describes and documents the ODBC data access classes, though in effect they work in exactly the same way as the SqlClient and OleDb classes.

```
<%-- .NET Framework version 1.0 --%>
<%@Import Namespace="System.Data"%>
<%@Import Namespace="Microsoft.Data.Odbc"%>
```

In version 1.1 of the .NET Framework, the ODBC classes **are** included, and do not have to be downloaded separately. However, an important point to note is that the namespace name has changed between versions 1.0 and 1.1. The namespace for the original (Beta) version you download separately is Microsoft.Data.Odbc, whereas in version 1.1 it is System.Data.Odbc. This means that you must change any Import directives that specify the namespace when you move your pages or applications from version 1.0 to version 1.1:

```
<%-- .NET Framework version 1.1 --%>
<%@Import Namespace="System.Data"%>
<%@Import Namespace="System.Data.Odbc"%>
```

The GetNewsListDR Function

The GetNewsList stored procedure is executed from within a function named
GetNewsListDR, declared in the home.aspx "Home" page. This function is shown in the
next listing, and you can see that it uses standard ADO.NET data access techniques:

home.aspx

```
   function to get list of new items for Repeater control
Function GetNewsListDR() As SqlDataReader
  Try
    Dim sqlConnect As SqlConnection = New SqlConnection(sConnect)
    Dim sProcName As String = "GetNewsList"
    Dim sqlComm As SqlCommand = New SqlCommand(sProcName, sqlConnect)
    sqlComm.CommandType = CommandType.StoredProcedure
    sqlConnect.Open()
    Return sqlComm.ExecuteReader(CommandBehavior.CloseConnection)
  Catch
    Return Nothing
  End Try
End Function
```

This code creates a new SqlConnection object using the connection string that
you previously placed in a page-level variable named sConnect (you'll see where this
is done shortly). Then it defines the name of the stored procedure you want to call,
and creates a new SqlCommand object using this name and the SqlConnection object.
The CommandType for the SqlCommand object is set to CommandType.StoredProcedure. This
makes access more efficient as ADO.NET then knows what the command itself represents—a stored procedure and not a table name or SQL statement.

To get the data from the database, open the connection and call the ExecuteReader
method of the SqlConnection object. This returns a SqlDataReader object that points to
the results set generated by the stored procedure, ready for use in the page. Simply
return this SqlDataReader as the result of your function.

The CommandBehavior Parameter for the ExecuteReader Method

Notice that I include the value CloseConnection for the CommandBehavior parameter in
the call to the ExecuteReader method. This is extremely important, because the underlying connection to the database remains open after you return the DataReader from
the function to the calling routine. It has to be open so that the data can be accessed.
However, once you've finished with the DataReader, the connection will remain open
until explicitly closed, wasting precious resources.

When you specify the value CloseConnection for the CommandBehavior parameter,
the DataReader will automatically close its underlying connection to the database
when the DataReader itself is destroyed (when it goes out of scope in your page, or
when you destroy it explicitly by setting it to Nothing in VB.NET or null in C#).

Data Binding the Repeater Control

So, now that you've got a function that returns a DataReader, all you need to do is bind the DataReader it returns to the ASP.NET Repeater control in the sample page. It will then generate the output to fill the "News" section (you'll look at the declaration of the Repeater control in the next section).

There is a page-level variable named sConnect declared within the server-side <script> section of the page (you saw this being used in the GetNewsListDR function earlier on):

home.aspx

```
<script runat="server">
' page-level variable to hold database connection string
Dim sConnect As String
```

In the Page_Load event handler, set this variable to the value of the connection string for the XroxCars database. The connection string is stored in the appSettings section of the two web.config files used for the site (in the xroxcars and cookieless-xroxcars folders):

web.config

```
<configuration>
  <appSettings>
    <add key="XroxCarsConnectString"
         value="server=localhost;database=XroxCars;uid=anon;pwd=;" />
  </appSettings>
</configuration>
```

So, to get the connection string from within any page, all you need to do is reference the AppSettings collection of the default ConfigurationSettings object that is exposed by the page:

home.aspx

```
Sub Page_Load()
  ...
  ... other code to get user ID, etc. goes here
  ...
  ' get database connection string from web.config
  sConnect = ConfigurationSettings.AppSettings("XroxCarsConnectString")
  ...
```

Then you can use the DataReader you get back from the GetNewsListDR method as the DataSource of the Repeater control, and call the DataBind method to display the data:

```
...
' set DataSource for "news" list and data-bind it
repNews.DataSource = GetNewsListDR()
repNews.DataBind()
...
... other non-relevant code here, omitted for clarity
...
End Sub
```

Choosing the Appropriate ASP.NET "List" Control

As you can see from Figure 4-10 the output you're looking for in the "News" list is simply a series of separate paragraphs, each containing the précis of the new items in the database (taken from the NewsPrecis column of the tblNews table).

ASP.NET provides several types of "list" controls that you can use to generate repeated content from a range of data sources. We use a range of list controls in the pages of the Xrox Car Company site. Choosing which control to use involves thinking about what you actually want the control to achieve. Table 4-2 showing all of the "list" controls should help. While the first four controls are relatively obvious in the way they are used, the last three often do need some extra consideration when selecting which is the most appropriate.

Table 4-2. The List Controls Provided with ASP.NET

Control	Useful when you need to ...
CheckBoxList	... create a list of check boxes, from which more than one can be selected.
RadioButtonList	... create a list of radio or option buttons, from which only one can be selected.
DropDownList	... create a drop-down selection list, from which only one item can be selected and you want to minimize the space used on the page.
ListBox	... create a list where more than one item is visible. Can be configured so that users can select only one item, or so that they can select more than one item.
Repeater	... repeat any type of content that you specifically define, without the control applying any of its own structuring or formatting to the content. The Repeater is simpler, lighter, and more efficient than the DataList or DataGrid, but with fewer features. Templates are used to define the format and layout of the content, and any line breaks, paragraph divisions, and so forth, must be specifically declared within these templates.

Table 4-2. The List Controls Provided with ASP.NET (continued)

DataList   ... lay out content in the cells of a table, or repeated across or down the page in columns. It is a powerful list control, which is one step up from the Repeater in complexity and in use of resources. By default it lays out the content generated for each item in the data source within one cell of an HTML `<table>`, though it can also be used like the Repeater (without generating a `<table>`–called "flow layout" mode). It also provides a header and footer that can be formatted separately, and it can lay content out vertically or horizontally in columns when in "table layout" mode.

DataGrid   ... build an HTML table where each value is in a separate column, so that it looks like a grid. It provides the most control over content, and the most extra features. As well as headers and footers, the control can divide the list of items across multiple pages, provide automatic inline editing features, easily link code to events raised by controls in each row, and even automatically generate the columns based on the data source contents. A wide range of formatting options allows attractive layouts to be constructed.

From Table 4-2, it's pretty easy to see that the best choice for our "News" list is a Repeater control. You can define all the content and formatting within the control's templates—as you'll see when you explore the code for the "Home" page shortly.

The Static Section of the "News" List

Before looking at the repeater control in the page, however, the following listing shows the outline of the "News" section and the static content it contains. You can see the anchor named news for our "skip to" link. For the headings and text in the first paragraph of this section I used a combination of CSS styles (defined as the class attribute of the `<span>` elements) and `<font>` elements to format the content. Because the `<span>` elements are inside the `<font>` elements, the CSS styles take precedence in browsers that support CSS. For other browsers and clients, the `<font>` elements still provide a close approximation of the desired formatting:

```
...
<td width="25%" rowspan="2" bgcolor="#ffffaa" valign="top">
  <a name="news" />
  <font face="Arial,Helvetica,sans-serif" size="4" color="#b50055">
  <span class="large-red-text"><b>* Buy online now!</b></span><br />
  </font><font face="Tahoma,Arial,Helvetica,sans-serif" size="2">
  <span class="body-text">Select your car, choose the extras you
    require, and place your order online now! Or
  </span>
```

```
<a class="std-link" href="compare.aspx">compare our models</a>
<span class="body-text"> to make sure you choose the right
  car for you!</span><br /><br />
...
... Repeater control declaration goes here
...
... Controls for the mailing list section go here
...
</td>
...
```

You'll be looking at how the mailing list controls work (declared at the end of this section of code) in the next chapter. Now you move on and look at the "News" Repeater control declaration.

The ASP.NET Repeater Control for the "News" List

A Repeater control provides no "structure" of its own (it doesn't create an HTML table, or even separate the items with a <br /> element). This means that you must specify how to display the items within the data source of the control, using at least an <ItemTemplate> section.

> **NOTE** *The Repeater control supports five templates, for the header, footer, item, alternating item, and separator. For a full reference to the Repeater control, see the .NET SDK. The relevant pages for versions 1.0 and 1.1 are:*
> ms-help://MS.NETFrameworkSDK/cpref/html/
> frlrfSystemWebUIWebControlsRepeaterPropertiesTopic.htm
> ms-help://MS.NETFrameworkSDKv1.1/cpref/html/
> frlrfSystemWebUIWebControlsRepeaterPropertiesTopic.htm

The ASP.NET Repeater control used to display the list of "News" items is shown in the next code listing. The contents of the <ItemTemplate> section are automatically repeated for each item in the data source (once for each row in the rowset exposed by the DataReader). Within this template use an ASP.NET Hyperlink control for the news item title (displaying the text as a hyperlink) followed by a normal HTML <span> element that contains the précis of the item. After this comes the **[read more]** hyperlink, which is created by another ASP.NET Hyperlink control, within a <span> element that specifies the format of the text and the square brackets:

```
<asp:Repeater id="repNews" runat="server">
  <ItemTemplate><font face="Tahoma,Arial,Helvetica,sans-serif" size="2">
    <b>
    <asp:Hyperlink runat="server" CssClass="std-link"
      Text='<%# Container.DataItem("NewsTitle") %>'
```

```
            NavigateUrl='<%# DataBinder.Eval(Container.DataItem, "NewsID", _
                                "readnews.aspx?id={0}") %>' />
        </b><br />
        <span class="body-text"><%# Container.DataItem("NewsPrecis") %>
          ... </span>
        <font size="1"><span class="small-text">
          [<asp:Hyperlink runat="server" CssClass="small-link"
                          Text='read more'
          NavigateUrl='<%# DataBinder.Eval(Container.DataItem, "NewsID", _
                                "readnews.aspx?id={0}") %>' />]
        </span></font><br /><br /></font>
      </ItemTemplate>
  </asp:Repeater>
```

Notice that the complete output for each of the rows (the content of the
<ItemTemplate> section) is wrapped in a <font> element that defines the format and
appearance of the text for clients that don't support CSS. However, within the <font>
and </font> tags of this element, each <span> element has its class attribute set so
that browsers that do recognize CSS will use this to format and style the output.

The [read more] text is one size smaller than the rest of the text, achieved with
a nested <font> element with the attribute size="1" (the font face is inherited from
the enclosing <font> element), or by the CSS styles small-text and small-link that are
applied as the class attributes of the enclosed <span> elements.

The <ItemTemplate> content ends with two <br /> elements. Remember that, as
the Repeater control does not generate any layout information, you have to specify it
all yourself within the templates you define for the control. The two <br /> elements
used here are inserted into the HTML output after the rest of the content is generated
by the <ItemTemplate> for each row or item in the data source.

Data Binding Syntax in a List Control Template

To get the values from the data source rowset into the page, use the special data
binding syntax shown in the previous listing. There are two basic approaches for
working with data that is exposed as a rowset, as is the case with the DataReader
object. You can specify the data source column name directly, or you can use the Eval
method of the DataBinder object to extract and optionally format the data.

The simplest approach is to specify the column name directly, using the syntax:

```
<%# Container.DataItem("column-name") %>
```

In the listing above, I use this statement directly (within the <span> element that
specifies the text formatting and style) to provide the précis of the news item, specifying the column NewsPrecis:

```
<%# Container.DataItem("NewsPrecis") %>
```

You can also use this syntax within the declaration of an attribute for a control, for example I use it to set the Text property of the first Hyperlink control to the value of the NewsTitle column in the rowset:

```
<asp:Hyperlink runat="server" CssClass="std-link"
                Text='<%# Container.DataItem("NewsTitle") %>'
                ...
```

> **NOTE** *Notice that you have to use double quotes around the column name within the data-binding block (the statement or code within the <%# and %> delimiters). So, when you use this to specify the value of an attribute for the control, you must use single quotes around the complete block.*

However, if you want to format the values contained in the rowset when they are displayed, you can use the Eval method of the DataBinder object that is exposed by the list control itself. This method takes two or three parameters. The first is a reference to the data source item (Container.DataItem–the same as was used directly in the previous example), and the second is the name of the column within this row or item that you want to display:

```
<%# DataBinder.Eval(Container.DataItem, "column-name") %>
```

The optional third parameter is a "format string" that defines how the output will appear. You can use standard format strings as defined within .NET, with {0} being the placeholder for the value. For example, to format a number as currency, you could use:

```
<%# DataBinder.Eval(Container.DataItem, "column-name", " {0:C}") %>
```

> **NOTE** *See the .NET SDK topic:*
> ms-help://MS.NETFrameworkSDK/cpguidenf/html/cpconformattingtypes.htm or
> ms-help://MS.NETFrameworkSDKv1.1/cpguidenf/html/cpconformattingtypes.htm
> *for more details about the format strings that can be used.*

Where the Eval method is really useful is when you need to build up a string value that contains the value of a column. In the example, you want the URL of the hyperlink to be the page readnews.aspx, with the id of the current item appended to the query string. For this you can use the format string "readnews.aspx?id={0}". The {0} part will be replaced by the value of the column when the data is bound:

```
<asp:Hyperlink runat="server" CssClass="std-link"
              Text='<%# Container.DataItem("NewsTitle") %>'
              NavigateUrl='<%# DataBinder.Eval(Container.DataItem, "NewsID", _
                                              "readnews.aspx?id={0}") %>' />
```

Exactly the same approach is taken to set the NavigateUrl property of the second hyperlink in the <ItemTemplate>, which generates the **[read more]** link. The only difference here is that the text for the link is the same for each item. Notice how you avoid extra white space around the hyperlink by carefully placing the square brackets and closing </font> and </span> tags:

```
...
<font size="1"><span class="small-text">
[<asp:Hyperlink runat="server" CssClass="small-link"
      Text='read more'
      NavigateUrl='<%# DataBinder.Eval(Container.DataItem, "NewsID", _
                                      "readnews.aspx?id={0}") %>' />]
</span></font><br /><br /></font>
```

> **NOTE** *Remember that the content of the data-binding block is code that is executed when the binding takes place. So if you break the block across more than one line in VB.NET, you have to include the line continuation character, as shown above. In C#, this is not, of course, required.*

> **NOTE** *Also in C#, because there is no implicit type conversion, it's common practice to use the Eval method for all data-binding statements, and avoid the simpler syntax you used earlier in VB.NET. The Eval method is marginally less efficient than directly specifying the column name, but the advantage of the automatic output-formatting feature generally outweighs this.*

The List of Car Models

The main right-hand section of the "Home" page contains a list of the different vehicles that are available from the Xrox Car Company. For each one, I provide a small graphic image and the model name, both of which are hyperlinks that visitors can follow to see the standard features, configure the vehicle to suit their requirements, and discover how much it costs to purchase.

Under the image is the basic price for the vehicle, and below the model name in the right-hand column is a short description of the vehicle followed by a hyperlink where visitors can compare various features of the different vehicles (Figure 4-11).

The Xrox Wrampant

Our original and still the most popular sports car in our range. The Wrampant provides a unique combination of performance and comfort that most any driver. Happy around town, and yet with extra horses under the bonnet so that you can take advantage of the open road. With its 2 x 2 seat combination, and spacious luggage carrying features, it makes an ideal car for both short and long journeys. … [compare models]

Prices from $22,995.00

The Xrox Wranger

Whether you've got a big job to do, a lot of equipment to carry, or you just like to give the appearance of being a big-city farmer, the Wranger is the ideal truck for you. Hugely powerful, massively strong, and unbelievably reliable, it will easily handle everything you can throw at it. … [compare models]

Prices from $27,950.00

Figure 4-11. A section of the list of models on the "Home" page

Choosing the Appropriate List Control

As you can see from Figure 4-11, the goal was to create two distinct columns for this part of the page. The easiest way to achieve this is with a two-column table placed within the current cell of the main page structure table. If you had chosen a Repeater control, you would have to create this nested table yourself, by placing the <table> and </table> around the complete control declaration, and then creating each two-column row within the <ItemTemplate> section of the control.

The next choice would be a DataList control, as this can create a complete HTML table containing a single row for each item in the data source. However, this would have made it awkward to get the two-column layout, as you would then have to use the align attribute of each image to force the text to wrap to the right of it, and it would be very difficult to get the price below the image while guaranteeing that the layout remained constant irrespective of the browser window width.

Of course, you could create a two-column table within each cell that the DataList control creates. This involves using the ASP.NET Table, TableRow, and TableCell server controls, and setting the ExtractTemplateRows property of the DataList to True as well. Without this, the DataList control ignores any table elements that are placed within its templates. And doing it this way, you'd have ended up with tables nested three deep—the main structure table for the page would have a table generated by the DataList control inside the current cell. This table would consist of a single-cell row for each item, with a nested table inside each of these cells!

Instead, to best meet the layout requirements, the obvious choice here is a DataGrid control. This will create a table containing a row for each item in the data source, and each row will have the number of cells that you specify when you declare the DataGrid control in the page. You'll see what this declaration looks like shortly.

Changing the Behavior for Script-enabled Clients

One other aspect of this part of the page is that the way it works changes depending on whether the current user's browser supports client-side scripting or not. I decided that the hyperlinks in this section, which open the page where the user can configure the vehicle, should display that page in a separate browser window.

The reason is that this allows users to view and configure more than one vehicle at a time, and decide on the final configuration they require afterwards. There is some interesting debate among Web designers and users as to whether pop-up windows like this are acceptable, but there are several quite legitimate reasons for using them—and I feel this is one. Besides, it gives me the opportunity to demonstrate some extra features of ASP.NET Web Forms and server controls.

> **NOTE** *The "compare models" link opens its target page in the same window, and not in a new browser window like the other two hyperlinks for the image and the model name.*

So, if the current user's browser supports client-side scripting, use hyperlinks that execute a client-side script function to open a new browser window at a specific position, and with specific window furniture (menus, toolbars, and so on) that are specified in this client-side code. However, if the user's browser does not support client-side scripting, use a normal <a> element but with the target attribute set to "_blank" so that it opens within a new window. I'll look at how this is done at the end of this section of the chapter, after you've seen how to extract and display the data for this section of the page.

The Data Access Code for the "Car Models" List

You won't be surprised to learn that the code to extract the data for the list of models is almost identical to what was used to extract the list of "News" items in the previous section of this chapter. There is a stored procedure named GetModelList within the database, which accesses the tblCars table and extracts the required columns from each row. This stored procedure is executed from within a function named GetModelListDR, which returns a DataReader that is bound to the DataGrid control in our page.

The GetModelList Stored Procedure

In the GetModelList stored procedure, I extract the ID of each vehicle, the model name, and the short précis from the tblCar table. I also need the lowest price for this model so that it can display **"Prices from $xx,xxx.xx."** I get this using a sub-query that selects the lowest value for this model from the CarEnginePrice column of the tblCarEngines table, joining this table to tblCar on the CarID column. Finally, I order the results alphabetically by model name:

Stored procedure: GetModelList

```
SELECT CarID, Model, Precis,
(SELECT MIN(CarEnginePrice) FROM tblCarEngines
        WHERE tblCarEngines.CarID = tblCar.CarID) As Price
FROM tblCar ORDER BY Model
```

You could, of course, extract the rows in any other order you wish, for example by price (or price descending), by ID, or by adding a column to the table that specifies the order in which you want them to be displayed.

The GetModelListDR *Function*

Our GetModelListDR function looks just like the GetNewsListDR function I described for the "News" section of the page, and so I don't need to describe the workings again. The only difference is that it uses the GetModelList stored procedure this time:

home.aspx

```
' function to get details of car models for DataGrid control
Function GetModelListDR() As SqlDataReader
  Try
    Dim sqlConnect As SqlConnection = New SqlConnection(sConnect)
    Dim sProcName As String = "GetModelList"
    Dim sqlComm As SqlCommand = New SqlCommand(sProcName, sqlConnect)
    sqlComm.CommandType = CommandType.StoredProcedure
    sqlConnect.Open()
    Return sqlComm.ExecuteReader(CommandBehavior.CloseConnection)
  Catch
    Return Nothing
  End Try
End Function
```

Data Binding *the* DataGrid *Control*

You saw the relevant parts of the Page_Load event handler when looking at the "News" list earlier on. Code there declares and sets the value of the sConnect variable that holds the connection string. The only things you need to do otherwise are assign the DataReader that is returned from the GetModelListDR function to the DataGrid control, and then initiate the data-binding process:

```
Sub Page_Load()
  ...
  ... other code to get user ID, etc. goes here
  ...
  ... get database connection string from web.config as seen earlier
  ...
  ' set DataSource for "car models" list and data-bind it
  dgrModels.DataSource = GetModelListDR()
  dgrModels.DataBind()
End Sub
```

The DataGrid Control for the "Car Models" List

The declaration of the "models list" section of the page is shown in the next listing. You can see the table cell that is part of the main page structure table, together with the anchor that the "skip to" link at the top of the page points to. Below that, within the table cell, is the outline declaration of the DataGrid control that generates the list of models:

```
<tr>
  <td valign="top">
    <a name="models" />
    <asp:DataGrid id="dgrModels" runat="server" Width="100%"
                  Font-Name="Tahoma,Arial,Helvetica,sans-serif"
                  Font-Size="10"
                  BorderStyle="None"
                  GridLines="None"
                  CellSpacing="10"
                  CellPadding="10"
                  ShowHeader="False"
                  AutoGenerateColumns="False"
                  OnItemDataBound="SetNavigateUrl">
      <ItemStyle VerticalAlign="top" />
      <Columns>
        ... column declarations go here ...
      </Columns>
    </asp:DataGrid>
  </td>
</tr>
```

You can see that I've included values for quite a few attributes of this control. I've specified the font name (face) and size, turned off the display of borders and grid lines (the individual cell borders), set the cell spacing and padding to 10, and told the control not to display a header row.

The next attribute, AutoGenerateColumns="False", tells the control that you don't want it to create the columns automatically. The default, if not specified, is "True", which means that the control will automatically generate a column in the resulting grid (an HTML table) for each column or field it finds in the rows of the data source. To exert fine control over the output, without having a separate column for each field in the rowset, you should define the columns yourself.

The OnItemDataBound attribute specifies the name of an event handler that will be executed once for each row in the data source, after the control has figured out what values are in the data row but before it creates the output for that row. Use this event handler to modify the URL of the hyperlinks in the resulting page, depending on whether the current user's browser supports client-side script. You'll see how this is done later.

Specifying Styles and Templates

After the opening tag of the DataGrid control, you come to the elements that define the content and appearance of each section of the control's output. Any styling or other information you provide within the <ItemStyle> element is applied only to the rows in the resulting grid. There are equivalent elements to define the style and appearance of the alternating item rows, the header, the footer, the selected item row, and the row currently being edited (if there is one). You'll see examples of these elements and templates in later examples from other pages in the site.

Notice that I mentioned a "selected row" style. Both the DataList and DataGrid controls provide a SelectedIndex property. When the control generates its output, the row at the index specified in this property is rendered using the style values specified in the <SelectedItemStyle> element.

It's also possible to switch a row into "edit" mode in a DataList or DataGrid control by setting the EditItemIndex to a value greater than -1. In this case, the styles specified in the <EditItemStyle> element are used to render the output for the row at the specified index.

If you are using templates to create the output (as will always be the case with a DataList control), the contents of the <SelectedItemTemplate> are displayed instead of the <ItemTemplate> or <AlternatingItemTemplate> contents for the row at the SelectedIndex position. Likewise, the contents of the <EditItemTemplate> are displayed instead of the <ItemTemplate> or <AlternatingItemTemplate> contents for the row at the EditItemIndex position

> **NOTE** *For a full reference to the* DataGrid *control, see the .NET SDK page:*
> ms-help://MS.NETFrameworkSDK/cpref/html/
> frlrfSystemWebUIWebControlsDataGridPropertiesTopic.htm or
> ms-help://MS.NETFrameworkSDKv1.1/cpref/html/
> frlrfSystemWebUIWebControlsDataGridPropertiesTopic.htm

Specifying Column Information in a DataGrid Template

The final element shown in the previous listing is the <Columns> element, which contains the definitions of the columns you want the DataGrid control to display. This element and its content are only required because you have told the control that you don't want it to generate the columns automatically—you'll be doing that yourself.

When specifying the column information for a DataGrid control, you can take advantage of several ready-built column types. This is the "next step up" from having the control generate the columns automatically based on the structure of each data source item. It gives you more control over the appearance and formatting of the column and its values.

The column types you can use are:

- asp:BoundColumn–values are displayed as text in the output. If the EditItemIndex of the control is not -1, values from the row at that index position are displayed in text boxes.

- asp:HyperlinkColumn–values in this column are displayed as hyperlinks, and the target URL can be created dynamically from the value if required.

- asp:EditColumn–displays **Edit**, **Update**, and **Cancel** command links in this column for each row, depending on the value of the EditItemIndex property of the control (which specifies the row that is currently being edited if there is one).

- asp:ButtonColumn–displays a button in this column for each row. The caption and action of the button can be specified to create custom behavior for the grid.

There is also one more type of column, and this is used when you want absolute control over the content and appearance of the column:

- asp:TemplateColumn–all the information to generate the column is provided by declaring templates. These work in the same way as the templates for a DataList or Repeater control, and you can define the content to be displayed for this column in each row, each alternating row, the selected row, and the row currently being edited (if there is one).

I only want two columns for the sample DataGrid control—one for the graphic of the vehicle and price, and one for the name, description, and link to compare models. However, I need to build the content for these columns using data from several columns (or fields) in the data source rows. So I have to resort to using an asp:TemplateColumn column type for both of these columns.

The Graphic Image and Price Column

The next listing shows the first column declaration, within the <Columns> element of the DataGrid control. Only an <ItemTemplate> is needed for this column, as all the rows have the same format (I'm not formatting alternate rows in a different style). Within the <ItemTemplate> declare an ASP.NET Hyperlink control, followed by a <br /> element and a <span> where the price will be inserted:

```
<Columns>
  <asp:TemplateColumn>
    <ItemTemplate>
      <asp:Hyperlink id="lnkCarImage" runat="server" Target="_blank"
          ImageUrl='<%# DataBinder.Eval(Container.DataItem, _
                    "Model", "images/{0}150.gif") %>'
          ToolTip='<%# DataBinder.Eval(Container.DataItem, _
                    "Model", "The Xrox {0} in detail") %>'
```

```
              NavigateUrl='<%# DataBinder.Eval(Container.DataItem, _
                           "CarID", "cardetail-noscript.aspx?id={0}") %>' />
    <br />
    <span class="body-text">
       <%# DataBinder.Eval(Container.DataItem, "Price", _
                           "Prices from <b>${0:#,##0.00}</b>") %>
    </span></ItemTemplate>
  </asp:TemplateColumn>
```

> **NOTE** *You could, of course, provide an* <AlternatingItemTemplate> *as well if you wanted alternate rows to look different, and a* <SeparatorTemplate> *if you wanted to insert some HTML or other output between each row.*

The Hyperlink control is used to display a clickable graphic image, as I suggested was possible when you looked at the "links to other pages" section earlier in this chapter. The image is a picture of the vehicle, and the path and name of the appropriate image as the ImageUrl attribute of the Hyperlink control must be specified.

This is achieved by using the DataBinder.Eval method, as was done with the Repeater control earlier on in this chapter, and specifying as the format string the value "images/{0}150.gif". This will resolve to a value such as "images/Wrampant150.gif" when data binding takes place, and so the correct image will be used in the page for this row. Likewise, you specify the ToolTip attribute in the same way, using a format string that will give a result such as **"The Xrox Wrampant in detail."**

The NavigateUrl attribute is set in the same way, but this time it's bound to the CarID column and not the Model (name) column, and so will resolve to a value such as "cardetail-noscript.aspx?id=4" after binding is complete. As you've also included the attribute Target="_blank" in the Hyperlink declaration, the page cardetail-noscript.aspx will be opened in a new browser window.

Following the Hyperlink control and the <br /> element is a <span> element that uses the CSS style class named body-text, and which contains the value from the Price column of the data source. I use the format string "Prices from <b>${0:#,##0.00}</b>" within the Databinder.Eval method here to produce the formatted output you can see in Figure 4-12—it's permissible to include HTML in the format string and have it rendered by the client. Figure 4-12 also shows the value for the ToolTip attribute that was specified in the Hyperlink declaration.

Figure 4-12. The output generated by the DataGrid *for the model list*

Viewing the output that is generated for this column in the browser, you can see the results of the format strings you specified for the various properties of the Hyperlink control and the price. Notice that (as you discovered in Chapter 2) Internet Explorer generates a style attribute in the opening tag of the <table> element that the control creates (and which will hold all the rows from the data source):

Result in Internet Explorer 6 (with client-side scripting disabled)

```
<table cellspacing="10" cellpadding="10" border="0" id="dgrModels"
       style="border-style:None;font-family:Tahoma,Arial,Helvetica,sans-serif;
       font-size:10pt;width:100%;">
 <tr valign="Top">
  <td>
   <a id="dgrModels__ctl2_lnkCarImage" Target="_blank"
      title="The Xrox Wrampant in detail"
      href="cardetail-noscript.aspx?id=1">
    <img title="The Xrox Wrampant in detail"
         src="images/Wrampant150.gif" border="0" /></a><br />
   <span class="body-text">Prices from <b>$22,995.00</b></span></td>
```

However, as all the text generated by the control is within <span> elements, which each have a class attribute that defines the CSS styles for that text, the overall text styles specified in the opening <table> tag are ignored in browsers that support CSS.

In "down-level" clients, the DataGrid control does not create the style attribute for the opening <table> tag. Instead, it wraps the entire content of each column inside a <font> element that used the values specified in the attributes to the DataGrid control (remember that Font-Size="10", without any unit specifier such as px or em, is translated into <font size="2"> by the control):

Result in Netscape 6 (with client-side scripting disabled)

```
<table cellspacing="10" cellpadding="10" border="0" id="dgrModels"
       width="100%">
 <tr valign="Top">
  <td><font face="Tahoma,Arial,Helvetica,sans-serif" size="2">
   <a id="dgrModels__ctl2_lnkCarImage" Target="_blank"
      title="The Xrox Wrampant in detail"
      href="cardetail-noscript.aspx?id=1">
    <img title="The Xrox Wrampant in detail"
         src="images/Wrampant150.gif" border="0" /></a><br />
   <span class="body-text">Prices from <b>$22,995.00</b></span></font></td>
```

Other than that, the output is that same. And the same <span> elements with the same class attribute values ensure that the appearance is correct in any client that supports CSS.

The Name and Description Column

The column that displays the model name, description and **[compare models]** link is very similar in declaration and workings to the previous column you've been looking at. The model name is generated by an ASP.NET Hyperlink control, but this time using text as the link and not a graphic image. This is followed by a ‹br /› element, and the text description of the vehicle within a ‹span› element. After this comes another Hyperlink control, with the text **"compare models"** for every row:

```
<asp:TemplateColumn>
  <ItemTemplate>
    <b><font face="Arial,Helvetica,sans-serif" size="3">
    <asp:Hyperlink id="lnkCarName" runat="server"
        CssClass="large-link" Target="_blank"
        Text='<%# DataBinder.Eval(Container.DataItem, "Model", _
                            "The Xrox {0}") %>'
        NavigateUrl='<%# DataBinder.Eval(Container.DataItem, "CarID", _
                            "cardetail-noscript.aspx?id={0}") %>' />
    </b><br /></font>
    <span class="body-text"><%# Container.DataItem("Precis") %> ...
    </span><font size="1"><span class="small-text">
    [<asp:Hyperlink runat="server" CssClass="small-link"
      Text='compare models'
      NavigateUrl='<%# DataBinder.Eval(Container.DataItem, "Model", _
                            "compare.aspx?compare={0}") %>' />]
    </span></font></ItemTemplate>
  </asp:TemplateColumn>
</Columns>
```

Notice that I provide a CssClass attribute for the two hyperlinks, specifying the class names that I want placed in these elements (as the class attribute). However, to provide the correct appearance on non-CSS-enabled browsers, you also need to include the appropriate ‹font› elements. Wrap the model name in a ‹font› element with the size set to "3", and the **compare models** link in a ‹font› element with the size set to "1". In "down-level" clients, the DataGrid control itself will automatically wrap all this inside another ‹font› element (with the correct font face and with a font size of "2"). The result is shown in Figure 4-13.

The Xrox Wrampant
Our original and still the most popular sports car in our range. The
Wrampant provides a unique combination of performance and comfort that
will suit almost any driver. Happy around town, and yet with extra horses
under the bonnet so that you can take advantage of the open road. With its
2 x 2 seat combination, and spacious luggage carrying features, it makes an
ideal car for both short and long journeys. ... [compare models]

Figure 4-13. The formatted hyperlink for the model name

Looking at the HTML output that the DataGrid control generates for this column, you can see the effects of the CssClass attributes I added to the Hyperlink controls, and the extra <font> elements. In Internet Explorer 6 (and other "up-level" browsers), the control generates the following output, including a class attribute on each <a> element:

Result in Internet Explorer 6 (with client-side scripting disabled)

```
<td><b><font face="Arial,Helvetica,sans-serif" size="3">
 <a id="dgrModels__ctl2_lnkCarName" class="large-link" Target="_blank"
    href="cardetail-noscript.aspx?id=3">The Xrox Wranger</a></b>
 <br /></font>
 <span class="body-text">Whether you've got a big job to do ...
 </span><font size="1"><span class="small-text">
   [<a class="small-link" href="compare.aspx?compare=Wranger">
   compare models</a>]
 </span></font></td>
<tr>
...
... row for next car here ...
```

In "down-level" clients, the control generates a slightly different output. Inside the table cell you get the <font> element generated from the Font-Name and Font-Size attributes specified in the opening tag of the DataGrid control declaration. Inside this is the content specified in the template, and it is the same as that for "up-level" clients that you've just seen:

Result in Netscape 6 (with client-side scripting disabled)

```
<td><font face="Tahoma,Arial,Helvetica,sans-serif" size="2">
 <b><font face="Arial,Helvetica,sans-serif" size="3">
 <a id="dgrModels__ctl2_lnkCarName" class="large-link" Target="_blank"
    href="cardetail-noscript.aspx?id=3">The Xrox Wranger</a></b><br /></font>
 <span class="body-text"> Whether you've got a big job to do ...
 </span><font size="1"><span class="small-text">
   [<a class="small-link" href="compare.aspx?compare=Wranger">
   compare models</a>]
 </span></font></font></td>
</tr>
...
... row for next car here ...
```

So, as before, the appearance of the output in clients that support CSS is guaranteed by the fact that every visible element has a class attribute that specifies the CSS style you want to apply to that element. Outside these <a> and <span> elements are nested <font> elements that will provide a very similar appearance in clients that do not support CSS.

Handling the ItemDataBound *Event for a* DataGrid

The results I showed you being generated by the DataGrid control in the previous sections are what you will see in a browser or client that does not support client-side scripting, or which has it disabled. You'll recall that I want to change the way that the hyperlinks in the models list work for clients that do support client-side scripting:

- First, I want to open the new window using client-side script so that I can control the size, position, and window furniture.

- I'd also like to be able to prevent multiple instances of the same model window being opened, and instead use an existing window if the user selects the same model again. And, in this case, I want to bring the existing window to the front so that it is visible.

- Most important of all, I have to load a **different page** into the pop-up window if the visitor's browser *does* support client-side scripting. By default (as you saw above) I load the page cardetail-noscript.aspx. However, if they have client-side scripting enabled, I want to load the page cardetail.aspx instead.

When I declared the DataGrid control earlier on, I included a value for the OnItemDatabound attribute:

```
<asp:DataGrid id="dgrModels" runat="server" Width="100%"
              ...
              OnItemDataBound="SetNavigateUrl">
```

This value is the name of an event handler that will be executed each time the control processes a row from the data source. The control passes two parameters to the event handler—a reference to itself (the "sender"), and a DataGridItemEventArgs object. This object contains a wealth of information about the event that is occurring, including information about the type of row that is being bound, and a reference to the row in the data source that is providing the data for this output row.

The SetNavigateUrl *Event Handler*

The next listing shows the complete SetNavigateUrl event handler defined within the page. First check the page-level variable bCanScript, as this will only be True if the current client supports client-side scripting (this was set in the Page_Load event handler when testing for script support, as you saw in the previous chapter).

You also need to check that the event is being raised for an "item" row or an "alternating item" row. It's only these rows that will contain the hyperlink controls whose properties you want to modify. The DataGridItemEventArgs object passed to the event handler exposes information about the row in the DataGrid control as the Item property, and the type of row is stored in the ItemType property of the Item object:

```
Sub SetNavigateUrl(sender As Object, args As DataGridItemEventArgs)
  If bCanScript And (args.Item.ItemType = ListItemType.Item _
  Or args.Item.ItemType = ListItemType.AlternatingItem) Then
    ' it's a data row that is being bound so create appropriate
    ' URLs for hyperlinks and remove Target attributes
    ' use separate function to ensure session ID is munged into URL
    ' in case the page is running in "cookieless sessions" mode
    Dim sCarID As String = args.Item.DataItem("CarID")
    Dim sHref As String = "javascript:openWindow('" _
                        & InsertSessionId(Request.Path) _
                        & "/cardetail.aspx?id=" & sCarID _
                        & "', '" & sCarID & "')"
    ' update href in controls to new value
    CType(args.Item.FindControl("lnkCarImage"), _
                              Hyperlink).NavigateUrl = sHref
    CType(args.Item.FindControl("lnkCarImage"), _
                              Hyperlink).Target = ""
    CType(args.Item.FindControl("lnkCarName"), _
                              Hyperlink).NavigateUrl = sHref
    CType(args.Item.FindControl("lnkCarName"), _
                              Hyperlink).Target = ""

  End If
End Sub
```

Once it's decided that this row needs to be processed, inside the If...End If construct, create a String containing the appropriate value to use as the NavigateUrl of the hyperlinks in this row. It should be something like:

```
javascript:openWindow('cardetail.aspx?id=1', '1')
```

When the user clicks on such a link, the browser will execute the client-side function named openWindow, passing it the URL of the page you want to display with the ID of the current vehicle appended as the query string, and the ID of the vehicle as a separate parameter as well.

After you've created the string for the URL, access the two Hyperlink controls that are in the current row of the DataGrid by using the FindControl method of the current Item (the current row in the DataGrid) and by specifying the value of the id property for the control you want to find. You have to cast (convert) the returned object to the appropriate type (a Hyperlink object), and then you can set the NavigateUrl property to the new value:

```
CType(args.Item.FindControl("lnkCarImage"), _
                          Hyperlink).NavigateUrl = sHref
```

The two hyperlinks declared in the DataGrid also contain Target attributes, set to open the new page in a new browser window (Target="_blank"). However, when you use a function to open the new window, you need to remove these attributes. You do this by setting the Target property of the Hyperlink controls to an empty string:

```
CType(args.Item.FindControl("lnkCarImage"), _
                        Hyperlink).Target = ""
```

If you view the result created by the DataGrid in a script-enabled browser, you can see the effect this event handler has. The href attributes of the two <a> elements now have the new values, and there are no target attributes:

```
<a id="dgrModels__ctl2_lnkCarImage"
   title="The Xrox Wrampant in detail"
   href="javascript:openWindow('cardetail.aspx?id=1', '1')">
 <img title="The Xrox Wrampant in detail"
      src="images/Wrampant150.gif" border="0" /></a><br />
 <span class="body-text">Prices from <b>$22,995.00</b></span></td><td>
 <b><font face="Arial,Helvetica,sans-serif" size="3">
 <a id="dgrModels__ctl2_lnkCarName" class="large-link"
    href="javascript:openWindow('cardetail.aspx?id=1', '1')">
 The Xrox Wrampant</a></b><br /></font>
```

Of course, you also need to include the client-side openWindow function in the example page. This is declared within the <head> section of the home.aspx page (it is inserted into the page every time, irrespective of whether the client supports scripting or not). As there is no runat="server" attribute in the opening <script> tag, the script is simply sent to the client "as is":

```
<head>
...
<script language='JavaScript'>
<!--
function openWindow(sHref, sCarID) {
  // open cardetail.aspx page in new window and bring to front
  var newWin = window.open(sHref, 'WCCDetail' + sCarID,
   'scrollbars=yes,toolbar=no,location=no,resizable=yes,directories=no,'
   + 'status=no,menubar=no,width=635,height=550,top=5,left=5');
  newWin.focus();
}
//-->
</script>
</head>
```

Notice that I use the first parameter (sHref) to specify the page that will be loaded into this window. To prevent multiple instances of the same model being displayed in different windows, use the second parameter (sCarID) to specify the name of the window that you'll open. If a window with this name is already open, the browser automatically loads the page into this existing window instead of opening a new one.

However, in this case, the window that it uses may not be visible—it may be hidden behind other windows. So, in the last line of the function, bring it to the front and give it the "input focus" by calling its focus method.

> NOTE   *If you decided to allow users to open more than one instance of the window*
> *for each model, as they can when client-side scripting is not enabled, you would*
> *just change the window name parameter to the* window.open *method from*
> 'WCCDetail' + sCarID *to* '_blank'.

Session IDs for Cookie-less Sessions

You may have noticed in the SetNavigateUrl event handler, when you were creating
the string for the new URL, that you called a function named InsertSessionId, and
passed to it the virtual path to the current page:

```
Dim sCarID As String = args.Item.DataItem("CarID")
Dim sHref As String = "javascript:openWindow('" _
                    & InsertSessionId(Request.Path) _
                    & "/cardetail.aspx?id=" & sCarID _
                    & "', '" & sCarID & "')"
```

The reason is that the application is designed to work with both normal cookie-
based sessions, and with cookie-less sessions. In the latter case, the URLs in the page
must contain the session ID, "munged" into the URL. In cookie-less sessions mode,
ASP.NET automatically performs this "munging" for all hyperlinks in the page, as you
saw near the start of the previous chapter. However, when you are building URLs
dynamically in code, as in the SetNavigateUrl event handler, you have to perform your
own "munging."

While you could do this by querying the SessionID property of the user's Session
object, and performing some fairly simple string manipulation, there is an easier
way. The Response object exposes a method named ApplyAppPathModifier, which
returns the path to the current page with the session ID "munged" into it if the page
is running in "cookie-less session" mode. If not, it doesn't insert the session ID.

So, the InsertSessionID function can take the path passed to it as a parameter
and call the ApplyAppPathModifier method. This returns the same virtual path, but
with the session ID munged into it when running in "cookie-less sessions" mode.
However, you want to return just the path, and not the complete modified path and
file name. Remember that you pass to this function the virtual path to the current
page, so you need to strip off the page name before returning just the path:

```
Function InsertSessionId(sPath As String) As String
  ' function to insert SessionID into path if running in cookieless
  ' session mode, and return just the path with no filename
  ' does not insert session ID if not in "cookieless" mode
  Dim sResult As String = Response.ApplyAppPathModifier(sPath)
  Return sResult.Substring(0, sResult.LastIndexOf("/"))
End Function
```

The code in the SetNavigateUrl event handler can then add the name of the target page to the result, and use it to build the final URL—as you saw earlier.

Summary

In this chapter I started to build the example site "Home" page, keeping in mind all of the issues I discussed in previous chapters. In particular, I've tried to make the page work properly, and give the same appearance, in as many client browser types as possible by using a combination of CSS styles and the more traditional <font> elements.

I also put in quite a lot of effort to make the page accessible to users who suffer a disability, such as limitations in movement or vision, that require them to use specialist user agents rather than graphical browsers. I included all the features and followed all the guidelines discussed near the end of the previous chapter to make navigation within the site as easy as possible for users of text browsers and "page reader" clients.

The "Home" page is neatly divisible into several sections, and you looked at the way that the overall structure of the page and these sections is achieved. You also looked in depth at three of these sections: the links to other pages, the "News" section, and the list of vehicle models available from the Xrox Car Company.

I also spent time discussing how the various "list" controls provided with ASP.NET can be used to make building pages easier, and I showed how to use a Repeater and a DataGrid control in the "Home" page.

Finally, you discovered how to modify the pages to take into account features available on the client to which the page is served. By handling events raised by the list controls, you can selectively change the output generated by the control. I used this technique to modify the way that hyperlinks work in the page when the user's browser supports client-side scripting.

In all, the topics I covered were:

- The overall structure of the "Home" page

- How to specify the styles and appearance of the page, and each page section

- How to provide additional accessibility and navigation features for specialist clients

- The section containing the links to other pages

- The "News and Special Offers" section of the page

- The list of car models and descriptions

- How the page changes behavior for script-enabled and non-script-enabled clients

In the next chapter, I'll complete the exploration of the "Home" page by looking at the animated banner, the page footer, and the mailing list sections of the page.

Banners, Footers, and Email

IN THE PREVIOUS CHAPTER, you saw the basic structure of the "Home" page of the example site, and examined the three main sections of the page: the links to other pages, the list of "News" items, and the list of vehicle models available from the Xrox Car Company. However, there are three other features of the "Home" page that I didn't have room to cover in Chapter 4.

I'll look at these in more detail in this chapter, including the animated page banner, the page footer, and the way visitors can sign up for the mailing list. The first two of these topics introduces an extremely useful generic technique in ASP.NET—wrapping up reusable sections of code into **user controls**.

So, the topics for this chapter are:

- The animated banner used in most of the pages

- The page footer used in most of the pages

- How to add users to the mailing list in the "Home" page

I'll start with a look at the topic of user controls, which I take advantage of for the animated banner and page footer in the example site.

About ASP.NET User Controls

When I work with ASP.NET, I tend to use its in-built elements (server controls, the .NET Framework classes, and so on) for building my Web sites and Web applications without a second thought. After all, these elements provide the foundations of the whole ASP.NET postback architecture, and all of the advantages that this brings.

However, the server controls provided with ASP.NET are sometimes not exactly what you want, especially when you have some esoteric purpose in mind. Neither are they directly customized to suit your Web sites—which is not surprising, as they have to be generic in nature.

One solution is to write and compile your own server controls. However, custom server control creation, while not difficult to do, is a little complex—and the topic as a whole is outside the scope of this book. In the meantime, there is an easier way to build custom controls that can behave in a similar way to server controls, and it provides most of the features that server controls do as well. You can build **user controls**.

Reusable Code and Content

User controls can be extremely useful when building a Web site or Web application. They provide several advantages over "inline" code that occurs in every page:

- They are reusable—the same single source file that defines a control can be inserted dynamically at runtime into any number of pages, as long as they reside within the same ASP.NET application (they are all in the same virtual application root folder or subfolders of that root folder.

- They can contain anything that you can put into an ordinary ASP.NET page (.aspx), including HTML, text, other content, server-side script, client-side script, and so on.

- Their content becomes part of the hosting page, so you can refer to the controls, script functions, and other objects within the user control as properties of the control.

- They can expose custom properties as simple data types, or as objects (classes), allowing values to be passed into the user control dynamically each time it is instantiated in an ASP.NET page.

- Code within the user control can reference objects in the parent ASP.NET page that is hosting the user control, through the Parent property of the control.

- Output caching can be configured for just the control, separately from the ASP.NET page that hosts it. This allows the content of just the user control to be cached between requests in exactly the same way you use output caching in an ASP.NET page, but with the content of the hosting page being regenerated on each request.

Of all these advantages, the primary one is usually the ability to write one "page" (user control) and then use it in several other pages. If the control has to be fixed when a bug is found, or updated to suit new requirements, only that single file needs attention. Each page that uses it will pick up the new version the next time it is requested. And moving blocks of content and/or code out of an ASP.NET page and into a user control also makes the hosting page simpler and easier to manage and debug (Figure 5-1).

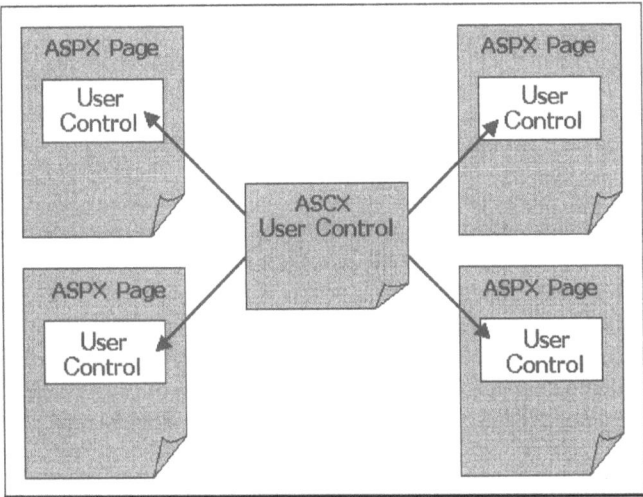

Figure 5-1. User controls can provide reusable content for more than one page.

Building a User Control

Building user controls is trivially easy, in fact a common approach is to discover some content in a page that you need to reuse, and just lift it out and convert it into a user control. Of course, those of us with a more organized approach to site and page design will already be aware of what user controls will be needed when designing the site (and there are a few pigs passing overhead right now!).

The only things that define a user control as being different from an ASP.NET page are the directive at the start of the file and the file extension. Instead of a Page directive, use a Control directive:

```
<%@Control Language="VB" %>
```

The file extension for a user control must be .ascx, although it can be placed in any folder within the virtual application where it is used. Unlike .NET assemblies (compiled .dll files), user controls *do not* have to reside in the bin folder.

You can use many of the same attributes within the Control directive of a user control as you do in an ASP.NET page, for example EnableViewState="True|False" and Debug="True|False", and these override the settings for the parent page. And you can include other directives as well. For example, as mentioned earlier, you can include an OutputCache directive:

```
<%@OutputCache Duration="60" VaryByParam="*" %>
```

You can also import namespaces from the .NET class library, or for custom components and assemblies that you create yourself:

```
<%@Import Namespace="System.Data.SqlClient" %>
<%@Import Namespace="MyAssembly.MyNewClass" %>
```

However, there are a couple of limitations on the things that can appear inside a user control:

- Do not include a server-side form (a `<form runat="server">` control), as there can only be one in an ASP.NET page, whereas several instances of a user control could be inserted into a single ASP.NET page. However, if only one instance of the control will ever be used in any ASP.NET page, you might want to break this rule.

- Do not include the `<html>`, `<head>`, and `<body>` elements, as these will generally be provided within the hosting ASP.NET page. However, if your control is used—for example—to create the complete `<head>` or `<body>` section of the page, and only one instance will ever be used in any ASP.NET page, you might want to break this rule.

The Contents of a User Control

So, what do you actually put into a user control? As I discussed earlier, you can put almost anything into one. A simple example is if you want to insert a corporate image and hyperlink into every page of a site. You could define the user control as:

```
<%@Control Language="VB" %>
<center>
<a href="http://mysite.com/about.aspx" title="About Us">
  <img src="corp-hq.jpg" alt="About us" border="0" />
</a>
<hr />
<a href="http://mysite.com/about.aspx" title="About Us">
  Read about our company ...
</a>
</center>
```

Then, when the CEO decides to change the text in the hyperlink to "Read all about our wonderful corporation," you only have to edit this `.ascx` file. All the pages that use it will display the new content when next requested.

A completely different way of using user controls is where they simply act as a way to centralize non-visible parts of a page, or even just server-side code blocks. For example, if you have a function that performs some complicated calculation, and you want to use it in several pages, you can create it as a user control like this:

```
<%@Control Language="VB" %>
<script runat="server">
Function CalculateSomethingDifficult(iInput As Integer) As String
  ...
  ... code to calculate and return the result ...
  ...
End Function
</script>
```

Now you can use this function as a method of the control—just like you would use a method of any other server control. And, of course, you can mix all kinds of content in a user control. The examples you'll see later in this chapter, which come from the example Xrox Car Company site, contain several different types of content as well as server-side code.

Exposing Properties from a User Control

One useful aspect of user controls is that they can expose properties—again, much like any other server control. There are two ways that you can expose properties: as a `Public` variable or by creating `Get` and `Set` methods within the control.

If you just want to expose a simple value type, such as an `Integer` or `String`, you can declare it within the user control as a `Public` variable, and even give it a default value:

```
<%@Control Language="VB" %>
<script runat="server">
Public MyProperty As String = "Not specified"

Sub Page_Load()
  ...
  ... use the value of the variable MyProperty here
  ...
End Sub
</script>

<p>Or even insert it into the output like this: <% = MyProperty %></p>
```

If the hosting ASP.NET page does not set the value of the property when it instantiates the user control, the value will be the default you provided: `"Not specified"`.

Alternatively, you can expose properties of objects within the user control. For example, if you have a text box with the `id` value `"MyTextbox"`, you can set up access to its properties like this:

```
<%@Control Language="VB" %>
<script runat="server">
Public Property TheText() As String
  Get
    Return MyTextbox.Text
```

```
    End Get
    Set
      MyTextbox.Text = value
    End Set
End Property
</script>

<asp:Textbox id="MyTextbox" runat="server" />
```

One final aspect of user controls that helps to demonstrate how powerful they can be is that you can even use templates within a user control to create a **templated user control**.

> **NOTE** *I don't cover this topic here, or use templated user controls in the example site, but you can read more about them in the .NET SDK here:* ms-help://MS.NETFrameworkSDK/cpguidenf/html/ cpconcreatingtemplatedusercontrol.htm.

Using a User Control in an ASP.NET Page

Having seen how to build user controls, you need to look at how to insert them into ASP.NET pages and then access them. User controls must first be registered in the ASP.NET pages that use them, with a Register directive. Specify the tag prefix and tag name that you'll use to identify the control and the path to the .ascx file that implements the control:

```
<%@Register TagPrefix="myprefix" TagName="mynewcontrol"
            Src="ascx/my-user-control.ascx"%>
```

Once it has been registered, insert the control into the page as an XML element, using the tag prefix and tag name you just specified. You can also give it an ID, so that you can refer to it afterwards in the code if required. Note that you must include the runat="server" attribute so ASP.NET knows that it has to process this element, and insert the user control into the page at this point:

```
<myprefix:mynewcontrol id="MyControl" runat="server" />
```

This is all that's required if the user control just contains HTML and static or dynamically generated content, and does not require any further interaction from us. The HTML and content will appear in the output at the point where you place the XML element you've just seen.

However, if the user control contains code that you want to access, for example a function that you want to use in your server-side code, refer to it using the ID of the user control. So, to call the CalculateSomethingDifficult function defined in an earlier example, you would use:

```
Dim sResult As String = MyControl.CalculateSomethingDifficult(42)
```

Setting Properties

If the user control exposes any properties, you can set these in the ASP.NET page that hosts the control. And it's done in exactly the same way as you would any other server control. For example, if the user control with the ID value "MyControl" exposes a String property named MyProperty, you can set the value when you insert the control into the page:

```
<myprefix:mynewcontrol id="MyControl" runat="server"
                       MyProperty="This value" />
```

If the user control also exposes an Integer property named MyNumber (or a property that is of any other simple value type), you still set it the same way, using attributes of the user control element:

```
<myprefix:mynewcontrol id="MyControl" runat="server"
                       MyProperty="This value" MyNumber="42" />
```

Furthermore, just as with the "standard" server controls, you can set the properties dynamically in your server-side code. This time, however, you should make sure that the values are of the correct data type (while VB.NET will convert most data types implicitly, C# does not):

```
MyControl.MyProperty = "Another value"
MyControl.MyNumber = 42
```

The Animated Page Banner

So, after a detour to talk about user controls, I can now get back to the Xrox Car Company site, and the remainder of the "Home" page that you started to look at in the previous chapter. I'll examine in detail how to implement the animated banner that appears at the top of the page when first opened in browsers such as Internet Explorer 4.0 and later, Netscape 4.0 and later, and Mozilla 1.0.

As you'll have guessed by now, the animated banner section of the page is a user control, and you insert it into each page as required. It exposes properties that you can set to manage the way that it behaves. As output, the user control generates a mixture of HTML and client-side script—depending on the type of client that is accessing the page in which the control is hosted.

To be able to modify its output, the user control contains server-side script that is executed each time it is instantiated in an ASP.NET page. This selects the appropriate sections of output for insertion into the hosting page. As part of this process, the server-side code also accesses an element within the hosting page itself.

Figure 5-2 shows what the banner looks like while the animation is running. The old car tows the "Xrox Car Company" logo onto the page, then trundles off to the right and disappears, after which the slogan appears.

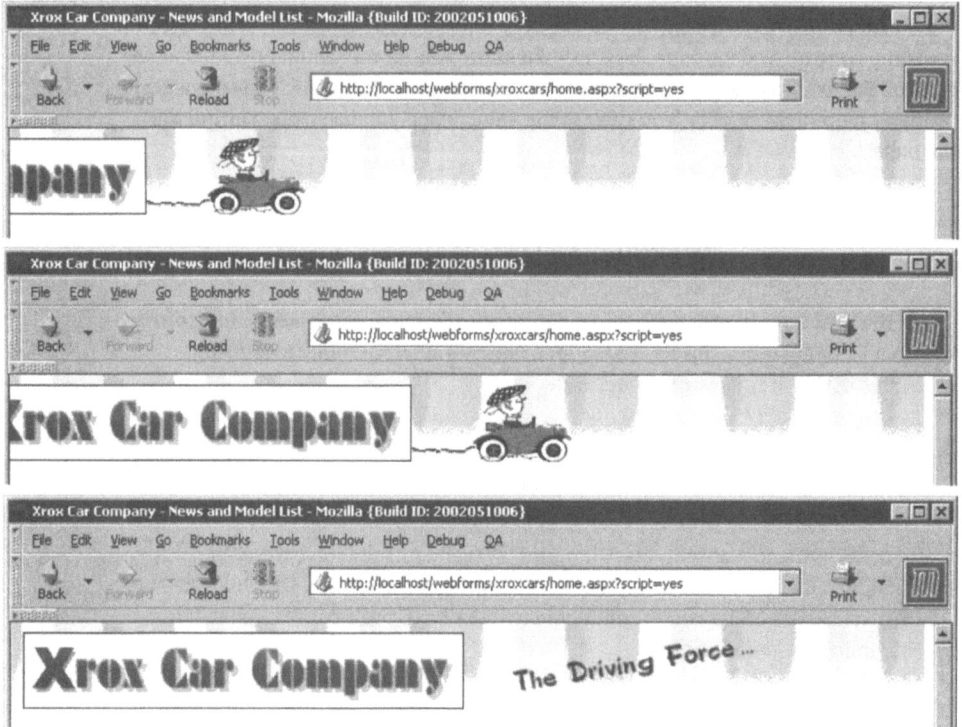

Figure 5-2. The animated "Home" page banner

Building the Animated Banner Control

To achieve the animation you see in Figure 5-2, you have to use different techniques in different browsers. You looked at the scripted animation techniques available in different browsers in Chapter 3, and I can summarize this as:

- Internet Explorer 6.x, Netscape 6.x, Mozilla 1.0, and Opera 6.x (in future revisions, when a bug in the absolute positioning feature is fixed) all support CSS2 and JavaScript 1.0. You can use standard HTML DOM2 methods along with CSS2 absolute positioning techniques to interact with the page content.

- Internet Explorer 4.x and above support Microsoft's version of Dynamic HTML (DHTML), and can execute JavaScript 1.0 using the built-in JScript interpreter. You can use DHTML methods against the MSHTML rendering engine to interact with the page content.

Netscape Navigator 4.x supports Netscape-specific Dynamic HTML features such as Layers, plus JavaScript 1.0. You use custom scripting techniques to interact with layers that contain fragments of the content.

To support all these browsers, you have to create content and client-side script that is specific to the three approaches for interacting with the page content. However, by covering all three approaches, you will be providing support for the vast majority of graphical clients that visit the site.

As you saw in Chapter 3, it's possible to write code that detects features of the browser it's running on, and executes the appropriate methods. However, this results in complicated code that is often hard to debug or to update as new browsers arrive. And if you have to include other content (in the example's case images, with the correct combination of attributes), it can be difficult to make it all work correctly in all the target browsers.

Instead, I chose to expose only browser-specific content and client-side script. The user control will only generate one of the three "sets" of output I defined earlier, depending on which client hits the page. I also want to ensure that the user only sees the animation once during each session, as it soon becomes boring if it's shown it on every page the user opens!

The Structure of the "Page Banner" User Control

The page banner user control, pagebanner.ascx, is stored in a folder named ascx under the main xroxcars and cookieless-xroxcars folders of the site. There is a lot of code in it, but it can be logically divided into five sections.

The first is the server-side code that exposes the properties of the control and implements a Page_Load event handler, and the HTML table in which the background image (bgmain.gif) and the images for the animation will be placed. After that come three separate sections that define the HTML and client-side code you send to each of the three different categories of client listed earlier, followed by another section that is sent to any other type of client.

The server-side code in the Page_Load event handler of the user control (which is executed when the page hosting the control is opened each time, just after that page's own Page_Load event handler) selects the appropriate one of these four sections, and displays in it the ASP.NET page that is hosting the user control. The following listing shows the contents of the sample's user control in outline, with the code that implements the functionality removed for clarity:

pagebanner.ascx (in outline)

```
<%@Control Language="VB" EnableViewState="False" %>
<script runat="server">
'property declarations
Public UAType As String = "Unknown"
Public UAVer As String = "Unknown"
```

```
            Public Animate As Boolean = False

            Private sBannerType As String = "Base"
            Sub Page_Load()
              ...
              ... code to select the appropriate section of output
              ...
            End Sub
            </script>
            <!-- start of table that holds the banner output -->
            <table id="tblBack"
                   background="images/bgmain.gif" style="width:100%"
                   width="100%" border="0" cellspacing="0" cellpadding="0">
            <tbody>
            <tr><td nowrap="nowrap">

            <asp:Literal id="blockIE4" runat="server" Visible="False">
            <!-- animated page banner for IE 4.x and 5.x only -->
              ...
              ... code and HTML to implement banner for IE 4.x and 5.x
              ...
            </asp:Literal>
            <asp:Literal id="blockStd" runat="server" Visible="False">
            <!-- animated page banner for IE 6.x, Nav 6.x and above -->
              ...
              ... code and HTML for IE 6.x, Netscape 6.x and Opera 6.x (when fixed)
              ...
            </asp:Literal>
            <asp:Literal id="blockN4" runat="server" Visible="False">
            <!-- animated page banner for N4.x only -->
              ...
              ... code and HTML to implement banner for Netscape 4.x
              ...
            </asp:Literal>
            <asp:Literal id="blockBase" runat="server" Visible="False">
            <!-- page banner with no animation -->
              <img src="images/wccheader.gif" width="370"
                   height="61" hspace="10" vspace="8" alt="Xrox Car Company" />
              <img src="images/force.gif" width="200"
                   height="40" hspace="20" vspace="5" alt="The Driving Force" />
            </asp:Literal>
            <!-- end of page banner table -->
            </td></tr>
            </tbody>
            </table>
```

You should be able to see from this listing that four <asp:Literal> controls are used to manage the output of the control. Each has a unique ID, and has its Visible property set to "False". So, unless you change this property to "True", the content of that Literal control will not be sent to the client. When you set the Visible property of a server control to "False", it does not create any output in the response sent to the client:

```
<asp:Literal id="blockIE4" runat="server" Visible="False">
  ... content here ...
</asp:Literal>
```

The ASP.NET Literal Control

The ASP.NET Literal control is a useful way to insert content into a page dynamically, or to remove it from a page programmatically. It's a relatively simple control, and the main advantage it provides is that it doesn't create any output of its own. Only the content of the control as defined for the Text property, or the HTML and other content declared between the opening and closing <asp:Literal> tags, is sent to the client.

The commonly used properties for the Literal control are shown in Table 5-1.

Table 5-1. The Commonly Used Properties of the Literal Control

Member	Description
Controls property	Returns a ControlCollection object that references all the child controls defined for this control.
EnableViewState property	Sets or returns a Boolean value indicating if the control will persist its viewstate, and the viewstate of any child controls it contains, between requests.
ID property	Sets or returns the programmatic identifier of the server control.
Page property	Returns a reference to the Page instance that contains this control.
Parent property	Returns a reference to the parent control for this control within the page's control hierarchy (if it has a parent).
Text property	Sets or returns the text and other content that the control will generate within the output if the Visible property is True.
Visible property	Sets or returns a Boolean value that indicates if the control will be rendered when the page is generated.
FindControl method	Searches through all the child controls of this control to find a specific one using its ID value.

> **NOTE** *A full list of the members for the* LiteralControl *can be found in the version 1.0 .NET SDK at:*
> ms-help://MS.NETFrameworkSDK/cpref/html/
> frlrfSystemWebUIWebControlsLiteralMembersTopic.htm
> *or, for version 1.1:*
> ms-help://MS.NETFrameworkSDKv1.1/cpref/html/
> frlrfSystemWebUIWebControlsLiteralMembersTopic.htm.

So, coming back to the user control, you can see that all you have to do is decide which section of the output you want to send to the client, and flip the Visible property to True for that section.

The Properties of the User Control

The sample user control exposes three properties, shown in the listing you saw earlier and repeated here. They are used to specify the manufacturer or name of the current client's browser, the major version, and to indicate if you want an animated or a static banner to be displayed:

```
Public UAType As String = "Unknown"
Public UAVer As String = "Unknown"
Public Animate As Boolean = False
```

There is also a Private (member) variable named sBannerType:

```
Private sBannerType As String = "Base"
```

This variable is used to indicate which section of content you want to send to your client, and the value placed in it is the ID of the Literal control that you want to make visible. This is done with code in the Page_Load event handler, which I'll be discussing shortly. The default value, Base, indicates that you'll send the non-animated version (shown at the end of the previous listing, and repeated here):

```
<asp:Literal id="blockBase" runat="server" Visible="False">
<!-- page banner with no animation -->
  <img src="images/wccheader.gif" width="370"
       height="61" hspace="10" vspace="8" alt="Xrox Car Company" />
  <img src="images/force.gif" width="200"
       height="40" hspace="20" vspace="5" alt="The Driving Force" />
</asp:Literal>
```

In this case, in conjunction with the table start and end declarations that are always present in the output of the user control, the client will receive the following content:

```
<table id="tblBack"
       background="images/bgmain.gif" style="width:100%"
       width="100%" border="0" cellspacing="0" cellpadding="0">
<tbody>
<tr><td nowrap="nowrap">
  <img src="images/wccheader.gif" width="370"
       height="61" hspace="10" vspace="8" alt="Xrox Car Company" />
```

```
    <img src="images/force.gif" width="200"
        height="40" hspace="20" vspace="5" alt="The Driving Force" />
</td></tr>
</tbody>
</table>
```

So, if you simply insert the page banner user control into a page, and do not set any of its properties, you get the static banner shown in Figure 5-3 sent to the client.

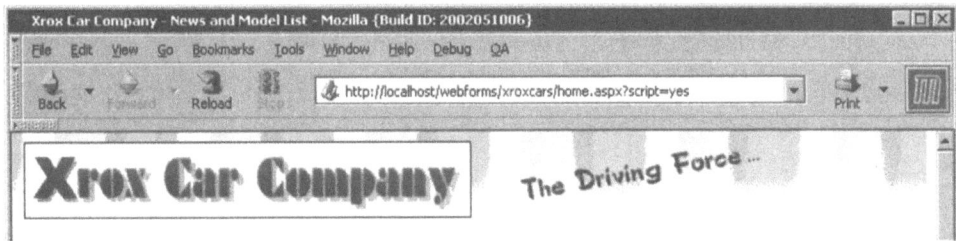

Figure 5-3. The static version of the page banner

The Page_Load *Event Handler*

When the user control loads, as a visitor requests the ASP.NET page that hosts it, the server-side code in the control's Page_Load event handler is executed. In this code, you can examine the values of the three properties that the control exposes, and set the page-level sBannerType variable to the appropriate value.

The first step is to see if you are going to generate an animated banner or not. If the Animate property is True, first examine the values of the UAType and UAVer properties to see which client the current page is being served to. For Internet Explorer 4.x or 5.x, set the private sBannerType variable to "IE4" and for Internet Explorer 6.x and later (which support CSS2), set it to "IE6":

```
Sub Page_Load()
  ' if Animate property is True get client type
  If Animate Then

    ' see if the current client is Internet Explorer
    If UAType = "IE" Then
      If (UAVer = 4 Or UAVer = 5) Then
        sBannerType = "IE4"
      End If
      If UAVer >= 6 Then
        sBannerType = "IE6"
      End If
    End If
```

If the current browser is a Netscape product, or one that does not provide manufacturer details directly (such as Mozilla), again check the major version number. If it's a version 4.x browser, set the sBannerType variable to "N4", while if it's version 5.x or later (Netscape 6.x has the user agent version string Mozilla/5.0, so is detected as version 5), set sBannerType to "N6":

```
' see if the current client is Navigator
If UAType = "Netscape" Then
  If UAVer = 4  Then    ' version 4 only
    sBannerType = "N4"
  End If
  If UAVer >= 5  Then   ' version 5/6+
    sBannerType = "N6"
  End If
End If
```

Finally, check to see if it's Opera 6.x or later. While this browser has problems with absolute positioning at the time of writing, Opera is actively looking into the problem and should have a fix available by the time you read this. So, detect it and set the sBannerType variable to "06" in this case:

```
' see if the current client is Opera
If (UAType = "Opera" And UAVer >= 6) Then
  sBannerType = "06"
End If
```

Selecting the Content Block to Send to the Client

Now that you have a definite fix on the current browser type, you can use a Select Case construct to choose the appropriate content block to make visible and send to the client. However, there is one more task that you have to perform if you want to use an animated banner.

You must add an onload attribute to the opening <body> tag in the page that hosts the user control. The value of this attribute must be the name of the client-side JavaScript function that you want to be executed when the page itself has finished loading on the client. In each page where the banner will be animated (in the sample's case, just the "Home" page), specify the <body> element as a server control:

```
<body id="BodyTag" runat="server" ... >
```

> **NOTE** *I discussed this near the start of Chapter 4, and explained that I would be adding an* onload *attribute to it from within a user control.*

To add the onload attribute, you need to get a reference to the <body> element in the hosting page. Access the Parent property of the control, which returns a reference to the Page object for the ASP.NET page that is hosting the control. Then use the FindControl method of the Page object to get a reference to the element with the ID "BodyTag":

```
Dim oBodyTag As HtmlGenericControl = Parent.FindControl("BodyTag")
```

Then it's simply a matter of adding the onload attribute. Use the Add method of the element's Attributes collection, specifying the attribute name and the value for that attribute. In this case, the value is "startAnimation()"—the name of the client-side script function that you'll place in the page, and that will provide the animation you want:

```
oBodyTag.Attributes.Add("onload", "startAnimation()")
```

So, in the Select Case statement, you can use the value you previously assigned to the variable sBannerType to decide which ASP.NET Literal control's content block should be visible for the current client, and add the onload attribute to the <body> tag as well if you are sending an animated banner:

```
' insert the appropriate block of code into the page
' currently Opera has a problem with positioning, but
' should be able to use blockStd section when fixed
' also add "onload" attribute to <body> tag in main page
Select Case sBannerType
  Case "IE4"
    Dim oBodyTag As HtmlGenericControl = Parent.FindControl("BodyTag")
    oBodyTag.Attributes.Add("onload", "startAnimation()")
    blockIE4.Visible = True
  Case "N6", "IE6"        ' plus Opera6 when fixed
    Dim oBodyTag As HtmlGenericControl = Parent.FindControl("BodyTag")
    oBodyTag.Attributes.Add("onload", "startAnimation()")
    blockStd.Visible = True
  Case "N4"
    Dim oBodyTag As HtmlGenericControl = Parent.FindControl("BodyTag")
    oBodyTag.Attributes.Add("onload", "startAnimation()")
    blockN4.Visible = True
  Case Else
    blockBase.Visible = True
End Select
...
```

If the Animate property is False, you don't need to do anything other than make the Literal control that contains the "Base" banner content visible:

```
      ...
   Else
      ' no animation required, show base version
      blockBase.Visible = True

   End If
End Sub
```

> **NOTE** Notice that the <body> element in any page where the banner will be ani-
> mated must be declared as a server control with the id of "BodyTag" for this to work.
> In other pages, where you don't animate the banner, there is no need for the <body>
> element to be a server control.

The Animation Content for CSS-enabled Clients

All that remains to look at in the banner is the content that you send to each of the
three types of client you are serving an animated version to. For any browser that
supports CSS2 and the HTML DOM version 2, you can use the content in the "standard" block—defined within the Literal control with an id value of "blockStd". The
next listing shows the first part of this content. It consists of five images, with a range
of attributes applied to each one:

```
<asp:Literal id="blockStd" runat="server" Visible="False">
<!-- animated page banner for IE 6.x, Nav 6.x and above -->
<!-- NOTE: also Opera6+ when positioning error is fixed -->
  <img src="images/bgsizer.gif" width="1px" height="83px" alt="" />
  <img id="CarImg" src="images/animtow1.gif"
       width="134px" height="61px" alt=""
       style="visibility:hidden; position:absolute; display:block;
              left:0px; top:8px" />
  <img id="CarImg2" src="images/animtow2.gif"
       width="134px" height="61px" alt=""
       style="visibility:hidden; position:absolute; display:block;
              left:0px; top:8px" />
  <img id="HeadImg" src="images/wccheader.gif"
       width="370px" height="61px" alt="Xrox Car Company"
       style="visibility:hidden; position:absolute; display:block;
              left:0px; top:8px" />
  <img id="Force" src="images/force.gif"
       width="200px" height="40px" alt="The Driving Force"
       style="visibility:hidden; position:absolute; display:block;
              left:420px; top:15px" />
```

The first image, bgsizer.gif, is used simply to force the HTML table that contains
the banner to be exactly 83 pixels high. It's a one-pixel-wide transparent GIF image, so
does not show up in the browser. Notice that the alt attribute is also set to an empty
string so that text-only browsers and page readers know that it should be ignored.

Next come the two "old car" images, one with a towrope and one without. These are actually three-frame animated GIF files that I built using Microsoft GIF Animator. They are absolutely positioned eight pixels down from the top of the page, and to the far left of the page. The CSS styles also specify that both images will be hidden when the page loads.

> **NOTE** *For information about Microsoft GIF Animator, see:*
> `http://www.microsoft.com/FRONTPAGE/previous/imagecomposer/page5.htm.`

After the "old car" images come the "Xrox Car Company" logo itself, and the image of the slogan "The Driving Force." The logo is positioned eight pixels down from the top of the page, and at the left side, while the slogan image is located at its final position. However, like the "old car" images, both are hidden when the page first loads.

Animating the Banner

Animation of the banner is implemented with client-side JavaScript code. The onload event of the page (defined in the <body> element, as you saw earlier) causes the function named startAnimation to be executed once the page has loaded into the user's browser. The next listing shows that function, complete with the rest of the client-side code.

There is a series of "global" variables defined in the client-side <script> section. In the startAnimation function I placed a "welcome" message in the browser's status bar, then set the global variables objCar and objHead as references to the two images I want to move across the screen first. I also set the initial positions of these images so that they will gradually appear at the left side of the page:

```
<script language="JavaScript">
<!--
//--- Version for IE 6.0 and higher, Netscape 6.0 and ---
//--- higher, Mozilla 1.0 and higher, plus Opera 6.0. ---
//--- Uses W3CDOM Level2 + CSS methods and properties ---
// declare the global variables
var objTimer;        // reference to window.setInterval timer
var objCar;          // reference to old car image
var objHead;         // reference to Xrox Car Co banner image
var bLoaded;         // flag to show if images are finished loading
var bSwapped;        // flag to show we've swapped to the 2nd car image
var iWindowWidth;    // width of client window
function startAnimation() {
  window.status = 'Welcome to the Xrox Car Company';
  objCar = document.getElementById('CarImg');
  iCarLeft = - 150;
```

```
objHead = document.getElementById('HeadImg');
iHeadLeft = -520;
bSwapped = false;  // using first car image
// need width of page to detect car reaching right-hand side
// table holding contents of page is sized to 100% of page width
// use this except in Navigator 4 where we have to use the
// innerWidth property of the window instead:
if (document.all)
  iWindowWidth = document.getElementById('tblBack').style.pixelWidth
else
  iWindowWidth = window.innerWidth;
// start the interval timer
objTimer = window.setInterval('moveImages()', 10);
}
```

As you can see towards the end of this code, I need to figure out the width of the browser window so that I can stop the animation when the car gets to the right side. In most CSS2-enabled clients I tried, the window object exposes a property named innerWidth that returns the width in pixels. However, Internet Explorer doesn't do this, so I used the width of the table within which I'm animating the images instead. Only Internet Explorer has a document.all collection (I discussed this in Chapter 3), and so I can detect IE by looking for this collection.

The final line of the code in the previous listing starts an interval timer running, and specifies that the function named moveImages should be executed every 10 milliseconds (effectively, this means as fast as the client can process the interval events).

Moving the Images

The moveImages function, which is responsible for the complete animation sequence, is shown next. In Internet Explorer, you can take advantage of a specific feature it provides to make sure that all the images have finished loading before starting the animation—check that the readyState property of the document object is "complete". This doesn't work in other clients, however, so check again for the presence of a document.all collection here.

Next, make the car and logo images visible, and see if the car has reached the right side of the window. If it has, stop the interval timer, hide the car image, change the status bar message, and display the "slogan" image by making it visible:

```
function moveImages() {
  // wait until all images have loaded (IE only)
  if ((document.all) && document.readyState != 'complete') return;
  // make the images visible, they're off screen
  objCar.style.visibility = 'visible';
  objHead.style.visibility = 'visible';
  if (iCarLeft > iWindowWidth - 135) {
    // car has got to right hand end
    window.clearInterval(objTimer);        // so stop timer
    objCar.style.visibility = 'hidden';    // and hide it
    window.status = 'Select a car for more information';
    // display the slogan image
```

```
  document.getElementById('Force').style.visibility = 'visible';
}
...
```

The two global variables declared earlier, iCarLeft and iHeadLeft, store the current position of the "old car" and logo images, and I set them to positions off to the left of the page when I first started the animation. So now, if the car has not yet reached the right side of the window, I need to move it right by one pixel. I also need to move the logo image right by one pixel if it has not yet reached its final position (10 pixels in from the left). All that's required is to increment the two global variables, and assign their new values to the left property of the images' style objects:

```
  ...
  else {
    // move the images
    iCarLeft += 1;
    objCar.style.left = iCarLeft;
    if (iHeadLeft < 10) {
      iHeadLeft += 1;
      objHead.style.left = iHeadLeft;
    }
    else {
        if (! bSwapped) {
          // swap to the second car image (no towrope)
          objCar.src = document.getElementById('CarImg2').src;
          bSwapped = true;
        }
    }
  }
}
//-->
</script>
</asp:Literal>
```

The other check to make, if the "Xrox Car Company" logo image *has* reached its final position, is if the car images have already swapped over so as to show the one *without* the towrope. The global variable bSwapped is initially set to false in the startAnimation function, but when the "Xrox Car Company" logo image reaches it final position (10 pixels in from the left of the window) I set it to true and then change the objCar variable to reference the other car image. Then this image is displayed instead of the one with the towrope.

The Animation Content for Internet Explorer 4.x and Later

The client-side code I used to animate the image in Internet Explorer 4.x and 5.x is almost the same as is used in CSS2-enabled clients, and which I've just been examining. These two versions implement Microsoft Dynamic HTML, which is actually very close to the final CSS2 recommendations. Many of the properties, methods, and techniques are the same, or extremely similar.

The reason that I provide a separate function for Internet Explorer 4.x and 5.x is that there is one fundamental difference between Microsoft DHTML and CSS2—the way that you get a reference to an element within the page. In DHTML you query the document.all collection, while in CSS2 (as you've just seen) you use the getElementById method of the document object (I discussed the decision to use two different versions of the server-side script code, rather than detecting the client type within this code, earlier in this chapter).

So, here's the listing of the functions I use for Internet Explorer 4.x and 5.x. The HTML content (the images) is identical to the CSS2 version of the banner, so I haven't repeated it here.

```
<script language="JavaScript">
<!--
//--- Version for Internet Explorer 4.x and 5.x only ---
//--- Uses IE-specific DHTML methods and properties  ---
// declare the global variables
var objTimer;       // reference to window.setInterval timer
var objCar;         // reference to old car image
var objHead;        // reference to Xrox Car Co banner image
var bLoaded;        // flag to show if images are finished loading
var bSwapped;       // flag to show we've swapped to the 2nd car image
var iWindowWidth;   // width of client window
function startAnimation() {
  window.status = 'Welcome to the Xrox Car Company';
  objCar = document.all['CarImg'];
  iCarLeft = - 150;
  objHead = document.all['HeadImg'];
  iHeadLeft = -520;
  bSwapped = false;  // using first car image
  // need width of page to detect car reaching right-hand side
  // table holding contents of page is sized to 100% of page width
  iWindowWidth = document.all['tblBack'].style.pixelWidth;
  // start the interval timer
  objTimer = window.setInterval('moveImages()', 10);
}
function moveImages() {
  // wait until all images have loaded (IE only)
  if ((document.all) && document.readyState != 'complete') return;
  // make the images visible, they're off screen
  objCar.style.visibility = 'visible';
  objHead.style.visibility = 'visible';
  if (iCarLeft > iWindowWidth - 135) {
    // car has got to right hand end
    window.clearInterval(objTimer);        // so stop timer
    objCar.style.visibility = 'hidden';   // and hide it
    window.status = 'Select a car for more information';
    // display the slogan image
    document.all['Force'].style.visibility = 'visible';
```

```
    }
    else {
      // move the images
      iCarLeft += 1;
      objCar.style.left = iCarLeft;
      if (iHeadLeft < 10) {
        iHeadLeft += 1;
        objHead.style.left = iHeadLeft;
      }
      else {
        if (! bSwapped) {
          // swap to the second car image (no towrope)
          objCar.src = document.all['CarImg2'].src;
          bSwapped = true;
        }
      }
    }
  }
}
//-->
</script>
```

The Animation Content for Netscape 4.x Only

In Netscape Navigator 4.x, the techniques used to animate the banner are very similar to those used in the two previous sections. However, elements cannot be referenced and manipulated in the same way. The only way to get the same type of effect is to place each image inside a separate <layer> element, and manipulate these instead. So, for a start, the HTML content you send to Navigator 4 has to be different:

```
<asp:Literal id="blockN4" runat="server" Visible="False">
<!-- animated page banner for N4.x only -->
  <img src="images/bgsizer.gif" width="1px" height="83px" alt="" />
  <layer id="HeadLayer" top="15px" left="-520px" visibility="hidden">
    <img src="images/wccheader.gif" width="370px" height="61px"
         alt="Xrox Car Company" />
  </layer>
  <layer id="CarLayer" top="15px" left="-150px" visibility="hidden">
    <img src="images/animtow1.gif" width="134px" height="61px" alt="" />
  </layer>
  <layer id="ForceLayer" top="25px" left="430px" visibility="hidden">
    <img src="images/force.gif" width="200px" height="40px"
         alt="The Driving Force" />
  </layer>
  <layer id="Car2Layer" top="15px" left="383px" visibility="hidden">
    <img src="images/animtow2.gif" alt="" />
  </layer>
```

I used the same bgsizer.gif image to force the table to be the correct height, but then each of the remaining images are placed within a separate <layer> element that is positioned on the page at the appropriate place, and hidden by setting the visibility attribute to "hidden" (note that I'm using attributes of the <layer> elements instead of selectors in a style attribute). I also have to use different values for the top property of each <layer> element, as the way that the layers are offset from the window is different to the way images are positioned in other browsers.

Moving the Layer Elements

In the code section, I again declare a series of "global" variables, but this time I have four that I'll use to reference the <layer> elements (rather than the image elements, as we did in the previous sections for other browsers). Then collect references to the appropriate <layer> elements by accessing the layers collection of the document object:

```
<script language="JavaScript">
<!--
//--- Version for Netscape Navigator 4.x only ---
//--- Uses Netscape-specific layers & methods ---
// declare the global variables
var objTimer;          // reference to window.setInterval timer
var layHead;           // reference to Xrox Car Co banner image layer
var layCar;            // reference to old car (with towrope) image layer
var layCar2;           // reference to old car (no towrope) image layer
var layForce;          // reference to slogan layer
var bSwapped;          // flag to show we've swapped to the 2nd car image
var iWindowWidth;      // width of client window

function startAnimation() {
  window.status = 'Welcome to the Xrox Car Company';
  layHead = document.layers['HeadLayer'];
  layCar = document.layers['CarLayer'];
  layCar2 = document.layers['Car2Layer'];
  layForce = document.layers['ForceLayer'];
  bSwapped = false;  // using first car image
  iWindowWidth = window.innerWidth;
  // start the interval timer
  objTimer = window.setInterval('moveImages()', 10);
}
```

Having started the interval timer running, react to each event it raises in the moveImages function as was done in the previous examples. While the overall process is much the same, there are slightly different values for the element positions in the various if...else constructs, and the visibility attribute has to be set directly for the <layer> elements (in the previous sections, as you'll recall, I set the visibility property of the style object). The other major difference is that the images are positioned using the moveToAbsolute method, rather than by setting the style.left property:

```
    function moveImages() {
      // make the images visible, they're off screen
      layCar.visibility = "visible";
      layHead.visibility = "visible";
      if (layCar.left > iWindowWidth - 50) {
        // car has got to right hand end
        window.clearInterval(objTimer);        // so stop timer
        layCar.visibility = 'hidden';          // and hide it
        window.status = 'Select a car for more information';
        layForce.visibility = "visible";       // show slogan
      }
      else {
        // move the images
        layCar.moveToAbsolute(layCar.left + 1, layCar.top);
        if (layHead.left < 20)
          layHead.moveToAbsolute(layHead.left + 1, layHead.top);
        else {
          if (! bSwapped) {
            // swap to the second car image (no towrope)
            layCar.visibility="hidden";
            layCar = layCar2;
            layCar.visibility="visible";
            bSwapped = true;
          }
        }
      }
    }
  //-->
  </script>
</asp:Literal>
```

Using the Animated Banner Control

Now that the banner control is complete, you can use it in the example pages. In the "Home" page, it will be animated where possible, but only when the visitor first hits this page. For subsequent hits, and in all other pages, only the static version of the banner will be shown.

As you saw when building the banner control, it exposes three properties:

pagebanner.ascx

```
'property declarations
Public UAType As String = "Unknown"
Public UAVer As String = "Unknown"
Public Animate As Boolean = False
```

In the "Home" page, first register the banner control using the Register directive:

```
home.aspx
<%@Register TagPrefix="wcc" TagName="pagebanner"
            Src="ascx/pagebanner.ascx"%>
```

Then, after the "skip to" links and before the start of the main page structure table, insert the banner control into the page:

```
<wcc:pagebanner id="ctlBanner" runat="server" />
```

Setting the Banner Control Properties

The next step is to set the properties of the banner control each time the page loads. In the Page_Load event handler of the "Home" page, home.aspx, collect the browser type and major version into two variables (you saw this in the previous chapter, when I was deciding which style sheet to send to the client).

Then you can check to see if the current browser supports client-side scripting, and if it is enabled, by checking the bCanScript variable. If this is False, you can't animate the banner. However, if bCanScript is True, you can use the values for the browser type and major version to set the properties of the banner control:

```
...
' get the browser type and version
Dim sUAType As String = Request.Browser("Browser")
Dim sUAVer As String = Request.Browser("MajorVersion")
...
' set properties of "pagebanner" user control
' if client supports scripting and it is enabled
If bCanScript Then
  ctlBanner.UAType = sUAType
  ctlBanner.UAVer = sUAVer

  ' check if user has seen animation in this session
  ' if not, show and set session value to indicate this
  If CType(Session("WccSeenAnimation"), Boolean) = False Then
    ctlBanner.Animate = True
    Session("WccSeenAnimation") = "True"
  End If

End If
...
```

To decide whether to animate the banner, check the user's ASP.NET session for a value named WccSeenAnimation. If this is False, set the Animate property of the banner to True and set the session value to True as well. The next time this page is loaded during the current session, the banner control will not be animated and the user will see the static version.

When you use the banner control in other pages, where it will never be animated, you don't have to bother with setting its properties. The default values within the control will automatically provide a static banner. So, for these pages, you only need to register the banner control with a register directive, and insert it into the page. For example, in the "Contact" page named `contact.aspx`, all you need is:

```
contact.aspx
<%@Register TagPrefix="wcc" TagName="pagebanner"
           Src="ascx/pagebanner.ascx"%>
...
...
<wcc:pagebanner id="ctlBanner" runat="server" />
```

The Page Footer Section

Every page in the example site displays a "standard" page footer section. This contains a set of text hyperlinks pointing to all the main pages on the site. This traditional type of page footer is the accepted way to provide alternate navigation features, plus the email address of the site's Webmaster for feedback purposes. Users generally expect to find something like this on Web sites, and many go straight to it if they can't easily and quickly find any other links to pages that they want. And so, while I've tried very hard to make our site easy to navigate, I still provide these links (Figure 5-4).

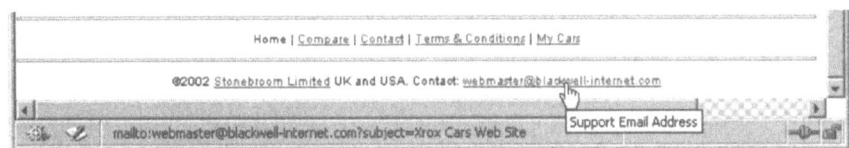

Figure 5-4. The page footer and text links

Notice that I also provide the pop-up tool-tips for the links, using the `title` attributes of the `<a>` elements that implement these links. You'll see this shortly.

In ASP 3.0 and earlier, it was a common technique to build page footers like this as Server-Side Include (SSI) files. These are just text files containing the HTML and any other required content, and they are inserted into the page using a `#include` directive. Although this approach still works fine in ASP.NET, the preferred method is to use a control of some type. It could be a server control, compiled into a DLL and placed in the `bin` folder or into the Global Assembly Cache (GAC). However, equally valid, is the approach I've taken here of building it as a **user control.**

Dynamic Hyperlinks in the Footer

One reason for using a control for the page footer can be seen in Figure 5-4. Remember that the accessibility guidelines I discussed in Chapter 3 suggest that self-referring links should be avoided. There should not be any link in a page that refers to this page, as it can cause confusion for visitors who are using specialist clients or user agents.

This means that for the footer of the sample's "Home" page, there should *not* be a hyperlink to the "Home" page. You can see from Figure 5-4 that this is the case in the sample page. I could, of course, omit this link—but leaving it in as text only (not a hyperlink) makes it obvious that this *is* the "Home" page.

So, you want to build a footer control that you can use in any page on the example site, but which shows the current page as text and not as a clickable hyperlink. My page footer user control does just this, as you'll see next.

Building the Page Footer Control

Like the page banner, the page footer section is implemented as a user control that you can insert into any page within the site (within the same virtual application). I use fairly basic HTML within the control for maximum compatibility with all clients, centering the content in the page with a `<center>` element, and setting the font face and size using the `<font>` element.

However, notice that each of the `<a>` elements in the list of links to other pages is a server control. By adding the `runat="server"` attribute, I'm telling ASP.NET to use the HtmlAnchor class (from the namespace `System.Web.UI.HtmlControls`) to implement this control. I also provide an `id` for each one that reflects the text content of the hyperlink.

After these links comes the copyright statement, followed by an ASP.NET `Hyperlink` control that creates the link containing the email address of the Webmaster. Notice that I don't specify values for the `NavigateUrl` (the `href` attribute) or the `Text` (the clickable content) for this control. I set these values at runtime using code in the `Page_Load` event handler:

footerlinks.ascx

```
<%@Control Language="VB" EnableViewState="False"%>
...
... server-side script section here ...
...
<center>
<hr size="1" />
<font id="fHOME" runat="server" size="1" face="Arial,sans-serif">
<a id="aHOME" href="../home.aspx" runat="server"
    target="_top" title="Home Page">Home</a> |
<a id="aCOMPARE" href="../compare.aspx" runat="server"
    target="_top" title="Compare Models">Compare</a> |
<a id="aCONTACT" href="../contact.aspx" runat="server"
    target="_top" title="Contact Details">Contact</a> |
```

```
<a id="aTANDC" href="../tandc.aspx" runat="server"
    target="_top" title="Terms/Conditions">Terms &amp; Conditions</a> |
<a id="aMYCARS" href="../secure/mycars.aspx" runat="server"
    target="_top" title="My Cars">My Cars</a>
</font>
<hr size="1"/>
<font size="1" face="Arial,sans-serif">&copy;2002 <a href="http://www.yoursirte.com/"
title="Your Site">Your Site</a>. Contact:
<asp:Hyperlink id="lnkWebmaster" runat="server" title="Support Email Address"
/></font>
</center>
```

I chose to use the HtmlAnchor controls for the text links here, rather than the ASP.NET Hyperlink, purely for efficiency reasons. As you'll see shortly, I need these to be server controls, but I don't need the extra complexity of the Hyperlink control. The HtmlAnchor is a simpler and lighter control, and performance of the site will benefit marginally from the reduced complexity.

> NOTE *I could have done the same with the link to the Webmaster, but the approach I've taken shows both techniques together so that you can compare the way the properties are set.*

The HtmlAnchor Control

The HtmlAnchor control inherits from the same base class (HtmlControl) as all the controls in the System.Web.UI.HtmlControls namespace, including the HtmlGenericControl you looked at in the previous chapter. However, because the HtmlAnchor control implements a specific HTML element (the <a> element), it has a few extra members that are specific to this type of element. In particular, it has four extra properties (Table 5-2).

Table 5-2. The Properties Specific to the HtmlAnchor Control

Member	Description
Href property	Sets or returns the URL that is used as the value of the href attribute when the element is rendered.
Name property	Sets or returns the text that is used as the value of the name attribute when the element is rendered.
Target property	Sets or returns the text that is used as the value of the target attribute when the element is rendered.
Title property	Sets or returns the text that is used as the value of the title attribute when the element is rendered.

> **NOTE** *A full list of the members for the* HtmlAnchor *can be found in the .NET SDK at:*
>
> ms-help://MS.NETFrameworkSDK/cpref/html/
> frlrfSystemWebUIHtmlControlsHtmlAnchorMembersTopic.htm
> ms-help://MS.NETFrameworkSDKv1.1/cpref/html/
> frlrfSystemWebUIHtmlControlsHtmlAnchorMembersTopic.htm

So, when an HtmlAnchor control is declared in the example page (simply by adding the runat="server" attribute to an <a> element), these properties can be set to specify the matching attribute values you want the rendered element to have. This is what I did in the code you saw earlier. For example, in the last link "My Cars" I specify the values for the href, target, and title:

```
<a id="aMYCARS" href="../secure/mycars.aspx" runat="server"
    target="_top" title="My Cars">My Cars</a>
```

> **NOTE** *Including the* target="_top" *attribute means that the new page will always open in the complete browser window, even if the current page is within a frameset.*

The Code for the Page Footer Control

The sample page footer control must have the ability to remove the hyperlink from one of the text links when it is inserted into a page. In fact, this is easy to do. Expose a property for the user control by defining a Public String variable named CurrentPageLink:

footerlinks.ascx

```
<script runat="server">
' control property set from ASPX page:
Public CurrentPageLink As String = ""
```

Then, in the Page_Load event handler for the control, find the control that implements this hyperlink, and remove the href attribute. This effectively renders the content of the control as text and not as a hyperlink. To remove an attribute from a control, you could access the Attributes collection using the attribute name:

```
MyAnchor.Attributes.Remove("href")
```

However, as the `href` attribute is exposed as the `Href` property of the control, it's easier to just set this property to an empty string. It gives us the same outcome—no `href` attribute:

```
MyAnchor.Href = ""
```

So, here's the `Page_Load` event handler so far. Convert the string supplied for the `CurrentPageLink` property of the control to uppercase, though this isn't strictly necessary as the `id` property is not case-sensitive, and prefix an `"a"` so that it will match the `id` value of the appropriate hyperlink. A `Try...Catch` construct prevents an error being raised if the value supplied in the `CurrentPageLink` property doesn't map to any of the hyperlinks:

footerlinks.ascx

```
Sub Page_Load()
  Try
    ' remove link for current page, leave as text
    Dim sCurrent As String = CurrentPageLink.ToUpper()
    CType(FindControl("a" & sCurrent), HtmlAnchor).Href = ""
    ' set the email address of the Webmaster
    ...

  Catch
  End Try

End Sub
```

Setting the Webmaster's Email Address

Next set the properties of the `Hyperlink` control that is used for sending email to the Webmaster. The email address of the Webmaster is stored in the `<appSettings>` section of the `web.config` file, in the root folder of the samples (as I've done with the connection string for the database—I discussed this technique in Chapter 4):

```
web.config
<appSettings>
  ...
  <!-- following is email address used as "From" in email messages -->
  <add key="XroxCarsWebmasterEmail" value="webmaster@your-own-site.com" />
  ...
<appSettings>
```

So all you have to do is extract this value from `web.config` and use it to create the values for the `Hyperlink` control's `NavigateUrl` and `Text` properties:

footerlinks.ascx

```
Sub Page_Load()
  Try
    ' remove link for current page, leave as text
    Dim sCurrent As String = CurrentPageLink.ToUpper()
    CType(FindControl("a" & sCurrent), HtmlAnchor).Href = ""
    ' set the email address of the Webmaster
    Dim sWebmasterEmail As String = _
              ConfigurationSettings.AppSettings("XroxCarsWebmasterEmail")
    lnkWebmaster.NavigateUrl = "mailto:" & sWebmasterEmail _
                                & "?subject=Xrox Cars Web Site"
    lnkWebmaster.Text = sWebmasterEmail
  Catch
  End Try

End Sub
</script>
```

Using the Page Footer Control

To use the footer control in the pages, all you need to do is register it and then insert it into the page at the point where you want the footer to appear (probably at the bottom of the page!). This is the Register directive:

```
<%@Register TagPrefix="wcc" TagName="footerlinks"
            Src="ascx/footerlinks.ascx"%>
```

When you insert the control into the page, you can specify the text of the link that you do *not* want to be displayed as a hyperlink. For example, in the "Home" page, use:

```
<wcc:footerlinks runat="server" CurrentPageLink="Home" />
```

In a page that is not referenced in the links within the footer control you can just insert the control without specifying a value for the CurrentPageLink property. All the text links will be displayed as hyperlinks in this case.

Adding Users to the Mailing List

The final section of the example "Home" page that you have not yet looked at in detail is the area below the list of news items where visitors can submit their email address to join the mailing list. I provide a text heading, a text box control with the caption "Your email address:", and a Go button to submit the value (Figure 5-5).

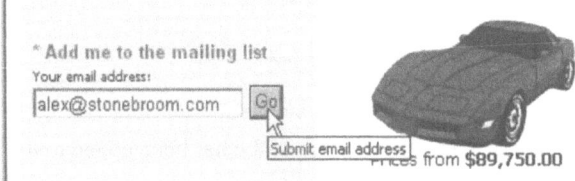

Figure 5-5. The controls to submit your email address

To try and avoid collecting invalid email addresses, it's a good idea to validate the format of the email address that the user enters. If the text box is empty, the page will display a message in the area below the four graphic links to other pages on the site telling the user that he or she must enter an email address. And if the user enters a value that doesn't appear to be a valid email address (it doesn't have the correct combination of "dots" and the "@" character), also display a warning (Figure 5-6).

You could not be added to the mailing list:
You must provide a valid email address in the text box

Figure 5-6. The result of entering an invalid address

Notice also that an asterisk appears next to the text box caption when the value is missing or in an incorrect format (as shown in Figure 5-7, where I omitted the "dot" before "com". OK, there is only one control on the page, so figuring out which one contains the invalid value doesn't require a diploma in computer science, but I'll show you later how you can achieve this effect very easily in your pages.

Figure 5-7. You forgot to include the "dot"!

In an "up-level" client, where client-side validation is being performed, this asterisk appears when the content of the text box is invalid and the user tabs to another control in the page, without requiring a postback to the server. The text error messages appear when the user attempts to submit the page by clicking the Go button—again without posting the page back to the server. However, this does not happen in "down-level" clients. The asterisk and the error message only appear after the page has been posted back to the server.

After a postback, and if the email address the user enters does appear to be valid, it's added to the database and the page displays a "thank you" message (Figure 5-8).

Compare   Contact Us   Conditions   My Cars

Thank you for joining our mailing list.

Figure 5-8. Confirmation that the address was accepted

The user also receives an email to confirm that he or she has been added to the mailing list (Figure 5-9).

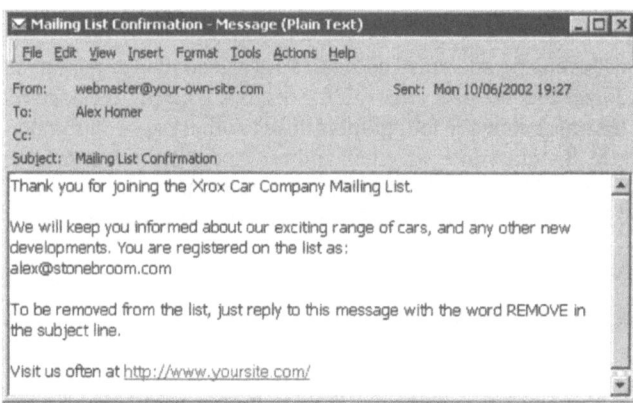

Figure 5-9. The emailed confirmation after joining the list

The Controls to Submit an Email Address

To create the section of the page that contains the captions, email address text box, and Go button, I used a mixture of ASP.NET server controls and ordinary HTML elements. The next code listing shows the source for this section of the page.

The heading "Add me to the mailing list" is declared within a `<span>` element that specifies the CSS class body-red-text, which defines the desired appearance for the text. However, for non-CSS browsers, I also wrap this in a `<font>` element that specifies the same font face, size, and color. Then the small text caption "Your email address:" is declared and formatted in the same way with a `<span>` and a `<font>` element.

Next come the two ASP.NET **validation controls** that I use to validate the email address. You'll look at these in more detail shortly. They are followed by an ASP.NET TextBox control and Button control:

```
<font face="Arial,Helvetica,sans-serif" size="2" color="#b50055">
<span class="body-red-text">
<b>* Add me to the mailing list</b></span></font><br />
<font size="1"><span class="small-text">
Your email address:</span></font>
```

```
<asp:RequiredFieldValidator id="valRequired" runat="server"
     ControlToValidate="txtMailList"
     ErrorMessage="* You must enter a value in the email address textbox"
     Display="dynamic">
     *
</asp:RequiredFieldValidator>
<asp:RegularExpressionValidator id="valRegExpr" runat="server"
     ControlToValidate="txtMailList"
     ValidationExpression=".*@.*\..*"
     ErrorMessage="* You must provide a valid email address in the textbox"
     Display="dynamic">
     *
</asp:RegularExpressionValidator><br /></font>
<font face="Arial,Helvetica,sans-serif" size="3">
<asp:TextBox id="txtMailList" Columns="20" runat="server"
              title="Enter your email address" />
</font>
<font face="Tahoma,Arial,Helvetica,sans-serif" size="2">
<asp:Button id="btnMailList" OnClick="AddToMailingList" Text="Go"
              runat="server" title="Submit email address" /></font>
```

There are a few things I need to point out here. Notice how I wrap the Textbox control in a <font> element that specifies a sans-serif-style font face, and size "3". Different browsers have different default fonts for the text controls on an HTML <form>, and different default widths for these controls. After some experimentation, I discovered that (at least in the various Windows-based browsers) this format creates a similar sized text box on all the clients I tested, and with similar sized text within the text box.

However, for the Go button (which ASP.NET renders as a standard HTML <input type="submit"> button, the best combination of font face and size to get the appearance I wanted appears to be that shown in the previous listing, a sans-serif font with size equal to"2".

Notice also how I provide title attributes for the text box and Go button (you can see the effect of the title attribute on the Go button in Figure 5-5). An alternative would be to set the ToolTip attribute or property, which achieves the same thing (it also generates a title attribute when rendered to the client). This technique provides an extra hint to users of specialist browsers as to what the controls are for, and is especially useful on complex forms.

ASP.NET Form Controls and the <form> Element

The various ASP.NET controls that implement HTML <form> control elements (such as text boxes, check boxes, lists, and so on) must be placed inside a server-side <form> section of the page—a <form> element with the runat="server" attribute. If not, the page produces a compilation error when you try to open it.

This makes sense because, although Internet Explorer will display ordinary HTML form controls (elements that are not server controls) without placing them on a <form>, most other browsers will not. They just ignore the element declarations, and the controls do not appear in the page.

However, it does mean that you have to use a server-side form (with the runat="server" attribute) if you want to use server controls. Why would you need to use a <form> without the runat="server" attribute? Well, there are a couple of scenarios. You might want to submit the values to a different page rather than post them back to the same page. The ASP.NET postback architecture prevents this with a server-side <form>.

Second, you might want to have more than one <form> on a page, perhaps submitting values to different pages, or submitting different sets of values. Again, the ASP.NET postback architecture does not allow this. There can only be one server-side <form> on a page. Neither of these is a common technique in most of our pages—so the postback architecture can be used and you can benefit from the advantages it provides.

However, one other scenario to bear in mind is if you are using non-server control elements such as an <input type="button"> or <input type="text">, and only interacting with them client-side (in other words, you are not submitting their values to the server). In this case you might prefer to put them on a <form> that does *not* contain a runat="server" attribute. But then you can't use server controls for these buttons or other control elements.

ASP.NET Validation Controls

I declared two ASP.NET validation controls in the previous listing, which will check the value that the user enters in the text box on the sample page. Validation of submitted values is something that you should always do, but it never seems to be as easy as you would expect.

The common approach is to validate the values with client-side script, to avoid a postback to the server if the value is obviously invalid. However, how many of us then *repeat the validation on the server* to check that a user is not trying to spoof the code by creating a page of his or her own that submits invalid values.

The validation controls are the most intelligent of all the controls supplied with ASP.NET. They can perform validation on the client in "up-level" browsers using client-side script that is automatically added to the page when it is processed by ASP.NET. And they always validate the values sent from the client on the server as well.

In "down-level" clients there is no client-side validation (at least in ASP.NET version 1.x, though it may be added in future releases). Instead, the validation is performed only on the server, and you can check that it succeeded in your code. The validation controls also provide the facility to disable client-side validation in "up-level" clients, or to disable validation altogether if required. And there is also a "validation summary" control that displays a list of all the validation errors found in the page. This is used to provide the error message you saw earlier in Figures 5-6 and 5.8.

A full list of the ASP.NET validation controls follows in Table 5-3.

Table 5-3. The ASP.NET Validation Controls

Validation Control	Description
`<asp:RequiredFieldValidator>`	Checks that the validated control contains a value. It cannot be empty. Can be used in conjunction with other validators on a control to trap empty values.
`<asp:RangeValidator>`	Checks that the value in the validated control is within a specified text or numeric inclusive range. If the validated control is empty, no validation takes place.
`<asp:CompareValidator>`	Checks that the value in the validated control matches the value in another control or a specific value. The data type and comparison operation can be specified. If the validated control is empty, no validation takes place.
`<asp:RegularExpressionValidator>`	Checks that the value in the validated control matches a specified regular expression. If the validated control is empty, no validation takes place.
`<asp:CustomValidator>`	Performs user-defined validation on an input control using a specified function (client-side, server-side, or both). If the validated control is empty, no validation takes place.
`<asp:ValidationSummary>`	Displays a summary of all current validation errors.

The Validation Control Members

With the exception of the `ValidationSummary` control, all validation controls inherit from the base class named `BaseValidator`, which is part of the class library namespace `System.Web.UI.WebControls`. The most commonly used properties and methods of the `BaseValidator` base class are described in Table 5-4.

Table 5-4. The Commonly Used Properties of the BaseValidator Control

Member	Description
`ControlToValidate` property	Sets or returns the ID of the input control containing the value to be validated.
`Display` property	Sets or returns a value indicating how the validation control will display its content. Can be `None` (not displayed), `Static` (hidden when value is valid), or `Dynamic` (removed from page when value is valid).
`EnableClientScript` property	Sets or returns a `Boolean` value indicating whether client-side validation is enabled where the client supports this.
`Enabled` property	Sets or returns a `Boolean` value indicating if validation will be carried out.

Table 5-4. The Commonly Used Properties of the BaseValidator Control (continued)

Member	Description
ErrorMessage property	Sets or returns the text of the error message that is displayed by the ValidationSummary control when validation fails.
IsValid property	Returns a Boolean value indicating if the value in the associated input control passed the validation test.
Text property	Sets or returns the text and/or HTML content of the control.
Validate method	Performs validation on the associated input control and updates the IsValid property.

The validation controls also expose properties and methods (and in one case an event) that are specific to that control type (Table 5-5).

Table 5-5. Validation Control-specific Properties, Methods, and Events

Control	Properties	Events
RequiredFieldValidator	InitialValue	- *none*
RangeValidator	MaximumValue, MinimumValue, Type	- *none*
CompareValidator	ControlToCompare, Operator, Type, ValueToCompare	- *none*
RegularExpressionValidator	ValidationExpression	- *none*
CustomValidator	ClientValidationFunction	OnServerValidate
ValidationSummary	DisplayMode, ShowHeaderText, ShowMessageBox, ShowSummary	- *none*

Most of the property names are self-explanatory, and I don't have room to examine them all in depth here. However, I'll show you how to use the RequiredFieldValidator and RegularExpressionValidator controls in the sample "Home" page next. You'll be looking at other ways you can use the validation controls later in the book when you see some pages from the Xrox Car Company site that use them.

NOTE   *A guide to the general techniques for using the validation controls can be found in the .NET SDK (depending on the version you are using) at:*
```
ms-help://MS.NETFrameworkSDK/cpguidenf/html/
cporiValidationWebServerControls.htm.
ms-help://MS.NETFrameworkSDKv1.1/cpguidenf/html/
cporiValidationWebServerControls.htm.
```
The reference section for each of the validation controls can be found within the System.Web.UI.WebControls *namespace of the class library section at:*
```
ms-help://MS.NETFrameworkSDK/cpref/html/
frlrfSystemWebUIWebControls.htm.
ms-help://MS.NETFrameworkSDKv1.1/cpref/html/
frlrfSystemWebUIWebControls.htm.
```

The Validation Controls in the "Home" Page

I've repeated the code I used to insert the two validation controls into the "Home" page in the next listing. You can see from this how I used the ControlToValidate property to connect the validation control with the control I want it to validate (the Textbox control with the ID of txtMailList).

It's quite acceptable to connect more than one validation control to another control on the page, in fact it's often required. Remember that only the RequiredFieldValidator detects an invalid value if the control is empty. The others only validate the contents if the control is not empty, so I often use a combination of the RequiredFieldValidator to check that a value has been entered, along with another validator to check that value:

```
<asp:RequiredFieldValidator id="valRequired" runat="server"
     ControlToValidate="txtMailList"
     ErrorMessage="* You must enter a value in the email address textbox"
     Display="dynamic">
     *
</asp:RequiredFieldValidator>
<asp:RegularExpressionValidator id="valRegExpr" runat="server"
     ControlToValidate="txtMailList"
     ValidationExpression=".*@.*\..*"
     ErrorMessage="* You must provide a valid email address in the textbox"
     Display="dynamic">
     *
</asp:RegularExpressionValidator><br /></font>
```

Set the ErrorMessage property in both of the controls in the example just shown. This defines the text that is displayed by the ValidationSummary control placed elsewhere in the page—you can compare this text with the error message in Figure 5-6 shown earlier in this section of the chapter. In the case of the RegularExpressionValidator, I also provided the regular expression that I wanted the user's value to be compared to. The example provides a rudimentary check for a valid email address.

> **NOTE** *A guide to the syntax and general techniques for using regular expressions*
> *can be found in the .NET SDK at:*
> ms-help://MS.NETFrameworkSDK/cpguidenf/html/
> cpconcomregularexpressions.htm
> ms-help://MS.NETFrameworkSDKv1.1/cpguidenf/html/
> cpconcomregularexpressions.htm

Displaying the Validation Control Content

The Display property of the validation controls specifies how the validation controls
will place the content of the control in the page, particularly when the value in the
control they are validating is valid. The content of the validation control is (as you'd
expect) the text and HTML placed between the opening and closing tags of the control. In the previous example, I used a single asterisk character.

When the value in the connected control is invalid, the validation control displays its content, by default in red (you can change the color, style, and size by
setting various properties or attributes of the control, such as ForeColor, Font-Size,
and so on, just as you would any other Web Forms control). So, the position of the
validation controls within the page defines where the content will be displayed. In
this example, they are placed after the caption for the text box, but before the text
box and <br /> element (see Figure 5-7).

When the value in the connected control is valid, the content of the validation
control is hidden. If the Display property of the validation control is set to "Static",
the space taken up by this content remains in the page—it is just hidden by setting
the CSS visibility selector to "hidden". This is useful when, for example, you place
a validation control in a table cell, as it will not change the layout of the table when
shown or hidden. However, if you set the Display property to "Dynamic", the validation
control actually removes the content from the page altogether by setting the CSS
display selector to "none" and so the layout of the page may change.

The ValidationSummary Control in the "Home" Page

To display the error messages from the validation controls when an invalid value is
submitted, use a ValidationSummary control. This is located in a table cell immediately
below the four graphic links to other pages in the example site, spanning the four
columns of the table that holds these images:

```
...
<tr>
  <td colspan="4" align="center">
  <font face="Arial,Helvetica,sans-serif" size="3" color="#b50055">
  <asp:ValidationSummary Font-Name="Arial,Helvetica,sans-serif"
      id="valSummary" cssClass="large-red-text" runat="server"
      HeaderText="<b>You could not be added to the mailing list:</b>"
      ShowSummary="true" DisplayMode="List" />
  <asp:Label id="lblMessage" cssClass="large-red-text" runat="server" />
  </font></td>
</tr>
...
```

When you declare the control, specify the formatting details in the same way as you have in other Web Forms controls, and in other parts of the page. Set the CssClass property to the name of the CSS class you want to use in CSS-enabled clients, and then specify the font details for other clients. Also, wrap the complete content of the table cell in a <font> element for non-CSS-enabled clients.

Notice the three other attributes I set for the ValidationSummary control. The HeaderText attribute defines the text shown above the list of errors collected from the other validation controls in the page, and the ShowSummary attribute specifies if these error messages will be displayed or not (so you can just show the header text if required). The DisplayMode attributes define how the list of errors is displayed. It can be "List" (the default, with line breaks between each one), "BulletList" (an HTML <ul> list), or "SingleParagraph" (with no line breaks). See Figure 5-6.

Underneath the ValidationSummary control is an ASP.NET Label control with the ID lblMessage. This is used this to display the error messages, or a "thank you" message if the user is successfully added to the mailing list. You'll see how to set the values for this Label control when you look at the code to add addresses to the database shortly.

Online Server Controls Examples

A useful way to see all of the validation controls in action in one page is to run the example I created some time ago for a different book. To save downloading all the samples and installing them on your machine (though you can if you wish), you can view them running on my server at http://www.daveandal.com/books/7035/. Select the Exploring Server Controls option, and open the Other Controls section of the menu to find the validation controls page (Figure 5-10).

Figure 5-10. An example page that demonstrates the Validation controls in action

This page allows you to experiment with many of the ASP.NET server controls, and there are examples on this site that you can play with to see all the others (such as the list controls) in action as well.

The Code to Handle Email Addresses

Having seen how to declare the validation controls in the sample page, you'll explore how to write the code that interacts with them. In fact, as you'll see, you don't have to do very much at all. The validation controls do all of the complicated work for you, and you are really just reduced to checking one property to see if the validation succeeded or not, then carrying out the actions required if validation did succeed.

So, the first section of code you need to look at in the "Home" page is the AddToMailingList event handler. When I declared the Go button, I specified the value AddToMailingList as the OnClick attribute:

```
<asp:Button id="btnMailList" OnClick="AddToMailingList" Text="Go"
            runat="server" title="Submit email address" />
```

All ASP.NET Web Forms server controls (from the namespace System.Web.UI.WebControls) implement the OnClick event as a **server-side** event. As I discussed way back in Chapter 1, these controls cannot provide the client-side onclick attribute. So, you can write a routine to handle this event on the server.

The first step is to see if the value submitted by the user is valid or not. While an "up-level" client will not allow the user to submit an invalid value (unless client-side scripting is disabled), a "down-level" one will. OK, so it automatically generates the error messages, but you still have to make sure that you only execute the code when all the values in the page *are* valid. You do this by checking the IsValid property of the current (default) Page object.

Using the Page.IsValid Property

If all the validation controls agree that the values in their connected controls are valid, the IsValid property of the Page object will be True, and you can execute some code that collects the email address for the text box, trims any spaces from the start or end of it, and then passes it to a function named UpdateMailingList:

```
' subroutine executed when the user submits an email
' address to add to the mailing list
Sub AddToMailingList(sender As Object, args As EventArgs)
  If Page.IsValid Then
    ' update database and display message
    Dim sMsg As String
    Dim sEmailAddr As String = txtMailList.Text.Trim()
    Select Case UpdateMailingList(sEmailAddr)
```

```
      Case 0
        sMsg = "You are already a member of our mailing list."
      Case 1
        sMsg = "Thank you for joining our mailing list."
        ' call routine to send email confirmation
        SendEmailConfirmation(sEmailAddr)
      Case Else
        sMsg = "* Sorry, you could not be added to the " _
             & "mailing list.<br />Please " _
             & "<a href='contact.aspx' title='contact us'>contact us</a>" _
             & " for more information"
    End Select
    lblMessage.Text = "<p><b>" & sMsg & "</b></p>"
  End If
End Sub
```

Depending on the value returned by the UpdateMailingList function, generate a suitable message as a String, and display it in the page by setting the Text property of the ASP.NET Label control named lblMessage that was placed underneath the ValidationSummary control. And if you do succeed in adding the user to the mailing list, call another routine named SendEmailConfirmation that, as you can probably guess, sends the confirmation email message you saw earlier when experimenting with the page.

The UpdateMailingList *Function*

When a user submits an email address to add to the mailing list, you must insert it into the database. The XroxCars database contains a table named tblMailingList, which contains two columns: a column named EmailAddr (the primary key and of type varchar) to hold the email address, and a datetime column named DateAdded to indicate when the address was added. The value for this column is set to the current date automatically when a new row is added because the function getdate() is specified as the default value within the definition of the table.

The database also contains a stored procedure named AddMailingListAddress. It accepts a varchar (String) as the first (input) parameter named Email, and sets the output parameter named Result to an integer value that depends on the outcome of the procedure. If the email address already exists in the table, the SELECT statement within the stored procedure (shown in the following code) will set the internal ROWCOUNT variable to one (1). The following IF statement will then fail, and the INSERT statement will not be executed. However, executing an IF statement has the side effect of resetting ROWCOUNT to zero, so in the last line the Result variable will be set to zero and returned from the stored procedure.

If the email address is not already in the database table, however, ROWCOUNT will be zero following execution of the SELECT statement, and so the stored procedure will execute the INSERT statement to add the email address to the database. This will set ROWCOUNT to one (1), and the value of the Result variable will also be set to 1:

AddMailingListAddress (stored procedure)

```
CREATE PROCEDURE AddMailingListAddress
@Email varchar(255), @Result int OUTPUT
AS
SELECT EmailAddr FROM tblMailingList WHERE EmailAddr = @Email
IF @@ROWCOUNT = 0
    INSERT INTO tblMailingList (EmailAddr) VALUES (@Email)
SELECT @Result = @@ROWCOUNT
GO
```

Of course, because the email address is the primary key of the table, you could just attempt an INSERT without bothering to check if it already exists. If it does, the INSERT will fail. However, although this saves executing two distinct operations within the stored procedure (a SELECT and an INSERT), the more systematic approach used here makes it easier to see what's going on, avoids raising an error, and will work without a primary key definition if required.

Executing the AddMailingListAddress *Stored Procedure*

The stored procedure AddMailingListAddress is executed within a function in the "Home" page named UpdateMailingList. The technique is similar to that used in the previous chapter to execute the stored procedures to get a list of "News" items and car models. However, now there are two parameters to contend with.

You can add parameters to a Command object in a range of ways—depending on what properties you need to set for these parameters. In this code I've chosen the simplest way to add parameters, by simply executing the Add method of the Parameters collection, and supplying the name of the parameter and the value. This method automatically figures out the data type of the value I provided, and creates a parameter of the correct type. All that remains is to tell it that the second parameter is an output parameter by setting the Direction property:

home.aspx

```
' function to add user's email address to mailing list
Function UpdateMailingList(sEmailAddr As String) As Integer
  ' database connection string already in sConnect from Page_Load event
  Dim sqlConnect As SqlConnection = New SqlConnection(sConnect)
  Try
    Dim sProcName As String = "AddMailingListAddress"
    Dim sqlComm As SqlCommand = New SqlCommand(sProcName, sqlConnect)
    sqlComm.CommandType = CommandType.StoredProcedure
    sqlComm.Parameters.Add("@Email", sEmailAddr)
    sqlComm.Parameters.Add("@Result", -1)
    sqlComm.Parameters("@Result").Direction = ParameterDirection.Output
    sqlConnect.Open
    sqlComm.ExecuteNonQuery()
    Return sqlComm.Parameters("@Result").Value
```

```
   Catch
      Return -1
   Finally
      sqlConnect.Close
   End Try
End Function
```

The code then executes the stored procedure (using the ExecuteNonQuery method because I don't want to return a rowset), and returns the value of the parameter named Result to the calling routine. If there is an error of any kind (which is trapped with a Try...Catch construct), the value -1 is returned instead. Depending on the value returned from the UpdateMailingList function, the code you looked at earlier in the AddToMailingList event handler for the Go button on the "Home" page will then create and display the appropriate message.

> **NOTE** *For a list of the six different overloads for the* Parameters.Add *method, see the .NET SDK topics:*
> ms-help://MS.NETFrameworkSDK/cpref/html/
> frlrfsystemdatasqlclientsqlparametercollectionclassaddtopic.htm
> ms-help://MS.NETFrameworkSDKv1.1/cpref/html/
> frlrfsystemdatasqlclientsqlparametercollectionclassaddtopic.htm

The SendMailUser *Control*

Sending an email message using the .NET Framework classes is easy, but there is one issue that I came across regularly while experimenting with these classes. If the code that uses these classes is not in a virtual application root folder (the root folder of an ASP.NET application), the process often proved to be unreliable.

While this isn't a problem in the "Home" page, which *is* in the root of the Xrox Car Company application, you'll also want to be able to send email messages from the My Cars page as you'll see described in Chapter 12. This page is in a subfolder named secure, and so it will suffer from the problem I've just mentioned.

To get round this, I created another **user control** that I can use to instantiate and execute the Framework classes I need to send an email message. Of course, I can't put this user control in the ascx subfolder where all the other user controls reside—I have to put it into the root folder of the application.

The next listing shows the complete sendmail.ascx user control I created. To use the objects and classes that send SMTP mail from within ASP.NET, I must import the System.Web.Mail namespace into the page, as you can see in the second line of this listing. I describe how the rest of code works in the following sections of this chapter:

```
sendmail.ascx
<%@Control Language="VB" EnableViewState="False"%>
<%@Import Namespace="System.Web.Mail"%>
```

```
<script runat="server">
' control properties set from ASPX page:
Public FromAddress As String = ""
Public ToAddress As String = ""
Public MessageSubject As String = ""
Public MessageBody As String = ""

' routine to send email message
Function SendEmail() As Boolean
  Try
    Dim oMessage As MailMessage = New MailMessage
    oMessage.From = FromAddress
    oMessage.To = ToAddress
    oMessage.Subject = MessageSubject
    oMessage.Body = MessageBody
    oMessage.BodyFormat = MailFormat.Text
    ' specify SMTP server name if required, default is "localhost"
    ' EDIT THIS LINE: SmtpMail.SmtpServer = "my-mail-server"
    ' send mail - requires local mail server to be available
    SmtpMail.Send(oMessage)
    Return True
  Catch
    Return False
  End Try
End Function
</script>
```

Exposing the Properties and Methods of the Control

The first few lines of code within the <script> section of the sendmail.ascx user control define the four Public String properties that I will specify values for when using this control. I expose the From and To addresses, the text for the subject line, and the text that will make up the body of the message.

The remainder of the code is a Public Function named SendEmail (exposed as a method of the user control) that sends the email message. I take the values of the four properties and use them to set the properties of the .NET MailMessage object I'm using to send the mail. I also specify that the format of the message (the BodyFormat property) is Text—though this is the default anyway. Finally, I call the Send method of the MailMessage object.

Using the SmtpMail *Class to Send the Message*

If you've worked with the CDONTS objects in earlier versions of ASP, you'll find that using the MailMessage object in ASP.NET is a very similar technique. CDO (Collaborative Data Objects) is a COM-based technology for interacting with SMTP mail systems in Windows, and the classes in the .NET System.Web.Mail namespace simply wrap these objects and make them available as .NET classes.

NOTE *Information about CDO for Windows 2000 can be found at:*
http://msdn.microsoft.com/library/en-us/cdo/html/_denali_cdo_for_nts_library.asp

Once the message has been created, you have to find a way to deliver it. I use the local SMTP Service that is installed as part of Internet Information Services on Windows Server 2003, Windows 2000 Server, Windows 2000 Advanced Server, and Windows 2000 DataCenter Server (it is not available in Windows 2000 Professional). Alternatively, arrange for a separate "smart host" to deliver the message instead.

Mail is sent using the `SmtpMail` object. The class that defines this object is static, and so you don't need to create a specific instance of it—you can just reference it directly. The `SmtpMail` object has one `Public` property, `SmtpServer`, which is used to specify the server that will deliver the message. If you are using the local SMTP Service, you can omit this property, or set it to `"localhost"` (the default):

```
' specify mail server to be used to deliver message
SmtpMail.SmtpServer = "localhost"
```

The `SmtpMail` object also exposes a `Public` method named `Send`, which is used to pass the message to the SMTP Service or other mail server that will deliver it. The sample "Home" page uses this code to send the message:

```
' send mail - requires mail server to be available
SmtpMail.Send(oMessage)
```

The `SendEmailConfirmation` *Routine*

So, in the "Home" page, you can create a suitable email message using the `sendmail.ascx` user control. Register this control at the top of the page, and then insert it right at the end of the page, just before the closing `</body>` tag. Give it an ID of `"ctlMail"`:

```
<%@Register TagPrefix="wcc" TagName="sendmail" Src="sendmail.ascx"%>
...
...
<!-- control containing the routine to send email messages -->
<wcc:sendmail id="ctlMail" runat="server" />
```

Now, in the `SendEmailConfirmation` routine within the "Home" page, you just have to build up a `String` holding the body of the message you want to send, and set the properties of the user control. Then you can call its `SendEmail` method to send the mail:

```
home.aspx
' routine to send email confirmation of addition to mailing list
Sub SendEmailConfirmation(sEmailAddr)
  Dim sMessage As String
  sMessage = "Thank you for joining the Xrox Car Company Mailing List." _
          & vbCrlf & vbCrlf _
          & "We will keep you informed about our exciting range of " _
          & "cars, and any other new developments. You are registered " _
          & "on the list as: " & vbCrlf & sEmailAddr & vbCrlf & vbCrlf _
          & "To be removed from the list, just reply to this message " _
          & "with the word REMOVE in the subject line." _
          & vbCrlf & vbCrlf & "Visit us often at http://www.yoursite.com/"
  ' use separate ASCX control to send the message
  ctlMail.FromAddress = _
          ConfigurationSettings.AppSettings("XroxCarsWebmasterEmail")
  ctlMail.ToAddress = sEmailAddr
  ctlMail.MessageSubject = "Mailing List Confirmation"
  ctlMail.MessageBody = sMessage
  ctlMail.SendEmail()
End Sub
```

Notice that I again use the value from web.config for the From address in the mail message, just as was used in the footerlinks.ascx user control you looked at earlier. It means that I only have to edit the value in the <appSettings> section of web.config to change the email address in both the footer of every page in the site and the "From" address for all email messages.

Configuration Issues for Sending Mail from ASP.NET

There are a few things to be aware of when you build ASP.NET pages that will send email messages:

- The behavior of the SmtpMail object depends on the configuration of your mail server, and depends on the CDO objects installed with Windows 2000 for its functionality. Strange errors and other effects can occur if this is not available or properly configured.

- The page containing the code that sends the message should be in a virtual application folder, and not just in a subfolder of the default Web site. While I have not been able to discover the exact reasons for this, I found that the SmtpMail.Send method can cause a "550 Cannot Relay for Domain" message when the folder containing the page was not configured as a virtual application.

- ASP.NET must have permission to access the SMTP Service. For the local SMTP Service, you must give the ASPNET account (or whichever account you are running the ASP.NET process under if you changed it from the default) at least Read and Write access to the inetpub\mailroot\pickup folder. I generally give the ASPNET account Read, Write, and Modify permission for mailroot and all its subfolders, so that ASP.NET can handle incoming mail as well.

- If you are delivering mail through a remote "smart host" mail server, you may have to configure it to allow ASP.NET to send a message to it, and also allow the machine that generates the message to relay through the smart host. The requirements depend on your network, mail server, security configuration, and the type of mail server you are using.

- Make sure that you use a valid email address for the From property of your messages. Some redirection servers and smart hosts perform a reverse lookup, and may reject messages that do not have a valid "from" address. The example page I provide in the samples for this book contains an invalid "from" address, which you should change to suit your own system.

> **NOTE** *A full reference to the MailMessage and SmtpMail classes can be found in the version 1.0 .NET SDK at:*
> `ms-help://MS.NETFrameworkSDK/cpref/html/frlrfSystemWebMail.htm`
> *or, for version 1.1:*
> `ms-help://MS.NETFrameworkSDKv1.1/cpref/html/frlrfSystemWebMail.htm`

Summary

In this chapter, you completed your tour of the "Home" page for the fictitious example "Xrox Car Company" Web site. While it has taken two whole chapters to do so, you covered a lot of ground in that time. In the previous chapter, you saw the design and implementation of the overall page structure, the way to apply styles and formatting, and how to extract content from the database and display it in the page.

In this chapter, you moved on to look at the concept of **user controls**, and how to build the two that provide the animated page banner and the intelligent page footer for the site. By exposing properties from these user controls, you can make them respond in various ways depending on the requirements of each page or specific situations. For example, the sample page banner provides different output depending on the type of client that the page is served to, and only creates the animated version when the user first visits the site.

You also looked at how to send email messages from the Web site in this chapter. Exploring the controls used to collect the information in the "Home" page led to a fairly in-depth discussion of the ASP.NET validation controls, as well as looking at the way to use the objects from the System.Web.Mail namespace to create and send email messages.

In all, the chapter covered:

- The animated banner used in most of the pages

- The page footer used in most of the pages

- How to add users to the mailing list in the "Home" page

In the next chapter, you'll leave our "Home" page behind and see some of the other pages that are implemented on the example site.

The Ancillary Pages

THE SAMPLE SITE'S "Home" page is now complete, and it's time to move on to look at some of the other pages. As you will guess, most of the techniques introduced in previous chapters are used in many, if not all, of the pages in the example site. This includes interacting with the user's session, formatting the output for a wide range of client types, and providing accessibility features to assist users of specialist types of client.

You saw that the "Home" page provides prominent links to four other pages, by way of the graphic buttons just below the banner at the top of the page. You'll be looking at three of these pages in this chapter, the "Compare Models," "Terms and Conditions," and "Contact" pages. These pages include features that are standard across most of the "ancillary" pages on the site, such as the links back to the "Home" page and other pages, as well as having the same overall layout (you'll be looking at the "My Cars" page in later chapters).

There are also two other pages that are opened from the "Home" page, but not from the graphical button links. These are the page that displays a complete "News" item (linked from the list of news précis in the left column of the "Home" page) and the "Model Details" page (linked from the vehicle image and name in the right-hand section of the "Home" page). You'll be looking at the first of these in this chapter, while you'll come back to the "Model Details" page later in this book.

So, this chapter examines:

- The general structure of the "ancillary" pages, including layout and navigation

- The "Terms and Conditions" and "Contact" pages

- When to use static as opposed to dynamic content

- The page that displays the individual "News" items

- The structure and workings of the "Compare Models" page

- How to create the display of model comparisons as an HTML table

I start with a look at the overall page structure of the ancillary pages.

The Structure of the Ancillary Pages

In Chapter 3, while discussing the guidelines for providing good accessibility on the Web pages for visitors who have restricted sight or movement, I pointed out that a great way to make a site easy to use was to have a common structure for the basic components or sections of every page. This makes it easier to find things like a menu bar, and to navigate between pages. And, as a bonus, it actually makes it easier for all visitors to use the site—they don't have to hunt around for links and content that is placed in different positions on each page.

The Overall Layout

All of the ancillary pages on the example site, with only a couple of minor exceptions, have a common layout for the page: a static banner, the link to the "Home" page and other pages, the content section, and the page footer, as shown in Figure 6-1.

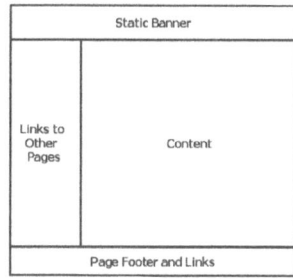

Figure 6-1. The four main sections of the anciliary pages in the site

"Terms and Conditions" and "Contact" Pages

As an example of the structure of the ancillary pages, Figure 6-2 shows the "Contact" page—you can see all the sections shown in Figure 6-1 within this page.

Figure 6-2. The "Contact" page

The HTML Table for the Ancillary Pages Structure

This overall layout is created with a standard HTML table, which includes three user controls that are common to all the ancillary pages. The page banner is the same user control named `pagebanner.ascx` that was used in the "Home" page, but now it is not animated. The page footer is the same user control named `footerlinks.ascx` that was used in the "Home" page, with the `CurrentPageLink` property set such that the current page is not a hyperlink.

The left-hand section containing the clickable image links is another user control—one that you haven't met so far. This control, named `mainlink.ascx`, is detailed later in this section of the chapter. Finally, the content of the page is displayed in the right side of the page, within a single cell of the HTML table.

So, to get the overall page structure, use the following abridged HTML declarations:

contact.aspx

```
<!doctype html public "-//W3C//DTD HTML 3.2 Final//EN">
<html>
<head>
<basefont size="2">
<link rel="stylesheet" type="text/css"
      href="stylesheets/wcc<% = sStyleSize %>.css" />
<title>Xrox Car Company—Contact Us</title>
</head>
<body leftmargin="0" rightmargin="0" topmargin="0"
      bgcolor="#ffffff" class="body-text">
<div style="position:absolute;height:0px;"><font size="1" color=#ffffff">

<!-- skip link for aural page readers -->
<layer visibility="hidden">
<a href="#content" style="color:#ffffff;font-size:1px;text-decoration:none">
<img width="1" height="1" hspace="0" vspace="0" src="images/_blnk.gif" border="0"
alt="Skip to Content" /></a>
</layer>
</font></div>
<wcc:pagebanner runat="server" /><br />
<table width="100%" border="0" cellspacing="0" cellpadding="10">
<tbody>
 <tr>
  <td valign="top" width="110px">
   <wcc:mainlink runat="server" CurrentPageLink="Contact" />
  </td>
  <td align="left">
   <a name="content" />
   <font face="Arial,Helvetica,sans-serif" size="4" color="#b50055">
   <p class="large-red-text"><b>Contact Us</b></p></font>
   <font face="Tahoma,Arial,Helvetica,sans-serif" size="2">
   <p class="body-text">
   <b>Xrox Car Company</b> is a fictitious organization created ...
```

```
      ...  page content goes here ...
    </p>
   </font>
  </td>
 </tr>
</tbody>
</table>

<wcc:footerlinks runat="server" CurrentPageLink="Contact" />
</body>
</html>
```

Looking through this, you should easily be able to pick out the important points:

- The page contains a section that declares the "skip to" link for aural page readers and text-only user agents, linking to the main "content" section of the page so that visitors can go straight to this section.

- The page banner user control is inserted into the page with the `<wcc:pagebanner>` element, as in the "Home" page, but doesn't need an `id` attribute as it's not going to be accessing the control in the server-side code.

- A two-column single-row HTML `<table>` contains the links to other pages, declared as the user control element `<wcc:mainlink>`, and the actual page content itself (our contact details) as text and HTML.

- Below the `<table>` is the user control that implements the "footer" links. This is inserted into the page with the `<wcc:footerlinks>` element, just as we did in the "Home" page, setting the `CurrentPageLink` property to the name of this page so that it is not included as a self-referencing hyperlink.

- The section containing the content uses both CSS styles and `<font>` elements to control the format and appearance of the text, as was done in the "Home" page of the site.

So, other than the content itself, which is simply inserted as text and HTML into the right-hand `<table>` cell, what haven't you seen before? There are a few lines of server-side code that you'll look at next. After that, the only thing that you need to examine in more detail is the `<wcc:mainlink>` user control—which you'll do in a short while.

The Code for the Ancillary Pages

There is very little code required in the "Contact" and "Terms and Conditions" pages. The only things you need to do are select the correct style sheet for the current browser type, and check that the user still has a current ASP.NET session available.

A page-level variable is declared to hold the part of the style sheet name that is extracted from the user's session (where it was stored by code in the "Home" page). In the Page_Load event handler, collect the value for this variable and then check to see if the code actually did find it. If not, you know that either the user's session has expired, or that the user entered the site at this page directly and not through the "Home" page. In either case, redirect the user to the page default.aspx, where the client detection process will be performed to reestablish the necessary session values:

contact.aspx

```
<script runat="server">
' ---------------------------------------------------------------------

' page-level variable to style sheet size
Dim sStyleSize As String = "Standard"

' ---------------------------------------------------------------------

Sub Page_Load()
  ' get style sheet size from Session
  sStyleSize = CType(Session("WccStyleSize"), String)

  ' if no value, session has expired or user entered
  ' site at page other than "Home" page
  If sStyleSize = "" Then
    Response.Clear()
    Response.Redirect("default.aspx")
  End If
End Sub

' ---------------------------------------------------------------------
</script>
```

The value for sStyleSize that is collected from the session is then used in the <link> element to select the correct style sheet:

```
<link rel="stylesheet" type="text/css"
    href="stylesheets/wcc<% = sStyleSize %>.css" />
```

Redirection When No Session Is Available

I discussed the decision to demand session support for the **Xrox Car Company** site when you looked at the design of the site as a whole, and again when I discussed the client detection process. As the design I've chosen will not work correctly without an ASP.NET session, I have to check that one exists each time a page that uses any values stored in the session is loaded.

In the case of the "Contact" and "Terms and Conditions" pages, the only value used is the style sheet name, and so the page would work without a session. The <link> element would fail to find a matching style sheet, and the <font> elements would provide the required formatting.

However, other pages in the site will not work correctly without session support, and will have to redirect the visitor to the default.aspx page if a current session is not available. I felt that it makes sense for all the pages to exhibit the same behavior.

The other issue here is where to redirect visitors to if session support is lost or a current session is not available. I chose to redirect them to the page default.aspx, which will then redirect them to the "Home" page after reestablishing the user ID, style sheet type, and client-side script support values in their session.

Likewise, if visitors have entered the site by loading one of the pages other than the "Home" page (via default.aspx) first, they will be seamlessly redirected to the "Home" page. This is not unusual behavior for a site that requires user interaction (try your own bank's online account management Web site for an example).

As an alternative to redirecting them to default.aspx, you could redirect them straight to home.aspx. Because there is no valid session available, the code in home.aspx will redirect them to the page no-sessions.htm. It displays details of why they are here, what might be the cause, and it provides a link to enter the site at the correct place— or to use the alternative cookie-less session version of the site instead (Figure 6-3).

Figure 6-3. The page that is displayed when session support is not available

Of course, if you redirect to default.aspx and the visitor's browser does not support cookies, the user will see this page anyway. The code in the "Home" pages causes this to happen, as you saw in Chapter 3. This is the reason that I decided to go with the "seamless" option of redirecting to default.aspx, as it probably gives a better user experience, and less of an impression that the site has "broken."

The MainLink User Control

The graphical links in the left-hand side of the "ancillary" pages are the same as those used near the top of the "Home" page, with the addition of a link back to the "Home" page itself. However, remember the accessibility guidelines that suggest you should never have a self-referring link in the pages (except when you need to post a <form> back to the server). So, you want to make sure that you only display links to other pages each time.

In the previous screenshot of the "Contact" page, you can see that the links there do not include the "Contact" clickable graphic button. However, Figure 6-4 shows that the "Terms and Conditions" page does have this link—but not a "Conditions" link.

Figure 6-4. The links that appear in the "Terms and Conditions" page

You can probably guess that the user control (mainlink.ascx) I used to implement these links works in much the same way as the footerlinks.ascx user control you examined in Chapter 5 (which implements the text links and copyright notice at the bottom of every page).

The visible content of the mainlink.ascx control is shown in the next listing. You can see that there are five <img> elements, nested inside five <a> elements. Notice that the <a> elements are server controls (implemented by the HtmlAnchor control you examined in the previous chapter), and that the id for each one contains the page name. However, the <img> elements are not server controls and have no id attribute:

mainlink.ascx

```
<%@Control Language="VB" EnableViewState="False" debug="True"%>
<a id="aHOME" runat="server" Title="Back to List of Models"
    href="../home.aspx">
 <img src="images/btn_home.gif" width="100" height="49"
      hspace="3" vspace="2" alt="Home Page" border="0" /></a>
<a id="aCOMPARE" runat="server" Title="Compare Vehicle Models"
    href="../compare.aspx">
 <img src="images/btn_compare.gif" width="100" height="49"
      hspace="3" vspace="2" alt="Compare Models" border="0" /></a>
<a id="aCONTACT" runat="server" Title="Contact and Feedback Details"
    href="../contact.aspx">
 <img src="images/btn_contact.gif" width="100" height="49"
      hspace="3" vspace="2" alt="Contact Us" border="0" /></a>
<a id="aTANDC" runat="server" Title="Terms and Conditions of Trading"
    href="../tandc.aspx">
 <img src="images/btn_tandc.gif" width="100" height="49"
      hspace="3" vspace="2" alt="Terms and Conditions" border="0" /></a>
<a id="aMYCARS" runat="server" Title="View My Cars and Configurations"
    href="../secure/mycars.aspx">
 <img src="images/btn_mycars.gif" width="100" height="49"
      hspace="3" vspace="2" alt="My Cars" border="0" /></a>
```

The Script Section

In the script section of the user control, declare a `Public` variable named `CurrentPageLink`, which acts as a property of the control. In the `Page_Load` event handler you can use this value to locate the appropriate `<a>` element and remove it from the output by setting its `Visible` property to `False`:

mainlink.ascx

```
<script runat="server">
' control property set from ASPX page:
Public CurrentPageLink As String = ""
Sub Page_Load()
  Try
    ' remove <a> from page—also removes child <img> element
    Dim sCurrent As String = CurrentPageLink.ToUpper()
    CType(FindControl("a" & sCurrent), HtmlAnchor).Visible = False
  Catch
  End Try

End Sub
</script>
```

When the page is executed, all the content of the page is built up into a "control tree"—a hierarchical tree of objects that represent every part of the page. The `<img>` element becomes part of the content of the `HtmlAnchor` control that represents the

<a> element (the <img> element is *not* a server control as it has no runat="server" attribute, and therefore cannot be a child control of the HtmlAnchor control). The result is that, when you remove the <a> element from the output, the <img> element disappears as well. So the page only contains the links that are not specified for the CurrentPageLink property.

Using the MainLink Control

You can use the mainlink.ascx control in exactly the same way as you did the footerlinks.ascx control. Register it in the page, and then insert it where you want the links to appear. As you insert it into the page, use an attribute to set the CurrentPageLink property of the control to the appropriate value that will hide the link for the current page:

tandc.aspx

```
<%@Register TagPrefix="wcc" TagName="mainlink" Src="ascx/mainlink.ascx" %>
...
<table width="100%" border="0" cellspacing="0" cellpadding="10">
<tbody>
 <tr>
  <td valign="top" width="110px">
    <wcc:mainlink runat="server" CurrentPageLink="TandC" />
  </td>
  <td align="left">
    <a name="content" />
    <p class="large-red-text"><b>Distance Selling Regulations</b></p>
    <p class="body-text">
      This paragraph sets out those items required pursuant to the ...
      ... page content goes here ...
    </p>
  </td>
 </tr>
</tbody>
</table>
```

NOTE *For a more complete discussion of user controls, see Chapter 5.*

Choosing Static or Dynamic Content

In the "Terms and Conditions" and "Contact" pages, I used static text and HTML to create the content (as displayed in the right section of the page). You can confirm this by viewing the ASPX source code for either of these pages. Using static text and HTML provides the best performance, as it is simply embedded into the compiled ASP.NET page and streamed to the client with the rest of the response.

However, this approach is really only acceptable when the content does not change over time, or when it changes only infrequently. Each change to the content means editing the page source directly. So it's worth looking at other ways that you could get this "content" into the page.

Making Static Content Dynamic

In the "Home" page, the content came from a database. There are tables containing lists of car models and news items that I want to display, and I did this using the various list controls that are provided with ASP.NET. And, of course, you'll see plenty more examples of this approach throughout the rest of the book.

The ASP.NET list controls provide not only an easy way to handle repeated values with only one relatively simple control declaration, but they also cope with the source data changing as regularly as is required. Each time the page is accessed, it collects the list of items from the database and builds the relevant section of the page dynamically.

So, if you only have one "thing" to display, rather than a list of items, should you still do it dynamically? As you'd expect, the typical programmer's response of "*it depends . . .*" is again likely. So, what does it really depend on? Here are a few pointers:

- How easy is it to update the source code for the page and post it to the live server? If you are using a staging server and some kind of content publishing system, there should be no problem.

- How complicated is the content? If it involves a lot of complex HTML and other data, it might be easier to write it directly in the page as static content rather than try to load it into a database table for dynamic insertion into the page at runtime.

- How easy is it to update the database, if you decide to store the content in this way? Do you need to provide "admin" pages that are used simply to update the database, and is the extra work involved for this worthwhile if the content changes only rarely?

- Are the servers under extreme loading, so that every extra bit of performance you can squeeze out of the pages is required to keep the site running well? While this seems like a good reason to use static content, investment in an extra server or two instead is probably quite justifiable—especially if you really do need to publish dynamic content.

- Are you using a multiple-server Web farm that runs against a single central database? In this case, unless the Web farm software includes features to replicate content between servers, pulling it from the central data store dynamically might be a good plan, and provide easier maintenance.

Dynamic Content Without a Database

Of course, even when the content is being loaded into the page dynamically, it doesn't always have to come from a database. It could be:

- **Stored as a text file**, which contains all the HTML and content required for that section of the page. We can read a text file from disk and stream it to the client as part of the response very easily using ASP.NET. You just call the WriteFile method of the Response object, passing in the physical path to the file you want to use:

```
Response.WriteFile("myfile.txt")
```

- **Declared within a User Control**, which is inserted into the page using a Register directive as you saw in the previous chapter. The content of the user control appears in the page wherever you place the element that you define for it:

```
<%@Register TagPrefix="wcc" TagName="pagecontent"
            Src="ascx/some-content.ascx" %>
  ...
  <wcc:pagecontent runat="server" />
```

- **Stored in an XML document**, and transformed into HTML and other content at runtime with an XSL or XSLT style sheet. There is even an ASP.NET control (the Xml control) that you can use to do this (you'll look at this control in more detail in Chapter 10, where I use it in the pages of the example site):

```
<asp:Xml id="ctlXml" runat="server"
         DocumentSource="content.xml"
         TransformSource="contentstyle.xslt" />
```

It could even come from another source such as a **Web Service**, which returns the HTML and content as a text stream (String) that is inserted into the page. However, this is probably not useful unless you absolutely must have the latest data, as it is likely to considerably reduce page performance. But it's another option if you really do need to go down this route.

Making Dynamic Content Static

There is also a converse situation that you meet quite often in Web sites containing a lot of dynamic content, where that content does not change very often. This is the situation where the data comes from a dynamic source, and it doesn't make sense to use static content in the form of HTML and text placed directly in the source of the page. But, if the data only changes infrequently (maybe once a week, once a month or even once a year), it would be nice to have a way to convert it to static content.

The laborious way to do this is to view the delivered page source in the browser, copy it as text, and paste it into the static page. However, this is not a solution that is generally likely to find favor. Instead, you can do much the same thing using code. In fact, I take advantage of this technique in several of my existing sites, as do many developers of other well-known commercial sites.

Often referred to as "bulk caching," "precaching," or "Web caching" in ASP 3.0 days, the technique is not really *caching* at all—at least not in any sense that it's understood with ASP.NET. All you need to do is run some code that requests the page, captures the response, and writes it to disk as an HTML page with the .htm file extension. The client then loads the .htm pages instead of the dynamic ones.

Of course, all the links in the generated pages must then point to the equivalent static .htm page, and not to the dynamic page that generates them. But, as long as the pages are written with this in mind, there's no problem.

Generating Static Pages with ASP.NET

The example that I used in Chapter 2 of this book to demonstrate how server controls react to different types of client uses techniques that can easily be adapted to generate static pages with ASP.NET. Although I didn't discuss how that example page actually works in Chapter 2, it's not difficult to see what it does from the following listing that shows the relevant techniques:

```
<%@Page Language="VB" %>
<%@Import Namespace="System.IO" %>
<%@Import Namespace="System.Net" %>

<script runat="server">
Sub Page_Load()
  ' create a Web Request object with a specified virtual path
  Dim sVPath As String = "http://localhost/test/input-page.aspx"
  Dim oWRequ As WebRequest = WebRequest.Create(sVPath)

  ' send the request and collect the response in a Stream object
  Dim oWResp As WebResponse = oWRequ.GetResponse()
  Dim oStream As Stream = oWResp.GetResponseStream()

  ' create a StreamReader to read the stream
  Dim oReader As New StreamReader(oStream, Encoding.ASCII)
  ' create a StreamWriter and use it to write the stream to a disk file
  Dim oWriter As NewStreamWriter(Server.MapPath("result.htm"))
  oWriter.Write(oReader.ReadToEnd())
  ' close all the objects
  oWriter.Close()
  oReader.Close()
  oWResp.Close()
End Sub
</script>
```

> **NOTE** *You'll find an example that uses very similar code to this in the* static-pages *subfolder of the sample files for this book.*

The WebRequest object fetches the page, and the entire content is written to disk as a file with the .htm file extension. This file can then be opened in a browser, and it is identical to the output of the dynamic page that it was created from. However, it avoids reexecuting the original page each time. The static page need only be generated when the data used in the dynamic page changes.

However, there are a couple of unfortunate side effects with this technique. If the page relies on values posted from a <form> or provided in the query string to change its behavior or output, static disk file generation is not going to be of any use. The .htm page cannot react dynamically to these values.

The other issue is that the page cannot react differently depending on the browser type that requests it. You'll recall that the ASP.NET Web Forms server controls change their output depending on whether the current request is from an "up-level" or a "down-level" client. By default, static .htm pages generated from a dynamic page using the code shown above will contain content suited to "down-level" clients only.

You can set the value of the UserAgent property of the WebRequest object, and have this value sent to the server as the USER_AGENT HTTP header. However, this is a property of the specific object type HttpWebRequest (not the generic WebRequest class), so you have to convert (cast) the object to the correct type first:

```
Dim sUAString As String = "Mozilla/4.0 (compatible; MSIE 6.0;)"
CType(oWRequ, HttpWebRequest).UserAgent = sUAString
```

> **NOTE** *If you prefer, you can use the specific objects like* HttpWebRequest *and* HttpWebResponse *in the code instead of the generic* WebRequest *and* WebResponse *objects and avoid the type cast.*

Now the dynamic page will think that the request came from Internet Explorer 6.0, and not the ASPX code that uses a WebRequest object, so the server controls in the requested page will create output suited to "up-level" clients instead.

Using ASP.NET Caching to Expose "Static" Pages

While creating static disk files is a useful technique in some situations, don't forget that ASP.NET also provides *real* caching—built right into the .NET Framework. I discussed this at some length towards the end of Chapter 2, when I looked at the effect it has on the output from the ASP.NET server controls.

An OutputCache directive such as the following tells ASP.NET to store the HTML and other content it generates in the local cache for the period (in seconds) specified in the Duration attribute. The following code caches the page for 24 hours, and you can use larger values to cache it even longer if required:

```
<%@OutputCache Duration="86400" VaryByParam="none" %>
```

On top of this, you can tell ASP.NET to only cache the "static" output for requests that have the same values within the HTTP headers. For example, as a "catch-all" that ensures the server sends a different page in response to each request that has different parameters (different <form> and/or query string values), you can use:

```
<%@OutputCache Duration="86400" VaryByParam="*" %>
```

And to make sure that it sends the correct output from server controls to each type of browser ("up-level" or "down-level") you can use:

```
<%@OutputCache Duration="86400" VaryByParam="*" VaryByCustom="browser" %>
```

I even demonstrated in Chapter 2 how you can create custom VaryBy values to minimize the number of different versions of the page that are cached. Look back there for more details if you need to refresh your memory.

This discussion also leads neatly to the next page I want to look at—the page to read the complete content of a "News" article. The content for this page is dynamic, being drawn from a database, so you need to consider how to get maximum performance and minimize loading on the server.

The "Read News Item" Page

In the "Home" page of the **Xrox Car Company** site, I provide a list of current news articles in the left column. The title of each one is a hyperlink, as is the **[read more]** link at the end of the article précis. Clicking one of these links opens the selected article in the main window so the visitor can read it.

The links are created within the templates I defined for the Repeater control that generates the list of articles. Create a URL for each hyperlink that points to the page readnews.aspx, and append the ID of that article to the query string. You can see the complete URL and query string (in this case `http://localhost/webforms/xroxcars/readnews.aspx?id=4`) in the status bar of the browser window in Figure 6-5.

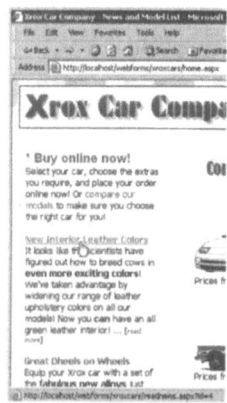

Figure 6-5. The link to open a news article, showing the query string that is used

The "Read News Item" page (readnews.aspx) that opens from these hyperlinks follows the same outline structure as the "Contact" and "Terms and Conditions" pages you looked at earlier. It has the same page banner, a set of clickable image links to other pages, and the same footer section containing the text links and copyright information. The title and content of the selected article are displayed in the right section of the page (Figure 6-6).

Figure 6-6. The "Read News Item" page

Before you look at the code that implements this page, I want to continue the discussion about using static or dynamic content by quickly reviewing the options available for inserting dynamic content into a page.

Inserting Dynamic Content into Pages

When you have decided that you want to include dynamic content, rather than using static HTML and text (as I did in the "Contact" and "Terms and Conditions" pages), you need to decide on the most appropriate technique for inserting that content into the page. You can still use the ASP 3.0 approach, but there are much better ways in ASP.NET. The following list explains the various options that are available.

- A traditional technique is to **write the content directly to the output** using a Response.Write statement at the point that you want the content to appear. This was a favorite approach in ASP 3.0, but is *not* recommended in ASP.NET. As the page is compiled into a class and then executed, Response.Write will probably not insert its output at the point you expect. It appears at the point where the statement is actually executed, and this is likely to be within an event handler, rather than during the procedural execution of the script in an ASP 3.0 page. For example, placing a Response.Write statement in the Page_Load event handler inserts the output before any other content—at the top of the page and before the opening <html> tag.

- You can still safely use the **ASP 3.0-style** <% =value %> **syntax** in the HTML section of the page, as was done with the style sheet name in the <link> element. This is actually Response.Write in disguise, but it is executed as the content is generated and the output appears at that point in the page. The only issue here is that the value must be a page-level variable, and not a variable that is defined inside an event handler such as Page_Load. In general, it is not a preferred approach—though it is acceptable when required (as described in Chapter 4, I used it in the <link> element to avoid having to declare it as a server control).

- You can use **data binding with a list control**, such as a Repeater, DataList, or DataGrid, if the data is stored in a suitable data source object (such as a DataReader, a DataSet, a collection, an array, or a HashTable). Even though there is only one "row" of data (containing, in the "News" page example, the title and the article content) this is still a perfectly valid approach. You only get one instance of the output that is declared in the list control's templates. If you want to place the values from this one "row" into a table, using a DataGrid makes it easy as it will generate the HTML <table>, <tr>, and <td> elements automatically. However, it does mean extra processing to instantiate the control and generate the output, which you can avoid using other techniques.

- You can use **simple single-value data binding**, either at Page level or to set the attribute or content of any control on the page. The result of a function or expression, or the value of a property, can be inserted directly into the page using a data binding statement such as <%# MyFunction() %>. Just remember to call the Page.DataBind() method in the Page_Load event handler as well. This approach is faster and more efficient than using a list control, and it also allows the value to be inserted into an element that is *not* a server control. For example, you can use syntax such as:

```
<span><%# MyFunction(parameter1, parameter2, ...) %></span>
<input type="text" value="<%# MyProperty %>">
```

- You can **set the property of a server control in the page** (usually the Text property or the InnerHtml property) to the value you want to display. This is the preferred approach in ASP.NET when you have single values to display, especially where they are text rather than individual numeric values. It is the most efficient approach, and is what I use in the "Read News" example page.

The HTML and Code for the "Read News" Page

As you've seen, the "Read News" page is fundamentally similar to the other ancillary pages in terms of structure, layout, and appearance. The HTML code that creates these features of the page is therefore much the same as in the "Terms and Conditions" and "Contact" pages.

readnews.aspx

```
<table width="100%" border="0" cellspacing="0" cellpadding="10">
<tbody>
 <tr>
  <td valign="top" width="110px">
    <wcc:mainlink runat="server" />
  </td>
  <td align="left" class="body-text">
    <a name="content" />
    <font face="Arial,Helvetica,sans-serif" size="4" color="#b50055">
    <p id="pNewsTitle" class="large-red-text" runat="server" />
    </font>
    <font face="Tahoma,Arial,Helvetica,sans-serif" size="2">
    <p id="pNewsText" class="body-text" runat="server" />
    </font>
  </td>
 </tr>
</tbody>
</table>
```

Because this page does not appear in the list of clickable graphic links generated by the user control mainlink.ascx, you don't have to set the CurrentPageLink property. Just insert the control and let it display all the links.

I've included two <p> elements in the page, specifying the CSS class that I want for them (they are also enclosed in the matching <font> elements as in the other ancillary pages). However, both of the <p> elements are server controls, because I've added the runat="server" attribute to them. This means that they will be implemented by ASP.NET as HtmlGenericControl objects, and so you can access their properties in the server-side code.

Getting the Content from the Data Store

But first, you need to get the dynamic content from the data source—in this case a SQL Server database. I've included a function in the page that calls a stored procedure named GetNewsItem within the database. This stored procedure returns the contents of all four columns in the row that has the ID value specified in the @ItemID parameter:

```
CREATE PROCEDURE GetNewsItem @ItemID int AS
SELECT * FROM tblNews
WHERE NewsID = @ItemID
```

I could, of course, just return the two columns I am using in the page—the page is not displaying the ID or the précis (from the column named NewsPrecis) at the moment, and this would make it marginally more efficient. However, as the unused items are just a number and a small text string, I decided to return all the columns here. This allows me to demonstrate a couple of ways that you can extract values from a DataReader, and also means that you can easily experiment and adapt the page to show the précis as well. Of course, if you know that a column will never be used in the page, you should not return it (especially if it is more than a few bytes).

The function GetNewsItemDR that calls this stored procedure is listed next. It works in the same way as the similar function I used in the "Home" page to get a list of all the "News" item précis, but this time I also have to provide a value for the @ItemID parameter:

```
  function to get selected news item from database
Function GetNewsItemDR(iItemID As Integer) As SqlDataReader
  Try
    Dim sConnect As String
    sConnect = ConfigurationSettings.AppSettings("XroxCarsConnectString")
    Dim sqlConnect As SqlConnection = New SqlConnection(sConnect)
    Dim sProcName As String = "GetNewsItem"
    Dim sqlComm As SqlCommand = New SqlCommand(sProcName, sqlConnect)
    sqlComm.CommandType = CommandType.StoredProcedure
    sqlComm.Parameters.Add("@ItemID", iItemID)
    sqlConnect.Open
    Return sqlComm.ExecuteReader(CommandBehavior.CloseConnection)
  Catch
    Return Nothing
  End Try
End Function
```

You can see that I specified the name of the stored procedure in the variable sProcName, created a Command object for this stored procedure, and set the CommandType. Then I created a new Parameter object using the Add method of the Parameters collection, setting the name to @ItemID and the value to that of the ID passed into this function as the iItemID parameter. The results of executing the stored procedure are then returned to the calling routine as a DataReader object.

Inserting the Content into the Page

The Page_Load event handler in the readnews.aspx page can use the GetNewsItemDR function to get a reference to a DataReader that will extract the values it needs. It also has to collect the style sheet type from the user's current ASP.NET session, or redirect the user to the default.aspx page if there is no existing session. However, this code is the same as you used in the other ancillary pages.

```
Sub Page_Load()
  ' get style sheet size from Session
  sStyleSize = CType(Session("WccStyleSize"), String)

  ' if no value, session has expired or user entered
  ' site at page other than "Home" page
  If sStyleSize = "" Then
    Response.Clear()
    Response.Redirect("default.aspx")
  End If
  ' get news item ID and display the contents
  Dim sNewsID As String = Request.QueryString("id")
  If sNewsID <> "" Then
    Dim dr As SqlDataReader = GetNewsItemDR(Integer.Parse(sNewsID))
    If dr Is Nothing Then
      pNewsText.InnerHtml = "Could not read from database"
    Else
      If dr.Read() Then
        pNewsTitle.InnerHtml = "<b>" & dr.GetString(1) & "</b>"
        pNewsText.InnerHtml = dr.GetString(3)
      End If
    End If
  End If
End Sub
```

The code first collects the value for the "News" item ID, passed to this page in a name/value pair named id appended to the query string. If there is a value here, it is converted to an Integer type using the shared Parse method, and passed to the GetNewsItemDR function.

If there was no error, a DataReader is returned and you can call the Read method of this DataReader to access the first (and only) row of data. The values of the second and fourth columns (at index 1 and 3 because the columns are indexed from zero) are then extracted to get the title and content of the "News" item. These values are inserted into the two <p> elements by setting their InnerHtml properties. In the case of the article title, the value is wrapped in a pair of HTML <b> elements.

> **NOTE** *I look at the use of the* DataReader.GetString *method in more detail shortly.*

Why Use <p> Elements?

To maximize the performance of the page, I used <p> elements rather than asp:Label controls, although these would work just as well. The HtmlGenericControl that implements the <p> elements is "lighter" than the Label control, because it doesn't perform the client detection and other clever styling stuff that the Web Forms Label control does. So there is a marginal performance benefit.

Similar justification could be applied to using a <div> or <span> element in the same way, depending on whether you want output to be "inline" or "block" in HTML/CSS terms. The <p> element provides a blank line above and below its content, which is what I wanted here. If I use <div> elements, the content will appear on separate lines but without the blank line between each <div>. And if I use <span> elements, the content will be wrapped in the current line without any line breaks or blank lines.

> **NOTE** *In the example, each paragraph within the content is itself wrapped in <p> elements, so the kind of element used in the page is not critical. However, if this was not the case, the choice of element would affect the layout of the page. Note that the HTML <p> element only generates a single line of white space before and after the content, irrespective of how many empty nested ones there may be in the page.*

Alternatively, I could have used an asp:Literal control here, like I did in the page banner control in Chapter 5. However, this doesn't have a class or CssClass property, so I would not be able to specify the CSS style class I want for the content of the control. Another possibility would be to create a suitable control dynamically, and then insert it into the page. Again, there is an extra overhead here, but it is a useful technique to be aware of. I'll demonstrate it later in this chapter when I look at the "Compare Models" page.

Before moving on, it's also worth mentioning how to access the contents of a DataReader when extracting values explicitly, as is done in this page (as opposed to data binding, where the values are "implicitly" extracted by the data binding process).

Extracting Values from a DataReader

The DataReader provides a wide range of methods that can be used to return data from it, and I used only the simplest in the "Read News" page. The values of a row in a DataSet table and in a DataReader are exposed as a collection of Item objects. You can access each Item by specifying the column name as a String, or the ordinal index as an Integer (with the first column being indexed as zero):

```
ItemValue = DataReader("column-name")
ItemValue = DataReader(column-index)
```

The value is returned in its native format, in other words as the data type that is defined for the column. So, if the column contains String values (column types char or varchar in SQL Server), both of the previous statements return a String.

However, the DataReader also provides methods that return specific data types from a column (but the column can only be specified by its index within the collection of columns, and not by column name). This sounds really useful until you realize that they don't actually perform any type conversion. For example, if you use the GetDateTime method, and the column is not of type datetime, then an error may occur (VB.NET *might* be able to implicitly convert it to suit the variable type you assign the result to, but C# will not).

```
DateTimeValue = DataReader.GetDateTime(column-index)
```

It also means that you have to check if the column contains <NULL> first using the IsDBNull method. If it does contain <NULL>, you'll get an error when you try and extract the value. However, the specific methods are marginally more efficient, and you may prefer to use them when you can be sure of the data type and the presence of a value in every row.

In earlier code I used the GetString method, and specified the indices of the columns I wanted:

```
pNewsTitle.InnerHtml = "<b>" & dr.GetString(1) & "</b>"
pNewsText.InnerHtml = dr.GetString(3)
```

DataReader *Methods That Return .NET Data Types*

A summary of the methods that return specific data types from a DataReader is shown in Table 6-1. These methods apply to both the SqlDataReader and OleDbDataReader objects (and to OdbcDataReader if you have installed the ODBC Data Provider for .NET v1.0, or if you are using v1.1 of the .NET Framework).

Table 6-1. The Methods of the DataReader That Return .NET Data Type Values

Method	Description
Get*xxx*	Returns a specific data type from a column of that type. The methods that are available are: GetBoolean, GetByte, GetChar, GetDateTime, GetDecimal, GetDouble, GetFloat, GetGuid, GetInt16, GetInt32, GetInt64, and GetString. The column must be specified by its integer index.
GetValue	Returns the value of the column specified by index, in its native format. Effectively the same as specifying the column index or column name only.
GetValues	Returns an array of Object types containing the column values in their native formats.
GetBytes	Reads a stream of bytes from within the specified column into a buffer (array), starting at the given buffer offset. You can also specify the start and end indices within the column to read only part of the content if required.
GetChars	Reads a stream of characters from within the specified column into a buffer (array), starting at the given buffer offset. You can also specify the start and end indices within the column to read only part of the content if required.

> **NOTE** *For a full description of all the members of the OleDbDataReader class, see the .NET SDK topics:*
> ms-help://MS.NETFrameworkSDK/cpref/html/
> frlrfSystemDataOleDbOleDbDataReaderMembersTopic.htm
> ms-help://MS.NETFrameworkSDKv1.1/cpref/html/
> frlrfSystemDataOleDbOleDbDataReaderMembersTopic.htm

DataReader *Methods That Return SQL Server Data Types*

The SqlDataReader object also implements methods that are specific to SQL Server native data types, allowing you to extract data into variables that are declared as these data types (using the types specified within the System.Data.SqlTypes namespace) (Table 6-2). These methods only apply to the SqlDataReader class.

Table 6-2. The Methods of the DataReader That Return SQL Data Type Values

Method	Description
GetSql*xxx*	Returns a specific SQL Server data type from a column of that type. The methods that are available are: GetSqlBinary, GetSqlBoolean, GetSqlByte, GetSqlDateTime, GetSqlDecimal, GetSqlDouble, GetSqlGuid, GetSqlInt16, GetSqlInt32, GetSqlInt64, GetSqlMoney, GetSqlSingle, and GetSqlString.
GetSqlValue	Returns the value of the specified column as a SqlDbType. Variant object.
GetSqlValues	Returns an array of Object types containing the column values in their native SqlType formats.

> **NOTE** *For a full description of all the members of the SqlDataReader class, see the .NET SDK topics:*
> ms-help://MS.NETFrameworkSDK/cpref/html/
> frlrfSystemDataSqlClientSqlDataReaderMembersTopic.htm
> ms-help://MS.NETFrameworkSDKv1.1/cpref/html/
> frlrfSystemDataSqlClientSqlDataReaderMembersTopic.htm

DataReader *Methods That Return Information About the Data*

The DataReader also provides four methods that are useful for finding out more about the data (Table 6-3). You can get the data type for a specific column, get the column name when you know the ordinal index within the row, or get the index when you know the column name. These methods apply to both the SqlDataReader object and the OleDbDataReader object (and to OdbcDataReader if you have installed the ODBC Data Provider for .NET v1.0, or if you are using v1.1 of the .NET Framework).

Table 6-3. The Methods of the DataReader That Return Information About the Data

Method	Description
GetDataTypeName	Returns a String containing the name of the data type for a column, as specified by its ordinal index within the row.
GetFieldType	Returns a Type object representing the data type of a column, as specified by its ordinal index within the row.
GetName	Returns a String containing the name of the column, as specified by its ordinal index within the row.
GetOrdinal	Returns an Integer that is the ordinal index of the column within the row, as specified by its column name.

The "Compare Models" Page

When I was designing the example site, I came up with the following rough sketch of the page where visitors can go to compare the performance and other features of all the vehicles. I decided that I'd provide a list of the models, some options on what type of comparison to carry out, and then show the results as a graphical chart of some type as you see in Figure 6-7.

Figure 6-7. The original sketch of the "Compare Models" page

Figure 6-8 shows the finished page on the site, and it follows the original design quite well. The chart you see is a GIF image that is generated dynamically by ASP.NET from the information in the database, every time the page is accessed. I've added to the original design by including the standard set of links to other pages on the site, positioned as in all the other ancillary pages. And I also added one other feature (just above the chart): the option to show the results as a **Table** instead of a **Chart**.

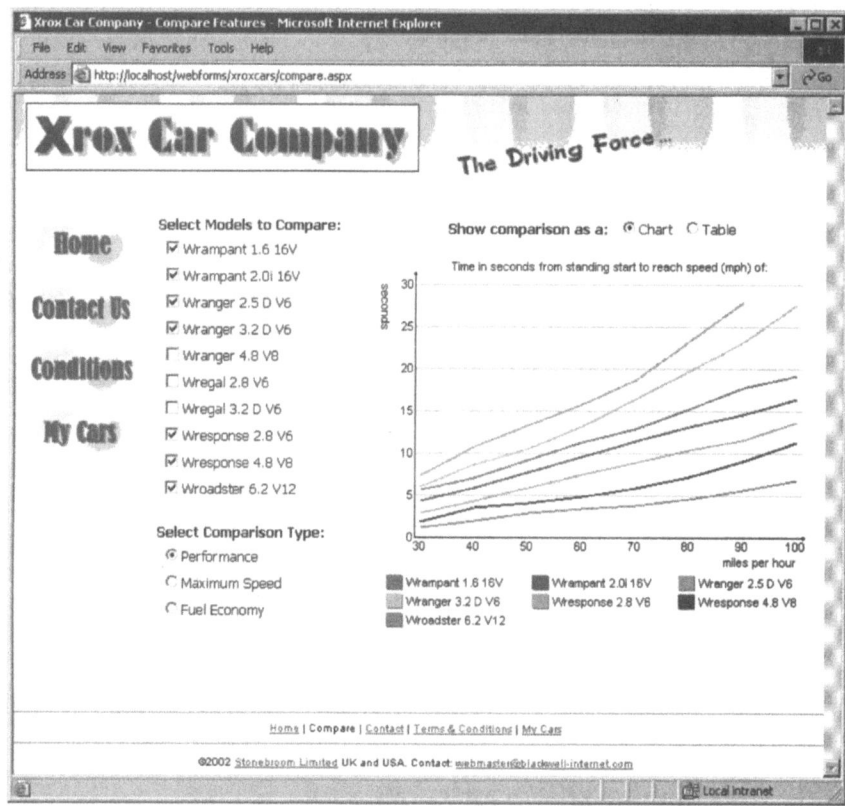

Figure 6-8. The completed version of the "Compare Models" page

Accessibility Issues with Complex Images

The Section 508 Guidelines on Accessibility to Information Technology suggest that you should provide alternative content for any element on a Web site that does not contain plain text. This is because most specialist browsers and user agents can only make sense of text, and not of any other types of content. In the discussion of this topic at the end of Chapter 3, I talked about fulfilling this requirement by adding alt and title attributes that describe the purpose or content of these non-text elements.

The second issue that comes into play, particularly when using charts and graphs, is the guideline that suggests no part of a site should rely solely on color for its meaning. Visitors may suffer from various levels of color blindness, applying to different sets of colors as well, so this guideline makes a lot of sense. In all of the pages up until now, color has been used only for aesthetic reasons, as you can see from the gray-scale screenshots in this book.

All of the precautions I've taken so far to comply with the guidelines are fine with things like text, hyperlinks, and simple images, but what happens when there is something like a chart or graph—as in the "Compare Models" page? The chart depends on colors to differentiate each line. And, for blind or partially sighted visitors, the chart is pretty much useless anyway. There's no way that any kind of user agent is going to be able to convert the information displayed in it to text or aural output.

Using a Long Description

The suggested technique for providing information that equates to the contents of a complex chart or graphic, where the alt attribute cannot reasonably contain this information, is to use the longdesc attribute and/or provide the same information in another format.

The longdesc attribute is part of the HTML 4.01 standard, and applies only to <img> elements. The W3C documentation for HTML 4.01 says that it is used to provide a "long description" of the image to which it is attached, which supplements the text in the alt attribute. This "long description" is the URL (or URI) of a page or text file that describes the content of the image in sufficient detail for the user to obtain as much information about the subject as is contained in the image. So, for a static image, it's possible to provide a long description quite easily.

However, it gets harder when generating images or other non-text content dynamically. Of course, using ASP.NET, or any other dynamic page creation technique, you can easily generate a description as a text string. As an example, if the data comes from a data table, you can iterate through the table building up a string that contains all the column values. Then you just have to assign the URL of this dynamic page to the longdesc attribute. Or you could use the longdesc attribute to point to a dynamic page that uses the same source data, but which writes it into the page as text or as an HTML table.

Of course, there are other possibilities as well. For example, you might use the longdesc attribute to link to a streaming media source that contains an aural description or commentary. Or you can link to a different site or resource that describes the object you feature in more appropriate ways.

Complex Images in Hyperlinks

One interesting issue arises when the image is used within a hyperlink, like this:

```
<a href="somewhere.aspx" title="go somewhere">
  <img src="image.gif" alt="go somewhere" longdesc="moredetails.aspx" />
</a>
```

A normal modern graphical browser may be aware of the longdesc attribute, but is unlikely to provide the user with any way to access it. However, specialist user agents should be able to do so (although few of them seem to at the moment), which means that they must find a way to present the link to the user so that he or she can make a choice—whether to load the page specified in the href attribute of the <a> element, or the page specified in the longdesc attribute of the <img> element.

Adding a "Long Description" Attribute with ASP.NET

In ASP.NET, you can generate image elements in a range of ways, other than using a normal (non-server control) <img> element. For example you might use the HtmlImage or the Web Forms Image server controls, or the Web Forms Hyperlink server control with an image specified for the ImageUrl property (as you do to display the vehicle images in the example "Home" page). However, none of these controls expose a property that you can set to insert a longdesc attribute.

Instead, with an HtmlImage or a Web Forms Image control, you can add a longdesc attribute using the Attributes collection that all ASP.NET server controls expose. If you have a control named MyImageControl, and you have a String variable named sDescription containing the URL of the "long description" page, you can add it as a longdesc attribute using:

```
MyImageControl.Attributes.Add("longdesc", sDescription)
```

However, as you discovered in Chapter 4, you can't add attributes to the <img> element that ASP.NET generates when you use a Web Forms Hyperlink control to display an image as a hyperlink. You can only add attributes to the enclosing <a> element, and in HTML this does not support the longdesc attribute. So, if you do need your complex graphics to be described by a "long description," but also act as a hyperlink (OK, so it's probably not a common scenario), then you must avoid using the ImageUrl property of the Hyperlink control, and use separate Hyperlink and Image controls, or <a> and <img> elements, instead.

Using a "D Link" Hyperlink

As most graphical browsers, and many other user agents, are not able to display or use the longdesc attribute value, other approaches are often used to provide alternative content formats for complex graphically presented information. The suggested technique, and the one most followed at the moment, is to use a "D Link."

A "D Link" is simply a hyperlink within the page containing the complex graphic or other non-text content that opens another page containing the text equivalent of this content. It is functionally equivalent to placing a URL in the longdesc attribute. Figure 6-9 shows how you might position a "D Link" that provides this textual equivalent content—the generally accepted position for such a link.

Figure 6-9. Providing a "D Link" to access alternative content

In fact, providing a "D Link" is actually a great idea as it can benefit all visitors, not just those with restricted sight. Because the hyperlink is visible in all browsers, any visitor can decide to view the text description if he or she prefers without requiring some specially equipped user agent to be able to decode the longdesc attribute. You'll see an example of how useful this technique is at the end of this chapter. Of course, this doesn't mean that you can forget longdesc altogether. It's easy enough to provide both, pointing them to the same URL.

Providing Alternative Content Formats

Having realized that I need to provide alternative content formats for complex images (usually a text description in the same page, or a separate page that contains the description), how do I do this in the "Compare Models" page? I don't use a "D Link" as such in the "Compare Models" page of the **Xrox Car Company** site.

Instead, I've built alternative content format presentation into the page as an integral feature. In fact, you've already seen the answer in the two option buttons above the chart in earlier screenshots. Selecting **Table** causes a postback to the server and produces the page you see in Figure 6-10.

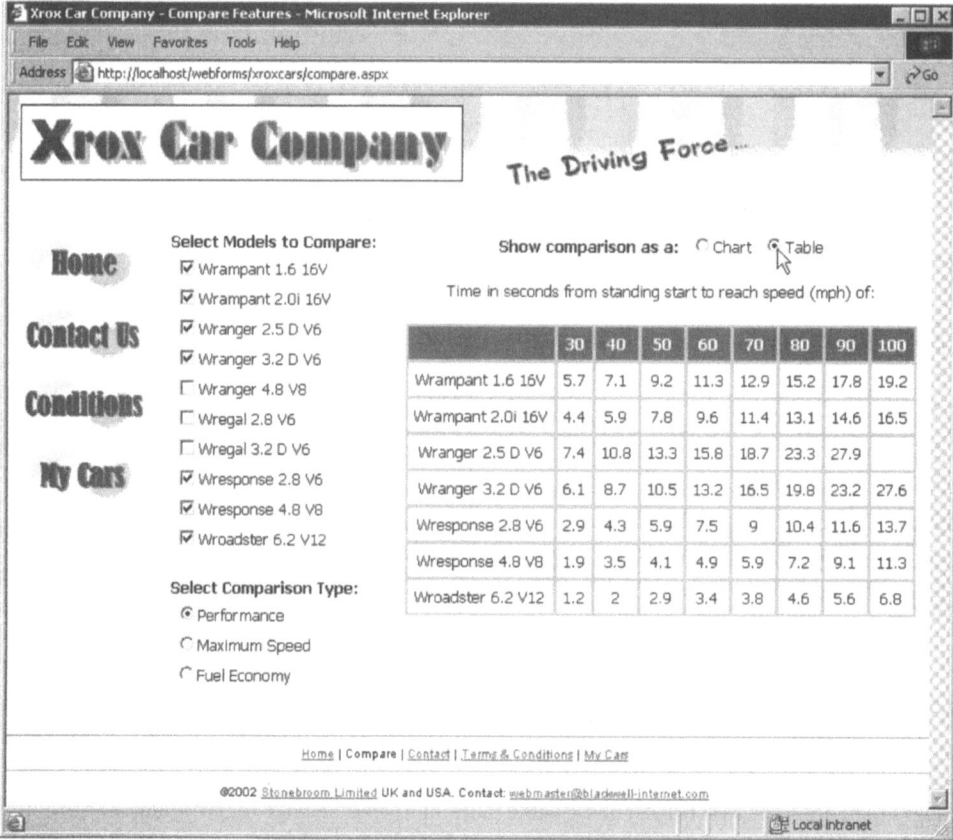

Figure 6-10. Presenting the data as a table instead of a chart

> **NOTE** *I could provide a [D] hyperlink next to the chart (when that mode is selected) that does the same thing as if I'd selected the* Table *option button. However, the option buttons and the page itself use the ASP.NET AutoPostBack feature. This means that the "D Link" would have to run some code to resubmit the form, because the values stored within the form controls are required to be able to build the table of values. And if the client does not support client-side scripting (many text-only browsers and specialist user agents do not), the "D Link" would have to be a Submit button instead.*

Building the "Compare Models" Page

The overall structure of the "Compare Models" page, the way that I select the appropriate style sheet, and the way that I redirect visitors to default.aspx if they have no current ASP.NET session are all very similar to the other ancillary pages. However, it's worth pointing out that I do need to provide an extra "skip to" link in this page, because it contains more than one obvious "content section" that visitors using text-based or aural page readers will want to be able to go straight to. Remember that each interaction with the controls on the example page will cause a postback to the server, and so a visitor using one of these specialist user agents will "start again" at the top of the page each time.

The "Skip To" Links

I provide two "skip to" links so that visitors can go straight to the area of the page that contains the "Select Models to Compare" controls (**Skip to Options**), or direct to the chart or the HTML table that contains the results of the comparison (**Skip to Result**):

compare.aspx

```
<div style="position:absolute;height:0px;"><font size="1" color=#ffffff>
<!-- skip link for aural page readers -->
<layer visibility="hidden">
<a href="#options" style="color:#ffffff;font-size:1px;text-decoration:none"><img
  width="1" height="1" hspace="0" vspace="0" src="images/_blnk.gif"
  border="0" alt="Skip to Options" /></a>
<a href="#result" style="color:#ffffff;font-size:1px;text-decoration:none"><img
  width="1" height="1" hspace="0" vspace="0" src="images/_blnk.gif"
  border="0" alt="Skip to Result" /></a>
</layer>
</font></div>
```

The Main Page Structure Table

The remainder of the page contains the usual page banner and page footer user controls, and the mainlink.ascx control that implements the list of graphical page links in the left-hand side of the page. However, the "content" section of the page is made up of two table cells in this case, rather than just the one I used in the other ancillary pages. The entire structure table is also wrapped in a server-side <form> so that the values of all the controls on the page can be posted back to the server:

```
<form runat="server">
<table width="100%" border="0" cellspacing="0" cellpadding="10">
<tbody>
 <tr>
  <td valign="top" width="105px">
    <wcc:mainlink runat="server" CurrentPageLink="Compare" />
  </td>
  <td align="left" valign="top" nowrap="nowrap">
```

```
    <a name="options" />
    ...
    ... controls to select comparison options go here
    ...
  </td>
  <td align="center" valign="top">
    <a name="result" />
    ...
    ... chart or HTML table containing results goes here
    ...
  </td>
 </tr>
</tbody>
</table>
</form>
```

Next I look at the contents of the second and third cells (the ones with the "skip to" anchors named options and result).

The Controls to Select the Comparison Type

The next code listing shows the HTML declarations I included in the "options" section of the page structure table. I have a couple of ordinary <span> elements that contain the headings for the two groups of controls, a CheckBoxList control to provide the selectable list of vehicle models, and a RadioButtonList that allows selection of one of the three types of comparison. Each element or server control has a class or CssClass attribute that specifies the CSS style to be applied, and the whole lot is enclosed in a <font> element to provide fallback for non-CSS browsers:

```
<font face="Tahoma,Arial,Helvetica,sans-serif" size="2">
<span class="body-text"><b>Select Models to Compare:</b></span>
<asp:CheckBoxList id="chkModels" CssClass="body-text"
                  Font-Size="10"
                  Font-Name="Tahoma,Arial,Helvetica,sans-serif"
                  AutoPostBack="True" runat="server" /><p />
<span class="body-text"><b>Select Comparison Type:</b></span><br />
<asp:RadioButtonList id="optCompareList" CssClass="body-text"
                  Font-Size="10"
                  Font-Name="Tahoma,Arial,Helvetica,sans-serif"
                  AutoPostBack="True" runat="server">
  <asp:ListItem Text="Performance" Selected="True" runat="server" />
  <asp:ListItem Text="Maximum Speed" runat="server" />
  <asp:ListItem Text="Fuel Economy" runat="server" />
</asp:RadioButtonList>
</font>
```

The details of the three option buttons I want in the RadioButtonList control are specified directly using ListItem controls, and I also indicate that I want the first one to be selected by default when the page is first loaded. However, I don't specify any content (ListItem controls) for the CheckBoxList. I'll be filling this "list" using server-side data binding in the Page_Load event, as you'll see when you look at the code in this page later.

Also notice that both the RadioButtonList and CheckBoxList controls include the AutoPostBack="True" attribute, so that the page will be submitted to the server each time the user changes the selections in either list—when adding or removing a vehicle from the list to compare, or when changing the comparison type.

The CheckBoxList *Control vs. the* RadioButtonList *Control*

The reasons for using these two controls are obvious if you have any experience of building user interfaces in a Web page. You want to allow users to select as many models for the comparison as they wish, and the traditional way to present this choice is with a list of check boxes. They can set (check) as many as they like.

However, I only want to generate a result for one of the three possible types of comparison. So I need to present a mutually exclusive set of options for this, and the traditional approach is with "radio buttons" (sometimes called "option buttons"). While it's possible to build pages that use the controls in a different way, it doesn't make sense to do so as it will tend to confuse users. They recognize that they can select more than one check box in a list, but only one radio button from a group.

The ASP.NET RadioButtonList and CheckBoxList controls actually enforce the standard and recognized approach when they are used. The output they produce in the rendered page limits you to using the controls in this way.

For example, the RadioButtonList control automatically sets the name attribute of each radio button element it generates to the same value—the value provided for the id attribute of the control. This causes them to be mutually exclusive when rendered in the browser. On the other hand, the CheckBoxList control creates a different name attribute for each check box element that it generates, using the value of the id that I provided and adding the index of the control within the list (Figure 6-11).

Select Models to Compare:
☑ Wrampant 1.6 16V
☑ Wrampant 2.0i 16V
☑ Wranger 2.5 D V6
☑ Wranger 3.2 D V6
☐ Wranger 4.8 V8
☐ Wregal 2.8 V6
☐ Wregal 3.2 D V6
☑ Wresponse 2.8 V6
☑ Wresponse 4.8 V8
☑ Wroadster 6.2 V12

Select Comparison Type:
⦿ Performance
○ Maximum Speed
○ Fuel Economy

Figure 6-11. The CheckBoxList and RadioButtonList controls

Getting the *Values of* CheckBoxList *and* RadioButtonList *Controls*

The other great thing about these "list" controls is that you can easily access them in server-side code to see which of the controls (radio buttons or check boxes) were selected when the page was posted to the server. The constituent controls for the lists have different id values within the rendered page (when viewed on the client), because this is a condition of the HTML standards. So, I could poke around in the Request.Form collection to see which ones are checked. But ASP.NET makes it much easier than that.

To get the index of the radio button that was selected when the page was posted to the server, you can simply query the SelectedIndex property of the RadioButtonList control. You can also get a reference to a ListItem object that represents the selected radio button from the SelectedItem property of the RadioButtonList control. The ListItem object exposes three useful properties:

- Text—returns the text caption of this item as a String

- Value—returns the value of this item (from the value attribute) as a String

- Selected—returns a Boolean value indicating if the item is checked (or selected)

So, to get the text caption of the selected radio button you can query the control like this:

```
sCaption = RadioButtonList.SelectedItem.Text
```

If you look up the SelectedIndex property for a CheckBoxList or RadioButtonList control in the .NET SDK, you'll find that it returns the index of the *first* selected item in a list control. With a RadioButtonList, there can only be one selected item, so there is no problem using the SelectedIndex property as was done in the preceding code example.

However, a CheckBoxList control allows the user to make multiple selections, and in this case you can't use the SelectedIndex property (unless you only want to get the index of the first one that is selected). Instead, you have to iterate through the Items collection that the CheckBoxList exposes and examine the Selected property of each ListItem control in this collection.

```
Dim lstItem As ListItem
Dim sMessage As String = ""
For Each lstItem In MyCheckBoxList.Items
  If lstItem.Selected Then
    sMessage &= lstItem.Text & " is selected.<br />"
  End If
Next
```

Of course, you can also iterate through the Items collection exposed by a RadioButtonList control if you wish, but this is only likely to be useful if you want to extract a list of the text captions for all the items. In fact you'll see this technique used when you look at the code in the "Compare Models" page shortly.

Getting List Control Values in ASP.NET Version 1.1

In version 1.1 of the .NET Framework, Microsoft added a new property, SelectedValue, to the ListControl base class in the System.Web.UI.WebControls namespace. This is the base class for four of the server controls that you can use in your ASP.NET pages: the DropDownList, CheckBoxList, RadioButtonList, and ListBox.

The SelectedValue property returns the Value property of the item currently selected in the control. So, for the RadioButtonList in the example page, the SelectedValue property would return a value such as "Performance" or "Maximum Speed". However, because I actually want the Integer index of the selected item, this is no help in this particular situation.

For list controls that can have more than one value selected; for example a CheckBoxList; ListBox or DropDownList that has multiple selection enabled; the SelectedValue property returns the value property of the first selected item. Again, this is no help in this situation, as I want to extract the values of all the selected items—not just the first one.

However, in many situations, you will find that the SelectedValue property is a useful short cut that lets you avoid referring to the SelectedItem.Text as I did in the previous section. Just bear in mind that this will prevent your page from working on version 1.0 of the Framework.

The Controls to Display the Results of the Comparison

The third cell of the page's structure table contains the two radio buttons where the user can choose to view the results as a chart or as a table. In this case, to show how it can be done, I've provided the two buttons as separate controls rather than using a RadioButtonList control. I've also included the AutoPostBack="True" attribute, as I did with the other controls on this page:

```
<font face="Tahoma,Arial,Helvetica,sans-serif" size="2">
<span class="body-text"><b>Show comparison as a:</b> </span>
<asp:RadioButton id="optShowChart" CssClass="body-text"
                 GroupName="ShowAs" AutoPostBack="True"
                 Text="Chart" Checked="True" runat="server" /> 
<asp:RadioButton id="optShowTable" CssClass="body-text"
                 GroupName="ShowAs" AutoPostBack="True"
                 Text="Table" runat="server" /><p />
...
</font>
```

The important point to note here is that I've set the GroupName attribute of both the RadioButton controls to the same value. This gives them the same name attribute when rendered in the browser, making them mutually exclusive.

> **NOTE** *Normally, the value provided for the* id *attribute of a server control is also rendered as the* name *attribute, and* id *attributes have to be different for every control on the page or ASP.NET will report a compilation error. The* RadioButtonControl *is the only control where you can specifically set a different value for the* id *and* name *(GroupName) attributes.*

The Controls to Display the Graphical Chart

Following the two radio buttons is an ASP.NET PlaceHolder control. This control does not itself create any output in the page, but simply acts as a container into which you can place other server controls dynamically at runtime. You'll be using it to insert an Image control that displays the graphical chart when the user selects this option with the radio buttons shown in the previous section of the page:

```
...
<!-- placeholder to hold image of results -->
<asp:PlaceHolder id="ctlPlaceholder" runat="server" />
...
```

The Controls to Display an HTML Table of the Results

Next comes a Label control used to display a caption for the table of results when this mode is selected, followed by a DataGrid control to display these results:

```
...
<!-- label to display caption and/or error messages -->
<asp:Label id="lblTableCaption" EnableViewState="False" runat="server" />
<p />
<!-- Datagrid to display results as a table -->
<asp:DataGrid id="dgrResult" EnableViewState="False" runat="server"
              Font-Size="10" Font-Name="Tahoma,Arial,Helvetica,sans-serif"
              BorderStyle="None" BorderWidth="1px" BorderColor="#DEBA84"
              BackColor="#DEBA84" CellPadding="5" CellSpacing="1">
  <HeaderStyle Font-Bold="True" ForeColor="#ffffff"
               BackColor="#b50055" HorizontalAlign="center" />
  <ItemStyle BackColor="#FFF7E7" HorizontalAlign="center" />
  <AlternatingItemStyle backcolor="#FFFFC0" HorizontalAlign="center" />
</asp:DataGrid>
...
```

You can see that a number of formatting options are specified in the DataGrid to give it an attractive appearance. It's often hard to figure out what values are needed for all these attributes to give the required result, and I "cheated" here by using a page designer tool to build the control declaration for me.

Microsoft has a free tool available called ASP.NET Web Matrix. This is a lightweight but extremely comprehensive and competent tool for building ASP.NET pages. It includes an **Auto Format** feature for the DataGrid and DataList controls that is just about identical to the one found in Visual Studio .NET. I used it to create a formatted DataGrid, then copied the resulting source code into the page and adjusted it to get the final appearance I wanted (Figure 6-12).

Figure 6-12. Applying styles to a table in ASP.NET Web Matrix

> **NOTE** *You can download Web Matrix from the ASP.NET community site at* http://www.asp.net/. *A useful introduction to Web Matrix is also available as a free PDF document from* http://www.daveandal.com/books/webmatrix/.

The Invisible Submit Button

The final control I include in this section of the page is a Submit button, implemented with an ASP.NET Button server control. I've specified AutoPostBack for all of the check boxes and radio buttons in the page, so that users only have to make a selection in the various controls on the page and it is refreshed from the server automatically. So why do I need a Submit button?

The reason is that I want the page to work without client-side scripting if possible—especially for text-based and aural page reader user agents that often do not provide this feature. In this case, I need a Submit button to post the page back to the server:

```
...
<!-- button to submit form if no client-side scripting -->
<p class="body-text">
<asp:Button id="btnGo" CssClass="body-text"
            Text="Compare..." Visible="False" runat="server" /></p>
</font>
```

Of course, as the Visible attribute is set to False, the button will not actually be included in the page sent to the client. However, in the Page_Load event handler, you can set the Visible property to True at run time if you detect that the current browser or user agent does not support client-side scripting.

The Code to Make It All Work

Having looked at the declaration of the HTML, content, and server controls that make up the "Compare Models" page, you can now move on and look at the server-side code that makes it all work. This page is opened from one of two links in the "Home" page. The first possibility is that it is opened from the link in the left-hand "News" section of that page. In this case, there is no query string appended to the URL, as you can see in the status bar of Figure 6-13.

Figure 6-13. Opening the "Compare Models" page from the link in the "News" section of the "Home" page

However, the "Compare Models" page can also be opened from the right-hand section of the "Home" page where the list of models is displayed. Following the description of each of the five base models is a [compare models] hyperlink. The data binding templates used in the DataList control that creates this section of the page adds the ID of each model to the query string of the URL for these links. You can see it in the browser's status bar in Figure 6-14.

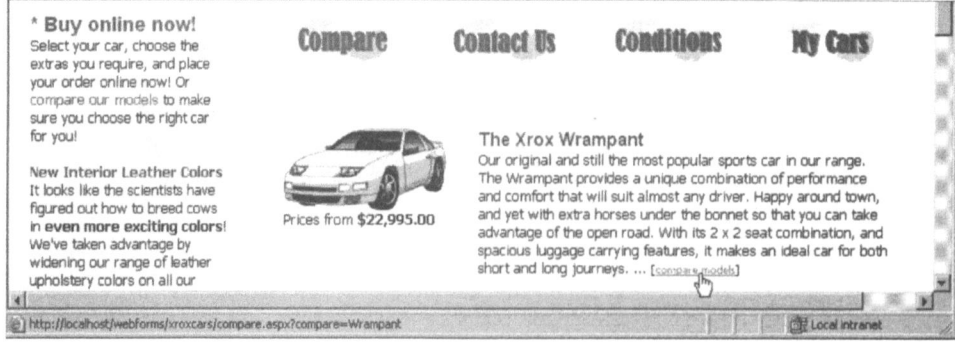

Figure 6-14. Opening the "Compare Models" page from a link in the "Model List" section of the "Home" page

Summarizing the Requirements

So, when the "Compare Models" page loads from one of these hyperlinks, I want the appropriate check boxes to be set automatically and to generate the comparison results. However, when the page is opened from the link in the "News" section, where there is no query string appended to the URL, I just want to display the page with no selections in the check boxes and no results displayed. So, I can summarize the requirements for the code as follows.

When the page first loads (this is not a postback), the code needs to:

- Collect the name of the style sheet for this client from the current ASP.NET session, or redirect the user to default.aspx if there is no value in the session (because it has expired or because the user entered the site at this page instead of the "Home" page).

- See if the client's browser supports scripting, and if not make the Submit button visible.

- Generate a list of values to populate the CheckBoxList with the combination of car models and engine types.

- Look for an ID value in the query string. If there is one, select the appropriate check boxes.

- Generate a chart (this is the default, rather than a table) showing the results of the comparison on Performance (again, this is the default). This only happens if one or more of the check boxes is selected.

When the user changes any of the values in the check boxes, or in either of the two radio button lists (and clicks **Compare** if client-side scripting is not available), a postback occurs. In this case, as the page loads, the code needs to:

- Collect the name of the style sheet for this client from the current ASP.NET session, or redirect the user to default.aspx if there is no value in the session.

- See if the client's browser supports scripting, and if not make the Submit button visible.

- See which type of display (**Chart** or **Table**) the user selected.

- Generate the chart or table showing the results of the currently selected comparison type, but again only if one or more of the check boxes is selected.

The Page-Level Variables

Several variables from within more than one function or routine in the page need to be accessed. Some of these variables are passed as parameters to the other routines, or returned directly as the result of a function. However, for the most commonly used values, declare them as page-level variables that will automatically be available within any routine in the page. For the style sheet name part, sStyleSize, this is actually a requirement because it is inserted into the page using the traditional ASP 3.0 technique with <% = sStyleSize %> as was done in the pages you looked at previously:

```
<script runat="server">
' page-level variable to hold database connection string
Dim sConnect As String

' page-level variable to style sheet size
Dim sStyleSize As String = ""

' page-level variable to hold client script ability
Dim bCanScript As Boolean

' page-level variable to hold text comparison description
Dim sCompareType As String = ""
```

The Page_Load *Event Handler*

Based on the requirements summary for the sample code you saw earlier, the next listing of the Page_Load event should immediately make sense. The database connection string is collected from web.config. The name part of the style sheet and the Boolean value that indicates if the current browser supports client-side scripting are then collected from the current ASP.NET session (remember that the code detected this and set the value in the default.aspx and "Home" pages when the visitor first entered the site).

If there is no ASP.NET session, perform the redirection to default.aspx, and if there is no client-side scripting support available make the Submit button visible in the page:

```
Sub Page_Load()
  ' get database connection string from web.config
  sConnect = ConfigurationSettings.AppSettings("XroxCarsConnectString")
  ' get style sheet size from Session
  sStyleSize = CType(Session("WccStyleSize"), String)

  ' if no value, session has expired or user entered
  ' site at page other than "Home" page
  If sStyleSize = "" Then
    Response.Clear()
    Response.Redirect("default.aspx")
  End If
  ' see if client supports client-side scripting
  bCanScript = CType(Session("WccCanScript"), Boolean)
```

```
' if not make "Compare" submit button visible
' because AutoPostBack will not work
If Not bCanScript Then
  btnGo.Visible = True
End If
...
```

Figure 6-15 shows the relevant section of the page when the client does not support client-side scripting. The page is still completely usable, except that visitors must click the **Compare** button after making their comparison selections.

Figure 6-15. The "Compare" button that appears when client-side scripting is not available

You could, of course, include this button in the page irrespective of the presence of client-side script support, but this is confusing for users. They might click the button after making a selection in one of the lists, and cause the page to be (partly) executed twice if client-side scripting is available. It also makes the whole thing a lot less intuitive and requires users to experiment to discover that they don't need to click the button (and, if not, why is it there?).

However, there is a flip side to consider. Would it be better to always show the **Compare** button and *not* use auto-postback? That way, users could make several changes in the lists of options without causing a postback and having to wait for the results of each individual selection. It really depends on how quickly the results get back to them. I chose the auto-postback scenario, but you might decide to use the other approach.

Checking for a PostBack

The next step in the Page_Load event is to see if this is a postback, or if it's the first time the page has been loaded. In both cases you may have to generate the chart or table of results (depending on the current selections made in the check boxes and radio buttons in the page), and there is also some extra work to do the first time the page is loaded.

I've written a couple of separate routines that, between them, carry out the bulk of the work of creating the page. A routine named ShowComparison is responsible for generating the results as a chart or table. It checks that at least one vehicle is selected, and takes into account the settings for the comparison type (performance, fuel consumption, or maximum speed) and the kind of result required (chart or table). I also have a separate function named GetModelListDR, which returns a DataReader containing the list of vehicle types and engine combinations to populate the list of check boxes.

So, in line with the outline specification of the code requirements for the Page_Load event handler, check the IsPostBack property to see if this request arises from the page being posted back. If it does, simply call the ShowComparison routine to generate the results:

```
...
If Page.IsPostBack Then
  ' generate chart for selected items
  ShowComparison()

Else
  ' first time page has loaded, not a postback, so
  ' set DataSource for "car models" list and data-bind it
  chkModels.DataSource = GetModelListDR()
  chkModels.DataTextField = "ViewName"
  chkModels.DataBind()

  ' see if a model was specified in query string
  ' if so, need to generate chart or table this time
  Dim sQuery As String = Request.QueryString("compare")
  If sQuery <> "" Then

    ' select the appropriate checkboxes
    Dim lstItem As ListItem
    For Each lstItem In chkModels.Items
      If lstItem.Text.IndexOf(sQuery) = 0 Then
        lstItem.Selected = "True"
      End If
    Next

    ' generate chart of comparisons
    ShowComparison()

  End If
End If
End Sub
```

If it is not a postback, the Else section of the preceding code is executed. In it the page calls the GetModelListDR function to get a DataReader that will extract the list of vehicles, and assigns this as the DataSource property of the CheckBoxList control. Specify that the column named ViewName should be used to provide the text captions for the check boxes, and call the DataBind method to display the results.

Managing and Using the Viewstate

By default the ASP.NET postback architecture automatically maintains the values of all server controls in a page between round-trips to the server through the *viewstate* (I discussed this topic in Chapter 1), unless I specifically "turn it off" for a page or for individual controls within the page. This includes the contents of "list" controls, such as the CheckBoxList control, and explains why it only needs to be populated when this is *not* a postback. When the page is posted back, ASP.NET automatically uses the viewstate to populate the values of the CheckBoxList control.

However, it's worth bearing in mind how this useful automatic feature will affect the contents of the page when using server controls. Two particular issues here are the way that it affects the Label and DataGrid controls used in the right-hand section of the page. The Label control is used to display captions or error messages each time the page loads, and you don't want this Label to remember any previous values. So, the EnableViewState="False" attribute is added to the control declaration to prevent this.

Even more important is the DataGrid that you use to display the results as a table when the user selects this option. The entire contents of the table are created dynamically from the database every time, and there is absolutely no reason why you would want the table to be repopulated with the previous values following a postback. So, again, the EnableViewState="False" attribute is included in the declaration of this control.

Just to give you an idea what effect this has, with the EnableViewState="False" attribute added to the DataGrid control, the viewstate that is included within the page (in the hidden-type input control that ASP.NET automatically generates within the <form> section) is around 850 characters when all 10 vehicles are selected. Without the EnableViewState="False" attribute (remember that the default is "True" if it is omitted), the viewstate grows to over 6,500 characters.

Generating all this extra unnecessary data for every page interaction puts more load on the server, and it also gets sent over the wire twice with every postback—once when the user interacts with the page and submits it, and again when the new page is delivered.

Setting the CheckBox Controls

I haven't quite finished with the Page_Load event handler yet. When this is not a postback, the page needs to collect any value that might be in the query string and set the appropriate matching check boxes. As you saw earlier, the query string can contain a name/value pair such as compare=Wregal if the user clicked one of the [compare models] links in the right-hand side of the "Home" page.

In this case, you need to iterate through the Items collection of the CheckBoxList control, and see if the caption (the Text property of the ListItem) starts with the model name contained in the query string. If it does, you can set (check) that check box by setting the Selected property of the corresponding ListItem to True. The relevant code is repeated here so that you can see what is happening:

```
' see if a model was specified in query string
' if so, need to generate chart or table this time
Dim sQuery As String = Request.QueryString("compare")
If sQuery <> "" Then
```

```
' select the appropriate checkboxes
Dim lstItem As ListItem
For Each lstItem In chkModels.Items
  If lstItem.Text.IndexOf(sQuery) = 0 Then
    lstItem.Selected = "True"
  End If
Next

' generate chart of comparisons
ShowComparison()

End If
```

If there is a value in the query string, after setting the appropriate check boxes, call the ShowComparison function to generate the results for the selected model in all available engine sizes.

> **NOTE** *If you are used to VBScript in ASP 3.0 and earlier, you may be wondering why I compare the result of the IndexOf method to zero (rather than one) when I want to find out if the match is at the beginning of the string. This is because the .NET language-agnostic IndexOf method treats strings as being zero-based rather than one-based.*

Getting the Car and Engine Data

Earlier, I mentioned the two routines I used in the Page_Load event handler. The ShowComparison routine is discussed in detail later in this chapter. Next, however, I want to show you how the other of these two routines works—namely the GetModelListDR function.

The database contains several tables that provide the information to drive the whole of the **Xrox Car Company** Web site. Of particular interest here are the three tables that contain the bulk of the information about the vehicles themselves. The table named tblCar contains the details that are specific to each vehicle model, such as the model name, number of doors, and so on. Meanwhile, the table named tblEngine contains details that are specific to each of the engines offered, such as the engine name (for example, "**6.8 V12**"), the cubic capacity, and the fuel type (Figure 6-16).

The third table shown in Figure 6-16, tblCarEngines, links the other two tables. Although there are only have five base vehicle models, most are available with more than one engine option. For example, the **Wregal** sedan is available with the 2.8 liter V6 gas/petrol engine or the 3.2 liter V6 diesel engine. The tblCarEngines table contains a row for each of the available vehicle/engine combinations, using the key values of the vehicle (CarID) and the engine (EngineID).

Figure 6-16. The tblCarEngines, tblCar, and tblEngines tables in the database

Notice also that the tblCarEngines table contains other information. Some details about a vehicle depend on both the model and the engine, and not on just one of these factors. Examples shown in Figure 6-16 are the performance, maximum speed, and fuel consumption. It's these values that I'll use in the charts and tables that compare the features of each vehicle.

The GetModelEngineCombinedList *Stored Procedure*

To populate the CheckBoxList that contains the list of all available cars with an entry for each engine option for every car, there needs to be a rowset that has a row for every possible valid combination of car and engine. However, there only needs to be a single column containing the text for the captions of the check boxes—as shown in Figure 6-17.

This caption is made up of the car model name and the engine name, which are in the two tables tblCar and tblEngine. So, the stored procedure has to JOIN these two tables with the tblCarEngines table, using the appropriate key columns (CarID and EngineID) in each table.

Select Models to Compare:

☑ Wrampant 1.6 16V

☑ Wrampant 2.0i 16V

☑ Wranger 2.5 D V6

☑ Wranger 3.2 D V6

☐ Wranger 4.8 V8

☐ Wregal 2.8 V6

☐ Wregal 3.2 D V6

☑ Wresponse 2.8 V6

☑ Wresponse 4.8 V8

☑ Wroadster 6.2 V12

Figure 6-17. The CheckBoxList and captions for each vehicle/engine combination

Having done so, it extracts and returns a single column named ViewName, containing text string values that are made up by concatenating the values of the Model column from the tblCar table, a space character, and the EngineName column from the tblEngines table. The rows are then sorted by model name and engine name:

```
CREATE PROCEDURE GetModelEngineCombinedList AS
SELECT ViewName = tblCar.Model + ' ' + tblEngine.EngineName
FROM (tblCar JOIN tblCarEngines ON tblCar.CarID = tblCarEngines.CarID)
     JOIN tblEngine ON tblEngine.EngineID = tblCarEngines.EngineID
ORDER BY tblCar.Model, tblEngine.EngineName
```

Populating the CheckboxList of Models and Engine Types

The stored procedure you've just looked at is used in the GetModelListDR function that provides the DataSource property of the CheckBoxList control. It is called in exactly the same way as the stored procedures used in the "Home" page. The page-level variable named sConnect contains the connection string, and it is used when the Connection object is created. From this you can create a Command object that references the stored procedure, and call its ExecuteReader method to return a DataReader:

```
' function to create list of models for CheckBoxList captions
Function GetModelListDR() As SqlDataReader
  Try
    Dim sqlConnect As SqlConnection = New SqlConnection(sConnect)
    Dim sProcName As String = "GetModelEngineCombinedList"
    Dim sqlComm As SqlCommand = New SqlCommand(sProcName, sqlConnect)
    sqlComm.CommandType = CommandType.StoredProcedure
    sqlConnect.Open
    Return sqlComm.ExecuteReader(CommandBehavior.CloseConnection)
  Catch
    lblTableCaption.Text = "Sorry, the database cannot be accessed."
    Return Nothing
  End Try
End Function
```

If there is an error, a simple text message is displayed in the Label control above the "results" chart or table.

Generating the Comparison Results

The "Compare Models" page now contains all the controls that the user can interact with, and the CheckBoxList showing the list of available model and engine combinations has been populated. The only feature of the page that you still need to explore is how to generate the table or graphical chart that displays the results of the selected comparison.

The ShowComparison Routine

The code in the Page_Load event handler I showed earlier calls a routine named ShowComparison when the page loads, and this does all the work of creating the chart or table of results. The first step is to see if any check boxes are selected, and you can easily do this by examining the `SelectedIndex` property of the `CheckBoxList` control. You'll recall that this returns the index of the first selected item in the list.

Which checkboxes are selected at the moment is of no concern; I only want to know if there are *any* selected. If none are selected, the `SelectedIndex` property returns `-1`, and in this case you can just exit from the routine:

```
' routine to show the comparison image or table
Sub ShowComparison()

  ' see if any checkboxes are selected
  ' if not just exit from routine
  If chkModels.SelectedIndex = -1 Then Exit Sub
  ...
```

However, if there are any selected, the code continues by collecting the type of comparison that the user specified in the three radio buttons (**Performance**, **Fuel Consumption**, or **Maximum Speed**). These three options are exposed by the `RadioButtonList` control named `optCompareList`, and you can get a `String` value that describes the comparison type by querying the `Text` property of the currently selected radio button. This returns the caption for that button, which you can use in the caption displayed above the results table, and in the `alt` attribute of the chart:

```
  ...
  ' get text comparison description
  sCompareType = optCompareList.SelectedItem.Text
  ...
```

> **NOTE** *Alternatively, if you are prepared to limit the application to running on ASP.NET version 1.1, you can just query the SelectedValue property of the* `RadioButtonList` *control:*
> `sCompareType = optCompareList.SelectedValue` ' version 1.1 only

Next, check to see which type of comparison is being performed. The two radio buttons above the chart or table are individual controls, rather than a `RadioButtonList` control, and have the values `optShowChart` and `optShowTable` for their `id` properties. So you can see if the **Chart** option was selected by examining the `Checked` property of this radio button directly:

```
  ...
  'see if we are generating a chart or a table
  If optShowChart.Checked Then
  ...
```

Creating the ASP.NET Image Element for the Chart

If the user is expecting the page to generate a chart, execute the code shown in the next listing. It creates a new ASP.NET Image element, and sets the ImageURL (which generates the src attribute) to the value returned by another function in the page named GetImageURL. You'll look at this function towards the end of this chapter, but for now just accept that it will provide a suitable value for the src property of the ‹img› element being created.

Next, the code sets the AlternateText property (which generates the alt attribute) to a string that includes the comparison type previously collected in the variable named sCompareType. Then it creates a string suitable for the longdesc attribute, and adds it to the Image element using the Add method of the Attributes collection, as I showed earlier in this chapter:

```
...
' insert new Image element for chart into page
' could pass values in session but using the
' query string is probably more efficient
Dim ctlImage As New Image()
ctlImage.ImageUrl = GetImageURL()
ctlImage.AlternateText = " Chart showing comparison of " & sCompareType
Dim sLongDesc As String
sLongDesc = "Use the option buttons located just before this " _
            & "chart to display the data as a text-based table."
ctlImage.Attributes.Add("longdesc", sLongDesc)
ctlPlaceholder.Controls.Add(ctlImage)
...
```

The final line in the preceding code then inserts this new Image element into the page as a child of the ASP.NET PlaceHolder control that was declared within the page. When the page is rendered, the PlaceHolder itself produces no output, but the Image element is rendered just like it would be if you had declared it directly within the HTML section of the page.

For example, if you select just the **Wranger 2.5 D V6** model, the content that is rendered to the client looks like this (the Image control adds the border="0" attribute automatically by default):

```
<!-- placeholder to hold image of results -->
<img longdesc="Use the option buttons located just before this chart to display the
data as a text-based table."
     src="compare-chart.aspx?ctype=0&amp;list=Wranger+2.5+D+V6"
     alt="Chart showing comparison of Performance" border="0" />
```

Meanwhile, the DataGrid control that is also declared in the page will only produce output when it is data bound, and so it will not appear when the **Chart** option is selected.

Creating the HTML Table of Results

However, if the user has selected the **Table** option rather than **Chart**, the `Else` section of
the `ShowComparison` function is executed instead. In it the page calls a function named
`GetCompareDR`, and assigns the `DataReader` it returns to the `DataSource` property of the
`DataGrid` in the right-hand side of the page, then calls the `DataBind` method:

```
   ...
  Else  'generate a table of the results
    ' Set DataSource and bind DataReader to DataGrid
    dgrResult.DataSource = GetCompareDR()
    dgrResult.DataBind()

  End If
End Sub
```

This is all you have to do to show the comparison data as a table, and you can
see that the result is well worth the small amount of effort involved (see Figure 6-10
earlier in this chapter).

But, of course, the interesting part comes in how to access the database to get
the values for the `DataGrid` control's `DataSource` property.

SQL Statement or Stored Procedure?

In all of the pages so far, a stored procedure within the database is used to extract the
rows that are bound to the various controls in the page. However, there are cases
where it makes sense to execute a SQL statement directly, rather than writing
a stored procedure. For example, if you want to extract different sets of columns, pass
in a varying number of parameters each time, carry out complex manipulation of the
values, or perform some non-standard type of formatting of the data, a suitable
stored procedure can soon become impossibly unwieldy. On top of this, the database
may not be able to precompile and optimize the procedure, reducing the benefits
that stored procedures can provide.

In this case, the `WHERE` clause that is needed to specify the rows wanted from the
`tblCarEngines` table will contain anything between 1 and 10 pairs of values (because
the user can select any number of vehicles for a comparison at one time). So you
would need a stored procedure to accept 10 pairs of parameters—the car model
name and engine name for each selected vehicle—and then test which of these
should be used in the `WHERE` clause. It makes much more sense to build the `WHERE`
clause dynamically within the ASP.NET code, and use it as part of the executed SQL
statement to get the desired results.

Generating the Required SQL Statement

I created a function named GetSqlStatement that returns the complete SQL statement that's needed to extract the required rows from the database. After declaring a couple of variables for use within the function, examine the SelectedIndex property of the RadioButtonList control that contains the three comparison options (**Performance, Fuel Consumption,** or **Maximum Speed**). Depending on the current selection in this list, generate a suitable "first section" of the SQL statement. And, as a by-product within the Select Case statement, create the matching caption to place in the Label control above the table of results, and then display it by assigning it to that control's Text property:

```
' function to create SQL statement to extract comparison values
Function GetSqlStatement() As String

  Dim sResult, sCaption As String
  ' see which comparison type is selected
  ' and create SELECT part of SQL statement
  Select Case optCompareList.SelectedIndex

    Case 0     ' compare Performance
      sCaption = "Time in seconds from standing start to reach speed of:"
      sResult = "SELECT [ ] = Model + ' ' + EngineName, " _
              & "[30] = Perf30, [40] = Perf40, [50] = Perf50, " _
              & "[60] = Perf60, [70] = Perf70, [80] = Perf80, " _
              & "[90] = Perf90, [100] = Perf100 " _
              & "FROM (tblCar JOIN tblCarEngines ON " _
              & "tblCar.CarID = tblCarEngines.CarID) " _
              & "JOIN tblEngine ON " _
              & "tblEngine.EngineID = tblCarEngines.EngineID WHERE "

    Case 1     ' compare Maximum Speed
      sCaption = "Maximum speed (mph) in each gear:"
      sResult = "SELECT [ ] = Model + ' ' + EngineName, " _
              & "[1st] = Speed1st, [2nd] = Speed2nd, [3rd] = Speed3rd, " _
              & "[4th] = Speed4th, [5th] = Speed5th, [6th] = Speed6th " _
              & "FROM (tblCar JOIN tblCarEngines ON " _
              & "tblCar.CarID = tblCarEngines.CarID) " _
              & "JOIN tblEngine ON " _
              & "tblEngine.EngineID = tblCarEngines.EngineID WHERE "

    Case 2     ' compare Fuel Consumption
      sCaption = "Fuel consumption (mpg) at a steady speed (mph) of:"
      sResult = "SELECT [ ] = Model + ' ' + EngineName, " _
              & "[30] = Fuel30, [40] = Fuel40, [50] = Fuel50, " _
              & "[60] = Fuel60, [70] = Fuel70, [80] = Fuel80, " _
              & "[90] = Fuel90, [100] = Fuel100 " _
              & "FROM (tblCar JOIN tblCarEngines ON " _
              & "tblCar.CarID = tblCarEngines.CarID) " _
              & "JOIN tblEngine ON " _
              & "tblEngine.EngineID = tblCarEngines.EngineID WHERE "
```

```
End Select
' set caption for table
lblTableCaption.Text = sCaption
...
```

You can see that the same `JOIN` is performed on the three tables as was done when getting the list of models for the check boxes earlier on. This is because you'll need to access the model name and engine name in the `WHERE` clause, as you'll see shortly. Also notice that the columns are renamed ("aliased" in SQL-Server terms), so that the names are suitable for use directly in the `DataGrid` control when displaying the results as a table.

The reason for this is that no templates have been declared for the `DataGrid` to control the way the data is presented (you can confirm this by looking back at the HTML section of the page shown earlier in this chapter). The `DataGrid` will be used to display three different sets of data, depending on the selected comparison type, and so the column headings can't be specified up front in the HTML declaration. It's easier to extract the data rows with appropriate column names than to add suitable templates to the `DataGrid` dynamically afterwards (though it is possible to do it this way if you prefer).

Notice that, to specify a column name that starts with a non-alphabetic character, you must enclose it in square brackets. I also wanted to leave the column heading above the vehicle name empty, so I used the HTML non-breaking space character ` ` for this column name—a useful trick when displaying data in a Web page.

Specifying the WHERE Clause

The final section of the `GetSqlStatement` routine is used to create the `WHERE` clause for the SQL statement. However, this is not quite as simple as it might at first appear. The `CheckBoxList` control does not have any facility to store values for each item in the list other than as the `Text` property of each `ListItem` control within the list. There is no way to set the `value` attribute of the individual check boxes that are generated by a `CheckBoxList`.

So, the only thing you can extract from each `ListItem` control is the value of the `Text` property, which is a combination of the model name and the engine name. You have to specify both of these in the `WHERE` clause, and match them to the values in the `Model` and `EngineName` columns of the `tblCar` and `tblEngines` tables. This is why the three-way `JOIN` you saw earlier in the SQL statement has to be performed.

This next listing shows the code used to create the `WHERE` clause. Iterate through the `Items` collection of the `CheckBoxList` control, and test each one to see if it is selected. If it is, extract the model name and the engine name from the `Text` property of that `ListItem`, and add a section to the `WHERE` clause for that particular vehicle:

```
...
' create WHERE clause section for each selected checkbox
Dim lstItem As ListItem
Dim sText, sModel, sEngine As String
```

```
For Each lstItem In chkModels.Items
  If lstItem.Selected Then
    sText = lstItem.Text
    sModel = sText.Substring(0, sText.IndexOf(" "))
    sEngine = sText.Substring(sText.IndexOf(" ") + 1)
    sResult &= "(Model = '" & sModel & "' AND EngineName = '" _
            & sEngine & "') OR "
  End If
Next
...
```

> **NOTE** *This does, of course, depend on the data content—it will fail if the model name contains a space. If you suspect that this is a possibility, and to provide more bulletproof code, you might prefer to use a specific delimiter character to separate the parts of the caption. Other techniques include building an array of the values, so that you can look them up in this array using the index of the checkbox.*

For each vehicle that is selected, this creates a matching section of the WHERE clause, for example:

```
"(Model = 'Wregal' AND EngineName = '2.8 V6') OR "
```

Then, after examining all the ListItem controls, strip off the extra OR, and add an ORDER BY clause that sorts the rows by model name and then by engine name:

```
  ...
  ' remove final "OR" from string
  sResult = sResult.SubString(0, sResult.Length - 4)

  ' add ORDER BY clause and return result
  Return sResult & " ORDER BY Model, EngineName"

End Function
```

Getting a DataReader *of Results for the* DataGrid

All that remains now is to execute the SQL statement just created to get the required rowset. This is done in the GetCompareDR function you saw being used earlier to set the DataSource property of the DataGrid. It is very similar to the other functions I used to get a DataReader, but this time I specify the SQL statement when creating the Command object rather than a stored procedure name, and tell the Command that it's a SQL statement by setting the CommandType property to the value Text:

```
          function to get DataReader of values for comparison table
Function GetCompareDR() As SqlDataReader

  Try
    Dim sqlConnect As SqlConnection = New SqlConnection(sConnect)
    ' get SELECT statement to extract the data
    Dim sSQL As String = GetSqlStatement()

    Dim sqlComm As SqlCommand = New SqlCommand(sSQL, sqlConnect)
    sqlComm.CommandType = CommandType.Text    ' SQL statement
    sqlConnect.Open
    Return sqlComm.ExecuteReader(CommandBehavior.CloseConnection)
  Catch
    lblTableCaption.Text = "Sorry, the database cannot be accessed."
    Return Nothing
  End Try
End Function
```

> **NOTE** *In fact, the default value for the* CommandType, *if you don't specify otherwise,*
> *is* CommandType.Text. *However, I prefer to specify it explicitly, as this makes it obvi-*
> *ous what's going on to anyone using the code.*

Creating the Chart Image URL and Query String

The one piece of code in the "Compare Models" page that you haven't looked at yet is
the GetImageURL function. You'll recall that I used this function to set the ImageUrl
property of the Image control (the src attribute of the <img> element) that is inserted
into the page when displaying the data as a chart rather than as a table.

The graphical chart is created as a GIF image by a separate ASP.NET page. This
means that all the values required must be passed to the ASP.NET page so that it can
create the appropriate chart. I'll discuss the reasons for using a separate page, what
other options are available, and some other ways to pass values between pages in the
Chapter 7 when you look at how to create the chart.

In the meantime, here's the code I used for the GetImageURL function. It works
much like the code I used to create the SQL statement's WHERE clause earlier on, but
this time the values are assembled into a format that is better suited for use in
a query string:

```
' function to generate URL and query string for image
Function GetImageURL() As String

  Dim sQuery As String = ""
  ' create a string for each selected checkbox
  Dim lstItem As ListItem
  Dim sText, sModel, sEngine As String
  For Each lstItem In chkModels.Items
```

```
      If lstItem.Selected Then
        sText = lstItem.Text
        sModel = sText.Substring(0, sText.IndexOf(" "))
        sEngine = sText.Substring(sText.IndexOf(" ") + 1)
        sQuery &= sModel & " " & sEngine & "*"
      End If
    Next
    ' remove final "*" from string
    sQuery = sQuery.SubString(0, sQuery.Length - 1)

    ' use string of models to build complete URL
    Return "compare-chart.aspx?ctype=" _
           & optCompareList.SelectedIndex.ToString _
           & "&list=" & Server.UrlEncode(sQuery)

End Function
```

At the end of the function, I build up the complete URL by appending the query string I've created to the name of the page that creates the chart (compare-chart.aspx) plus a name/value pair that specifies the selection type (using the SelectedIndex value I extracted earlier from the RadioButtonList). As an example of the result, when the user selects the first two of the **Wranger** models, the value that is returned from the function looks like this:

```
compare-chart.aspx?ctype=0&list=Wranger+2.5+D+V6*Wranger+3.2+D+V6
```

In the next chapter, I'll be looking at the way the charts you see in the "Compare Models" page as you select various types of comparison are created, as well as looking at how to create other types of chart. However, to finish off this chapter, I'll very briefly show you how the page works in a couple of specialist user agents that cannot handle graphics—and which benefit from the ability to display the data as an HTML table.

Testing for Accessibility

The "Compare Models" page I've created looks fine in all the graphical browsers that are usually used to test the pages. However, I really do need to test it in the other specialist and non-graphical user agents I want to support as well. So in the final section of this chapter, I'll show you how it works in the Lynx text-only browser and in the IBM Home Page Reader.

Using a Text-Only Browser

In Figure 6-18, I've opened the "Compare Models" page in Lynx from the **[compare models]** link in the "Home" page for the **Xrox Wrampant**. You can see the two "skip to" links I placed at the top of the page, with the **Skip to Result** link highlighted. The check boxes for each vehicle, and the first two of the comparison type radio buttons, can also be seen here.

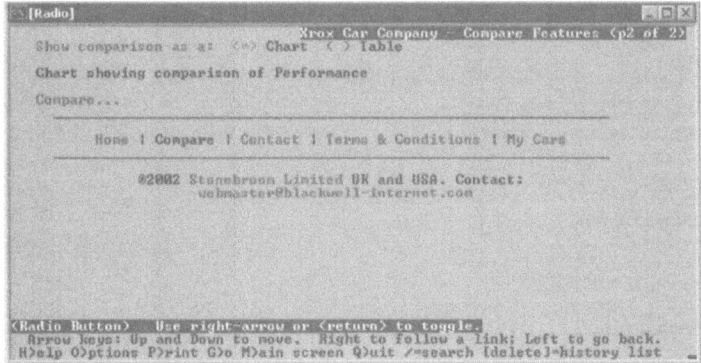

Figure 6-18. The "Compare Models" page displayed in the Lynx text-only browser

Following the **Skip to Result** link takes us to the radio buttons where you can select the way the comparison results should be displayed. By default the display is a chart, and you can see that the only thing visible in the text-only client is the alt text added to the <img> control that displays the chart (Figure 6-19).

Figure 6-19. How the chart appears in the Lynx text-only browser

However, selecting the **Table** option and then activating **the Compare** link displays the results as an HTML table, and you can see that Lynx exposes the contents in a useful and readable form—the page works fine and achieves the original aims (Figure 6-20).

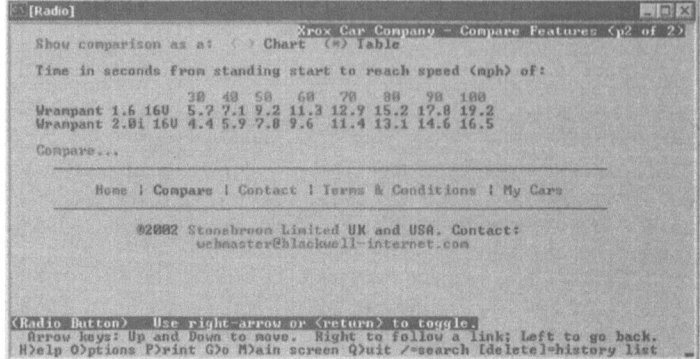

Figure 6-20. The results displayed as a table in the Lynx text-only browser

Using an Aural Page Reader

The next test for the page is in the IBM Home Page Reader, which you met in earlier chapters when I discussed the various types of specialist clients that we should all endeavor to support. This time I've hidden the graphical view and other windows, so only the text that is read to the user is visible. You can clearly see (in the section of the output that I've highlighted) the radio buttons to select a chart or table view of the results, followed by the alt text of the (default view) chart (Figure 6-21).

Figure 6-21. The "Compare Models" page displayed in the IBM Home Page Reader

However, selecting the **Table** option returns the values as an HTML table, and they are read to the user row by row (Figure 6-22).

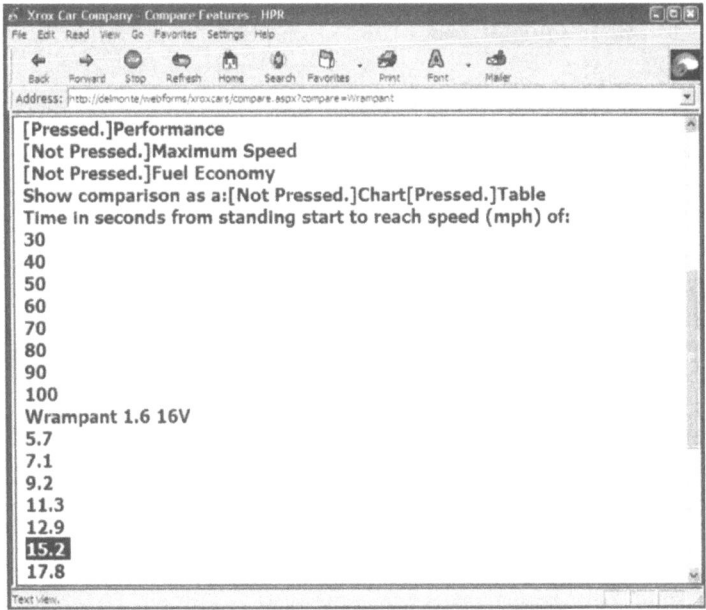

Figure 6-22. The table of results displayed in the IBM Home Page Reader

Returning to the longdesc Attribute

Of course, this is still not the optimal format of the values as far as aural devices are concerned. The user is presented with just strings of numbers, and it's hard to relate them to each other. A better solution is to use the longdesc attribute of the hyperlink that is displaying the chart, or a "D Link" next to the table, to present a more useful view of the data (as I discussed earlier in this chapter). Although not actually implemented in the example application, it is not hard to follow the guidelines I discussed to build a page that uses the same data and business logic, but presents it in a different format. For example, rather than binding the rows to a DataGrid to display them, you could iterate through the rows in code and generate a more user-friendly output format:

```
Dim sResult As String = ""     ' to hold the result string for display
...  generate the DataSet containing the results here ...
' get reference to table in DataSet
Dim tblResult As DataTable = dsResult.Tables("Compare")
```

```
Dim iColCount As Integer = tblResult.Columns.Count
Dim fValue As Double
Dim sValue As String

' iterate through data rows
For Each oRow As DataRow In tblResult.Rows

  sResult &= "Model: <b>" & oRow(0).ToString() & "</b><br />"
  ' iterate through the columns in the row, omitting the
  For iLoop As Integer = 1 To iColCount - 1

    Try    ' in case database value is <NULL>

      ' get value from column in this row
      fValue = oRow(iLoop)

      If sCompareIndex = 0 Then
        sValue = fValue.ToString("F1")
      Else
        sValue = fValue.ToString("F0")
      End If

      sResult &= tblResult.Columns(iLoop).ColumnName & " = " & sValue & "<br />"

    Catch
    End Try

  Next   ' column
  ' display string in a control on the page
  lblOutput.Text = sResult & "<p />"

Next   ' data row
```

Together with some simple logic to generate the page headings, you could then offer the user something like that shown in Figure 6-23. Notice the URL contains the same query string as is used to generate the chart itself.

Another interesting addition to the page might be to extend the checks done on the user's client or browser type, when that user first hits the site, to see if he or she is using a text-only client or a page reader. This isn't a trivial task, as the BrowserCapabilities routines provided by ASP.NET do not, by default, have the data available for this. However, if you could detect these types of client (perhaps by examining the user agent string available via the "USER_AGENT" value within the Request.ServerVariables collection), you could adapt the page's code so that the Table option is the default for these types of client instead of the Chart option.

Figure 6-23. An alternative view of the results in the IBM Home Page Reader

Summary

This is a relatively long chapter compared to most others in this book, and I used it to cover a lot of ground. Although the overall topics were few—looking at the ancillary pages of the example site, the general page structure, and the way the informational content is displayed—it did bring to light many areas where I felt that I should expand on the reasoning behind my design choices as well as show you the implementation details and the results.

For example, you looked in some detail at the choices made between static and dynamic content, and how you can implement this in various ways. I also focused in more detail than before on how you can insert content into a page at runtime, and discussed the ways you can use a DataReader to extract content from a database.

In several places throughout the chapter I also incorporated some pointers about maximizing accessibility in the pages, especially when using complex graphical images that contain information. This information is not generally available to users of non-graphical clients, and I showed you ways you can present it in other formats as well as a graphic or chart.

I finished the chapter by testing the "Compare Models" page in a couple of non-graphical clients to prove that the techniques I chose do work, including making the content available as a table instead of a graphical chart.

The topics covered were:

- The general structure of the "ancillary" pages, including layout and navigation

- The "Terms and Conditions" and "Contact" pages

- How to decide when to use static as opposed to dynamic content

- The page that displays the individual "News" items

- The structure and workings of the "Compare Models" page

- How to create the display of model comparisons as an HTML table

In the next chapter, I'll be completing the construction of the "Compare Models" page by showing you how the charts and graphs it displays are generated, along with a look at some other types of chart that you can create with ASP.NET and the .NET Framework classes.

Creating Graphs and Charts

In Chapter 6, I built the "Compare Models" page for the Xrox Car Company site. This page allows visitors to compare the vehicles Xrox sells in terms of their performance, fuel consumption, and maximum speed. The results of these comparisons can be displayed as a graphical chart or as an HTML table. I've already shown you how the table of results is created, but I didn't discuss how to create the chart that this page displays.

So, in this chapter, I'll continue where I left off, and look at how to use the drawing classes that are part of the .NET Framework to create the charts you see in the "Compare Models" page. This page only uses two basic types of chart: a line chart and a bar chart. However, before looking at these two specific examples, I'll show you a simpler type of chart. Probably the easiest type of chart to create is a pie chart, and I'll show you a generic example of this.

So, the topics for this chapter are:

- Looking at the various ways that you can generate graphics and images dynamically

- Exploring the ways that you can use these images in the example pages

- The .NET Framework classes that allow you to generate these graphics and images

- How to create a simple pie chart as a generic function

- How to create the line charts for the Xrox Car Company site

- How to create the bar chart for the Xrox Car Company site

I start with a look at the concept of using dynamically generated images.

Dynamically Generated Graphics and Images

One of the long-standing issues with designing attractive Web pages to display information is how to present information that is predominantly graphical in nature in such a way that it can be viewed in all kinds of browsers, running on all kinds of operating systems.

Some of the available techniques for displaying static and dynamically generated graphics in a Web browser are:

- Using a **Java Applet, a plug-in,** or an **ActiveX control** that runs on the client's machine and generates the output. The big issues here are compatibility with the operating system and browser and concerns over security. Allowing code that is downloaded from the Web to run on your machine, even when sand-boxed (in the case of Java Applets) is something many people prefer to avoid.

- Using some built-in feature, add-in, or component that is preinstalled with the browser, such as the Internet Explorer **Structural Graphics Control** intro-duced with IE4. The problem with this technique is that it is not cross-browser compatible.

- Using a standard graphics rendering language, such as **Virtual Modeling Language** (VML, as implemented in Internet Explorer 5.0) or the **W3C Scalable Vector Graphics** (SVG) recommendations. Again, the issue with these tech-niques is lack of general browser support.

- Animation techniques that use a language and technology such as **Macromedia Flash**. This is a powerful and useful way to present moving and interactive images. Though it has traditionally been used more for dramatic effect than actual information presentation, and is frowned on for this reason by many users, it can be used to create extremely useful presentations as well as static output. It can also be scripted so that the content is generated dynamically—for more details see the Macromedia site at http://www.macromedia.com/.

- Converting the output to a static presentation using something like the **Adobe Portable Document Format** (PDF). Like Flash and many of the other tech-niques listed above, this requires client-side installation of a plug-in that can handle the PDF file. However, users often accept it more readily than other techniques. PDF documents can be generated dynamically on the server in a range of ways, for example using components provided by companies like ActivePDF (http://www.activepdf.com/).

While all of these are perfectly acceptable techniques within the limitations that they incur, many developers still prefer to provide normal GIF or JPEG images that are inserted into the page using a standard <img> element. This approach is almost guaranteed to work in all graphical browsers. And, increasingly, there is support in browsers for a relatively new image format, called Portable Network Graphics (PNG). This format avoids the issues that arise from the GIF format being a commercially patented technology. However, for maximum compatibility with old browsers, the GIF format is still the order of the day.

So, if you are going to use a GIF (or other format) image to present information that changes over time, you need to generate this image dynamically. There is a wide range of components available for ASP and ASP.NET that can do this. For some exam-ples, check out:

- The ASP101 graphics components list at:

  `http://asp101.aspin.com/home/components/graphics`

- HotScripts image manipulation tools at:

  `http://www.hotscripts.com/ASP/Scripts_and_Components/Image_Manipulation/`

- And, of course, the component gallery on the Microsoft ASP.NET community site at:

  `http://www.asp.net/ControlGallery/default.aspx`

Of course, being a geek and an avid .NET developer, I chose to build my own graphics routines that use the .NET Framework classes. Before you see how, I'll look briefly at performance and caching issues with dynamic images, so you can see why I chose to use dynamically generated GIF images, and find out how to get them into the sample pages.

Performance and Caching

As well as choosing the technique for creating graphics and images based on my technology and language preferences, plus the support available in the various client types I want to service, it's worth considering the effect that this choice has on performance and server loading.

Generating an image or graphic dynamically, especially a complex one, obviously takes more effort than just referencing a disk file that contains the image. The techniques I examine in this chapter generate the image as a stream of bytes, using code running on the server, so there is a performance hit each time the graphic is generated. How much of a hit obviously depends on the complexity of the image, the efficiency of the algorithms in the code that creates it, and the raw speed of the language in which the code is written.

In other words, if you write the code in raw C or machine code, you're going to get better performance than using something like Visual Basic 6. However, in the new and exciting ".NET world," you can enjoy all the benefits of the Framework classes and runtime engine by using a managed language such as C# or VB.NET instead. OK, so the code won't be as fast as raw C, but it is still extremely efficient—as well as being a great deal easier to write.

Generating Graphics on the Client

To some extent you can minimize the performance hit by sending just the *instructions* for creating the image to the client, rather than the *complete data* for the image. In the case of line graphics, especially relatively simple ones such as charts or line drawings, this can reduce server loading and bandwidth usage because the instructions are generally smaller than the amount of data contained in the rendered image. This is, for example, the way that VML, Macromedia Flash, and the Microsoft Structured Graphics control work. The downside is that it compromises compatibility, and often accessibility as well, as none of the available techniques work on all kinds of client.

ASP.NET Caching for Images and Graphics

When using disk image files, referenced in the src attribute of an <img> element, the browser will usually cache the image file and reuse this where possible, rather than downloading the image every time. It just checks that the image is still "current" by comparing the "expires" date of the image in its cache with that on the server.

However, when you generate images dynamically, you lose this automatic support. It is possible to configure IIS to set the "expires" date and time for files so that even dynamic pages are cached. You can do the same by setting the Response.Expires property in the page code in both ASP and ASP.NET. Unfortunately, this usually breaks the page when different values appear in the Request.QueryString or Request.Form collections, as it doesn't allow the code to be reexecuted to take account of these values.

At this point you are probably jumping up and down and shouting "What about ASP.NET Output Caching?" A good point, but here there is a problem as well. Yes, ASP.NET can automatically reexecute the page if the values in the Request.QueryString or Request.Form collections differ. However, when it sends back a page from the Output Cache, it appears to always set the "content type" (the MIME type of the response) to "text/html"—assuming that the cached output is being used to generate the page in the browser.

While this is a reasonable assumption in most cases, it causes a problem when the ASP.NET code is generating a dynamic image that should have a different content type ("image/gif" or "image/jpeg", for example). Modern browsers will still display the image, but you can't always rely on this in other clients. It can also cause unpredictable behavior —for example, in Internet Explorer, when the user right-clicks to save the image as a file, it is saved as a .bmp file instead of a .gif or .jpg file. For these reasons, I chose to avoid using caching with the example pages.

Writing Images to Disk Files

If you find excessive server loading caused by repeated execution of the code that creates the image, you can to experiment with caching in your applications. Or, often an even better solution, write the images to disk files at specific intervals, or only when the source data changes, and use the appropriate file extension (.gif, .jpg, or whatever).

Using this approach, IIS will set the correct content type automatically, depending the file extension. Plus, the browser will cache the image as well, so you get the best of both worlds. In the section about saving a bitmap later in this chapter, I show how easy it is to create a disk file containing an image or graphic using the .NET Framework classes.

Using Dynamic Images in Web Pages

If you choose to present your graphical output as GIF or JPEG images, you can insert them into a page easily with an ordinary <img> element. Of course, as you discovered in the previous chapter, you still need to consider how to provide the equivalent information for clients using a browser that is not capable of displaying images, or visually impaired visitors to whom images are of no use anyway.

In these cases, you must be sure to include an alt attribute to indicate the content of the image, plus a longdesc attribute and/or a "D Link" to provide the same information contained in the image. However, all this is easy enough to implement, as you saw in the "Compare Models" page in Chapter 6.

Alternative Elements for Inserting Images

Other ways that you can insert images in a range of formats into a Web page are:

- **Using an <embed> element.** This was originally championed by Netscape in its Navigator browsers, and allows the insertion of documents in a wide range of formats. It depends on the appropriate plug-in being installed and available on the client's machine, though most popular plug-ins can be downloaded on demand if not already installed:

```
<embed src="myimage.gif" type="image/gif" height="100" width="150">
   The alternate text goes here for browsers
   that do not support embedded documents.
</embed>
```

- **Using an <object> element.** This is part of the recommendations for HTML 4.01, and was originally introduced by Microsoft in its Internet Explorer 3.0 browser. Most commercial browsers now support it, though the actual implementation and workings vary widely. It can be used to insert all kinds of document, including an image:

```
<object data="myimage.gif" type="image/gif" height="100" width="150">
   The alternate text goes here for browsers
   that do not support the <object> element.
</object>
```

In Internet Explorer 3.0 and later, using the <object> element, the image is inserted into a frame of the specified size, with scrollbars that allow the visitor to move the image around and view all of it if it is larger than the specified size. This might be useful in some situations, but will not work in many other browsers. The same effect can also be obtained in CSS2-enabled browsers using the CSS overflow and clip style selectors.

Using Multiple Static Image Files

When you want to display an image that can change depending on the selections made by the visitor, or in response to some outside factor (for example, a sun or cloud on a site that contains weather forecasts) a common technique is to have a series of images available and use code to choose the appropriate one.

So, for example, there could be a series of images of the cars on the Xrox Car Company site, each in a different color. When the user selects a color, just change the src of the <img> element dynamically in the code to display the correct image. You can do this on the server in ASP.NET simply by assigning the value to the ImageUrl property of a Web Forms Image control, or to the src property of an HtmlImage control.

You can also do this client-side for most recent browsers. Access the <img> element and simply assign the URL of the image file you want to display to the src attribute—effectively this is what was done in the animated page banner you looked at in Chapter 5. As a simple example, in a browser that supports DOM2 and CSS2 techniques, you can use something like this:

```
document.getElementById('CarImg').src = 'newimage.gif';
```

You'll also see another trick in Chapter 8, where I use a GIF image containing sections that are marked as transparent. In this case, I can change the appearance of the image by simply changing the background color of the surface on which it's displayed.

However, none of these techniques use images that are created dynamically—they are all just different ways of using multiple *static* images. It is an easy way to achieve the desired result, but it becomes more and more cumbersome as the number of images required grows.

What you'll be exploring in this chapter is actually generating the image itself dynamically. Before you do, however, there is one other minor topic you should consider. How are values passed into the page or object that creates the image?

Passing Values to an Image-Generation Page

If you are creating an image where the content of that image depends on some values specified at runtime, you need to be able to pass these values into the page or component that is creating the image. In ASP 3.0, when I use a custom or commercial component to create an image, I usually do so by instantiating the component within a page and then setting the appropriate properties.

But even here, the page that creates the image is separate from the page in which it is displayed. The client requests this page after the page containing the <img> element has finished loading, and the data returned by the second page is loaded into the <img> element and displayed. So I still need to be able to pass values from the first page into this second page (the one that creates the image) to indicate what I want the image to contain (Figure 7-1).

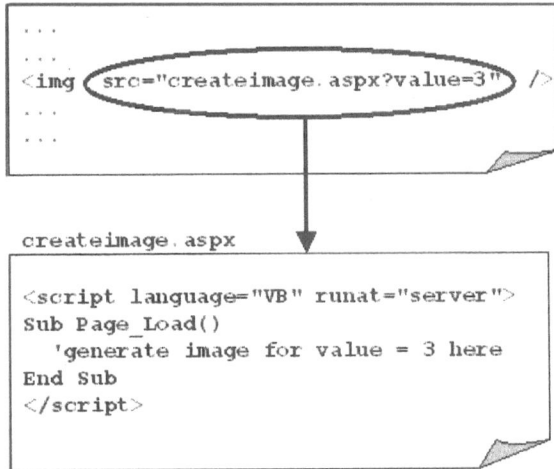

displayimage.aspx

```
. . .
. . .
<img  src="createimage.aspx?value=3"  />
. . .
. . .
```

createimage.aspx

```
<script language="VB" runat="server">
Sub Page_Load()
   'generate image for value = 3 here
End Sub
</script>
```

Figure 7-1. Passing values to an image-generating page in the query string

In the preceding example, and in the "Compare Models" page in the previous chapter, I chose to pass the values using the query string. However, there are other options. You might be tempted to try passing them as the values in a <form> that is posted to the chart generation page. However, the target page is linked via the src attribute of an <img> element, and so this will not work. The only way to do this would be to use the Server.Execute method to execute the page within the execution cycle of the current page.

Another option would be to store the values in the user's ASP.NET session, and then retrieve them in the target page. This is quite acceptable if you ensure that the client you are serving the pages to can support ASP.NET sessions (as I do in the Xrox Car Company site). The downside is that it can make it harder to see what's happening when experimenting, testing, and debugging the page because the values must be retrieved from a valid session each time.

However, the query string is generally the simplest option, and it means that that the target page (which creates the image) can include the EnableSessionState="False" directive to minimize server loading. The actual URL used is not visible in the browser, except when viewing the source of the page, and hence will not confuse visitors even if it's a complex set of values.

The only real issue here is keeping the total length (the full path of the page plus the query string) below the maximum that the browser and server can accept. The usual working value for this is 1,024 characters, so you should not run into problems unless you have an inordinately large number of parameters to pass to the image generation page.

The .NET Framework Drawing Classes

As the topic of this chapter is generating images with the .NET Framework classes, it's high time you actually started to investigate these classes. The root namespace is System.Drawing, and there are several other ancillary namespaces that include classes designed for more specific tasks or advanced image manipulation. Table 7-1 summarizes all relevant the namespaces.

Table 7-1. The Framework Namespaces Related to Drawing and Creating Images

Namespace	Description
System.Drawing	Provides access to the basic graphics functions used in GDI+, including bitmaps, brushes, pens, colors, points, and rectangles. Within this namespace is the Graphics class, which exposes most of the basic methods for drawing onto a bitmap.
System.Drawing.2D	Provides extra classes and enumerations for two-dimensional vector graphics use, including the classes required for generating gradient fills.
System.Drawing.Imaging	Provides advanced features for interacting with bitmaps and images, creating color palettes, specifying image formats, and managing image encoding.
System.Drawing.Text	Provides advanced font handling and management classes, allowing interaction with collections of installed fonts.
System.Drawing.Printing	Provides the classes required to manage printing of graphics, including access to all the necessary printer functions and settings.
System.Drawing.Design	Provides the classes required for developing design-time extensions to the UI, for example when creating custom classes and controls for use in Visual Studio .NET.

The System.Drawing *Class*

When creating reasonably simple GIF or JPEG images such as are used in the Xrox Car Company site, I mainly used the classes from the System.Drawing namespace only. Table 7-2 summarizes the most commonly used classes, indicating what they are used for.

Table 7-2. The Commonly Used Classes in the System.Drawing *Namespace*

Class	Description
Bitmap	The drawing surface on which the graphics tools will be used, and which stores the graphic image. Exposes methods to save the bitmap in a range of formats, and to interact with the bitmap on a pixel-by-pixel basis.
Graphics	This is the main tool for drawing on a bitmap. It provides methods to draw straight and curved lines; plus outlined or filled circles, ellipses, pie "slices," rectangles, polygons, and so on. It also exposes a series of methods to transform, rotate, and scale sections of a bitmap.
Pen	Used to draw lines and curves. The width and color can be specified.
Brush	Used to fill shapes and draw text. This is a base class—the concrete classes that inherit from it are SolidBrush, TextureBrush, and LinearGradientBrush, allowing a range of fill styles to be used.
Color	Defines a color for a brush or pen, and provides methods to define the color in a range of different ways.
Rectangle	Defines a rectangular region within the bitmap, where the top, left, width, and height are specified as Integer values.
RectangleF	A Rectangle structure that uses floating-point (Single) values for the dimensions and coordinates instead of Integer values.
Font	Specifies the font style, size, and weight to be used when drawing text onto a bitmap.
StringFormat	Specifies the alignment and other features of the text that is drawn onto a bitmap, including tabs, digit substitution, and hot-key indicators.

> **NOTE** *A full reference to the* System.Drawing *namespace is provided in the .NET version 1.0 SDK at:*
> ms-help://MS.NETFrameworkSDK/cpref/html/frlrfSystemDrawing.htm *or in the version 1.1 SDK at:*
> ms-help://MS.NETFrameworkSDKv1.1/cpref/html/frlrfSystemDrawing.htm

It's All Very Simple

All this looks complicated, but in fact the principle is very simple. Just use a Pen or Brush object to draw the image elements onto a Bitmap object. You can think of the Graphics object as being the "hand" that does the drawing, by creating the lines, fills, text, and other elements (Figure 7-2).

Figure 7-2. A conceptual view of the drawing process

In more technical terms, the process is:

- Create a Bitmap—this represents the drawing surface

- Create a Graphics object based on the bitmap—this represents the "hand" that manipulates the drawing tools

- Create a Pen—this is used to draw lines.

- Create a Brush—this is used to fill shapes and draw text strings

- Call the methods of the Graphics object to create the required content using the Pen and Brush objects

- Call the Save method of the Bitmap object to output the finished image

- Dispose of the objects

The next listing shows the outline code required in an ASP.NET page to generate a GIF image. Notice that I set the correct ContentType for the response, so that the client knows that it is a GIF image. While Internet Explorer will automatically display the result as an image without this, some other browsers will not:

```
' set content-type of response so client knows it is a GIF image
Response.ContentType="image/gif"

' create a new bitmap
Dim oBitMap As New Bitmap(iWidth, iHeight)
```

```
' create new graphics object to draw on bitmap
Dim oGraphics As Graphics = Graphics.FromImage(oBitMap)

'create a solid brush for writing text and filling shapes
Dim oBrush As New SolidBrush(Color.Yellow)

'create a red pen for drawing lines
Dim oPen As New Pen(Color.Red, 1)

...
...
'code here to draw the individual elements onto the bitmap
...
...

' write bitmap to response
oBitmap.Save(Response.OutputStream, ImageFormat.Gif)

' dispose of objects
oPen.Dispose()
oBrush.Dispose()
oGraphics.Dispose()
oBitmap.Dispose()
```

So, if it's as easy as this, I should have no problem generating my charts. In the remainder of this chapter, I'll show you a generic example for creating a pie chart, and then examine the page I used in the Xrox Car Company site to generate the model comparison charts.

Creating a Simple Pie Chart

Probably the easiest kind of chart to generate dynamically is a pie chart. The Graphics object exposes methods that generate an outlined or a filled "pie slice," so all you need to do is call these methods for each row in the data to generate a complete pie chart. However, you also need to add the "key box" for each slice in the chart, indicating what that slice represents.

The finished chart is shown in the Figure 7-3. I'm charting the popularity of each vehicle model from the Xrox Car Company site. I've chosen to make the chart as attractive as possible by adding shadows to the various elements of the chart. This makes the code a little more complicated, but is well worth the extra effort. Without it, the chart looks quite flat and amateurish.

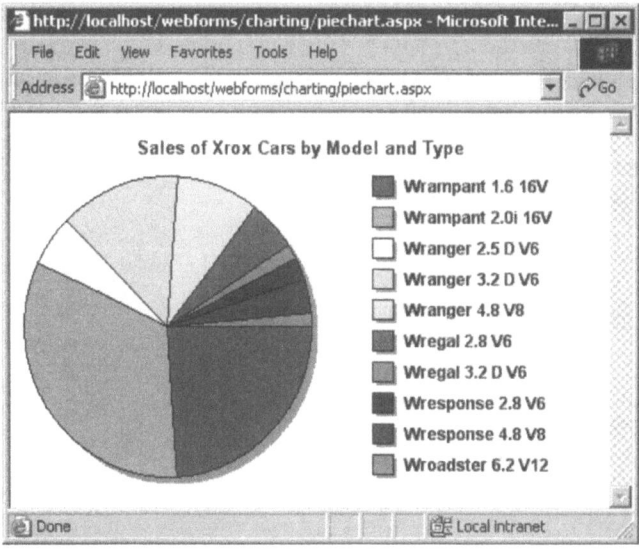

Figure 7-3. The result from the pie chart example

> **NOTE** *You'll find this example in the* charting *subfolder of the samples provided for this book. You can obtain the sample files from* http://apress.com *or from* http://www.daveandal.com/books/7868/, *where you can run them online as well.*

Providing the Data Source

In most cases, the data to build a chart like this will come from a database or perhaps an XML document, though it could, of course, be an array or a collection of some type. All you need are two items of information for each of the rows or objects that you want to include in the chart: the text string that describes the data item and the value itself.

The most likely data source will be a database of some kind, as in the example charts used in the Xrox Car Company site. What's important is that the data must be available in a way that allows the "rows" or "items" to be accessed more than once. You need to iterate through the data at least twice, and so you can't use the forward-only DataReader as the data source directly.

Instead, the best choice for accessing a database when creating charts is to use a DataSet. You can then pass the table from the DataSet that contains the information (as a DataTable object) to the charting routine. You can even extract a specific set of rows as a DataRowCollection and pass this to the routine. Furthermore, if the data is stored in an XML file rather than in a database, you can easily load it into a DataSet using the ReadXml method of the DataSet object.

Another approach is to make the data available as an Array or a Collection. Of these, the Array is perhaps the most obvious, and you can easily create an array in code with the values you need if the source of the data is not a relational data store such as a SQL database. Plus, if the data is only available as a DataReader object, you can use the GetValues or GetSqlValues methods of the DataReader to return an Array containing the values. I discussed these methods briefly in the previous chapter.

Finally, if the data is created programmatically, you might create a custom class that holds the two values you need for each slice of the pie chart, and then use a collection based on this custom class as the data source for the charting routine.

In the pie chart example page, I'm using a DataSet as the data source. However, to keep this demonstration of using the System.Drawing classes as simple as possible, I'm not fetching this data from a database. Instead, I just create the rows individually within the code. You'll see how next.

Creating the DataSet *for the Pie Chart Example*

The example page charts the proportion of sales for each vehicle model. So I need a table in the DataSet that contains the vehicle name and the number of that model sold. Note that this figure is *not* a percentage of the total number sold. It's extremely unlikely that any database would store percentages of the total for any specific quantity, because it would need to be recalculated for all the rows every time one quantity changed. Or, in terms of the example, the value for every row would have to be recalculated whenever a vehicle is sold.

The following listing shows the code I used to create the DataSet and table, returning it as the result of a function named GetDataSet. I created the empty DataSet object, added a new DataTable to it, and defined two columns in this table. Then I can add rows to the table by specifying the values for these two columns (to avoid unnecessary repetition, I don't show the code for every row here):

piechart.aspx

```
' function to create a DataSet containing a few values
Function GetDataSet() As DataSet

  ' create a new DataSet object and a new table
  Dim dsResult As New DataSet()
  Dim tblData As New DataTable("Data")
  dsResult.Tables.Add(tblData)

  ' define two columns (fields) within the table
  tblData.Columns.Add("Caption", System.Type.GetType("System.String"))
  tblData.Columns.Add("Value", System.Type.GetType("System.Double"))
  'declare a variable to hold a DataRow object
  'fill in the values and add to table then repeat
  Dim oRow As DataRow = tblData.NewRow()
  oRow("Caption") = "Wrampant 1.6 16V"
  oRow("Value") = 277
  tblData.Rows.Add(oRow)
```

```
oRow = tblData.NewRow()
oRow("Caption") = "Wrampant 2.0i 16V"
oRow("Value") = 381
tblData.Rows.Add(oRow)

...
... repeat for other eight rows
...


   Return dsResult    ' return DataSet
End Function
```

The Pie Chart Example Page

I've attempted to provide a routine that is reasonably generic in the pie chart example. However, to make all the possible features of the chart configurable through parameters to a method would mean a large number of parameters would be required. I chose just to expose four parameters to the "generic" routine: the DataSet, the bitmap width and height, and the text for the caption at the top of the chart. So, I can call the routine using something like:

```
DrawPieChart(dsMyDataSet, 420, 250, "A Test Pie Chart")
```

To make the chart more configurable, you could expose things like the offset of the shadows for the elements, the size and color of the text, the alignment of the "key" boxes and text, the spacing between the chart and the "key" boxes, and so on. However, this may not be the best approach in most practical situations.

In most cases, the variables I've just mentioned are not that important—they are not a vital part of the result I'm hoping to achieve. Using some sensible hard-coded values for these variables within the routine is fine. It also marginally improves the efficiency of the code by reducing the variable references and subsequent calculations required to position each element.

Of course, when you come to build your own charts and graphs, you might decide to make more features configurable via parameters, depending on your requirements. However, as you'll see towards the end of the chapter, I actually reduced the level of configurability in the line charts that are a part of the Xrox Car Company site.

Adding the Import Directives

Before doing any drawing in the example ASP.NET page, I need to import the namespaces that are required. I only need the System.Drawing namespace for most of the tasks, however there are a couple of classes in the System.Drawing.Imaging namespace that I can also take advantage of. And, because I'm using a DataSet in the code, I also need the System.Data namespace:

```
<%@Page Language="VB" %>
<%@Import Namespace="System.Drawing" %>
<%@Import Namespace="System.Drawing.Imaging" %>
<%@Import Namespace="System.Data" %>
```

Instead of importing a namespace, I can refer to the classes within it directly by specifying the full class path within the .NET Frameworks namespace hierarchy. In fact, I do this in a later example where I make use of the LineCap enumeration to add an arrowhead to the end of the axis lines. LineCap is part of the System.Drawing.Drawing2D namespace, but rather than importing the whole namespace I specify the full namespace and class name when I use it:

```
oPen.EndCap = System.Drawing.Drawing2D.LineCap.ArrowAnchor
```

This makes the code wordier, and I use this approach only when referring to an item that appears once or twice in a page. Any more than that and it probably makes more sense to import the namespace into the page. Importing a namespace does not make the page any "heavier" or any less efficient because the compiler only includes references to the classes actually used in the page, and not the complete namespace. You can use either approach in your code—I am simply demonstrating both here.

The Page_Load *Event Handler*

The next part of the code in the pie chart example page is the Page_Load event handler. All I do here is set the ContentType of the response, specify the caption for the chart, and call the DrawPieChart routine to create the chart. I pass to it the DataSet returned from the GetDataSet method you looked at earlier, and the width and height for the chart:

```
Sub Page_Load()
  ' set content-type of response so client knows it is a GIF image
  Response.ContentType="image/gif"

  ' specify the caption text for the chart
  Dim sCaption As String = "Sales of Xrox Cars by Model and Type"
  ' call routine to draw the pie chart - specify width and height
  ' for image that is created and the caption for top of image
  DrawPieChart(GetDataSet(), 420, 250, sCaption)

End Sub
```

The DrawPieChart routine creates the bitmap and draws the chart on it, and then saves the result to the response (as you saw earlier in the outline of the process). Despite the fact that the browser accessed an ASP.NET (.aspx) page, it will think that the response is a normal GIF image (which, of course, it is) and will display it as an image. Of course, there is no HTML or other content in the page, as we must only send the client data that is generated by the Bitmap object.

Drawing Text on a Bitmap

Within the DrawPieChart routine, you'll need to write text strings onto the bitmap. In fact this is often the most complex part of creating a chart. The Graphics object exposes a method called DrawString, which takes as parameters:

- The text to write as a String.

- A Font object that defines the font to be used.

- A Brush object that defines the color and fill for the text. This is usually a SolidBrush object, though a TextureBrush or LinearGradientBrush can be used instead.

- A Point or RectangleF object that indicates the position of the text, or the *X* and *Y* coordinates of the starting position for the text.

- A StringFormat object that defines the alignment and various other attributes (such as digit substitution, trimming, and the hotkey character) for the text.

If you provide a starting point for the text, using a Point object or the *X* and *Y* coordinates, you lose some control over the actual alignment. I find that it's generally easier to use a RectangleF to define the area where the text should appear, and then control its position within this rectangle using the alignment properties of the StringFormat object passed as the last parameter:

```
oGraphics.DrawString(sText, oFont, oBrush, oRect, oFormat)
```

Alternatively, you may prefer to calculate the start position for the text and use one of the other overloads of the DrawString method:

```
oGraphics.DrawString(sText, oFont, oBrush, iTop, iLeft, oFormat)
```

Or, to create a Point object that defines the *X* and *Y* position:

```
oGraphics.DrawString(sText, oFont, oBrush, oPoint, oFormat)
```

Note that the StringFormat parameter is optional (in the sense that there are overloads of the DrawString method that do not accept this parameter), so you could just use:

```
oGraphics.DrawString(sText, oFont, oBrush, oPoint)
```

NOTE *A full reference to the* DrawString *method is provided in the version 1.0 .NET SDK at:*
```
ms-help://MS.NETFrameworkSDK/cpref/html/
frlrfsystemdrawinggraphicsclassdrawstringtopic.htm
```
or in the version 1.1 SDK at:
```
ms-help://MS.NETFrameworkSDKv1.1/cpref/html/
frlrfsystemdrawinggraphicsclassdrawstringtopic.htm
```

A Custom Routine to Draw Text Strings

It's clear from the preceding discussion that it's quite a lot of work to draw a text string on the bitmap—creating the necessary objects and then calling the DrawString method. For this reason, I built a generic routine that I can use to draw text strings. As well as accepting a reference to the current Graphics object that I'm using to create the bitmap content, it allows me to specify the other variables like the text itself, the rectangle in which it is drawn (using four integer values), the font style and size, the color, and the alignment:

```
' routine to draw text string in rectangle on bitmap
Sub DrawText(oGraphics As Graphics, iTop As Integer, _
             iLeft As Integer, iWidth As Integer, _
             iHeight As Integer, sText As String, _
             Optional eFontStyle As FontStyle = FontStyle.Regular, _
             Optional iFontSize As Integer = 8, _
             Optional sColor As String = "Black", _
             Optional eAlign As StringAlignment = StringAlignment.Near, _
             Optional eFlag As StringFormatFlags = Nothing)
    ...
```

Many of the parameters are optional, and are set to the basic commonly used values, so you often only need to specify the first six parameters. Notice the last parameter named StringFormatFlags. This is used to set the Flags property of the StringFormat object used to control the layout of the text within the rectangle. Among the extra controls it allows me to apply are whether the text should wrap within the rectangle, and whether any excess content should be clipped at the boundaries.

The value for this property of the StringFormat object is an integer made up by ANDing values from the StringFormatFlags enumeration. I really only included this so that I could take advantage of another value it exposes—DirectionVertical. I need this to place the text string vertically next to the *Y*-axes when I create line charts.

Within the DrawText routine, create a RectangleF object using the top, left, width, and height parameter values, and then create a new Font object using the font name, size, and style parameter values:

```
...
' create the rectangle to hold the text
Dim oRect As New RectangleF(iTop, iLeft, iWidth, iHeight)

' create a Font object for the text style
Dim oFont As New Font("Arial", iFontSize, eFontStyle)
...
```

> **NOTE** *There are actually 13 different constructors for a* Font *object, taking a range of different parameters. You'll find a full list in the version 1.0 .NET SDK at:* ms-help://MS.NETFrameworkSDK/cpref/html/frlrfSystemDrawingFontClassctorTopic.htm *or in the version 1.1 SDK at:* ms-help://MS.NETFrameworkSDKv1.1/cpref/html/frlrfSystemDrawingFontClassctorTopic.htm

Formatting and Drawing the Text

Next, I created a new StringFormat object and specified the necessary alignment. I only exposed the horizontal alignment in the parameters to the custom DrawText routine, allowing text to be left-aligned, right-aligned, or centered within the rectangle. It's also possible to vertically align the text within the rectangle, but I always use StringAlignment.Center here. I can vary the vertical position of the text when I call the custom routine by changing the height of the rectangle.

```
...
'create the format object to define the format and style
Dim oFormat As New StringFormat(eFlag)
oFormat.Alignment = eAlign        ' horizontal alignment
' always center vertically within rectangle area
oFormat.LineAlignment = StringAlignment.Center
...
```

One interesting point is that the values used to horizontally align text are not the same as you might expect. For left-to-right (Western-style) text, use StringAlignment.Near to align the text at the left of the enclosing rectangle, and StringAlignment.Far to align it to the right. For text that is written from right-to-left (which is specified by setting the Flags property of the StringAlignment object to StringFormatFlags.DirectionRightToLeft), the behavior is reversed. And the LineAlignment property, which controls vertical alignment, uses the same enumeration values, with Near being at the top of the rectangle, and Far being at the bottom of the rectangle.

Finally, I can create a SolidBrush object of the appropriate color, and then draw the text onto the bitmap:

```
...
' create a brush object and draw the text
Dim oBrush As New SolidBrush(Color.FromName(sColor))
oGraphics.DrawString(sText, oFont, oBrush, oRect, oFormat)

End Sub
```

Using the Custom DrawText Routine

To use the DrawText function, you must specify at least the first six parameters—the Graphics object reference, the rectangle boundaries, and the text string to draw. The other parameters can be omitted to use their default values. So, to draw a caption centered at the top of the chart, you can use:

```
DrawText(oGraphics, 0, 0, oBitMap.Width, 20, "My New Pie Chart")
```

If you want to control the font style, size, color, and alignment, just add these parameters when calling the function:

```
DrawText(oGraphics, 0, 0, oBitMap.Width, 20, "My New Pie Chart", _
         FontStyle.Bold, 10, "Red", StringAlignment.Center)
```

To draw text vertically, as you'll see in the line charts you create later in this chapter, specify the value StringFormatFlags.DirectionVertical for the final parameter. You can omit any intermediate parameters that you don't want to set specific values for, and the default values are used (Figure 7-4).

Figure 7-4. Drawing text vertically on a BitMap

```
DrawText(0, 20, 12, 230, "seconds", , , , , _
         StringFormatFlags.DirectionVertical)
```

Creating and Using Colors in Images

I'm going to need a range of colors for the chart. Probably the best way to do this is to create an Array of the colors I want to use, so that I can extract different ones as I iterate through the rows in the data source. In the example page, I create an Array of Color objects (rather than text color names as String variables).

Following is the code for the GetColorArray function in the example page. I only need 10 colors, because the example will only have 10 rows in the data source (one for each vehicle model in the DataSet table). However, you must make sure that there are sufficient colors for the maximum number of data rows or items you expect your own charting routines to handle—this routine will provide different colors for up to 20 data rows:

```
Function GetColorArray() As Color()
  ' declare an Array for 20 colors
  Dim aColors(19) As Color

  ' fill the array of colors for chart items
  ' use browser-safe colors (multiples of #33)
  aColors(0) = Color.FromArgb(204, 0, 0)      'red
  aColors(1) = Color.FromArgb(255, 153, 0)    'orange
  aColors(2) = Color.FromArgb(255, 255, 0)    'yellow
  aColors(3) = Color.FromArgb(0 ,255, 0)      'green
  aColors(4) = Color.FromArgb(0, 255, 255)    'cyan
  aColors(5) = Color.FromArgb(51, 102, 255)   'blue
  aColors(6) = Color.FromArgb(255, 0, 255)    'magenta
  aColors(7) = Color.FromArgb(102, 0, 102)    'purple
  aColors(8) = Color.FromArgb(153, 0, 0)      'dark red
  aColors(9) = Color.FromArgb(153, 153, 0)    'khaki
  aColors(10) = Color.FromArgb(0, 102, 0)      'dark green
  aColors(11) = Color.FromArgb(51, 51, 102)    'dark blue
  aColors(12) = Color.FromArgb(102, 51, 0)     'brown
  aColors(13) = Color.FromArgb(204, 204, 204) 'light gray
  aColors(14) = Color.FromArgb(0, 0, 0)        'black
  aColors(15) = Color.FromArgb(102, 204, 255) 'sky
  aColors(16) = Color.FromArgb(255, 204, 255) 'pink
  aColors(17) = Color.FromArgb(255, 255, 204) 'chiffon
  aColors(18) = Color.FromArgb(255, 204, 204) 'flesh
  aColors(19) = Color.FromArgb(153, 255, 204) 'pale green

  Return aColors
End Function
```

Color Modes and Color Palettes

Notice that I do *not* use the standard .NET color names here. There is an issue with using the standard colors when creating GIF images in .NET, and in fact whenever I use colors in a Web page. It's easy to assume that every client I serve pages to has its system display set up in "true color" mode—so it can display a minimum of 32,000 colors ("high color" mode).

In these modes, almost any color I use will be displayed without being dithered. They will appear as solid colors in the browser. However, some people still work in 256-color mode, and in this case the colors will be dithered —which can make the output look quite ugly.

And while it's very easy to forget about the problems of 256-color display with modern browsers, you'll come down to earth with a bump when you use .NET to generate GIF images. The standard method of encoding the bitmap you create when saving it as a GIF uses only the standard "browser-safe" range of 216 standard colors. Any other colors are dithered, producing a non-solid appearance in all browsers (irrespective of the system display settings) that is often unacceptable. An enlarged view of the output when using a different color (in this case "Khaki") shows the result (Figure 7-5).

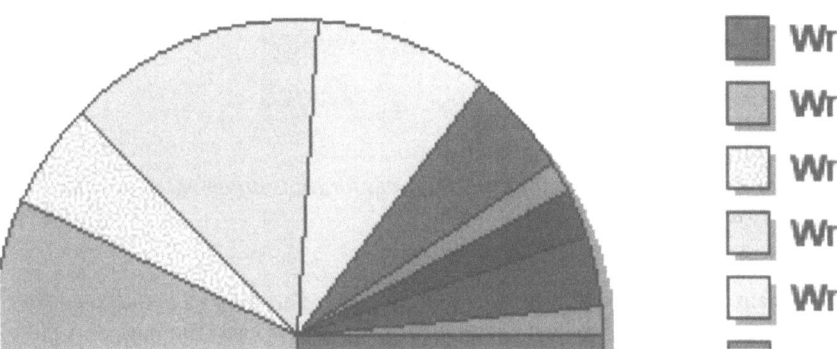

Figure 7-5. The fixed 256-color pallette can dither non-standard colors

One way around this is to define the palette that the bitmap uses by creating a new ColorPalette object and adding the colors you want to it. It's not trivial, but certainly an option. However, it doesn't solve the client-side issue. Just because I've generated the image with a specific color doesn't mean that the browser will be able to display it without dithering. If the user's system is configured in 256-color mode, it might not be able to display the color anyway—or it might be dithered when another window that uses a different palette is brought to the foreground, causing annoying color shifts as users work with the pages in the site.

Another option is to use different encoding for the bitmap when you save it. Options include PNG and JPEG. As I mentioned earlier, support for PNG format is less universal in older browsers, so a JPEG is probably a better choice. However, the default high compression ratio that the standard encoding uses for JPEG output produces a rather "muddy" and ill-defined output—even tinting the white background a light sepia color (Figure 7-6).

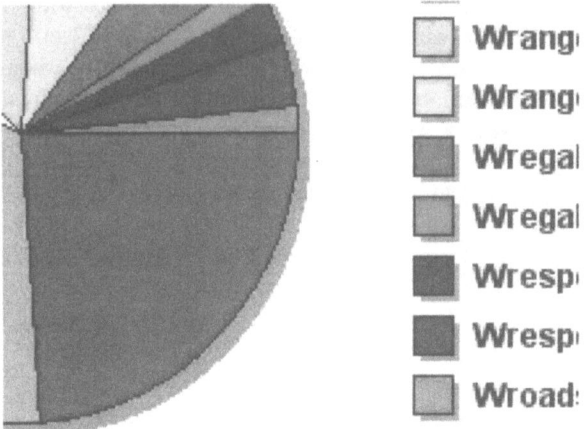

Figure 7-6. The standard compression settings for JPEG images can cause the image to appear "muddy."

Again, there is a code-intensive solution that references an instance of the appropriate Encoder class, and changes the properties to suit the image's requirements. However, after much experimentation, I found that the best solution to get maximum compatibility with all clients is to stick to using GIF images with the 216 browser-safe colors. For images that are "pictures" rather than bitmaps (for example, an idyllic country scene taken with a digital camera, rather than a chart like I'm using here) JPEG is a better option, and you'll need to interact with the encoder to get the optimum results.

The Browser-Safe and Standard Colors

I've discussed the requirement to use only the 216 browser-safe colors in your pages and images. But what are these colors? The simple answer is that they use values for their Red, Green, and Blue (RGB) components that are all multiples of the hexadecimal value #33 (51 in decimal). This allows an even spread of colors, as #33 is an integer divisor of the maximum value #FF (255 in decimal).

There are several sites on the Web that provide lists of these colors (I mentioned the W3C site in Chapter 3); however, I've included a page that does this (and more) with the samples for this book. After all, it's not hard to calculate what they are!

The colors that are classed as "browser-safe" are things like #003366 or #cc9966. What's really unfortunate is that only eight of these possible combinations of RGB values exactly match the standard "known" colors defined by name in .NET. This is why I define the colors using RGB values in the example page. The only colors that do match exactly are:

NET Name	Black	Blue	Lime	Cyan	Red	Magenta	Yellow	White
RGB Value	#000000	#0000ff	#00ff00	#00ffff	#ff0000	#ff00ff	#ffff00	#ffffff

The example page I've provided builds up a series of HTML tables that show the 216 colors as they appear in your browser, the decimal and hexadecimal values of each of the three components of the color (the RGB values), and the equivalent .NET color name if one exists. You can access this page (color-list.aspx in the charting subfolder of the samples) from the opening menu of the sample files (Figure 7-7).

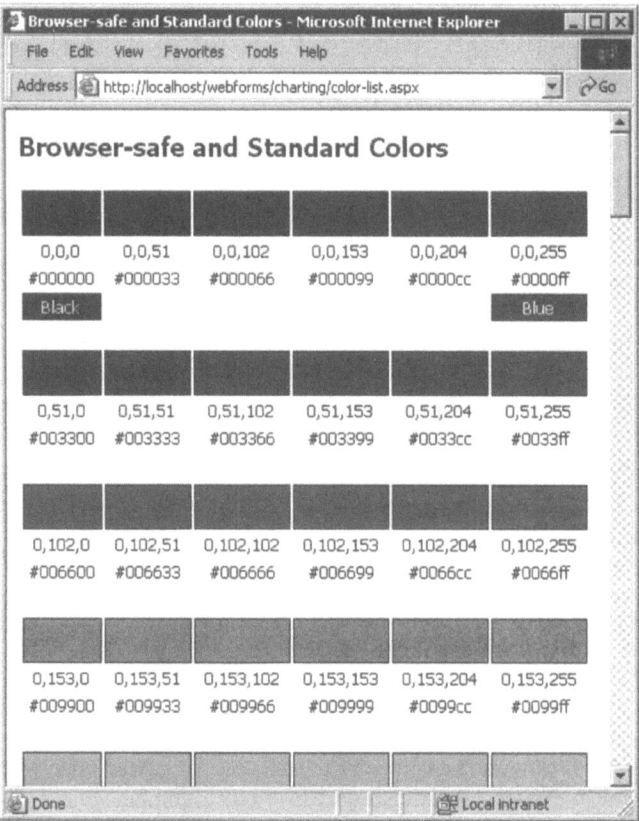

Figure 7-7. The browser-safe colors example page

How the Browser-Safe Colors Page Works

The Browser-Safe Colors page you see in Figure 7-7 appears to be quite simple. Each of the three components of the color that make up the RGB definition can have one of six values (#00, #33, #66, #99, #cc, or #ff). So all you need are 36 (6 x 6) tables that each display the six possible values for one of the components. However, rather than create 36 tables manually, it makes sense to allow ASP.NET to generate them dynamically for you.

So, in the HTML section of the page include the page title and some styling information for the text, followed by an ASP.NET PlaceHolder control where you'll insert our dynamically generated table:

```
<!-- placeholder to hold table of results -->
<asp:PlaceHolder id="ctlPlaceholder" runat="server" />
```

Then, in the Page_Load event handler, create the table and add it to the Controls collection of the PlaceHolder control (I used this technique in the previous chapter to insert an Image control into a page dynamically):

color-list.aspx
```
Sub Page_Load()
  ...
  ... code to create an ASP.NET Table control named oTable here
  ...
  ctlPlaceholder.Controls.Add(oTable)
End Sub
```

Creating the Arrays of Colors

Before I start, I need to create two arrays to hold the colors I'll be displaying and examining in the code. There are 168 "known" (named) colors defined in .NET, and I can create an array of these by iterating through them from zero to YellowGreen (the last KnownColor, as they are stored in the Color structure enumeration alphabetically). For each color I create a Color object using the static FromKnownColor method:

```
' array to hold list of 168 "known" colors
Dim aKnownCols(167) As Color
Dim eValue As KnownColor
For eValue = 0 To KnownColor.YellowGreen
  aKnownCols(eValue) = Color.FromKnownColor(eValue)
Next
...
```

I create an array of the browser-safe colors using three nested For...Next loops, with the "step" value set to #33 (51 decimal). For each of the 216 (6 x 6 x 6) combinations, I create the equivalent Color object by calling the static FromArgb method of the Color object:

```
...
' array to hold list of 216 browser-safe colors
Dim aSafeCols(215) As Color
Dim rValue, gValue, bValue As Integer
Dim iPointer As Integer = 0
For rValue = 0 To 255 Step 51
  For gValue = 0 To 255 Step 51
    For bValue = 0 To 255 Step 51
      aSafeCols(iPointer) = Color.FromArgb(rValue, gValue, bValue)
      iPointer += 1
    Next
  Next
Next
...
```

Creating the Rows for Each Table

Now I declare the variables I'll need within the code. To display a cell with the correct background color, I'll set the BackColor property of that Cell object. As there is no other content in the cell, I'm using a string of large font non-breaking spaces (sColorCell) to ensure that the cell is large enough to show the color.

Then I can create five new TableRow objects that I'll add to the table once I've finished "filling them in." I also specify the horizontal alignment for the three rows that will contain text:

```
...
' declare variables, we'll create 5 rows simultaneously
Dim oRow1, oRow2, oRow3, oRow4, oRow5 As TableRow
Dim oCell As TableCell
Dim oColor, oKnown As Color
Dim sDecimalVals, sHexVals, sKnown As String

' to create empty cell with colored background
Dim sColorCell As String
sColorCell = "<font size=5>       </font>"

' create empty Table object and five Row objects
Dim oTable As New Table
oRow1 = New TableRow()
oRow2 = New TableRow()
oRow3 = New TableRow()
oRow4 = New TableRow()
oRow5 = New TableRow()

' set horizontal alignment for three rows
oRow2.HorizontalAlign = HorizontalAlign.Center
oRow3.HorizontalAlign = HorizontalAlign.Center
oRow4.HorizontalAlign = HorizontalAlign.Center
...
```

One of the great things about creating tables dynamically with the Web Forms controls is that you can generate multiple table rows at one time, as I'm doing in this example (the fifth row is empty, and is just there to add vertical white-space between each set of color rows). After all the rows are complete, just add them to the Table object in the correct order. Where different types of output are displayed for each color in different rows of the table, it means that you can iterate through the

0,0,255
#0000ff
Blue

Figure 7-8. The cells for one color in the browser-safe colors page

array of colors once only, creating all the rows in one pass, rather than having to iterate through the array once for each row as you would if you were generating output directly to the response (as for ASP 3.0) (see Figure 7-8).

> **NOTE** *You can do much the same using the* HtmlTable, HtmlTableRow, *and* HtmlTableCell *controls from the* System.Web.UI.HtmlControls *namespace. However, we chose to use the Web Forms equivalents (*Table, TableRow, *and* TableCell*) from the* System.Web.UI.WebControls *namespace here, as they provide easier control of the format and layout.*

Creating the Cells for Each Table Row

Now I can iterate through the safe colors in the aSafeCols array. I build up a String for the values in decimal and in hexadecimal (the format string "x2" indicates that the value should be formatted as two hexadecimal characters, using lowercase letters for values above 9):

```
...
' iterate through array of safe colors
For Each oColor In aSafeCols

  ' create the strings showing decimal and hex RGB values
  sDecimalVals = oColor.R.ToString() & "," & oColor.G.ToString() _
                 & "," & oColor.B.ToString()
  sHexVals = "#" & oColor.R.ToString("x2") & oColor.G.ToString("x2") _
             & oColor.B.ToString("x2")
  ...
```

Next, check to see if the current color is the same as any of the standard .NET "known" colors. Iterate through the aKnownCols array to check if the RGB value of each color is identical to the RGB value of the current browser-safe color. If it is, I set the String value sKnown to the .NET known color name. If not, it remains empty:

```
...
' see if this color is same as any standard color by iterating
' through "known" colors array and comparing ARGB values.
' not breaking at first match avoids returning "system" colors
' such as "DialogText" and "WindowTitleBarText" which come first
sKnown = ""
For Each oKnown In aKnownCols
  If oKnown.ToArgb = oColor.ToArgb Then
    sKnown = oKnown.Name
  End If
Next
...
```

Displaying the Color and Color Details

It's time to start generating the cells for the rows. I do this by creating a new `TableCell` object, and adding a `LiteralControl` to its `Controls` collection. The parameter to the `LiteralControl` is the text string I want to display in that cell. For the first cell, this is the `String` I declared earlier in the page, which inserts a series of large non-breaking space characters. Then I can display the actual color by setting the background color of the cell to this color. I also give the cell a black one-pixel-wide solid border (by specifying the value 1 for the `Pixel` method of the static `Unit` object), before adding it to the first of the five rows:

```
...
' create a new cell, and add LiteralControl containing value
oCell = New TableCell()
oCell.Controls.Add(New LiteralControl(sColorCell))

'set properties for this cell, and add to row 1
oCell.BorderColor = Color.Black
oCell.BorderStyle = BorderStyle.Solid
oCell.BorderWidth = Unit.Pixel(1)
oCell.BackColor = oColor
oRow1.Cells.Add(oCell)
...
```

Next come the two cells that contain the RGB values in decimal and hexadecimal. Each is placed in a `LiteralControl` within a new `TableCell` object, and these two cells are added to the second and third of the `TableRow` objects:

```
...
' repeat for cells containing decimal and hex RGB values
oCell = New TableCell()
oCell.Controls.Add(New LiteralControl(sDecimalVals))
oRow2.Cells.Add(oCell)
oCell = New TableCell()
oCell.Controls.Add(New LiteralControl(sHexVals))
oRow3.Cells.Add(oCell)
...
```

Next I create the cell for the fourth of the rows. If the current color is one of those that matches the "known" .NET colors, the string sKnown will not be empty, and so I can insert the color name into this cell. I then create a new `Color` object with this name, and use it to change the background color of this cell—adding a black border as I did earlier. I also change the foreground color of this cell to white if this color has values less than 124 (decimal) for its red and green components, so the text will show up.

If the current color is not a "known" color, just leave the cell empty. It will generate only the <td></td> tags in this case, preserving the layout of the table when rendered in the browser. In either case, this section of code is completed by adding the cell to the fourth of the new `TableRow` objects, and then creating an empty cell and adding it to the fifth `TableRow` object:

```
...
' create cell for matching "known" color if there is one
oCell = New TableCell()
If sKnown <> "" Then
  oCell.Controls.Add(New LiteralControl(sKnown))

  ' create color object using "known" color name
  oKnown = Color.FromName(sKnown)
  oCell.BackColor = oKnown
  oCell.BorderColor = Color.Black
  oCell.BorderStyle = BorderStyle.Solid
  oCell.BorderWidth = Unit.Pixel(1)

  ' see if we need to use white text on this background
  ' color when displaying color name in cell
  If oKnown.R < 124 And oKnown.G < 124 Then
    oCell.ForeColor = Color.White
  End If

End If
' add "known color" cell to row 4
oRow4.Cells.Add(oCell)

' create cell in row 5 to provide space between color rows
oCell = New TableCell()
oCell.Controls.Add(New LiteralControl(" "))
oRow5.Cells.Add(oCell)
...
```

Starting a New Row

I want to start a new row each time the blue component of the color value reaches 255—as it will with every sixth color, because I set the blue component of the colors in the array in the innermost of the three nested loops when I filled the array. When it does reach 255, I add the five rows I've been creating to the table, and then create five new ones and set the horizontal alignment as I did before. Then I can go back and process the next color in the array.

After I've processed all the colors, and the table is complete, I insert it into the PlaceHolder control defined in the HTML section of the page. When ASP.NET renders the page to the client, the newly filled Table control will generate a normal HTML table:

```
...
' if Blue element of color has reached 255 start a new row
' add five existing rows to table, create new ones and set
' horizontal alignment for the three of them holding text

If oColor.B = 255 Then
  oTable.Rows.Add(oRow1)
  oTable.Rows.Add(oRow2)
  oTable.Rows.Add(oRow3)
```

```
      oTable.Rows.Add(oRow4)
      oTable.Rows.Add(oRow5)
      oRow1 = New TableRow()
      oRow2 = New TableRow()
      oRow3 = New TableRow()
      oRow4 = New TableRow()
      oRow5 = New TableRow()
      oRow2.HorizontalAlign = HorizontalAlign.Center
      oRow3.HorizontalAlign = HorizontalAlign.Center
      oRow4.HorizontalAlign = HorizontalAlign.Center
    End If

  Next
  ' table complete, so insert into page within PlaceHolder control
  ctlPlaceholder.Controls.Add(oTable)

End Sub
```

So, having taken a detour to look at browser safe colors, color palettes, and image formats, and seen how to create HTML tables dynamically with ASP.NET, I'll come back to our pie chart example.

The Generic Pie Chart Routine

The "generic" DrawPieChart routine takes as parameters a DataSet containing the source data, the width and height of the chart to create, and the caption to place at the top of the GIF image that it generates. Earlier, in the Page_Load event handler, I called the DrawPieChart routine using:

```
DrawPieChart(GetDataSet(), 420, 250, sCaption)
```

In this section of the chapter, you'll see how the DrawPieChart routine works. I start by creating a BitMap object, a Graphics object, a new black Pen object and a new white SolidBrush object—exactly as I demonstrated earlier in this chapter in the outline description of the process of drawing using the .NET Framework classes.

The default for a new BitMap object is for all the pixels to be set to zero, giving a completely black bitmap. So the first thing I do after creating the various objects I'll need is to draw a filled rectangle the same size as the bitmap with the new white SolidBrush object (in the last line of the following listing) so that I have a white background to work on:

piechart.aspx
```
Sub DrawPieChart(dsData As DataSet, iWidth As Integer, _
                 iHeight As Integer, sCaption As String)
  ' create a new bitmap
  Dim oBitMap As New Bitmap(iWidth, iHeight)
```

```
' create new graphics object to draw on bitmap
Dim oGraphics As Graphics = Graphics.FromImage(oBitMap)

'create a black pen for drawing lines and draw border
Dim oPen As New Pen(Color.Black, 1)

'create a solid brush for the background and fill it
Dim oBrush As New SolidBrush(Color.White)
oGraphics.FillRectangle(oBrush, 0, 0, oBitMap.Width, _
                        oBitMap.Height)
...
```

Next I can add the chart caption, centered at the top of the bitmap and allowing 20 pixels for the height of the rectangle in which the text is placed. I use a bold 10px font:

```
...
' draw caption centered at top of bitmap using routine in this page
DrawText(oGraphics, 0, 0, oBitMap.Width, 20, sCaption, _
        FontStyle.Bold, 10, , StringAlignment.Center)
...
```

Calculating the Position of the Main Chart Elements

Now I create some variables I'll need, and calculate the position of the various elements of the example chart based on the size of the bitmap being created. I get an array of colors using the routine you saw earlier, and then specify the vertical spacing for the top of the "pie" itself, allowing room for the chart caption. Then I calculate the diameter of the "pie," allowing room for the caption above it and the shadow below it (Figure 7-9):

```
...
' fill the array of colors using routine later in page
Dim aColors() As Color = GetColorArray()

' vertical space for chart caption
Dim iCaptionHeight As Integer = 30

' variable to hold size of space above pie chart if it is
' smaller than available height of bitmap.
' Used to center it vertically with "key" boxes and text
Dim iPieTopOffset As Integer = iCaptionHeight

' calculate dimensions of pie chart, allowing space
' for "key" text as 0.4 of width on right of chart
' and for shadow - which is 5 pixels below chart
Dim iPieDiameter As Integer = oBitMap.Height _
                              - iCaptionHeight - 6
...
```

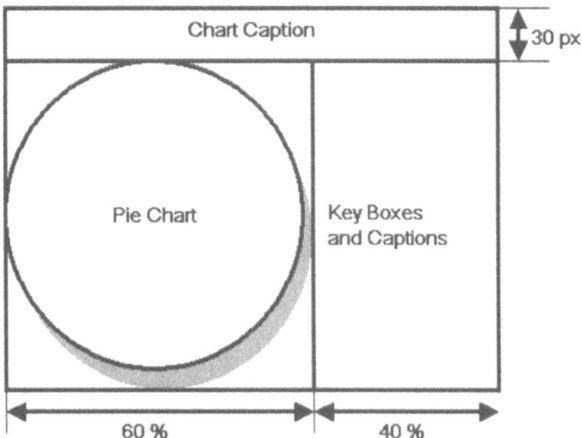

Figure 7-9. The layout proportions for the chart and captions

However, as the "pie" is circular, I need to make sure that I have enough room for it and the "key" boxes and individual value captions (located on the right of the "pie"). I decided that the "pie" should only take up 60 percent of the horizontal width of the bitmap, so I check for this and adjust the diameter of the "pie" if required (and adjust the vertical offset as well in this case, to keep it vertically aligned with the "key" boxes alongside it):

```
...
If iPieDiameter > (oBitMap.Width * 0.6) Then
  iPieDiameter = oBitMap.Width * 0.6
  iPieTopOffset = ((oBitMap.Height - iPieDiameter) \ 2) _
                  + iCaptionHeight
End If
...
```

Creating Rectangles and Drawing Shadows

Now I'm ready to start drawing some shapes. I create two rectangles—one for the "pie," and one offset by 5 pixels vertically and horizontally for the shadow. Then I can change the color of the SolidBrush to dark gray and fill the shadow using the FillEllipse method of the graphics object. This method sizes the ellipse to fit inside the rectangle I pass as the second parameter and, as the width and height are the same, I get a circle:

```
...
' create rectangles for chart and shadow background
Dim oRectPie As New Rectangle(0, iPieTopOffset, _
                              iPieDiameter, iPieDiameter)
```

```
Dim oRectShadow As New Rectangle(5, iPieTopOffset + 5, _
                                    iPieDiameter, iPieDiameter)
' create color for shadows to objects
Dim cShadow As Color = Color.FromArgb(153, 153, 153)

' set brush color and draw circle for shadow
oBrush.Color = cShadow
oGraphics.FillEllipse(oBrush, oRectShadow)
...
```

> **NOTE** *There are also overloads of the* FillEllipse *method that accept four* Integer *or four* Single *values, instead of a rectangle object. And there is a* DrawEllipse *method that draws an outlined ellipse or circle using a* Pen *object instead of a brush object, with the size specified in the same way as for the* FillEllipse *method.*

Next, I get a reference to a DataRowCollection that references all the rows in the single table of the source DataSet. Then I calculate the left position of the "key" boxes, which will be 45 pixels to the right of the "pie." The vertical spacing between these boxes is the height of the bitmap minus the caption height, minus 15 pixels to allow a little extra space and room for the shadows, divided by the number of intervals between them (I use integer division here as I want an integer result). This interval is the number of source data rows minus one:

```
...
' get reference to collection of data rows
Dim colRows As DataRowCollection
colRows = dsData.Tables(0).Rows

' calculate left position of "value key" boxes
Dim iKeyBoxLeft As Integer = iPieDiameter + 45

' calculate vertical spacing for "value key" boxes
Dim iKeyBoxSpace As Integer _
    = (oBitMap.Height - iCaptionHeight - 15) \ (colRows.Count - 1)
...
```

Declaring More Variables and Totaling the Rows

I need to store several values as I iterate through the rows in the data source, so I declare the variables for these values next. Notice that I use floating-point values for several of these variables. If the fSliceStart and fSliceDegrees values are forced to Integer values, the slices may not be exactly the right "width," and not fully fill the pie chart (you'll see where these variables are used very soon). The other variables hold values from the data rows, and so (depending on the values I'm charting) these might not be Integer values:

```
...
' declare variables we'll need
Dim oRow As DataRow                 ' reference to data row
Dim iRowIndex As Integer = 0        ' index for current row
Dim fSliceStart As Single = 0       ' start degrees of slice
Dim fSliceDegrees As Single         ' number of degrees for slice
Dim iKeyBoxTop As Integer           ' vertical offset of "key" box
Dim fTotalValue As Double = 0       ' total of all values in table

' variables to hold values extracted from rows
Dim sSliceCaption As String
Dim fSliceValue As Double
...
```

I also need to find the total value of all the rows, so that I can work out what ratio of the total each "slice" of the pie chart represents. I iterate through the rows summing the values from the second column (which contains the value), using a Try...Catch construct just in case there is a NULL value in any row:

```
...
' calculate total of all values in data table
' iterate through the rows in the table
For Each oRow In colRows
  Try
     fTotalValue += oRow(1)
  Catch
  End Try
Next
...
```

Drawing the Pie Slices

At last I'm ready to start drawing the "slices" of the pie chart, and for this I need to iterate through the rows again. For each row, I calculate the top position of the "key" box using the spacing value calculated earlier, and the row index that was set to zero when this variable was originally declared. Then I can set the color of the Brush, and draw a filled rectangle that creates the shadow for the "key" box. I hard-coded the size (15 pixels wide by 14 pixels high):

```
...
' now ready to draw the pie chart itself
' iterate through the rows in the table again
For Each oRow In colRows

  ' calculate vertical position of "key" box
  iKeyBoxTop = iCaptionHeight + (iKeyBoxSpace * iRowIndex)
```

```
' draw shadow for "key" box
oBrush.Color = cShadow
oGraphics.FillRectangle(oBrush, iKeyBoxLeft + 3, iKeyBoxTop + 3, 15, 14)
...
```

The next step is to collect the values from the current data row, again using a Try...Catch construct as a precaution against NULL values in the row:

```
...
' get values from data row
Try
  sCaption = oRow(0)
  fSliceValue = oRow(1)
Catch
  sCaption = "Error"
  fSliceValue = 0
End Try
...
```

The DrawPie *and* FillPie *Methods*

To draw a pie slice I use the DrawPie and FillPie methods of the Graphics object. Both of these can take a Rectangle object as their second parameter, the start position for the slice in degrees for the third parameter, and the number of degrees that the slice should take up as the fourth parameter.

So now I have to establish the number of degrees that this pie "slice" will take up. I calculate the ratio of the total value for this "slice," and then multiply by 360 to get a value in degrees. Then I can add the color for this "slice" from the array of Color objects (using the row index variable) into the Brush, and draw the "slice." I first call the FillPie method with the Brush to create the colored "slice," followed by a call to the DrawPie method. This uses the black Pen to draw an outline on top of the "slice," giving a nice clean edge between the individually colored slices:

```
...
' convert to number of degrees for this value
fSliceDegrees = (fSliceValue / fTotalValue) * 360

' set brush color from array of colors
oBrush.Color = aColors(iRowIndex)

' draw filled pie slice and then outline in black
oGraphics.FillPie(oBrush, oRectPie, fSliceStart, fSliceDegrees)
oGraphics.DrawPie(oPen, oRectPie, fSliceStart, fSliceDegrees)
...
```

> **NOTE** *There are also overloads of the* DrawPie *and* FillPie *methods that accept parameters defining the top, left, width, and height instead of using a* Rectangle *object.*

Adding the Key and Caption

Now it's time to add the "key" box for this "slice," using the same color as I used to fill the "slice," and then outline the box with the black pen. I've already calculated the position. Draw the text for this value to the right of the "key" box using the DrawText routine, placing it 7 pixels to the right of the box (22 pixels minus the width of the box). The width of the rectangle into which the text is drawn is calculated by subtracting the left position of the box and the 22-pixel offset from the width of the bitmap. The height of the text rectangle is the same as the box, so the text is centered vertically against the box:

```
...
' draw filled "key" rectangle and then outline in black
oGraphics.FillRectangle(oBrush, iKeyBoxLeft, iKeyBoxTop, 15, 14)
oGraphics.DrawRectangle(oPen, iKeyBoxLeft, iKeyBoxTop, 15, 14)
' draw caption text next to "key" box
DrawText(oGraphics, iKeyBoxLeft + 22, iKeyBoxTop, _
        oBitMap.Width - iKeyBoxLeft + 22, 14, sCaption, _
        FontStyle.Bold, 9)
...
```

I'm only writing the text caption here, but you might like to add more information. For example, you might add the actual value of this "slice" as a number to the text string. And, because you already know the total values for all the "slices" of the pie, you can easily add the percentage as a number as well. I do this on one of my Web sites when displaying the relative number of visitors from each country that visit the site (by measuring and analyzing the language setting of their browsers (see Figure 7-10).

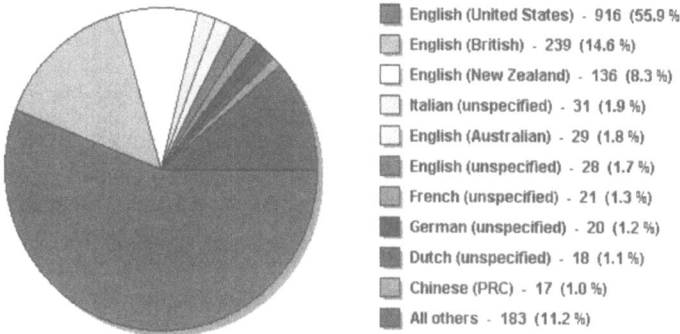

User Languages for Visitors to our Site Last Week

- English (United States) - 916 (55.9 %)
- English (British) - 239 (14.6 %)
- English (New Zealand) - 136 (8.3 %)
- Italian (unspecified) - 31 (1.9 %)
- English (Australian) - 29 (1.8 %)
- English (unspecified) - 28 (1.7 %)
- French (unspecified) - 21 (1.3 %)
- German (unspecified) - 20 (1.2 %)
- Dutch (unspecified) - 18 (1.1 %)
- Chinese (PRC) - 17 (1.0 %)
- All others - 183 (11.2 %)

Figure 7-10. An example of including multiple values in the captions for each key

Completing the Loop

Before starting the next slice, I need to do a couple of things. The start position (in degrees) of the first slice is zero, so this slice is drawn starting at 3 o'clock and going clockwise. However, the next slice must start at the end of the previous one, so I add the number of degrees for the current slice to the starting position. I also increment the row index variable so that the positions and colors for the next slice are set correctly. Then I can go round and process the next row:

```
...
' save start position for next slice and increment row index
fSliceStart += fSliceDegrees
iRowIndex += 1

Next
...
```

Once all the rows are processed, all that remains is to save the bitmap to the response so that it is sent to the browser, and to destroy the objects that have been used. In ASP.NET the objects are disposed of when page execution ends, but it is always good practice to do this explicitly:

```
...
' write bitmap to response
oBitmap.Save(Response.OutputStream, ImageFormat.Gif)

' dispose of objects
oPen.Dispose()
oBrush.Dispose()
oGraphics.Dispose()
oBitmap.Dispose()

End Sub
```

A Note About Saving a Bitmap

Notice that I saved the bitmap in the preceding code directly to the current ASP.NET Response object. The output of the Bitmap object's Save method is a Stream, and so you can save the image data to any kind of object that accepts a Stream (in the preceding code I used Response.OutputStream).

However, the other obvious requirement is to be able to save the bitmap as an image file to the server's disk. The Save method has an overload that saves the data as a disk file, and all you need to do is specify the full physical path and file name:

```
oBitmap.Save("c:\temp\piechart.gif", ImageFormat.Gif)
```

This might be useful if you want to create the images for your site only at specific intervals, perhaps to save on server loading if the values you are charting do not change very often.

The Vehicle Comparison Charts

Having seen how to create a pie chart, I can now move on and show you how the comparison charts I use in the Xrox Car Company site are generated. The techniques are much the same as I used in the pie chart example, in particular the way that I create BitMap and Graphics objects, draw on the BitMap, and output the results to the browser. Where the pages really differ are in the set of drawing commands I use, and the way I calculate the values required to position each element of these charts.

The code in the "Compare Models" page creates a complete URL for the chart image, including the name of the page that creates the image (compare-chart.aspx) and a query string that defines the comparison type and the list of models to include in the chart. For example, if the user selects the Performance comparison option for the two Wregal models, the URL used to load the chart image will be:

```
compare-chart.aspx?ctype=0&list=Wregal+2.8+V6*Wregal+3.2+D+V6
```

The ctype value is the index of the selected comparison radio button, so zero is performance, one is maximum speed, and two is fuel economy. The list value is just a list of the selected model names (taken from the check box captions), delimited with an asterisk character. The URLEncode method I used when creating the query string replaces any spaces with a "plus" sign.

Getting the Values and Data for the Chart

Before even thinking about generating a chart, the appropriate data from the XroxCars database must be extracted. In the Page_Load event handler collect the value of ctype from the query string, and check that it is a valid value. If not call a separate routine named DrawErrorMessage, which uses a very similar DrawText routine to that used in the pie chart example to output the error message in bold red text (as the current Graphics object is held in a page-level variable in this example, you don't need to pass it to the DrawText routine).

However, if you do get a valid value, collect the value for list from the query string. Providing that this is not empty, call a routine named DrawChart located elsewhere in this page:

compare-chart.aspx
```
' extract from Page_Load() event handler
...
' get comparison type from query string
sCompareIndex = Request.QueryString("ctype")
If sCompareIndex >= "0" And sCompareIndex <= "2" Then

  ' get model list from query string
  sModelList = Request.QueryString("list")
  If sModelList <> "" Then
    DrawChart()
  Else    ' no vehicle list in query string
```

```
      DrawErrorMessage("No vehicles specified")
    End If

  Else    ' no comparison type in query string
    DrawErrorMessage("Comparison type incorrect or not specified")
  End If
  ...
```

Creating the SQL Statement

It's necessary to create suitable SQL statements that will extract the values for each
of the three types of chart. You'll recall that you had to do the same in the "Compare
Models" page to get the data for our table view of the comparison results. The only
real difference between the first part of this routine and the one used in the "Compare
Models" page is that slightly different names are assigned to some of the columns:

```
Function GetSqlStatement() As String
  Dim sResult As String
  ' see which comparison type is selected
  ' and create SELECT part of SQL statement
  Select Case sCompareIndex

    Case 0     ' compare Performance
      sCaption = "Time in seconds from standing start to reach speed of:"
      sResult = "SELECT Caption = Model + ' ' + EngineName, " _
              & "[30] = Perf30, [40] = Perf40, [50] = Perf50, " _
              & "[60] = Perf60, [70] = Perf70, [80] = Perf80, " _
              & "[90] = Perf90, [100] = Perf100 " _
              & "FROM (tblCar JOIN tblCarEngines " _
              & "ON tblCar.CarID = tblCarEngines.CarID) " _
              & "JOIN tblEngine " _
              & "ON tblEngine.EngineID = tblCarEngines.EngineID WHERE "

    Case 1     ' compare Maximum Speed
      sCaption = "Maximum speed (mph) in each gear:"
      sResult = "SELECT Caption = Model + ' ' + EngineName, " _
              & "[1st gear] = Speed1st, [2nd gear] = Speed2nd, " _
              & "[3rd gear] = Speed3rd, [4th gear] = Speed4th, " _
              & "[5th gear] = Speed5th, [6th gear] = Speed6th " _
              & "FROM (tblCar JOIN tblCarEngines " _
              & "ON tblCar.CarID = tblCarEngines.CarID) " _
              & "JOIN tblEngine " _
              & "ON tblEngine.EngineID = tblCarEngines.EngineID WHERE "
    Case 2     ' compare Fuel Consumption
      sCaption = "Fuel consumption (mpg) at a steady speed (mph) of:"
      sResult = "SELECT Caption = Model + ' ' + EngineName, " _
              & "[30] = Fuel30, [40] = Fuel40, [50] = Fuel50, " _
              & "[60] = Fuel60, [70] = Fuel70, [80] = Fuel80, " _
              & "[90] = Fuel90, [100] = Fuel100 " _
              & "FROM (tblCar JOIN tblCarEngines " _
```

```
            & "ON tblCar.CarID = tblCarEngines.CarID) " _
            & "JOIN tblEngine " _
            & "ON tblEngine.EngineID = tblCarEngines.EngineID WHERE "

   End Select
   ...
```

However, now you need to create the WHERE clause for the SQL statement that is being generated. The list of vehicles to include in the chart was extracted from the query string earlier in the code, and assigned to the String variable named sModelList. Each vehicle name is delimited with an asterisk character, and so you can convert this String into a String Array using the Split method. Then iterate through the array extracting the individual vehicle names and building up the WHERE clause:

```
  ...
  ' create WHERE clause section for each value in query string
  ' split list into an array, then extract each value
  Dim aList() As String = sModelList.Split("*")
  Dim sItem, sModel, sEngine As String
  For Each sItem In aList
    sModel = sItem.Substring(0, sItem.IndexOf(" "))
    sEngine = sItem.Substring(sItem.IndexOf(" ") + 1)
    sResult &= "(Model = '" & sModel & "' AND EngineName = '" _
               & sEngine & "') OR "
  Next
  ' remove final "OR" from string
  sResult = sResult.SubString(0, sResult.Length - 4)

  ' add ORDER BY clause and return result
  Return sResult & " ORDER BY Model, EngineName"

End Function
```

As an example, this is the SQL statement that is generated when the "performance" option is specified and compares four of the vehicles:

```
SELECT Caption = Model + ' ' + EngineName, [30] = Perf30, [40] = Perf40, [50] = Perf50,
   [60] = Perf60, [70] = Perf70, [80] = Perf80, [90] = Perf90, [100] = Perf100
FROM (tblCar JOIN tblCarEngines ON tblCar.CarID = tblCarEngines.CarID)
   JOIN tblEngine ON tblEngine.EngineID = tblCarEngines.EngineID
WHERE (Model = 'Wrampant' AND EngineName = '1.6 16V')
   OR (Model = 'Wrampant' AND EngineName = '2.0i 16V')
   OR (Model = 'Wranger' AND EngineName = '4.8 V8')
   OR (Model = 'Wregal' AND EngineName = '3.2 D V6')
ORDER BY Model, EngineName
```

There is the same GetCompareDS function in the compare-chart.aspx page as there is in the "Compare Models" page. It uses the preceding GetSqlStatement function to get the appropriate SQL statement, and returns a DataSet containing the results.

Drawing the Appropriate Chart

The DrawChart routine that is executed from the Page_Load event handler simply calls the GetCompareDS function, and extracts the single table named Compare from the resulting DataSet. Then, providing there were some rows found, it calls a routine just like the one used in the pie chart example to get an array of colors for the chart:

```
' routine to draw chart on bitmap
Sub DrawChart()

  ' get DataSet containing rows to chart
  Dim dsResult As DataSet = GetCompareDS()

  ' get reference to table in DataSet
  Dim tblResult As DataTable = dsResult.Tables("Compare")

  ' exit from routine if there was an error
  If tblResult Is Nothing Then Exit Sub

  ' exit if there were no rows found
  If tblResult.Rows.Count = 0 Then
    DrawErrorMessage("No matching vehicles found")
    Exit Sub
  End If

  ' fill the array of colors for each item
  FillColorArray()
  ...
```

Next I decide which chart I am going to create. I've written two routines, named DrawLineChart and DrawBarChart. I use the first of these for the "performance" and "fuel economy" line charts, and the other for the "maximum speed" bar chart.

The DrawLineChart routine expects six parameters that define the low and high values for the Y-axis, the interval between each value on this axis, the caption for this axis, the caption for the X-axis, and the DataTable that contains the values to be used when generating the chart.

The DrawBarChart routine expects only three parameters. These define the interval between each value on the X-axis, the caption for the X-axis, and the DataTable that contains the values to be used when generating the chart.

The caption for the chart is held in a page-level variable named sCaption, and this is drawn onto the bitmap after executing the appropriate one of our two chart generation routines to create the main section of the chart:

```
  ...
  ' decide which type of chart to draw and
  ' pass in suitable parameter values
  Select Case sCompareIndex
```

```
   Case 0     ' compare Performance
     DrawLineChart(0, 30, 5, "seconds", "miles per hour", tblResult)
   Case 1     ' compare Maximum Speed
     DrawBarChart(10, "miles per hour", tblResult)
   Case 2     ' compare Fuel Consumption
     DrawLineChart(0, 55, 5, "miles per gallon", "miles per hour", _
                   tblResult)
 End Select
   ' draw text caption onto chart
   DrawText(35, 0, 365, 12, sCaption)

End Sub
```

So, all that remains now is to see how the DrawLineChart and DrawBarChart routines work. They take advantage of many of the techniques I used to create the pie chart earlier in this chapter. I'll show you the line chart first, and then the bar chart later on.

Drawing the Line Chart

The DrawLineChart routine in the example page is used to draw both the "performance" and the "fuel economy" line charts. These are very similar, the only differences (apart from the actual plotted values) being the set of "tick" values on the Y-axis and the caption of the Y-axis. Figure 7-11 shows an example of the "performance" chart with all 10 vehicles included in the comparison. You can see that the parameter values I used when I called this routine give Y-axis values that go from 0 to 30 seconds, spaced every 5 seconds.

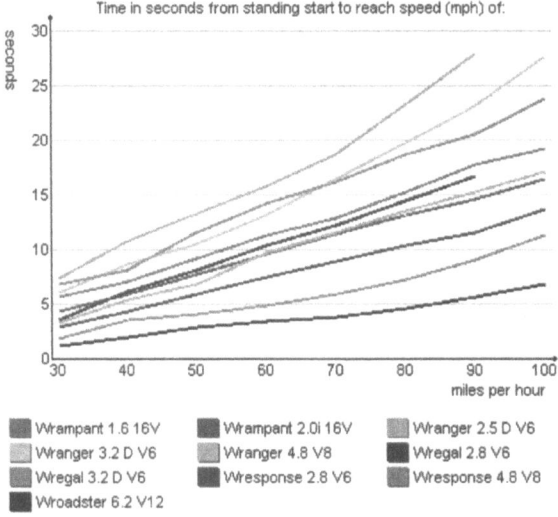

Figure 7-11. The completed performance chart

The same routine, when creating the "fuel economy" chart, generates a *Y*-axis using the different values that are provided for these parameters. The values are from 0 to 55 miles per gallon, spaced every 5 miles per gallon (Figure 7-12).

Figure 7-12. The completed fuel economy chart

Declaring the Variables You'll Need

Start the DrawLineChart routine by declaring the necessary variables. Integer variables hold the position of the text caption and the "key" boxes for each vehicle (which appear below the *X*-axis of the chart). There are also Integer variables to hold the start and end positions of each "value line" segment being drawn onto the chart. These are followed by a String to hold the description (caption) for each value, and a floating-point variable to hold the actual value. The last two variables are used to reference the rows and columns in our source data table:

```
Sub DrawLineChart(iYMinVal As Integer, iYMaxVal As Integer, _
                  iYInterval As Integer, sYAxisText As String, _
                  sXAxisText As String, oXData As DataTable)

    ' variables required within routine
    Dim iLoop, iTextPos, iKeyXTop, iKeyXLeft As Integer
    Dim iLineXStart, iLineYStart, iLineXEnd, iLineYEnd As Integer
    Dim sValue As String
    Dim fValue As Single
    Dim oRow As DataRow
    Dim oCol As DataColumn
    ...
```

Creating Arrow Caps for the Axes

Each axis has an arrowhead at the "high value" end. You can create these quite easily by assigning the value `LineCap.ArrowAnchor` to the `EndCap` property of the `Pen` object used to draw the line (you can also add various line caps to the start of the line as well, by specifying the `StartCap` property of the `Pen` object). The `LineCap` enumeration is part of the `System.Drawing.Drawing2D` namespace, and as this hasn't been imported into the page, you have to specify the namespace when you reference the enumeration.

Once you've set the `EndCap` property of the `Pen`, you can call the `Graphics` object's `DrawLine` method to draw the *X*- and *Y*-axes for the chart. Notice that (as I discussed earlier) the position and size of the elements of the chart have been hard-coded, because I always want it to be the specific size I defined—I won't be using it as a "generic" routine:

```
...
'create arrow-head end point for pen and draw axes lines
oPen.EndCap = System.Drawing.Drawing2D.LineCap.ArrowAnchor
oGraphics.DrawLine(oPen, 35, 250, 399, 250)    ' X Axis
oGraphics.DrawLine(oPen, 35, 250, 35, 10)      ' Y Axis
oPen.EndCap = Nothing
...
```

After drawing the lines, set the `EndCap` property of the `Pen` to Nothing (null in C#) so that the arrowhead will not appear on the lines you draw from now on.

> **NOTE** *Like the other methods in the* System.Drawing *namespace that I've used, the* DrawLine *method has several overloads. I used the one that accepts four* Integer *values here, and I'll use the one that accepts four* Single *values later in the code. There are also overloads that accept two* Point *objects (which define the start and end points of the line) rather than four individual coordinates.*

Drawing the Y-Axis Values

Now the position of each "tick" value for the *Y*-axis can be calculated and drawn onto the chart. Calculate the number of "tick" values there will be, taking into account the start, end, and interval values specified in the parameters to this routine. From this, you can calculate the spacing in pixels between each "tick" value (the chart is 230 pixels high), and the value that this represents in the units used within the data row:

```
...
' now add text and caption to Y (vertical) axis
' calculate spacing in pixels and value of each increment
Dim iYValCount As Integer = ((iYMaxVal - iYMinVal) / iYInterval) + 1
Dim iYSpacePX As Integer = 230 \ (iYValCount - 1)
Dim fYSpaceValue As Single = (iYMaxVal - iYMinVal) / (iYValCount - 1)
...
```

Then it's just a matter of iterating through the number of values just calculated, working out the vertical position of each value on the axis, and drawing the text to show this value. The bottom of the *Y*-axis is 255 pixels down the bitmap, and by subtracting the index within the loop for this value, multiplied by the value per "tick" on the axis, I get the vertical position. Notice that I draw the text aligned to the right (StringAlignment.Far). While this position is stored in the variable, draw a light gray horizontal line across the chart as well:

```
...
' for each value on Y axis
For iLoop = 0 To iYValCount - 1

  ' calculate value to display
  sValue = (iYMinVal + (iLoop * fYSpaceValue)).ToString()

  ' calculate vertical position and write text
  iTextPos = 244 - (iLoop * iYSpacePX)
  DrawText(11, iTextPos, 25, 12, sValue, , , , StringAlignment.Far)

  ' draw light gray horizontal line if not on X axis
  If iLoop > 0 Then
    oPen.Color = Color.FromArgb(204, 204, 204)   'light gray
    oGraphics.DrawLine(oPen, 36, iTextPos + 6, 395, iTextPos + 6)
  End If

Next
' write Y axis caption vertically aligned left (top)
DrawText(0, 20, 12, 230, sYAxisText, , , , StringAlignment.Near, _
        StringFormatFlags.DirectionVertical)
...
```

At the end of the loop, once I've drawn the "tick" values for the *Y*-axis, I add the text description for this axis using the value passed into this routine as a parameter. The combination of the values StringAlignment.Near and StringFormatFlags.DirectionVertical causes the text to be drawn vertically, starting at the top of the rectangle defined with the first four parameters.

Drawing the X-Axis Values

The next step is to draw the "tick" values onto the *X*-axis. This is a bit easier, because the values themselves appear in the rows of the data source table as the names of the columns (excluding the first, which contains the text description of the values in each row). So I can find out how many there are by querying the Count property of the table's Columns collection and subtracting one. From this I can calculate the pixel spacing per "tick" value, by dividing the number of values into the size of the *X*-axis (355 pixels).

Then iterate through the Columns collection of the table starting at the second column (at index 1), and extract the column name. The horizontal position is calculated using the index of the loop and the spacing between each "tick" value, and the column name is drawn at this point just below the *X*-axis. I specify the value `StringAlignment.Center` when calling the `DrawText` routine, so the text will be horizontally centered on the point just calculated:

```
...
' now ready to start X (horizontal) axis text and captions
' calculate spacing in pixels of values on X axis
' use DataColumns collection, but not first column (car name)
Dim iXValCount As Integer = oXData.Columns.Count - 1
Dim iXSpacePX As Integer = 355 \ (iXValCount - 1)

' for each value on X axis
For iLoop = 0 To iXValCount - 1

  ' get column name to display
  sValue = oXData.Columns(iLoop + 1).ColumnName

  ' calculate horizontal position and write text
  iTextPos = 15 + (iLoop * iXSpacePX)
  DrawText(iTextPos, 252, 50, 12, sValue, , , , StringAlignment.Center)

Next
' write X axis caption aligned right
DrawText(40, 264, 355, 15, sXAxisText, , , , _
          StringAlignment.Far)
...
```

As before, once I've finished drawing the "tick" values, I add the caption for this axis just below these values. Because I used the value `StringAlignment.Far` in this call to the `DrawText` routine, the text is right aligned under the axis.

Drawing the Value Lines

Now I can draw the "value" lines onto the chart. Set the `Pen` width to two pixels, and calculate the multiplier for the *Y*-axis. I'll use this to convert each value in the data rows into the number of pixels above the *Y*-axis for that point. I also declare an index variable to use in the loop, just as I did in the pie chart example:

```
...
' now ready to draw lines of values for each row in data table
' set line width in pen to 2 and set start color
oPen.Width = 2

' calculate multiplier for Y values per pixel
Dim fYMultiplier = iYSpacePX / fYSpaceValue

' set the index of the current data row
' used to set colors and "key" positions
Dim iRowIndex As Integer = 0
...
```

327

So, now I can start to iterate through the rows in the table, setting the color of the Pen for each one using the array of colors, so the line for each vehicle is drawn in a different color. Then the start position of the first line segment for this row at the left-hand end of the X-axis can be set, and I can calculate the Y value for this point by multiplying the row value minus the start value of the Y-axis by the multiplier I calculated earlier, giving the number of pixels above the X-axis. To position this point on the chart, I also need to subtract the value I've just calculated from 250 (the vertical position of the X-axis):

```
...
' iterate through data rows
For Each oRow In oXData.Rows

  ' set pen color from array of colors
  oPen.Color = aColors(iRowIndex + 1)

  ' set starting values for line points for each row
  iLineXStart = 40
  iLineYStart = 250 - ((oRow(1) - iYMinVal) * fYMultiplier)

  ...
```

Now I know where the line for this row will start, and I can iterate through the rest of the columns in this row. In other words, I start at the third column, indexed 2, because this contains the end point for the first line segment—I've already located the starting point for the first line segment.

For each accessed column, the horizontal position of the current line segment end point is calculated. Then I extract the row value and calculate the vertical position. In both cases I use the same formula as I did in the previous section of code. However, here I use a Try...Catch construct when extracting the value, because I know that some vehicles will not have values in some columns (for example, two of the vehicles are not capable of reaching 100 mph, so the line for these must stop at the previous "tick" value on the X-axis).

Once I've got the position of the end of the line segment, I can draw it onto the chart using the DrawLine method of the Graphics object:

```
...
' iterate through the columns in the row, omitting the
' first one which contains the vehicle name
For iLoop = 1 To iXValCount - 1

  'set the end X position of the line
  iLineXEnd = 40 + (iLoop * iXSpacePX)

  Try   ' in case database value is <NULL>
    ' get value from column in this row
    fValue = oRow(iLoop + 1)

    'calculate end Y position of line from value
    iLineYEnd = 250 - ((fValue - iYMinVal) * fYMultiplier)
```

```
        ' draw the line on the chart
        oGraphics.DrawLine(oPen, iLineXStart, iLineYStart, _
                           iLineXEnd, iLineYEnd)
    Catch
    End Try
    ...
```

The one other task within this loop, before I go on to draw the next line segment for this vehicle, is to save the end point coordinates of the current line segment. This is the starting point for the next line segment for this vehicle.

```
    ...
    ' save current position for start of next line segment
    iLineXStart = iLineXEnd
    iLineYStart = iLineYEnd

Next
...
```

Drawing the "Key" Boxes and Descriptions

Once all the line segments for this vehicle are drawn, and before I move to the next row in the table, I must add the "key" box and text to the bottom of the chart. There is room for three of these "key" boxes and text across the width of the chart, and I've allowed room for four vertically. This means I can get up to 12 values in this area of the chart (in the example site, there are 10) (see Figure 7-13).

Figure 7-13. The "key" boxes below the chart

The position of these "key" boxes is hard-coded into the routine, with the top left position of the first at *X*=9, *Y*=284. The space between them is 136 pixels horizontally and 17 pixels vertically, so I can calculate the position of the current one like this:

```
    ...
    ' now add the "key" box and vehicle name
    ' calculate left and top positions for current row
    iKeyXTop = 284 + ((iRowIndex \ 3) * 17)
    iKeyXLeft = 9 + ((iRowIndex Mod 3) * 136)
    ...
```

By using integer division by three against the loop index for the vertical position, I know that it will only move the "key" box down to the next row for every third one. Likewise, by using Mod 3 when calculating the horizontal position, I know that it will return to zero for every third value of the loop index.

Now that I know the position of the "key" box for the current row I can draw it onto the bitmap. I set the color of the page-level Brush to light gray and draw the shadow rectangle offset by one pixel horizontally and vertically, then set it to the current color for the value in this row and draw the colored box on top of this shadow.

To finish I draw the text collected from the first column of this row (the vehicle description) next to the "key" box, and then increment the row index variable, before going back to process the next row (the next vehicle) in the source data table:

```
' set brush color and draw shadow for box
oBrush.Color = Color.FromArgb(102, 102, 102)
oGraphics.FillRectangle(oBrush, iKeyXLeft + 1, iKeyXTop + 1, 15, 13)

' set brush color and draw box and text
oBrush.Color = aColors(iRowIndex + 1)
oGraphics.FillRectangle(oBrush, iKeyXLeft, iKeyXTop, 15, 13)
DrawText(iKeyXLeft + 18, iKeyXTop, 115, 14, oRow(0).ToString(), _
        , , , StringAlignment.Near)
'increment row index ready for next row
iRowIndex += 1

    Next
End Sub
```

That's it for the line chart, and—as you've seen—you can use this routine for both the performance and fuel economy charts in the Xrox Car Company site.

Drawing the Bar Chart

The one type of chart that I haven't examined yet is the bar chart. I use this type of chart in the "Compare Models" page to show the maximum speed in each gear for the vehicles Xrox Cars sells. I chose to use a horizontal bar chart because the text descriptions for each vehicle fit better against the Y-axis, while the short "miles per hour" values fit better on the X-axis. However, the technique for creating this type of chart is much the same as for a vertical bar chart, and you should have no problem converting the code if you prefer that type of chart.

Figure 7-14 shows the "maximum speed" comparison chart when all the vehicles are selected. A semi-3D effect is achieved by drawing a shadow under each bar, as well as under the "key" boxes as was done in the previous line chart example. Notice that not all vehicles have the same number of gears.

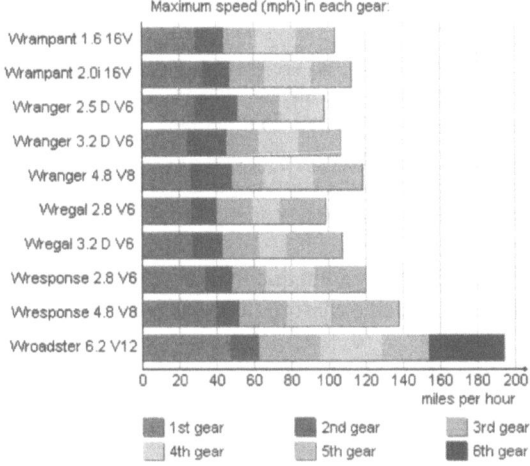

Figure 7-14. The completed maximum speed chart

Unlike the line charts (where the maximum values of the axes stayed the same irrespective of which vehicles were selected, here I want to change the maximum value of the X-axis depending on the maximum speed of the selected vehicles. For example, when the visitor selects only some of the slower vehicles, the maximum value on the X-axis drops from 200 mph to 120 mph (or less if the visitor only selects the smallest engine version of the Xrox Wranger).

I also have to adjust the width and position of the bars as the number of selected vehicles changes, otherwise the bars will only fill the top part of the chart and this looks extremely odd. Figure 7-15 shows both this change in bar width and the change in the maximum X-axis value.

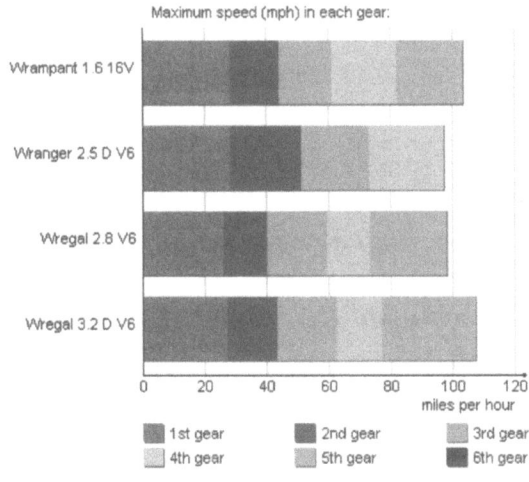

Figure 7-15. The maximum speed chart when only four vehicles ae selected

The Routine Parameters and Variable Declarations

As I mentioned earlier, the routine that creates the bar chart takes only three parameters. You can see them in the next listing. The *X*-axis always starts at zero, and the maximum value is calculated from the rows in the table, so it depends on which vehicles are selected in the "Compare Models" page. This means that I only need to pass in the interval I want to use for the *X*-axis values, the caption for the chart, and the source data table (in fact, as I'm only generating one type of chart here, I could have hard-coded the caption into the routine).

The following listing shows the routine declaration and the variable declarations. The list of variables I use is very similar to the line chart routine you've just seen:

```
Sub DrawBarChart(iYInterval As Integer, sXAxisText As String, _
                 oXData As DataTable)
  Dim oRow As DataRow
  Dim oCol As DataColumn
  Dim iLoop, iTextPos, iKeyXTop, iKeyXLeft As Integer
  Dim iRectXStart, iRectYStart, iRectWidth, iRectHeight As Integer
  Dim sText As String
  ...
```

Drawing the Axes and "Key" Boxes

The next step is to draw the axes, using an arrowhead LineCap as before:

```
...
'create arrow-head end point for pen and draw axes lines
oPen.EndCap = System.Drawing.Drawing2D.LineCap.ArrowAnchor
oGraphics.DrawLine(oPen, 120, 261, 399, 261)   ' X Axis
oPen.EndCap = Nothing
oGraphics.DrawLine(oPen, 120, 17, 120, 261)    ' Y Axis
...
```

> **NOTE** *It is possible to vary the size and style of the arrowhead if you are not satisfied with the defaults, but this involves creating a custom* LineCap *object and setting its properties before assigning it to the* CustomEndCap *or* CustomStartCap *property of the Pen object. For more details about creating custom* LineCap *objects, see the .NET SDK topic:*
> ms-help://MS.NETFrameworkSDK/cpref/html/
> frlrfsystemdrawingdrawing2dcustomlinecapclasstopic.htm *or*
> ms-help://MS.NETFrameworkSDKv1.1/cpref/html/
> frlrfsystemdrawingdrawing2dcustomlinecapclasstopic.htm

Because I know that there can be a maximum six gears, I can draw the six "key" boxes first; using the first six colors in the array of Color objects. The text descriptions for each one are the names of the columns in the source data table, omitting the first column as this contains the vehicle description that will be displayed next to the *Y*-axis.

For each of the six "key" boxes, I extract the column name into a String variable, and then calculate the top and left position using the same technique as was used in the line chart routine to get two rows of three "key" boxes. After this I can set the Brush color to light gray and draw the shadow rectangle, then set the color to the appropriate one for this loop index and draw the colored rectangle. I finish off within the loop by drawing the text description (the column name) next to this "key" box:

```
...
' draw the "key" boxes for each of the 6 possible
' values (gears) using column names from DataTable
For iLoop = 0 To 5

  ' get column name to display
  sText = oXData.Columns(iLoop + 1).ColumnName

  ' calculate position
  iKeyXTop = 295 + ((iLoop \ 3) * 17)
  iKeyXLeft = 120 + ((iLoop Mod 3) * 110)

  ' set brush color and draw shadow for box
  oBrush.Color = Color.FromArgb(102, 102, 102)
  oGraphics.FillRectangle(oBrush, iKeyXLeft + 1, iKeyXTop + 1, 15, 13)

  ' set brush color and draw box and text
  oBrush.Color = aColors(iLoop + 1)
  oGraphics.FillRectangle(oBrush, iKeyXLeft, iKeyXTop, 15, 13)
  DrawText(iKeyXLeft + 18, iKeyXTop, 115, 14, sText, _
          , , , StringAlignment.Near)
Next
...
```

Calculating the X-Axis Values

The *X*-axis for the example bar chart is harder to build than the previous line chart example, because I don't have the predefined maximum value available as a parameter. I have to calculate it from the values in the data rows. So I start by iterating through all the columns in all the rows to get the maximum value from any column in any row:

```
...
' next, find maximum value from all rows
Dim iValue, iRowsMax, iMaxValue As Integer
For Each oRow In oXData.Rows
  For iLoop = 1 To oXData.Columns.Count - 1
    Try
      iValue = oRow(iLoop)
```

```
            If iValue > iRowsMax Then
                iRowsMax = iValue
            End If
        Catch
        End Try
    Next
Next
...
```

Now I round up this maximum value to the next whole interval (the interval is specified as a parameter to this routine) by adding on the interval value, using integer division by the interval value, then multiplying by the interval again. From this value I can work out the number of values that will appear on the axis, and the spacing for these values in pixels (the *X*-axis is 270 pixels long):

```
...
' round up to next iYInterval
iMaxValue = ((iRowsMax + iYInterval) \ iYInterval) * iYInterval

' calculate number of values and pixel spacing
Dim iXValCount As Integer = (iMaxValue \ iYInterval) + 1
Dim iXSpacePX As Integer = 270 \ (iXValCount - 1)
...
```

The only problem now is that, if the maximum value is high and the "tick" value spacing specified in the parameter to this routine is low, there may be more "tick" values than will fit on the axis without overlapping—or looking "odd" by being too close together. I decided that the minimum spacing between "tick" values should be 25 pixels, and so I check if this is the case with the results I've calculated so far:

```
...
' see if the captions will overlap
While iXSpacePX < 25

    ' double the interval size
    iYInterval = iYInterval * 2

    ' recalculate values based on this interval size
    iMaxValue = ((iRowsMax + iYInterval) \ iYInterval) * iYInterval
    iXValCount = (iMaxValue \ iYInterval) + 1
    iXSpacePX = 270 \ (iXValCount - 1)

End While
...
```

If there are too many values, double the interval that was provided as a parameter to the routine and then recalculate the maximum value (to take into account the new interval value), the number of values, and the pixel spacing. It's most likely that I'll only have to do this once, but by enclosing it all in a While...End While construct, I know that the interval will always be doubled enough times to give the spacing I want.

Drawing the X-Axis Values

Finally, now that I have all the preliminary values I need, I can iterate through the number of "tick" values and draw them just below the X-axis. The technique is much the same as was used in the line chart example earlier on, so I'm not detailing all the steps again. The value 96 you see hard-coded here is the horizontal position of the pixel just to the right of the Y-axis, where the "tick" values for the X-axis start and go along horizontally. Meanwhile, 263 is the vertical offset of the X-axis from the top of the bitmap:

```
...
' for each value on X axis
For iLoop = 0 To iXValCount - 1

  ' get value to display along axis
  iValue = iYInterval * iLoop

  ' calculate horizontal position and write text
  iTextPos = iLoop * iXSpacePX
  DrawText(96 + iTextPos, 263, 50, 12, iValue.ToString(), _
           , , , StringAlignment.Center)
  ' draw light gray vertical line if not on Y axis
  If iLoop > 0 Then
    oPen.Color = Color.FromArgb(204, 204, 204) 'light gray
    oGraphics.DrawLine(oPen, 120 + iTextPos, 17, 120 + iTextPos, 260)
  End If

Next
' write X axis caption aligned right
DrawText(40, 274, 355, 15, sXAxisText, , , , _
         StringAlignment.Far)
...
```

Within the loop, you can see that there is a vertical line on the chart at each "tick" value, rather like there was in the line chart. There they were horizontal lines, but vertical lines suit the horizontal bar chart better. Once all the "tick" values have been drawn, the last line of the preceding code adds the text description (caption) for the X-axis just below them.

Drawing the Y-Axis Values

Before I can start drawing the Y-axis values or the bars themselves, I have to carry out more calculations. First, I need the multiplier that determines the way the code translates the values in the data rows to pixel values. This can be obtained by dividing the width of the chart (270 pixels) by the maximum value on the X-axis.

Then, having declared the row index variable, I calculate the number of pixels that each horizontal bar of the chart can take up on the *Y*-axis (iYSpacePX) by dividing the chart height (240 pixels) by the number of rows in the data source:

```
...
' calculate multiplier for X values per pixel
Dim fXMultiplier = 270 / iMaxValue

' create index for row to set vertical position
Dim iRowCount As Integer = 0

' calculate vertical space for each row on Y axis
Dim iYSpacePX As Integer = 240 / oXData.Rows.Count
...
```

I now know how much vertical space each bar can use (it depends, of course, on the number of bars—which equates to the number of vehicles selected). However, I want to leave some space between them so that the light gray vertical "tick lines" will be visible. So, I make each of the bars three-quarters (75%) of the available space (iYBarHeight), and center them vertically within the available space by offsetting them by 12.5% (iYBarAbove):

```
...
' make each bar 3/4 of available space to provide
' gap between each one so scale rules are visible
Dim iYBarHeight As Integer = iYSpacePX * 0.75
Dim iYBarAbove As Integer = iYSpacePX * 0.125
...
```

Drawing the Bars onto the Chart

At last I can start to draw the bars onto the chart. I iterate through the rows in the source data table, calculating the vertical position of the bar by multiplying the vertical space available by the row index and adding 18 pixels to allow for the caption at the top of the chart. Then I can draw the text description of the vehicle at this vertical offset, right aligning it against the *Y*-axis. The description comes from the first column of the data row:

```
...
' iterate through data rows
For Each oRow In oXData.Rows

   ' calculate vertical position for row values
   iRectYStart = 18 + (iRowCount * iYSpacePX)

   ' draw the vehicle name (caption) left of Y axis
   DrawText(0, iRectYStart, 118, iYBarHeight + iYBarAbove, _
            oRow(0).ToString(), , , , StringAlignment.Far)
   ...
```

I want to draw a shadow for the bar to give a 3D effect. However, I also need to think about how I'll create each different colored rectangle segment of the bar (each color indicating the maximum speed in a particular gear). It's possible to start with first gear, and then draw subsequent rectangles starting from where the previous one ended—rather like I did when drawing the line segments in the previous example.

However, it is easier to draw each bar starting from the *Y*-axis, horizontally across the chart to its full actual value. This means that I don't have to keep track of the end of each bar, or subtract the previous data row value from the next one to get the correct size for the bar. As long as I draw the bars for the highest values first, and work backwards to the lowest value, each one will overlay correctly so that I get the result I want (Figure 7-16).

Wrampant 1.6 16V

Figure 7-16. Overlaying the color blocks in the bar chart

I also need to draw the shadow for the bar before drawing any of the segments. However, I only want to draw this for the largest segment (though you might like to try it with each segment for an even more exciting 3D effect). So I declare a Boolean variable that will indicate if I've already drawn the shadow. Remember that some vehicles will not have values for the fifth or sixth gear columns in the data row, so I can't just draw the shadow for the first column I process:

```
...
' flag so that shadow is only drawn once
Dim bDrawShadow As Boolean = True
...
```

Now I can iterate through the columns in the current data row, starting from the last one (Columns.Count - 1) and stepping backwards to the second column (at index 1—remember that the first column is the text description of the vehicle). I collect the value of this column, within a Try...Catch construct because there may not be a value for this gear for this vehicle, and apply the value multiplier to get the length of the bar in pixels.

Before drawing the bar, I check if the shadow has been drawn yet, and if not I do it now using the current bar length value. I offset it by one pixel vertically and horizontally, and clear the shadow flag so that it won't be drawn again. After that, I can set the appropriate color for the Brush and draw the colored bar segment:

```
...
' iterate through the columns of this row
For iLoop = (oXData.Columns.Count - 1) To 1 Step -1
  Try
    iValue = oRow(iLoop)
    iRectWidth = iValue * fXMultiplier
```

```
        If bDrawShadow Then
          ' if this is the first value box for this row
          ' then set brush color and draw shadow for bar
          oBrush.Color = Color.FromArgb(102, 102, 102)
          oGraphics.FillRectangle(oBrush, 121, iRectYStart + iYBarAbove, _
                                  iRectWidth + 1, iYBarHeight + 1)
          bDrawShadow = False    ' clear flag
        End If
        ' set brush color and draw value bar
        oBrush.Color = aColors(iLoop)
        oGraphics.FillRectangle(oBrush, 121, iRectYStart + iYBarAbove, _
                                iRectWidth, iYBarHeight)
      Catch
      End Try

    Next
    ...
```

Having processed each column in this data row, I can now increment the row index variable, and process the row for the next vehicle:

```
    ...
    iRowCount += 1
  Next
End Sub
```

And that's it. The result is the attractive bar chart you saw earlier. It might seem like a long-winded and complicated process, but remember that it's just a matter of calling a few simple methods of the Graphics object to draw lines, ellipses, circles, rectangles, and text.

The hard part is calculating the positions of each element of the chart. One technique I used was to create a static view of the chart by drawing the elements manually in a paint program of some type—I used PaintShop Pro (from http://www.jasc.com/) but Windows Paint will do just as well. Once you've roughed out the chart, you can quite easily measure the positions and offsets of the various parts of the chart in pixels.

Summary

In this chapter, I showed you how to build the attractive and interactive charts that I used in the "Compare Models" page of the fictitious Xrox Car Company site. However, I started the chapter with a more general discussion of when and how you might consider using images or graphics that present information, rather than just being there for decorative effect. I also considered some of the options available for creating dynamic images, such as the performance comparison charts.

I followed this by looking at the easiest type of chart to create—the pie chart. Using some hard-coded values, I generated an attractive pie chart with "key" boxes to describe each value. And, in the middle of this, I wandered off to look at how to build tables dynamically using the ASP.NET `Table`, `TableRow`, and `TableCell` server controls. While it might seem a little out of place here, I used this technique to discuss and demonstrate the browser-safe colors that you will probably want to stick to when generating GIF images with the .NET Framework `System.Drawing` classes.

The final sections of the chapter were devoted to the Xrox Car Company comparison charts. I built and discussed a line chart and a bar chart, both of which can accept a varying number of data rows as the source for the chart. The bar chart also scales the axes automatically to cope with varying maximum values within the data.

In summary, this chapter:

- Looked at the various ways that graphics and images can be generated dynamically

- Explored the ways to use these images in the example pages

- Described the .NET Framework classes that allow generations of these graphics and images

- Showed how to create a simple pie chart as a generic function

- Showed how to create the line charts for the Xrox Car Company site

- Showed how to create the bar chart for the Xrox Car Company site

In the next chapter, I start to look at another of the interactive and dynamic pages on the Xrox Car Company site. I'll show you how to build the page that allows users to configure a vehicle online.

Interactive Web Forms

SO FAR, THE PAGES I've created for the Xrox Car Company example site have been marginally interactive, in that they allow visitors to view performance details of the vehicles, select items such as News articles, and join the mailing list. However, when it comes to building pages that collect information, particularly multiple items such as the configuration of a vehicle, you need to provide much more in the way of interactivity.

As you'll see in this chapter, ASP.NET makes creating these kinds of pages much easier than it was in previous versions of ASP. The built-in features such as maintenance of viewstate, and the postback architecture, remove the need for a lot of code that you would have had to write in, say, ASP 3.0.

My aim in this chapter is to build a page that allows visitors to configure any of the vehicles to their exact requirements, and then save this configuration as a quote so that they can place an order for that vehicle either immediately or at some point in the future. At the same time, I want to make the page as attractive and interesting as possible, tempting them to explore the various vehicles that Xrox Cars offers.

Of course, it's important to start by looking at the overall requirements, and coming up with a design for the page that provides all the desired features. So, before starting to build the actual page that is part of the application, I'll explore some of the concepts and design decisions to help you understand how you can apply the same techniques to your own sites.

The aims of this chapter are to look at:

- How well the final page meets the original design requirements

- The Model Details page in outline, to understand how it is created

- The structure of the Model Details page, to understand how it works

I start with an overview of the requirements, and see how well I've met these requirements. This will also help to familiarize you with the way that the page works, making it easier to follow the detailed descriptions of the techniques I use that come later on in this and the next chapter.

Meeting the Design Requirements

In Chapter 1, I showed you the basic design for the Xrox Car Company site, and the rough sketches I created. The final site construction is based on these sketches and requirements, and follows them quite closely. Some of the original ideas have evolved into something more practical as construction was under way, but in general I have produced a close representation of both the appearance and the process that I originally planned. And, no, I didn't cheat and draw the sketches after the site was finished!

The Original Design

The original design for the site includes a page where users can go to see more details about each model, and configure it to suit their personal requirements. As they do so, the page displays the total price for that configuration—including any monthly finance terms they select. At the same time, a picture of the vehicle changes to reflect their color choice.

Selecting a Color for the Vehicle

The first of the original sketches I drew is shown again next; describing the section of the page where users specify the color they want (Figure 8-1).

Figure 8-1. The original sketch of the color selection page

Some of the features of this page have been omitted in the final site. As far as implementation is concerned, a Reviews section would probably have mirrored the operation of the News feature that is available from the Home page, and therefore would have demonstrated nothing new unless it was extended to accept user reviews and act as a list server.

The option of a two-tone "paint job" has also been dropped; mainly because it again would add nothing extra to the techniques I'm attempting to demonstrate. I've also moved the display of the price to the upper section of the page. However, all the other original design features are in place and working, as you can see in Figure 8-2, which is taken from the final application.

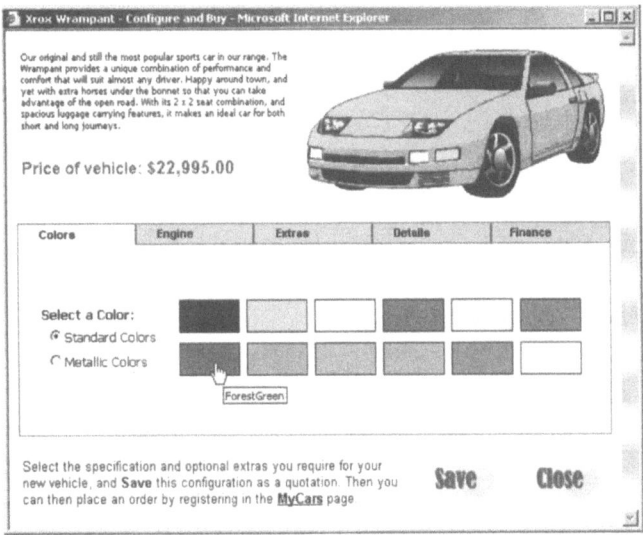

Figure 8-2. The completed color selection page within the application

Selecting the Engine for the Vehicle

The second part of the Model Details page allows users to select the engine they prefer. All the vehicles can be provided with a choice of at least two different engines, and some with more than this. My original sketch is shown in Figure 8-3.

Figure 8-3. The original sketch of the engine selection page

Figure 8-4 shows the section of the final application where the choice of engine is made. Again, it closely follows the original design concept, displaying details of the engines and indicating those of the currently selected engine by highlighting that row in the table.

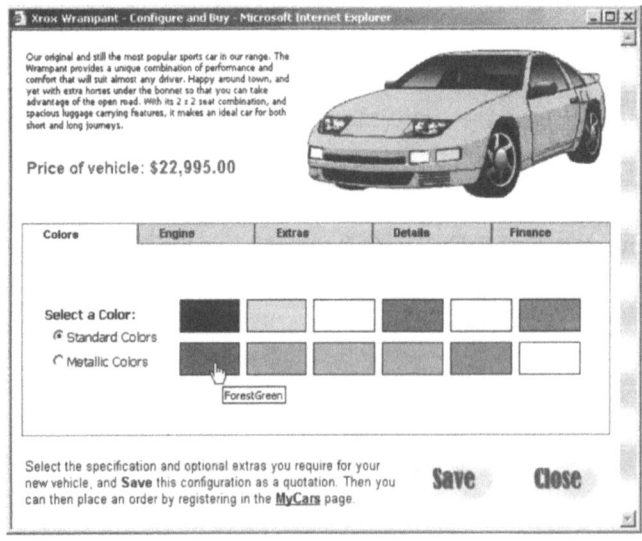

Figure 8-4. The completed engine selection page within the application

Comparing Figure 8-4 with Figure 8-3, you can see the effect on the price of select-ing the larger engine. As with computers, you have to pay to get the extra performance! You may also notice that Figure 8-4 shows the page displayed in Mozilla 1.0, whereas the previous one showed Internet Explorer 6. The appearance of the common content is just about identical. This was an early design decision in that I attempted to provide the best support I could for all kinds of client browser.

Selecting the Optional Extras for the Vehicle

The third section of the page allows visitors to select from a range of optional extras. Figure 8-5 is the original sketch.

Figure 8-5. The original sketch of the optional extras selection page

While I originally envisaged using a mixture of drop-down lists and option buttons, I ended up implementing a somewhat simpler interface. Each vehicle in the range can be equipped with a selection of optional extras, depending on the model. The page on the example site lists these options, and allows a visitor to select which he or she requires. As users select each one, the price is updated to reflect the new total (Figure 8-6).

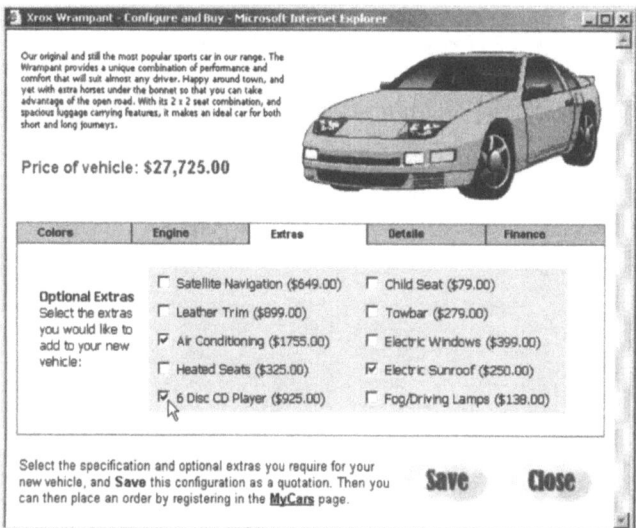

Figure 8-6. The completed optional extras selection page within the application

Viewing the Standard Features of the Vehicle

The fourth section of the Model Details page allows visitors to examine the list of standard features for each vehicle. There is no requirement for interactivity in this section, as it is used simply to display information (Figure 8-7).

Figure 8-7. The original sketch of the standard features page

However, as you can see in the finished page (Figure 8-8), I provide the information as a pair of collapsible "tree view" lists. Each contains a subset of the standard features for this model, and the lists can be expanded to show these details:

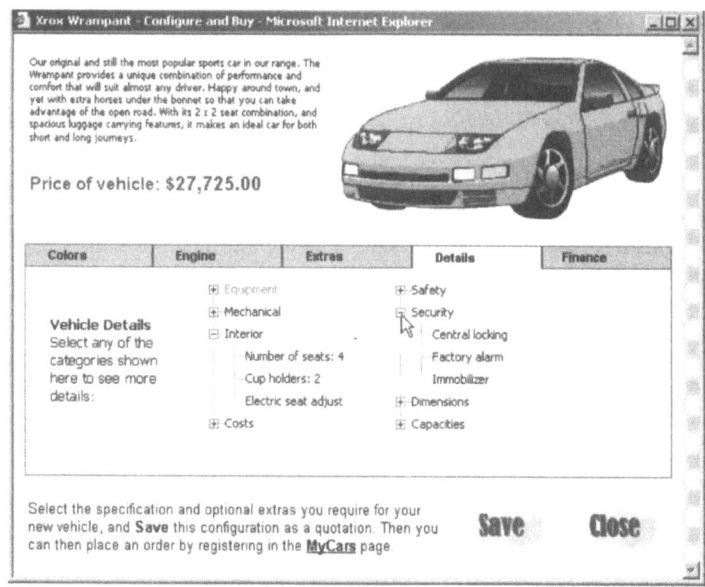

Figure 8-8. The completed standard features page within the application

Selecting a Finance Package for the Vehicle

The final section of this page allows visitors to select a monthly payment finance package that suits them. The original design envisaged two options—specifying the number of months or allowing the page to calculate the number of months given the desired monthly payment (Figure 8-9).

Figure 8-9. The original sketch of the finance details page

Again, I implemented this feature almost exactly as in the design sketch. Figure 8-10 shows this page after the user has selected the number of months required and clicked the Calculate button.

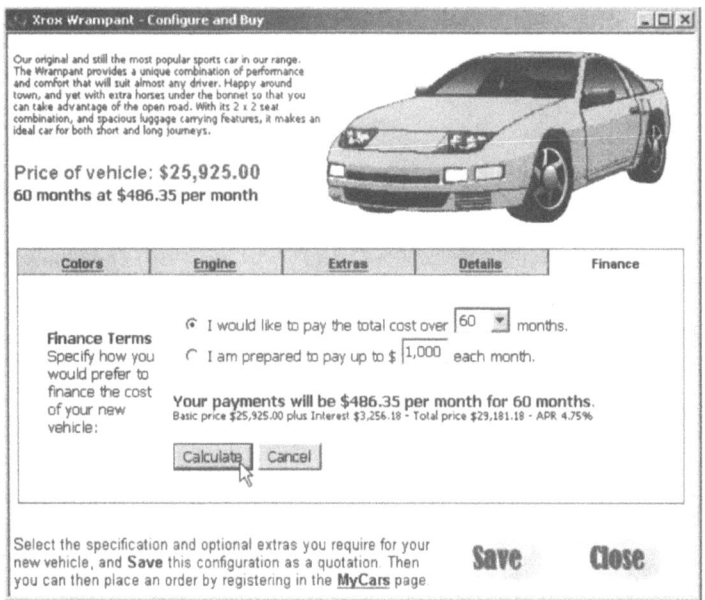

Figure 8-10. The completed finance details page within the application

Notice that Figure 8-10 shows the page in Opera 6.02, rather than Internet Explorer. Other than some very minor page layout details, the result is the same as that you get in Internet Explorer, Netscape 6, and Mozilla.

Supporting "No-Script" Clients

One other point of the original design is that I wanted to provide full support for non-script-enabled and non-graphical clients, as well as for traditional Web browsers. Figure 8-11 shows what this page looks like when using a browser that does not support client-side script (or, in this case, has it disabled):

Figure 8-11. The model details page for "no-script" clients

You can see that now all (five) sections of the page are displayed, separated by horizontal rules, rather than as a "tabbed dialog" page. Without client-side script support, the techniques that I use to create the tabbed dialog effect will not work. And I also have to provide Submit buttons (with the caption "Update") so that the user's configuration selections can be posted to the server for processing. Rather than just one at the bottom of the page, I chose to include an Update button within each section of the page to make it more intuitive.

Supporting "Text-Only" Clients

As well as non-script-enabled clients, I also want to support (as far as possible) text-only and other non-graphical clients. Figure 8-12 shows part of the same page displayed in Lynx—a text-only browser that I demonstrated in earlier chapters. Although the hyperlinks do not show up well when printed in black and white, you should be able to see from the figure that users can select the color, the engine, and the optional extras for a vehicle, as well as selecting the desired finance package (not shown in this screenshot).

Figure 8-12. The model details page displayed in a text-only browser

There are a couple of issues with Lynx, mainly caused by the fact that I am attempting to display this page in a separate window from the Home page and the other pages on the site. Lynx opens all pages in the same "window," and not in a new instance of the browser. I'll come back to this topic shortly when I examine how the page works with non-script-enabled clients.

Supporting "Page-Reader" Clients

As with the other pages in the site, I've tried to provide a good level of support for visitors who use specialist user agents, such as an aural browser like the IBM Home Page Reader. Figure 8-13 shows the part of the page where the user selects the color for the vehicle. I've reduced the size of the top graphical section of the display so that you can see the text that is extracted from the page and read to the user.

Figure 8-13. The model details page displayed in a page reader client

From my experiments, with the screen turned off, I found that I could still specify all the options and use all the other controls on this page.

Saving Quotations and Closing the Window

Once the visitor has finished configuring a chosen model, I allow the user to save the configuration to the server as a quotation—without having to "log on." Afterwards the visitor can register with the site, or log in if he or she has previously registered, view this quotation, and place an order based on it. This can be done immediately or at a later date, because the page saves all the quotes for when the user comes back to the site another time. You can see the instructions and the Save button in Figure 8-14.

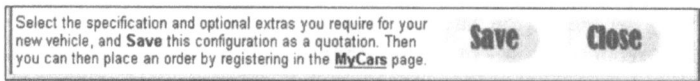

Figure 8-14. Saving the current configuration of a vehicle as a quotation

For client-script-enabled clients, the MyCars link can be used to go directly to the page that displays this user's quotes and previous orders. This page is displayed in the main window, and not in the current Model Details window. The link automatically closes the current window at the same time. This gives a reasonably seamless feel to the interface, rather like a traditional Windows executable application would. The Close link automatically closes the Model Details window, but does not change the page that is displayed in the main window.

When client-side scripting is not available, the way that the Model Details window is displayed and behaves in this respect is different. You can't use client-side code to open the window in the first place, or to control the size and position (as you saw in Chapter 4 when you looked at the code in the Home page that opens this window).

The lack of client-side script support also means that I can't provide a Close link, or automatically change the page that is displayed in the main window when the Save link is clicked. In this case, I still display the Save link, but no Close link, and the instructions are slightly different. The user has to manually close this window in the traditional way using the buttons on the title bar (Figure 8-15).

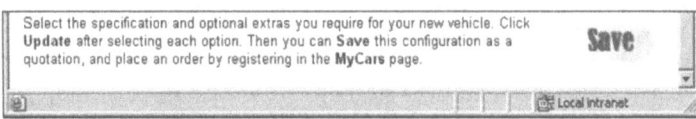

Figure 8-15. Saving a quotation in non-script clients

The Navigation Issue in Lynx

The one issue that the site does not address for navigation from the Model Details page back to the other pages in the site is when I view the site using a text-only client such as Lynx. Many of these types of client display all the pages they load in the same window (in fact Opera can be configured to do the same). So in these cases, you should provide a link that simply navigates to the Home page (or some other page, as required) and opens it in the same window.

But I don't want to do this if the Model Details page is displayed in the new (pop-up) window that is part of the design. I could add some clever client-side script that detects whether this is a pop-up window or the only window, and then provide a suitable link. But without client-side script support (such as in Lynx), I can't implement this either.

However, users can simply navigate back to the Home page by entering the URL of the site into their browser, and then go to the MyCars page from there to view a quote they have just received. As long as their browser supports cookies, or they have already registered and have a login ID and password, they will be connected to their new and existing quotations and orders. OK, so it's not a great site design feature, but it is the only option I can offer in this case.

The Model Details Page in Outline

Having seen the page in action, and discussed some of the technical issues that arise from trying to mirror the original design specifications, I'll move on and look at the page in more detail. In this section I'll give you an overview of the operation of the page, and show how to use the query string, the postback architecture of ASP.NET, and ASP.NET sessions to preserve data and pass it between requests to give optimum performance across all the different types of supported clients.

Opening the Model Details Page

You'll recall from the discussion of the Home page that the links there to open the Model Details page change depending on whether the current client supports client-side scripting or not. If they do support scripting, the page `cardetail.aspx` (in the same folder as the Home page) is opened into a new (pop-up) window using client-side script. This allows the window size and position to be controlled—I placed it in the top left and made it around 630 pixels wide and 550 pixels high.

This means that it will fit nicely onto the screen in 800 x 600 resolution and above (the usual minimum these days for most graphical script-supporting clients). On a 640 x 480 resolution screen it will be too long, but the full width of the title bar, and the buttons at the top right of this, will be visible. So the user can resize the window to suit his or her preferences. Scroll bars will be displayed automatically if required.

> **NOTE** *See Chapter 4 for more information and a code listing showing how the Home page opens the Model Details window.*

The Home page also makes sure that, when client-side scripting is supported, there is only one instance of the Model Details window open for each vehicle model (clicking the same model in the Home page again just brings the existing Model Details window for that vehicle to the front). Of course, you may choose to allow multiple windows for the same vehicle to exist simply by changing the code. However, it does demonstrate a technique that you might want to adopt in your applications.

If the current browser does *not* support scripting, however, you can do no more than just open the page in a new window (you can't control the window size or specify what "window furniture" it will contain either). So there could be multiple windows for the same model in this case, but it makes no difference to how the code works in the Model Details page. The other point is that there is a different page to implement the Model Details for non-script-enabled clients, named (not surprisingly) `cardetail-noscript.aspx`.

The only other feature of the way the Model Details pages is loaded is that I include a query string in the URL when the page opens, which specifies the ID of the selected vehicle. So, in the Model Details pages, I can detect which vehicle I need to fetch data for, and then display it within the page. You'll see how to use this when you look at the code for these pages later in this chapter.

Using the Postback Architecture

Continuing the overview, let me show you how I actually manage the data about the selected vehicle, and how the page interacts with users as they configure this vehicle. The advantages that the ASP.NET postback architecture brings (as I discussed in many places in earlier chapters) means that I can just about leave the page to look after maintaining the user's selections all by itself.

I've enabled viewstate for the Model Details pages (in the Page directive), so all the values that the user enters, the content of the labels and text boxes, the current selection in the lists and option buttons, and the general "state" of the page, will all be persisted between requests without me having to write any code at all.

Compare this to what would be required in (for example) ASP 3.0, JSP, or Perl, where you would have to save the values from around 20 different types of HTML "form" controls in the user's session or in a database with each request, and then extract them all and use these to populate the controls correctly for the response. Simply adding an extra control to the page in these other environments can produce a lot of extra work, while in ASP.NET it's all handled automatically!

A Schematic of the Whole Process

Figure 8-16 shows in overview the process of managing the data in the Model Details page. When the page is first opened, I use some stored procedures to interrogate the database and build a DataSet that contains all the information required for this page. This process is quite resource intensive, and so I cache the DataSet in the user's session afterwards. This means that I don't need to go back to the database and re-create it with each postback.

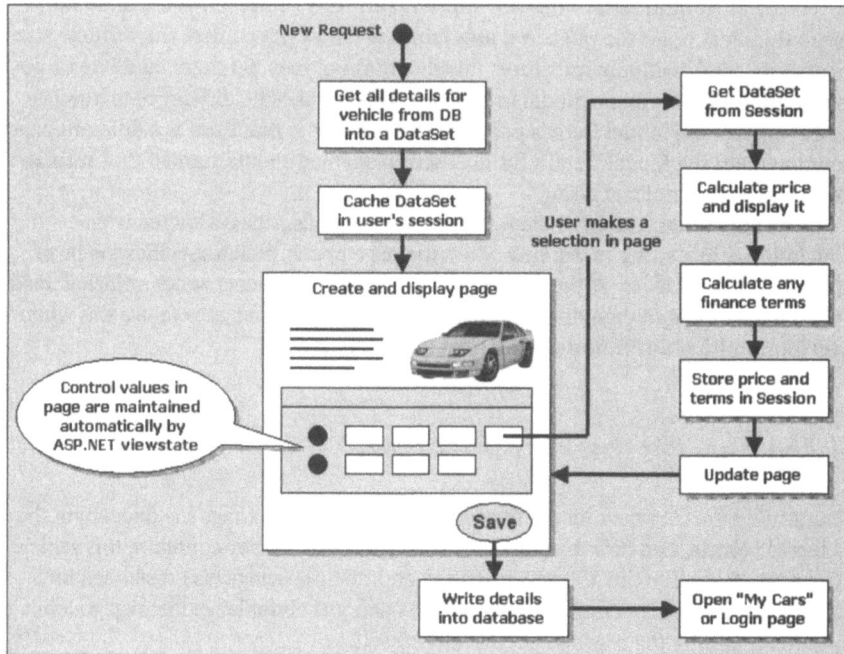

Figure 8-16. Managing the data in the Model Details page

> **NOTE** *Recall that I am insisting that the client supports sessions. I do this either through the use of cookies or by redirecting the client to a copy of the application that uses the ASP.NET cookie-less session feature.*

Calculating the Price and Finance Terms

As the user interacts with the controls on the page, it is posted back to the server each time (with a couple of exceptions if the client is Internet Explorer 5.5 or later, as you'll see). With each postback, depending on which control caused the postback, I can calculate the price for the vehicle and update the display to reflect this.

However, I only display the finance terms (the number and amount of each monthly payment) when a user specifically clicks the Calculate button in that part of the page. Each time the price of the vehicle is recalculated the previous finance terms are cleared. I could, of course, recalculate these as well each time the price changes, but there is an issue in that the price might exceed the limits I've defined for the maximum number of payments if the user has specified their maximum monthly payment amount. By forcing them to go back and recalculate it, I also have the option to comply with possible legal requirements by displaying the interest rate and amount each time.

Storing the Price and Finance Terms

After I have calculated the total price for the vehicle, and possibly the finance terms as well, I need to cache these somewhere where I can get at them again when the user decides to save the current configuration as a quotation. I could always extract them from the label controls where they are displayed, but this gets clunky because I am building up a string containing several values in the case of the finance terms, as shown in Figure 8-17.

Figure 8-17. The controls for seleccting a finance package

Instead, I chose to store the values in an array, and cache this array in the user's session. It can easily be extracted so that I can work with the content (reading and updating it) with each request.

Detecting Control Events and Updating the Page Content

Then, after all the calculations are done, I can update the relevant parts of the page. In some cases, this may involve setting other values, such as selecting a row in the Engines table or changing the color of the car image at the top of the page—it depends on which control caused the postback. Again, this is where ASP.NET makes life easy, as each control on the page can raise its own specific event on the server as it processes the request.

So, for example, I can write an event handler that is invoked only when the option buttons for the type of color (Standard or Metallic) are clicked. OK, so the Page_Load event is also called with every postback, but I use this to my advantage by running code that I need to execute in every page load in the Page_Load event handler, and then any control-specific code in the handler for that control's own postback event (such as OnClick or OnCheckedChanged).

Later, you'll see all the event handlers I use, along with the remainder of the code and content in this page. However, there is one other feature of ASP.NET that I also find extremely useful in interactive pages, and which I take advantage of in the Model Details page. This is the auto-postback feature.

Using Auto-Postback to Drive the Page

Most Web users are familiar with the auto-postback effect in a Web page, where simply making a selection in a list or checking a check box causes the page to be submitted to the server. In ASP.NET, this process can be implemented just by adding the `AutoPostback="True"` attribute to any of the interactive controls such as a check box, an option button, a drop-down list, or in fact any other type of list such as a `CheckBoxList` control or a `RadioButtonList` control. I discussed this technique in detail in earlier chapters.

Of course, I have a problem with auto-postback when there is no client-side scripting support, but I've already described how to use multiple "submit" buttons on the `cardetails-noscript.aspx` page to get around this. I'll also look at this topic in a little more depth later in this chapter.

What Happened to the Frames?

In the original design, you may recall that I considered using HTML frames within the Model Details page to allow the price and finance terms to be calculated in the background. Many sites use this technique, including well-known ones such as Dell Computers. An "options" page (which can be a dynamic `.asp` or a static `.htm` page) contains a series of controls on an HTML `<form>`.

The `target` attribute of this `<form>` specifies a separate frame within the same browser window, and so any page generated in response to the form being submitted is displayed in the other frame. The current page that contains the `<form>` continues to be displayed. This means that, as the user makes selections and clicks a Submit button (or client-side script in the page submits the form automatically as they select from the lists of options), the other frame can be repeatedly reloaded to show the current price.

Why haven't I adopted this useful-sounding technique here? The answer is that ASP.NET effectively prevents you from taking this approach unless you are prepared to abandon the comforting and extremely supportive environment of the postback architecture. For the automatic maintenance of viewstate to work, I have to use a server-side `<form runat="server">`. This means that I must post each page back to itself every time, as the server-side `<form>` demands this and prevents us from specifying a different value for the `action` attribute. I can't submit the `<form>` to a different page.

OK, so I can still set the `target` attribute so that the page loads into a different frame, then post back to the same page and use some clever detection code (probably via a value placed into a `hidden`-type control on the form) that causes just the price to be displayed in the second frame.

However, having said all that, You have already seen that most of the actions that the user takes when interacting with the page require a postback to the server to update the page. And any actions that don't require a postback do not affect the price anyway, so there is no advantage to using a separate frame. This is why I ultimately chose to use just a single page in the Model Details window.

Implementing a "Tabbed Dialog"

My design calls for a "tabbed dialog" appearance in the Model Details page, and you can see from the earlier figures that I have accomplished this for all the modern graphical script-enabled browsers such as Internet Explorer, Mozilla, Opera, and (not shown so far) Netscape. To achieve this I used two of the special controls that are part of the Internet Explorer Web Controls Pack. This pack contains several extremely useful controls that are designed for use in both ASP.NET, and client-side in Internet Explorer 5.5 and later.

About the IE Web Controls

The Internet Explorer team at Microsoft has been providing special tools and components for use client-side with IE for some time. Many of the controls were installed automatically with previous versions of Internet Explorer, such as the Structural Graphics control for drawing vector graphics in the page, a range of Data Source Controls for interacting with Remote Data Services and XML files to display data in the page, and several multimedia controls such as graphics filters and the Time control.

However, the IE Web Controls represent a breakthrough in that they are designed to interface directly with ASP.NET and produce compatible output on all kinds of browsers—not just Internet Explorer. They include a set of components (Hyper-Text Components or HTCs) that are downloaded to the client as well as a set of server control classes that are installed into the .NET Framework on the server.

The IE Web Controls pack includes:

- The **MultiPage** control, which allows you to create several separate sections of a page and have just one of these sections displayed at a time.

- The **TabStrip** control, which provides the "tab" effect you see in the earlier figures to represent a tabbed dialog in a Web page.

- The **TreeView** control, which can display an expandable and collapsible list of values or links.

- The **Toolbar** control, which can be used to create a Windows-style toolbar within a Web page.

I use the first three of these controls in the example application, and you'll see more about these when you look at the code in more detail later in this and the next chapter. The controls do make it extremely easy to add these kinds of features to a page, and in Internet Explorer 5.5 and later, they provide superb client-side interactivity that can reduce the number of postbacks to the server. The bonus is that they are backwards compatible as well, so while the performance (and in some cases the appearance) is downgraded in clients other than IE 5.5 and later, they still function as expected.

> **NOTE**   *You can obtain the IE Web Controls from the MSDN Web site at:*
> `http://msdn.microsoft.com/downloads/samples/internet/`
> `asp_dot_net_servercontrols/webcontrols/Default.asp`
> *or individually from the ASP.NET site at*
> `http://www.asp.net/IEWebControls/Download.aspx?tabindex=0&tabid=1.`
> *Be sure to select the option(s) that install both the ASP.NET Server controls and the DHTML client-side Behavior components. The text in the download page suggests that controls will only work with version 1.0 of ASP.NET, though I have not experienced any issues using them with version 1.1 applications.*

Fallback Support for Older Browsers

In Internet Explorer 5.5 and later, the TabStrip control uses an HTC that is loaded from the server and instantiated client-side within the page. This HTC integrates directly and automatically with the MultiPage control, which is another HTC that is loaded from the server and instantiated client-side. You can switch from one "tab" or "page" to another without any postback to the server being required, because the details of all the tabs and their content are stored within the client-side page.

Of course, none of this is going to work in other browsers. However, in this case, the controls detect that a different client is in use and automatically provide "standard" HTML output (as an HTML `table`) that displays just the current "tab" and its content. When the user clicks a different tab heading, a postback to the server causes the contents of the tab the user selected to be displayed instead. As you saw in earlier figures, this works fine in browsers such as Mozilla and Opera 6.

However, one other point to watch out for is that the TabStrip uses Cascading Style Sheets (CSS 1.0) to control the positioning, font style, display of borders, and shading. Figure 8-18 shows the Model Details page displayed in Netscape Navigator 4.5, and you can see that its lack of full CSS support means that the appearance is less than optimal. However, as long as I choose the background colors for the tabs carefully, the output is still reasonably close to the design requirements. And, other than using images to create the appearance of the tabs, there isn't much else I could do to get a "tabbed dialog" effect anyway:

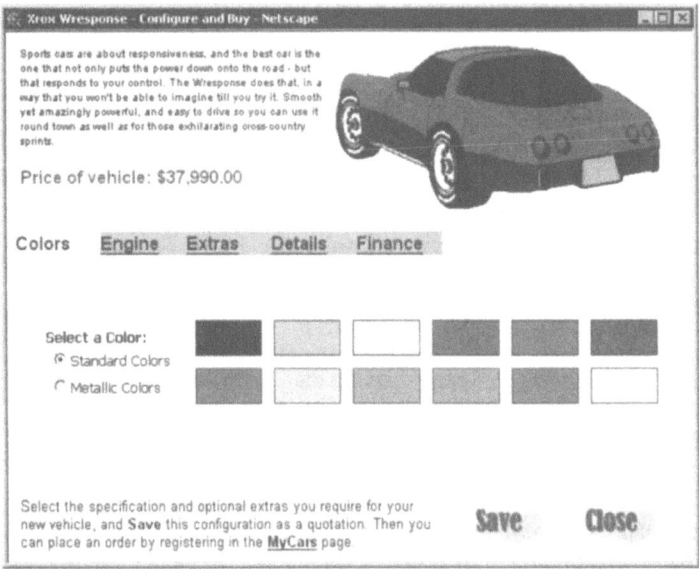

Figure 8-18. The output from the TabStrip control in Netscape Navigator 4.5

Coping Without Client-Side Scripting Support

You saw in earlier discussions and figures that I implemented two different pages for the Model Details—one that requires client-side scripting to be available and one that does not. I discussed some of the reasons I chose this approach, and what the differences in the pages are. For completeness, I'll summarize the differences here, as they relate to many of the topics I've been discussing so far.

Table 8-1 shows the differences between the two Model Details pages, how this affects the original design requirements, and how to work around the limitations that the lack of client-side scripting imposes.

Table 8-1. Comparing Script-Enabled and Non-Script-Enabled Capabilities

Task	Description	With Client Script	Without Client Script
Opening the Model Details window.	I want to open the Model Details window at a specific position and size, and reuse the appropriate window.	Code demonstrated in Chapter 4 uses the client-side `window.open` and `focus` methods.	Set `target` attribute of hyperlink to `"_blank"` to open page in a new window.
Closing the Model Details window.	There are several occasions where the page that is displayed in the main window changes in response to events in the Model Details window, such as when a quotation is saved.	Change the value of `location.href` for the main window (`window.opener`) to display the required page, then call the client-side `window.close` method of this window.	Can't be done without using named frames in each window. Not implemented in the example application so the user has to manually close the Model Details window and navigate to the main window.
Displaying the "tabbed dialog" and individual "tabs" and their content.	The TabStrip control requires client-side script support in all cases.	Control automatically provides suitable output depending on client type.	Can't be done when using the TabStrip control, so they are all displayed in one long page.
Automatic postback as the user interacts with controls in the page.	Makes the page more responsive by updating it when a control is clicked or a value changed.	Add the ASP.NET `AutoPostback` attribute to relevant control declarations.	Use multiple Submit buttons (with the caption Update) within the page.
Setting option buttons in response to text entry or list selection.	Used in the Finance section to set the appropriate option button when selecting the calculation method.	Client-side event handler for the `OnChange` and `OnKeyDown` events sets the `checked` property of the relevant option button.	Can't be done, though page is still usable without this.

You'll see the `cardetail-noscript.aspx` page in the next chapter, once you've seen how the version that requires client-side script works. You'll discover that the bulk of the page content and code is identical, and there are only a few changes I have to make to cope with the lack of client-script support. Of course, this is because I originally designed the page to be implementable without client-side script. I look at this issue next.

Client-Side Versus Server-Side Page Updates

Modern browsers have great support for building dynamic pages that don't require regular postbacks to the server. Since the days of Internet Explorer 4 (and, to some extent, Navigator 4), you've been able to use Dynamic HTML in conjunction with client-side script to change the appearance and content of a page while loaded into the browser. With the advent of the "version 6" browsers, CSS 2.0 provides the same kinds of features. So, in my Model Details page, why haven't I implemented more of this kind of approach to reduce server postbacks and provide a smoother and more responsive user experience? The reasons for this are fourfold:

- It's extremely hard to create dynamic pages that depend on client-side features, and that will work in different types of browsers. You saw this when I was building the animated page banner back in Chapter 5.

- I can't provide support for older browsers and non-graphical clients and page readers, which either don't support Dynamic HTML or the very nature of its use makes it irrelevant (for example, in a "page reader").

- The processes I need to carry out in calculating the price and finance terms are complex, and not easy to accomplish in client-side script alone. I would also have to remote all the data and algorithms required to perform the calculation to the client each time.

- I am using many of the ASP.NET server controls to reduce development time and effort, and to provide the appearance and functionality I want. With a few minor exceptions, these depend on a postback to the server to work properly.

All of this doesn't mean that you should always avoid client-side processing. In some cases it can provide a real benefit. There are many techniques that are available for remoting data to a client and processing it there, although I don't. Nor do I have room to cover the techniques here.

An Example—Changing the Color of the Car

As an example of the decision process I went through, one of the features of the Model Details page is that it changes the color of the car displayed at the top right of the page as you select a color from the list in the first page of the tabbed dialog. Rather than have multiple images in all the possible colors, I "cheated" by using a single GIF image where the bodywork of the vehicle is transparent. The image is displayed in the cell of an HTML table, and I just have to change the background color of the cell to display the car in a different color. Figure 8-19 shows the results in Netscape 6.0.

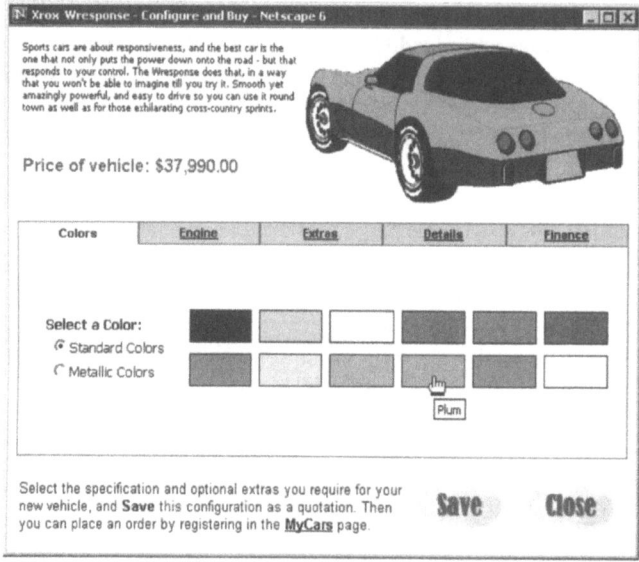

Figure 8-19. The color of the car image changes as each color is selected

Almost all graphical Web browsers, including some very old ones, allow you to specify the background color of a cell using the bgcolor attribute, so this technique is reasonably universal for all graphical clients. However, some browsers (notably Internet Explorer 4 and later, Netscape 4 and later, and the version 6 browsers) allow you to change the value of the bgcolor property of a table cell while the page is displayed in the browser, and they render this color immediately.

This means that you could execute some client-side code in response to the user selecting a color and avoid a postback to the server. It would work in most of the common browsers in use today, and give a more responsive interface because the user would see the result immediately. However, there are a few reasons I chose not to go down this route:

- It won't work if the browser does not support client-side scripting, so I'd have to code two different processes—one client-side and one server-side, or a combination of the two. This isn't too difficult, but it makes maintenance harder in the long run.

- The syntax for accessing elements in a page varies in different types of clients; for example, Netscape 4 and IE 4 are different from each other, and both are different from the CSS 2.0 techniques supported by version 6 browsers. So I'd need multiple versions of the client-side script code.

- I would still have to do some client detection if I wanted to support old browsers that do not allow the bgcolor attribute to be set, and force a postback to the server.

- I may need to change the price of the vehicle. The metallic colors add a premium to the cost of the vehicle, and so I would have to provide client-side code to handle price recalculations as well.

The Conclusion

While you can see that I have tended towards using server-side processing and postbacks in the sample application, this doesn't mean that you should always go down this route. Client-side script support is extremely useful in many circumstances, as you can see from the earlier comparisons of the two versions of the Model Details page that I implemented.

So don't be put off by my decision here to stay with mainly server-side processing. Remember that I still use client-side script for several features of the page; much of it is implemented automatically by the ASP.NET server controls and the IE Web Controls. Furthermore, many of the basic client-side-script-driven techniques that I do implement in the page, such as automatic postback of a <form> and setting the checked property of options buttons, use JavaScript code that is fully cross-browser compatible.

Saving Quotations and Orders

As well as allowing the user to see details of the vehicles Xrox Cars offers, and the price for their chosen configuration, the Model Details page has to be able to save that user's quotation for later use (and, hopefully, conversion into an order!). This is done by writing all the details of the current configuration (all the selections made in the Model Details page) into the database (Figure 8-20).

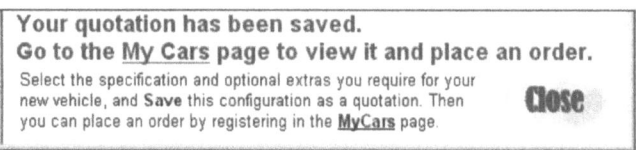

Figure 8-20. The result of saving a quotation to the database

You'll recall that I established a unique User ID for all visitors to the site, and stored this in their ASP.NET sessions. Each page checks that a session exists and takes action to reestablish one if there isn't one present when that page loads (by redirecting the user to default.aspx where the User ID is created again). You saw the code to do all this when you looked at the client-detection routines and the Home page, back in Chapters 3 and 4.

So, knowing that users will have a unique User ID stored in their sessions, all I have to do is include this ID in the quote stored in the database. When users come back to the site, I can connect them to any existing quotations they have received. In fact, any orders they place are stored in the same table, with just a single "flag" value indicating if it is a quotation or an order. This means that I can display a user's quotations and/or orders whenever I want.

The "flag" value also allows me to "expire" quotations. I could delete any quotation rows automatically if they were more than, say, 14 days old, by executing a suitable SQL statement or stored procedure either when the My Cars page is displayed, or (even better) by running a separate executable application or service at specific intervals such as once a day.

You'll see the process of writing the configuration to the database as a quotation in this and the next chapter, as you examine the Model Details page. Then, in later chapters, you'll look at the way that I authenticate users and allow them to log in and view their existing quotations and orders.

The Structure of the Model Details Page

So, having spent half a chapter in general overview, you should now have a good understanding of what the Model Details page does—at least in outline. In the remainder of this chapter and throughout the next one, you'll see the code I use to create the page, and the ASP.NET processing that makes it all work. You'll look at the version for script-enabled clients first, and then I'll show you the way I change the page to work with non-script-enabled clients towards the end of Chapter 9.

The overall layout of the page source is similar to what I used in most of the other pages on the example site. I start with the Page directive, which specifies that I want viewstate to be available and implemented in this page, and that I want to be able to read and write data in the user's ASP.NET session.

This is followed by the Import directives for the namespaces I'll need in the page. I included the System.Data and System.Data.SqlClient namespaces so that I can access the SQL Server database, and I need the System.Drawing namespace so that I can work with the colors defined for each car model. You'll see how and why later:

cardetail.aspx
```
<%@ Page Language="VB" EnableViewState="True" EnableSessionState="True" %>
<%@ Import Namespace="System.Data"%>
<%@ Import Namespace="System.Data.SqlClient"%>
<%@ Import Namespace="System.Drawing" %>
...
```

Importing and Registering the IE Web Controls

I also have to import and register the namespace that implements the IE Web Controls I used in this page. This is not a default ASP.NET namespace, so I have to include the

Register directive to specify details of the assembly and the tag prefix I'll use when I declare the controls in the page. Note that the Assembly attribute value must all be on one line, and not broken over two lines as I've had to do here in the code listing:

```
...
<%@ Import Namespace="Microsoft.Web.UI.WebControls" %>
<%@ Register TagPrefix="ie" Namespace="Microsoft.Web.UI.WebControls"
    Assembly="Microsoft.Web.UI.WebControls, Version=1.0.2.226,
    Culture=neutral, PublicKeyToken=31bf3856ad364e35" %>
<!-- note that preceding Assembly attribute must be all on one line -->
...
```

> **NOTE** *The values you see in the* Register *directive are provided in the documentation for the controls, and will probably vary in later versions of these controls.*

After this comes the ASP.NET script section where the code to implement the page interactivity is located. You'll be looking at this code in detail later in this chapter and the next:

```
...
<script runat="server">
...
... ASP.NET server-side code goes here ...
...
</script>
```

The HTML Section of the Page

The visible content of the page comes next. There is the same selection of elements at the beginning of the page as for most other pages, though I don't use the animated page banner in this page. However, I do include a "skip to" link for text-only and page-reader clients, which points to an anchor element located in the main section of the page.

Notice that I also use the same technique as in other pages to insert the correct style sheet name into the <link> element, and I have an empty server-side <title> element that I'll fill with the vehicle name in the ASP.NET code as the page loads:

```
<!doctype html public "-//W3C//DTD HTML 3.2 Final//EN">
<html>
<head>
<basefont size="2" face="Tahoma,Arial,Helvetica,sans-serif">
<link rel="stylesheet" type="text/css"
        href="stylesheets/wcc<% = sStyleSize %>.css" />
<title id="elmTitle" runat="server" />
</head>
<body bgcolor="#ffffff" class="body-text">

<div style="position:absolute;height:0px;"><font size="1" color=#ffffff>
<!-- skip link for aural page readers -->
<layer visibility="hidden">
<a href="#content" style="color:#ffffff;font-size:1px;text-decoration:none"><img
width="1" height="1" hspace="0" vspace="0" src="images/_blnk.gif" border="0" alt="Skip
to Content" /></a>
</layer></font></div>
<form runat="server">
...
... dynamic page content goes here...
...
</form>
</body>
</html>
```

The remainder of the page is a single server-side `<form>` section, within which the rest of the dynamic and static content is located. This content is in five sections:

- The model description, price, and image

- The TabStrip control

- The MultiPage control

- A Label for displaying information and error messages

- The instructions for saving quotes, and the Save and Cancel buttons

I discuss each of these sections in turn.

The Model Description, Price, and Image

The top section of the example page contains nothing unexpected; simply an HTML table that displays the model description (précis) and the image. I use an asp:Label for the description and extract the text from the database and insert it into this Label during the Page_Load event. The image of the car is placed into a cell in the right-hand column that spans two rows using an asp:Image control. I set the ImageUrl property of this control during the `Page_Load` event to load the appropriate image depending on which vehicle was selected in the Home page:

```
<!-- model description and image -->
<table border="0" cellspacing="5" cellpadding="0">
<tr>
<td valign="top"><font face="Arial,Helvetica,sans-serif" size="1">
  <asp:Label class="fixed-small-text" id="lblPrecis" runat="server" />
  </font></td>
<td rowspan="2" id="tclColor" bgcolor="white" nowrap="true" runat="server">
  <asp:Image id="imgCar" runat="server" /></td>
</tr><tr>
<td><font face="Arial,Helvetica,sans-serif" size="3" color="#b50055"><b>
  Price of vehicle:
  $<asp:Label id="lblPrice" CssClass="large-red-text" runat="server" /></b>
  </font><font face="Arial,Helvetica,sans-serif" size="2"><br />
  <b><asp:Label id="lblTerms" CssClass="body-text"
                Text=" " runat="server" /></b>
  </font></td>
</tr>
</table><p />
<a name="content" />
...
```

Notice that I set the background color of the cell containing the car image to "white". You'll see why in more detail in the next couple of chapters when you see how I calculate the price of the vehicle and save a quotation for it. Basically, I need to be able to extract the color name from the `BgColor` property of this cell in the server-side code (this is why it is also defined with the `runat="server"` attribute, so that it is implemented as a server control).

The lower cell in the left-hand part of the table shown in the preceding code listing contains two `asp:Label` controls where I'll display the current price of the vehicle, and any finance terms that the user has specified. Notice that I use the same technique as in other pages you've seen previously to control the font, size, and color—I specify the CSS class name in the `Label` control, then wrap it in `<font>` tags for clients that don't understand CSS. After the end of the table is the "skip to link" anchor that allows users to go straight to the page content (Figure 8-21).

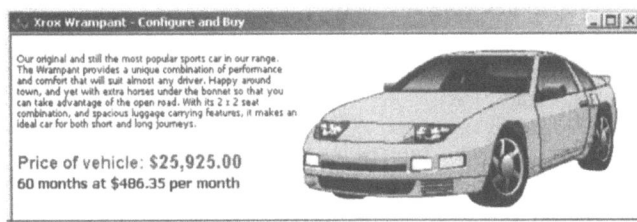

Figure 8-21. The car image, précis, price, and finance details

The "Tabbed Dialog" Section

The main interactive section of the example page is implemented as a "tabbed dialog" in script-enabled browsers, and for this I've used the TabStrip and MultiPage controls from the IE Web Controls pack that I discussed earlier in this chapter.

To control the position of the "tabbed dialog" on the page, I enclose it all inside a two-row single-column HTML table. The first row of the table contains the TabStrip control that implements the individual outlined tab labels, and the second row contains the MultiPage control that manages the display of the appropriate set of controls depending on which tab is selected (Figure 8-22).

Figure 8-22. The TabStrip *and* MultiPage *controls in the color selection page*

The TabStrip Control

The following code listing shows the declaration of the TabStrip control within the first row of the table:

```
...
<!-- tab strip control -->
<table border="0" width="100%" cellpadding="0" cellspacing="0">
 <tr>
  <td>
   <ie:TabStrip id="tsCarDetail" runat="server"
       style="width:100%"
       TargetID="mpCarDetail"
       TabDefaultStyle="background-color:#cccccc; border-width:1px;
                        border-style:solid; border-color:#666666;
                        font-weight:bold; text-align:center;
                        font-family:Arial,Helvetica,sans-serif;
                        font-size:11px; height:21; width:79;"
       TabHoverStyle="color:#ff0000; text-decoration:underline;
                      background-color:#cccccc;"
       TabSelectedStyle="background-color:#ffffff; border-bottom:none"
       SepDefaultStyle="background-color:#ffffff; border-top:none;
                        border-left:none; border-right:none">
```

```
        <ie:Tab Text="Colors" />
        <ie:Tab Text="Engine" />
        <ie:Tab Text="Extras" />
        <ie:Tab Text="Details" />
        <ie:Tab Text="Finance" />
      </ie:TabStrip>
    </td>
  </tr><tr>
    ...
```

To insert the TabStrip control into the page, I simply declare it just like I would any other ASP.NET server control—except that I use the tag prefix ie I registered for the IE Web Controls earlier in the page. Then I can set the attribute values to specify the appearance I want for the control. I'm using only a small selection of the available attributes for this example, taking advantage of many of the sensible defaults that the control implements.

The values I've used create a horizontal tab strip (the default type) that fills the width of the enclosing table cell (style="width:"100%"). The tabs can alternatively be aligned vertically if required. The appearance of each tab is controlled by the various xxxxStyle properties, such as TabDefaultStyle, TabHoverStyle, and TabSelectedStyle. The style properties specified for the TabDefaultStyle attribute are inherited by the style attributes for the other parts of the control (hover, selected, separator, and so on) so I don't have to repeat these.

Then, within the TabStrip element itself, I specify the tabs that I want to appear using individual Tab elements, and the Text that I want to appear on each of these tabs. Figures 8-22 and 8-23 show the result for the values I've used in the declaration of the TabStrip control.

Figure 8-23. The output generated by the TabStrip *control*

Using Images with a TabStrip Control

An alternative approach is to use images to create the visible appearance for the tabs and the separators between them, and these are specified using a separate set of attributes; DefaultImageUrl, SepDefaultImageUrl, SepHoverImageUrl, and so on. Then I can declare a different image to be used on each tab, for example:

```
<ie:TabStrip id="tabWithImages" runat="server"
             SepDefaultImageUrl="center-default.gif"
             SepSelectedImageUrl="selected-centre.gif">
  <ie:TabSeparator DefaultImageUrl="left-tab-edge.gif"
                   SelectedImageUrl="selected-left-tab-edge.gif" />
  <ie:Tab DefaultImageUrl="tab1-image.gif"
          SelectedImageUrl="tab1-selected-image.gif" />
  <ie:TabSeparator/>
  <ie:Tab DefaultImageUrl="tab2-image.gif"
          SelectedImageUrl="tab2-selected-image.gif" />
  <ie:TabSeparator/>
  <ie:Tab DefaultImageUrl="tab3-image.gif"
          SelectedImageUrl="tab3-selected-image.gif" />
  <ie:TabSeparator DefaultImageUrl="right-tab-edge.gif"
                   SelectedImageUrl="selected-right-tab-edge.gif" />
</ie:TabStrip>
```

I don't have room here for a complete reference to the TabStrip or MultiPage controls, but you can access the documentation for them from the link that is added to your Start menu when you install the controls.

The IE Web Controls can be instantiated both from within ASP.NET, as I'm doing, and directly within a page on the client just as you can instantiate any other HTC. Therefore there are two sets of references to the controls—the ASP.NET references for the server-side .NET assembly "wrapper," and the client-side HTC references for the controls themselves. Both are available online at MSDN. Go to:

http://msdn.microsoft.com/library/default.asp?url=/workshop/webcontrols/
webcontrols_entry.asp

The MultiPage Control

The second row of the table that I "opened" in the previous code listing contains the MultiPage control. This control manages all the content that I want to display on all the "tabs" of the tabbed dialog, with each page being declared within a separate PageView element. All these PageView elements are enclosed within the MultiPage element itself.

The following listing shows the declaration of the MultiPage control, with the HTML content of each "tab" omitted to make it easier to see how the control itself is declared within the page. I'll come back and look at the content of each "tab" later:

```
...
<!-- multipage control -->
<td nowrap="nowrap">
  <ie:MultiPage id="mpCarDetail" runat="server"
                style="border-width:1px; border-style:solid;
                       border-color:#666666; border-top:none">
    <ie:PageView id="mpColors">
      <!-- controls for "Colors" tab go here -->
    </ie:PageView>
```

```
      <ie:PageView id="mpEngine">
        <!-- controls for "Engine" tab go here -->
      </ie:PageView>
      <ie:PageView id="mpExtras">
        <!-- controls for "Extras" tab go here -->
      </ie:PageView>
      <ie:PageView id="mpDetails">
        <!-- controls for "Details" tab go here -->
      </ie:PageView>
      <ie:PageView id="mpFinance">
        <!-- controls for "Finance" tab go here -->
      </ie:PageView>
    </ie:MultiPage></td>
  </tr>
</table>
...
```

Notice how the `style` attribute I used with this control adds a border around three sides of the control, but omits it from the top. This is what produces the "tabbed dialog" appearance in the page. However, bear in mind that the `TabStrip` and `MultiPage` controls are inserted into rows of a table, and so it's vital to prevent white space appearing between them, thus ruining the border effect. For this reason, in my opening `<table>` tag, I set the `cellpadding` and `cellspacing` attributes to zero:

```
<table border="0" width="100%" cellpadding="0" cellspacing="0">
```

Linking the *TabStrip* and *MultiPage* Controls

The preceding declarations insert the two controls, the `TabStrip` and `MultiPage`, into the page and I get the appearance I want automatically. However, how do I switch between the "tabs" and show the appropriate content in the `MultiPage` control when the user clicks one of the tabs? One way is to react to the `SelectedIndexChange` event that the `TabStrip` control raises when a tab is clicked. I can do this on the server or on the client.

> **NOTE** *Notice that the event name does not follow the normal pattern for other ASP.NET controls—it does not end with "d" like, for example, the OnCheckedChanged event of the ASP.NET CheckBox control.*

By handling the `SelectedIndexChange` event for the `TabStrip` control, I can determine which tab was clicked by examining the `SelectedIndex` property of this control. Then I can tell the `MultiPage` control to display the content of the appropriate "tab" or "page" section by setting its `SelectedIndex` property to the required index value.

However, when I use TabStrip and MultiPage controls together, as in the example, I don't have to do even this minor amount of work to integrate the two controls. If you look back at the listing of the TabStrip declaration, you'll see that I specified the ID of the MultiPage control in the TargetID attribute of the TabStrip control:

```
TargetID="mpCarDetail"
```

This means that the two controls are automatically linked together. As long as there is the same number of "tabs" (Tab elements) defined for the TabStrip as there are "pages" (PageView elements) for the MultiPage control, it will all work seamlessly without any intervention. Clicking the first "tab" displays the first "page" content, clicking the second "tab" displays the second "page" content, and so on.

So, all I have to do now is specify the content for each page. Though it might seem to be a rather strange order for doing things, I'm going to postpone looking at the content of each "tab" for now, and move on to look at the remainder of the HTML in this page. I'll come back and look at each "tab" in more detail at the start of Chapter 9, and examine the ASP.NET code that is used to implement the operation of the controls in each tab. This saves you from having to keep referring back to a listing in this chapter as I discuss the code; and, anyway, there's a lot more to cover before you start looking at this code.

What Output Do the TabStrip and MultiPage Controls Create?

The easiest way to understand what the TabStrip and MultiPage controls actually do is to look at the output they create in the browser. You can do this in most browsers by right-clicking the page and selecting View Source, or by using the Source option from the View menu.

In Internet Explorer 5.5 and later, the ASP.NET server controls that implement the TabStrip and MultiPage create XML elements within the page. These XML elements contain the data (content) that the client-side HTC controls use to generate the visible appearance for the page. The section of the output created by the TabStrip control is shown in the following code listing:

Output from the TabStrip control in Internet Explorer 5.5 and later
```
<?XML:NAMESPACE PREFIX="TSNS" /><?IMPORT NAMESPACE="TSNS"
IMPLEMENTATION="/webctrl_client/1_0/tabstrip.htc" />
<TSNS:TabStrip id="tsCarDetail" selectedIndex="0" targetID="mpCarDetail"
tabDefaultStyle="background-color:#cccccc;border-width:1px;border-style:
solid;border-color:#666666;font-weight:bold;text-align:center;
font-family:Arial,Helvetica,sans-serif;font-size:11px;height:21;width:79;"
tabHoverStyle="color:#ff0000;text-decoration:underline;
background-color:#cccccc;" tabSelectedStyle="background-color:#ffffff;
border-bottom:none;" sepDefaultStyle="background-color:#ffffff;
border-top:none;border-left:none;border-right:none;"
onSelectedIndexChange="JScript:document._ctl0.__tsCarDetail_State
__.value=event.index" onwcready="JScript:try{document._ctl0.__tsCarDetail_State
__.value=selectedIndex}catch(e){}" style="width:100%">
```

```
    <TSNS:Tab>Colors</TSNS:Tab>
    <TSNS:Tab>Engine</TSNS:Tab>
    <TSNS:Tab>Extras</TSNS:Tab>
    <TSNS:Tab>Details</TSNS:Tab>
    <TSNS:Tab>Finance</TSNS:Tab>
</TSNS:TabStrip>
```

You can see that the `<?IMPORT...>` element in the first line of the preceding code references the HTC file `tabstrip.htc`, which is located in the `webctrl_client` folder of the example Web site. Installing the IE Web Controls automatically creates this folder for each Web site on the machine, and installs the HTC files into it. From there, the HTC files are downloaded to the client and instantiated within the page to process the XML content you see in the preceding listing. If I subsequently create a new Web site on the server, I have to copy this folder to it if I want to use the IE Web Controls in this new site.

The `MultiPage` control behaves much the same way. The following listing shows an abridged version of the output it creates, and again you can see the reference to the HTC file—in this case `multipage.htc`. Notice that all of the "tab" or "page" sections are sent to the client within the XML output. This allows it to display any of the pages, and switch between them, without requiring a postback to the server each time:

Output from the MultiPage control in Internet Explorer 5.5 and later
```
<?XML:NAMESPACE PREFIX="MPNS" /><?IMPORT NAMESPACE="MPNS"
IMPLEMENTATION="/webctrl_client/1_0/multipage.htc" />
<MPNS:MultiPage id="mpCarDetail" selectedIndex="0"
onSelectedIndexChange="JScript:document._ctl0.__mpCarDetail_State
__.value=event.selectedIndex" style="border-width:1px; border-style:solid;
border-color:#666666; border-top:none">
  <MPNS:PageView id="mpColors">
    <!-- section for "Colors" tab -->
    ... HTML elements as defined in ASP.NET page appear here ...
  </MPNS:PageView>"
  <MPNS:PageView id="mpEngine">
    <!-- section for "Engine" tab -->
    ... HTML elements as defined in ASP.NET page appear here ...
  </MPNS:PageView>
  ... other page sections here ...
</MPNS:MultiPage>
```

The TabStrip *and* MultiPage *Controls in Down-level Clients*

In all other browsers and clients, where the HTC model is not supported (including IE 5.0, where HTC support is not robust enough for these controls), the `TabStrip` and `MultiPage` server controls generate standard HTML output. The output generated by the `TabStrip`, when the first "tab" is selected, looks like what you see in the following code (for clarity, I'm only showing the output for the first two "tabs" here):

Output from the TabStrip control in all other browsers and clients

```
<table cellspacing="0" cellpadding="0" border="0" id="tsCarDetail"
style="width:100%">
<tr>
<td nowrap height="21" width="79" bgcolor="#ffffff" style="color:#000000;
border-width:1px;border-style:solid;border-color:#666666;font-weight:bold;
text-align:center;font-family:Arial,Helvetica,sans-serif;font-size:11px;
height:21;width:79;background-color:#ffffff;border-bottom:none;">
<font face="Arial,Helvetica,sans-serif" color="#000000"><b>Colors</b>
</font></td>
<td nowrap bgcolor="#cccccc" height="21" width="79"
style="color:#000000;background-color:#cccccc;border-width:1px;
border-style:solid;border-color:#666666;font-weight:bold;text-align:center;
font-family:Arial,Helvetica,sans-serif;font-size:11px;height:21;width:79;">
<font face="Arial,Helvetica,sans-serif" color="#000000"><b><a
href="javascript:document._ctl0._tsCarDetail_State_.value='1';
_doPostBack('tsCarDetail','1')"><font color="#000000">Engine</font></a>
</b></font></td>
... other "tab" definitions go here ...
</tr>
</table>
```

You can see that the result is an HTML table, with the style of each cell set so that the appropriate borders are visible. However, the background color of the "tabs" is set using the bgcolor attribute of that cell, which is why Navigator 4 can display the tabs in different background colors even though it does not process the CSS styles (look back at the screenshot of Navigator 4 in the earlier section about the IE Web Controls to see what I mean).

The MultiPage control also generates standard HTML output in browsers and clients other than IE 5.5 and later. Only the content for one "tab" or "page" is visible because that's all the control creates output for:

Output from the MultiPage control in all other browsers and clients

```
<table id="mpCarDetail" width="100%" style="border-width:1px;
border-style:solid; border-color:#666666; border-top:none">
  <tr>
    <td id="mpColors" valign="top">
      <!-- section for "Colors" tab -->
      ... HTML elements as defined in ASP.NET page appear here ...
    </td>
  </tr>
</table>
```

You can see that these clients must use a postback to the server to display a different page. So the result, compared to Internet Explorer 5.5 and later, is a reduction in responsiveness due to the repeated postbacks. On a slow connection this difference is quite noticeable, but there is no other way to reliably achieve the required result with all other client types.

The postback is caused by the JavaScript URL defined as the value of the href attribute for each of the links on the "tabs" in the output of the TabStrip control, for example:

```
<a href="javascript:document._ctl0._tsCarDetail_State_.value='1';
_doPostBack('tsCarDetail','1')"><font color="#000000">Engine</font></a>
```

This code uses the same client-side script function (named _doPostBack) as the ASP.NET AutoPostback feature that I discussed in previous chapters, which submits the form to the server. This is why, even when running in "down-level" mode with clients other than Internet Explorer 5.5 and later, the controls still require client-side script support to be available.

The Information and Error Messages Label

After the "tabbed dialog" comes a Label control where I can display error message or information to the users as they interact with the page. Hopefully, they will only see "information" messages, and the most likely one is the confirmation that I success-fully saved their chosen vehicle configuration as a quote.

The code for the Label is simple enough, specifying the font details and CSS class I want to apply to it. Notice that I also disable viewstate for the Label, so that any messages are not persisted across postbacks:

```
...
<!-- label to display information and error messages -->
<font face="Arial,helvetica,sans-serif" size="3" color="#b50055"><b>
<asp:Label id="lblMessage" EnableViewState="False" class="large-red-text"
           runat="server" /></b></font>
...
```

Figure 8-24 shows the Label after the user has saved a quotation. Notice that the Save button has disappeared now, and only the Close button is visible. I show you the code that creates these buttons next.

Figure 8-24. The information and links in the page after a quotation has been saved

The Instructions, Save, and Close Buttons

The final section of the page contains the instructions for saving a quote, and the Save and Close buttons—as you've seen in several earlier figures. The instructions are simply static text defined within an HTML table cell, except that it contains a hyperlink that executes a JavaScript function named mainWindowPage when clicked. This is the same href value as I used in the "information" text (shown in Figure 8-24) when a quote is saved. I'll come back and look at this function shortly:

```
...
<!-- "save quote" and "window close" buttons -->
<table border="0" width="100%">
 <tr>
  <td><font face="Arial,helvetica,sans-serif" size="2">
    Select the specification and optional extras you require for your new
    vehicle, and <b>Save</b> this configuration as a quotation. Then you
    can place an order by registering in the
    <a href="javascript:mainWindowPage('secure/mycars.aspx', true)">
      <font color="#000000"><b>MyCars</b></font></a>
    page.</font></td>
  ...
```

After the instructions comes the cell that contains the Save and Close buttons. The Save button is not visible by default (the Visible attribute is set to "False"). The button is, of course, an image, and I am using an <input type="image"> control to display it. This means that it will be implemented by ASP.NET as an HtmlInputImage control (as was used in the Home page), and so I have to define the name of the function in the ASP.NET code that will run server-side when the button is clicked as the OnServerClick attribute:

```
  ...
  <td align="right" nowrap="nowrap">
    <input id="btnSave" type="image" src="images/btn_save.gif"
           Visible="False" runat="server" width="100" height="49"
           border="0" OnServerClick="SaveCarDetails"
           alt="Save specification as a quote for future reference" />
    <a href="javascript:window.close()">
      <img src="images/btn_close.gif" border="0"
           width="100" height="49" alt="Close this window" /></a></td>
  </tr>
</table>
```

The last part of the code above implements the Close button. In this case I simply place the image inside an ordinary client-side HTML <a> element, with the href set to a JavaScript URL that closes the current window. There is no need to interact with this control on the server, so I can reduce the processing overhead for the page by *not* defining it as a server control (I omit the runat="server" attribute).

The Client-Side `mainWindowPage` *Function*

The two hyperlinks to the My Cars page you saw earlier, in the instructions for saving a quote and in the message that indicates that the quotation was successfully saved, call a client-side JavaScript function named `mainWindowPage`. The hyperlinks pass two values to this function as parameters: the URL of the page that should be displayed in the main windows of the site, and a `Boolean` value to indicate if the Model Details window should be closed (`true`) or left open (`false`):

```
javascript:mainWindowPage('secure/mycars.aspx', true)
```

The function itself is shown in the following code listing, and you can see that it is simple enough. The Model Details page was opened from a link in the main window (on the Home page), and the browser automatically maintains a reference to this window as the `opener` property of the current (Model Details page) `window` object:

```
function mainWindowPage(sHref, bClose) {
  window.opener.location.href = sHref;
  if (bClose) window.close();
}
```

So, now I can change the page that is displayed in the main window by setting the `href` property of that window's `location` object to the URL I want to display. Then, if the value of the second parameter to the `mainWindowPage` function is `true`, I call the `close` method of the current window.

Using the ASP.NET `RegisterClientScriptBlock` *Method*

However, if you look at the HTML section of the Model Details page, you'll find that this function is not declared there. This is because I inserted it into the page using a method of the ASP.NET `Page` object called `RegisterClientScriptBlock`. This method is a useful way to insert client-side script code into the output that is sent to the client. The ASP.NET code I used to generate the Model Details page contains, within the `Page_Load` event handler, the following code:

In the `Page_Load` *event handler*

```
' create the client-side script block for the control events in the page
Dim sScript as String = "<script language='JavaScript'>" & vbCrlf _
  & "<!--" & vbCrlf _
  & "function setOptionButtons(sName) {" & vbCrlf _
  & "  document.forms[0].elements[sName].checked = true;" & vbCrlf _
  & "}" & vbCrlf _
  & "function nodeExpanded(oSender) {" & vbCrlf _
  & "  var clickedNode = oSender.clickedNodeIndex;" & vbCrlf _
  & "  var colNodes = oSender.getChildren();" & vbCrlf _
```

```
& "   for (var i = 0; i < colNodes.length; i++) {" & vbCrlf _
& "     if (colNodes[i].getNodeIndex() != clickedNode)" & vbCrlf _
& "       colNodes[i].setAttribute('expanded', false);" & vbCrlf _
& "   }" & vbCrlf _
& "}" & vbCrlf _
& "function mainWindowPage(sHref, bClose) {" & vbCrlf _
& "   window.opener.location.href = sHref;" & vbCrlf _
& "   if (bClose) window.close();" & vbCrlf _
& "}" & vbCrlf _
& "//-->" & vbCrlf _
& "<" & "/" & "script>"

' register it so that it is inserted into the page
If(Not IsClientScriptBlockRegistered("JSBlock")) Then
  RegisterClientScriptBlock("JSBlock", sScript)
End If
```

This code creates a String named sScript that contains the client-side script
I want to include in the page, and then passes it to the RegisterClientScriptBlock
method. This method automatically inserts a complete and new client-side <script>
section into the output, just after the opening tag of the server-side <form> section
that must also exist in the page. At the same time, it registers this script section
with the Page object using the name that I specified in the first parameter to the
RegisterClientScriptBlock method—in this case JSBlock.

Obviously the preceding code creates more than just the mainWindowPage function
that you looked at earlier. The other two functions, setOptionsButtons and nodeExpanded
are used in other parts of the Model Details page, and you'll see how in the next
chapter.

OK, so far this does nothing more than what you could achieve by simply placing
the JavaScript (or VBScript) directly into the HTML section of the page (traditionally
I would put it in the <head> section). So in general, when you only want to insert
a single specific script section into a page, you would do so by coding it directly into
the page. However, the RegisterClientScriptBlock method comes into its own when
you create user controls or custom server controls, where multiple instances of that
control might be inserted into the final ASP.NET page. In this case, you can prevent
more than one instance of the client-side code section being inserted into the page,
which would cause a client-side script error and prevent the page from working
properly.

The RegisterClientScriptBlock method uses the name (or key) you allocate to
the script section to identify it. So you can prevent it being inserted into the page
more than once by using the IsClientScriptBlockRegistered method and specifying
this key, as shown in the preceding code. Now only the first instance of a control will
actually insert the client-side code, and subsequent instances will not—no matter
how many exist on the page.

Other ASP.NET "Register" Methods

The Page object also exposes some other similar methods that might be useful when
building user controls and custom server controls. Table 8-2 is a brief summary, and

you can find out more about all of them from the System.Web.UI.Page section of the .NET SDK.

Table 8-2. Methods of the Page Class for Inserting and Managing Client-Side Script

Method	Description
RegisterClientScriptBlock	Registers with the specified name (key) a client-side script section that will be inserted into the page, directly after the opening <form> tag.
IsClientScriptBlockRegistered	Returns True if a client-side script section registered with the specified name (key) has already been inserted into the page.
RegisterStartupScript	Registers with the specified name (key) a client-side script section that will be inserted into the page, directly before the closing <form> tag.
IsStartupScriptRegistered	Returns True if a startup script section registered with the specified name (key) has already been inserted into the page.
RegisterOnSubmitStatement	Registers with the specified name (key) a client-side code statement (or series of statements) that will be added to the opening <form> tag as an attribute. The name of the attribute must be specified, for example "submit".
RegisterHiddenField	Registers with the specified name (key) an <input type="hidden"> control that will be inserted into the page. The name of the field and its value must be specified.

> **NOTE** *For more details about these and the other methods and properties of the* Page *object, see the version 1.0 SDK documentation at:*
> ms-help://MS.NETFrameworkSDK/cpref/html/frlrfSystemWebUIPageMembersTopic.htm
> *or in version 1.1 of the SDK at:*
> mshelp://MS.NETFrameworkSDKv1.1/cpref/html/
> frlrfSystemWebUIPageMembersTopic.htm

Summary

In this chapter, I began our tour of the Model Details page from the Xrox Car Company Web site. This is by far the most complex part of the site. It allows visitors to view detailed information about each vehicle, and configure it by selecting the color, engine type, optional extras, and finance package that best suits them. At the same time, the page displays the current all-inclusive price, a breakdown of the finance rates, total interest, and monthly payments required.

So the page has to provide a great deal of interactivity, as well as being intuitive and attractive. I feel that I've met the original design brief, and produced a page that works well, is relatively efficient in operation, and is easy to use.

But so far, I've only really scratched the surface. I've only looked in detail at the simple parts of the page (the image and description at the top, and the instructions, information, and Save/Close buttons section at the bottom). However, I have also sorted out how I'll provide the "tabbed dialog" appearance using two of the controls from the IE Web Controls pack.

In all, the aims of this chapter were to look at:

- How well the final page meets the original design requirements

- The Model Details page in outline, to understand how it is created

- The structure of the Model Details page, to understand how it works

In the next chapter I move on to look first at the data that drives the page, and then at the code and content I use to implement each of the five "pages" that are displayed in turn within the "tabbed dialog." And, of course, I still have to figure out what I need to do differently to make the page work with browsers that do not support client-side scripting.

The Interactive
Model Details

CHAPTER 8 INTRODUCED YOU to the most complex of the pages in the example Xrox Car Company Web site, where visitors can view details of the vehicle range, select the color, engine type, optional extras, and finance package that they require, and then save this configuration as a quotation. Now that you have a good understanding of what the page does, and you have seen an overview of the structure of the page, you can move on and look at how it actually works.

My aim in this chapter is to look first at the data that drives the page, and then at the code I use to present this data to visitors who view the page with a script-enabled browser. I'll also show you the event handlers I use to make the page react to visitor interaction. However, I don't have room to cover all the code in the Model Details page in this chapter, so I'll save the tasks of calculating the price and the finance terms for the vehicle, and saving a quotation, for Chapter 10.

In this chapter, the topics covered are:

- The data that drives the Model Details page

- How to extract this data for use in the page

- How to present the data to visitors in the five distinct sections of the page

- How to react to events that occur for the controls in these sections

I start with a look at the parts of the database that are involved in this process, and the way I extract this data for use in the page.

The Data for the Model Details Page

Before you look at the ASP.NET code in the Model Details page, I need to show you in more detail the database that drives the site. It contains all the data about the vehicles; plus the colors, engines, and optional extras that are available for each one. So, before you can really understand the code that presents and manipulates this data, you need to see how the data is stored, and how to extract it in a suitable format for use in the Model Details page.

The Vehicle Details Database Tables

You've looked at some of the tables in the database in previous chapters, as I've created procedures and functions that extract the data and display it. However, to help tie it all together, Figure 9-1 shows all the tables that are related to storing information about each vehicle, each quotation or order that I store for these vehicles, and the users who generated these quotations and orders. It also shows the relationships between the tables.

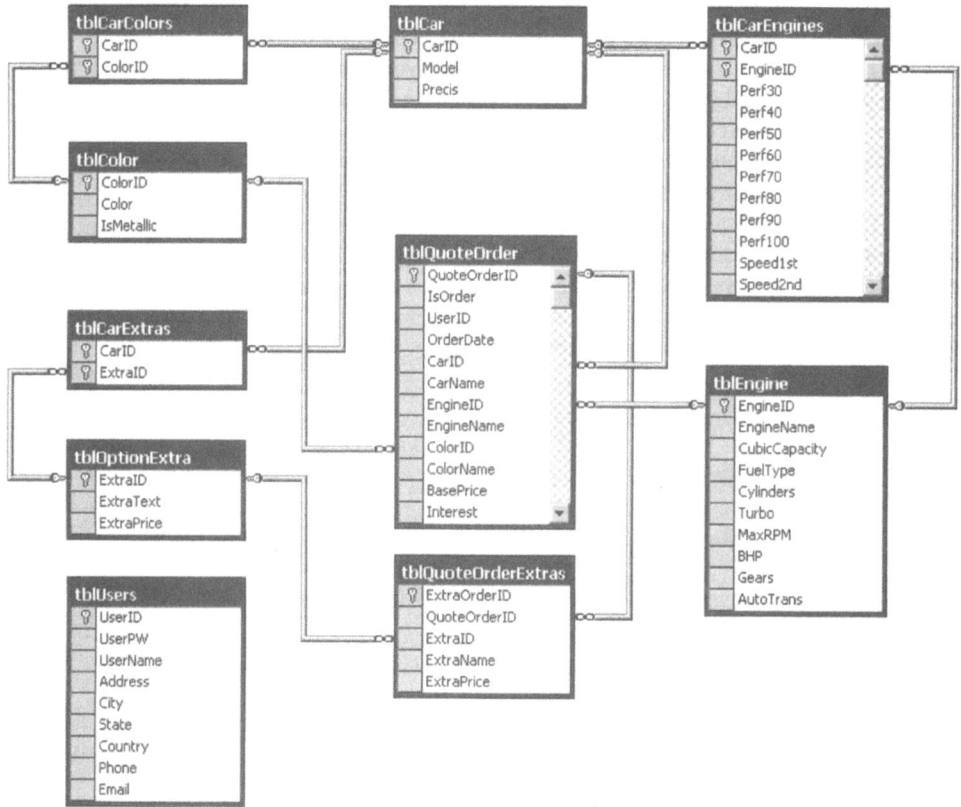

Figure 9-1. The database tables used in the Model Details page

> **NOTE** *Not all 25 columns in the* tblCarEngines *table are visible in this diagram. As well as those you see there are four more* Speedxxx *columns, eight* Fuelxxx *columns, and a final column named* CarEnginePrice *that contains the price for each available car/engine combination. Likewise, three columns are not visible for the* tblQuoteOrder *table. These are* TotalPrice, PaymentMonths, *and* PaymentAmount.

While it looks a little complicated, the structure I've chosen is the only really sensible way to approach the issue of allowing each vehicle to have a choice of engines, colors, and extras. The intermediate tables (tblCarColors, tblCarEngines, and tblCarExtras) simply link each vehicle with the color, engine, or optional extras that are available for that vehicle. In database terms, they resolve the many-to-many relationships that arise in situations like this—for example each car is available in more than one color, while each color is available for more than one car.

Each quotation or order consists of a single row in the tblQuoteOrder table, plus zero or more linked rows in the tblQuoteOrderExtras table that indicate the optional extras the customer selected. Notice the IsOrder column in the tblQuoteOrder table, which is used to indicate if this is an order or a quotation.

The other point worth mentioning is that the tblUsers table is not related through a foreign key constraint to any other table. Quotations might be stored against an anonymous User ID if the visitor has not previously registered or logged into the site. These IDs will not exist in the tblUsers table, preventing the tblUsers and tblQuoteOrder tables from being linked.

NOTE *You'll see details of the design and operation of the user "login" features of the example site in Chapter 11.*

But in the Real World...

This database is fine for the example application, but of course it doesn't provide the features you would probably need in a "real-world" site. The Xrox Cars site doesn't actually process orders or collect payment information (mainly because there aren't any real cars to sell), but where this kind of "back-end" processing is required it will probably involve a lot more in the way of data collection and storage.

However, the aim of this book is to demonstrate interface design and construction in ASP.NET, not back-end data processing, so I make no apologies for stopping where I have with the example site. It's for the same reason that I do not use a separate data layer or middle tier in the application—I just access the stored procedures that expose the data directly from the ASP.NET pages.

The Stored Procedures for the Model Details Page

The Model Details page requires access to almost all of the data in the tables shown earlier, with the exception of the tblUsers table that stores details of each visitor as he or she registers with the site. This table is used only during the registration process, and in the My Cars page that you'll be looking at in Chapter 12.

I could extract this data directly from the database every time the page is opened, but I decided that for my requirements it makes more sense (as I discussed in Chapter 8) to extract it once, and then store it in the user's ASP.NET session. The best way to do this is to use a DataSet object, and take advantage of the ability it provides to store multiple tables within a single DataSet.

Extracting the Vehicle Details

I need a table that contains the basic details about each car/engine combination for the model the user has chosen. For example, if the user selected the Xrox Wregal by clicking it in the Home page, there are three car/engine combinations that are available for this model and the first stored procedure will need to extract these three rows from the database.

To do this I have to join the tblCar and tblEngine tables. However, as this is a many-to-many relationship, I must perform two joins. The tblCar table is joined to the tblCarEngines table, which is in turn joined to the tblEngine table. This also gives us access to the CarEnginePrice column in the tblCarEngines table, which I'll need in the page (Figure 9-2).

Figure 9-2. The tables containing the vehicle details

The stored procedure is shown next. It accepts a single parameter that is the ID of the vehicle for which I'm displaying the details. Notice that I use a CASE statement within the SQL to return the text strings "Yes" or "No" for the columns that are effectively Boolean values (SQL Server bit columns). This makes it look a lot nicer when I display the results using data binding in the example page:

```
CREATE PROCEDURE GetAllCarDetails @CarID int AS
SELECT tblCar.CarID, Model, Precis, tblEngine.EngineID, EngineName,
  CubicCapacity, FuelType, Cylinders, MaxRPM, BHP, Gears, CarEnginePrice,
  Turbo = CASE Turbo WHEN 1 THEN 'Yes' ELSE 'No' END,
  AutoTrans = CASE AutoTrans WHEN 1 THEN 'Yes' ELSE 'No' END
FROM (tblCar JOIN tblCarEngines ON tblCar.CarID = tblCarEngines.CarID)
  JOIN tblEngine ON tblEngine.EngineID = tblCarEngines.EngineID
WHERE tblCar.CarID = @CarID
```

From this stored procedure I get the details of the car model (the ID, model name, and précis), the engine details (ID, name, and technical data), and the price for that car/engine combination.

Extracting the List of Available Colors

Another task is to collect a list of colors that are available for the selected model. I can do this by joining the tblCar table to the tblColor table, using the intermediate table tblCarColors. Again I use a single parameter (the Car ID) to select the appropriate vehicle. I return the color ID and name, plus the bit column value that indicates if this is a metallic color or not:

```
CREATE PROCEDURE GetAllCarColors @CarID int AS
SELECT tblCarColors.ColorID, tblColor.Color, tblColor.IsMetallic
FROM (tblCar JOIN tblCarColors ON tblCar.CarID = tblCarColors.CarID)
  JOIN tblColor ON tblCarColors.ColorID = tblColor.ColorID
WHERE tblCar.CarID = @CarID
```

Extracting the List of Available Extras

I also need a list of the optional extras that are available for the selected vehicle to build the Extras section of the page. Not all of the optional extras are available with all vehicles. Again, I have to join three tables—in this case tblCar, tblOptionExtra, and the intermediate tblCarExtras table. I provide the Car ID value as the single parameter to the stored procedure, and return the ID, name, and price of the available optional extras, plus a text string that is a combination of the name and price to display as the caption of each check box:

```
CREATE PROCEDURE GetAllCarExtras @CarID int AS
SELECT tblOptionExtra.ExtraID, tblOptionExtra.ExtraText,
       tblOptionExtra.ExtraPrice,
       DisplayText = ' ' + RTRIM(tblOptionExtra.ExtraText) + ' ($'
       + CONVERT(varchar(10), tblOptionExtra.ExtraPrice) + ')   '
FROM (tblCar JOIN tblCarExtras ON tblCar.CarID = tblCarExtras.CarID)
  JOIN tblOptionExtra ON tblCarExtras.ExtraID = tblOptionExtra.ExtraID
WHERE tblCar.CarID = @CarID
```

This gives me all the information I require about the vehicle itself, but there is one other set of values that I also need. These values are used to calculate the monthly payments when the user specifies the desired finance package.

The Finance PMT Values Table

One table that is not shown in the earlier schematics, but which relates to the data used in the Model Details page, is the list of values to calculate the monthly payment amount required over a specified term to cover the cost of the selected vehicle plus the interest that is added during that term. This is referred to as a PMT (payment over a fixed term at a fixed interest rate) calculation.

You can find formulas for performing this calculation on the Web, though I usually take advantage of the PMT function in programs like Excel to perform this kind of calculation when working with Office-style documents. Within the .NET Framework, the Pmt function is implemented as part of the Visual Basic .NET namespace, and so can be used instead. Interestingly, however, there is no equivalent in C#.

I chose to take an approach that uses the VB.NET Pmt function, and demonstrates a few other techniques that you might find useful as well. In particular, I use the global.asax file to execute some code when the application starts, and fill a database table named tblFinancePMTData with a list of values from which I can calculate the payment terms for any vehicle as the application runs.

Using global.asax to Handle Application-level Events

Like "classic" ASP, ASP.NET allows you to execute code in response to several "application-level" events, outside the pages that make up the parts of the site that the user sees. The file global.asax works in almost exactly the same way as global.asa does in ASP 3.0 and earlier. In it are defined event handlers that are executed in response to the events raised within the application as it starts, runs, or ends.

The events I can handle include these five, which are generally the most commonly used in applications:

- Application_Start occurs when the application first starts up, such as when the site is first accessed, or when the web.config file in the root folder of the application is edited. For legacy support, Application_OnStart is included as an alternative for this event.

- Application_End occurs when the application stops, for example when the last active session expires or when the web.config file is edited and before a new instance of the application starts. For legacy support, Application_OnEnd is included as an alternative for this event.

- Session_Start occurs when a user who does not have an ASP.NET session already active requests any ASP.NET page within the application. For legacy support, Session_OnStart is included as an alternative for this event.

- Session_End occurs when a session expires, either after the timeout specified in machine.config or web.config, or when the Session.Abandon method is called. For legacy support, Session_OnEnd is included as an alternative for this event.

- Application_Error occurs when an ASP.NET compilation or runtime error is detected within the application. Details of the error can be obtained by using the Server.GetLastError method.

Remember that the global.asax file *must* be placed in the root folder of an ASP.NET application. It will not be executed if this is not the case.

> **NOTE** *ASP.NET can spawn new instances of an application when errors occur in the default instance, and in response to changes in memory availability or (depending on the settings in the* machine.config *file) after a specified number of hours or number of hits. The* Application_Start *and* Application_End *events are raised whenever this occurs. If possible, ASP.NET maintains a separate instance of the "old version" of the application until all active sessions have expired, redirecting existing users to this instance so that their session values are preserved.*

Running Code on Application Startup

From the previous section, it is obvious that the example page can handle the Application_Start event and use it to pre-fill the tblFinancePMTData table with the list of values needed to calculate the finance payments. I store the current finance interest rate for the site in the <appSettings> section of the web.config file, just as I do with the database connection string. When I edit web.config, the application is automatically restarted, and so the new rate is used to refill the tblFinancePMTData table with the correct values each time.

web.config

```
<configuration>
  <appSettings>
    ...
    <!-- change following to adjust finance interest rates -->
    <add key="XroxCarsInterestRate" value="4.75" />
    ...
  </appSettings>
  ...
</configuration>
```

So, in the global.asax file, I start by importing the namespaces I'll need to access the database. I also import a couple of extra namespaces, which I'll use to write status messages to the event log and a text log file when the database is updated:

global.asax

```
<%@Application Language="VB" %>
<%@Import Namespace="System.Data" %>
<%@Import Namespace="System.Data.SqlClient" %>
<%@Import Namespace="System.Diagnostics" %>
<%@Import Namespace="System.IO" %>
...
```

Then I declare a couple of application-level variables that I'll use within the event handlers—the name of the event log I'll write to and the path and name of the log file I'll be updating:

```
...
<script runat="server">
Dim sLogName As String = "XroxCarCompany"
Dim sLogFile As String = "C:\Temp\XroxCarCoLog.txt"
...
```

The Application_Start *Event Handler*

Next comes the event handler for the Application_Start event. After declaring some local variables I need in this event handler, I extract the current interest rate and the database connection string from web.config:

```
...
Sub Application_Start(Sender As Object, E As EventArgs)
  ' code that runs on application startup
  ' update database table containing calculated PMT values
  ' for calculating vehicle finance payments
  Dim sInterestRate, sStoredProc, sConnect, sMessage As String
  Dim fInterestRate, fPMTResult As Double
  Dim fPaymentPer1000 As Decimal
  Dim iMonth As Integer

  ' get values from web.config file
  sInterestRate = ConfigurationSettings.AppSettings("XroxCarsInterestRate")
  sConnect = ConfigurationSettings.AppSettings("XroxCarsConnectString")
  ...
```

Now I can update the database. I have a stored procedure in the database named UpdatePmtFinanceData that accepts a number of months and a decimal payment value. The payment value is the amount required to pay off a loan of $1000.00 plus interest at the current rate, over the specified number of months. So, for example, if the number of months is 36, the value is the monthly payment required to pay off a $1000.00 loan plus the interest over 36 months. I can use this payment amount to calculate the payment required for any vehicle later on by simply multiplying the payment by the car price divided by 1000.

The following listing shows the UpdatePmtFinanceData stored procedure. If the table is empty it inserts the row, or updates an existing row if there is already one present:

```
CREATE PROCEDURE UpdatePmtFinanceData @Months int, @Payment decimal(9,2)
AS
UPDATE tblFinancePMTData SET Payment = @Payment WHERE Months = @Months
IF @@ROWCOUNT = 0
  INSERT INTO tblFinancePMTData (Months,Payment) VALUES (@Months,@Payment)
```

Calculating the Payment Amounts

Returning to the event handler, all I have to do to fill the table is execute this stored procedure once for every monthly period over which I want to allow users to extend their loans. In my case, the range is from 6 to 120 months in six-month intervals. The techniques I use to execute the procedure are exactly the same as I've used in all other example pages. After establishing a connection to the database, I use a For..Next construct with a Step value of 6, and then call the VB.NET Pmt function with the appropriate values to get the result. I round it to two decimal places, then set the parameters for the stored procedure and execute it:

```
...
' declare stored proc name and data access objects
sStoredProc = "UpdatePmtFinanceData"
Dim sqlConn As New SqlConnection(sConnect)
Dim sqlComm As New SqlCommand(sStoredProc, sqlConn)
sqlComm.CommandType = CommandType.StoredProcedure
Try
    ' parse interest rate into a Double
    fInterestRate = Double.Parse(sInterestRate)

    ' open database connection
    sqlConn.Open()

    ' calculate payment rate per $1000 at six-month intervals
    For iMonth = 6 To 120 Step 6
        fPMTResult = - Pmt(fInterestRate / 1200, iMonth, 1000, 0)
        fPaymentPer1000 = Decimal.Round(CType(fPMTResult, Decimal), 2)
        ' set parameters and call stored proc to update database table row
        sqlComm.Parameters.Clear() sqlComm.Parameters.Add("@Months", iMonth)
        sqlComm.Parameters.Add("@Payment", fPaymentPer1000)
        sqlComm.ExecuteNonQuery()
    Next
    ...
```

The VB.NET PMT Function

The VB.NET Pmt function expects up to five parameters:

```
Pmt(interest-rate, #periods, present-value, [future-value], [due-date])
```

- interest-rate is a Double that specifies the interest rate per period. In the example case this is per month, so I divide the value (for example 4.75) by 1200 to get a percentage value per month (for example 0.00396).

- #periods is a Double that specifies the number of payments that are required or the number of periods over which the loan will run.

- present-value is a Double that specifies the present value (or lump sum) that must be paid, excluding interest. Effectively it is the value of the goods to the seller when the sale takes place.

- future-value (optional) is a Double that specifies the value or balance left after all the payments have been made. To completely pay off the loan, the value of this parameter must be zero, and this is the default that is assumed if you omit this optional parameter.

- due-date (optional) is a Microsoft.VisualBasic.DueDate object that specifies when payments are due, and can be DueDate.EndOfPeriod if payments are due at the end of the payment period, or DueDate.BegOfPeriod if payments are due at the beginning of the period. It is an optional argument, and DueDate.EndOfPeriod is assumed if omitted.

The return value of the function is a Double that specifies the amount for each payment. In accountancy terms this is a debit against the loan, and so is returned as a negative number. This is why I reverse the sign before I insert it into the database table.

> **NOTE** *A full reference to the* Pmt *function can be found in the .NET version 1.0 SDK at:* ms-help://MS.NETFrameworkSDK/vblr7net/html/vafctPmt.htm *or in the version 1.1 SDK at:* ms-help://MS.NETFrameworkSDKv1.1/vblr7net/html/vafctPmt.htm

Writing Status Messages to the Event Log and a Text Log File

After all values have been inserted into the tblFinancePMTData table, I write a status message to both the event log and a text log file so that the administrator can check that the process is working properly. I use the same two routines within the global.asax page for this as I did in the Application_Start event handler. Because I wrapped the database update code in a Try...Catch construct, I can output the appropriate message:

```
    ...
    ' write a "succeeded" message to error log
    sMessage = "Updated FinancePMTData values in database"
    WriteEventLogMessage(sLogName, sMessage, EventLogEntryType.Information)
    WriteErrorFileMessage(sLogFile, sMessage)
  Catch
    ' write a "failed" message to error log
    sMessage = "Unable to update FinancePMTData values in database"
    WriteEventLogMessage(sLogName, sMessage, EventLogEntryType.Error)
    WriteErrorFileMessage(sLogFile, sMessage)
  Finally
    sqlConn.Close()    ' close the database connection
  End Try
End Sub
```

The WriteEventLogMessage *Routine*

The WriteEventLogMessage routine I've included in this page is shown in the following code listing. One issue is that the ASP.NET account, under which the example pages run by default, does not have permission to create a new Event Log, and so the code will always fail. If you want to use the Event Log to record application events and errors, you could run this page once under the context of an administrative-level account to create the Event Log. Or, you could write a simple executable application that does the same and run it from the command line under the context of an administrative-level account. Once the new Event Log has been created, ASP.NET should be able to write events to it:

```
Sub WriteEventLogMessage(sLogName As String, sMessage As String, _
                         eType As EventLogEntryType)
  Try
    ' write a string message to the system's Event Log
    ' create the event log if it does not already exist
    ' however the ASPNET account must have relevant
    ' permissions for this to work—it does not by default
    If (Not EventLog.SourceExists(sLogName)) Then
      EventLog.CreateEventSource(sLogName, sLogName)
    End if
    ' write event to log
    Dim oLog as New EventLog
    oLog.Source = sLogName
    oLog.WriteEntry(sMessage, eType)
  Catch
  End Try

End Sub
```

> **NOTE** *A full reference to the* EventLog *class can be found in the .NET version 1.0 SDK at:*
> ms-help://MS.NETFrameworkSDK/cpref/html/
> frlrfsystemdiagnosticseventlogclasstopic.htm
> *or in the version 1.1 SDK at:* ms-help://MS.NETFrameworkSDKv1.1/cpref/html/
> frlrfsystemdiagnosticseventlogclasstopic.htm

The WriteErrorFileMessage *Routine*

More generally useful is the ability to write messages to a text log file as the application runs. The WriteErrorFileMessage routine shown in the following code listing does just that, taking the file path and the text of the message as parameters. I use a StreamWriter to append the text to the log file. The second parameter to the StreamWriter constructor determines if new text will be appended to the file (True), or if it will replace the existing file content (False). Then I call the WriteLine method, passing it the current date and time (using the Now function) and the text of the message I want to write to the file:

```
Sub WriteErrorFileMessage(sFilePath As String, sMessage As String)
  ' write a string to the text log file sFilePath
  ' creates the file if it does not already exist
  Dim oWriter As StreamWriter
  Try
    oWriter = New StreamWriter(sFilePath, True)
    oWriter.WriteLine(Now().ToString & "-" & sMessage)
  Catch
  Finally
    oWriter.Close()    ' remember to close it afterwards
  End Try
End Sub
```

Just make sure on your server that the folder you specify for the log file (in this case C:\Temp\) does already exist, and that the ASP.NET account has permission to write to it.

> **NOTE** *A full reference to the* StreamWriter *class can be found in the .NET version 1.0 SDK at:*
> ms-help://MS.NETFrameworkSDK/cpref/html/
> frlrfSystemIOStreamWriterMembersTopic.htm
> *or in the version 1.1 SDK at:* ms-help://MS.NETFrameworkSDKv1.1/cpref/html/
> frlrfSystemIOStreamWriterMembersTopic.htm

Running Code When an Application Error Occurs

One other feature of the global.asax file that I use in the example application is the ability to handle the Application_Error event. I use this event to execute the WriteEventLogMessage and WriteErrorFileMessage routines that you've just seen, and thereby provide a log of application errors (compilation and run-time errors that occur in any of the pages in the application).

All that's involved is to extract the error details, create a suitable String value, and then pass it to the two methods that record the error. I can call the Server.GetLastError method to get a reference to a standard Exception object that represents the error, and use the ToString method to get the complete error details as a String.

```
Sub Application_Error(Sender As Object, E As EventArgs)
  ' code that runs when an unhandled error occurs
  Dim sMessage As String = Server.GetLastError().ToString()
  WriteEventLogMessage(sLogName, sMessage, EventLogEntryType.Error)
  WriteErrorFileMessage(sLogFile, sMessage)
End Sub
```

The GetFinancePMTRates Stored Procedure

After that diversion to look at global.asax, I can now show you the last of the stored procedures needed for the Model Details page. I want to extract all the payment data from the `tblFinancePMTData` table in the database, so that I can load it into the `DataSet` I'm using to power the Model Details page.

The stored procedure itself is as simple as you would expect. It just selects and returns all the rows from the `tblFinancePMTData` table:

```
CREATE PROCEDURE GetFinancePMTRates AS
SELECT Months, Payment FROM tblFinancePMTData ORDER BY Months
```

Fetching and Storing the Data for the Page

Now that all the necessary stored procedures are in place, you can see the code that builds the `DataSet` I'll be using to drive the Model Details page. The function `GetCarDetailsDS` takes the ID of the vehicle on display, and returns a `DataSet` object. The listing that follows shows the first part of this function:

cardetail.aspx

```
Function GetCarDetailsDS(sCarID As String) As DataSet
  ' to hold DataSet for the results
  Dim dsCarDetail As DataSet = Nothing

  ' to hold Session key for DataSet
  Dim sSessionKey As String = "XroxCar" & sCarID & "Details"
  ...
```

I've already decided that I'll store the `DataSet` in the user's ASP.NET session after extracting it for the first time, so I need to create a suitable session key value. I may be storing more than one `DataSet` if the user is viewing the details of several cars, so the session key must include the car ID. In the preceding code, you can see how I create this session key. The resulting key for the vehicle with ID value 3, for example, will be `"XroxCar3Details"`.

Accessing the Database and Filling the DataSet

Once you know the session key, you can try and extract the `DataSet` from the session. If this is the first time the user has accessed the Model Details page for this model, the `DataSet` will not be in the user's session. At this point in the `GetCarDetailsDS` function the variable `dsCarDetail` will still be `Nothing` (null in C#), and so the next line of code tests for this:

```
  ...
  'try and get DataSet from user's Session
  dsCarDetail = CType(Session(sSessionKey), DataSet)
  If dsCarDetail Is Nothing Then    'not in Session-get from database
    ...
```

If my dsCarDetail variable is Nothing, I know that I'll have to go off to the database and fill the DataSet. First I declare the names of the four stored procedures that I described earlier in this chapter, and then collect the database connection string from the web.config file. I also create the Connection and Command objects I'll need, and specify the CommandType as I've done in many previous examples:

```
...
' to hold stored procedure names
Dim sCarProcName As String = "GetAllCarDetails"
Dim sColorProcName As String = "GetAllCarColors"
Dim sExtrasProcName As String = "GetAllCarExtras"
Dim sFinancePMTProcName As String = "GetFinancePMTRates"
Dim sConnect As String = _
      ConfigurationSettings.AppSettings("XroxCarsConnectString")
Dim sqlConn As New SqlConnection(sConnect)
Dim sqlComm As New SqlCommand(sCarProcName, sqlConn)
sqlComm.CommandType = CommandType.StoredProcedure
...
```

Now I can create a new empty DataSet, and specify the single parameter of the Command using the Car ID value that is passed to the GetCarDetailsDS function. Then it's just a matter of opening the database connection and executing the Fill method four times, changing the value of the CommandText (the stored procedure name) each time.

However, before executing the final call to the Fill method, I have to remove the parameter from the Command object because the GetFinancePMTRates stored procedure does not accept any parameters. I can do this by calling the Clear method of the Command object's Parameters collection:

```
...
Try
   ' create a new empty DataSet for the results dsCarDetail = New DataSet()
   ' and fill it from the database
   sqlComm.Parameters.Add("@CarID", sCarID)
   Dim daCarDetail As New SqlDataAdapter(sqlComm)
   sqlConn.Open()
   daCarDetail.Fill(dsCarDetail, "CarDetails")
   sqlComm.CommandText = sColorProcName
   daCarDetail.Fill(dsCarDetail, "CarColors")
   sqlComm.CommandText = sExtrasProcName
   daCarDetail.Fill(dsCarDetail, "CarExtras")
   sqlComm.CommandText = sFinancePMTProcName
   sqlComm.Parameters.Clear()
   daCarDetail.Fill(dsCarDetail, "FinancePMTRates")
   ...
```

This creates a DataSet containing four tables:

- CarDetails contains a row for each car/engine combination for this vehicle model

- CarColors contains a row for each color that is available for this vehicle model

- CarExtras contains a row for each optional extra that is available for this model

- FinancePMTRates contains the rows required to calculate the finance payments

Saving the DataSet in the Session

Now that the DataSet is ready for use, it can be saved in the user's ASP.NET session, ready for the next (postback) request. The remainder of the code is the Catch and Finally sections of the Try...Catch construct I'm using to trap any database access errors, followed by the statement that returns the DataSet (or Nothing if there was an error). Notice that I have to call the Close method of the Connection after I have finished with it. I opened the connection explicitly earlier so the Fill method will not close it when it completes each time:

```
    ...
    'save DataSet in Session for next postback
    Session(sSessionKey) = dsCarDetail

  Catch
    Return Nothing
  Finally
    sqlConn.Close()
  End Try

  End If
  Return dsCarDetail
End Function
```

> **NOTE** *If the connection is closed when* Fill *is called, it is opened automatically (implicitly) by the* Fill *method and then closed again immediately afterwards. This is a considerable waste of processing resources when you are filling more than one table, and to get the best performance you should open the connection first (before the first call to the* Fill *method) and then close it again after the last call to the* Fill *method.*

Of course, as the data within the DataSet is the same for each user, and only depends on the CarID value (the selected model), you could store it in the Application object rather than in the user's Session. This would mean that the DataSet for each model would remain in the Application until it is restarted, whereas the ones in each user's Session disappear automatically when the session ends. If you have data that does not depend on the actual user, then you might like to consider testing this alternative approach to see if it reduces server loading and improves performance in your own application.

The Code in the Model Details Page

Before I show you the main interactive "tabbed dialog" sections of the Model Details page, you should examine the code in the Page_Load event handler to see how the page behaves, and what it does, when first loaded and during each postback.

I have a few page-level variables declared within the page, outside any event handlers. These variables hold values such as the style sheet size (as used in all other sample pages), the ID of the selected vehicle, a reference to the DataSet holding the data to populate the page, and a variable to hold the ID of the current visitor (used when it's time to save a quotation for that visitor).

There is also an array of string values that I use to hold the calculated price and finance terms in the user's ASP.NET session, and a String to hold the session key that I use when storing this array in the user's session:

cardetail.aspx

```
' page-level variable to style sheet size
Dim sStyleSize As String = "Standard"

' page-level variable to hold current car ID
Dim sCarID As String

' page-level variable to hold DataSet of values from database
Dim oCarsDS As DataSet
' page-level variable to hold User ID for links to My Cars page
Dim sUserID As String
' page-level array to hold current car price and finance terms
' (0) = Basic Price including extras and color option
' (1) = Annual interest rate applicable to purchase
' (2) = Interest amount included in Total Price
' (3) = Total Price including interest for finance plan (if selected)
' (4) = Number of months for finance plan (if selected)
' (5) = Monthly payment amount for finance plan (if selected)
Dim aCurrentPrice(5) As String
' page-level variable to hold Session key for prices array
Dim sPricesSessionKey As String
```

The Page_Load Event Handler

In the Page_Load event itself, I start by generating the client-side event handlers that I'll be using in the page. I discussed the use of the RegisterClientScriptBlock method and the client-side mainWindowPage function at the end of the previous chapter, and I'll discuss where the other two client-side functions (setOptionButtons and nodeExpanded) are used later in this chapter:

```
Sub Page_Load()
  ' create the client-side script block for the control events in the page
  Dim sScript as String = "<script language='JavaScript'>" & vbCrlf _
    & "<!--" & vbCrlf _
    & "function setOptionButtons(sName) {" & vbCrlf _
    & "  document.forms[0].elements[sName].checked = true;" & vbCrlf _
    & "}" & vbCrlf _
    & "function nodeExpanded(oSender) {" & vbCrlf _
    & "  var clickedNode = oSender.clickedNodeIndex;" & vbCrlf _
    & "  var colNodes = oSender.getChildren();" & vbCrlf _
    & "  for (var i = 0; i < colNodes.length; i++) {" & vbCrlf _
    & "    if (colNodes[i].getNodeIndex() != clickedNode)" & vbCrlf _
    & "      colNodes[i].setAttribute('expanded', false);" & vbCrlf _
    & "  }" & vbCrlf _
    & "}" & vbCrlf _
    & "function mainWindowPage(sHref, bClose) {" & vbCrlf _
    & "  window.opener.location.href = sHref;" & vbCrlf _
    & "  if (bClose) window.close();" & vbCrlf _
    & "}" & vbCrlf _
    & "//-->" & vbCrlf _
    & "<" & "/" & "script>"

  ' register it so that it is inserted into the page
  If(Not IsClientScriptBlockRegistered("JSBlock")) Then
    RegisterClientScriptBlock("JSBlock", sScript)
  End If
  ...
```

Checking for an Active Session

Next, as in the other example pages, I need to confirm that a session is currently active for this user. I extract the value for the style sheet size from the session and check that I actually did get something. If not, I have to redirect the user to default.aspx to restart the session and reestablish the user ID and style sheet size.

However, as the Model Details page is running in a pop-up window that is opened from the Home page in the main window, I need to do a little extra work compared to the action taken in the other pages. I have to change the URL of the main window to load the default.aspx page and then close the Model Details window.

Of course, if you remember what you read towards the end of Chapter 8 (when I discussed the links to the My Cars page) you'll realize how I achieve this. I just output some client-side script that changes the location.href property for the main window (the opener property of the current window) to default.aspx, and call the close method of the current window. As this client-side script is not inside a function, but "inline" in the page, it is executed automatically as soon as the client's browser receives it:

```
...
' get style sheet size from Session
sStyleSize = CType(Session("WccStyleSize"), String)
' if no value, session has expired or user entered
' site at page other than "Home" page
If sStyleSize = "" Then

  ' write client-side code that reloads Home page and closes
  ' window to browser, plus message for non-script clients
  Dim sReload As String = "<html><body>" & vbCrlf _
    & "<script language='JavaScript'>" & vbCrlf _
    & "<!--" & vbCrlf _
    & "window.opener.location.href = 'home.aspx';" & vbCrlf _
    & "window.close();" & vbCrlf _
    & "//-->" & vbCrlf _
    & "<" & "/" & "script>" & vbCrlf _
    & "<center><b>Your session has expired.</b><p />" _
    & "<b>Please close this window and reload the Home page</b>" _
    & "</center></body></html>"

  ' then prevent rest of page from being processed
  Response.Write(sReload)
  Response.Flush()
  Response.End()
  Exit Sub

End If
...
```

Notice at the end of this code, after sending the script to the client, I prevent the server-side code from executing any further and flush the contents of the ASP.NET output buffer to the client.

Collecting the DataSet

If there is an active session, the next step is to collect the DataSet containing the data needed to build the page. I also collect the current user ID from the session (because I now know that there is an active session), and store it away in the page-level variable for later use. Then I need to find out which model was selected and extract this value from the query string—it is placed there by the links in the Home page that open this page:

```
...
' get UserID from Session
sUserID = CType(Session("WccUserID"), String)

' get car ID from query string
sCarID = Request.QueryString("id")
If sCarID > "" Then
  ...
```

Providing there is a Car ID, I can now call the `GetCarDetailsDS` function I examined earlier to get the `DataSet`. If it is not available, I display a message and exit:

```
...
' get DataSet from function elsewhere in this page
' we'll also need it almost every time a postback occurs
oCarsDS = GetCarDetailsDS(sCarID)
If oCarsDS Is Nothing Then
   lblMessage.Text = "Sorry, the database cannot be accessed."
   btnSave.Visible = False
   Exit Sub
End If
...
```

Collecting the Price and Finance Terms

You saw in the page-level declarations that I have an array to hold the price of the current configuration of the vehicle, plus the details of the currently selected finance package. I store this array in the user's session between postbacks (this is easier than trying to extract the values from the controls on the page each time).

As with the `DataSet` containing the details of the vehicle, I have to build a session key that denotes the ID of the vehicle so that I can store an array for each model if the user is configuring more than one at a time. However, this is only valid for the script-enabled version of the page, because the Home page prevents visitors from opening more than one pop-up Model Details window for the same model of vehicle.

In the version of the page for non-script-enabled clients, I'll have to handle the case where a visitor could be configuring more than one instance of the same vehicle, in which case using only the Car ID to differentiate the session-level variables is not a safe or valid approach—it would cause all instances of the page to use the same array values.

And, if I later decide to allow users to configure more than one instance of the same vehicle in the script-enabled version (by changing the code in the Home page that opens the Model Details window), I would face the same problem. So, I might as well provide robust code in both versions of the page to make maintenance easier and avoid any possibility of an error in the future.

To achieve this I create a unique (random) session key to use for each array. However, the next question is where do I store this key so that I can get at it each time the page is loaded? I obviously can't keep it in the user's session, because that would defeat the whole object of the process. I could add it to the query string, but that means I would have to create it in the Home page rather than here.

Saving Values in the Viewstate of the Page

One great way to persist page-specific values across a postback is to use the *viewstate* of the page. Storing `String` values in the viewstate is easy. It works just like storing them in an ASP.NET session. I insert a value into the viewstate using:

```
ViewState("key-name") = value
```

and I extract it using:

```
value = CType(ViewState("key-name"), String)
```

Storing other data types (such as numbers) requires converting them to their String representation, but this is easy enough to do using the ToString method when they are stored, and the Parse method when they are extracted.

Viewstate is useful at times like this because the values are stored within the page and not on the server, which makes it a great approach for *page-instance-specific* values. When values are *not* specific to the page instance, and you can guarantee session support (as in the sample application), storing them in the session is often a better approach because it saves them being round-tripped to the client.

In the case of the prices array, I could, of course, just store the values themselves as individual values in the viewstate. Remember, however, that this adds to the page size, and so large or complex data structures (such as the DataSet that contains all the vehicle details), or values that can't easily be converted into a String, are not good candidates for storing in the viewstate. The technique I demonstrate here of using the session to store the data and the viewstate just to store the session key is probably more efficient.

So, returning to the Page_Load event handler, I check if this is a postback or if it's the first time the page has been loaded. If it is a postback, I collect the key for the price and finance terms array from the viewstate and use it to access and collect the array:

```
...
If Page.IsPostback Then
  ' get key for Prices array from the page ViewState
  sPricesSessionKey = CType(ViewState("PriceArrayKey"), String)
  ' get array of current prices and finance terms from Session
  aCurrentPrice = CType(Session(sPricesSessionKey), String())
...
```

If this is the first time that the page has been loaded, there are different tasks to complete. First create the key for the prices array and store it in the viewstate of the page. Then generate a random number and use it in conjunction with the Car ID—an example key might be something like "WCCPricesKey3-814".

Then I can populate the controls on the page by calling two routines that are defined elsewhere: ShowCarDetails and CalculateCarPrice. You'll recall that I only need to populate the controls on the page the first time it loads, as the current values selected by a visitor will be maintained by the viewstate when a postback occurs:

```
...
Else
  ' create random key for storing price/finance terms array in
  ' user's session for this instance of the page, just in case
  ' they are configuring multiple instances of the same vehicle
  Dim oRand As New Random()
```

```
        sPricesSessionKey = "WCCPricesKey" & sCarID & "-" _
                    & oRand.Next(0, 999).ToString()
        ' store this key in the ViewState of the page
        ViewState("PriceArrayKey") = sPricesSessionKey
        ' display details of this vehicle
        ShowCarDetails(sCarID)
        ' calculate and display price for default configuration
        CalculateCarPrice()
      End If
    End If
  End Sub
```

I discuss the ShowCarDetails and CalculateCarPrice routines in detail in Chapter 10.

The Model Details "Tab" Pages in Detail

At last I have everything in place to start examining the code for the five "tabbed dialog" page sections of the Model Details page. You've seen an outline view of the page in the previous chapter, and the HTML declarations that implement the parts of the page outside the "tabbed dialog." And now you've also seen how the necessary data is accessed and stored in a DataSet ready for use. So now let me show you the remaining code. I start with the section that displays the colors available for the current vehicle.

The Color Selection Section

The first of the five "tabs" contains a list of all the colors that are available for the current vehicle. There are two ranges of colors, standard and metallic, and the option buttons on the left allows visitors to choose which color range they want to select from. A pop-up ToolTip shows the color name when the mouse pointer hovers over a color (Figure 9-3).

Figure 9-3. Selecting a color for the vehicle

You'll recall that each of the "tabbed dialog" sections is enclosed in a PageView element that is part of the IE Web Controls MultiPage control declaration. Inside the PageView I declare a three-column single-row HTML table to hold the dialog content.

The left-hand cell contains a small transparent image that is resized to force the "tab" to be the correct vertical height (you'll see this technique in all the "tab" sections). The next cell contains the two option buttons, which are created with a RadioButtonList control containing an explicit declaration of the two buttons as ListItem controls:

```
<ie:PageView id="mpColors">
<!-- section for "Colors" tab -->
<table border="0" cellpadding="6">
  <tr>
    <td><img src="images/_blnk.gif" border="0"
             width="1" height="170" alt="" /></td>
    <td><font face="Tahoma,Arial,Helvetica,sans-serif" size="2">
      <span style="body-text"><b>Select a Color:</b></span><br />
      <asp:RadioButtonList id="optColorType"
                           OnSelectedIndexChanged="SelectColorType"
                           Font-Name="Tahoma,Arial,Helvetica,sans-serif"
                           Font-Size="10"
                           AutoPostBack="True'
                           CssClass="body-text" runat="server">
        <asp:ListItem Text="Standard Colors" Value="optColStandard"
                      Selected="True" />
        <asp:ListItem Text="Metallic Colors" Value="optColMetallic" />
      </asp:RadioButtonList></font>
    </td>
    ...
```

By default, I set (select) the Standard Colors option when the page first loads, but the actual selection after a postback will depend on the last setting chosen by the user, as stored in the viewstate for the page. You can also see that I set AutoPostBack to True for the RadioButtonList control so that a click automatically posts the page back to the server. And I specify a server-side event handler named SelectColorType for the OnSelectedIndexChanged attribute, so it will be executed when an option button is clicked. You'll see all this code later.

Displaying the Color Blocks

The main issue in this section of the page is how to display blocks of color in such a way that the user can click one to select it. I could create the same outward appearance using an HTML table, setting the background color of each cell to the appropriate color. However, this leaves no easy way to react to a "click" event, because only Internet Explorer 4.0 and later, and the CSS2-enabled "version 6" browsers recognize this event for a table cell.

Instead I chose to use standard <input type="image"> controls, with the image being a GIF file of the appropriate color. Originally, when I experimented with stretching a single-pixel-size image to the required display size using the width and height attributes, I found that browser support for this was extremely variable. In particular, Opera failed to resize the image.

However, Opera is in fact behaving correctly, because HTML 4 does not define width and height attributes for an <input> element. A click on an <input type="image"> control submits the <form> on which the control is declared to the server for processing, including the x and y coordinates of the mouse pointer within the image. So, if you think about it, how would rescaling an image affect these if you were allowed to do so? Should the coordinates be the actual position in pixels on the scaled image, or the equivalent position on the original-sized image?

So, the images I display are sized to the required final dimensions for the page, and stored in the /images/colors/ folder of the site. There is one for each color listed in the tblColor table. While having to deliver all these images to the client might seem to be a waste of bandwidth, there is really no other cross-browser compatible solution. In any case, each image file is only 122 bytes (I used a bitmap editor to reduce the number of colors in the image to a minimum), and they will be cached on the client after the first access to the page.

The following listing shows the remainder of the Colors "tab." You can see that I use a DataList control with the RepeatLayout, RepeatDirection, and RepeatColumns attributes set so that I get a six-column wide table with the color blocks laid out horizontally:

```
...
<td><font face="Tahoma,Arial,Helvetica,sans-serif" size="2">
  <asp:DataList id="dlsColors" runat="server" CellSpacing="5"
                RepeatLayout="Table" RepeatDirection="Horizontal"
                RepeatColumns="6">
    <ItemTemplate>
      <input type="image" id="imgColor" runat="server"
             OnServerClick="SelectColor"
             Src='<%# DataBinder.Eval(Container.DataItem, "Color",
                                     "images/colors/{0}.gif") %>'
             Alt='<%# Container.DataItem("Color") %>'
             Width="60" Height="30" Border="1"
             Title='<%# Container.DataItem("Color") %>'
             Style="border-width:1px;border-style:solid;
                    border-color:Black;" />
    </ItemTemplate>
  </asp:DataList></font>
</td>
</tr>
</table>
</ie:PageView>
```

The ItemTemplate for the DataList generates the <input type="image"> element for each color using data binding. These elements have a range of attributes set so that the correct image is displayed, and a pop-up ToolTip is created for all types of clients. Because I include the attribute Border="1", I'll get an outline (albeit a blue "hyperlink" one) in browsers that do not support CSS. However, for those that do, the Style attribute I've also included overrides this to add a one-pixel wide black border around each image (useful when the image is white!).

Where Do the Colors Come From?

In case you haven't noticed yet, I should admit that I cheated a little in selecting the colors that are available for the vehicles. I used the .NET Framework standard colors, allowing the code to automatically generate the appropriate color for the large car image at the top of the Model Details page. You'll see this code later.

To assist in generating the images for the color blocks, and to view the available .NET Framework colors, I used a modified version of the "color listing" page that I introduced in Chapter 7. That page, color-list.aspx in the charting subfolder of the samples, was designed to show the browser-safe colors. However, in the example application I've abandoned that approach for the car colors—most car buyers are not interested in whether their new vehicle is a browser-safe color, but whether it looks nice.

The page dotnet-color-list.aspx is also in the charting subfolder of the samples, and it displays all the .NET standard colors with their names and RGB values (in hex and decimal). The first few colors are the standard "Windows furniture" colors such as Desktop, ActiveCaption, and WindowText. After that come the 140 other standard colors. The code is much the same as was used in the color-list.aspx page, so I am not listing or describing it again here (Figure 9-4).

Figure 9-4. The example page displaying the standard .NET range of colors

Populating the Page Heading and Colors Section

The ShowCarDetails routine that is called from the Page_Load event handler is responsible for populating the five "tabbed dialog" sections. However, it also fills in a couple
of items at the top of the Model Details page. I've listed the first part of the routine
next, and I'll be working through it section by section as you look at each of the
"tabs" in the page.

    The routine starts by getting references to each of the tables (DataTable objects)
within the DataSet that holds all the data for this page. Then it gets a reference to the
first row in the CarDetails table. This table contains a row for each car/engine combination for this model, but the model name and précis are the same in all the rows
because they all refer to the currently selected model.

    So, using the values in this row, I can fill in the précis and get the model name.
From the model name I can figure out which image to load, and add the appropriate
alt attribute to it. I also set the text of the <title> element (the element with the id
value elmTitle) so that the title bar of the pop-up window shows the model name:

ShowCarDetails subroutine

```
' routine to show selected car details
Sub ShowCarDetails(sCarID As String)

  ' get references to the tables in the DataSet
  Dim oDTCar As DataTable = oCarsDS.Tables("CarDetails")
  Dim oDTColor As DataTable = oCarsDS.Tables("CarColors")
  Dim oDTExtras As DataTable = oCarsDS.Tables("CarExtras")
  Dim oDTFinance As DataTable = oCarsDS.Tables("FinancePMTRates")
  ' fill in Precis and image of car
  Dim oDR As DataRow = oDTCar.Rows(0)
  lblPrecis.Text = oDR("Precis").ToString()
  Dim sCarName As String = oDR("Model").ToString()
  imgCar.ImageUrl = "images/" & sCarName & "300.gif"
  imgCar.AlternateText = "The Xrox " & sCarName
  elmTitle.InnerText = "Xrox " & sCarName & " - Configure and Buy"
  ...
```

Displaying the Appropriate Set of Colors

Now I can get a reference to a DataView object for the CarColors table in the DataSet.
This table contains all the available colors, both standard and metallic ranges, and so
I need to decide which ones should be displayed. I can find the current selection by
examining the value of the RadioButtonList control named optColorType (the Standard
Colors and Metallic Colors option buttons).

    By good fortune, rather than forward planning, the SelectedIndex property of the
RadioButtonList control returns the same value as I use in the table to denote the
color range (zero for standard colors and one for metallic colors). I can apply a filter
to the rows in the DataView, so that only the appropriate colors are included, by using
this value when I set the RowFilter property. Then I bind the filtered DataView to the

DataList control named dlsColors that displays the color blocks. After the DataList output has been generated I remove the row filter to allow any other code that needs to access the data to do so:

```
...
' fill the DataList of colors depending on setting of
' the Standard/Metallic radio buttons
Dim oDTView As DataView = oDTColor.DefaultView
oDTView.RowFilter = "IsMetallic = " & optColorType.SelectedIndex
dlsColors.DataSource = oDTView
dlsColors.DataBind()
oDTView.RowFilter = ""
...
```

It's good practice to remove a RowFilter after use, as it can cause hard-to-find bugs in your code if you later reuse the DataView (or the underlying table) without remembering to remove the filter first.

Reacting to Events in the Colors Section

The code you've just seen will populate the DataList control named dlsColors with the standard colors when the page is first loaded. However, the page must handle both a "click" event arising from a visitor selecting a different color, and a "change" event that arises when the user clicks on the option buttons to switch from standard colors to metallic colors or vice versa.

The attributes I declared on the RadioButtonList control that implements the two option buttons specify that a postback will occur when an option is selected, and that the event handler named SelectColorType will be executed when this happens. All the SelectColorType event handler has to do is change the list of colors that are displayed in the DataList control. Effectively it's a copy of the code I just looked at:

```
' routine to show range of colors when a Standard/Metallic is selected
Sub SelectColorType(oSender As Object, oArgs As EventArgs)
  ' get reference to table in the DataSet
  Dim oDTColor As DataTable = oCarsDS.Tables("CarColors")
  ' fill the DataList of colors depending on setting of
  ' the Standard/Metallic radio buttons
  Dim oDTView As DataView = oDTColor.DefaultView
  oDTView.RowFilter = "IsMetallic = " & optColorType.SelectedIndex
  dlsColors.DataSource = oDTView
  dlsColors.DataBind()
  oDTView.RowFilter = ""

End Sub
```

Meanwhile, the attributes I declared on the DataList itself specify that a postback will occur when a color block is clicked (each one is an <input type="image"> element), and that the event handler named SelectColor will be executed when this happens. In this case, I just have to accomplish two things. I need to update the color of the car image at the top of the page, and I do this by simply changing the background color of the table cell that contains it.

As I mentioned in Chapter 8, each car image I use in this page is a GIF image where the bodywork of the vehicle is transparent. So the background color shows through, and it looks like the color of the vehicle has changed. In reality, however, you would probably want to display a more tempting (and better quality) image of the vehicle. You could just as easily change the src of the element containing the car image to load a different full-color image instead.

The only other step required for the SelectColor event handler is to recalculate the price. There is a price premium for the metallic colors, and so the current price might be incorrect if the user has switched from a standard to a metallic color, or vice versa. To recalculate the price I just have to execute the same CalculateCarPrice routine as I did when I first loaded the page (and which I'll discuss in Chapter 10):

```
' routine to select the color chosen by the user and update car image
Sub SelectColor(oSender As Object, oArgs As ImageClickEventArgs)
   tclColor.BgColor = oSender.Alt
   CalculateCarPrice()
End Sub
```

The Engine Selection Section

The second "tab" in the sample page displays the list of available engines. The option buttons at the left of the "tab" allow visitors to select an engine from the list, and the table on the right indicates which one is selected by highlighting it. Notice the text strings in the Turbo and Auto columns that I created within the stored procedure you looked at earlier (Figure 9-5).

Colors	Engine	Extras	Details	Finance

Select an Engine:	Capacity	Fuel Type	Cyls	Turbo	Max RPM	BHP	Gears	Auto
○ 1.6 16V	1,599cc	Gas/Petrol	4	No	6,800	94	5	No
● 2.0i 16V	1,998cc	Gas/Petrol	4	No	7,200	103	5	Yes

Figure 9-5. Selecting an engine for the vehicle

The HTML for this part of the page again uses an HTML three-column single-row table (as do all the "tabs"). Again the left-hand cell contains the image that sets the height of the "tab," and the next cell contains a RadioButtonList control—much like the Colors section you just saw. However, this time the data to generate the list comes from the database and is set dynamically when the page loads. So the RadioButtonList control contains no ListItem elements:

```
<ie:PageView id="mpEngine">
<!-- section for "Engine" tab -->
<table border="0" cellpadding="6">
  <tr>
    <td><img src="images/_blnk.gif" width="1" height="170" alt="" /></td>
    <td><font face="Tahoma,Arial,Helvetica,sans-serif" size="2">
      <span style="body-text"><b>Select an Engine:</b></span><br />
      <asp:RadioButtonList id="optEngine"
                           OnSelectedIndexChanged="SelectEngine"
                           Font-Name="Tahoma,Arial,Helvetica,sans-serif"
                           Font-Size="10" AutoPostBack="True"
                           CssClass="body-text" runat="server"/>
    </font>
  </td>
  ...
```

Again I use AutoPostBack to automatically submit the page to the server in response to a click on the option buttons. This executes a server-side event handler named SelectEngine, which looks after highlighting the appropriate row in the table next to the option buttons and recalculating the vehicle price.

The Engine Details (DataGrid) Table

The right-hand table of engine details is also generated with server-side data binding, and to get the format, layout, and appearance I want, I used a DataGrid control this time. It is better suited to a purely columnar layout than other list controls. However, rather than allowing it to generate the columns automatically, I have specified these using BoundColumn controls. I want to change the column headings from those used in the database tables to something more appropriate (although I could have done this in the stored procedure, of course). I also specify the display format of the data in two of the columns:

```
    ...
    <td><font face="Tahoma,Arial,Helvetica,sans-serif" size="2">
      <asp:DataGrid id="dgrEngine" runat="server"
                    AutoGenerateColumns="False" CellPadding="4"
                    Font-Size="10" Font-Name="Tahoma,Arial,Helvetica,sans-serif"
                    HeaderStyle-HorizontalAlign="center"
                    HeaderStyle-BackColor="#b50055"
                    HeaderStyle-ForeColor="#ffffff"
                    HeaderStyle-Font-Bold="True"
                    ItemStyle-HorizontalAlign="center"
                    SelectedItemStyle-BackColor="#ffffcc">
        <Columns>
          <asp:BoundColumn HeaderText="Capacity" DataField="CubicCapacity"
                           DataFormatString="{0:#,###0cc}" />
          <asp:BoundColumn HeaderText="Fuel Type" DataField="FuelType" />
```

```
            <asp:BoundColumn HeaderText="Cyls" DataField="Cylinders" />
            <asp:BoundColumn HeaderText="Turbo" DataField="Turbo" />
            <asp:BoundColumn HeaderText="Max RPM" DataField='MaxRPM'
                             DataFormatString="{0:#,###0}" />
            <asp:BoundColumn HeaderText="BHP" DataField="BHP" />
            <asp:BoundColumn HeaderText="Gears" DataField="Gears" />
            <asp:BoundColumn HeaderText="Auto" DataField="AutoTrans" />
          </Columns>
        </asp:DataGrid></font>
      </td>
    </tr>
</table>
</ie:PageView>
```

Populating the Engine Section

The ShowCarDetails routine executed when the page first loads continues by populating the controls for the Engine section of the page. Using the reference to the
CarDetails table that I obtained at the start of this routine, I can bind the data directly
to the RadioButtonList control named optEngine that implements the list of option
buttons for the engine types.

I want to display the engine name and use the ID of the engine as the value of
each option button. I achieve this by specifying the appropriate column names from
the DataSet table as the DataValueField and DataTextField property values:

ShowCarDetails subroutine (continued)

```
...
' fill RadioButtonList with available engines
optEngine.DataSource = oDTCar
optEngine.DataValueField = "EngineID"
optEngine.DataTextField = "EngineName"
optEngine.DataBind()
...
```

I also need to populate the table that displays the technical details of each
engine. The CarDetails table in the DataSet contains all the information on each
engine, so I can use this table again. I just have to bind it to the DataGrid control
named dgrEngine.

There are two more tasks. I want to be able to call the CalculateCarPrice routine
when the page first loads, before the user has made any selections, so that the user
can see the price of the basic model. So I must set the option buttons to specify one
of the engines, and I chose to select the first one—which should be the smallest and
the least expensive. I also select the corresponding row in the DataGrid table by setting its SelectedIndex property to zero as well:

```
...
' fill the DataGrid with the details of each engine
dgrEngine.DataSource = oDTCar
dgrEngine.DataBind()
```

411

```
' and select the first engine in these two lists
optEngine.SelectedIndex = 0
dgrEngine.SelectedIndex = 0
...
```

Reacting to Events in the Engine Section

The only event that the Engine section of the page can raise is the selection of a different engine. The AutoPostBack attribute causes a postback to occur when this happens, and the OnSelectedIndexChanged attribute will cause the event handler named SelectEngine to be executed. All this does is set the SelectedIndex property of the DataGrid to the same value as the SelectedIndex of the RadioButtonList so that the correct row is highlighted, and then calls the routine to recalculate the price of the vehicle:

```
' routine to select row in DataGrid when an engine is selected
Sub SelectEngine(oSender As Object, oArgs As EventArgs)
  dgrEngine.SelectedIndex = optEngine.SelectedIndex
  CalculateCarPrice()
End Sub
```

The Optional Extras Selection Section

The third "tab" is the Extras page, which shows the optional extras that are available for this vehicle. I've implemented it as a series of check boxes, and users can select as many as they wish from the list (Figure 9-6).

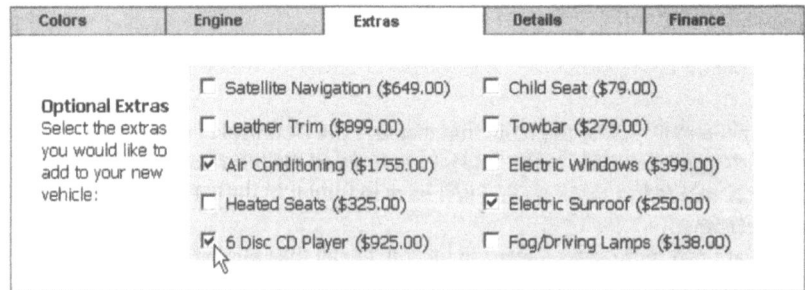

Figure 9-6. Selecting the optional extras for the vehicle

The HTML content of this "tab" is relatively simple. There is some declarative text in the left-hand table cell, and a CheckBoxList control in the right-hand section. The captions for each check box are created through server-side data binding. As you'll recall, I carried out some text manipulation within the SQL of the stored procedure (described earlier in this chapter) to build these captions.

As in the previous two "tabs," I set AutoPostBack for the CheckBoxList, and specified that the server-side event handler named SelectExtras will execute when a postback occurs. And, as in the Colors "tab," I use the RepeatLayout, RepeatDirection, and RepeatColumns attributes to get a two-column table—though this time I lay out the controls in that table vertically rather than horizontally:

```
<ie:PageView id="mpExtras">
<!-- section for "Extras" tab -->
<table border="0" cellpadding="6">
  <tr>
    <td><img src="images/_blnk.gif" width="1" height="170" alt="" /></td>
    <td valign="top">
      <font face="Tahoma,Arial,Helvetica,sans-serif" size="2">
      <p> </p><span style="body-text"><b>Optional Extras</b><br />
      Select the extras<br />you would like to<br />add to your new<br />
      vehicle:</span></font>
    </td>
    <td nowrap="nowrap">
      <font face="Tahoma,Arial,Helvetica,sans-serif" size="2">
      <asp:CheckBoxList id="chkExtras"
                        OnSelectedIndexChanged="SelectExtras"
                        RepeatLayout="Table"
                        RepeatColumns="2" RepeatDirection="Vertical"
                        Font-Name="Tahoma,Arial,Helvetica,sans-serif"
                        Font-Size="10" CellPadding="3" BackColor="#ffffcc"
                        AutoPostBack="True" CssClass="body-text" runat="server">
      </asp:CheckBoxList></font>
    </td>
  </tr>
</table>
</ie:PageView>
```

Populating the Extras Section

As the ShowCarDetails routine runs when the page first loads, the next part is responsible for populating the list of optional extras. I use the reference to the CarExtras table in the DataSet that I obtained at the start of this routine to bind that table to the CheckBoxList control named chkExtras. I use the value of the column that I created within the stored procedure (DisplayText) as the caption, so that each check box displays the "extra" name and price, followed by a couple of   non-breaking space characters to separate the two columns:

ShowCarDetails subroutine (continued)

```
...
' fill the CheckBoxList with list of available extras
chkExtras.DataSource = oDTExtras
chkExtras.DataTextField = "DisplayText"
chkExtras.DataValueField = "ExtraID"
chkExtras.DataBind()
...
```

You can see in the preceding code that I attempt to bind the ID of each of the optional extras to the value property of each check box. However, as you discovered in the Compare Models page in Chapter 7, this doesn't actually do anything. When I use a CheckBoxList control, the value attributes are never set. This is because their "value" can't sensibly be accessed following a postback because of the way these controls work within the browser. You'll see how I have to work around this when you look at the routine to calculate the car price in the next chapter.

Reacting to Events in the Extras Section

When visitors check or uncheck any of the boxes in the CheckBoxList control, the AutoPostBack and OnSelectedIndexChanged attribute values I specified cause a postback to occur, and the routine named SelectExtras is executed on the server. All I need to do here is recalculate the car price to take into account the change in the optional extras specified by the visitor:

```
' routine to update price as optional extras are selected
Sub SelectExtras(oSender As Object, oArgs As EventArgs)
  CalculateCarPrice()
End Sub
```

The Standard Features (Details) Section

The fourth "tab" does not provide any features for selecting options for the vehicle, but is still interactive. It contains two expandable "tree view" lists that display categorized information about the vehicle. I wanted to prevent the user from changing the layout of the page by expanding these tree views beyond the current size of the "tab" section, and thereby increasing its height, so I have used some code that automatically collapses any other open "node" when you open a different one (Figure 9-7).

Figure 9-7. Viewing the standard features of the vehicle

The HTML declaration for this page shows the two "tree view" controls. These are implemented using two instances of the TreeView control from the IE Web Controls pack that I discussed in Chapter 8.

The IE Web Controls TreeView Control

This is the third of the four controls from the IE Web Controls pack that I use in the example application. It saves an inordinate amount of development time when building applications because, like the TabStrip and MultiPage controls I discussed in Chapter 8, the TreeView control automatically adapts its behavior to suit the client browser in use. All I have to do is declare the control and specify the source of the data that will be displayed within it.

The TreeView control expects the source data to be declared as a series of <treenode> elements within the source code, or supplied as an XML document or disk file. In Internet Explorer 5.5 and above, the XML or declarative data is sent to the client, along with an XML element that instantiates the treeview.htc behavior component on the client. In other browsers, the server-side TreeView control generates an HTML table containing images, text, and hyperlinks that provide the same visual appearance.

The Declarative Source Format for a TreeView Control

To declaratively define the nodes for a TreeView control, I use syntax such as the following:

```
<ie:treeview runat="server">
  <ie:treenode text="First top-level node">
    <ie:treenode text="First child node" />
    <ie:treenode text="Second child node" />
  </ie:treenode>
  <ie:treenode text="Second top-level node">
    <ie:treenode text="First child node" />
    <ie:treenode text="Second child node" />
  </ie:treenode>
</ie:treeview>
```

The nodes can be nested to any depth, though I have only shown two levels in the preceding example. The text attribute obviously defines the text that will appear for each item in the tree. To react to a user clicking on any node, all I have to do is handle the events that this raises (on the server or on the client).

Data-Binding an XML Data Source File to a TreeView *Control*

When the TreeView control is instantiated within an ASP.NET page I can use server-side data binding to an XML document to build the visible output for the client, rather than having to declare it inline as in the previous example. The next listing shows the XML document format that is required (remember that XML is case-sensitive for element and attribute names!). This is one of the XML files I use as the source for the Details page in the Xrox Car Company site:

```
<?xml version="1.0"?>
<TREENODES>
  <TreeNode Text="Equipment">
    <TreeNode Text="Power Steering" />
    <TreeNode Text="Cruise control" />
    <TreeNode Text="Tinted windows" />
  </TreeNode>
  <TreeNode Text="Mechanical">
    <TreeNode Text="Front wheel drive" />
    <TreeNode Text="Anti-lock brakes" />
  </TreeNode>
  <TreeNode Text="Interior">
    <TreeNode Text="Number of seats: 4" />
    <TreeNode Text="Cup holders: 2" />
    <TreeNode Text="Electric seat adjust" />
  </TreeNode>
  <TreeNode Text="Costs">
    <TreeNode Text="Insurance rate: 9" />
    <TreeNode Text="Cost per mile: $ 0.89" />
    <TreeNode Text="Service 12,000 miles" />
  </TreeNode>
</TREENODES>
```

To perform the server-side data binding, I just have to assign the URL of this document to the TreeNodeSrc property of the TreeView control and call the DataBind method:

```
tvwDetails.TreeNodeSrc = "xmldata/tvdata.xml"
tvwDetails.DataBind()
```

Alternatively, I can assign a String that contains valid XML, rather than a String that specifies the URL of an XML file on disk or at another location, to the TreeNodeSrc property. Another approach is to use XSLT to transform an existing XML document into the correct valid format for the TreeView control. The TreeNodeSrc property is set to the URL of, or a String containing, the XML document as before; and the TreeNodeXsltSrc property is set to the URL of, or a String containing, an appropriate XSLT style sheet.

Reacting to TreeView Events

When the user clicks a text item in the tree view, the OnSelectedIndexChange event fires. I can get the index of the node that was clicked by examining the NewNode property of the TreeViewSelectEventArgs object that is passed to the event handler, and the index of the node that was previously selected from the OldNode property.

```
Sub MyTreeView_Select(oSender As Object, oArgs As TreeViewSelectEventArgs)
   intOldNodeIndex = oArgs.OldNode
   intNewNodeIndex = oArgs.NewNode
   ... etc ...
End Sub
```

There are also OnExpand, OnCollapse, and OnCheck events that are raised when the user expands a closed node, collapses an open node, or clicks the check box for a node (the nodes of a tree view can be displayed as check boxes). These events all expose a TreeViewClickEventArgs object to their event handler:

```
Sub MyTreeView_Event(oSender As Object, oArgs As TreeViewClickEventArgs)
   intNodeIndex = oArgs.Node
   ... etc ...
End Sub
```

To select a node in the tree view, all I have to do is set the SelectedNodeIndex property of the TreeView control.

> **NOTE** *A full reference to the* TreeView *control, and the other controls in the IE Web Controls pack, can be found using the link that they add to your Start menu when installed, or directly from:* http://msdn.microsoft.com/library/default.asp?url=/ workshop/webcontrols/webcontrols_entry.asp

The HTML for the Details Section

I am using two TreeView controls to create the appearance and data content for the Details section of the example page. In the next listing of the HTML section of the page source, you can see these two controls. Because I use server-side data-binding to populate them, there is no declarative content here.

Notice how I specify the style for each node. As I am simply displaying text (rather than using the nodes as hyperlinks), I don't want them to change color when the mouse hovers over them or when they are selected, so I set the HoverStyle and SelectedStyle style selectors to the same values as the default for all other nodes, as follows:

```
<ie:PageView id="mpDetails">
<!-- section for "Details" tab -->
<table border="0" cellpadding="6">
  <tr>
    <td><img src="images/_blnk.gif" width="1" height="170" alt="" /></td>
    <td valign="top">
      <font face="Tahoma,Arial,Helvetica,sans-serif" size="2">
      <p> </p><span style="body-text"><b>Vehicle Details</b><br />
      Select any of the<br />categories shown<br />here to see more<br />
      details:</span></font>
    </td>
    <td>   </td>
    <td valign="top">
      <font face="Tahoma,Arial,Helvetica,sans-serif" size="2">
      <span style="body-text">
      <ie:TreeView id="tvwDetailsLeft" runat="server"
                   OnExpand="NodeExpanded"
                   DefaultStyle="font-family:Tahoma,Arial,Helvetica,
                                 sans-serif;font-size:11px;"
                   HoverStyle="color:#000000;background:#ffffff;"
                   SelectedStyle="color:#000000;background:#ffffff;" />
      </span></font></td>
    <td>   </td>
    <td valign="top">
      <font face="Tahoma,Arial,Helvetica,sans-serif" size="2">
      <span style="body-text">
      <ie:TreeView id="tvwDetailsRight" runat="server"
                   OnExpand="NodeExpanded"
                   DefaultStyle="font-family:Tahoma,Arial,Helvetica,
                   sans-serif;font-size:11px;"
                   HoverStyle="color:#000000;background:#ffffff;"
                   SelectedStyle="color:#000000;background:#ffffff;" />
      </span></font></td>
  </tr>
</table>
</ie:PageView>
```

Another point to note is that I *do not* include the AutoPostBack attribute for the TreeView controls, but I have included the OnExpand attribute. In the code listing coming shortly, you'll see that I set the SelectExpands property of the controls to True, but only if the current browser *is not* Internet Explorer 5.5 and later. This seemingly random pattern of settings actually provides exactly the behavior I want. You see why next.

The Behavior of the TreeView *Controls in the Model Details Page*

If you've experimented with the example site, you'll have seen that the TreeView control behaves in such a way that, in browsers *other than* Internet Explorer 5.5 and later, you can open a top-level node by clicking either the "box" next to that node or the text of the node itself. The nodes are not hyperlinks, so there can be no confusion about whether this action will navigate to another page or just open the node to display its child nodes. However, in Internet Explorer 5.5 and later you have to click the "box" next to the node—clicking the node text has no effect in this case.

Second, you can only open one of the top-level nodes at a time. Opening a top-level node automatically closes any other top-level node that may be open in that control. I do this to prevent the height of the "tabbed dialog" section changing—as it will if more than one top-level node is open at the same time.

To achieve the "automatic opening" of a top-level node, I just have to set the SelectExpands attribute or property of the TreeView control to True. The control looks after generating all the appropriate code automatically. To achieve the "automatic collapse" of other top-level nodes, I have to react to the OnExpand event and use some code to collapse all the other top-level nodes.

Unfortunately, this combination of settings causes errors in Internet Explorer 5.5 and later, where the output is being created by the treeview.htc control on the client. I discovered that I could work around the problem by only allowing a click on a node to expand that node (SelectExpands) for browsers other than IE 5.5 and later. This is why the behavior is different for the different browsers.

In fact it turns out not to be a major problem because, in IE 5.5 and later, the text nodes are not underlined, so they do not look like hyperlinks. In other browsers that do underline the text nodes, such as Navigator 4 and 6, Mozilla, and Opera, clicking the text node causes it to expand.

Finally, to prevent Internet Explorer from submitting the page when a node is clicked, I have to omit the AutoPostBack attribute (as you saw in the preceding code above). I don't want to handle this event, so there is no reason to post back in this case. Of course, for other browsers, I do need a click on a node to cause a postback—this is the only way that the appearance of the tree can be updated. But this happens automatically for these types of browser anyway (each node is a hyperlink that submits the page), even when AutoPostBack is False.

So, in summary, the code needs to:

- Handle the OnExpand event for all browsers to collapse any other open top-level nodes. In IE 5.5 and later I do this client-side using some JavaScript code that interacts with the client-side treeview.htc component. For all other browsers, I handle the event server-side and interact with the ASP.NET TreeView control. So I add the attribute OnExpand="NodeExpanded" to the declaration of the control, as you saw in the preceding code. However, in IE 5.5 and later, I modify this value later in the run-time code so that it raises the event client-side.

- Set the SelectExpands property of the TreeView controls to True, but only for browsers other than Internet Explorer 5.5 and later.

You'll see how I achieve all this, and the server-side and client-side event handlers I use later in the chapter.

Populating the Details Section

So, let me show you how I populate the TreeView controls in the example. I am using static XML disk files to fill the controls, but there is no reason why the data could not be extracted dynamically from a database instead. I could load it into a DataSet and export it as XML, or load it directly from the database into an XmlDataDocument and extract it that way.

I have 10 XML files located in the xmldata subfolder of the application, two for each of the car models offered. One file contains the Equipment, Mechanical, Interior, and Costs top-level headings and child nodes for the left-hand TreeView control, and the other contains the Safety, Security, Dimensions, and Capacities top-level headings and child nodes for the right-hand TreeView control.

You saw an example of these files earlier in this section of the chapter. The names of these XML files indicate which control they are aimed at, and the model to which they apply. For example, the file for the left-hand control for the vehicle with ID value 4 is named tvdata-left-4.xml.

Before I can bind the XML data to the TreeView controls, however, I have to sort out the issue of assigning the correct attributes to them. The first stage in this part of the ShowCarDetails routine is to figure out if I am talking to IE 5.5 and later. I can do this by looking at the property values exposed by the Request.Browser object:

ShowCarDetails subroutine (continued)

```
...
If (Request.Browser.Browser = "IE") _
And (Request.Browser.Version >= "5.5") Then
   ...
```

At this point I know that I am dealing with IE 5.5 or later, and so I can add the client-side event handler attributes to the TreeView controls. Setting the OnExpand property (directly in code, or through the OnExpand attribute as I've done in the page) specifies how the ASP.NET server-side TreeView control behaves when the OnExpand event occurs.

However, I can add an onexpand attribute to the client-side element that is created by the TreeView control, without affecting the server-side behavior, by referencing the Attributes collection of the control directly. I set the attribute value so the TreeView control executes a client-side event handler named nodeExpanded, and passes a reference to the client-side TreeView component to it:

```
...
' set up client-side event handlers for the onexpand event by
' adding attributes directly to tree-view control outputs
tvwDetailsLeft.Attributes.Add("onexpand", "nodeExpanded(this)")
tvwDetailsRight.Attributes.Add("onexpand", "nodeExpanded(this)")
...
```

However, if the current browser is not IE 5.5 or later, I set the SelectExpands property (as discussed earlier):

```
...
Else  ' not IE 5.5 or above
   ' specify that we want the entries to auto-expand when clicked
   ' (setting these caused some versions of IE to misbehave)
```

```
    tvwDetailsLeft.SelectExpands = True
    tvwDetailsRight.SelectExpands = True

  End If
  ...
```

The final steps required are to assign the appropriate XML files to the two controls, depending on which vehicle model is displayed, and then call the DataBind method for each control. Notice that I do all this inside a Try...Catch construct so that I can trap an error if the XML file does not exist or cannot be loaded:

```
  ...
  ' specify XML source files for two Details tree-view controls
  ' and call DataBind—works just like ASP.NET list controls
  Try
    tvwDetailsLeft.TreeNodeSrc = "xmldata/tvdata-left-" & sCarID & ".xml"
    tvwDetailsLeft.DataBind()
    tvwDetailsRight.TreeNodeSrc = "xmldata/tvdata-right-" & sCarID & ".xml"
    tvwDetailsRight.DataBind()
  Catch
    lblMessage.Text = "Error loading XML source for tree-view controls."
  End Try
  ...
```

Reacting to Events in the Details Section

The only remaining task is to handle the events that are raised when the user expands a top-level node in either list. Both TreeView controls call the same event handler, but this may be the client-side version or the server-side version—depending on which browser is hosting the page. For browsers other than IE 5.5 and later, this server-side event is executed by ASP.NET:

```
Sub NodeExpanded(oSender As Object, oArgs As TreeViewClickEventArgs)
  ' iterate through all the top-level child nodes of the control
  Dim oTopNode As TreeNode
  For Each oTopNode In oSender.Nodes

    ' if it is not the node that was just expanded, collapse it
    If Not oTopNode Is oSender.GetNodeFromIndex(oArgs.Node) Then
      oTopNode.Expanded = False
    End If

  Next
End Sub
```

As this event handler is used by both TreeView controls, I need to be able to detect which one the event relates to. This is easy to do because the first parameter to the event handler (oSender) is a reference to the control that raised the event. In the code you can see that I simply iterate through all top-level nodes of the TreeView control, as exposed through the Nodes collection of the control.

For each node, I check if this is the one that was clicked. The only really unfamiliar aspect of programming the TreeView control is that the TreeViewClickEventArgs.Node property returns the index of the node, and not (as you may expect) a reference to a Node object. This is probably because the control is running client-side, and references cannot be passed back to the server.

However, a reference to any Node object can be obtained using the GetNodeFromIndex method of the TreeView control. So I can compare each top-level Node object in the TreeView.Nodes collection with the Node object that caused the event to occur, and set the Expanded property to False for all the nodes that did not cause this event to collapse them.

The Client-Side nodeExpanded *Event Handler*

The previous server-side event handler takes care of collapsing the nodes in browsers other than IE 5.5 and later. However, in IE 5.5 and later I have specified that an OnExpand event should execute the client-side event handler named nodeExpanded. The client-side attribute that is added to the TreeView controls is:

```
onexpand="nodeExpanded(this)"
```

You'll recall from the end of Chapter 8, and earlier in this chapter, that I used the RegisterClientScriptBlock method to insert three client-side functions into the page. The nodeExpanded event handler is one of these functions:

```
function nodeExpanded(oSender) {
  var clickedNode = oSender.clickedNodeIndex;
  var colNodes = oSender.getChildren();
  for (var i = 0; i < colNodes.length; i++)
    if (colNodes[i].getNodeIndex() != clickedNode)
      colNodes[i].setAttribute('expanded', false);
  }
}
```

I am now working client-side directly with the treeview.htc control so, as you can see, the methods and properties that are available are different. However, it should be clear from this code that I am doing the same thing as was done in the server-side event handler.

After collecting the index within the collection of top-level nodes of the node that was clicked, I can get a collection of these top-level nodes using the getChildren method of the TreeView control itself. Then I iterate through this collection setting the expanded attribute of each node except the current one to false.

Remember that the data to populate the TreeView controls on the client, in IE 5.5 and later, is sent to the client as an XML document. As you may have noticed, if you are familiar with coding against the XML DOM, the techniques used client-side to interact with the control are effectively the same as those used to interact directly with the equivalent XML document.

The Finance Package Selection Section

The final "tab" on the Model Details page allows the visitor to select a finance package and see the payment terms for the vehicle they are currently configuring (Figure 9-8).

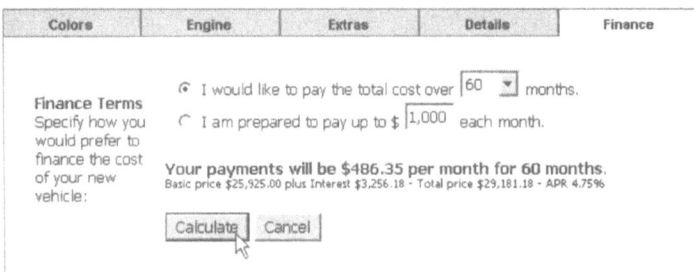

Figure 9-8. Selecting a finance package for the vehicle

The HTML that creates this "tab" section is shown in the following listing. There seems to be a lot of code, but most of it is layout and formatting information. The important parts are the two RadioButton controls for selecting the payment type, the DropDownList and TextBox to specify either the number of months or the maximum monthly payment, and the two Button controls to Calculate or Cancel the finance package:

```
<ie:PageView id="mpFinance">
<!-- section for "Finance" tab -->
<table border="0" cellpadding="6">
  <tr>
    <td><img src="images/_blnk.gif" width="1" height="170" alt="" /></td>
    <td valign="top">
      <font face="Tahoma,Arial,Helvetica,sans-serif" size="2">
      <p> </p><span style="body-text"><b>Finance Terms </b><br />
      Specify how you<br />would prefer to<br />finance the cost<br />
      of your new<br />vehicle:</span></font>
    </td>
    <td><font face="Tahoma,Arial,Helvetica,sans-serif" size="2">
      <span style="body-text">  
      <asp:RadioButton id="optByMonths" GroupName="optFinanceMethod"
          Checked="True" Text="" CssClass="body-text" runat="server"
          ToolTip="Select payment over a specified number of months" />
      I would like to pay the total cost over
      <asp:DropDownList id="lstFinanceMonths" CssClass="body-text"
          OnChange="setOptionButtons('optByMonths')" runat="server" />
      months.<br />  
```

```
                    <asp:RadioButton id="optByAmount" GroupName="optFinanceMethod"
                        Text="" CssClass="body-text" runat="server"
                        ToolTip="Select payment of a specified monthly amount" />
                    I am prepared to pay up to $
                    <asp:TextBox id="txtMonthPayment" Text="1,000" Columns="4"
                        MaxLength="7" CssClass="body-text" runat="server"
                        OnKeyDown="setOptionButtons('optByAmount')"
                        ToolTip="Enter the monthly payment amount" />
                    each month.<p />
                    <asp:Label id="lblFinanceResult" CssClass="body-text"
                        runat="server" />
                    <br /></span></font>
                    <font face="Tahoma,Arial,Helvetica,sans-serif" size="1">
                    <asp:Label id="lblFinanceInfo" CssClass="small-text" runat="server"
                        Text="Select payment options you prefer and click Calculate" />
                    <p /></font>
                    <font face="Tahoma,Arial,Helvetica,sans-serif" size="2">
                    <span style="body-text">
                    <asp:Button id="btnCalculate" Text="Calculate"
                        OnClick="ShowFinanceTerms" CssClass="body-text"
                        ToolTip="Calculate the options selected above" runat="server" />
                    <asp:Button id="btnCancel" Text="Cancel" Enabled="False"
                        OnClick="ClearFinanceTerms" CssClass="body-text"
                        ToolTip="Cancel existing finance package" runat="server" />
                    </span></font>
                </td>
            </tr>
        </table>
    </ie:PageView>
```

Enabling and Disabling Buttons and Other Controls

You can see that the final control on this page, the Cancel button named btnCancel, is
disabled by default when the page first loads. This is because there is no finance
package specified, and it makes it obvious to the user that this is the case. It will be
enabled once the user specifies the desired finance terms, so that he or she can cancel the finance package later if required.

When you take advantage of this technique in your pages, just bear in mind that
many older browsers do not recognize the disabled attribute (which is how ASP.NET
disables buttons and other HTML controls). So you should never rely on a control
being disabled. For example, your code should always be able to cope with a button
being clicked, and the subsequent server-side event handler being executed, even
when you have disabled that button.

Populating the Finance Section

Because the ShowCarDetails routine runs when the Model Details page first loads, all
I have to do is populate the drop-down list of months. This is done using server-side

data binding, as with most of the other list controls on the page. I already have a reference oDTFinance to the DataTable in the DataSet that contains the PMT payment information I need to populate the control. I specify that the list should display the number of months, and use the payment information as the value of each item in the list:

ShowCarDetails subroutine (continued*)*

```
...
' fill the DropDownList with months for Finance page
lstFinanceMonths.DataSource = oDTFinance
lstFinanceMonths.DataTextField = "Months"
lstFinanceMonths.DataValueField = "Payment"
lstFinanceMonths.DataBind()

' select the "36 months" entry as the default
lstFinanceMonths.SelectedIndex = 5

End Sub
```

The only other task, at the end of the preceding code, is to select the entry for 36 months, which is probably the most appropriate default value. This entry is the sixth one (at index 5) and I select it by setting the SelectedIndex property of the DropDownList control.

Reacting to Events in the Finance Section

You may have noticed in the HTML listing for this section of the page that none of the controls carry the AutoPostBack attribute. This is because I only want to post the page for processing when one of the buttons is clicked. These buttons are rendered as <input type="submit"> controls, and so they will always initiate a postback when clicked.

The events I specify for these controls are defined in the OnClick attributes. The OnClick events are raised server-side because these are ASP.NET Button controls:

```
<asp:Button id="btnCalculate" Text="Calculate"
            OnClick="ShowFinanceTerms" CssClass="body-text"
            ToolTip="Calculate the options selected above" runat="server" />
<asp:Button id="btnCancel" Text="Cancel" Enabled="False"
            OnClick="ClearFinanceTerms" CssClass="body-text"
            ToolTip="Cancel existing finance package" runat="server" />
```

You'll see the ShowFinanceTerms and ClearFinanceTerms event handlers in the next chapter when you discover how I calculate the price of a vehicle and the finance terms for it.

Reacting to Client-Side Events in the Finance Section

Although I don't want a postback to occur for any of the controls in this section of the page, other than the Calculate and Cancel buttons, I do want to execute some *client-side* code when two events occur. To provide a more intuitive and usable interface, I want the option buttons that select the finance package type to automatically reflect the users' actions when they interact with the drop-down list or the text box on the page.

In other words, selecting a number of months in the drop-down list should automatically select the first option, whereas typing into the text box should automatically select the second option. I achieve this by using some simple client-side code in the page. The DropDownList control named lstFinanceMonths has this attribute added to it in the declaration you saw earlier:

```
OnChange="setOptionButtons('optByMonths')
```

and the TextBox named txtMonthPayment has this attribute:

```
OnKeyDown="setOptionButtons('optByAmount')
```

So selecting a different value in the drop-down list, or typing in the text box, will execute the client-side setOptionButtons function. This is the third of the functions you saw being inserted into the page earlier with the RegisterClientScriptBlock method:

```
function setOptionButtons(sName) {
  document.forms[0].elements[sName].checked = true;
}
```

All this function does is take the name of the control that is passed to it as a parameter, and set the checked property of that control. So the appropriate option button is selected depending on whether the event is raised by the drop-down list or by the text box.

Summary

With this look at the five "tabbed dialog" sections, the several distractions you've encountered, and side streets you've traveled on the way, you have completed almost all the investigations into the design, construction, and interactivity of the Model Details page.

In the previous chapter you looked at the page in outline and I discussed how easy it is to build this kind of page when you take advantage of the ASP.NET features like viewstate support and the postback architecture. In this chapter, you've looked at the data I use to drive the page, the way to extract it, and the way to use it to populate the controls on the page. You also looked in detail at most of the event handling code—both server-side and client side—that makes the page interactive.

Along the way you've examined the design of the database tables, the stored procedures that extract the data, and the function that builds this data into a `DataSet` that is cached in the user's session. You also looked at using the `global.asax` file to run code when an application starts or when an error occurs.

Then, while exploring the five "tabs" on the example page where most of the interactivity is centered, I discussed the `TreeView` control from the IE Web Control pack, and you saw how you can often react to events both server-side and client-side depending on the browser type and capabilities.

In all, the topics covered were:

- The data that drives the Model Details page

- How to extract this data for use in the page

- How to present the data to visitors in the five distinct sections of the page

- How to react to events that occur for the controls in these sections

In the next chapter, you'll complete your look at the Model Details page by seeing how to calculate prices and finance terms, and how to save quotations for use later.

Car Prices
and Quotations

CHAPTER 9 LOOKED IN DETAIL at the data I use to drive the Model Details page, and the code I use to populate the controls on the page. I also showed you how the viewstate automatically preserves the "state" or settings of all the controls, so that you only need to populate the controls once and then write simple handlers to react to events that are raised as visitors interact with the page.

The aim of this chapter is to complete your study of the Model Details page. You'll look at how to calculate the price of the vehicle, the finance terms, and then how to save all this information as a quotation. You also need to see how the page designed for non-script-enabled client browsers works, and how different it is from the one I've been building for script-enabled clients.

So, the topics you'll be looking at are:

- How to calculate the price of a vehicle as the user configures it

- How to calculate the finance terms for a vehicle

- How to save the configuration as a quotation

- How the non-script-enabled version of the page works

I start by showing you how to calculate the current cost of a vehicle, including all the extras, as the user configures it.

Calculating the Price of the Vehicle

In the two previous chapters, you've seen how the Model Details page in the Xrox Car Company sample Web site allows visitors to configure the vehicles by selecting the color, engine type, and optional extras they require. As they do so, the current "all inclusive" price is displayed in the page. And if users specify a finance package, the payment terms and other details are displayed (Figure 10-1).

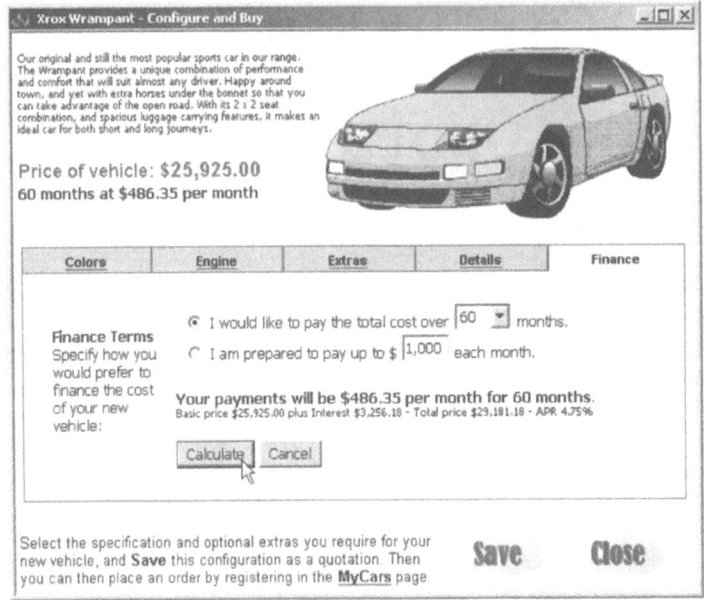

Figure 10-1. Displaying the details of the selected finance package

In this first section of the chapter, you'll look at how to calculate and display the price of the vehicle in its current configuration, and then later you'll look at the code that calculates and displays the finance terms.

All the work of calculating the price of the vehicle takes place in one routine in the page, named CalculateCarPrice. As you saw in the previous chapter, it is executed as soon as the page is loaded to show the price of the standard (default) configuration. It is also executed by any event handlers that affect the price as users make their selections in the page, such as specifying a color from a different range (standard or metallic), choosing an engine, or adding optional extras.

The CalculateCarPrice Routine

The CalculateCarPrice routine is listed next, broken down into the separate stages that I discuss individually to make it easier to follow. I start by declaring a single variable to hold the running total as the calculations are performed:

cardetail.aspx

```
Sub CalculateCarPrice()
' routine to update price displayed in window when any options are changed
  Dim fPrice As Decimal = 0
  ...
```

Clearing Any Existing Finance Terms

Before I start calculating the price, I remove any existing finance terms from the stored array. I do this because the new price is most likely to be different from the existing price after the calculation is complete, and so any existing finance terms will be incorrect. In previous chapters, I discussed whether I should just recalculate the finance terms as well, but the issue I came across is that the new price may be greater than is valid for the user's currently selected finance package. If the user specified a maximum monthly payment, it might not be enough to cover the combined purchase price and interest within the maximum period allowed for loan repayments (120 months).

There is a separate routine that I can use to clear any existing finance terms (you'll see this in detail later in this chapter), and I can just call this directly. However, the routine is actually an event handler—it is executed in response to the user clicking the Cancel button in the Finance section of the page. So I must provide the two parameters for the "sender" and "event arguments" that all ASP.NET event handlers expect to receive. As the ClearFinanceTerms event handler doesn't actually use the parameters, I can safely specify Nothing for these (or null if writing the code in C#):

```
...
' clear any existing finance terms from array and page
ClearFinanceTerms(Nothing, Nothing)

' hide Save button for quotations
btnSave.Visible = False
...
```

I also hide the Save button at the bottom of the page, which is implemented as an <input type="image"> control, while the calculation is performed. If there is no error, I can show it again before returning from this routine. However, it does mean that if an error should occur and this routine ends prematurely (in other words, I can't create a valid quotation) the Save button will not be available.

Notice that I choose to hide this button rather than attempt to "disable" it. As I discussed in the previous chapter, not all browsers can disable controls—so you may decide it is better to hide them (remove them from the page) instead.

Getting the Price for the Current Car/Engine Combination

Now it is time to start calculating the price of the vehicle. Within a Try...Catch construct, which will catch any data access error, I create a filter string that will select the appropriate row from the CarDetails table in the DataSet. I have to specify the car ID and the engine ID values, as the table contains a row for each car/engine combination available for this model.

Then I get a reference to the CarDetails table, which (as you saw in the previous chapter) is generated from joining the tblCar, tblCarEngines, and tblEngine tables. I apply the filter using the Select method, which returns an array of DataRow objects, and then extract the price from the CarEnginePrice column of the first DataRow in the array. This row is, of course, the single matching row within the table:

```
...
Try
  ' create suitable filter to get appropriate row from tblCarEngines
  Dim sFilter As String = "CarID = " & sCarID & " AND EngineID = " _
                          & optEngine.SelectedItem.Value
  ' get reference to table in DataSet and select matching row
  Dim oDTCar As DataTable = oCarsDS.Tables("CarDetails")
  Dim aRows As DataRow() = oDTCar.Select(sFilter, "")

  ' extract price for this car/engine combination
  fPrice = aRows(0)("CarEnginePrice")
  ...
```

DataTable.Select *vs.* DataView.RowFilter

As an aside, it's worth pointing out the two different ways that the code in the Model Details page has "filtered" rows in a table to select a subset. In the previous chapter, when I populated the controls in the ShowCarDetails routine, I had cases to deal with where I had to select a subset of the rows in a table before binding the data to a list control.

An example of this is when the code displays the available colors for a vehicle where I have to filter the data depending on whether I am displaying colors from the standard or the metallic range. In that example, I created a DataView based on the table, and then filtered the rows that are available by setting the RowFilter property:

```
Dim oDTView As DataView = oDTColor.DefaultView
oDTView.RowFilter = "IsMetallic = " & optColorType.SelectedIndex
dlsColors.DataSource = oDTView
dlsColors.DataBind()
oDTView.RowFilter = ""
```

I remarked that I needed to remove the filter afterwards so other routines that accessed the table would be able to see all the rows. This is because a DataView is just what the name implies—an alternative view of (or series of references to) the data in the original table. Effectively, the row filter is applied to the table as well.

However, in this chapter I've used a different approach to get a subset of rows from a table, without creating a DataView at all. The Select method of the DataTable object returns an array of references to the rows in the table that match a given criteria, but without applying any kind of filter to the table. It also allows me to sort the rows that are returned into a different order. For example:

```
Dim oDTCar As DataTable = oCarsDS.Tables("CarDetails")
Dim sFilter As String = "CarID = " & sCarID
Dim sSort As String = "CarEnginePrice DESC"
Dim aRows As DataRow() = oDTCar.Select(sFilter, sSort)
```

The Select method approach is handy when you want to select several sets of rows at a time, or when you only want to access the data using code. However, I can't bind the ASP.NET list controls to an array of DataRows (such as is returned from the Select method), so the use of a DataView and a RowFilter is the appropriate technique when using server-side data binding.

Adding the Extra Cost for a Metallic Color

Next, I must check to see if the user has selected a metallic color, as there is a price premium for these colors. The actual premium value is stored within the <appSettings> section of the web.config file, located in the root folder of the application (or, in this case, the root folder where you installed the samples):

web.config

```
<configuration>
  <appSettings>
    ...
    <!-- change following to adjust premium price for metallic paint -->
    <add key="XroxCarsMetallicPaint" value="375.00" />
    ...
  </appSettings>
</configuration>
```

> **NOTE** *The* web.config *file (introduced with ASP.NET) is a great way to store values that you need to access within an application. It's easy to edit them at a later date, and this action automatically causes ASP.NET to restart the application. All the pages will then use the new value. As you saw in previous chapters, I use this technique to store the database connection string, as well as several other "global" values that are required in the application.*

Back in the code of the Model Details page, I first have to find out which color the user has selected before I can tell if it is a metallic color or not. You saw in the previous chapter that the selected color is used to set the BgColor property of the table cell that displays the image of the car, in the top right of the page. In the HTML declaration of this cell I include the attribute bgcolor="White" (all cars are available in white) as the default.

The table cell is defined as a server control (it has an ID of tclColor and includes the runat="server" attribute), so the background color setting is automatically maintained across postbacks by ASP.NET through the viewstate. So I can extract the color name directly in the server-side code by accessing this element's BgColor property. I use it to create a filter that will select this row from the CarColors table in the DataSet, and then call the Select method to return only this matching row:

cardetail.aspx

```
...
' create suitable filter to get appropriate row from tblColors
' using color name set in background of car image cell
sFilter = "Color = '" & tclColor.BgColor & "'"

' get reference to table in DataSet and select matching row
Dim oDTColors As DataTable = oCarsDS.Tables("CarColors")
aRows = oDTColors.Select(sFilter, "")
...
```

The CarColors table is created by a stored procedure (which was examined in the previous chapter) that joins the tblCar, tblCarColors, and tblColor tables. As well as including the color ID and price, the stored procedure also extracts the SQL Server bit column named IsMetallic from the tblColor table. So I can check the value of this column in the selected row to see if this is a metallic color. A SQL Server bit column value is treated as being True (value 1) or False (value 0), so I can use the following code to perform my test:

```
...
' if it is a metallic color, add on the premium for this
If aRows(0)("IsMetallic") Then
  Try
    fPrice += Decimal.Parse(ConfigurationSettings.AppSettings
                                    ("XroxCarsMetallicPaint"))
  Catch
    lblMessage.Text = "Error in metallic paint premium in web.config"
    lblPrice.Text = "* Error *"
    Exit Sub
  End Try
End If
...
```

If the column does contain 1 (True), I extract the price premium from the web.config file and parse it into a Decimal, then add it to the variable named fPrice that contains the running total for this vehicle. I do all this inside a Try...Catch construct to trap any error that might arise if the web.config entry is missing or not in the correct format. If there is an error, I display the message in the "message" Label control at the bottom of the page, display the text *Error* in the price Label control at the top of the page, and exit from the routine (Figure 10-2).

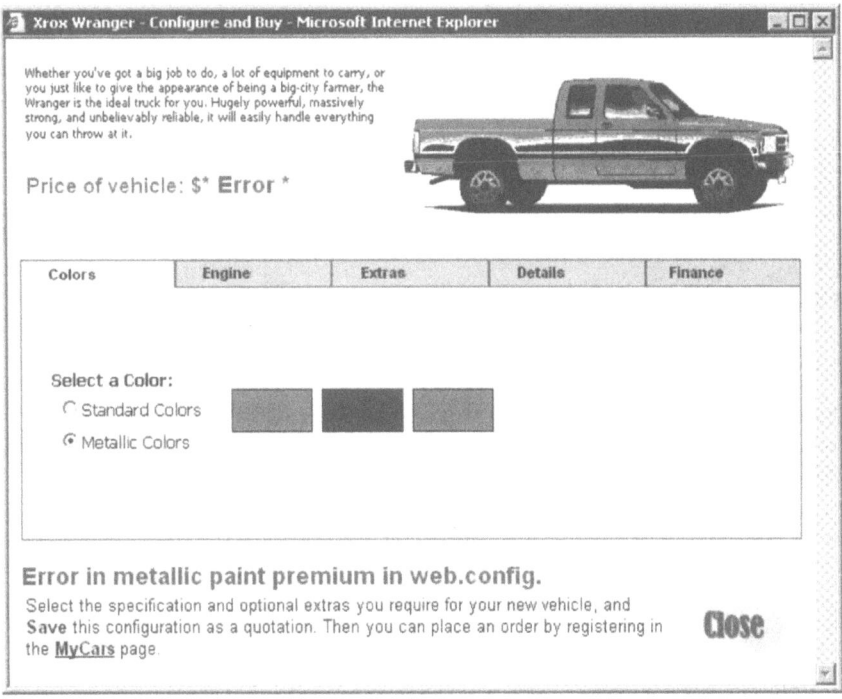

Figure 10-2. Displaying an error when there is no value in web.config

> **NOTE** *Of course, in a real-world application, you'll probably want to use a less developer-centric error message for these kinds of errors!*

Adding the Cost of Optional Extras

If the user has selected any optional extras for the vehicle, these must be added to the price. The DataSet contains a table named CarExtras that is created by the stored procedure I examined in Chapter 9, and this table is used to populate the list of optional extras. The stored procedure joins the tblCar, tblCarExtras, and tblOptionExtra tables, exposing the ID, name, and price of all the optional extras that are available for the current vehicle.

You'll recall that this stored procedure also generates a column named DisplayText that contains a combination of the name and price for these optional extras. I use this column to populate the captions for the check boxes where users select the options they require (Figure 10-3).

Figure 10-3. The check boxes for selecting the required optional extras

So the next step is to see which of these check boxes were "ticked." The check boxes are created by an ASP.NET CheckBoxList control, which means that I can use a For...Each construct to iterate through the Items collection and test each one to see if the Selected property is True:

```
...
' get reference to tblOptionExtra in DataSet
Dim oDTExtras As DataTable = oCarsDS.Tables(« CarExtras »)

' iterate through the list of Extras to see which are selected
Dim oItem As ListItem
For Each oItem In chkExtras.Items
  If oItem.Selected Then
    ...
```

If the Selected property of a check box is True, I need to get the price for this optional extra from the CarExtras table in the DataSet, and add it to the running total variable fPrice. The only problem here is that, although the DataValueField property of the CheckBoxList control was set to the column that contains the ID of the optional extras when the control was populated, there is no value property available for the individual check boxes (i.e., for the ListItem controls that make up the list).

Instead, to create a suitable filter for the table I either have to parse the name of the optional extra out of the caption text (the DisplayText column value) and use this to filter the ExtraText column, or use the entire caption text to filter the DisplayText column. This second alternative seems to be the most obvious approach, and is the one I've taken.

So, I create the filter I need and get a reference to the row that matches this filter. The price is extracted from the ExtraPrice column in the matching row and added to the running total. Then I can see if any other check boxes are selected:

```
    ...
    ' although we specified the ExtraID column as the DataValueField property
    ' of the CheckBoxList control, it does not render any value attributes.
    ' Instead have to look up the selected items in the original DataSet
    ' using the DisplayText value from the caption of each button and then
    ' extract the Price column value - alternatively I could parse it out of
```

```
        ' the Text property (the caption) of the selected item
        ' create suitable filter to get appropriate row from tblOptionExtra
        sFilter = "DisplayText = '" & oItem.Text & "'"
        aRows = oDTExtras.Select(sFilter, "")
        fPrice += aRows(0)("ExtraPrice")

      End If
    Next

  Catch
    lblMessage.Text = "Sorry, the database cannot be accessed."
    lblPrice.Text = "* Error *"
    Exit Sub
  End Try
  ...
```

At the end of the preceding code, you can see the Catch section of the Try...Catch construct. I just display suitable messages in the price Label control at the top of the page and in the "message" Label control at the bottom of the page.

Storing the Total Price in the Prices Array

The final task in the CalculateCarPrice routine is to store the price I've just calculated in the array of prices and finance terms that I cache in the user's session. This means that, when the user places an order, it doesn't have to be recalculated—I can just use the values that were calculated the last time the user changed any of the configuration selections.

The array I use can contain up to six values. This is the page-level declaration of the array in the code of the page:

```
' page-level array to hold current car price and finance terms
' (0) = Basic Price including extras and color option
' (1) = Annual interest rate applicable to purchase
' (2) = Interest amount included in Total Price
' (3) = Total Price including interest for finance plan (if selected)
' (4) = Number of months for finance plan (if selected)
' (5) = Monthly payment amount for finance plan (if selected)
Dim aCurrentPrice(5) As String
```

The Page_Load event handler extracts this array from the user's session into the aCurrentPrice variable each time the page is posted back to the server, so I can set or update the current price in the array by converting it to a String using the ToString method. As I do so, I format it so it can be displayed directly in the My Cars page you'll see in Chapter 12:

```
  ...
  ' store total price including extras in array
  aCurrentPrice(0) = fPrice.ToString("#,##0.00")
  ...
```

I also need to store this array back in the user's session ready for the next postback. The session key is already stored in another page-level variable, named sPricesSessionKey. Then the last two tasks to complete the routine are to display the price I just calculated in the Label control at the top of the page, and to show the Save button so the user can save this configuration as a quotation if desired:

```
...
' update Session with new array values
Session(sPricesSessionKey) = aCurrentPrice

' display price in page
lblPrice.Text = fPrice.ToString("#,##0.00")

' show Save button
btnSave.Visible = True

End Sub
```

Calculating the Finance Terms

The Finance "tab" on the Model Details page allows users to specify how they want to pay for their vehicle. There are two options—they can specify the number of months over which they want to spread the cost of the vehicle by selecting a value between 6 and 120 from the drop-down list, or they can type in the maximum monthly payment that they want to make (Figure 10-4).

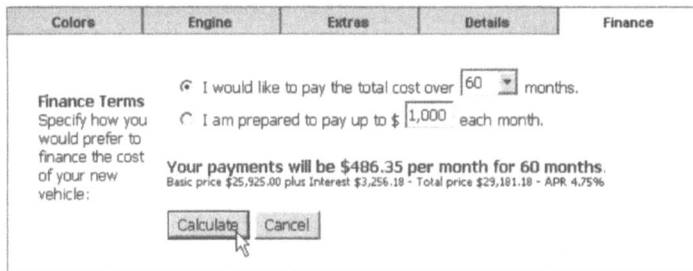

Figure 10-4. Specifying and calculating the required finance terms

Clicking Calculate then works out the total interest, the monthly payment required, and total price. This is displayed, together with the interest rate that was used in the calculation, within the Finance "tab." It is also displayed (not shown here) just below the price of the vehicle near the top of the page. You can see this in Figure 10-1 (near the start of this chapter).

Clicking the Cancel button simply removes the selected finance package and clears the Label controls that display the payment terms. The Calculate button is disabled (in browsers that support this feature) when there is no finance package currently selected.

Calculating the finance terms involves three routines:

- The ShowFinanceTerms routine is responsible for displaying the results of the calculation, and manipulating the buttons on the page.

- The CalculateFinanceTerms function does the actual mathematical part of the task. It is called from the ShowFinanceTerms routine.

- The GetNumberPayments function, given a maximum monthly payment value, returns the number of months over which that payment will be required. It is called from the CalculateFinanceTerms function.

You'll look at each of these routines next.

The ShowFinanceTerms *Routine*

The first step in calculating the payment terms for the selected finance package is to clear any existing values from the last calculation. This is accomplished using the ClearFinanceTerms routine in the same way as was done when calculating the price of the vehicle earlier in this chapter:

```
Sub ShowFinanceTerms(oSender As Object, oArgs As EventArgs)
' routine to display finance terms for "Calculate" button
  ' clear any existing finance terms from array and page
  ClearFinanceTerms(Nothing, Nothing)
  ...
```

Then I can call the separate CalculateFinanceTerms function in the example page to calculate the payment terms. This function fills in the values in the prices array, and returns an empty String as the result if everything succeeds without any errors. If this is the case, I can build up three text strings from the values in this array and display them in the page.

The Label control named lblTerms is located just below the car price, near the top left of the page. The two Label controls named lblFinanceResult and lblFinanceInfo are located just above the Calculate and Cancel buttons in the Finance "tab" of the page:

```
  ...
  ' call function to calculate finance terms values
  ' returns error message, or empty string if all OK
  Dim sError As String = CalculateFinanceTerms()
  If sError = "" Then
```

```
' display the results in the page
lblTerms.Text = aCurrentPrice(4) & " months  at $" _
  & aCurrentPrice(5) & " per month"
lblFinanceResult.Text = "<b>Your payments will be $" _
  & aCurrentPrice(5).ToString() & " per month for " _
  & aCurrentPrice(4).ToString() & " months</b>."
lblFinanceInfo.Text = "Basic price $" & aCurrentPrice(0) _
  & " plus Interest $" & aCurrentPrice(2) & "–Total price $" _
  & aCurrentPrice(3) & "–APR " & aCurrentPrice(1) & "%"
...
```

I also enable the Cancel button so users can remove this finance package selection if they wish, and I make sure that the Save button is visible:

```
...
' enable the button to cancel these terms
btnCancel.Enabled = True

' show Save button
btnSave.Visible = True
...
```

> **NOTE** *If the previous calculation of the car price (as opposed to this calculation of the finance terms) had failed, the* CalculateFinanceTerms *function will also fail when it tries to parse and use the value for the vehicle price that is stored in the array (it will return the string* "*Error*" *in this case), and so the Save button will not be visible.*

Handling an Error in the Calculation

If the CalculateFinanceTerms function encounters an error, the String value it returns (which was stored in the variable named sError at the start of this ShowFinanceTerms routine) will be the error message. So, in this case, the code simply removes any existing values for the finance terms from the Label controls on the page and hides the Save button. Notice that I place a non-breaking space into the Label at the top of the page, which prevents any shift in the layout of the table that contains the vehicle price and the finance terms:

```
...
Else
  ' display the error details in the page
  lblTerms.Text = " "
  lblFinanceResult.Text = "<b>" & sError & "</b>"
  lblFinanceInfo.Text = ""
```

```
    ' hide Save button
    btnSave.Visible = False


  End If
End Sub
```

The CalculateFinanceTerms *Function*

Having seen how the ShowFinanceTerms routine listed earlier handles the display of the
finance terms, now you'll examine the CalculateFinanceTerms function, which actually
does the real work of calculating the payments required for the selected finance package.

I start by declaring a few variables that I'll need, and then collect the interest
rate from web.config. You saw how it is stored there when you looked at filling the
tblFinancePMTData table in Chapter 9. If the interest rate cannot be extracted and
parsed into a Decimal, the code simply exits from the function and returns an appropriate error message:

```
Function CalculateFinanceTerms() As String
' function to calculate payment terms from current user selections
  Dim fInterestRate As Single
  Dim fBasePrice, fTotalInterest, fMonthlyPayment As Decimal
  Dim fTotalPrice, fPaymentPer1000 As Decimal
  Dim iMonths As Integer

  ' get interest rate from web.config file
  Try
    fInterestRate = _
    Decimal.Parse(ConfigurationSettings.AppSettings("XroxCarsInterestRate"))
  Catch
    Return "Interest Rate Error in web.config file"
  End Try
  ...
```

Now the routine can get the total price for the vehicle configuration the user
specified from the first row of the prices array, where it was stored when the price
was calculated and displayed. Again, any error attempting to retrieve it and parse it
into a Decimal type results in an error message being returned to the
ShowFinanceTerms routine.

ShowFinanceTerms routine:

```
  ...
  ' get basic price including extras from prices array
  Try
    fBasePrice = Decimal.Parse(aCurrentPrice(0))
  Catch
    Return "Basic Price Error in Session Array"
  End Try
  ...
```

Processing the "Maximum Monthly Payment" Finance Package

The next step is to see which type of finance package is being calculated. If the option button named optByAmount is checked, the routine is calculating the terms where the user has specified the maximum amount they wish to pay per month. So the first step in this case is to collect the value the user entered into the text box control named txtMonthPayment. I attempt to parse it into a Decimal, and any error is reported back to the ShowFinanceTerms routine:

```
...
' see which payment option is selected
If optByAmount.Checked Then    ' paying a specified amount each month
  Try
    ' get monthly payment from text box as a Decimal number
    fMonthlyPayment = Decimal.Parse(txtMonthPayment.Text)

  Catch
    Return "The value for the monthly payment is not a valid number."
  End Try
...
```

Provided that the value the user entered is a valid number I can now call another function named GetNumberPayments, located elsewhere in this page, to get the number of months required to pay off the specified total at the current interest rate. The first parameter is the price of the vehicle, and the second is a variable that was declared at the top of this function. The GetNumberPayments function updates this value (I pass it ByRef, as you'll see when you come to look at this function), and it also updates all the finance terms in the prices array:

```
...
' calculate the number of payments required and other values
' parameter fMonthlyPayment is ByRef and will be updated within
' the function to show actual payment required
iMonths = GetNumberPayments(fBasePrice, fMonthlyPayment)
...
```

The return value of the GetNumberPayments function is the number of months required, or zero if an error occurs during the calculation. So I can check if there was a problem by examining this returned value, and display a suitable message. I actually check that the result is not more than 120 as well, because I want to limit the number of payment months to this maximum value:

```
...
' see if the resulting term is acceptable
If (iMonths = 0) Or (iMonths > 120) Then
  Return "The monthly payment specified is not sufficient " _
      & "to repay the loan."
End If
...
```

> **NOTE** *In fact, in this example, the* GetNumberPayments *function cannot return any value greater than 120 because the* tblFinancePMTData *table does not contain any rows with "number of months" values above this. It will always return zero if the maximum payment specified is less than the minimum value in the table rows. However, if the table did contain more rows, this check would be required.*

Processing the "Number of Months" Finance Package

Now you've seen how to calculate the number of months for a loan given a minimum monthly payment (although you still have to look at the GetNumberPayments function that the previous section of the code uses). If the option button named optByAmount is *not* checked, however, the routine has to perform the opposite calculation. I need to work out how much the monthly payments will be given the number of months over which the loan should extend.

In this case, the first step is to get the number of months selected by the user, and the equivalent payment amount per $1000, from the drop-down list named lstFinanceMonths. I get the number of months (as displayed by the list) by parsing the Text property of the ListItem object that is returned as the SelectItem of the list control. The "payment per $1000" figure comes from the Value property of the same ListItem object. This is because, when I populated the list, I declared the DataTextField and DataValueField properties as the Months and Payment columns of the tblFinancePMTData table.

> **NOTE** *If you are running the application only under ASP.NET version 1.1, you can use the* SelectedValue *property of the* lstFinanceMonths *list instead of parsing the* SelectedItem.Value *property. However, to get the text of the currently selected entry in the list you still need to access the* SelectedItem.Text *property. The only time you can get the text of the selected item from the* SelectedValue *property is when the list control has the same values for the* Text *and* Value *properties of each list item (or there is no* Value *property specified, in which case the* Text *property is also returned as the value).*

As you've seen before, I use a Try...Catch construct to trap any number parsing errors, though the fact that I extract the values from a pre-populated drop-down list suggests that they will only ever contain valid numbers, and this might be seen as overkill:

```
...
Else    ' paying over a specified number of months

  Try

    ' get values from drop-down list
    iMonths = Int32.Parse(lstFinanceMonths.SelectedItem.Text)
    fPaymentPer1000 = Decimal.Parse(lstFinanceMonths.SelectedItem.Value)
```

```
            ' calculate payment for this vehicle price
            fMonthlyPayment = fPaymentPer1000 * fBasePrice / 1000

        Catch
            Return "The value for the number of months is not a valid number."
        End Try

    End If
    ...
```

In the preceding code, you can see how easy it is to use the "payment per $1000" figure and the price of the vehicle to calculate the actual monthly payment amount for this vehicle. However, if there is an error, the routine just exits from this function and returns a suitable error message.

Calculating the Interest and Filling the Prices Array

Now that I know the monthly payment required, whichever finance package is selected, I can calculate the other values that make up the complete finance package. The total price is just the number of payments multiplied by the number of months, and the interest part of the loan is the total price minus the actual price of the vehicle including any extras that were specified:

```
    ...
    ' calculate total price
    fTotalPrice = fMonthlyPayment * iMonths
    fTotalInterest = fTotalPrice - fBasePrice
    ...
```

The final steps are to update the prices array with the values that were just calculated, and the interest rate that was extracted from web.config earlier in this routine. Then I save the array back into the user's ASP.NET session, and return an empty String to indicate that the process succeeded:

```
    ...
    ' fill in the finance terms section of the array of values
    aCurrentPrice(1) = fInterestRate.ToString()
    aCurrentPrice(2) = fTotalInterest.ToString("#,##0.00")
    aCurrentPrice(3) = fTotalPrice.ToString("#,##0.00")
    aCurrentPrice(4) = iMonths.ToString()
    aCurrentPrice(5) = fMonthlyPayment.ToString("#,##0.00")

    ' update Session with new array values
    Session(sPricesSessionKey) = aCurrentPrice

    Return ""    ' empty string indicates all worked OK
End Function
```

The GetNumberPayments *Function*

The third and final routine that is used when calculating the finance terms is the GetNumberPayments function. This function accepts the price of the vehicle as the first parameter, and a Decimal variable as the second parameter. This parameter is declared as ByRef (by reference), so the function will receive a reference to the actual variable as declared in the calling routine rather than a copy of the value. This means that it can access and change the original value, and the calling routine will see this updated value:

```
Function GetNumberPayments(fBasePrice As Decimal, _
                            ByRef fMonthlyPayment As Decimal) As Integer
' get number of payments required given desired monthly payment
' by searching through PMT values in DataSet table
' Note that fMonthlyPayment parameter is ByRef and the value will
' be updated within function to actual payment required
...
```

I start the process of finding the number of months required by declaring a variable that will hold the "payment per $1000" that is equivalent to the values in the tblFinancePMTData table column named Payment. Remember that the values in this column are what would be required to pay off a loan of $1000.00, and so I have to convert these values into "real" payments that take into account the value of the car.

I get the value for fPaymentPer1000 by multiplying the maximum monthly payment that the user specified by 1000, and then dividing that by the value of the vehicle the user wants to buy. Doing it this way means that I don't have to convert every value extracted from the tblFinancePMTData table into a "real" payment—I just compare it to the fPaymentPer1000 variable instead:

```
...
Dim fPaymentPer1000 As Decimal
' calculate the maximum payment per 1000 acceptable to client
fPaymentPer1000 = fMonthlyPayment * 1000 / fBasePrice
...
```

Finding the Matching Table Row

To find the nearest payment that is less than the maximum specified by the user, I could iterate through the ListItem controls in the drop-down list. After all, it contains all the values from the tblFinancePMTData table. However, it's faster and more efficient to search in the copy of this table (named FinancePMTRates) that is already cached in the DataSet. I can use a filter to select the rows and then read the values directly.

So, the next step in this function is to create the filter, specifying that the value of the Payment column payment should be less than the value of the fPaymentPer1000 variable. I also specify that the results should be sorted in descending order by payment value, which means that the first row in the array of rows returned after

applying the filter will be the highest value that is less than the maximum specified
by the user:

```
...
' create suitable filter and sort criteria to get array of rows
' where first contains highest acceptable payment per 1000
Dim sFilter As String = "Payment <= " & fPaymentPer1000
Dim sSort As String = "Payment DESC"
...
```

I now apply this filter to the FinancePMTRates table in the DataSet and get back the
array of matching rows. The required "payment per $1000" is the value of the Payment
column in the first row, and I just have to convert it into a "real" payment for the vehicle by multiplying by the cost of the vehicle and then dividing by 1000:

```
...
Try
   ' get reference to table in DataSet and select matching rows
   Dim oDTFinance As DataTable = oCarsDS.Tables("FinancePMTRates")
   Dim aRows As DataRow() = oDTFinance.Select(sFilter, sSort)
   ' calculate payment for this vehicle price using actual
   ' payment required from second column of data row
   fMonthlyPayment = aRows(0)("Payment") * fBasePrice / 1000
   ...
```

Now that I know what the actual payment will be, I can extract the number of
monthly payments that will be required to fully cover the loan from the same row.
I return this value as the result of the function, but remember that I've also set the
value of the fMonthlyPayment parameter of this function (in the preceding code), so
this will be available to the calling routine as well:

```
   ...
   ' extract number of months from first column of row
   Return aRows(0)("Months")

Catch
   ' return zero if cannot calculate the result
   ' will occur if payment is too low (no data rows selected)
   Return 0

End Try
End Function
```

At the end of this code, you can see that I catch any error and return zero as the
result of the function. This is most likely because no row was found with a low enough
payment to match the one specified by the user. In other words, the payment the
user specified is not enough to cover the loan over the maximum term for which
there are rows in the FinancePMTRates table.

The ClearFinanceTerms *Routine*

The previous sections of this chapter have covered all the code that I use to calculate the finance terms for the Model Details page. There is just one other routine connected with the Finance "tab" on the page—the ClearFinanceTerms event handler. This routine is executed when the Cancel button in the Finance "tab" is clicked, and it just has to remove any existing finance terms.

This is easy enough to do. I just clear all the rows in the prices array except the first one (at index zero), as it contains the last calculated price for the vehicle. Then I can save the array in the user's session, clear the Labels on the page that show the finance terms, and disable the Cancel button. Notice that I use the Label above the Calculate and Cancel buttons to display brief instructions—it prevents the page from looking too "empty":

```
' routine to clear any current finance terms for "Cancel" button
Sub ClearFinanceTerms(oSender As Object, oArgs As EventArgs)
  ' clear the finance terms section of the array of values
  aCurrentPrice(1) = ""
  aCurrentPrice(2) = ""
  aCurrentPrice(3) = ""
  aCurrentPrice(4) = ""
  aCurrentPrice(5) = ""

  ' update Session with new array values
  Session(sPricesSessionKey) = aCurrentPrice

  ' clear any current finance terms text from page
  lblTerms.Text = " "
  lblFinanceResult.Text = "Select the payment options you prefer " _
                  & "and click <b>Calculate</b>."
  lblFinanceInfo.Text = ""
  ' disable the "Cancel" button
  btnCancel.Enabled = False

End Sub
```

> **NOTE** *Remember that I suggested you write all your event handlers in such a way that they can still safely be executed if a button or other control that is supposed to be disabled causes a postback. The* ClearFinanceTerms *routine meets this criterion.*

Saving the Configuration As a Quotation

And so I come to the final section of code in the Model Details page. As you will see when you experiment with this page, visitors can save their current configuration of any vehicle, including the selected color, engine type, optional extras, and finance terms as a quotation. These details are stored in a pair of tables in the database, and can be viewed in the My Cars page that you'll be looking at in Chapter 12. Any of these quotations can be converted into an order at any time, in the same page.

So, I'll show you how I save the configuration to the database as a quotation. First, let me start with a reminder of the database tables that are involved in the process.

The Saved Quotes and Orders Tables

The example database contains two tables that I use to store a quotation or an order for any of the vehicles. The parent table, tblQuoteOrder, contains all the relevant details of the vehicle itself. This includes the ID and name of the model, the engine and the color selected by the user, and the price and any finance terms that were specified.

The related child table named tblQuoteOrderExtras contains details of any optional extras that were added to the vehicle. As there could be zero or more of these, I use a child table that has a one-to-many relationship with the parent table (Figure 10-5).

Figure 10-5. The tables to store quotations and orders

The relationship between the parent and child rows is through the primary key of the tblQuoteOrder table, the column named QuoteOrderID, and the matching foreign key column in the tblQuoteOrderExtras table. The UserID column in the tblQuoteOrder table identifies which user saved this quotation.

You'll notice that the tables are not fully normalized in that there is "redundant" information stored in them. For example, I store the names of the vehicle, engine, color, and optional extras, as well as their ID values. In theory I can always look up the names in the other tables of the database given the ID values—for example, I can find the vehicle name from the tblCar table given the car ID.

However, I chose the less normalized approach for a couple of reasons:

- If the rows or column values in the original tables change, for example a car is no longer available and is removed, or the name is changed, I would not be able to find a match. OK, so good database management suggests that I should never remove rows like this, and instead flag them as "unavailable" or "not current" to allow the joins to still work. But, my approach makes sure that the original value is available at any point in the future.

- It makes it a lot easier and is more efficient when displaying the data, as you'll see in the My Cars page you look in Chapter 12. I don't have to create multiple table joins to get the names of the car, engine, color, or optional extras.

Updating the Data Within a Transaction

The design of the two tables you've just looked at means that, to save a quotation, all I have to do is add the appropriate rows to these tables. I add one row per quotation to the tblQuoteOrder table, and zero or more related rows to the tblQuoteOrderExtras table depending on which (if any) optional extras are specified by the user.

Because I may have to update two tables to achieve the desired result (and there may be more than one update to the tblQuoteOrderExtras table if the user specifies more than one optional extra), it's wise to consider using a *transaction* to make sure that the process either completes or fails as a single operation. In other words, either all the updates succeed, or they all fail.

If only some of the updates succeed, I leave the tables in an undefined state where the content is invalid. For example, if I insert a row in the parent table, but one or more updates to the child table fail, I have not saved the quotation accurately.

Using a transaction means that I can either commit all the updates in one go, once I am certain that they all succeeded, or roll them all back if any one stage of the process fails so that the tables remain in their original state.

There are three basic types of transaction that I can use:

- **Database Server Transactions** are usually stored procedures that themselves contain the transaction statements. I pass in as parameters all the data required to perform all the updates on all the tables, and the stored procedure manages the entire process. It contains statements that execute the BEGIN TRANSACTION command before the updates are applied, and then either COMMIT TRANSACTION or ROLLBACK TRANSACTION after the updates have been applied—depending on whether they were all successful or not.

- **Distributed Transactions** are usually managed by external software or services (such as the Windows Transaction Service) that manages transactions across different databases, which can be located on separate servers. These servers can be geographically separated from each other.

- **Connection-based Transactions** are managed by the data access software that applies the updates, rather than by the database or a separate service. This is the type of transaction I'm using in the example. ADO.NET provides great support for these types of transactions.

The big advantage of using connection-based transactions is that I don't have to pass in all the values for all the updates in one go. In my example, I don't know beforehand how many "optional extra" rows I'll need to insert into the tblQuoteOrderExtras table, and so it would be hard to write a stored procedure that accepted the appropriate number of values.

By using a connection-based transaction, I can execute different stored procedures, and execute them as many times as required, within the transaction. Then, once I know the outcome of all the updates, I can decide whether to commit all of them, or roll them all back. And as soon as one update fails, I can abandon the process and roll back all previous updates.

Saving a Quotation

To see how the Model Details page saves a quotation, I'll show you the SaveCarDetails routine next. This is called when the user clicks the Save button in the page. It does all the work of saving the quotation to the database and displays status messages to the user.

The plan is to first collect all the information required for the parent tblQuoteOrder table and then insert this row. However, the QuoteOrderID primary key column in this table is of type IDENTITY (sometimes called an AutoNumber column), and so the value is created automatically by the database when a new row is inserted. I can't specify a value for this column.

However, I need to insert the value that the database generates for the QuoteOrderID column into each row I add to the tblQuoteOrderExtras child table. This is required to create the relationship between the new quotation and any child "optional extra" rows for that quotation.

So, the stored procedure I use to insert the parent row in the tblQuoteOrder table must return the value of the QuoteOrderID column. After checking that the new row was successfully inserted, I can use this value in the rows I add to the tblQuoteOrderExtras child table.

The only additional point is that there are two other columns in the tblQuoteOrder table that I do not insert values for. Within the database table definition, the IsOrder column has a default value of zero specified. When I insert a new quotation, this default value indicates that this row is a quotation and not an order. The column named OrderDate also has a default value, in this case created by the function GETDATE(). So the new row will automatically have the current date and time inserted into the OrderDate column—I don't have to set it.

The Stored Procedures for the SaveCarDetails Routine

To add a new row to the tblQuoteOrder table, I use the stored procedure named InsertNewQuote. This is shown next, and you can see that it expects me to provide as parameters values for all 12 columns for which default values are not specified:

```
CREATE PROCEDURE InsertNewQuote
@UserID varchar(20), @CarID int, @CarName varchar(50),
@EngineID int, @EngineName varchar(10), @ColorID int,
@ColorName varchar(50), @BasePrice money, @Interest money,
@TotalPrice money, @PaymentMonths money, @PaymentAmount money,
@QuoteOrderID int OUTPUT
AS
```

```
INSERT INTO tblQuoteOrder(UserID, CarID, CarName, EngineID,
    EngineName, ColorID, ColorName, BasePrice, Interest,
    TotalPrice, PaymentMonths, PaymentAmount)
VALUES (@UserID, @CarID, @CarName, @EngineID,
    @EngineName, @ColorID, @ColorName, @BasePrice, @Interest,
    @TotalPrice, @PaymentMonths, @PaymentAmount)
SELECT @QuoteOrderID = @@IDENTITY
```

Notice also that the stored procedure declares an OUTPUT parameter named @QuoteOrderID. The last line of the procedure selects the value of the IDENTITY column named QuoteOrderID for the most recently inserted row in the current (connection) session. This is the value needed to create the links between this new row and any rows inserted into the tblQuoteOrderExtras child table.

The process of inserting optional extra rows into the tblQuoteOrderExtras table is much simpler. The primary key in this table is also an IDENTITY column (named ExtraOrderID), and so I don't need to insert a value for this column. Therefore the InsertNewQuoteExtraLine stored procedure takes only four parameters, and inserts a new row using these values. The first parameter is the QuoteOrderID value returned from the previous stored procedure:

```
CREATE PROCEDURE InsertNewQuoteExtraLine
@QuoteOrderID int, @ExtraID int, @ExtraName varchar(50), @ExtraPrice money
AS
INSERT INTO tblQuoteOrderExtras(QuoteOrderID, ExtraID, ExtraName, ExtraPrice)
VALUES (@QuoteOrderID, @ExtraID, @ExtraName, @ExtraPrice)
```

The SaveCarDetails *Routine*

The SaveCarDetails routine starts by collecting the values that are needed to insert a row into the parent table. To make it easier to see what's going on, I save all the values in local variables before attempting to call the stored procedures. Many of the values I need are stored in page-level variables, or in the prices array that was saved in the user's session. Much of the process is just converting these values to the correct data type. For example, the CarID column in the database is of type int (a 32-bit Integer value), whereas the sCarID variable contains a String:

```
Sub SaveCarDetails(oSender As Object, oArgs As ImageClickEventArgs)
    ' routine to save current configuration of vehicle in database
    ' collect the values we'll need for the tblQuoteOrder table
    Dim sAnonUserID As String = CType(Session("WccUserID"), String)
    Dim iCarID As Integer = Int32.Parse(sCarID)
    ...
```

There is a reference to the DataSet containing the tables I used to populate the controls on the page in the ShowCarDetails routine available in the page-level variable named oCarsDS, so I can also get some of the values I need from this. For example, the name of the current vehicle comes from the first row of the CarDetails table in this DataSet:

```
...
Dim sCarName As String = oCarsDS.Tables("CarDetails").Rows(0)("Model")
...
```

Fetching the Price and Finance Values

The price and payment information needed for the stored procedure parameters can be extracted from the aCurrentPrice array in the user's session, where this data is stored as the user configures a vehicle. The "base price" is the total price of the vehicle including the user's choice of color, engine, and optional extras. I get this from the first row of the array, where it was saved by the CalculateCarPrice routine you looked at earlier. I also assign this value to the dTotalPrice variable, which is used to set the @TotalPrice parameter to the stored procedure. If there is no finance package selected, the total price is the same as the base price:

```
...
Dim dBasePrice As Decimal = Decimal.Parse(aCurrentPrice(0))
Dim dTotalPrice As Decimal = dBasePrice
...
```

Now you can check to see if the user specified a finance package. The code looks at the third row in the prices array (at index 2) for a value. This is where the total amount of interest is stored if the user has selected either of the two finance packages. If this value is not empty (remember that it's a String array), the values from the array for the total interest amount, the total price including the interest, the number of monthly payments required, and the monthly payment amount are extracted:

```
...
Dim dInterest, dPaymentAmount As Decimal
Dim iPaymentMonths As Integer
If aCurrentPrice(2) <> "" Then
  dInterest = Decimal.Parse(aCurrentPrice(2))
  dTotalPrice = Decimal.Parse(aCurrentPrice(3))
  iPaymentMonths = Int32.Parse(aCurrentPrice(4))
  dPaymentAmount = Decimal.Parse(aCurrentPrice(5))
End If
...
```

Fetching the Engine and Color Details

The next step is to collect the engine details. The ASP.NET viewstate automatically maintains the values of all the controls in the page as the user interacts with them, and all that's needed to get the values for the engine ID and name is to query the RadioButtonList that specifies the engine type. The SelectedItem property of that control returns a reference to the currently selected ListItem object in the list, and the values of the Text and Value properties can be extracted from this:

```
...
Dim iEngineID As Integer = optEngine.SelectedItem.Value
Dim sEngineName As String = optEngine.SelectedItem.Text
...
```

Getting the color details is just a little more difficult. I get the color name from the BgColor property of the table cell that holds the image of the vehicle, and use this to create a filter that I can use in the Select method against the CarColors table. The color ID is then extracted from the single row that is returned:

```
...
' extract color from DataSet as in CalculateCarPrice routine
Dim sColorName As String = tclColor.BgColor
Dim sFilter As String = "Color = '" & sColorName & "'"
Dim aRows As DataRow() = oCarsDS.Tables("CarColors").Select(sFilter, "")
Dim iColorID As Integer = aRows(0)("ColorID")
...
```

Preparing to Execute the Stored Procedures

Now I have all the values I need to insert the new quotation row, I specify the names of the stored procedures I'll be using and create the Connection and Command objects needed to execute these stored procedures. This is just like what I've done in many earlier example pages and routines:

```
...
' specify the stored procedure names
Dim sSaveQuote As String = "InsertNewQuote"
Dim sSaveExtraLine As String = "InsertNewQuoteExtraLine"
```

```
' create connection and command objects
Dim sConnect As String = _
                ConfigurationSettings.AppSettings("XroxCarsConnectString")
Dim sqlConn As New SqlConnection(sConnect)
Dim sqlComm As New SqlCommand(sSaveQuote, sqlConn)
sqlComm.CommandType = CommandType.StoredProcedure
...
```

Starting a Transaction

Before going any further, I have to set up the transaction that will make sure I get
a valid result across the two tables after inserting the new quotation and any related
optional extra rows. I declare a variable to hold a SqlTransaction object (there are
OleDb and Odbc versions of this object available as well if you are not using SQL
Server). Then I start a Try...Catch construct:

```
...
' declare a variable to hold a Transaction object
Dim oTransaction As SqlTransaction

Try
  ...
```

I can only start a new transaction against an open connection, so I open the database connection next and then call the BeginTransaction method to start the transaction.
A reference to the transaction is returned, which is saved in the oTransaction variable:

```
...
' open connection and start a transaction
sqlConn.Open()
oTransaction = sqlConn.BeginTransaction()
...
```

Although I now have a transaction available for the connection, it will not be
used by default. I have to specify which Command objects will use it by assigning it to
their Transaction property. This approach allows me to have more than one transaction in place for a connection if required (I can also nest transactions). So I can assign
each Command to the appropriate transaction. However, in the code I only need one
transaction, and I assign this to the Command object next:

```
...
' attach transaction to Command object
sqlComm.Transaction = oTransaction
...
```

Adding the `InsertNewQuote` *Stored Procedure Parameters*

Now the necessary parameters for the first stored procedure can be added to the
`Command` object's `Parameters` collection, using the values collected earlier in this routine. Notice how `@QuoteOrderID` is specified as an `OUTPUT` parameter:

```
...
' add parameters to Command
sqlComm.Parameters.Add("@UserID", sAnonUserID)
sqlComm.Parameters.Add(« @CarID », iCarID)
sqlComm.Parameters.Add("@CarName", sCarName)
sqlComm.Parameters.Add("@EngineID", iEngineID)
sqlComm.Parameters.Add("@EngineName", sEngineName)
sqlComm.Parameters.Add("@ColorID", iColorID)
sqlComm.Parameters.Add("@ColorName", sColorName)
sqlComm.Parameters.Add("@BasePrice", dBasePrice)
sqlComm.Parameters.Add("@Interest", dInterest)
sqlComm.Parameters.Add("@TotalPrice", dTotalPrice)
sqlComm.Parameters.Add("@PaymentMonths", iPaymentMonths)
sqlComm.Parameters.Add("@PaymentAmount", dPaymentAmount)
sqlComm.Parameters.Add("@QuoteOrderID", 0)
sqlComm.Parameters("@QuoteOrderID").Direction _
                                 = ParameterDirection.Output
...
```

Executing the `InsertNewQuote` *Stored Procedure*

I can now execute the `InsertNewQuote` stored procedure to add the new quotation row
to the `tblQuoteOrder` table. The `ExecuteNonQuery` method will return 1 if the insert succeeds, and if not I create a new `Exception` object and `Throw` it. This causes the execution
to pass to the `Catch` part of the `Try...Catch` construct, with the string I provide when
I create the `Exception` as the error message:

```
...
' execute the stored procedure
If sqlComm.ExecuteNonQuery() <> 1 Then
  ' throw an Exception to display error message
  Throw New Exception("* Could not insert new Quote into database.")
End If
...
```

However, if the stored procedure did succeed in adding the new row, the `OUTPUT`
parameter named `@QuoteOrderID` will contain the row key value from the `QuoteOrderID`
column of the row just inserted. I save this in a variable named `iQuoteID`:

```
...
' get value of new quote ID from parameters
Dim iQuoteID As Integer = sqlComm.Parameters("@QuoteOrderID").Value
...
```

Adding the* InsertNewQuoteExtraLine *Stored Procedure Parameters

Now I'm ready to add the rows to the tblQuoteOrderExtras child table, using the stored procedure named InsertNewQuoteExtraLine. I change the CommandText property of the command to this stored procedure name, clear the Parameters collection of the existing parameters I used for the InsertNewQuote stored procedure, and add the four parameters I have to provide to the InsertNewQuoteExtraLine stored procedure.

The first parameter is the value of the primary key column named QuoteOrderID in the parent tblQuoteOrder table for the new quotation row I just inserted. However, I set the other three parameters to "dummy" values here. I did this because I want to be able to change the values of the parameters as I iterate through the list of optional extras for this quotation, rather than adding and removing them each time:

```
...
' change stored procedure name for updating Extras table
sqlComm.CommandText = sSaveExtraLine

' clear parameters collection and add parameters for Extras table
sqlComm.Parameters.Clear()
sqlComm.Parameters.Add("@QuoteOrderID", iQuoteID)
sqlComm.Parameters.Add("@ExtraID", 0)
sqlComm.Parameters.Add("@ExtraName", "")
sqlComm.Parameters.Add("@ExtraPrice", 0)

' get reference to tblOptionExtra in DataSet
Dim oDTExtras As DataTable = oCarsDS.Tables(« CarExtras »)
...
```

The final line of the preceding code listing gets a reference to the "optional extras" table named CarExtras in the cached DataSet because I'll need this to get information about each optional extra when I insert the rows into the tblQuoteOrderExtras table.

Iterating Through the Selected Optional Extras

Now I can see which optional extras the user specified for the vehicle. I iterate through the collection of ListItem objects for the CheckBoxList control named chkExtras that implements the list of optional extras in the example page. For any of these that are selected, the InsertNewQuoteExtraLine stored procedure must be executed to add a row to the tblQuoteOrderExtras table.

So, inside the For Each...Next construct I create a filter that will select the matching row from the CarExtras table in the DataSet. Then, using the Select method with this filter string, I can extract the values for this optional extra from the row and use them to set the values of the parameters for the stored procedure:

```
...
' iterate through the Extras selected in the page and
' see if each one is selected in turn
Dim oItem As ListItem
For Each oItem In chkExtras.Items
  If oItem.Selected Then

     ' get a reference to the matching row in the DataSet
     sFilter = "DisplayText = '" & oItem.Text & "'"
     aRows =  oDTExtras.Select(sFilter, "")

     ' set value of last three parameters
     sqlComm.Parameters("@ExtraID").Value = aRows(0)("ExtraID")
     sqlComm.Parameters("@ExtraName").Value = aRows(0)("ExtraText")
     sqlComm.Parameters("@ExtraPrice").Value = aRows(0)("ExtraPrice")
     ...
```

Next, I execute the stored procedure and check the return value just as I did when I was inserting the new quotation row. If there is an error, the return value will not be 1, and I create an Exception and Throw it to abort the process:

```
   ...
   ' execute the stored procedure
   If sqlComm.ExecuteNonQuery() <> 1 Then
     ' throw an Exception to display error message
     Throw New Exception("* Could not insert new Optional " _
                       & "Extra row into database.")

   End If
  End If
Next
...
```

Committing or Rolling Back the Transaction

If all the updates completed without an error, I can commit them by calling the Commit method of the Transaction object I attached to the connection. However, an Exception will already have been raised if any of them failed. In this case, I call the Rollback method of the Transaction object to undo all the database updates and display the error message from the Exception:

```
 ...
 ' no errors, so commit all the updates
 oTransaction.Commit()

Catch objError As Exception
  'error encountered so roll back all the updates
  oTransaction.Rollback()
```

```
    'display error details
    lblMessage.Text = "* Error while inserting Quote. " _
                        & objError.Message
    Exit Sub  ' and stop execution
Finally
    sqlConn.Close()
End Try
...
```

And, of course, I have to close the database connection after I've finished. I do this in the `Finally` section of the `Try...Catch` construct—as you can see in the preceding code. And, in case you are concerned that the connection doesn't get closed when an error occurs, you'll be pleased to know that the code in the `Finally` block runs even when exiting from the routine using the `Exit Sub` statement.

Displaying the Result

Now I can display a message indicating that the quotation was saved, and how the user can view it. Notice that the message I display contains a JavaScript URL that calls the client-side `mainWindowPage` function. As you saw in Chapter 8, this function can be used to close the Model Details window and show a specific page in the main window of the site—in this case the My Cars page:

```
...
' display "OK" message and link to "My Cars" page
Dim sQUOT As String = Chr(34)
lblMessage.Text = "Your quotation has been saved.<br />" _
                & "Go to the <a href=" & sQUOT _
                & "javascript:mainWindowPage('secure/mycars.aspx', true)" _
                & sQUOT & "><font color=" & sQUOT & "#b50055" & sQUOT _
                & ">My Cars</font></a> page to view it and place an order."
' hide the Save button
btnSave.Visible = False

End Sub
```

The final step (in the preceding code) is to hide the Save button, helping to indicate that the quotation was saved and preventing the user from saving the same quotation twice. Of course, if the user changes the configuration, the price will be recalculated and the Save button will reappear. So users can save multiple quotations for the same vehicle if required (Figure 10-6).

> **Your quotation has been saved.**
> Go to the <u>My Cars</u> page to view it and place an order.
>
> Select the specification and optional extras you require for your new vehicle, and
> **Save** this configuration as a quotation. Then you can place an order by registering in **Close**
> the <u>MyCars</u> page.

Figure 10-6. The result of saving the current configuration as a quotation

And with this, you've completed studying the script-enabled version of the Model Details page. The only remaining task in this chapter is to look at how to provide a version of this page that works in browsers and other user-agents that do not support client-side scripting.

The No-Script Version of the Page

As I've discussed at various points throughout the previous two chapters, the cardetail.aspx page relies on client-side script support for several of its functions:

- The TabStrip control can't be used without client-side script support, because this is required for the postback hyperlinks to operate.

- While the MultiPage control will still work (in that it will generate the appropriate output for the section of the page below the "tabs"), the automatic interaction with the TabStrip control does not operate. So there is no obvious way to specify which section of output to create. Visitors would have to force a reload of the whole page using a Submit button each time they wanted to view a different section.

- I can't depend on AutoPostBack to work for any controls, so the page will not be submitted automatically when the user makes a selection in a RadioButtonList or CheckBoxList control in the Colors, Engine, and Extras sections of the page.

- The TreeView control in the Details section of the page will not work, as it also requires client-side script support for the postback hyperlinks to operate.

- The client-side setOptionButtons function I use to select the appropriate option button in the Finance page when users select from the drop-down list containing the number of months, or types their maximum monthly payment amount in the text box, will not work.

- I can't use code to change the page that is displayed in the main window of the site (the client-side mainWindowPage function), so I can't automatically redirect users to default.aspx if their session has expired, or to the My Cars page after saving a quotation.

- The Close button will not work, as it uses script to execute the client-side window.close method.

However, all the other features of the page do work, including selecting a color and a finance package, as these use Submit buttons (the color blocks, you'll recall, are <input type="image"> controls, which effectively are Submit buttons).

Avoiding the `TabStrip` *and* `MultiPage` *Controls*

The list of things that do not work without client-side script seems formidable, but in fact it's not hard to solve all these problems, or at least "make do" and still provide a usable interactive page. I can't do much about the `TreeView` and `MultiPage` controls, and so (as you saw in Chapter 8), I decided to show all of the interactive sections of the page in one go. Figure 10-7 shows the top section of the `cardetail-noscript.aspx` page, and Figure 10-8 shows the bottom half of the same page.

Figure 10-7. The upper section of the Model Details page for non-script-enabled clients

> NOTE   *In this case, I'm displaying the page in Mozilla, and I simply used the Edit |*
> *Preferences dialog to turn off client-side JavaScript before opening the site. I also*
> *tested the page in a completely non-script browser (Amaya from W3C at*
> `http://www.w3.org`). *Despite a few layout problems and the different appearance*
> *for the controls, it provides a very similar output to the figures shown here.*

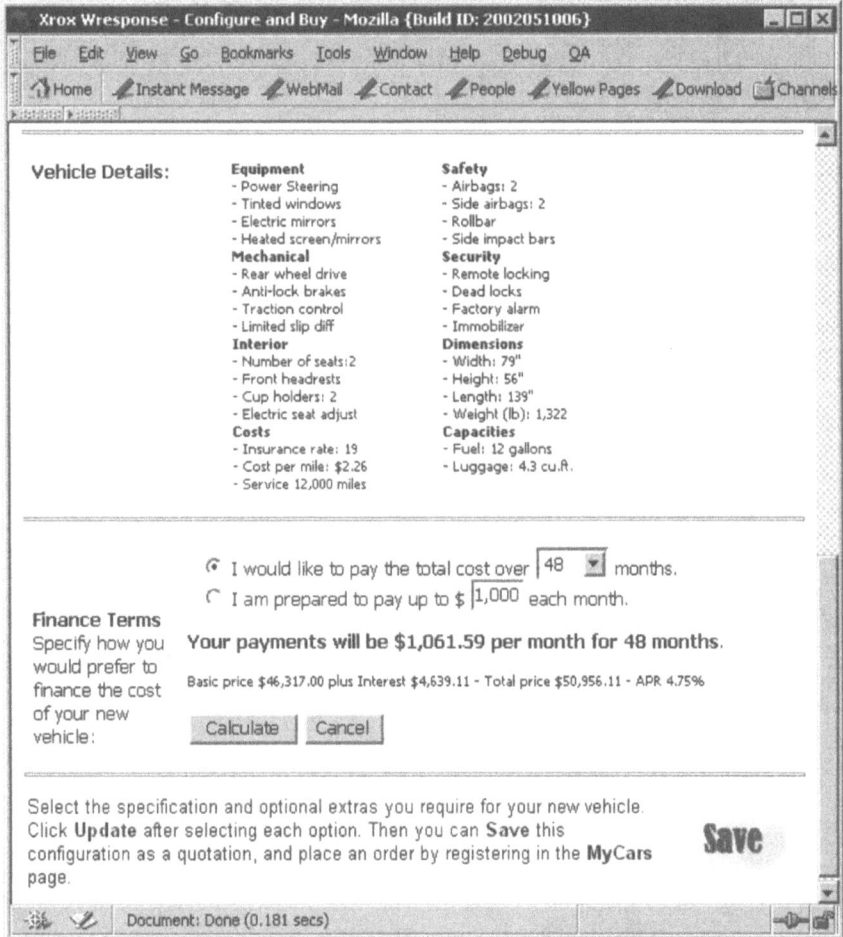

Figure 10-8. The lower section of the Model Details page for non-script-enabled clients

Custom MultiPage Effects

You could create your own MultiPage control, of course, possibly by wrapping the controls for each "tab" page in an asp:Panel control or a similar container control. Then you would set the Visible property to True for the section of controls you want to include, and False for the others.

Even when controls carry the attribute Visible="False" (or have their Visible property set to False), they are still part of the Page object that ASP.NET is processing on the server. It's just that they are not rendered as part of the output to the client. So the viewstate for hidden controls is still maintained across postbacks, even when they are not included in the client-side rendition of the page.

Another approach would be to build an HTML table (perhaps using asp:Table elements like I did in the color-list.aspx page), putting each set of controls into a separate row. Then you could show and hide the appropriate rows by setting their Visible property in your server-side code.

My Solution—Use Hyperlinks and Horizontal Rules

In the example no-script page, as you've seen, I abandon the concept of a "tabbed" dialog effect and display all the configuration sections in the page every time. I replaced the TabStrip control with a series of hyperlinks that target anchor elements within the page. So clicking the Colors link simply scrolls the page to the Colors section, clicking the Engine link scrolls the page to the Engines section, and so on:

cardetail-noscript.aspx

```
<hr size="1" />
<a href="#Colors"><font face="Arial,Helvetica,sans-serif"
    size="2" color="#000000"><b>Colors</b></font></a>  
<a href="#Engine"><font face="Arial,Helvetica,sans-serif"
    size="2" color="#000000"><b>Engine</b></font></a>  
<a href="#Extras"><font face="Arial,Helvetica,sans-serif"
    size="2" color="#000000"><b>Extras</b></font></a>  
<a href="#Details"><font face="Arial,Helvetica,sans-serif"
    size="2" color="#000000"><b>Details</b></font></a>  
<a href="#Finance"><font face="Arial,Helvetica,sans-serif"
    size="2" color="#000000"><b>Finance</b></font></a>
<hr size="1" />
...
```

Then, to separate each section, I placed horizontal rules in the page where previously the PageView elements ended and the next PageView element started. You can also see the anchors for the "page section" hyperlinks here:

```
...
<!-- section for "Colors" tab -->
<a href="Colors" />
... content of Colors "tab" here ...
<hr size="1" />

<!-- section for "Engines" tab -->
<a href="Engine" />
... content of Engine "tab" here ...
<hr size="1" />
... etc ...
```

Working Around the Lack of AutoPostBack

Without client-side script support, I can't depend on AutoPostBack to automatically submit the page to the server as the user interacts with the controls. Instead, I insert a normal `<input type="submit">` button within each section of the page, with the caption Update and a suitable pop-up ToolTip created by the `title` attribute:

```
<input id="btnUpdate1" type="submit" runat="server"
       value="Update" OnServerClick="NoScriptUpdate"
       title="Calculate and Update the price and other details" />
```

The `OnServerClick` attribute points to a server-side event handler named `NoScriptUpdate` that I've added to the page:

```
Sub NoScriptUpdate(oSender As Object, oArgs As EventArgs)
  CalculateCarPrice()
End Sub
```

All this does is force the price of the vehicle to be updated. The "change" event handlers that I include in the list controls on the page are still defined. For example, I still have the attribute `OnSelectedIndexChanged="SelectExtras"` on the `CheckBoxList` control that implements the list of optional extras for the vehicle.

Without `AutoPostBack`, of course, these "change" events are not immediately raised on the server when an item is selected, but they are still raised when a postback does occur. So they will still execute and update the page just as they do in the script-enabled version.

Replacing the `TreeView` Control

I can't use a `TreeView` control without client-side script support because the nodes are hyperlinks that execute a client-side JavaScript URL function to cause the selected nodes of the tree to be expanded and contracted. Instead, I chose to display all the data from the source XML files as hierarchical lists (Figure 10-9).

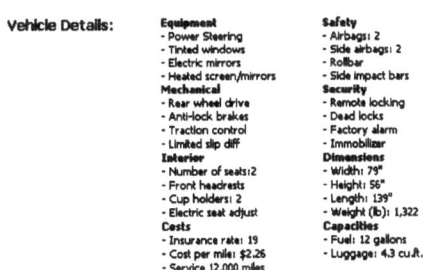

Figure 10-9. Displaying the standard features in non-script-enabled clients

Because there is no longer a fixed-size "tabbed dialog," the length of the lists is not really important. To display the XML content, I take advantage of another control that I briefly mentioned in Chapter 6—the ASP.NET `Xml` server control.

The ASP.NET Xml Web Forms Control

The ASP.NET Xml control is designed to make it easy to display XML in a Web page, or the result of transforming XML into another format (usually HTML) with an XSL or XSLT style sheet. The control has only a few properties that are associated with generating output (Table 10-1).

Table 10-1. The Properties of the ASP.NET Xml Server Control

Property	Description
Document	A reference to an XmlDocument object that contains the XML document to display or transform.
DocumentContent	A string containing the text of the XML document to display or transform.
DocumentSource	A string that contains the physical or virtual path to the XML document to display or transform.
Transform	A reference to an XslTransform object that contains the XSL or XSLT style sheet to use for transforming the XML document before displaying it.
TransformSource	A string that contains the physical or virtual path to the XSL or XSLT style sheet to use for the transformation.
TransformArgumentList	A reference to an XsltArgumentList object that contains the arguments to be passed to the style sheet.

When the control comes to render its content to the output, any required XSL or XSLT transformation takes place automatically. So all I have to do is specify the XML and XSLT documents that I want to use, and the control does the rest.

In the HTML section of the page, I removed the declaration of the two TreeView controls from the Details "tab," and replaced them with two asp:Xml controls:

```
<!-- section for "Details" tab -->
<table border="0" cellpadding="6">
  <tr>
    <td valign="top"><a name="Details" />
      <font face="Tahoma,Arial,Helvetica,sans-serif" size="2">
      <span style="body-text"><b>Vehicle Details:</b></span></font></td>
    <td>   </td>
    <td valign="top">
      <font face="Tahoma,Arial,Helvetica,sans-serif" size="1">
      <span style="small-text">
      <asp:Xml id="xmlDetailLeft" runat="server" />
      </span></font></td>
    <td>   </td>
```

```
    <td valign="top">
      <font face="Tahoma,Arial,Helvetica,sans-serif" size="1">
      <span style="small-text">
      <asp:Xml id="xmlDetailRight" runat="server" />
      </span></font></td>
  </tr>
</table>
```

Populating the Xml Controls

One point to watch out for, however, is that the control properties and its output are not maintained automatically in the viewstate of the page, so I have to specify the properties of the control each time the page loads. Therefore, I added this code to the Page_Load event so that it runs every time the page loads:

```
...
' specify XML source files and the matching XSLT
' stylesheets for the two asp:Xml controls
' have to do this on every page load as the result
' is not persisted in the viewstate
Try
  xmlDetailLeft.DocumentSource = "xmldata/tvdata-left-" & sCarID & ".xml"
  xmlDetailLeft.TransformSource = "xmldata/cardetail.xslt"
  xmlDetailRight.DocumentSource = "xmldata/tvdata-right-" & sCarID & ".xml"
  xmlDetailRight.TransformSource = "xmldata/cardetail.xslt"
Catch
  lblMessage.Text = "Error loading XML data for car details."
End Try
...
```

The XML Documents and the XSLT Style Sheet

You looked at the XML documents that contain the vehicle details in Chapter 9. The document format is like that shown in the following code listing:

tvdata-left-1.xml

```
<?xml version="1.0"?>
<TREENODES>
  <TreeNode Text="Equipment">
    <TreeNode Text="Power Steering" />
    <TreeNode Text="Cruise control" />
    <TreeNode Text="Tinted windows" />
  </TreeNode>
  <TreeNode Text="Mechanical">
    <TreeNode Text="Front wheel drive" />
    <TreeNode Text="Anti-lock brakes" />
  </TreeNode>
```

```
<TreeNode Text="Interior">
  <TreeNode Text="Number of seats: 4" />
  <TreeNode Text="Cup holders: 2" />
  <TreeNode Text="Electric seat adjust" />
</TreeNode>
<TreeNode Text="Costs">
  <TreeNode Text="Insurance rate: 9" />
  <TreeNode Text="Cost per mile: $ 0.89" />
  <TreeNode Text="Service 12,000 miles" />
</TreeNode>
</TREENODES>
```

To transform this into a hierarchical list is easy using XSLT. I don't have room for an XSLT primer here, so you may have to go off and consult other suitable books if you are not familiar with it. The example XSLT style sheet, named cardetail.xslt, contains a template that matches the root of the XML document (match="/"). This template then selects all the TreeNode elements in the document that are child nodes of a TREENODES element (remember that XML is case-sensitive). These TreeNode elements represent the top-level headings, and the template that matches them outputs the value of the Text attribute wrapped in HTML <b> and </b> tags and followed by a <br /> element.

Then it selects all the TreeNode child nodes of the current top-level node, and applies a template to these. The only template that matches in this case is the last one (match="*"). In this template the content of the Text attribute is output without the HTML <b> and </b> tags, indented by preceding it with a hyphen, and followed by a <br /> element:

cardetail.xslt

```
<?xml version='1.0'?>
<xsl:stylesheet xmlns:xsl="http://www.w3.org/1999/XSL/Transform" version="1.0">
<xsl:template match="/">
  <xsl:apply-templates select="child::TREENODES/child::TreeNode"/>
</xsl:template>
<xsl:template match="TREENODES/child::TreeNode">
  <b><xsl:value-of select="attribute::Text" /></b><br />
  <xsl:apply-templates select="child::TreeNode"/>
</xsl:template>
<xsl:template match="*">
 -<xsl:value-of select="attribute::Text" /><br />
</xsl:template>
</xsl:stylesheet>
```

Because of the recursive nature of the process in XSLT, the result is that the child nodes of each top-level node are processed immediately after that top-level node, and before the next top-level node. So, the output is what you saw in Figure 10-9.

Managing Without the `setOptionButtons` *Function*

The three remaining issues to face when there is no client-side script support are relatively minor, and have little effect on the way the page behaves. The omission of the `setOptionButtons` routine that automatically selects the appropriate option button in the `Finance` section of the page simply means that users have to remember to select the required option when they select the number of months or enter their maximum payment amount, and before they click the Calculate button (Figure 10-10).

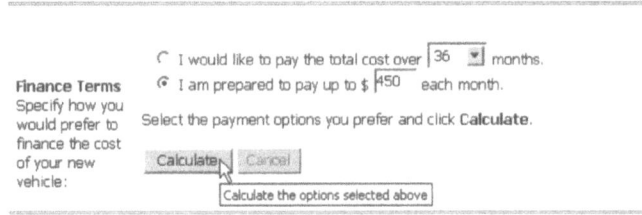

Figure 10-10. The finance package selection controls

Managing Without the `mainWindowPage` *Function*

One area that does lose some useful functionality without client-side script support is being able to manage navigation from the Model Details window to another window. There are a couple of times when this is really useful:

- If the user has "lost" their current session (by not accessing a page within the timeout period), I have to redirect them to the `default.aspx` page to start a new session and collect (or generate) the user ID. But this page needs to open in the main window, not in the pop-up window that contains the Model Details page.

- When users save a quotation (and in the instructions at the foot of the window) it's nice to be able to provide a link that opens the My Cars page in the main window and closes the Model Details window.

You can't do any of this without client-side scripting. In response to the "lost" session, all you can do is display a message to the user explaining how to start a new session.

```
' get style sheet size from Session
sStyleSize = CType(Session("WccStyleSize"), String)
```

```
' if no value, session has expired or user entered
' site at page other than "Home" page
If sStyleSize = "" Then

  ' write message for non-script clients
  Dim sReload As String = "<html><body><center>" _
    & "<b>Your session has expired.</b><p />" _
    & "<b>Please close this window and reload the Home page</b>" _
    & "</center></body></html>"

  ' then prevent rest of page from being processed
  Response.Write(sReload)
  Response.Flush()
  Response.End()
  Exit Sub

End If
```

> **NOTE** *Even though you can't open the Model Details window from the main window as a pop-up, the pop-up window does remember who its parent is (this is where the value for the* window.opener *property comes from). However, I can't do anything about it without script support.*

As to the issue of the navigation to the My Cars page, all I can do here is again provide a helpful message without the hyperlinks. And, as the page is likely to be longer than the user's screen depth, he or she won't be able to see the bottom of the page after a postback to save a quotation. Therefore I display the information (or error) message at the top of the page instead (Figure 10-11).

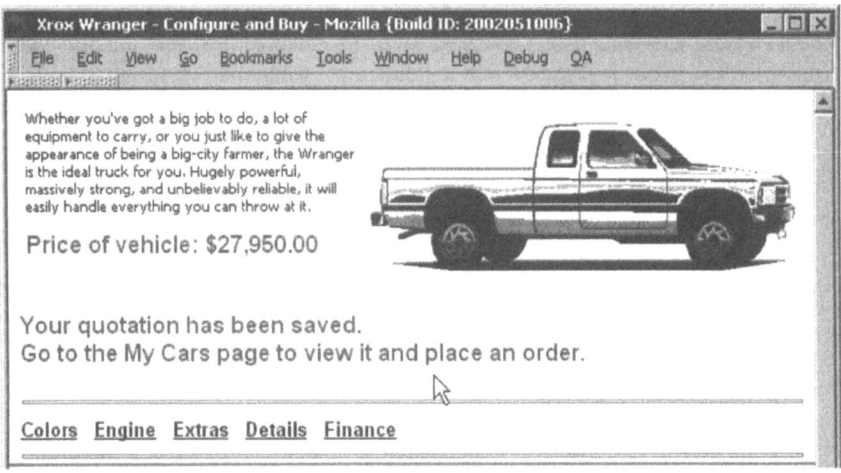

Figure 10-11. The message after saving a quotation in the non-script-enabled version of the application

Managing Without a Close Button

Well, what can I say? How will you manage without a Close button? Just hope that the user is clever enough to use the normal Windows "close" button at the top right of the window. If you think it's necessary, you can always put some text in the page to remind them of this.

Summary

At last you've covered all aspects of the Model Details page. While devoting three chapters to a single Web page might seem excessive, I've tried to provide the information in a way that makes it easy to understand what the page does, how it works, and why I designed and built it the way I did.

The previous two chapters covered this overview and looked at the basic page structure, including exploring the database used to power the application, as well as a detailed look at how the bulk of the code that provides the interactive interface works.

This chapter has been devoted to a more narrow range of topics. You looked at how to calculate the price of a vehicle, including all the user selections such as the color range, engine type, and optional extras. I also showed you how to calculate the payment terms for the selected finance package.

Then you moved on to look at how I save the current vehicle configuration to the database as a quotation. In this part of the chapter I included an aside to discuss the use of transactions to protect the validity of a database during updates, and you saw how you can implement connection-based transactions using ADO.NET.

Finally, the chapter explored the differences between the two versions of the Model Details page—one that is designed for script-enabled browsers, and one that is designed to work as well as possible in non-script-enabled browsers and other user-agents.

The topics at the chapter covered were:

- How to calculate the price of a vehicle as the user configures it

- How to calculate the finance terms for a vehicle

- How to save the configuration as a quotation

- How the non-script-enabled version of the page works

Having saved a quotation for a vehicle to the database, the next stage in the example application is to see how the user can view that quotation and place an order for the vehicle. All this is accomplished in the My Cars page, but before you can get there you have to think about the other requirements of most Web applications—allowing users to register, and managing authentication and authorization through a "login" feature.

The Login and Register Page

WITH THE COMPLETION OF THE Model Details page in Chapter 10, visitors to the example Xrox Car Company site can now see the range of vehicles, compare vehicle performance, check out the features of each model, and configure them to suit their requirements. They can also save this configuration as a quotation. However, there is one more feature of the site that you haven't yet explored.

I want to allow my visitors to come back at any time and view the quotations they have saved. I also want them to be able to place an order for a vehicle based on a quotation they received. And, having purchased one or more vehicles from Xrox Cars, I'd like them to be able to see their purchase history as well.

OK, so selling cars over the Web is not a common activity (though it is happening), although the features I've just been discussing are in common use on most e-commerce sites today. The quotation is just a glorified "shopping cart," and the ability to view previous order history is available at most sites. So, while my example may appear a little esoteric, it is close to the actual "real world" requirements for many sites. In this and the next chapter, you'll see how I implement these features in the Xrox Car Company site.

In this chapter, the aim is to look at:

- The ASP.NET and other techniques used for authentication and authorization

- How to identify "anonymous" users as they browse and then log into the site

- How to collect and store information about visitors when they register

- How to force users who have already registered to provide "logon" details

- How the "login and register" page in the example Xrox Car Company site works

I start with a brief review of the way Web servers and the example site normally deal with "anonymous" visitors. This involves three technical terms, which I'll define and describe first—Authentication, Authorization, and Impersonation.

Web Site Users and Identities

Most Web sites are designed to allow users to visit without having to present any credentials. This is ideal, because usually you want to encourage as many visitors as possible to come to your sites (and buy something as well, if that's the purpose of the site). So, most visitors are "anonymous," in that they do not have to provide any information about their identity before they can view the pages.

Of course, as with most Web sites out there, not all of the pages are suitable for anonymous access. Where you allow users to place an order, download information, access resources they are supposed to pay for, or even administer the site itself, they are often forced to identify themselves so that you can see if they should be permitted to carry out these actions.

The topic of identifying users and allowing only certain users to access specific resources involves three topics that are fundamentally separate, but which become intertwined when implementing restricted access to Web pages:

- **Authentication** is the process of discovering the **identity** of a user, either automatically by using some persistent identification feature (such as a cookie or a client certificate) or by prompting the user to provide some recognizable information or characteristic. This information or characteristic could be a user name and password, a smart card, a fingerprint scan or a scan of the retina of the user's eye, or whatever else you may have seen in recent sci-fi movies. As long as it is something only that particular user can provide, you can use it for authentication.

- **Authorization** follows from authentication. Once you know exactly who a user or visitor is, you can decide if that visitor should be allowed to access the requested resource. Information about who can access what resources can be stored in a variety of ways. For a Windows disk file, or many other Windows resources, it is an Access Control List (ACL) that is defined within the operating system. For other resources, the list of users and their individual permissions (such as READ and/or WRITE) can be stored in a database or in some other storage system such as an XML document, Active Directory, and so forth.

- **Impersonation** is related to authentication, in that it allows a user to access resources as though he or she were someone else. An obvious example is the "anonymous user" account that Internet Information Server uses to access resources on behalf of visitors to a Web site who are not individually authenticated. You'll look at this topic in more detail soon.

This book is not about Web server or Web site security, and so I will not be discussing all the related topics in detail. However, you will look at how I use the three features for controlling access that I just listed—both generally and in relation to the Xrox Car Company site.

Authentication

The first step in implementing any kind of restricted access to resources or a Web site is to be able to identify each user when that user sends a request for a resource. Even when you allow anonymous access to resources, the browser or user-agent automatically sends some information about the user to the server. This includes things like:

- The IP address of the user's browser, proxy server, or ISP, so that you can send the response back.

- The user-agent string that identifies what type of browser or user-agent software the user is using, so that you can send back appropriate content to suit the visitor's browser.

- The various content types that the user's browser will accept, such as HTML, images, and so on. Again, this allows the server to tailor the output to suit that type of client.

What the browser doesn't do by default is send details of the actual user, for example the user's name and address or email address. Neither does it automatically send a user name and password that allows me to uniquely identify the *user* (rather than the browser). If I want this to happen, I have to specifically set up the server or configure the site to not accept "anonymous" visitors (and hence prompt for the user's credentials).

In the Xrox Car Company site, you'll recall that I allocate each user an ID when that user first comes to the site. This is done in `default.aspx`, and the ID is stored in the user's ASP.NET session, and in a persistent cookie that is stored on the user's machine. If the user has visited the site before, I look in the cookie for this ID (in the code in `default.aspx`), and reuse this for all subsequent visits. If this is the user's first visit to the site (or if they have destroyed the cookie since the last visit or are using a different machine), I create a new "anonymous" ID for that visitor.

So, each user can be identified by the user ID I allocated. However, as you can see from the preceding discussion, this is not really any use in *authenticating* a user. It may indicate that the user has been here before (if there is a cookie with the ID in it), but that really only identifies the machine where I stored it. It could be a different person who is using the machine this time.

So, to actually identify the user, I have to force them to provide some form of unique characteristic that I can check against a list of existing users. In the example case, I use the most common technique—I ask for a combination of user name and password. Once the user provides these, I can look the user up against the database of registered users, and identify that user uniquely.

Authorization

While authentication allows the site to identify users, I also need to see if they are allowed to access the resource they requested. In the Xrox Car Company site there is only one level of authorization. If a user can be authenticated, that visitor can access the My Cars page. If the user cannot be authenticated, that person has to register and provide the details the site needs for authentication in the future. Once this is done, the user becomes authorized to access the My Cars page.

In most Web sites, this level of authorization is sufficient for the "public" parts of the site. However, you may also have areas of the site that are not available to registered users. For example, if your site administration tasks (adding new items, setting prices, and suchlike) are performed via pages in the site, then you will definitely want to limit access to a more controlled subset of users.

In terms of "registration" for these users, it is likely to be the site administrator who creates the list of users who will have access, and even what level of access each one should have. Some may be able to upload new content, while others will only be able to view reports on the site's performance. In many ways, this is similar to the concept of Windows' own file access security, where some users may have "read/write" permission while others might only have "read" permission.

For the example site, the list of users who will have access to the My Cars page is held in the database. The user name and the password (encrypted to prevent anyone being able to view the table contents and see the passwords) are stored in a table. The table also contains the registered details of each user, such as the user's name, address, email address, and so on. I collect all this information from visitors when they register (Figure 11-1).

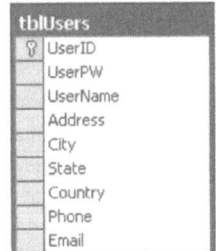

Figure 11-1. The Users table in the database

Impersonation

I've talked about "anonymous" access to the site, but you are no doubt aware that nobody can actually access resources on a server without being identified first. Then that visitor must access the resources under the context of an existing account that is valid on the machine, or valid on the domain to which the machine belongs. When you specify the entry for Everyone in the security dialogs in Windows, what you are actually saying is "every existing valid account."

To allow users who are not authenticated to access content on a Web site anonymously, Internet Information Server (IIS) up to and including version 5.0 uses its own account—by default named IUSR_*machinename*—to access the resources on behalf of the anonymous or unauthenticated user. In other words, the user is being impersonated as the IUSR account. There is also an account named IWAM_*machinename* that is used for out-of-process execution, for example to execute components installed in Windows Component Services (or MTS under Windows NT4).

In ASP.NET, the IUSR and IWAM accounts continue to exist as before. However, unlike ASP 3.0 and earlier, all access to pages or resources that are processed by the ASP.NET Framework is (by default) under the context of an account named ASPNET. So my ASP.NET pages and other ASP.NET resources are accessed with the user being impersonated as the ASPNET account.

Note that the ASPNET account is only used for ASP.NET resources. So, for example, .doc, .zip, image files, and many other types of files are accessed under the context of the IUSR account and not the ASPNET account unless you specifically configure ASP.NET to handle these types of files (in IIS Manager, open the App Mappings page from the Configuration button in the Home Directory page of the Properties dialog for the site). So any access limitations you want to specify for these types of file must be done against the IUSR account.

In some cases I still use the IUSR and ASPNET accounts to access restricted resources, and use custom security methods or the built-in methods that are provided by ASP.NET to limit access. So the user is still being impersonated by that account. In other cases, I might abandon impersonation and force the user to provide details of a Windows account on the machine or domain that does have access permission for the requested resource.

In the Xrox Car Company site I allow the default impersonation in IIS to be used, and access pages and resources under the context of the IUSR and ASPNET accounts. I identify users through ASP.NET Forms Authentication, and then control access to resources with the associated built-in authorization features of ASP.NET. These two topics are the main focus of the later sections of this chapter.

IIS 6.0 and Windows Server 2003

While all of the preceding is true for IIS 4.0 and IIS 5.0, as installed with Windows NT, Windows 2000, and Windows XP, the new version of IIS supplied with Windows Server 2003 (IIS 6.0) works in a slightly different way. By default, it runs Web sites within *Application Pools*, and the worker processes used for accessing resources run under the context of an account named NETWORK SERVICE. This provides a better level of security, as it has a lower overall level of permissions on the server than the LOCAL SYSTEM account that worker processes use for ASP.NET in IIS 4.0 and IIS 5.0.

Windows Server 2003 creates an account group called IIS_WPG, of which the IWAM_*machinename*, LOCAL SERVICE, NETWORK SERVICE, and SYSTEM accounts are automatically members. It means that that you can use this group to configure access to resources for ASP.NET running under the default configuration of IIS 6.0. Alternatively, you can just assign the permissions for resources directly to the NETWORK SERVICE account if you prefer more fine-grained control.

Also bear in mind that you can configure IIS 6.0 to run in a special "compatibility" mode called *IIS 5.0 Isolation Mode* (in the Service tab of the Properties dialog for the Web Sites entry in IIS Manager). In this case, IIS 6.0 runs ASP.NET just like it does under IIS 5.0, and the accounts used and permission settings you make are the same as in IIS 5.0. So, the ASPNET account is used for ASP.NET resources, and the IUSR_*machinename* account is used for other resources. And an account named IWAM_*machinename* is used for out-of-process execution of components in this mode, just as in IIS 5.0.

> **NOTE** *For more information of the IIS and ASP.NET security model in Windows Server 2003, open the Help file from IIS Manager and navigate to the section: Server Administration Guide | Security | Access Control | Web Site Permissions.*

Permissions for the Anonymous Accounts

The "anonymous" accounts I discussed earlier have only limited access to resources on the machine, providing a basic level of security so that visitors can only access the resources I specify (usually just the content of the Web site) and any required components and temporary folders. By default, the IUSR and IWAM account can only read files and execute specified components. If you want to be able to write to the server's disk from within a Web page, or access another service such as SMTP, you have to manually add this permission to the IUSR (and/or IWAM) accounts.

The ASPNET and NETWORK SERVICE accounts have similar permissions to the IUSR and IWAM accounts, with a few extra added to allow them to access the .NET Framework class files and other folders these accounts use. So, to write to the server's disk from an ASP.NET page, for example, you have to give the ASPNET or the NETWORK SERVICE account (depending on which version of IIS you are using) the relevant "write" or "modify" permissions.

ASP.NET Authentication Methods

ASPNET provides three types of authentication and authorization. Table 11-1 shows these types, together with the default of using only the features of IIS itself. I'm only going to be discussing Forms authentication in depth in this book, but I will briefly indicate how the other types work so that you can see if they better suit your requirements.

Table 11-1. The Authentication Methods Available in ASP.NET

Type	Name	Description
Windows built-in authentication	Windows	The initial authentication is performed by IIS through Basic, Digest, or Integrated Windows authentication. The requested resources are then accessed under the context of the account that the user presents credentials for. The web.config file can specify the accounts that are valid for the whole or parts of the application.
Passport-based authentication	Passport	This option uses a centralized Web-based authentication service provided by Microsoft that offers single-sign-on (SSN) and core profile services for member sites.
Forms-based authentication	Forms	Unauthenticated requests are automatically redirected to an HTML form page using HTTP client-side redirection. This is similar to custom authentication methods used in previous versions of ASP, but it provides much of the functionality as part of the framework of ASP.NET. The user provides login credentials and submits the form. If the application authenticates the request, the system issues a cookie that contains the credentials (in fact, a key for reacquiring the identity). The client browser then sends the cookie with all subsequent requests, and the user can access the application while this cookie is retained. Access to requested resources takes place within the context of the ASPNET or NETWORK SERVICE account, depending on which version of IIS you are using.
Default (IIS) authentication	None	*The default.* Impersonation can still be used, but access control is limited to that specified within IIS. Resources are accessed under the context of the special ASP.NET process account, or the IUSR account if impersonation is enabled.

To specify the type of authentication I want to use in an ASP.NET virtual application or virtual directory I provide the Name shown above in the <authentication> section of the web.config file for that site or directory:

```
<configuration>
...
<system.web>
  <authentication mode="Windows|Passport|Forms|None">
    authentication options used for the application
  </authentication>
  <authorization>
    users and roles that have access to the application
  </authorization>
  <identity>
    if application should run under a different account
  </identity>
</system.web>
...
</configuration>
```

The other two elements shown here within the <system.web> section of web.config are used to specify how access control should be carried out. The <authorization> section is used to specify which users or groups can and cannot access the application. The <identity> section is used to specify if impersonation is enabled—in other words, whether to run under the user (or IUSR) account, the special ASPNET or NETWORK SERVICE process account, or a different account that you specify.

Windows Authentication

If you want each user to be authenticated against an existing Windows account, the best choice is Windows authentication. Simply configure machine-level or domain-level accounts in Windows using the built-in account management tools. Users provide their user name and password when they access the restricted pages in the site. In fact, if they have logged onto their local machine with these credentials, they are used automatically without the logon dialog appearing.

Obviously, this approach is not usually suitable for a public Web site, as you would then have to set up domain or local accounts within Windows for each user. Besides which, many browsers (other than Internet Explorer 5 and later) cannot use the Digest authentication method that is required. Windows authentication is more suited to an intranet situation, or perhaps an extranet where you have only a limited set of users and can specify which browser they use to access the site.

Setting Up Windows Authentication

To set up an application or a section of an application to use Windows authentication, you simply specify this authentication mode and then turn on impersonation within the <identity> element:

```
<configuration>
...
<system.web>
  <authentication mode="Windows" />
  <identity impersonate="true" />
</system.web>
...
</configuration>
```

Now, each user will access resources under the context of the account with which he or she was authenticated by IIS.

Passport Authentication

Microsoft provides a "Passport Service" that can be used to authenticate users on any passport-enabled site, anywhere on the Internet. When users log onto a participating site, their browser or user agent sends their credentials to the passport service, which authenticates them and places a secure cookie on their machine. Then, when a user accesses another participating site, the browser presents this cookie to the passport service to prove that the user has already been authenticated. The passport service then indicates who that user is to the new site so the visitor can be properly authorized—that is, the new site can check if this user has permission to access the requested resource.

The power of the passport service is that a user can present the same credentials to any participating site, while only having to log in once during a session. When the user's browser is closed, or the user indicates that he or she wishes to log off, the cookie is destroyed. The user must then log on again to re-access resources on any of the participating sites.

Setting Up Passport Authentication

To set up passport authentication you must subscribe to the "Passport Service," and install special software on your Web server to allow the process to work. Full details are available from http://www.microsoft.com/netservices/passport/. Once you've installed the software and subscribed to the service, you configure passport authentication in the web.config file:

```
<configuration>
...
<system.web>
  <authentication mode="Passport">
    <passport redirectUrl="internal|url" />
  </authentication>
</system.web>
...
</configuration>
```

The `<passport>` element supports a single attribute named `redirectUrl`. The default value (before you install and configure passport authentication) is `internal`, which means that unauthenticated requests receive a generic error message created by your server. Any other string is assumed to be the URL of the passport service that unauthenticated requests will be redirected to for authentication.

Forms Authentication

Where the highest levels of security are not required, Forms-based authentication (sometimes referred to as cookie-based authentication) automates many of the tasks that you would normally perform yourself in earlier versions of ASP to build custom authentication solutions. Forms-based authentication also removes the unintuitive Windows Logon dialog, allowing you to replace it with an attractive custom form, or integrate the login controls (basically two text boxes and a button) into existing pages.

The forms authentication process generates a secure cookie when the user logs into the application, and sends it to the client. Then, if this cookie is present in subsequent requests, you know that the user has already been authenticated. The cookie contains the user's identity, and ASP.NET can check that this user is authorized to access the requested resource. If the user does have authorization, it returns this resource (for example, by executing an ASP.NET page). If not, access is denied.

If the cookie is not present in the request headers, the user is automatically redirected to a custom login page that you create yourself. Users enter their credentials into this login page and submit them to the application where these credentials are automatically checked to authenticate the users. If they are recognized, an authentication cookie is added to the headers and the request is sent to the next stage of the process. ASP.NET checks to see if each user is authorized to access the requested resource requested, and if so sends it to that user. If not, access is denied.

Setting Up Forms-based Authentication

Like all other ASP.NET security settings, Forms-based authentication is configured within the `web.config` file for an application or a virtual directory. The `<authentication>` section carries the value `Forms` for the `mode` attribute, and within the element itself I add more elements to specify how the authentication of users will be carried out:

```
<configuration>
...
<system.web>
  <authentication mode="Forms">
    <forms name="cookie-name"
           path="cookie-path"
           loginurl="url"
           protection="All|None|Encryption|Validation"
           timeout="number-of-minutes" >
      <credentials passwordFormat="Clear|SHA1|MD5">
        <user name="user-name" password="user-password" />
```

```
            <user name="user-name" password="user-password" />
            ... more users listed here ...
        </credentials>
      </forms>
   </authentication>
   <machineKey validationKey="AutoGenerate|key"
               decryptionKey="AutoGenerate|key"
               validation="SHA1|MD5"/>
</system.web>
...
</configuration>
```

The attributes of the <forms> element define:

- The name that will be assigned to the cookie.

- The path for which the cookie is valid. This is usually set to "/" to indicate the complete site. If not, and the site contains links that are not in the correct letter case (for example, an <a> element with href="mypage.aspx" where the actual page name is MyPage.aspx), the cookie will not be returned by some browsers. This will cause the login form to be displayed again.

- The loginurl that specifies the virtual path to the login form page.

- The protection level required for the cookie. The settings are: All (the default), which uses both data validation (based on the <machineKey> element) and encryption (Triple DES if available and if the key is at least 48 bytes long); None (should be used only for personalization purposes); Encryption (the cookie is encrypted but data validation is not performed); Validation (validation is performed but the cookie is not encrypted).

- The timeout in minutes before the cookie expires on the user's machine and the server.

Within the <forms> element is:

- An optional <credentials> element that specifies the encryption algorithm used to encrypt the user's password in the web.config file. Within this element there can be a series of optional <user> elements that between them specify the users who will be able to access the protected resources.

You can also specify an optional <machineKey> element within the <system.web> section, which specifies the keys and method to be used to encrypt the cookie contents. In general I omit this element, and allow a key to be created automatically. However, it can be useful in a situation like a Web farm, where you want all machines to use the same key. The key length must match the number of characters required for the encryption level and method that is used. This entry in the default machine.config file specifies that the keys are auto-generated:

```
<machineKey validationKey="AutoGenerate"
            decryptionKey="AutoGenerate"
            validation="SHA1" />
```

So, an example `web.config` file for Forms authentication might look like the following. Remember that the `<credentials>` and `<machineKey>` sections are optional. The example also lists some users, and you can see that their passwords are encrypted:

```
<configuration>
...
<system.web>
  <authentication mode="Forms">
    <forms name="MyNewApp" path="/" loginUrl="/main/login.aspx"
           protection="All" timeout="30" >
      <credentials passwordFormat="SHA1">
        <user name="billjones"
              password="87F8ED9157125FFC4DA9E06A7B8011AD80A53FE1" />
        <user name="marthasmith"
              password="93FB8A49CC350BAEB2661FA5C5C97959BD328C50" />
        <user name="joesoap"
              password="5469541CA9236F939D889B2B465F9B15A09149E4" />
      </credentials>
    </forms>
  </authentication>
  <!-- keys usually only specified for a Web farm -->
  <machineKey validationKey="3875f9...645a78ff"
              decryptionKey="3875f9...645a78ff"
              validation="SHA1" />
</system.web>
...
</configuration>
```

> **NOTE** *The `<identity>` element is not used in Forms-based authentication.*

Hard-coding user details into the `web.config` file (within the `<credentials>` section) is fine if you only have a few users, or perhaps where you use generic accounts such as "admin" or "user" where all users in that "group" log in with the same credentials. However, it soon becomes cumbersome when you have lots of users, or when you need to change the user list or user passwords regularly. In this case, it's better to use another technique for storing the list of users and their passwords. As you'll see later in this chapter, I prefer to use a database to store these details instead.

Specifying Users and Groups

The previous examples all show how you can use the built-in features of ASP.NET to authenticate users. However, you also want to be able to authorize them, by limiting access to resources to specific users. This is done within the `<authorization>` section of the web.config file, with a series of `<allow>` and `<deny>` elements. The general form of each of these elements is highlighted in the following listing:

```
<configuration>
...
<system.web>
  <authentication mode="Windows|Passport|Forms|None">
    authentication options used for the application
  </authentication>
  <authorization>
    <allow roles="comma-separated list of Windows account group names"
           users="comma-separated list of Windows user account names"
           verb="GET|POST|HEAD" />
    <deny roles="comma-separated list of Windows account group names"
           users="comma-separated list of Windows user account names"
           verb="GET|POST|HEAD" />
    users and roles that have access to the application
  </authorization>
  <identity>
    if application should run under a different account
  </identity>
</system.web>
...
</configuration>
```

The `<allow>` and `<deny>` element must contain either a roles or a users attribute. It does not have to contain both, and the verb attribute is always optional. To specify a domain user account, include the domain name followed by a backslash and the user name, for example MyDomainName\MyUserName. There are also special values that refer to Windows built-in account groups, such as Everyone, BUILTIN\Administrators, and so on.

To specify a local (machine) account just use the machine name in place of the domain name. There is no way to specify a domain account without the actual domain (there is no short-cut that means "use the local domain"), so you have to edit the list if you change the domain name or move the application to another domain.

There are also two special symbols that you can use:

- An asterisk (*) means all users, roles, or verbs, depending on which of these attributes it is used in.

- A question mark (?) means "anonymous access." In the case of Windows and Forms-based authentication, this is the account set up in IIS for anonymous access. This character can only be used within the users attribute.

You'll see the way I use the last of these special symbols in the Xrox Car Company site later on in this chapter.

Specifying HTTP Access Types

You can also use the `<allow>` and `<deny>` elements to control the type of HTTP action that a user can take when accessing an application or directory by using the `verb` attribute:

```
<configuration>
...
<system.web>
  <authorization>
    <allow verb="GET" users="*" />
    <allow verb="POST" users="MyDomainName\MyAccount" />
    <deny verb="POST" users="*" />
  </authorization>
</system.web>
...
</configuration>
```

This example allows the domain-level account named MyAccount to send POST requests to the application (submit an HTML form), but all other users are only be able to send GET requests. And, of course, I can combine this access control setting with the list of groups and users, by adding the `verb` attribute to the previous example that used the `roles` and `users` attributes.

Avoiding Nested ASP.NET Applications

ASP.NET does not allow you to share resources between different applications. This includes things like assemblies in the `bin` directory, user controls, session state, and so on. Neither can you carry session state into a separate application using the `Server.Transfer` method. This limitation even applies when you "nest" applications—in other words when you make a subfolder within an existing virtual application directory into a virtual application directory. Although the new application is nested within the existing one, the restrictions on accessing resources applies between these two applications.

However, (as you saw earlier) if you use a `web.config` file that includes the `<authentication>` element, you must place this in the root folder of an ASP.NET application. So, to limit access to a specific subfolder using this approach would mean that this subfolder has to be a separate nested ASP.NET application. But even if this folder is nested within the existing application, the two applications will not be able to share values, assemblies, or user controls.

Thankfully, you can easily get round this problem. The `<authentication>` and `<authorization>` sections *can* be in the same `web.config` file if you are limiting access to all the pages in all folders of the application. They can instead be placed in *separate* `web.config` files, in different folders, if you only want to limit access to certain folders and not all of them.

While the web.config file containing the <authentication> element *must always* be in a virtual application folder (the application root directory or the root folder of the Web site), web.config files containing the <authorization> element can be placed in any subfolder. They do not have to be placed in a virtual application folder. This means that you avoid the need for nested applications, and you can share all the resources across all the pages in all the subfolders.

Xrox Cars Login and Register Process

I use Forms-based authentication in the example application, so that I can force users to be authenticated before they get access to the My Cars page, where they can view previous quotations and place an order. To implement this, I have a subfolder named secure that contains the My Cars page. It also contains the "logon" page (named login.aspx) that allows the user to log in and be authenticated.

The next schematic shows the layout of the site and the relevant web.config files. All the pages that can be accessed anonymously, without logging on, are in the root folder of the site (plus a few other subfolders that contain the user controls, images, and XML data files) (Figure 11-2).

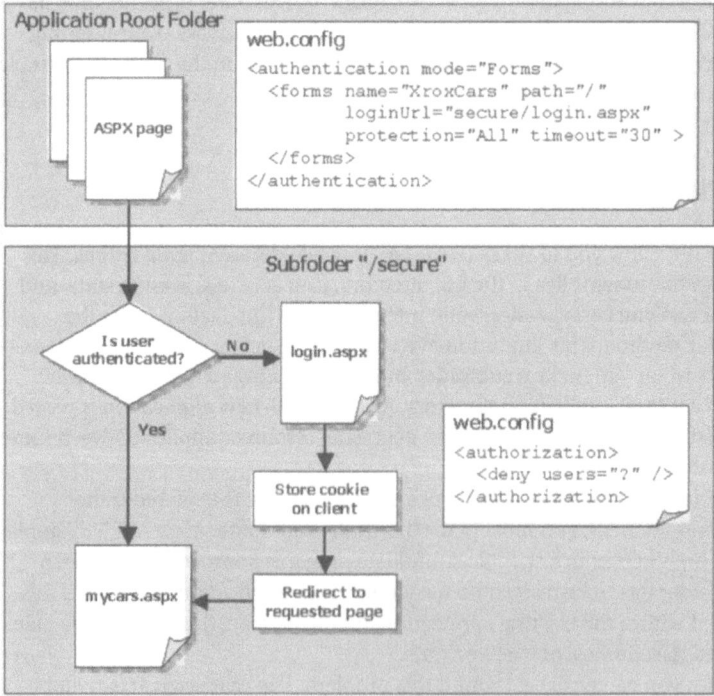

Figure 11-2. The login process and the relevant web.config files

The Root Folder `web.config` File

The root folder named xroxcars of the sample application contains the following web.config file (I've omitted the <session> element that defines the way that sessions are supported from this listing for clarity):

```
<configuration>
  <system.web>
    <!-- specify that we will use Forms authentication -->
    <authentication mode="Forms">
      <forms name="XroxCars" path="/" loginUrl="secure/login.aspx"
             protection="All" timeout="30" >
      </forms>
    </authentication>
  </system.web>
</configuration>
```

I'm using Forms-based authentication, and I specify that the name of the application is XroxCars. This name is used in the cookie I send to the client following successful authentication. I also specify that the cookie should apply to the complete site, so that it is sent back to the server with every request to a page from the site. In theory, I could specify only the secure subfolder here, but (as I discussed earlier) it is generally more reliable to specify the whole site and thereby make sure that the cookie is always returned.

The loginUrl value is the path (relative to the location of the web.config file) of the page that visitors use to provide their login credentials. I also specify that I want all normal encoding techniques to be used to protect the cookie contents, and that the cookie will expire in 30 minutes. So, if the user does not access a restricted page within 30 minutes, he or she will effectively be logged out automatically.

You'll notice that I don't specify a list of users in the <authentication> section of the web.config file. I could, and then ASP.NET would automatically check to see if the credentials provided are acceptable or not. However, I want to be able to add new users automatically and store more details about each one, without having to keep updating the web.config file (remember that each change to it will force a restart to the application). So, instead, I keep the user details in a database table, and perform the authentication checks myself.

The "secure" Subfolder `web.config` File

The Forms authentication settings I specified in the root folder of the application (Xroxcars) apply to all the folders and subfolders within our application—the entire Xrox Car Company site. However, the default authorization settings (in machine.config) allow all users—anonymous or otherwise—to access all ASP.NET resources in these folders.

To protect a specific subfolder, all you need to do is specify the authentication options required for that folder in a web.config file located there. In the xroxcars/secure subfolder, I have the following web.config file:

```
<configuration>
<system.web>
  <authorization>
    <deny users="?" />
  </authorization>
</system.web>
</configuration>
```

This prevents anonymous access to ASP.NET resources located in this folder. The special symbol "?" simply means "anonymous users." Now any visitor who wants to access the My Cars page must be authenticated first, and then authorized by ASP.NET.

Looking at the lower section of Figure 11-2, you can see that the Forms authentication process will automatically redirect unauthenticated users to the page named login.aspx. In that page, the task is to decide if the user is to be allowed access, and if so tell ASP.NET to generate the appropriate cookie and then redirect the user to the page originally requested (mycars.aspx).

> **NOTE** *Remember that all the ASP.NET authentication and authorization processes only apply to resources that are accessed by ASP.NET. In other words, they only prevent anonymous access to file types that are mapped to the ASP.NET process in IIS Manager. By default, this does not include things like* .htm, .inc, .pdf, .doc *and* .zip *files, and so on.*

Authentication for Cookie-less Clients

Of course, while I've been getting excited about how easy all this is to achieve in ASP.NET, there is one other scenario to consider. The site demands session support from users, and I implement this using cookie-less sessions (URL munging) for clients that don't support cookies. But what happens to Forms-based authentication when there is no client-side cookie support? The answer is simple—it doesn't work.

> **NOTE** *For this reason, the* web.config *file in the root folder of the cookie-less version of the application* (cookieless-xroxcars) *does not contain an* <authentication> *or* <authorization> *section. And there is no* web.config *file in the* cookieless-xroxcars/secure *subfolder.*

In this case I have to provide some other mode of authentication and authorization. In the cookieless-xroxcars folder of the examples is the version of the Xrox Car

Company application that works with clients that don't support cookies (or have them disabled). Here, I use one of the more traditional techniques for limiting user access and forcing visitors to log on before accessing restricted content.

Custom Authentication and Authorization Techniques

Before the advent of ASP.NET, most Web sites had evolved techniques for forcing users to register and then log on before being allowed to access specific resources. The common techniques all use some "token" value that indicates if a user has been authenticated, and this value is stored between page requests in a cookie, the query string, a hidden <form> control, or in the user's ASP.NET session.

The "token" value is generated and persisted (using whichever technique is chosen from the preceding list) once the user has logged in. As each page is requested, a process (usually part of each page) checks that a suitable value exists to indicate that the user was authenticated, and optionally checks to see if this user is authorized to view the page or resource. If authorized, the user receives the page or resource. If not, the user is redirected to the login page.

Of course, when you think about it, this is just what ASP.NET Forms authentication does. Only it hides a lot of the difficult parts of the process and makes it much easer to implement. I don't need to worry about creating a suitable cookie or testing to see if it exists.

But when you have to manage without cookies, you have to do all this work yourself. You also have to find somewhere else to persist the "token" value. You could add it to the query string as a name/value pair, but that makes it easy for a user to bookmark the page complete with the authentication "token," and so the user can avoid logging on at a later date. It's also easy for users to break in without being authenticated by simply typing the value themselves, so you would be forced to use some dynamic or random value that changes every time to prevent this.

Alternatively, and a little safer (but not much) is the use of a hidden-type HTML control to hold the "token" value. However, while this is not immediately visible (and so it is not stored in Web server, proxy server, and router logs like the query string!) this can still leave you wide open to spoofing attacks by people who just build their own pages with the "token" inserted into a hidden-type control using the value attribute.

Instead, where I am guaranteed session support (as in the Xrox Car Company site), the best option is to store the "token" that indicates successful authentication in the user's session. That way it is never sent across the network, it will disappear when the user's session expires, and overall is generally a great deal more secure than the query string or <form> controls approach (Figure 11-3).

Figure 11-3. Storing an authentication token in the user's session

I still use the same login page to collect the values, and the same techniques to authenticate the user against the contents of the example database table. The only differences are in the way the "token" that indicates successful authentication is stored. You'll see how I implement this cookie-less approach when you look at the login.aspx page in detail soon.

The Process Step-By-Step

While I use two different techniques to perform the authentication and authorization process in the example site (depending on whether the client support cookies, as I've just been discussing), the process as a whole is the same. In this section, I'll pull together all the aspects and requirements so that you can see exactly what the login and register page must achieve. First I summarize the steps, and then look at the whole thing in more detail. Figure 11-4 is the obligatory schematic.

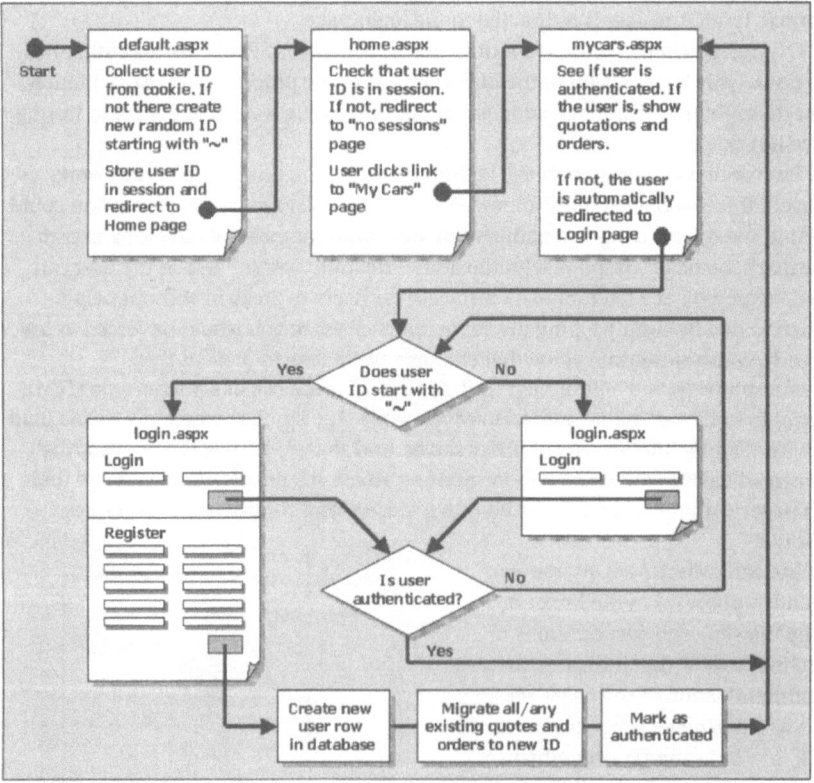

Figure 11-4. The authentication process for the Xrox Car Company site

The process steps are also summarized in a little more detail in the next section, which should help to make it clearer:

- In default.aspx, either collect the existing ID from a cookie sent with the request when the user first enters the site, or generate a new random user ID if there is no cookie. The user ID is then stored in the user's ASP.NET session.

- In the Home page, check that there is a user ID in the session. If not, redirect the user to a page that indicates the problem, and asks the user to either enable cookies or use the alternative cookie-less version of the application.

- When the user attempts to access a page in the secure folder (mycars.aspx), check to see if the user has been authenticated (in other words, has the user logged on to the application yet?). In the "standard" version of the application, ASP.NET Forms-based authentication does this for you. In the cookie-less version, look for a session value to indicate this.

- If the user has been authenticated, display the visitor's quotations and orders and allow the user to place an order.

- If not yet authenticated, redirect the user to the Login page. Here check to see if an "anonymous" User ID is in use. Anonymous user IDs (ones generated randomly the first time the user visits the site or if there is no existing cookie containing a user ID) start with the "~" character.

- If this is an anonymous user ID, the page displays both the "login" controls and the "register" controls. If the user has already registered, but "lost" the cookie containing the user ID, he or she can enter the details of the account that was created when that user registered, and log on using this. Or the user can register if he or she has not done so before (Figure 11-5).

- If this is not an anonymous user ID, you know that the user has already registered and so you just display the "login" controls (See Figure 11-6).

If the login succeeds (meaning that the user is authenticated), he or she is redirected to the My Cars page. If the login fails, I just redisplay the same set of controls on the login page again.

If the user registers (rather than logging in using an existing account), I create a row in the tblUsers table in the database. Then I have to check if the user has any quotes already stored against this anonymous user ID, and if so migrate these across to the new permanent user ID. I also mark them as being authenticated (using the ASP.NET Forms authentication methods or by writing the token to the session) before redirecting the user to the My Cars page.

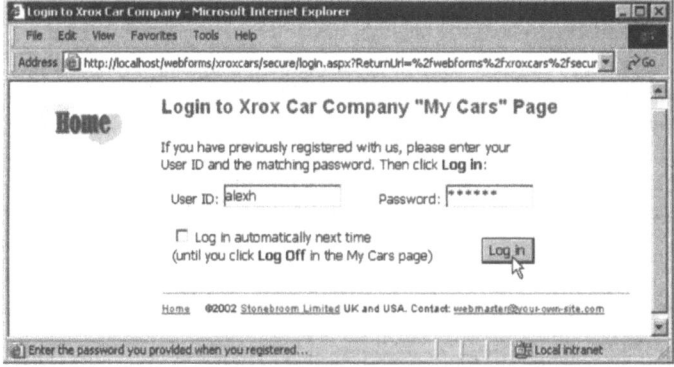

Figure 11-5. The login page for an anonymous visitor

Figure 11-6. The login page for a registered user

Why Use Anonymous User IDs?

You'll notice that some of the complexity in this process is caused by the fact that I use an anonymous user ID to start with. Then, in some cases, I have to switch over to accessing the restricted My Cars page under the context of a different user. The reason for this is that I wanted to delay presenting the user with a login dialog for as long as possible.

It can be off-putting, when you are browsing a site, to be forced to register before you can examine the products and decide what to buy. Most modern sites avoid this by allowing you to fill your shopping cart without having to register or log in. Only when you get to the checkout is this required.

This is the approach I've taken, and you can see that—while it adds some complexity—it's not really that hard to do. Visitors can browse the range of vehicles, view the details of each one, configure them to suit their requirements, and save one or more quotations if they wish. All this is possible with an anonymous user ID or a registered user ID.

The main point is to use some value for the automatically allocated anonymous ID that makes it easy to differentiate from a registered user ID. I could, of course, look to see if the user was already registered by scanning the database table, and present a register screen if that user is not found. However, I felt that my approach was easier and more efficient in the long run, avoiding database lookups where possible.

Storing the user ID in a cookie on the user's machine (where cookies are supported) also allows us to automatically pick it up whenever the user accesses the site, and display it in the login page so that the user only has to type his or her password. OK, you may decide for security reasons *not* to pre-fill the user ID text box, but that depends on your requirements for the site and whether you think that the risk it adds outweighs the benefit to the user.

Why Use a Combined Login and Register Page?

You can also see that I use a combined "login" and "register" page. Many sites implement different pages for these two features, so that every user sees the login page first. This login page contains a link to a separate page where the user can register if that user hasn't done so before. If you implement custom input validation techniques client-side, using separate pages is often easier to manage. It also means that you can submit the user's value to different pages if required—one for logging in and a different one for registering.

However, there is the postback architecture in ASP.NET. It does its utmost to persuade you to submit pages back to themselves for processing, rather than to a different "handler" page. Meanwhile, you can benefit from the extra capabilities that the ASP.NET server controls provide to make the work of handling the user input, validating it, and storing it much easier.

There are a couple of downsides to this approach, however—although I work around them in the example site. As you'll see later on, I've had to abandon client-side validation because I can't decide which "set" of controls the user will fill in when first loading the page. The user might have "lost" the user ID cookie, but remember the login details. In this case that user would enter these details and click Login. However, the same user might not have registered before, and so will use the other "set" of controls and click Register. With ASP.NET client-side validation enabled, one "set" of controls will always be invalid, preventing the page from being submitted.

Second, having two "submit" buttons (Login and Register) on the same page can cause some confusion if the user presses the Return key instead of clicking the appropriate button. In traditional ASP pages, you can use separate <form> sections with only one submit button on each <form>. The browser submits the <form> that contains the input focus when the **Return** key is pressed; so (assuming that the user typed values into one of the text boxes on that form before pressing the **Return** key) the appropriate one is submitted

However, ASP.NET only allows you to include one server-side <form> section in a page, so both controls are on the same form. Only the first one (in the order of the HTML declarations) can be "pressed" using the **Return** key, so if the user fills in the "register" section controls and presses **Return** there will be an error because this user has effectively clicked the Login button.

In the login.aspx page you get around this (where possible) by disabling the buttons using interactive client-side script to achieve the same effect. When the user types in a text box, the Submit button is disabled for the other "set" of controls. You'll see how when you look at this page in detail next.

The Login and Register Page

In this section of the chapter, you'll explore the workings of the "login and register" page in detail. I start by giving you a quick look at the HTML declarations, and a discussing of the way I use the ASP.NET Validation controls to check the user's input. Then I'll move on and show you the code in the page that makes it all work.

The HTML Page Declarations

Basically, the structure of the "login and register" page (login.aspx) is simple. Use exactly the same formatting, style sheet declaration, and "skip to" links as I did in the pages you've seen in previous chapters. In the login.aspx page, the main difference is within the single server-side ASP.NET <form> section. Here you have a two-column single-row table that contains the link back to the Home page in the left-hand column, and all remaining page content in the right-hand column. The login and register controls make up this content, consisting of:

- A section containing the user name and password text boxes and Login button for visitors that have already registered

- A section containing an ASP.NET ValidationSummary control that displays any validation errors

- A section containing an ASP.NET Panel control that encloses the text boxes and Register button for visitors who have not previously registered

An outline view of the page structure follows:

login.aspx

```
...
<form runat="server">
<table width="100%" border="0" cellspacing="0" cellpadding="10">
<tbody>
 <tr>
  <td valign="top" width="110px">
    <a Title="Back to List of Models" href="../home.aspx">
     <img src="../images/btn_home.gif" width="100" height="49" hspace="3"
          vspace="2" alt="Home Page" border="0" /></a>
  </td>
  <td align="left">
    <a name="content" />
    <font face="Arial,Helvetica,sans-serif" size="4" color="#b50055">
    <p class="large-red-text">
      <b>Login to Xrox Car Company "My Cars" Page</b></p></font>
    <!-- "Login" controls for existing user -->
    <!-- HTML and validation controls go here -->
    <!-- summary of validation errors -->
    <!-- ASP.NET ValidationSummary control here -->
    <asp:panel id="pnlRegister" Visible="False" runat="server">
      <!-- "Register" controls for new user -->
      <!-- HTML and validation control declarations here -->
      <!-- not visible by default, displayed as required -->
    </asp:panel>
  </td>
 </tr>
</tbody>
</form>
...
```

The ASP.NET Validation Controls

I'm using the ASP.NET Validation controls to check the user's input and make sure that it complies with the "rules" I established. For example, a user ID must be between 4 and 20 characters in length and cannot contain any spaces. These controls make it really easy to perform both server-side and client-side validation in an ASP.NET page.

However, as I noted towards the end of the previous section of this chapter, I am not using client-side validation at all. This is because I have two distinct "sections" of input controls on the page, and the user can fill in either section. The validation controls can only be enabled and disabled when a postback occurs, but if client-side validation is enabled the user won't be able to submit the page without filling in values for both sets of controls.

It also means that I have to "manually" enable and disable the validation controls server-side, as well as validating the controls individually, rather than relying on the automatic validation that occurs by default (like I did when validating an email address in the Home page). However, this approach demonstrates just how versatile the controls are, and how you can use them in a range of situations for specific and non-standard validation requirements.

The "Login" Section of the Page

The top section of the page contains the two text boxes where users can log in if they have previously registered. There are two validation controls attached to each of these text boxes, one to force a value to be entered (a RequiredFieldValidator control) and one to check that the entry meets the criteria for that field (a RegularExpressionValidator control). I also specify a range of attributes for each of the text boxes to make it easier for the user to see what I expect them to enter into that text box. The following listing shows the introductory text for this section of the page, and declarations for the first (User ID) text box:

```
<!-- "Login" controls for existing user -->
<font face="Tahoma,Arial,Helvetica,sans-serif" size="2">
<span class="body-text">
If you have previously registered with us, please enter your<br />
User ID and the matching password. Then click <b>Log in</b>:</span>
<table cellpadding="5" cellspacing="5" border="0">
 <tr>
  <td colspan="2" align="center" nowrap="nowrap">
   <font face="Tahoma,Arial,Helvetica,sans-serif" size="2">
   <span class="body-text">User ID:</span>
   <asp:TextBox id="txtLogonUserID" CssClass="body-text"
        TabIndex="1" Columns="15" runat="server"
        ToolTip="Enter your registered user ID"
        onkeypress="disableSubmit('Register')"
        onfocus="javascript:window.status='Enter registered userID'" />
   <asp:RequiredFieldValidator id="valRequLogonUserID" runat="server"
        ControlToValidate="txtLogonUserID" Display="dynamic"
        ErrorMessage="You must provide your User ID">
     *
   </asp:RequiredFieldValidator>
   <asp:RegularExpressionValidator id="valRegexLogonUserID" runat="server"
        ControlToValidate="txtLogonUserID" Display="dynamic"
        ValidationExpression="\S{4,20}"
        ErrorMessage="User ID must be 4 - 20 characters with no spaces">
     *
   </asp:RegularExpressionValidator>    
   ...
```

The TextBox *Control Attributes*

Among the attributes for the text boxes you can see that I specify:

- The TabIndex, allowing us to control the order that the input focus moves through the controls when the user presses the **Tab** key.

- The number of Columns (the physical size of each text box).

- The ToolTip that provides the pop-up tool-tip when the mouse hovers over the control.

- A value for the onkeypress event handler attribute, which executes the client-side JavaScript function named disableSubmit when the user types in this text box. You'll look at this function later.

- A value for the onfocus event handler attribute, which executes a JavaScript URL statement that displays a useful tip in the status bar of the browser when this control receives the input focus.

The Validation Control Attributes

The attributes included for the validation controls depend on the type of control. For the RequiredFieldValidator you must specify the ControlToValidate attribute to indicate which control you want to validate, and the ErrorMessage to display when the content is invalid. You also specify that the Display of the content of the control (an asterisk) should be "dynamic", so that it does not take up space on the page when the input control content is valid.

For the RegularExpressionValidator you also provide the ControlToValidate, Display, and ErrorMessage attribute values. You also have to provide a value for the ValidationExpression attribute to define what content is valid. As you saw in the Home page, this value is a regular expression that evaluates to True or False, depending on the contents of the validated control. The regular expression, "\S{4,20}", specifies that the value must be between 4 and 20 non-space characters.

NOTE *A guide to the syntax and general techniques for using regular expressions can be found in the version 1.0 .NET SDK at:*
ms-help://MS.NETFrameworkSDK/cpguidenf/html/
cpconcomregularexpressions.htm
or in the version 1.1 SDK at:
ms-help://MS.NETFrameworkSDKv1.1/cpguidenf/html/
cpconcomregularexpressions.htm

The Password Text Box and Validation Controls

The next listing shows the section that declares the Password text box and associated validation controls. You can see that it is virtually the same as the previous declaration for the User ID controls, with the notable difference that this time the TextMode attribute is added and set to "Password" so that the control displays asterisks as the user enters his or her password (it is rendered on the client as an `<input type="password">` control):

```
...
<span class="body-text">Password:</span>
<asp:TextBox id="txtLogonPWord" CssClass="body-text"
     TabIndex="2" TextMode="Password" Columns="10" runat="server"
     ToolTip="Enter the password you provided when you registered"
     onkeypress="disableSubmit('Register')"
     onfocus="javascript:window.status='Enter password provided ...'" />
<asp:RequiredFieldValidator id="valRequLogonPWord" runat="server"
     ControlToValidate="txtLogonPWord" Display="dynamic"
     ErrorMessage="You must provide your password">
  *
</asp:RequiredFieldValidator>
<asp:RegularExpressionValidator id="valRegexLogonPWord" runat="server"
     ControlToValidate="txtLogonPWord" Display="dynamic"
     ValidationExpression="\S{4,20}"
     ErrorMessage="Password must be 4-20 characters with no spaces">
  *
</asp:RegularExpressionValidator></font>
 </td>
</tr>
...
```

Allowing Persistent Authentication

Next comes the declaration of the check box (captioned Log in automatically next time). This allows users to persist the login even when they leave the site, close their browser, and then come back another time:

```
...
<tr>
 <td align="left" nowrap="nowrap">
  <font face="Tahoma,Arial,Helvetica,sans-serif" size="2">
  <span id="spnHideChecbox" runat="server">
  <asp:CheckBox id="chkPersist" CssClass="body-text" TabIndex="3"
       runat="server" />
  Log in automatically next time<br />
  (until you click <b>Log Off</b> in the My Cars page)</span></font>
 </td>
 ...
```

By default, a user's authenticated "session" expires automatically when the login timeout value is reached, or when the browser closes. In both cases, the cookie containing the authentication token is destroyed. However, you can cause the cookie to be stored on the user's machine with a long timeout (5 years), so that the user can return to the site and be automatically authenticated without having to log in again.

Only when you specifically destroy the cookie (or if the user destroys it) does that user need to log in again. You'll see how to destroy the cookie and "log off" the user when you look at the My Cars page in Chapter 12.

Persistent logins can present a security risk (a different user could access the site from this user's machine, or even hijack the cookie by copying it to another machine), but they are useful in applications where the security level requirement is low. I include the feature here mainly to demonstrate how it is achieved, should you wish to incorporate it into your pages.

The Login Button and Message Label

The final two controls in this section of the page are the Login button and a Label where the status messages are displayed (for example, if there is a data access problem). Validation errors are not displayed here—that's the job of the ValidationSummary control you'll see shortly.

The Button control that implements the Login button is shown next, and you can see that I again include a ToolTip and TabIndex attribute. The OnClick attribute specifies that the server-side event handler named DoLogin will be executed when the button is clicked.

```
...
<td align="right" valign="bottom">
 <font face="Tahoma,Arial,Helvetica,sans-serif" size="2">
 <asp:Button id="btnLogon" Text="Log in" CssClass="body-text"
      runat="server" ToolTip="Log in to view the My Cars page"
      TabIndex="4" OnClick="DoLogin" /></font>
 </td>
</tr>
...
```

The message label completes this section of the page. I turn off viewstate support so that any error messages will not be persisted across postbacks and confuse the user:

```
...
<tr>
 <td colspan="2" align="center" nowrap="nowrap">
 <font face="Tahoma,Arial,Helvetica,sans-serif" size="2">
 <b><asp:Label id="lblLoginMsg" CssClass="body-text"
         EnableViewState="false" runat="server" /></b></font>
 </td>
 </tr>
</table>
...
```

Figure 11-7 shows the Login section of the page, with the ToolTip for the button and the status message from the password text box visible.

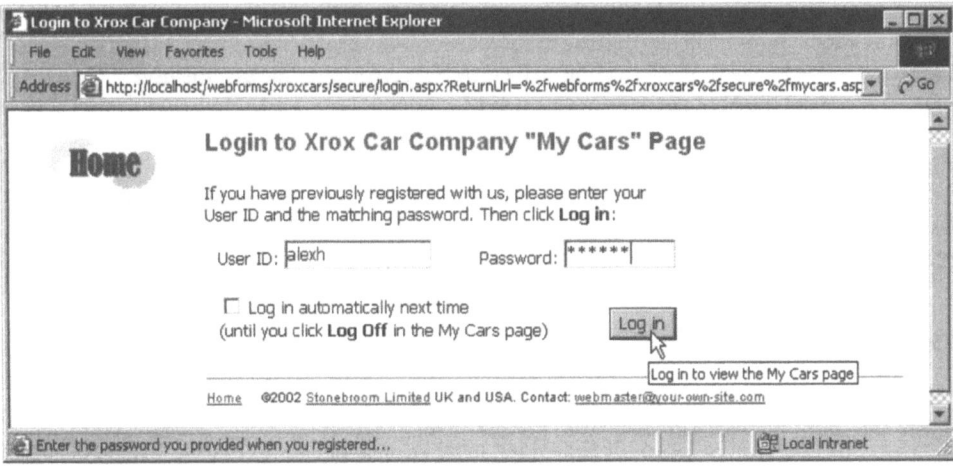

Figure 11-7. Logging in to the Xrox Car Company site

The ValidationSummary Control

The page contains two separate sections of controls, but only one ValidationSummary control. This will display validation errors from whichever section of the page the user submitted (Login or Register). Therefore I placed it between the Login and Register sections so the content is always displayed near any controls that may contain an error.

The only attribute I provide for the ValidationSummary control is the HeaderText to display above the list of validation errors:

```
...
<!-- summary of validation errors -->
<font face="Tahoma,Arial,Helvetica,sans-serif" size="2">
<asp:ValidationSummary id="valSummary" runat="server"
    HeaderText="<hr /><b>Sorry, your values cannot be accepted.</b><br />
             The following errors were found. Please check<br />
             the values you entered (marked with '*')</b>" />
</font>
...
```

The "Register" Section of the Page

The Register section of the page contains many more controls than the Login section, but the declarations are just about identical. For each text box I specify the Columns,

TabIndex, ToolTip, onkeypress, and onfocus attributes just as before. There are also (with one exception) the same two validation controls per text box—a RequiredFieldValidator and a RegularExpressionValidator.

The next listing shows the declaration of the introductory text for this section, followed by the User ID text box and associated validation controls. Notice that this section of the page is enclosed in an ASP.NET Panel control (which creates a <div> or a <table> depending on the client type). I set the Visible attribute to False for this Panel, so the content will not be included in the page by default. When I want to display the Register controls, I just have to set the Visible property to True at run time:

```
...
<asp:panel id="pnlRegister" visible="False" runat="server">
<!-- "Register" controls for new user -->
<hr size="1" /><p />
<font face="Tahoma,Arial,Helvetica,sans-serif" size="2">
<span class="body-text">
If you <b>have not</b> previously registered with us, you can do so
now.<br />Please complete the form below, indicating the User ID
and password<br />you want to use to access this site in future.
Then click <b>Register</b>:</span>
<table cellpadding="5" cellspacing="5" border="0">
 <tr>
  <td colspan="4" align="left" nowrap="nowrap">
    <font face="Tahoma,Arial,Helvetica,sans-serif" size="2">
    <span class="body-text">User ID (minimum 4 characters,
    no spaces):</span>
    <asp:TextBox id="txtUserID" CssClass="body-text"
        TabIndex="5" Columns="15" runat="server"
        ToolTip="Enter a User ID (4 to 20 characters, no spaces)"
        onkeypress="disableSubmit('Logon')"
        onfocus="javascript:window.status='User ID to log on in future'" />
    <asp:RequiredFieldValidator id="valRequUserID" runat="server"
        ControlToValidate="txtUserID" Display="dynamic"
        ErrorMessage="You must provide a User ID">
      *
    </asp:RequiredFieldValidator>
    <asp:RegularExpressionValidator id="valRegexUserID" runat="server"
        ControlToValidate="txtUserID" Display="dynamic"
        ValidationExpression="\S{4,20}"
        ErrorMessage="User ID must be 4-20 characters with no spaces">
      *
    </asp:RegularExpressionValidator></font>
  </td>
 </tr>
 ...
```

Comparing Control Values

To save space and repetition, I haven't listed all the other control declarations here. However, there are a few points worth noting. There is a text box for users to enter the password they want to use, and another one to confirm this password by entering it again.

The second of these text boxes has a RequiredFieldValidator attached to force a value to be entered, but instead of a RegularExpressionValidator I attach a CompareValidator control that compares the values in the two text boxes. To achieve this, I just set the ControlToCompare attribute to the ID of the first text box, and specify that the comparison Type is to compare the two values as strings:

```
<asp:CompareValidator id="valCompPWordCheck" runat="server"
    ControlToValidate="txtPWordCheck" Display="dynamic"
    ControlToCompare="txtPWord" Type="String"
    ErrorMessage="Password and confirmation do not match">*
</asp:CompareValidator></font></td>
```

Other Regular Expressions

The regular expression I used for the user ID and password is of the form "\S{4,20}". This specifies that the value must contain non-space characters (and be between 4 and 20 characters long in this case). However, when validating other controls, such as the name, address, and so forth, I want to allow spaces to be included in the value. So, in these controls, I specify a regular expression of the form ".{4,20}" instead. The full stop means "any alphanumeric character" rather than "any non-space alphanumeric character."

When validating the email address in the Home page I used a fairly simple regular expression:

```
".*@.*\..*"
```

This basically limits entries to [*any alphanumeric characters*]@[*any alphanumeric characters*].[*any alphanumeric characters*]. So, many non-valid values could be entered, though it does ensure that I get something that resembles an email address. If you want to be more specific, and lock down the possible range of values that can be entered, you can use one of the many regular expressions that are listed on different Web sites, or are in common use. This one more closely limits acceptable values to the standard formats for an email address:

```
"([a-zA-Z0-9_\-\.]+)@(([a-zA-Z0-9\-]+\.)+)([a-zA-Z0-9]{2,4})"
```

The Register Button and Message Label

Finally, the Register section contains a Button control to submit the page and a Label control to display messages—much like you saw earlier in the Login section. The Button control calls a server-side event handler named DoRegister when clicked:

```
  ...
  <td colspan="2" align="right" nowrap="nowrap">
   <font face="Tahoma,Arial,Helvetica,sans-serif" size="2">
   <asp:Button id="btnRegister" Text="Register" CssClass="body-text"
       runat="server"
       ToolTip="Click to register details and access the My Cars page"
       TabIndex="15" OnClick="DoRegister" />
   </font>
  </td>
 </tr><tr>
  <td colspan="4" align="center" nowrap="nowrap">
   <font face="Tahoma,Arial,Helvetica,sans-serif" size="2">
   <b><asp:Label id="lblRegisterMsg" CssClass="body-text"
         EnableViewState="false" runat="server" /></b></font>
  </td>
 </tr>
</table>
</asp:panel>
...
```

Figure 11-5, which you saw earlier, shows the page when the current user has a temporary user ID. The controls to register are visible this time.

The Client-Side Script Functions

It's a nice touch in a page where users have to enter values to set the input focus to the first control on the page, ready for them to start typing. And if there might be an existing value in that control, it's even nicer to select it so that they can just type a new value without having to delete the existing one, or press Tab to go to the next control.

The <body> element in my page defines a client-side event handler named setUserIDFocus that will be executed when the page has finished loading:

```
<body ... onload="setUserIDFocus()">
```

This function simply moves the input focus to the first User ID text box on the page, using the focus method, and then selects the entire content of that control to give the effect I want:

```
<script language="JavaScript">
<!--
function setUserIDFocus() {
  var txtUserID = document.forms[0].elements['txtLogonUserID'];
  txtUserID.focus();
  txtUserID.select();
}
...
```

Disabling the Submit Buttons

I discussed earlier, when explaining why I include both the Login and Register sections in the same page, how having two Submit buttons on the same <form> can cause confusion if the user presses the **Return** key instead of clicking the appropriate Submit button. To solve this, I include a client-side function in the example page that disables the Submit button for the section that the user is not interacting with.

All the text boxes in the Login section of the page contain the following onkeypress attribute, which executes the client-side function named disableSubmit when the user types in the text box. They pass in a String that indicates which section the user is interacting with:

```
onkeypress="disableSubmit('Logon')"
```

Likewise, all the text boxes in the Register section contain this onkeypress attribute:

```
onkeypress="disableSubmit('Register')"
```

The disableSubmit function simply has to detect which section is being used, and then enable and disable the appropriate Submit buttons by setting their (client-side HTML) disabled property. Notice that I check if the controls actually exist on the page first to prevent a script error. While the Login button should always exist, the Register button may not be included if this user already has a permanent user ID:

```
...
function disableSubmit(sAction) {
  var btnLogin = document.forms[0].elements['btnLogon'];
  var btnRegister = document.forms[0].elements['btnRegister'];
  if (btnRegister == null) return;
  if (sAction == 'Logon') {
    btnRegister.disabled = false;
    btnLogin.disabled = true;
  }
  else {
    btnLogin.disabled = false;
    btnRegister.disabled = true;
  }
}
//-->
</script>
```

Not all browsers support disabling of controls, and so the function will have no effect in these browsers. However, it does work in Internet Explorer 4 and later. And, because the disabled property is part of the specification for controls in the HTML DOM version 2 and CSS2, it works in the "version 6" browsers from Mozilla, Netscape, and Opera (Opera does not "gray out" disabled buttons, but it does prevent them from being used).

The ASP.NET Server-Side Code

Having seen the HTML and client-side code in the "login and register" page, the next step is to look at the server-side ASP.NET code that it contains. I declare three page-level variables to hold values that I'll use throughout the page. The sStyleSize and sConnect values are used in exactly the same way as in other pages you've already looked at. The user ID will be extracted from the user's session and stored in the sUserID variable:

```
' page-level variable to hold style size
Dim sStyleSize As String = "Standard"

' page-level variable to hold current user ID
Dim sUserID As String

' page-level variable to hold DB connection string
Dim sConnect As String
```

The Page_Load Event Handler

When the page loads, the first thing to do is ensure that I still have an active ASP.NET session. I do this in the same way as I've done in other pages you've seen by testing for the presence of the current user ID in the session (recall that I stored it there in default.aspx when the user first entered the site). If it's not there, I know that the session has expired, and so I redirect them to default.aspx to reestablish it:

```
Sub Page_Load()
  ' get current UserID from Session
  sUserID = CType(Session("WccUserID"), String)
  If sUserID = "" Then

    ' not in Session so browser does not support
    ' sessions or did not load default.aspx first
    Response.Clear()
    Response.Redirect("../default.aspx")
    Response.End()

  End If
  ...
```

Next, I extract the style sheet size from the user's session so that it can be inserted into the <link> element to select the correct style sheet (as in all the earlier pages you've examined). Then I can extract the connection string for the database from the web.config file:

```
...
' get style sheet size from Session
sStyleSize = CType(Session("WccStyleSize"), String)
' get database connection string from web.config
sConnect = ConfigurationSettings.AppSettings("XroxCarsConnectString")
...
```

Displaying the Register Section

Next, I decide if I need to display the section containing the Register controls.
Anonymous user IDs (for visitors who have not yet registered) start with "~", so
I just have to check for this. For an anonymous ID I make the Panel containing
the Register controls visible. For a permanent user ID, I hide the Panel and pre-fill
the User ID text box with the value I extracted from this user's session earlier on:

```
...
' if this is a temporary login name, may need to register
If sUserID.Substring(0, 1) = "~" Then
  ' make register controls visible
  pnlRegister.Visible = True

Else
  ' hide register controls
  pnlRegister.Visible = False

  ' display this user's ID in login text box
  txtLogonUserID.Text = sUserID

End If
...
```

Of course, if a user chooses as a permanent ID one that starts with this character,
that user will always see the Register controls, but it seems to be an unlikely situation
so I don't check for it. If you want to prevent this, just change the regular expression
in the validation control for the txtUserID text box to prevent a user from choosing
one that starts with "~".

Disabling the Validation Controls

I've already decided that I will have to "manually operate" the validation controls to
allow the page to contain two distinct sets of controls, only one set of which may be
filled with valid values each time. So, in the Page_Load event handler, I disable the
controls completely by turning off client-side validation and server-side validation
for every control in the page.

One nice feature when using the ASP.NET validation controls is that the Page object
exposes a collection of all the validation controls (Page.Validators), which allows me to
easily iterate through them. This saves me from having to iterate through all the controls in the Page.Controls collection and check to see if each one is a validation control
or not.

For each validation control found, I set the `EnableClientScript` and `Enabled` properties to `False`:

```
...
' disable client-side validation and disable the default
' automatic validation to allow page to be submitted
' when only some of the controls are visible/filled
Dim oValidator As BaseValidator
For Each oValidator In Page.Validators
  oValidator.EnableClientScript = False
  oValidator.Enabled = False
Next
...
```

Of course, I could have disabled client-side validation for the controls by including the attribute `EnableClientScript="False"` in the control declarations. However, I have to iterate through them to set the `Disabled` property each time, because I change this value elsewhere in the page. It will be maintained in the viewstate otherwise.

Adapting the Page for Cookie-Less Clients

The last task in the `Page_Load` event handler is a minor diversion to ensure that I cope correctly with clients that do not support cookies. If I am using cookie-less sessions, I must set the "authenticated" flag value in the session to indicate that the user is not currently authenticated. Also, because I can't use cookies, I cannot offer persistent authentication. So I hide the check box where the user would normally be able to select this option:

```
...
' see if we are using cookie-less sessions
If Session.IsCookieless Then

  ' set authentication flag in session to "no"
  ' set to "yes" after successful login/registration
  Session("WCCUserAuthenticated") = "no"
  ' hide the persistent cookie auto-logon option
  ' as this only applies to Forms-based authentication
  spnHideChecbox.Visible = False
End If
End Sub
```

The DoLogin Event Handler

When the user enters the user ID and password for an existing "account" in the top section of the page, and clicks the Login button, the `DoLogin` routine is executed. In it, I first have to validate the values the user entered, and I do this by manipulating the validation controls that were declared within this section of the page.

I used a specific set of ID values for these validation controls, as you can confirm from the listings I showed you earlier. The validation controls in the Login section have the string "Logon" in their control ID: for example valRequLogonUserID and valRequLogonPWord. The controls in the register section do not contain this string.

So I can iterate through the Page.Validators collection and examine the ID of each one to see if it contains this string. If it does, I first have to enable it, and then call its Validate method to perform the validation:

```
Sub DoLogin(oSender As Object, oArgs As EventArgs)
' check if User ID and password exist in database
' and redirect them to the "My Cars" page if valid
  Dim oValidator As BaseValidator
  Dim sValidatorID As String
  For Each oValidator In Page.Validators
    sValidatorID = oValidator.ID
    If sValidatorID.IndexOf("Logon") > 0 Then

      ' this is a validator for the "Login" controls
      ' so enable it and perform validation
      oValidator.Enabled = True
      oValidator.Validate()

    End If
  Next
  ...
```

Now the IsValid property of the Page object will be set depending on the results of the validation, but only for any enabled validation controls. So, the next step is to see if there were any validation errors. If there were, the ValidationSummary control will display the values of the ErrorMessage property for each enabled validation control, and I don't have to do any more. The page will be redisplayed with the errors visible to the user ready for corrective action.

If there were no validation errors, I can continue and check if this user can be authenticated. However, the AuthenticateUser routine (which is located elsewhere in this page, and described in detail later) returns the permanent user ID of the current user by updating the sUserID variable to this value.

This means that—if the user has already registered, but has entered the site without the cookie that holds his or her permanent user ID—that user will currently have a temporary "anonymous" user ID in the session and in the variable sUserID. So if the user saved any quotations before reaching the login page, these quotations will have been saved using the anonymous ID. It means that I need to save this ID in another variable so that I can migrate these quotations across to the user's permanent user ID afterwards:

```
  ...
  ' see if validation controls indicate that all values
  ' in appropriate set of controls on page are valid
  ' if not, page will display validation errors
  If Page.IsValid Then
```

```
' if user has already registered but entered site this time
' with a temporary UserID we need to save this temporary ID
' so that we can migrate any quotes they received before
' switching over to their registered user name
Dim sAnonID As String = ""
If sUserID.Substring(0, 1) = "~" Then
  sAnonID = sUserID
End If
...
```

Now I can call my AuthenticateUser routine, and if it returns True I know that the user was successfully authenticated. Then, if the user was using an anonymous temporary ID, I call another routine in the page named MigrateExistingRows. This simply swaps the user ID value of any rows that contain this user's anonymous ID to the registered permanent user ID:

```
...
If AuthenticateUser() Then
  ' after authentication sUserID contains registered User ID
  ' if they were using an anonymous ID then now need to migrate
  ' any existing quotes to registered user ID they provided
  If sAnonID > "" Then
    MigrateExistingRows(sAnonID, sUserID)
  End If
  ...
```

All that remains now is to redirect the user to the My Cars page. If this user is using cookie-less sessions, it means that ASP.NET Forms authentication is not actually being used. So I have to create my own routine to mark such users as being authenticated and then redirect them to the My Cars page. You'll see this routine, named RedirectFromCookielessLoginPage, described shortly:

```
...
' redirect to page originally requested (mycars.aspx)
' depends on what session support we are using
If Session.IsCookieless Then
  ' using custom session-based authentication
  RedirectFromCookielessLoginPage(sUserID)
Else
...
```

However, if the user is using Forms authentication, I have a couple of things to do. I have to make sure that the cookie stored on this visitor's machine contains the current registered User ID (in case the user "lost" the original cookie and is using a temporary one). A routine named UpdateUserIDCookie that I've included in my page does this, and I provide the user ID I want to store in the cookie as a parameter.

Then I can simply call the RedirectFromLoginPage method of the FormsAuthentication object, providing as the first parameter the ID of the user I want to be marked as authenticated. This method creates the ASP.NET authentication cookie and places it on the client, then redirects the user to the page that was originally requested. In my case, this will be the My Cars page. Notice that I specify the value of the "persistent authentication" check box as the second parameter when I call this method. If this is True (checked), a long-term *persistent* cookie will be created instead of a short-term *session* cookie that expires when the browser is closed or the timeout period ends:

```
...
Else
   ' using Forms-based authentication
   ' update cookie to reflect current user name
   UpdateUserIDCookie()
   ' redirect to page they originally requested
   ' create persistent cookie if selected in page
   FormsAuthentication.RedirectFromLoginPage(sUserID, _
                                              chkPersist.Checked)
   End If
 End If
End If
End Sub
```

The DoLogin event handler that I've just been looking at uses four other routines to perform its magic. I described briefly what these routines do in the previous section, and I'll look at each one in more detail next. The four routines are:

- AuthenticateUser, which searches in the tblUsers table for an existing user ID and password combination, and returns the actual user ID from the database if a match is found.

- MigrateExistingRows, which changes the value of the user ID in the tblQuoteOrders table from a temporary anonymous user ID to the correct permanent registered user ID for all rows that match a specified anonymous user ID.

- RedirectFromCookielessLoginPage, which marks a user as being authenticated, and then redirects the user to the My Cars page. It is used when the browser does not support cookies.

- UpdateUserIDCookie, which simply writes a new cookie to the client's machine containing the specified user ID.

Authenticating an Existing User

The AuthenticateUser routine is shown next. In it I first collect the user ID from the text box on the page and remove any leading or trailing spaces. In theory the validation controls will prevent the user from entering any spaces, but it does no harm to be sure! Then I specify the name of a stored procedure in the database that will select the matching user, and create the connection and command objects as usual—setting the CommandType to indicate that I'm using a stored procedure:

```
Function AuthenticateUser() As Boolean
' check if this UserID/password is valid

    ' get login User ID specified in form controls
    ' and remove any stray spaces from start and end
    Dim sLogonID As String = txtLogonUserID.Text
    sLogonID = sLogonID.Trim()
    ' specify the stored procedure name
    Dim sProcName As String = "AuthenticateUser"

    ' create connection and command objects
    Dim sqlConn As New SqlConnection(sConnect)
    Dim sqlComm As New SqlCommand(sProcName, sqlConn)
    sqlComm.CommandType = CommandType.StoredProcedure
    ...
```

The stored procedure I use, named AuthenticateUser, is relatively simple. It expects to be supplied with two parameters—the user ID and password—and it returns from the database the value of the user ID for the row that contains the specified user ID and password. This means that, if the user enters a user ID in a different letter case (they are not case-sensitive), it will be returned in the correct case:

```
CREATE PROCEDURE AuthenticateUser
@UserID varchar(20), @UserPW varchar(255) AS
SELECT UserID FROM tblUsers WHERE UserID = @UserID AND UserPW = @UserPW
```

> **NOTE** *By default SQL Server and most other databases are not case-sensitive when selecting or matching text values. However, if you have installed and/or configured your database to run in case-sensitive mode, the user ID will be case-sensitive unless you add code to convert it to a specific case (probably all lowercase) when storing and retrieving it each time.*

Encrypting the Password

So now you can think about where the other parameter for the stored procedure, the user's password, comes from. I am storing the passwords in the database in encrypted form, and so I have to encrypt the password that the user entered into the text box before I can use it as a parameter for the stored procedure, and in the WHERE clause of that stored procedure.

The delightfully named HashPasswordForStoringInConfigFile method of the FormsAuthentication object can convert a text string into the equivalent SHA1 or MD5 *hash* equivalent value, and this is how I convert the user's password. The great thing about using encrypted hash values is that they are automatically case-sensitive, so (for example) the hash for "Alex" is completely different from the hash for "alex". Therefore the password check is case-sensitive because I am actually comparing two hash values in the stored procedure's WHERE clause.

The next line of the AuthenticateUser routine creates the password hash, and then I can add the parameters I need to the Command object's Parameters collection:

```
...

' create SHA1 hash of password provided (could use "MD5" instead)
Dim sPWHash As String
sPWHash = FormsAuthentication.HashPasswordForStoringInConfigFile _
                                    (txtLogonPWord.Text, "SHA1")
' add the parameters to the Command object
sqlComm.Parameters.Add("@UserID", sLogonID)
sqlComm.Parameters.Add("@UserPW", sPWHash)
...
```

As a brief diversion here, it's worth mentioning one problem that does arise when storing passwords only in "hashed" form. A hash is a mathematical function that is easy to perform one way (creating the hash) but extremely difficult to perform the other way (extracting the original value from the hashed value). This is intentional, as it is the whole reason for using a hash to encrypt the value.

However, many sites offer a "Forgot your password?" feature that emails the account password to the email address that the account is registered for. I could email my users the encrypted hash but that would be no help, as they could not tell from that what the original password was. And neither can I, so I can't offer this kind of feature. All I could do is implement some system for allowing them to provide a new password and then update the database table with the hash of this password.

Executing the Stored Procedure

Now I can execute the stored procedure. I know that it returns a rowset that should contain only one row, and that row has a single column (the user ID). So, for speed and efficiency, I can use the ExecuteScalar method rather than creating and returning a DataReader object. The ExecuteScalar method returns just the value of the first column in the first row of the resulting rowset.

Therefore, if the result returned by ExecuteScalar is the same as the value of the user ID stored in the sUserID variable, I know that the user exists and provided the correct password. All I then have to do is update the page-level sUserID variable to the actual (letter-case correct) user ID, and store it in the user's ASP.NET session as well. Then I can return True to indicate successful authentication. However, if I don't get a match on the user ID and password, I display a message in the Label control in this section of the page and return False:

```
...
Try
  ' execute the stored procedure
  sqlConn.Open()
  If sqlComm.ExecuteScalar() = sLogonID Then
    ' found matching row so use new logon as UserID and update session
    sUserID = sLogonID
    Session("WCCUserID") = sUserID
    Return True
  Else
    ' no matching row found
    lblLoginMsg.Text = "* Invalid User ID or password, try again..."
    Return False
  End If
Catch objError As Exception
  'display error details
  lblLoginMsg.Text = "* Error while accessing database.<br />" _
                     & objError.Message & "<br />" & objError.Source

  Return False
Finally
  sqlConn.Close()
End Try
End Function
```

The remainder of the code is the Catch section of the Try...Catch construct (where I display the error details), and the Finally section that closes the database connection irrespective of whether there was an error or not.

Migrating Existing Quotations to the New User ID

The next routine I use in the DoLogin event handler is responsible for migrating any existing quotes that have been saved with an anonymous user ID to the user's permanent registered user ID. For this I use a simple stored procedure named MigrateQuotes, which accepts two parameters—the old (anonymous) and the new (registered) user ID:

```
CREATE PROCEDURE MigrateQuotes
@AnonUserID varchar(20), @NewUserID varchar(20) AS
UPDATE tblQuoteOrder SET UserID = @NewUserID WHERE UserID = @AnonUserID
```

> **NOTE** *The related child table named* tblQuoteOrderExtras *is linked to the* tblQuoteOrder *table by a primary key/foreign key constraint. The primary key of the* tblQuoteOrder *table is an* IDENTITY *value that is created automatically, and not the user ID (which could occur many times in the* tblQuoteOrderExtras *table). Therefore the user ID is not included in the* tblQuoteOrderExtras *table, and so I don't need to update any rows in this table.*

511

The `MigrateExistingRows` routine receives the two values I need when it is called, and returns a `Boolean` result to indicate success or failure. All the code uses well-tried techniques that are identical to many other routines you've seen in other pages of the example site.

As there could be zero or more existing quotations for this user, I can't use the number of rows that were updated to check for success or failure of the stored procedure. However, it will raise an error if the update process itself fails (for example, if you do not grant the correct permissions or the connection fails). So I return `True` if the `ExecuteNonQuery` method does *not* cause an error, or `False` if it does:

```
Function MigrateExistingRows(sAnonID As String, sNewID As String) _
                                                  As Boolean
' migrate existing quotes in database for anonymous user
' to the new user ID they specified when registering
  ' specify the stored procedure name
  Dim sProcName As String = "MigrateQuotes"

  ' create connection and command objects
  Dim sqlConn As New SqlConnection(sConnect)
  Dim sqlComm As New SqlCommand(sProcName, sqlConn)
  sqlComm.CommandType = CommandType.StoredProcedure

  ' add parameters to Command
  sqlComm.Parameters.Add("@AnonUserID", sAnonID)
  sqlComm.Parameters.Add("@NewUserID", sNewID)

  Try
    ' execute the stored procedure
    sqlConn.Open()
    sqlComm.ExecuteNonQuery()
    Return True

  Catch objError As Exception
    Return False
  Finally
    sqlConn.Close()
  End Try
End Function
```

Redirecting Cookie-less Clients

When dealing with clients that do not support cookies, I can't use ASP.NET Forms authentication. So I have to build my own version of the `RedirectFromLoginPage` method that the `FormsAuthentication` object exposes (and that I use in the `DoLogin` event handler for clients that do support cookies).

The custom `RedirectFromCookielessLoginPage` routine is called after I have authenticated a user, and its task is to mark the user as being authenticated and then redirect the user to the appropriate page. All that's involved is to store the token value "yes" in the `WCCUserAuthenticated` session variable, then perform the redirection:

```
Sub RedirectFromCookielessLoginPage(sUserID As String)
' custom routine to redirect client to mycars.aspx page after
' successful authentication when using cookieless sessions
   ' set session flag to indicate registration succeeded
   Session("WCCUserAuthenticated") = "yes"
   Response.Clear()
   Response.Redirect("mycars.aspx")
   Response.End()

End Sub
```

Notice that I hard-coded the page URL for redirection within the code because I know that I will only ever redirect to the My Cars page. This is the only page (other than the "login and register" page) in the secure folder, and the only one for which access is restricted and authentication is required.

This is in contrast to the FormsAuthentication.RedirectFromLoginPage method, which automatically redirects users to the page they originally requested (the one that they were trying to view when they were redirected to the "login" page). When this redirection to the login page takes place, the URL of the original page is appended to the query string, and so the RedirectFromLoginPage method can tell which page it needs to redirect the user to after successful authentication. You can see this in the Address bar in Figure 11-8.

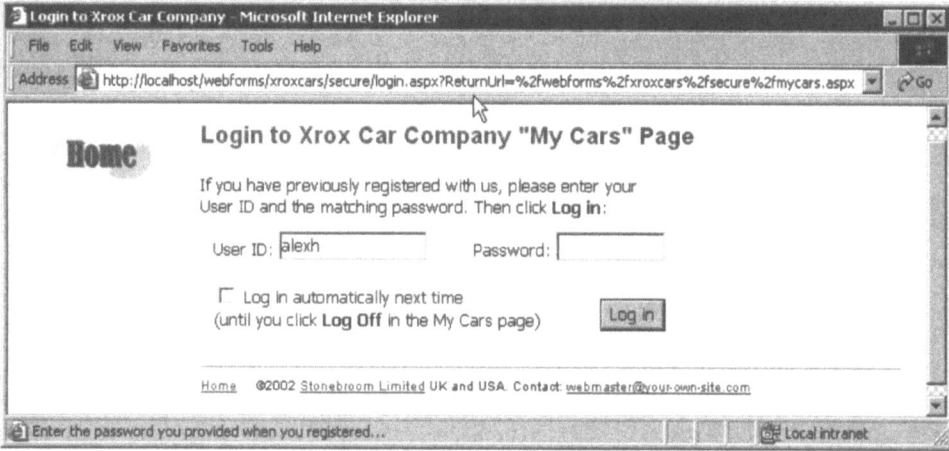

Figure 11-8. The redirection details stored within the page URL

I could, of course, replicate this behavior in the custom RedirectFromCookielessLoginPage routine if required. I would have to add the URL of the current page to the query string in the page that causes the login page to be loaded (in my case the My Cars page), but this can easily be extracted from the `Request.Path` property. Then, in the `RedirectFromCookielessLoginPage` routine, I could extract this URL from the query string and perform the appropriate redirection.

Updating the User ID Cookie

The final routine that I call from the `DoLogin` event handler is responsible for writing the cookie containing the user ID to the client's machine. If I have changed the user ID from an anonymous one to a registered one as the user logged into the site, I have to do this so that the user's next visit will take place under the context of the correct user ID.

The code is just the same as I used to create the cookie in the `default.aspx` page. I create a new `HttpCookie` object, setting the name and value within the constructor, and then specify that it should apply to the entire site and that it should not expire for five years. Then I add it to the cookies collection for this page:

```
Sub UpdateUserIDCookie()
' write new cookie with UserID to client's browser
  Dim oCookie As New HttpCookie("WccUserID", sUserID)
  oCookie.Path = "/"
  Dim dNow As DateTime = Now()
  oCookie.Expires = dNow.AddYears(5)
  Response.Cookies.Add(oCookie)

End Sub
```

> **NOTE** *Remember that this cookie is not the same as the authentication cookie that is created automatically by the Forms authentication process. The cookie I create in the preceding routine only contains the user ID, and is used to persist it between visits to the site.*

The DoRegister Event Handler

The other event handler in the page, `DoRegister`, is executed when the user clicks the Register button rather than the Login button. The task here is more complex, because I have to:

- Validate the registration values that the user entered

- Insert the new user into the database

- Migrate any existing quotes to the new user ID

- Mark the user as being authenticated

- Redirect the user to the My Cars page

Luckily (or perhaps due to good design!), I already have routines that I can use to perform several of these tasks. I used these in the DoLogin event handler you've just been looking at.

Validating the User's Values

The first step in the DoRegister event handler is much the same as you saw in the DoLogin event handler. I validate the values that the user entered, but this time for the controls in the lower (Register) section of the page. The technique is just the same, but I test for validation control IDs that do *not* contain the string "Logon":

```
Sub DoRegister(oSender As Object, oArgs As EventArgs)
' runs when the "Register" button is clicked
' add user to database, migrate any existing quotes
' and redirect them to the "My Cars" page
  ' cause appropriate set of validation controls to
  ' check the values of the controls on the page
  Dim oValidator As BaseValidator
  Dim sValidatorID As String
  For Each oValidator In Page.Validators
    sValidatorID = oValidator.ID
    If sValidatorID.IndexOf("Logon") < 0 Then

      ' this is a validator for the "Register" controls
      ' so enable it and perform validation
      oValidator.Enabled = True
      oValidator.Validate()

    End If
  Next
  ...
```

Now I can see if validation succeeded, and if so I save the temporary anonymous user ID just as I did in the DoLogin event handler:

```
  ...
  ' see if validation controls indicate that all values
  ' in appropriate set of controls on page are valid
  ' if not, page will display validation errors
  If Page.IsValid Then

    ' save existing "anonymous" user ID
    Dim sAnonID As String = sUserID
    ...
```

Inserting the New User Details

Next I attempt to insert the new user's details into the tblUsers table in the database. I use a separate routine named InsertNewUser (elsewhere within this page), which returns True or False depending on whether the new values can be inserted. You'll look at this routine later:

```
...
If InsertNewUser() Then
  ...
```

Providing that I did successfully add the new user to the database, I can now migrate any existing quotations he or she may have saved to their new registered user ID. I use the same MigrateExistingRows routine as I did in the DoLogin event handler, and specify the old and new user ID values as parameters:

```
...
' inserted new user into tblUsers in DB so now
' update any existing quotes for old temporary
' anonymous user ID to new registered user ID
MigrateExistingRows(sAnonID, sUserID)
...
```

The remainder of the DoRegister routine is again remarkably similar to the DoLogin routine you saw earlier. If the client does not support cookies I use the custom RedirectFromCookielessLoginPage routine to update the "authenticated flag" value in this user's session and then redirect the user to the My Cars page.

If the client does support cookies (and therefore supports Forms-based authentication), I update the cookie and call the RedirectFromLoginPage method of the FormsAuthentication object to mark the user as being authenticated and redirect this user to the My Cars page. Notice that this time I specify the value False for the persistent login parameter to the RedirectFromLoginPage method, as this is safer. The user can decide to switch on persistent login when he or she next logs into the site if desired:

```
...
' redirect to page originally requested (mycars.aspx)
' depends on what session support we are using
If Session.IsCookieless Then
  ' using custom session-based authentication
  RedirectFromCookielessLoginPage(sUserID)
Else
  ' using Forms-based authentication
  ' update cookie to reflect new user name
  UpdateUserIDCookie()

  ' do not create persistent authentication cookie this time
  FormsAuthentication.RedirectFromLoginPage(sUserID, False)
End If
```

```
    Else
      'display error details
      lblRegisterMsg.Text = "* The User ID you specified is already in use"
    End If
  End If
End Sub
```

Inserting a New User into the Database

The only remaining section of code in the "login and register" page that I haven't discussed yet is how to insert a new user into the tblUsers table of the database. As you'll be expecting by now, I use a stored procedure to perform the row insert. This stored procedure, named InsertNewUser, accepts nine parameters that are equivalent to the nine columns in the table for which I must provide values:

```
CREATE PROCEDURE InsertNewUser
@UserID varchar(20), @UserPW varchar(255), @UserName varchar(50),
@Address varchar(60), @City varchar(30), @State varchar(20),
@Country varchar(30), @Phone varchar(20), @Email varchar(50) AS
INSERT INTO tblUsers(UserID, UserPW, UserName, Address,
                        City, State, Country, Phone, Email)
VALUES (@UserID, @UserPW, @UserName, @Address,
        @City, @State, @Country, @Phone, @Email)
```

I execute this stored procedure using the ExecuteNonQuery method of the Command object, just as I've done so many times before in other pages. The only twist here is that I need to create the appropriate "hash" of the password before I add it to the Parameters collection:

```
Function InsertNewUser() As Boolean
' add a new user to the database


  ' specify the stored procedure name
  Dim sProcName As String = "InsertNewUser"

  ' create connection and command objects
  Dim sqlConn As New SqlConnection(sConnect)
  Dim sqlComm As New SqlCommand(sProcName, sqlConn)
  sqlComm.CommandType = CommandType.StoredProcedure

  ' create SHA1 hash of password provided (could use "MD5" instead)
  Dim sPWHash As String
  sPWHash = FormsAuthentication.HashPasswordForStoringInConfigFile _
                                            (txtPWord.Text, "SHA1")
  ' get proposed new UserID from text box
  Dim sNewUserID As String = txtUserID.Text
```

```
' add parameters to Command
sqlComm.Parameters.Add("@UserID", sNewUserID)
sqlComm.Parameters.Add("@UserPW", sPWHash)
sqlComm.Parameters.Add("@UserName", txtName.Text)
sqlComm.Parameters.Add("@Address", txtAddr.Text)
sqlComm.Parameters.Add("@City", txtCity.Text)
sqlComm.Parameters.Add("@State", txtState.Text)
sqlComm.Parameters.Add("@Country", txtCountry.Text)
sqlComm.Parameters.Add("@Phone", txtPhone.Text)
sqlComm.Parameters.Add("@Email", txtEmail.Text)
...
```

I then execute the stored procedure, and if the result is one (one row was updated) I know that the process was successful and I can return True. Otherwise, or if there is an error, I return False. Then, in the Finally block, I just have to close the database connection:

```
...
Try
  ' execute the stored procedure
  sqlConn.Open()
  If sqlComm.ExecuteNonQuery() = 1 Then

    ' new user insert succeeded so update session and variables
    sUserID = sNewUserID
    Session("WCCUserID") = sNewUserID
    Return True

  Else
    Return False
  End If

Catch objError As Exception
  Return False
Finally
  sqlConn.Close()
End Try
End Function
```

Summary

Another long chapter, and more complicated concepts and code—or so it may seem. In fact, the techniques I've used in this chapter are not really that complicated, but they can seem confusing at first. ASP.NET Forms authentication is extremely powerful (I've really only shown you the simplest ways of using it here), and saves a lot of work on your behalf when writing code. Once you become familiar with the process it forces you to follow, it all makes a great deal of sense.

In this chapter, I started by reviewing the basic concepts of access control, in particular how they relate to a Web site. I followed this with a brief summary of the ASP.NET authentication and authorization configuration options, before concentrating in more detail on how Forms-based authentication works and how I use it in the example Xrox Car Company site.

Forms-based authentication is a great time-saver, but falls down if there is no support for cookies in the client. However, I discussed other "traditional" ASP techniques for controlling access, and for checking if a user has been authenticated, and used one of these techniques (storing a "flag value" in the user's session) in the example site. You saw how you can interweave it with Forms-based authentication to get the best of both worlds.

I also discussed how you can work with the ASP.NET validation controls in a more controlled and specific way to achieve "managed" validation where a page contains more than one set of input controls that must be validated. And, related to this discussion, you saw how to get around a couple of problems caused by only having one <form> section on a page, instead of separate ones as was the traditional approach in ASP 3.0 and earlier.

Finally, I worked through the code for the "login and register" page in the example site, showing you how it all fits together—and demonstrating a few other tips on the use of encrypted passwords, and providing persistent login rather than having the authentication expire when the browser is closed or the session times out.

The topics discussed in this chapter were:

- The ASP.NET and other techniques I used for authentication and authorization

- How to identify "anonymous" users as they browse and then log into a site

- How to collect and store information about visitors when they register

- How to force users who have already registered to provide "logon" details

- How the "login and register" page in the example Xrox Car Company site works

In the next and final chapter, you look at the remaining page in the example site where the users can view their quotations and place orders for vehicles. It's the pinnacle I've been working towards (and the one feature that would pay for the site if it wasn't a fictional example!).

Quotations and Orders

IN THIS FINAL CHAPTER, you'll look at the one remaining page of the Xrox Car Company that I haven't yet discussed. The My Cars page allows visitors to see quotations they have saved, and place an order for a vehicle based on one of these quotations. Of course, placing an order in a "real world" site usually involves a great deal of "back-end" processing such as verifying payment details, registering the order, and updating the customer's account details.

This book's aim has been to show how you can use ASP.NET Web Forms and server controls to build interfaces, so I will not be looking at this "back-end" processing. I'll take a shortcut to placing an order, with a simple update to the database. However, you will see how you can use ASP.NET to build a useful and informative interface easily, including how to bind the list controls that are provided with ASP.NET to sets of nested data, as well as to simple data tables.

So, the aims of this chapter are to show:

- How to bind related sets of data to a range of list controls

- How to easily display hierarchical data in nested form

- How I built the My Cars page

- How to handle the placing of an order for a vehicle

I start by showing you the concepts of binding to related and hierarchical sets of data.

Binding List Controls to Related Data

ASP.NET provides a useful range of server controls that can display lists, using a data source that contains repeated "rows" or "items" of data. Examples that you've already seen in this book include the CheckBoxList, RadioButtonList, DropDownList, Repeater, DataList, and DataGrid.

Binding to a Single Data Source

In all of the previous examples that use these list controls, I bound the control to a single data source such as a DataTable or DataView. Then, in some of the examples, I interacted with the control by hooking into the ItemDataBound event and used code in this event handler to read, modify, and even insert new content into the output for the control for one or more of the "rows" it creates.

For example, in the Home page, I interact with the DataGrid control to change the URL of the hyperlinks in the output generated by this control. This allows me to detect if the current user's browser supports client-side scripting—and, if so, change the URLs so they use a JavaScript function to open the new window rather than a traditional hyperlink:

home.aspx

```
Sub SetNavigateUrl(oSender As Object, oArgs As DataGridItemEventArgs)
  If bCanScript And (oArgs.Item.ItemType = ListItemType.Item _
  Or oArgs.Item.ItemType = ListItemType.AlternatingItem) Then

    ' it's a data row that is being bound so create appropriate
    ' URLs for hyperlinks and remove Target attributes
    Dim sCarID As String = oArgs.Item.DataItem("CarID")
    Dim sHref As String = "javascript:openWindow('" _
                          & InsertSessionId(Request.Path) _
                          & "/cardetail.aspx?id=" & sCarID _
                          & "', '" & sCarID & "')"

    ' update HRef in controls to new value
    CType(args.Item.FindControl("lnkCarImage"), Hyperlink).NavigateUrl = sHref
    CType(args.Item.FindControl("lnkCarImage"), Hyperlink).Target = ""
    CType(args.Item.FindControl("lnkCarName"), Hyperlink).NavigateUrl = sHref
    CType(args.Item.FindControl("lnkCarName"), Hyperlink).Target = ""
  End If
End Sub
```

However, while this might just seem like a useful technique for modifying the content of a control, it is actually a lot more useful and powerful than that. It allows me to interact with the content of the "template" section that generates the output in its entirety. I can insert new controls, show and hide existing controls, update almost any of the properties of existing controls, and thereby change the output that the list control generates in almost any way I like.

Binding Nested List Controls

From the preceding discussion, you can probably see how you can use this technique to display related or nested data within an ASP.NET list control. During the ItemDataBound event, you can interact with other list controls that are declared within the templates of the main list control (or generated dynamically), binding them to the appropriate data source and even selecting the appropriate value(s) within these nested list controls.

To see what I mean, you'll soon see an example that is not actually part of the Xrox Car Company site. However, to give you a flavor for where I'm going, take a look at Figure 12-1 of the My Cars page in the Xrox Car Company site. Within the list I display a list of the optional extras that were specified for each vehicle when the quotation was saved. However, these optional extras are in a related child table, and not in the table containing the quotations. To create this nested (hierarchical) display, I have to interact with the list control that creates the page content during the ItemDataBound event.

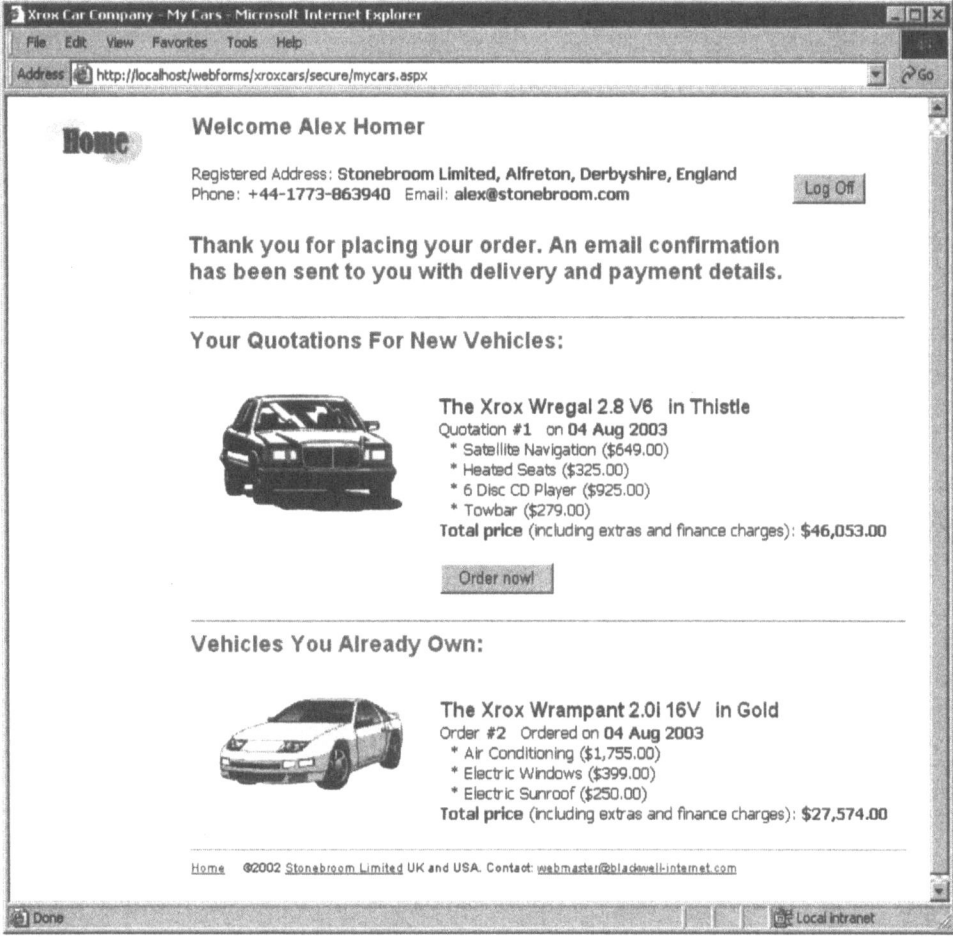

Figure 12-1. The My Cars page from the Xrox Cars sample site

An Example of Nested Bound Controls

To help you understand how you can data-bind nested list controls that are located within another list control, I've provided a simple example page named `nested-binding.aspx`. You'll find this in the `nested-binding` subfolder of the sample files for this book. It demonstrates how three different types of ASP.NET list control can be used within a `DataGrid` control, though the principles are applicable to any other combination of list controls.

Figure 12-2 shows the final page. I've placed a `DataGrid` control on the page, and you can see that it contains three columns: Select Engine, Select Extras, and Select Color. Each of the three rows in the `DataGrid` contains three list controls: a `RadioButtonList`, a `CheckBoxList`, and a `DropDownList`. The third column in each row also contains an ASP.NET `Image` control. The `Image` control reflects the selection in the `DropDownList` control above it.

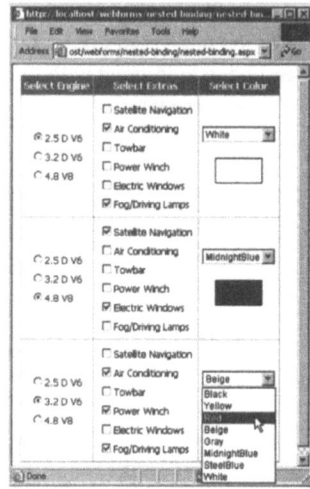

Figure 12-2. The nested data binding example page

> **NOTE** *I am* not *handling postbacks in this page, so selecting in the list controls has no effect. The aim of this example is to demonstrate how to construct these nested lists. There is a server-side* <form> *in the page, but this is only because it is required when I use the* CheckBoxList, RadioButtonList, *and* DropDownList *controls.*

The DataGrid Declaration

The declaration of the `DataGrid` control contains the styling information, and sets the `AutoGenerateColumns` attribute to `False` because I want to generate custom column content. The `<Columns>` element contains the definition of the columns I want to display, and in this case you can see that I've used three `TemplateColumn` elements to define the three columns I want:

nested-binding.aspx

```
<asp:DataGrid id="dgrNesting" runat="server"
    AutoGenerateColumns="False"
    CellPadding="4" Font-Size="10"
    Font-Name="Tahoma,Arial,Helvetica,sans-serif"
    HeaderStyle-HorizontalAlign="center" HeaderStyle-BackColor="#b50055"
    HeaderStyle-ForeColor="#ffffff" SelectedItemStyle-BackColor="#ffffcc"
    ItemStyle-HorizontalAlign="center" HeaderStyle-Font-Bold="True">
```

```
<Columns>
  <asp:TemplateColumn HeaderText="Select Engine">
    <ItemTemplate>
      <asp:RadioButtonList style="font-size:12px"
            id="radEngine" runat="server" />
    </ItemTemplate>
  </asp:TemplateColumn>

  <asp:TemplateColumn HeaderText="Select Extras">
    <ItemTemplate>
      <asp:CheckBoxList style="font-size:12px"
            id="chkExtras" runat="server" />
    </ItemTemplate>
  </asp:TemplateColumn>

  <asp:TemplateColumn HeaderText="Select Color">
    <ItemTemplate>
      <asp:DropDownList style="font-size:12px"
            id="selColor" runat="server" /><p />
      <asp:Image id="imgColor" border="1" runat="server" />
    </ItemTemplate>
  </asp:TemplateColumn>

</Columns>
</asp:DataGrid>
```

The content of each column is just an empty list control of the appropriate type,
a RadioButtonList, a CheckBoxList, or a DropDownList. The third column also contains
an Image control with no value set for the ImageUrl (the source of the image to display). I'll fill the lists, select some values at random, and set the ImageUrl property of
the Image control within the event handler that I attach to the DataGrid control.

The Data Sources for the Lists

I've reused part of the code that builds the DataSet from the Model Details page in
this example. The DataSet I generate contains three tables: CarDetails contains
a list of car/engine combinations, CarExtras contains a list of extras that are available for the selected vehicle, and CarColors contains a list of the colors that are
available for the selected vehicle.

When I generate the DataSet within the Page_Load event, I specify the value "5"
for the CarID so that I get back a DataSet containing the three rows that define the
three possible car/engine combinations for the Xrox Wranger truck, and the extras
and colors available for this vehicle:

```
Sub Page_Load()
  ' get DataSet from function elsewhere in this page
  oCarsDS = GetCarDetailsDS("5")
  ...
```

Then I can bind the default view of the CarDetails table (a DataView object) to the main DataGrid control named dgrNesting:

```
...
' display details of this vehicle
dgrNesting.DataSource = oCarsDS.Tables("CarDetails").DefaultView
dgrNesting.DataBind()
End Sub
```

However, this only gives me an empty DataGrid, as you can see in Figure 12-3. The RadioButtonList and CheckBoxList controls have no content (no ListItems, because I have not specified a DataSource), and so they generate no visible output. The DropDownList does appear, but again it has no content so the list is empty. And, because I didn't specify the ImageUrl for the Image control, this shows no image.

Figure 12-3. The result of the initial data binding process

Handling the OnItemDataBound Event

What I need to do now is handle the ItemDataBound event, just as I did in several examples in earlier chapters that used list controls. I add an event handler named FillLists to the page, and specify that this should be executed when each row in the DataGrid is data-bound to the source data, by adding it to the declaration of the DataGrid (highlighted in the next listing):

```
<asp:DataGrid id="dgrNesting" runat="server"
    AutoGenerateColumns="False"
    CellPadding="4" Font-Size="10"
    Font-Name="Tahoma,Arial,Helvetica,sans-serif"
    HeaderStyle-HorizontalAlign="center" HeaderStyle-BackColor="#b50055"
    HeaderStyle-ForeColor="#ffffff" SelectedItemStyle-BackColor="#ffffcc"
    ItemStyle-HorizontalAlign="center" HeaderStyle-Font-Bold="True"
    OnItemDataBound="FillLists">
```

Now, in the FillLists event handler, I can interact with the controls in each row of the DataGrid as the DataBind method I execute in the Page_Load event handler binds these rows to the source data from the CarEngines table. The next listing shows the first part of the declaration of the FillLists event handler. As in earlier examples, I must make sure that I only execute code in response to the event when the source of the event is an Item or an AlternatingItem row (even if I don't specify an AlternatingItem template in the definition of a list control, the event is still raised as an AlternatingItem row event for alternate rows):

```
Sub FillLists(oSender As Object, oArgs As DataGridItemEventArgs)
' runs when the OnItemDataBound event occurs
' used to bind nested list controls and select values
' in this example, values selected at random but could come from rows

  ' make sure its an Item or AlternatingItem row
  If oArgs.Item.ItemType = ListItemType.Item _
  Or oArgs.Item.ItemType = ListItemType.AlternatingItem Then
    ...
```

Referencing the Nested List Controls

The next step involves getting references to the controls in the current row of the DataGrid—in other words the row that is currently being bound to the main CarDetails data source. I use the FindControl method of the current Item (the row being bound, as exposed by the Item property of the DataGridItemEventArgs object that is passed to the event handler), and specify the ID of the control I want to find:

```
    ...
    ' get references to the three list controls and Image in this row
    Dim oRadioList As RadioButtonList _
          = CType(oArgs.Item.FindControl("radEngine"), RadioButtonList)
    Dim oCheckList As CheckBoxList _
          = CType(oArgs.Item.FindControl("chkExtras"), CheckBoxList)
    Dim oDropList As DropDownList _
          = CType(oArgs.Item.FindControl("selColor"), DropDownList)
    Dim oImage As Image = CType(oArgs.Item.FindControl("imgColor"), Image)
    ...
```

Binding the Nested List Controls

Now I can bind the list controls in this row to the relevant data sources. The RadioButtonList control that shows the list of engines can be bound to the same CarDetails table as the parent dgrNesting list control, as this will provide the three engine types for this vehicle.

I use the DataTextField and DataValueField properties to set the captions of the radio buttons and their values, just as I have in earlier examples, and then call the DataBind method to display the data. The fact that I'm now inside the event handler for the ItemDataBound event, rather than in the Page_Load event handler for a single control located directly on the page (as I've used in earlier examples) makes no difference. It works in just the same way:

```
    ...
    ' set DataSource and DataBind the RadioButtonList control
    oRadioList.DataSource = oCarsDS.Tables("CarDetails").DefaultView
    oRadioList.DataTextField = "EngineName"
    oRadioList.DataValueField = "EngineID"
    oRadioList.DataBind()
    ...
```

Likewise, I can bind the other list controls to the appropriate data sources. I bind the list of optional extras to the CarExtras table, and the list of available colors to the CarColors table. Again I specify the DataTextField so that the controls know which column contains the text to display, and for the DropDownList control I also specify the DataValueField property (remember that the CheckBoxList control does not actually use the DataValueField property, as you discovered in earlier examples):

```
...
' set DataSource and DataBind the CheckBoxList control
oCheckList.DataSource = oCarsDS.Tables("CarExtras").DefaultView
oCheckList.DataTextField = "ExtraText"
oCheckList.DataBind()
' set DataSource and DataBind the DropDownList control
oDropList.DataSource = oCarsDS.Tables("CarColors").DefaultView
oDropList.DataTextField = "Color"
oDropList.DataValueField = "ColorID"
oDropList.DataBind()
...
```

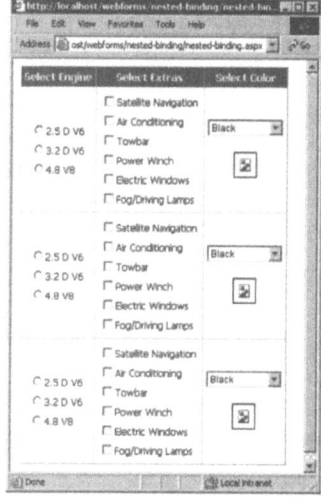

This is all I need to do to populate the three list controls in the page. Figure 12-4 shows the results. Of course, I haven't specified the ImageUrl of the Image control in each row, so this still doesn't display anything. And the lists are all "unselected" or set to the first value in the data source, as so far I haven't specified what value these controls should have.

Setting the Values of Nested List Controls

So, the next step is to look at how to set the values of the controls in each row. You have probably figured this out already, but I'll work through the code I used just to confirm this. I first have to decide what the values of each control should be.

Figure 12-4. The result after populating the list controls in each row

In applications that allow users to edit data, the values of the controls in each row will be the current values in the source data row.

For example, if the DataGrid was displaying a list of customers, a drop-down list of country names should be set to the name of the country in the database table for that customer. The users can change this, but if they don't the page reflects the underlying data—which is what you would expect.

The value of the underlying data in the row that is currently being bound can be obtained within the ItemDataBound event from the DataItem property that is exposed by the arguments to the event handler. In the Xrox Cars Home page, for instance, I extracted the value of the CarID from the current row (which I used to build the href for each link) as the DataGrid was being data bound using:

home.aspx

```
Dim sCarID As String = oArgs.Item.DataItem("CarID")
```

> **NOTE** *You'll find plenty of examples of using these techniques to display and allow the user to update data in my sister book,* ASP.NET Distributed Data Applications *(ISBN 1-86100-318-9, see* http://www.daveandal.com/books/4923/ *or* http://www.apress.com/ *for more details).*

In this example, however, I just generate random values for the list controls to demonstrate the techniques for setting the control values. I generate five integers, with their ranges of value depending on the maximum number of items in each list control (note that the Random.Next method returns an Integer that is *less than* the value of the second parameter):

nested-binding.aspx

```
...
' create random values for the controls
Dim iEngine As Integer = oRandom.Next(0, 3)
Dim iExtra1 As Integer = oRandom.Next(0, 6)
Dim iExtra2 As Integer = oRandom.Next(0, 6)
Dim iExtra3 As Integer = oRandom.Next(0, 6)
Dim iColor As Integer = oRandom.Next(0, 8)
...
```

Selecting Based on a SelectedIndex *Value*

If the value I have can be treated as the SelectedIndex of the nested control, it's easy to set the control value. I just assign it to the SelectedIndex property of the control:

```
...
' select RadioButton in "Engines" RadioButtonList control
oRadioList.SelectedIndex = iEngine
...
```

This will often be the case if the control uses a set of consecutive zero-based values from a table designed to contain control values, as in the list of engines in the Model Details page. And, in a RadioButtonList, I can only select one item. However, in a CheckBoxList I might want to select more than one item. This could be the case if the values come from a linked child table, as with the optional extras for the vehicles. In this case, I can set the Selected property of the matching ListItem controls within the Items collection of the control, based again on their index within the control:

```
...
' select three CheckBoxes in "Extras" CheckBoxList control
oCheckList.Items(iExtra1).Selected = True
oCheckList.Items(iExtra2).Selected = True
oCheckList.Items(iExtra3).Selected = True
...
```

For a drop-down list, I use the same technique as the RadioButtonList. Like the RadioButtonList, the DropDownList control only allows one item to be selected—so I can set the SelectedIndex property of the control directly:

```
...
' if we know the SelectedIndex value
oDropList.SelectedIndex = iColor
...
```

However, if I was using a ListBox control rather than a DropDownList control, and the declaration included the attribute SelectionMode="Multiple", users would be able to select more than one item, as with a CheckBoxList. In this case, to set multiple values in the event handler, I'd use the same technique as shown earlier for the CheckBoxList control—setting the Selected property of the appropriate ListItem objects within the control's Items collection.

Selecting Based on a Value That Appears in the Control

Often, the value I want to select in a nested list control is not equivalent to the SelectedIndex of the control. This is regularly the case when I get the value from the underlying DataRow that the current template row is based on. The value I want to select may, for example, be the Text of the ListItem object within a DropDownList control, or (more likely) the Value of that ListItem object.

To do this, I have to iterate through the control's Items collection and examine each ListItem to see if the Value (or Text) matches the value I want to select. When I find a match, I set the Selected property of that ListItem object:

```
...
' select item(s) in a list control by iterating through values to find
' a match for a specific value if it is one of those shown in the list
Dim oItem As ListItem
For Each oItem In oDropList.Items
  If oItem.Value = iColor Then oItem.Selected = True
Next
...
```

Setting the ImageUrl of the Image Control

The final step in the event handler in this example sets the ImageUrl property of the Image control in the third column of the DataGrid control to the same color as is selected in the DropDownList of colors above it.

Code that ran earlier within this event handler (as shown previously) set the SelectedIndex of the DropDownList to the (random) color value I require. To show how I can access the nested controls in exactly the same way as I do when they are not within another list control, I now extract the color name from the DropDownList control—simply by using the SelectedItem property to return a reference to the currently selected item in the list, and then accessing the Text property of this item. This returns the name of the color, and I can use it to build the URL of the image I want to display:

```
...
' get text from drop-down list and use to set Image source
Dim sColorName As String = oDropList.SelectedItem.Text
oImage.ImageUrl = "../xroxcars/images/colors/" & sColorName & ".gif"

  End If
End Sub
```

The final result is shown in Figure 12-2, which you saw earlier, and you can see that it does provide some great ways to display data in list form.

Binding to Hierarchical Data

So far, I've demonstrated how I can use list controls (and other controls) nested within a parent list control, and access these nested controls to fill them with data, select values, and set their properties. However, there is another specialist situation I often have to handle that is related to the techniques you've just seen.

In fact "related" is a good term to use, because the example you've just seen uses only "*un*-related" data as a source for the list controls. Each control is bound to a set of data that is unrelated to the data used for the parent list control. OK, so I used the same data for the parent control and one of the nested list controls in the previous example, but only because that table contained the data required for both list controls.

Another common scenario when data binding list controls to data is when the data consists of *related rows*. For example, it could be a list of orders and a list of the lines for each order. Or, in the Xrox Car Company example (as you saw in Chapter 10 and repeated in Figure 12-5), I have a table containing a list of quotations and a related child table containing the list of optional extras for all the quotations.

Each optional extra row in the table named tblQuoteOrderExtras is related to only one quotation row in the table tblQuoteOrder. Of course, there could be (and is likely to be) more than one optional extra for any single quotation, giving a one-to-many relationship between the tblQuoteOrder table and the tblQuoteOrderExtras table (Figure 12-5).

Figure 12-5. The related tables containing the quotation and order data

This type of data is often referred to as *hierarchical*, probably because—when listed in the page—the parent and child rows are nested to form a hierarchy of information (Figure 12-6).

Figure 12-6. Hierarchical listing of the related quotation and order data

Hierarchical Binding in the My Cars Page

As you've seen, the My Cars page in the Xrox Car Company site displays the details of each user's quotations and previous orders in a hierarchical format. I'll use this page to demonstrate how I perform this kind of data binding, though you can easily adapt the technique to suit your own requirements.

As with the nested binding examples I showed you earlier, the declaration of the controls to perform hierarchical binding is simple enough. I have a parent list control, which must support templates, and one or more nested child list controls. In the My Cars page, I use Repeater controls for both the parent and the nested child rows.

The big differences between nested and hierarchical data binding are in the content of the DataSet I use as the data source for the controls, and the way I extract the rows that form the data source for the nested child control.

Specifying a DataRelation *Within a* DataSet

In the ItemDataBound event handler, at the point where I come to bind the nested list control, I need to extract the set of child data rows from the DataSet that are related to the current parent row (the row being bound to the parent list control). To achieve this, I must specify a relationship between the two data tables that I placed in the DataSet.

ADO.NET allows you to place more than one DataTable into a DataSet, and then optionally create relationships between these tables (DataRelation objects). When you create a relationship, the existing rows are automatically examined to ensure that they can be related without causing an error. For example, there must be only one parent row for every child row, the parent rows must be uniquely identifiable on their primary key, and there cannot be any "orphan" child rows that have no related parent row.

The constructor for a DataRelation object specifies the name of the relationship, and references to the columns in the parent and child tables that implement this relationship:

```
Dim MyRelation As New DataRelation("name", parent-column, child-column)
```

Then I add the new relationship to the Relations collection of the DataSet object:

```
DataSet.Relations.Add(MyRelation)
```

Extracting the Related Child Rows

Once there is a relationship in place within the DataSet, I can use it to extract related child rows given a parent row. This requires the parent row to be available as a DataRowView object. The ItemEventArgs object that is passed to the event handler as a parameter contains a reference to the data row that is currently being bound to the parent list control, as the Item.DataItem property, and I can convert this into a DataRowView. In VB.NET, as you've seen in previous examples, I use a CType statement:

```
MyDataRowView = CType(oArgs.Item.DataItem, DataRowView)
```

In C#, I can do it like this:

```
DataRowView MyDataRowView = (DataRowView)oArgs.Item.DataItem;
```

Once I've got a DataRowView, I can use its CreateChildView method to get a DataView instance based on the related child table, which contains only the related child rows. I specify as a parameter to the CreateChildView method the name of the relationship I want to use:

```
MyChildDataView = MyDataRowView.CreateChildView("relation-name")
```

Then I can bind this DataView to the nested list control in the current row. This list control will display only the rows in the child table that are related to the row currently being displayed by the parent list control. Exactly what I'm after! You'll see this code in use in the following description of the My Cars page.

Building the My Cars Page

The remainder of this chapter is devoted to looking at the structure, content, and code that makes up the My Cars page. Here I display the user's quotations and existing orders in two lists, with the user's name and address details at the top of the page. For any quotation the user has received, he or she can place an order simply by clicking the "Order now!" button (Figure 12-7).

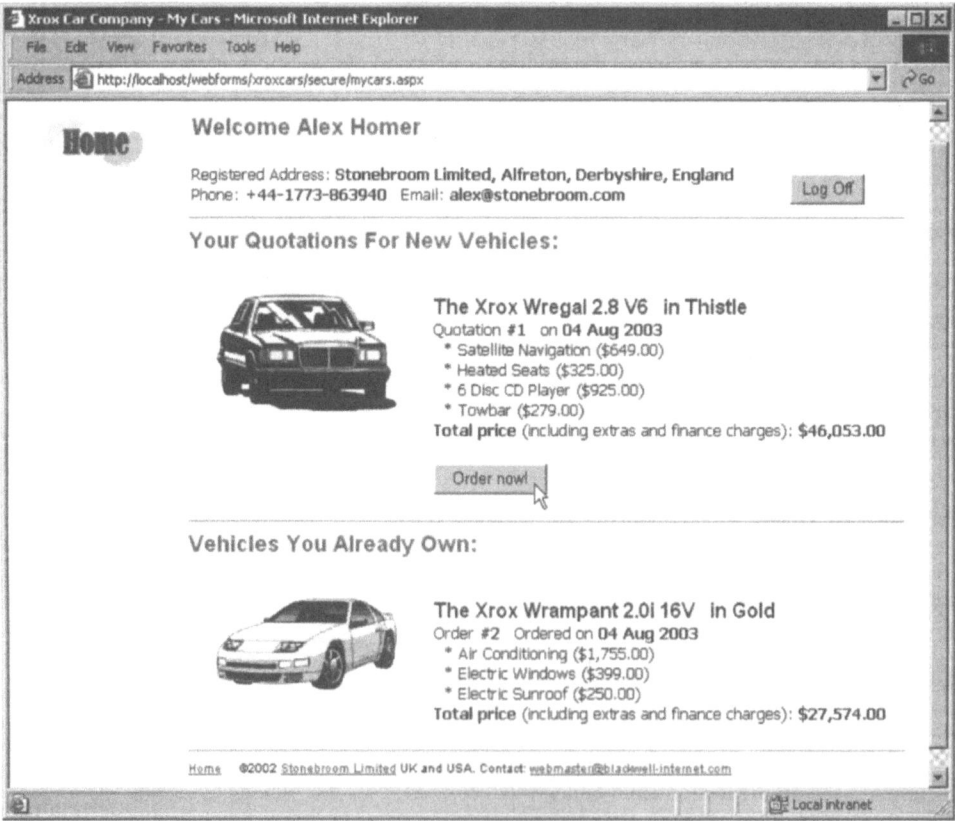

Figure 12-7. Placing an order against an existing quotation

The HTML for the My Cars Page

Much of the outline structure of this page is the same as the pages you've seen in earlier chapters, so I won't be listing and describing all the ways that I specify the style information, the "skip to" links, or the link back to the Home page. Instead, I'll concentrate on what is actually different from the other pages you've seen.

The entire content of the page is wrapped in a server-side <form> so that I can perform postbacks when the user places an order. Inside this <form> is a two-column, single-row HTML table that controls the layout of the content. The left-hand cell contains just the link back to the Home page. The right-hand cell contains the user's address details and the Log Off button, plus the two lists of quotations and previous orders.

Here's an outline of the HTML for the <form> section, with the section for the user's name and address, the Log Off button, and the templates for the list controls removed for clarity:

mycars.aspx

```
...
<form runat="server">
<table width="100%" border="0" cellspacing="0" cellpadding="10">
<tbody>
 <tr>
  <td valign="top" width="110px">
    <!-- link to Home page here -->
  </td>
  <td align="left">

    <!-- user's name/address details and Log Off button here -->
    <!-- message for feedback when placing an order here -->
    <!-- caption for list of quotes here -->
    <!-- list of quotes -->
    <asp:Repeater id="repQuotes" runat="server"
        OnItemDataBound="QuotesListDatabound" OnItemCommand="PlaceOrder">
      ...
      ... templates here...
      ...
    </asp:Repeater>
    <!-- caption for list of orders here -->
    <!-- list of orders -->
    <asp:Repeater id="repOrders" runat="server"
        OnItemDataBound="OrdersListDatabound">
      ...
      ... templates here...
      ...
    </asp:Repeater>
    <!-- page footer here -->
  </td>
 </tr>
</tbody>
</table>

</form>
...
```

The Name and Address Details, and Log Off Button

The top part of this section of the page contains an HTML table where a "welcome" message is displayed that includes the user's name, the registered address details, and the button to log off and destroy the cookie (including a persistent cookie) that performs authentication when using ASP.NET Forms authentication. If the current session is supported by the ASP.NET cookie-less sessions mechanism, the Log Off button will destroy the existing authentication flag that is stored in the user's session instead (Figure 12-8).

Welcome Alex Homer

Registered Address: **Stonebroom Limited, Alfreton, Derbyshire, England**
Phone: +44-1773-863940 Email: **alex@stonebroom.com**   Log Off

Figure 12-8. The details of the user and the Log Off button at the top of the page

The section of HTML that generates this part of the page is listed next. You can see the two ASP.NET Label controls I use. The Label control with the ID of lblHeading displays the "welcome" text, and the Label with ID value lblDetail displays the two lines containing the user's address details, phone number, and email address.

Then comes the `<input type="submit">` button that I use to implement the Log Off button. I chose to use an HtmlInputButton control here, but I could equally well have used an ASP.NET Button control instead. Notice that the OnServerClick attribute is specified so that the event handler named DoSignOut will execute when the button is clicked (causing a postback to the server):

```
...
<!-- user's name/address details and Log Off button -->
<table border="0" width="95%">
 <tr>
  <td align="left"><a name="content" />
    <font face="Arial,Helvetica,sans-serif" size="4" color="#b50055"><b>
    <asp:Label id="lblHeading" CssClass="large-red-text"
         runat="server" /></b></font><p />
    <font face="Tahoma,Arial,Helvetica,sans-serif" size="2">
    <asp:Label id="lblDetail" CssClass="body-text" runat="server" />
    </font>
  </td>
  <td align="right" valign="bottom">
    <font face="Tahoma,Arial,Helvetica,sans-serif" size="2">
    <input type="submit" Value="Log Off" runat="server"
         OnServerClick="DoSignOut"
         title="Log off and cancel automatic logon for this site" />
    </font>
  </td>
 </tr>
</table>
...
```

The Messages Label

Next I have a Label that I use to display status and error details. For example, after the user places an order, I display the message you see in Figure 12-9.

Thank you for placing your order. An email confirmation has been sent to you with delivery and payment details.

Figure 12-9. The Label that confirms an order has been placed

The Label control declaration includes the CSS style definition for large red text, and I've enclosed it in a <font> element for older browsers (as I've done throughout the application):

```
...
<!-- message for feedback when placing an order -->
<font face="Arial,Helvetica,sans-serif" size="4" color="#b50055"><b>
<asp:Label id="lblMessage" CssClass="large-red-text"
    EnableViewState="False" runat="server" /></b></font>
...
```

The Caption for the Quotations Section

The remaining two sections of the HTML implement the two lists—one for quotations and one for orders. They are fundamentally similar, so I'll just show you the quotations list and then point out the differences when you come to the list of orders.

The quotations list is preceded by a Label control that contains the horizontal rule to separate the page content, and the caption for the list. Initially it has the Visible attribute set to False so that the horizontal rule and caption are not displayed in the page. I can change this later in the code, when I see if there are any quotations to show:

```
...
<!-- caption for list of quotes -->
<asp:Label id="lblQuotesHeading" CssClass="large-red-text"
    Visible="False" EnableViewState="False"
    runat="server"><hr size="1" />
  <font face="Arial,Helvetica,sans-serif" size="4" color="#b50055">
  <b>Your Quotations For New Vehicles:</b>
</asp:Label></font><p />
...
```

Figure 12-10 shows the caption, followed by the output from the first of the Repeater controls.

Your Quotations For New Vehicles:

The Wrox Wregal 2.8 V6 in Thistle
Quotation #25   on 02 Sep 2002
    * Satellite Navigation ($649.00)
    * Heated Seats ($325.00)
    * 6 Disc CD Player ($925.00)
    * Towbar ($279.00)
Total price (including extras and finance charges): **$51,837.26**
Basic price $46,053.00 plus $5,784.26 interest.
Terms: 60 monthly payments of $863.95

> Order now!

Figure 12-10. The section of the page that shows quotations

The List Control for the Quotations Section

The list shown in Figure 12-10 (OK, so there's only one quotation in the list, but there could be several) is implemented by the following HTML declaration of the Repeater control. I start by declaring the attributes that will cause two event handlers to be executed—one when each item in the list is bound to the source data (OnItemDataBound) and one that is executed when any control within the rows of the list causes a postback to the server (OnItemCommand):

```
...
<!-- list of quotes -->
<asp:Repeater id="repQuotes" runat="server"
     OnItemDataBound="QuotesListDatabound"
     OnItemCommand="PlaceOrder">
  ...
```

The HeaderTemplate *Section*

Next, I declare the templates that will create the visible output from the source data. I want to generate an HTML table that will contain all the items in the list, with each item in a separate row of this table. So I start with a HeaderTemplate, which generates the opening <table> element:

```
...
<HeaderTemplate>
  <table border="0" cellpadding="7" cellspacing="7">
</HeaderTemplate>
...
```

The ItemTemplate *Section*

Each row of the output is generated by successive iterations of the ItemTemplate, and in this template I create the table row. I place an image of the current vehicle in an

ASP.NET Image control within the first cell of this row, using the Eval method to create the appropriate ImageUrl and ToolTip attributes:

```
...
<ItemTemplate>
  <tr>
   <td valign="top">
     <asp:Image runat="server" hspace="10"
          ImageUrl='<%# DataBinder.Eval(Container.DataItem, _
                          "CarName", "../images/{0}150.gif") %>'
          ToolTip='<%# DataBinder.Eval(Container.DataItem, _
                          "CarName", "The Xrox {0}") %>' />
   </td>
   ...
```

Next comes the second cell of the table row for this item in the list. In it I have a series of elements that generate the output containing the model name, engine name, and color name. The quotation number, date, and order ID follow. All these values are taken from the rows of the parent table named tblQuoteOrder (via a stored procedure that you'll see later):

```
...
<td valign="top">
  <font face="Arial,Helvetica,sans-serif" size="3">
  <b>The Xrox <%# Container.DataItem("CarName") %>
  <%# Container.DataItem("EngineName") %>   in
  <%# Container.DataItem("ColorName") %></b></font><br />
  <font face="Tahoma,Arial,Helvetica,sans-serif" size="2">
  Quotation #<b>
  <asp:Label id="lblOrderID">
    <%# Container.DataItem("QuoteOrderID") %>
  </asp:Label></b>  
  on <b><%# DataBinder.Eval(Container.DataItem, "OrderDate", _
                          "{0:dd MMM yyyy}") %></b><br />
  ...
```

The Nested Repeater *Control for the Optional Extras*

Now I come to the interesting part. To display the list of optional extras in this quotation, I use a nested Repeater control. This is declared next, and you can see that I use an ItemTemplate that outputs the details of the optional extras in the data source that it will be bound to. These details are in the related child table named tblQuoteOrderExtras, and again are extracted from the database by a stored procedure that you'll see later:

```
...
<!-- list of extras for each vehicle -->
<asp:Repeater id="repQuoteLines" runat="server">
```

```
            <ItemTemplate>
                * <%# Container.DataItem("ExtraName") %>
              ($<%# DataBinder.Eval(Container.DataItem, "ExtraPrice", _
                                    "{0:#,##0.00}") %>)<br />
            </ItemTemplate>
          </asp:Repeater>
          ...
```

The Price and Finance Details

After I've listed all the optional extras for this quotation, I add more values from the main tblQuoteOrder table columns. I display the total price, followed by a Label control that wraps the basic price, interest, number of months, and monthly payment details. This Label control has the attribute Visible="False", so these values will not be visible unless I change the Visible property to True in the code. I'll do this only if there are finance terms saved for the quotation:

```
          ...
          <b>Total price</b> (including extras and finance charges):
          <b>$<%# DataBinder.Eval(Container.DataItem, "TotalPrice", _
                            "{0:#,##0.00}") %></b><br />
          <asp:Label id="lblFinance" Visible="False" runat="server">
            Basic price $
            <%# DataBinder.Eval(Container.DataItem, "BasePrice", _
                            "{0:#,##0.00}") %> plus
            $<%# DataBinder.Eval(Container.DataItem, "Interest", _
                            "{0:#,##0.00}") %> interest.<br />
            Terms: <%# Container.DataItem("PaymentMonths") %>
            monthly payments of
            $<%# DataBinder.Eval(Container.DataItem, "PaymentAmount", _
                            "{0:#,##0.00}") %>
          </asp:Label><p>
          ...
```

The Order now! Button

The final control in the ItemTemplate is the Order now! button. I specify a ToolTip for this button, and then set the CommandName attribute to the ID of the current quotation. When I handle events raised by controls within a list control (such as the Repeater control), I can use the CommandName and CommandArgument properties to pass text values to the event handler.

In general, I use this feature to pass the row key for the current row so that, within the event handler, I can identify which row caused the event to occur. You'll see how I retrieve this value when I look at the event handler for the ItemCommand event later in this chapter:

```
    ...
    <asp:Button id="cmdOrder" Text="Order now!" runat="server"
        ToolTip="Place an order for this vehicle now"
        CommandName='<%# Container.DataItem("QuoteOrderID") %>' />
    </p></font>
  </td>
  </tr>
</ItemTemplate>
 ...
```

The FooterTemplate *Section*

The final template in the Repeater control declaration is the FooterTemplate section. This just has to output the closing `</table>` tag for the table I've been creating within the main (parent) Repeater control:

```
  ...
  <FooterTemplate>
    </table>
  </FooterTemplate>
</asp:Repeater>
  ...
```

The Orders Section

The next section of the example page is the list of existing orders for the user. Most of the declaration of the caption and the Repeater controls is the same as in the quotations section, with a few minor differences. For example, I don't want to remind customers how much interest they paid when they bought their last car, so I don't show the breakdown of the finance terms. Neither, for obvious reasons, do I want to show the Order now! button (Figure 12-11).

Vehicles You Already Own:

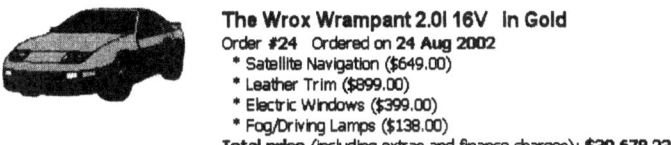

The Wrox Wrampant 2.0l 16V in Gold
Order #24   Ordered on 24 Aug 2002
    * Satellite Navigation ($649.00)
    * Leather Trim ($899.00)
    * Electric Windows ($399.00)
    * Fog/Driving Lamps ($138.00)
Total price (including extras and finance charges): **$30,678.23**

Figure 12-11. Displaying details of vehicles that the user already owns

In the code declarations for the orders section I have a different event handler attached to the ItemDataBound event, and I do not define an event handler attribute for the ItemCommand event (there are no controls in this list that can cause a postback):

```
...
<!-- list of orders -->
<asp:Repeater id="repOrders" runat="server"
     OnItemDataBound="OrdersListDatabound">
     ...
     ... as shown for quotations list control
     ...
```

I still have a nested "child" Repeater for the list of optional extras, but there are no bound controls for the finance terms in the ItemTemplate section of the main "parent" Repeater:

```
...
<!-- list of extras for each vehicle -->
<asp:Repeater id="repOrderLines" runat="server">
  <ItemTemplate>
      * <%# Container.DataItem("ExtraName") %>
    ($<%# DataBinder.Eval(Container.DataItem, "ExtraPrice", _
                          "{0:#,##0.00}") %>)<br />
  </ItemTemplate>
</asp:Repeater>
<b>Total price</b> (including extras and finance charges):
<b>$<%# DataBinder.Eval(Container.DataItem, "TotalPrice", _
                       "{0:#,##0.00}") %></b><br />
</font>
  </td>
 </tr>
</ItemTemplate>
...
```

The Code for the My Cars Page

In the <script> section of the page, I declare the customary variables to hold the style sheet size, the current user ID, and the database connection string. I also have a variable to hold the DataSet containing all this user's quotation and order details that I extract from the database:

```
...
' page-level variable to hold style size
Dim sStyleSize As String = "Standard"

' page-level variable to hold current user ID
Dim sUserID As String

' page-level variable to hold DB connection string
Dim sConnect As String
```

```
' page-level variable to user and order details DataSet
Dim dsDetails As DataSet
...
```

Before looking at the Page_Load event handler, however, you'll see how I extract the details of the users and their quotations and orders from the database and fill the DataSet that I use throughout the remainder of the page.

Generating the DataSet *of User Details*

I need to create three tables of data within the DataSet. These are:

- Details of this user from the tblUsers table—the user's registered name and street address, phone, and email address. This table within the DataSet is named UserDetail.

- A list of quotations and orders from the tblQuoteOrder table for this user. This table within the DataSet is named Orders.

- A list of all the optional extras for all this user's quotations and orders, taken from the tblQuoteOrderExtras table. This table within the DataSet is named OrderLines.

The Stored Procedures to Extract the Data

I use three stored procedures to extract the data I need from the database. To get the user details for the UserDetail table, I select all the columns from the tblUsers table in the database for the row with the matching UserID:

```
CREATE PROCEDURE GetUserDetails @UserID varchar(20) AS
SELECT * FROM tblUsers WHERE UserID = @UserID
```

To extract the list of quotations and orders for the Orders table, I select all the columns from the tblQuoteOrder table in the database for all rows with the matching UserID:

```
CREATE PROCEDURE GetUserOrders @UserID varchar(20) AS
SELECT * FROM tblQuoteOrder WHERE UserID = @UserID ORDER BY OrderDate DESC
```

To extract the list of optional extras for all the user's quotations and orders, for the OrderLines table in the DataSet, I need to join the tblQuoteOrder and tblQuoteOrderExtras tables on the QuoteOrderID value. This allows me to select the columns I want from the tblQuoteOrderExtras table in the database for all rows where the parent row in the tblQuoteOrder table contains a matching UserID:

```
CREATE PROCEDURE GetUserOrderLines @UserID varchar(20) AS
SELECT tblQuoteOrder.QuoteOrderID, ExtraName, ExtraPrice
FROM tblQuoteOrder JOIN tblQuoteOrderExtras
  ON tblQuoteOrder.QuoteOrderID = tblQuoteOrderExtras.QuoteOrderID
WHERE UserID = @UserID
```

The GetUserDetailsDS Function

The function named GetUserDetailsDS, which uses these three stored procedures and
returns a DataSet, is very similar to previous examples. I define the stored procedure
names, create the Connection and Command objects, set the single @UserID parameter for
the stored procedures, and then fill the DataSet with the three tables returned by
these stored procedures:

```
Function GetUserDetailsDS() As DataSet
  ' function to get current user's details as a DataSet
  ' to hold DataSet for the results
  Dim dsUserDetail As DataSet = Nothing

  ' to hold stored procedure names
  Dim sDetailsProc As String = "GetUserDetails"
  Dim sOrdersProc As String = "GetUserOrders"
  Dim sOrderLinesProc As String = "GetUserOrderLines"

  Dim sqlConn As New SqlConnection(sConnect)
  Dim sqlComm As New SqlCommand(sDetailsProc, sqlConn)
  sqlComm.CommandType = CommandType.StoredProcedure
  sqlComm.Parameters.Add("@UserID", sUserID)

  Try
    ' create a new empty DataSet for the results
    dsUserDetail = New DataSet()

    ' and fill it from the database
    Dim daUserDetail As New SqlDataAdapter(sqlComm)
    sqlConn.Open()
    If daUserDetail.Fill(dsUserDetail, "UserDetail") = 1 Then

      ' found details for a single user as expected so fill other
      ' tables in DataSet with all quotation and order details
      sqlComm.CommandText = sOrdersProc
      daUserDetail.Fill(dsUserDetail, "Orders")
      sqlComm.CommandText = sOrderLinesProc
      daUserDetail.Fill(dsUserDetail, "OrderLines")
      ...
```

Creating the Relationship Between the Tables

However, before I finish, I must add the DataRelation to the DataSet that will allow me
to extract the related child rows for each parent row when I come to bind the nested

Repeater controls in the lists of quotations and orders. I need a relationship between the parent Orders table and the child OrderLines table in the DataSet.

I showed you how this is done earlier in the chapter. In this example, the new relationship is named relOrders, and I specify references to the QuoteOrderID column of the parent and child tables as the second and third parameters to the DataRelation constructor. Then I add the new relationship to the DataSet object's Relations collection:

```
    ...
    ' create relationship between Orders and OrderLines tables
    ' and add it to the DataSet object's Relations collection
    Dim oRelation As New DataRelation("relOrders", _
        dsUserDetail.Tables("Orders").Columns("QuoteOrderID"), _
        dsUserDetail.Tables("OrderLines").Columns("QuoteOrderID"))
    dsUserDetail.Relations.Add(oRelation)
  Else
    dsUserDetail = Nothing
  End If
Catch
  dsUserDetail = Nothing
Finally
  sqlConn.Close()
End Try
' return DataSet—will be Nothing if there was an error
Return dsUserDetail

End Function
```

Now (as you can see in the preceding code) I can return the DataSet, or return Nothing if there was an error. I also have to remember to close the database connection. I opened it myself, so it remains open when the three calls to the Fill method have completed.

There is no point in storing the DataSet in the user's ASP.NET session, as I did in the Model Details page, because it is only used once—to fill the lists of quotations and orders. If there is a postback to the server, it's because the user placed an order. In this case the data in the database will change, and so I will have to refill the DataSet anyway.

The Page_Load Event Handler

Now that you know where the data comes from, I'll show you the remaining code routines in the My Cars page. The Page_Load event handler has several tasks to carry out, including some you've seen in many of the other pages. This includes setting the correct value for the CSS style sheet, checking if an ASP.NET session exists for this user, and collecting the database connection string from web.config:

```
Sub Page_Load()
  ' get style sheet size from Session
  sStyleSize = CType(Session("WccStyleSize"), String)

  ' if no value, session has expired or user entered
  ' site at page other than "Home" page
  If sStyleSize = "" Then
    Response.Clear()
    Response.Redirect("../default.aspx")
    Response.End()
  End If

  ' get connection string from web.config
  sConnect = ConfigurationSettings.AppSettings("XroxCarsConnectString")
  ...
```

Checking If the User Has Been Authenticated

Now I can make sure that the user was authenticated. I set a Boolean flag variable to
False as the default, then check which kind of session support I am using. If this
user's browser or user-agent does not support cookies, and is using the cookie-less
version of the application, I check if the user was authenticated by looking in the
ASP.NET session for the authentication value WCCUserAuthenticated="yes".

If I find this, I can set the "authenticated" flag to True and collect the ID of this
user from the session variable named WCCUserID. This value was stored there in the
Login page. If I don't find the authentication value in the session, I redirect the user
to the Login page instead:

```
  ...
  ' flag for checking if user is authenticated
  Dim bAuthenticated As Boolean = False

  ' check what type of session support we are using
  If Session.IsCookieless Then

    ' cookie-less sessions, so look in session
    If CType(Session("WCCUserAuthenticated"), String) = "yes" Then
      bAuthenticated = True
      sUserID = CType(Session("WCCUserID"), String)
    Else    'not authenticated
      Response.Clear()
      Response.Redirect("login.aspx")
      Response.End()
    End If
  ...
```

Alternatively, if the user's browser or user-agent does support cookies, I know
that the ASP.NET Forms authentication system was used to authenticate the user,
and that there is a valid ASP.NET authentication cookie on his or her machine. If not,

the user would have been automatically redirected to the Login page, and would not have gotten this far.

Once the user has been authenticated in this way, I can take advantage of another feature of the ASP.NET security model. I can access the default User object for this page instance, and from its Identity.Name property get the ID that was used for authentication. This is the user ID value I'll be using later in the page code:

```
...
Else
  ' get name of authenticated current user from Forms
  ' authentication system—User ID can be extracted from
  ' the User object implemented by Forms authentication
  bAuthenticated = User.Identity.IsAuthenticated
  sUserID = User.Identity.Name

End If
...
```

Setting the Webmaster Email Address

In the other site pages, I take advantage of the custom user control I built to create the page footer containing the links to other pages and the link to send email to the Webmaster of my site. However, in the My Cars page I only have a single link—to the Home page—and so I have implemented the page footer directly within the HTML declaration of this page. This means that I need to extract the email address of the Webmaster from the web.config file and set the NavigateUrl and Text of the hyperlink in the page footer when the page loads:

```
...
' set the email address of the Webmaster in the page footer
Try
  Dim sWebmasterEmail As String = _
                 ConfigurationSettings.AppSettings("XroxCarsWebmasterEmail")
  lnkWebmaster.NavigateUrl = "mailto:" & sWebmasterEmail _
                              & "?subject=Xrox Cars Web Site"
  lnkWebmaster.Text = sWebmasterEmail
Catch
End Try
...
```

Displaying the Page Content

Now I can display the main content of the My Cars page. I check that the user was authenticated (in theory I know that this will be the case, but it is worth checking to be sure in case someone changed the web.config file).

If this page load is not occurring through a postback (in other words, it's the first time that the page has been loaded), I can collect the DataSet of values using the GetUserDetailsDS function you've just been looking at. Providing that it returns a DataSet, I can then call two other routines in the page to display the content:

```
    ...
  If bAuthenticated Then
    If Not Page.IsPostback Then
      ' this is the first time the page has been loaded
      ' get user's details and quotes from database
      dsDetails = GetUserDetailsDS()
      If dsDetails Is Nothing Then
        lblDetail.Text = "<b>* Could not access database.</b>"
      Else
        ' display registered user's details, quotes, and orders
        DisplayUserDetails(dsDetails)
        DisplayUserVehicles(dsDetails)
      End If
    End If
  Else
    lblDetail.Text = "<b>* Not authenticated</b>"
  End If
End Sub
```

If I don't get a DataSet back, or if the user was not authenticated, I just display suitable messages in the lblDetail control on the page instead.

Displaying Details of the User

The first of the routines I call from the Page_Load event, DisplayUserDetails, simply extracts the user's registration details from the single row (at index zero) in the UserDetail table of the DataSet, and builds up a couple of String values containing these details. These String values are then inserted into the two Label control in the top section of the page:

```
Sub DisplayUserDetails(dsDetails As DataSet)
  ' extract user's name/address/etc from DataSet
  ' and display them at the top of the page

  Dim drDetails As DataRow = dsDetails.Tables("UserDetail").Rows(0)
  lblHeading.Text = "Welcome " & drDetails("UserName")
  lblDetail.Text = "Registered Address: <b>" _
    & drDetails("Address") & ", " & drDetails("City") _
    & ", " & drDetails("State") & ", " _
```

```
   & drDetails("Country") & "</b><br />Phone: <b>" _
   & drDetails("Phone") & "</b>   Email: <b>" _
   & drDetails("Email") & "</b>"

End Sub
```

Displaying Details of the User's Vehicles

The second of the routines I call from the Page_Load event handler is DisplayUserVehicles. To display the details of the user's quotations and orders, I have to bind the data in the Orders table of the DataSet to the two Repeater controls on the page. To decide if a row in the Orders table is a quotation or an order, all I have to do is filter the table on the IsOrder column, which is set to one for an order or zero for a quotation.

So, after getting a DataView from the DefaultView property of the table, I apply a filter to it that selects only the rows that have zero for the IsOrder column. Then I can check to see if there are any quotations by examining the Count property of the DataView. If there are one or more quotations, I make the horizontal rule and the large red text caption for this table visible (you'll recall that these are declared within the Label control with ID value lblQuotesHeading):

```
Sub DisplayUserVehicles(dsDetails As DataSet)
   ' extract lists of quotes and orders for this user from
   ' DataSet and display in Repeaters in this page

   ' get a filtered DataView of just the quotations
   Dim dvQuotes As DataView = dsDetails.Tables("Orders").DefaultView
   dvQuotes.RowFilter = "IsOrder = 0"
   If dvQuotes.Count > 0 Then

      ' at least one quote so make Quotes heading visible
      lblQuotesHeading.Visible = True

   End If
   ...
```

Then I can bind the filtered DataView to the Repeater control to display the quotations. Remember that I only bind the parent Repeater to the data extracted from the Orders table here. I will fill in the nested list of child optional extra rows in the ItemDataBound event handler, as you'll see shortly:

```
   ...
   ' bind quotations Repeater control to display them
   repQuotes.DataSource = dvQuotes
   repQuotes.DataBind()
   ...
```

Then I can repeat the process to display any orders for this user. This time the row filter selects only rows that have the value one in the IsOrder column:

```
...
' get a filtered DataView of just the orders
dvQuotes.RowFilter = "IsOrder = 1"
If dvQuotes.Count > 0 Then

    ' at least one order so make Orders heading visible
    lblOrdersHeading.Visible = True

End If
' bind orders Repeater control to display them
repOrders.DataSource = dvQuotes
repOrders.DataBind()

End Sub
```

The ItemDataBound Event Handlers

The routine I've just looked at is responsible for binding the two "parent" Repeater controls on the page to the list of quotations and orders in the Orders table of the DataSet. However, when I declared these two Repeater controls, I specified event handlers for their OnItemDataBound attributes.

So, when the ItemDataBound event occurs as each row is bound to the source data, the event handlers will be invoked. I have defined two different event handlers, named QuotesListDatabound and OrdersListDatabound. While they are fundamentally similar, they have to access different sets of controls. I could have used some If...Then constructs within a single event handler to work with both lists, but this would have made it harder to see what's happening.

Handling the ItemDataBound Event for the Quotations List

In the QuotesListDatabound event handler, I first check that I am reacting to the event only for an Item or an AlternatingItem row. I have two distinct tasks to accomplish in this event handler. I want to show the contents of the Label control that contains the finance details if the user specified these when saving the quotation. I also have to get the appropriate set of "optional extra" rows from the DataSet and bind these to the nested "child" Repeater control.

To see if the user saved any finance details with the quotation, I can check the value of the PaymentMonths column in the Orders table. If it is greater than zero, there are details to show so I set the Visible property of the Label control that contains the finance details for this row of the Repeater output:

```
Sub QuotesListDatabound(oSender As Object, oArgs As RepeaterItemEventArgs)
  ' runs for each row in Quotes Repeater as it is databound
  ' see if it is an item or alternating item row
  If oArgs.Item.ItemType = ListItemType.Item _
  Or oArgs.Item.ItemType = ListItemType.AlternatingItem Then

    ' show Finance terms section only if not zero
    If oArgs.Item.DataItem("PaymentMonths") > 0 Then
      CType(oArgs.Item.FindControl("lblFinance"), Label).Visible = True
    End If
    ...
```

Now I can get the list of optional extras for this quotation. As you saw in the earlier sections of this chapter, I need to convert the DataRow that is exposed by the Item.DataItem property of the arguments to the event handler into a DataRowView, and then execute its CreateChildView method to get a DataView containing the related child rows from the OrderLines table in the DataSet.

So, I start by getting a reference to the nested "child" Repeater control using the FindControl method (the ID of the Repeater control is repQuoteLines). Then I pass the name of the DataRelation in the DataSet to the CreateChildView method. The resulting DataView is assigned to the DataSource property of the Repeater control. A call to the DataBind method of this control is enough to cause it to display these rows:

```
    ...
    ' get DataView of related child rows from OrderLines table
    ' (tblQuoteOrderExtras in database) and bind to nested Repeater
    ' control that appears in each row of the parent Repeater
    Dim oLinesRep As Repeater _
        = CType(oArgs.Item.FindControl("repQuoteLines"), Repeater)
    oLinesRep.DataSource = CType(oArgs.Item.DataItem, _
                                 DataRowView).CreateChildView("relOrders")
    oLinesRep.DataBind()
  End If
End Sub
```

Handling the ItemDataBound *Event for the Orders List*

The event handler named OrdersListDatabound for the Repeater control that displays the list of orders is shown in the next listing. I don't display the finance terms when I list a user's existing vehicle orders, so I don't need to worry about showing these. I just have to bind the nested "child" Repeater control in each row of this list, in exactly the same way as I did in the previous code listing:

```
Sub OrdersListDatabound(oSender As Object, oArgs As RepeaterItemEventArgs)
  ' runs for each row in Orders Repeater as it is databound
  ' see if it is an item or alternating item row
  If oArgs.Item.ItemType = ListItemType.Item _
                Or oArgs.Item.ItemType = ListItemType.AlternatingItem Then
    ' get DataView of related child rows from OrderLines table
    ' (tblQuoteOrderExtras in database) and bind to nested Repeater
```

```
       ' control that appears in each row of the parent Repeater
       Dim oLinesRep As Repeater _
                        = CType(oArgs.Item.FindControl("repOrderLines"), Repeater)
       oLinesRep.DataSource = CType(oArgs.Item.DataItem, _
                                    DataRowView).CreateChildView("relOrders")
       oLinesRep.DataBind()
    End If
End Sub
```

Logging Out of the Application

I include a feature in the My Cars page that allows a user to "log out" of the application if desired. You'll recall that the ASP.NET Forms authentication mechanism places a *session cookie* on the user's machine. This cookie contains encoded authentication information, which allows the user to access pages that are not available to anonymous visitors. When the user closes his or her browser (or when the authentication session times out) this cookie disappears, and the user has to log in again when next visiting the site.

Users can also specify that I should place a *persistent cookie* on their machine, by ticking the "Log in automatically next time" check box on the Login page. This cookie survives the user closing his or her browser, and allows that user to access the protected pages without having to log in again next time.

However, it's good practice to allow users to "log off" if they wish—especially if they are going to be leaving their machine running or allow other people to use it. And, if they have previously specified the "persistent cookie" option, they can destroy this cookie by logging off.

If the user's browser does not support cookies, however, I am performing all of the authentication tasks myself, and storing an authentication flag value in the user's ASP.NET session. In this case, clicking the Log Off button simply has to clear this flag value within the session, requiring the user to log on again when coming back to the My Cars page.

The Log Off Button Code

As you've seen in the earlier figures, I provide a Log Off button near the top of the My Cars page. When clicked, this button causes a postback to the server and executes a routine named DoSignOut. While I could test what kind of session support is in use, I chose to simply execute all of the tasks required to log out a user for both kinds of sessions—it only involves a few lines of code in all.

To destroy the Forms authentication cookie, I just call the SignOut method of the FormsAuthentication object. To clear the cookie-less sessions authentication flag, I just set the session variable WCCUserAuthenticated to "no". Then, irrespective of the type of session support in use, I have to redirect the user to the appropriate page outside the secure folder of the application. I chose to redirect users to the Home page:

```
Sub DoSignOut(objSender As Object, objArgs As EventArgs)
  ' runs when the "Log Off" button is clicked
  ' destroy the users authentication cookie
  FormsAuthentication.SignOut()

  ' clear authenticated flag in session
  Session("WCCUserAuthenticated") = "no"

  ' redirect them to the Home page
  Response.Clear()
  Response.Redirect("../home.aspx")
  Response.End

End Sub
```

Placing an Order

When the user clicks the Order now! button in any of the quotation rows (if there are any displayed), a postback is initiated and the event handler named PlaceOrder is executed. I defined this event handler in the OnItemCommand attribute of the Repeater control that displays the list of quotations. When this event occurs, I want to convert the current quotation (the one containing the Order now! button that was clicked) into an order.

I use a simple stored procedure to convert a quotation into an order. It just has to set the IsOrder column value of the specified row in the tblQuoteOrder table in the database to one. I pass the order ID into the stored procedure as a parameter:

```
CREATE PROCEDURE ConvertToOrder @QuoteOrderID int AS
UPDATE tblQuoteOrder SET IsOrder = 1 WHERE QuoteOrderID = @QuoteOrderID
```

I call this stored procedure from the PlaceOrder event handler. The first step here is to figure out which quotation I want to convert into an order. You'll recall that I set the CommandName property of the Order now! buttons in the Repeater declaration using the following code:

```
<asp:Button id="cmdOrder" Text="Order now!" runat="server"
    ToolTip="Place an order for this vehicle now"
    CommandName='<%# Container.DataItem("QuoteOrderID") %>' />
```

The highlighted line shows that each Order now! button will have as its CommandName the ID of the order for the row it is located within. To get this value within the event handler, I query the CommandSource property of the arguments passed into the routine. This returns a reference to the control that caused the postback, and I convert this to a Button object then access the CommandName property. This returns a String value, but I want an Integer to pass to the stored procedure, so I have then to parse it to an Int32 type:

```
Sub PlaceOrder(oSender As Object, oArgs As RepeaterCommandEventArgs)
  ' simple routine to convert a Quote into an Order
  ' in reality would probably collect payment information first

  ' get order ID from routine arguments
  Dim sOrderID As String = CType(oArgs.CommandSource, Button).CommandName
  Dim iOrderID As Integer = Int32.Parse(sOrderID)
  ...
```

Executing the Stored Procedure

Now I can define the name of the stored procedure, create the Connection and Command objects, specify the parameter I require, and execute the stored procedure just as I've done in many previous examples:

```
  ...

  ' to hold stored procedure name
  Dim sProcName As String = "ConvertToOrder"

  Dim sMessage As String
  Dim sqlConn As New SqlConnection(sConnect)
  Dim sqlComm As New SqlCommand(sProcName, sqlConn)
  sqlComm.CommandType = CommandType.StoredProcedure
  sqlComm.Parameters.Add("@QuoteOrderID", iOrderID)

  Try
    sqlConn.Open()
    If sqlComm.ExecuteNonQuery() = 1 Then
      ...
```

Displaying the Results

If the stored procedure succeeds in updating one row in the table, I know that the quotation has been converted into an order. The next thing is to redisplay the page content to show that this is the case. However, because the stored procedure has changed the content of the database, I have to reload the DataSet by calling the same GetUserDetailsDS function as I did in the Page_Load event handler when I first loaded the page. Then I can execute the DisplayUserVehicles routine again with the new DataSet to display the updated information:

```
      ...
      ' update to an order from a quote succeeded
      ' get DataSet with updated values and display them
      dsDetails = GetUserDetailsDS()
      DisplayUserVehicles(dsDetails)
      ...
```

Next I inform the user that the order has been placed by sending an email message, using a separate routine named SendEmailConfirmation within this page. I just provide the OrderID and it does the rest—you'll see how shortly. Then I create a suitable message to display in the page, depending on the outcome of the database update:

```
    ...
    ' send email confirmation of order
    SendEmailConfirmation(sOrderID)
    sMessage = "<p>Thank you for placing your order. " _
               & "An email confirmation<br />" _
               & "has been sent to you with delivery and " _
               & "payment details.</p>"

  Else
    sMessage = "* Sorry, this quotation could not be located."
  End If
Catch
  sMessage = "* Sorry, the database could not be accessed."
Finally
  sqlConn.Close()
End Try
' display message in Label on page
lblMessage.Text = sMessage

End Sub
```

At the end of this code, after making sure that the database connection is closed, I display the message I created in the Label control between the two Repeater controls on the page (you can see it in Figure 12-12—in this case the list of quotations is now empty).

Sending Order Confirmation Email Messages

After an order has been successfully placed, the My Cars page displays a message and sends the user an email to confirm this. You can see this message in Figure 12-12, where I have just placed an order for the Xrox Wregal 2.8 V6 in Thistle, with a few optional extras.

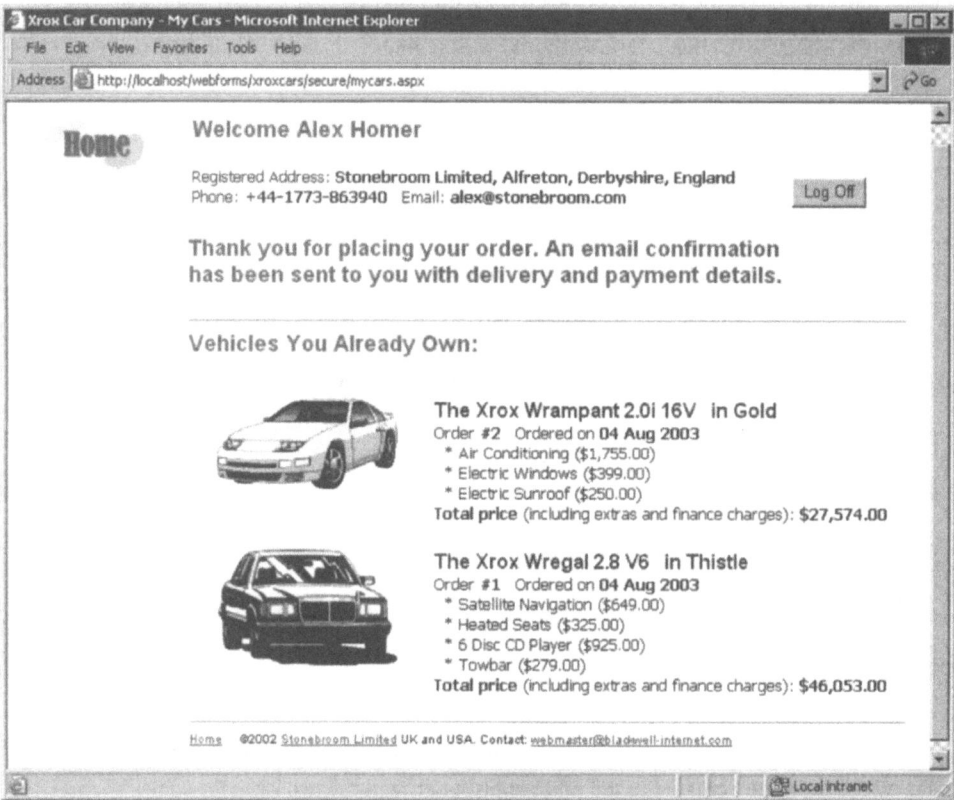

Figure 12-12. The confirmation message after an order has been placed

To send the confirmation email, I take advantage of the same `sendmail.ascx` user control that I use in the Home page to send confirmation messages to visitors when they join the mailing list.

> NOTE   *As discussed in previous chapters, I discovered that the ASP.NET classes, which interact with the CDO objects in Windows 2000, sometimes fail to send the message when the page is placed in a folder that is not an application root directory, and so I placed the* `sendmail.ascx` *user control in the root folder of the application.*

I register the `sendmail.ascx` control at the top of the My Cars page:

```
<%@Register TagPrefix="wcc" TagName="sendmail" Src="../sendmail.ascx"%>
```

Then I insert it just before the closing `</body>` tag:

```
<!-- control containing the routine to send email messages -->
<wcc:sendmail id="ctlMail" runat="server" />
```

Now I can use it just like I did in the Home page by setting the FromAddress, ToAddress, MessageSubject, and MessageBody properties, and then calling the SendEmail method.

Creating the Confirmation Email Message

The message I create is reasonably complex because I want to include all the order details, including a list of the optional extras and the finance terms. I build up the message body as a series of String values, and then concatenate them with the remaining text to form the complete message.

So, first I collect the user's registered details from the UserDetail table in the DataSet:

```
Sub SendEmailConfirmation(sOrderID As String)
  ' routine to send email confirmation of placing an order
  Try
    ' build parts of message as strings
    ' get user details from single row of UserDetail table in DataSet
    Dim drDetails As DataRow = dsDetails.Tables("UserDetail").Rows(0)
    Dim sUser As String = "Name: " & drDetails("UserName") & vbCrlf _
      & "Address: " & drDetails("Address") & vbCrlf _
      & "City: " & drDetails("City") & vbCrlf _
      & "State: " & drDetails("State") & vbCrlf _
      & "Country: " & drDetails("Country") & vbCrlf _
      & "Phone: " & drDetails("Phone") & vbCrlf _
      & "Email: " & drDetails("Email") & vbCrlf
    ...
```

Next, I filter the Orders table to select just the order specified in the parameter passed to the SendEmailConfirmation routine. In this case I'm using the Select method of the table to return an array containing the single row I want at index zero:

```
    ...
    ' create a criteria and select the matching row in the Orders table
    ' in the DataSet, then extract order details
    Dim sFind As String = "QuoteOrderID = " & sOrderID
    Dim arrOrders As DataRow() = dsDetails.Tables("Orders").Select(sFind)
    Dim drOrder As DataRow = arrOrders(0)
    ...
```

Using the values in this row, I build the next String containing the date, the order number, the model name, the engine name, and the color of the vehicle:

```
...
Dim dDate As DateTime = drOrder("OrderDate")
Dim sOrder As String = "Order #" & drOrder("QuoteOrderID") _
  & " placed on " & dDate.ToString("dd MMM yyyy") & vbCrlf
Dim sModel As String = "Model: The Xrox " & drOrder("CarName") _
  & vbCrlf & "Engine: " & drOrder("EngineName") & vbCrlf _
  & "Color: " & drOrder("ColorName") & vbCrlf
...
```

Listing the Optional Extras

Now I want a list of optional extras. I create a suitable filter to select the rows from
the OrderLines table that have the current OrderID value, and then (providing that
I found some rows) iterate through them adding each one to the String that
describes the vehicle:

```
...
' select the matching rows in the OrderLines table
' in the DataSet, then extract "extras" details
Dim fPrice, fInterest, fPayment As Decimal
Dim drOrderLine As DataRow
arrOrders = dsDetails.Tables("OrderLines").Select(sFind)
If arrOrders.Length > 0 Then
  sModel &= "Optional extras included in your order:" & vbCrlf
  For Each drOrderLine In arrOrders
    fPrice = drOrderLine("ExtraPrice")
    sModel &= "* " & drOrderLine("ExtraName") & " ($" _
            & fPrice.ToString("F2") & ")" & vbCrlf
  Next
End If
...
```

Showing the Price and Finance Details

The next part of the email message is the price and any saved finance terms. I can collect
all this information from the row referenced by the drOrder variable, which I set when
I was extracting the model details earlier in the code. To see if there were any finance
terms saved with the quotation I just have to check the value of the PaymentMonths column, as I did when displaying the quotation details earlier in the page:

```
...
fPrice = drOrder("TotalPrice")
Dim sPrice As String = "Total Price including extras " _
                       & "and finance charges: $" _
                       & fPrice.ToString("#,##0.00") & vbCrlf
If drOrder("PaymentMonths") > 0 Then
  fPrice = drOrder("BasePrice")
  fInterest = drOrder("Interest")
```

```
    fPayment = drOrder("PaymentAmount")
    sPrice &= "Basic price: $" & fPrice.ToString("#,##0.00") _
      & " plus $" & fInterest.ToString("#,##0.00") _
      & " interest." & vbCrlf & "Terms: " _
      & drOrder("PaymentMonths").ToString() & " monthly payments of $" _
      & fPayment.ToString("#,##0.00") & vbCrlf
  End If
  ...
```

Building the Message Body and Sending the Message

With all the parts of the message body complete, I can build up the final message as a String named sMessage. Then I set the FromAddress property of the user control to the email address of the Webmaster (again extracted from web.config), set the ToAddress property to the user's email address (extracted from the "user details" table row), set the MessageSubject property to a suitable value, and assign the sMessage string to the MessageBody property. To send the message I just have to call the SendEmail method of the user control:

```
    ...
    Dim sMessage As String = "Thank you for placing your order with the " _
        & "Xrox Car Company." & vbCrlf & vbCrlf _
        & "Your order details are:" & vbCrlf & vbCrlf _
        & sOrder & vbCrlf & sUser & vbCrlf _
        & sModel & vbCrlf & sPrice & vbCrlf _
        & "We will contact you as soon as your vehicle " _
        & "is ready for delivery and arrange payment " _
        & "and shipping details." & vbCrlf & vbCrlf _
        & "NOTE: Xrox Car Company is a fictitious organization " _
        & "designed only to promote this book. " _
        & "For more details see http://www.daveandal.net/books/7868/"

    ' use ASCX control in root folder of application to send the message
    ctlMail.FromAddress _
                = ConfigurationSettings.AppSettings("XroxCarsWebmasterEmail")
    ctlMail.ToAddress = drDetails("Email")
    ctlMail.MessageSubject = "Xrox Car Company Order Confirmation"
    ctlMail.MessageBody = sMessage
    ctlMail.SendEmail()
  Catch
  End Try

End Sub
```

As a result of ordering the vehicle you saw in Figure 12-12, I get an email confirmation that looks like Figure 12-13.

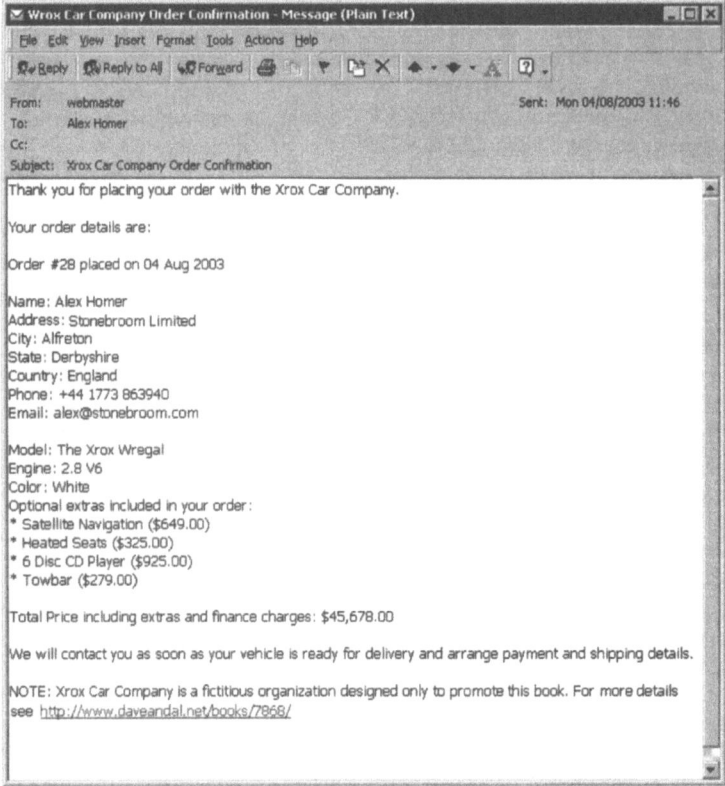

Figure 12-13. The confirmation email sent after placing an order

All I have to do now is write even more books so that I can pay the monthly premium.

Summary

In this final chapter, you've completed your study of both the Xrox Car Company example site, and the techniques you saw me use within it to build interactive and attractive user interfaces with ASP.NET. Hopefully you can now see why I believe that ASP.NET, with its postback architecture, automatic page state maintenance, huge range of useful server controls, and the backing of the whole .NET Framework class library, makes it the obvious choice for developing modern Web applications.

In this chapter, I concentrated on the remaining page of the site, the My Cars page where a visitor can view quotations he or she saved, and place orders for the exciting range of vehicles that are on offer. I demonstrated a few new techniques including binding unrelated and related sets of data to nested list controls. I also showed you how you can interact with the Forms authentication system I introduced in Chapter 11 to protect pages from unauthorized access.

The topics for this chapter were:

- How to bind related sets of data to a range of list controls

- How to easily display hierarchical data in nested form

- How I built the My Cars page

- How to handle placing an order for a vehicle

So, now it's your turn to take up your ASP.NET server and build great Web sites and Web applications.

Index

Panel server control
 browser compatibility with, 74–76
 in down-level clients, 76–78
parent rows, 532–533
passport-based authentication, 476,
  478–479
passwords
 confirming, 499–500
 encrypting, 509–510
 forgotten, 510
 specifying characters for, 500
 text box and validation controls for,
  496
payments
 calculating amount of car, 390–392
 clearing values from last calculation,
  439
 extracting current interest rate and
  database connection string, 390
Pen object, 291–292
performance
 client-side processing for improved,
  27
 dynamic graphics and, 285
 maximizing when using sessions, 91
 <p> elements for, 244
 sending ASP.NET compiled pages to
  client, 7
Performance line chart, 323–324
permissions for anonymous users,
  475–476
per-session cookies, 105
persistent authentication, 496–497
persistent cookies, 105
pie charts, 293–318
 adding import directives for,
  296–297
 color in images, 301–311
 creating DataSet for, 295–296
 drawing text strings on bitmap,
  298–301
 generic DrawPieChart routine,
  311–318
 illustrated, 294
 overview, 293
 Page_Load event handler for,
  297–298
 providing data source for, 294–296
 selecting configurable features for,
  296
 See also DrawPieChart routine
piechart.aspx
 code for, 295–296
 DrawPieChart routine, 311–318
Pmt function, 388, 391–392
PNG format, 303

populating
 CheckBoxList with car and engine
  types, 267–268
 color selection tab, 407
 engine selection tab, 411–412
 finance package tab, 424–425
 My Cars page list controls, 528
 optional extras tab, 413–414
 page heading for Model Details page,
  407
 standard features tab, 419–421
 XML controls, 465
postback architecture
 about, 5, 9–10
 advantages of, 11
 auto-postbacks, 358
 checking postback to Compare
  Models page, 263–264
 client-side script function for
  postback, 68
 confirming acceptance of email
  addresses, 207–208
 designing server-side postbacks, 535
 emulating individual control events,
  11–12
 postbacks when placing orders,
  553–555
 saving session data with postbacks,
  355
 server-side and client-side event
  handling with, 12–14
 using, 355–358
 viewstate, 16–17, 265, 401–403
 working around lack of
  AutoPostBack, 462–463
predefined font sizes, 113–114
Preferences dialog box, 100, 104
preventing
 anonymous users, 485–486
 page reloads, 18–19
price arrays, 444
prices
 adding cost for metallic color,
  433–435
 calculating vehicle, 356, 429–438
 collecting, 401–403
 displaying total, 540
 fetching finance values and,
  452–453
 limitations in background
  calculations, 358
 showing in confirmation message,
  558–559
 storing, 357, 437–438
 See also CalculateCarPrice routine;
  finance terms

forums.apress.com

JOIN THE APRESS FORUMS AND BE PART OF OUR COMMUNITY. You'll find discussions that cover topics of interest to IT professionals, programmers, and enthusiasts just like you. If you post a query to one of our forums, you can expect that some of the best minds in the business—especially Apress authors, who all write with *The Expert's Voice™*—will chime in to help you. Why not aim to become one of our most valuable participants (MVPs) and win cool stuff? Here's a sampling of what you'll find:

DATABASES
Data drives everything.

Share information, exchange ideas, and discuss any database programming or administration issues.

INTERNET TECHNOLOGIES AND NETWORKING
Try living without plumbing (and eventually IPv6).

Talk about networking topics including protocols, design, administration, wireless, wired, storage, backup, certifications, trends, and new technologies.

JAVA
We've come a long way from the old Oak tree.

Hang out and discuss Java in whatever flavor you choose: J2SE, J2EE, J2ME, Jakarta, and so on.

MAC OS X
All about the Zen of OS X.

OS X is both the present and the future for Mac apps. Make suggestions, offer up ideas, or boast about your new hardware.

OPEN SOURCE
Source code is good; understanding (open) source is better.

Discuss open source technologies and related topics such as PHP, MySQL, Linux, Perl, Apache, Python, and more.

PROGRAMMING/BUSINESS
Unfortunately, it is.

Talk about the Apress line of books that cover software methodology, best practices, and how programmers interact with the "suits."

WEB DEVELOPMENT/DESIGN
Ugly doesn't cut it anymore, and CGI is absurd.

Help is in sight for your site. Find design solutions for your projects and get ideas for building an interactive Web site.

SECURITY
Lots of bad guys out there—the good guys need help.

Discuss computer and network security issues here. Just don't let anyone else know the answers!

TECHNOLOGY IN ACTION
Cool things. Fun things.

It's after hours. It's time to play. Whether you're into LEGO® MINDSTORMS™ or turning an old PC into a DVR, this is where technology turns into fun.

WINDOWS
No defenestration here.

Ask questions about all aspects of Windows programming, get help on Microsoft technologies covered in Apress books, or provide feedback on any Apress Windows book.

HOW TO PARTICIPATE:
Go to the Apress Forums site at **http://forums.apress.com/**.
Click the New User link.